The Economics
of
Banking, Liquidity,
and Money

The Economics
of
Banking, Liquidity,
and Money

Peter M. Garber
BROWN UNIVERSITY

Steven R. Weisbrod
WEISBROD GROUP, LTD.

D. C. Heath and Company
Lexington, Massachusetts   Toronto

Address editorial correspondence to:
D. C. Heath
125 Spring Street
Lexington, MA 02173

Book design: Ann Turley
Cover design: Dustin Graphics
Cover photograph: Photo Courtesy of The Harwood Company, Oakland, CA.

Published simultaneously in Canada.

International Standard Book Number: 0-669-27272-8

Library of Congress Catalog Number: 91-75588

10 9 8 7 6 5 4 3 2 1

To the

Instructor

The major financial and monetary debate over the past decade has changed its focus from the traditional issue of how monetary policy affects the economy to how financial innovation affects the stability of the monetary system. For example, we have seen that the demand for the basic monetary aggregates has become difficult to predict because of changes in the way businesses make payments. This change has resulted from technological improvements and the globalization of financial markets, both of which have increased the liquidity of financial markets. Technological innovations have permitted financial arbitrage across a wide range of previously independent markets. The speed at which transactions can be settled has greatly reduced the demand for bank deposits as a means of payment. Major market participants effectively trade obligations to pay for securities instead of using bank deposits.

These developments have made securities markets more liquid and capital cheaper, but they have also increased risk. In this new environment, we have seen wholesale failures among financial institutions unprecedented since the Great Depression.

We believe a successful course in money and banking must provide the student with a framework for understanding how our monetary and financial system has evolved and on what it depends to remain in good working order. Two financial events, one well-publicized and the other little-noticed, which occurred just as this book was going to press, illustrate how rules and institutions provide support for market liquidity. The well-known event was the scandal at Salomon Brothers over violation of rules governing trading in the government securities market. The little-noticed event was news that on August 7, 1991, major New York banks borrowed over $3 billion from the Federal Reserve's discount window to cover loans to Wall Street security dealers who could find no other source of credit to finance their inventory on that particular day. The demand for bank loans sent the interbank interest rate, the fed funds rate, soaring to 30 percent.

Liquid markets require confidence among participants that the game is being played by the rules. If a market participant is able to impose large losses on other traders by violating trading rules, immediate settlement in securities will appear risky. Inventors will spend more time evaluating the behavior of their trading partners, and while they are evaluating, they will hold bank deposits. As a result, securities markets will become less liquid, and the cost of illiquidity will be borne by the economy in the form of higher capital costs.

Investors in liquid markets also must have confidence that they can settle their transactions in the form of bank deposits, if, for whatever reason, they should desire to do so. This means that the banking system must be able to provide liquidity assurance in an emergency; government-run central banks have become the major suppliers of this assurance. In the United States the central bank guarantees settlement of transactions occurring over its electronic payments system. It also ensures that the supply of reserves necessary to create additional bank deposits is somewhat elastic. The jump in the fed funds rate to 30 percent illustrates how uncertainty can lead to a major increase in the demand for bank loans and hence reserves.

The rules and the guarantees of a modern financial system have fostered lower capital costs and wider access to financial markets. However, they have also provided incentives for some parties to try to force others to absorb more risk than they bargained for and have encouraged investments in risky projects. Naturally, some of the risky projects made feasible by the greater liquidity in capital markets have failed, and taxpayers have had to foot the bill.

Surely, economists and noneconomists alike would point to the consequences of the liquidity revolution as the major monetary and financial event of recent times. Yet, we do not know of another money and banking textbook that addresses the causes of this revolution, the institutional and legal arrangements necessary for a modern financial system to function, and the gains and losses that have accrued to the world economy as a result of all these changes. This fundamental gap in the choice of material around which to design a money and banking course motivated the writing of this textbook.

The book is organized to provide the student with an understanding of the process of liquidity creation. First we consider the organization of securities markets. We discuss arbitrage, market makers, exchanges, and settlement procedures as methods of making securities markets more liquid. However, investors need to have money available to them as an alternative to settlement in securities if they are to maintain confidence in the liquidity of the system. It is this consideration that motivates our discussion of money. We show how creation of a monetary standard and settlement in money has costs and how these costs are spread throughout the economy. The banking system exists to reduce the cost of settling transactions in money.

In modern economies, a government-owned central bank is the liquidity-provider of last resort to the banking system. As a consequence, the central bank bears risks for which it tries to obtain compensation. Thus the central bank has incentives to prevent liquidity costs from being reduced too drastically; this is the reason why central banks often impose reserve requirements on banks. We consider market reaction to the costs that regulators attempt to impose on the system. These reactions are the source of financial innovation. Finally, we discuss regulatory supervision aimed at restraining financial market innovation.

We have not followed the tradition of exhaustively discussing various theories about how monetary expansion affects real output and the price level, although we include a chapter on this subject. However, in the course of the book, we define a major role for the central bank as provision of liquidity to securities markets — that is, acting as market maker in cash. If the central bank successfully identifies liquidity problems, temporary expansion of reserves can have a salutary effect on the economy. An example of this would be Fed expansion during the stock market crash of 1987. Security transactions can be settled without a drastic decline in securities prices, which would have a negative effect on confidence and real output. On the other hand, if the central bank mistakes a change in real securities values for a liquidity problem, it will end up subsidizing risky projects; and, if these projects do not pay off, inflation will result.

We believe the student can best learn the mechanics of financial innovation and how it affects the economy through problem solving. In the study guide that accompanies the text, we have tried to create extended problems that let students discover for themselves how financial innovation occurs, whom it benefits, and who potentially pays the costs.

SPECIAL TEXT FEATURES

Each chapter includes boxed applications that illustrate themes in the text discussion. Overall, the text includes more than 60 boxes, ranging from the impact of leverage on management control to the Panamanian banking crisis, the effect of shorter check clearing times, and the junk bond market in chaos.

Key terms in the text discussion are printed in boldface; they are also listed at the end of the chapter to facilitate student review and then are formally defined in the Glossary at the end of the text.

The chapter ends with a brief Conclusion, the list of key terms, and ten to fifteen exercises designed to encourage analytical thinking. Further readings of special interest to students are also included.

An unusual end-of-text feature is full solutions to half the text questions. These solutions, which can be found after Chapter 21, often expand on the topic under consideration.

THE SUPPLEMENTS PACKAGE

Each chapter in the Study Guide begins with an overview of the chapter. Also, as described earlier, the Study Guide emphasizes extended problems that guide the student into a fuller understanding of financial issues. Solutions to these problems are included. Each chapter also provides about 15 true-false questions and as many multiple-choice questions. These more conventional questions are also answered with full commentary, so that the student can use the Study Guide to obtain a thorough review of the text.

INSTRUCTOR'S GUIDE AND TEST BANK

This manual provides full solutions to the remaining text questions. The Test Bank portion includes approximately 850 multiple-choice questions. The questions are also available in computerized form for IBM and Macintosh systems.

ACKNOWLEDGMENTS

In a task of this size, the authors shoulder only a part of the burden. Many others ease the way. In particular, George Lobell long ago encouraged us to start this project in his Johnny Appleseed rounds through the country's economics departments and then pushed it through to completion. Patricia Wakeley, our development editor, accelerated the evolution of our prose toward readability and gave us constant insights into organization. Carolyn Ingalls, our production editor, bridged the gap from word processor to final product.

Several colleagues read and criticized various chapters at key stages in the development of the text. These include

Andrew Atkeson, *University of Chicago*

David Folkerts-Landau, *International Monetary Fund*

Michele Fratianni, *Indiana University*

Dale Henderson, *Board of Governors of the Federal Reserve*

David Humphrey, *Federal Reserve Bank of Richmond*

Howard Lee, *Weisbrod Group*

Seonghwan Oh, *UCLA*

Deborah S. Prutzman, *Paul, Weiss, Rifkind, Wharton, & Garrison*

We are also grateful for the numerous helpful comments provided by manuscript reviewers. These included

Stuart Allen, *North Carolina State University*

Christine Amsler, *Michigan State University*

Dwight Blood, *Brigham Young University*

William N. Butos, *Trinity College*

David W. Findlay, *Colby College*

Joseph G. Haubrich, *University of Pennsylvania*

Lora P. Holcombe, *Auburn University*

Jaap Koelewijn, *Free University, Amsterdam*

Patricia C. Mosser, *Columbia University*

Dale K. Osborne, *University of Texas–Dallas*

Thomas Palley, *Amherst College*

Arthur J. Raymond, *Tufts University*

Robert Schweitzer, *University of Delaware*

George Sofianos, *New York Stock Exchange*

A. Charlene Sullivan, *Purdue University*

Daniel T. Walz, *Trinity University*

Don Wells, *University of Arizona*

Finally, our thanks go to Robert Reville and Arindam Mitra, graduate students at Brown University, who helped us to compose and answer many of the problems in the text.

P. M. G.
S. R. W.

To the Student

Financial markets and financial institutions form essential elements of any industrial market economy. They are the conveyor belt for moving resources from the hands of those who wish to save to those who wish to borrow. More importantly, financial institutions supply the services through which almost all payments are made for goods and services; and they are at the center of the trading of securities, which are claims on cash payments.

This book is designed to help you to understand the connection among all these activities. We look extensively at how these activities combine to reduce the cost of switching savings from one form to another or to consumption. Our guiding principle will be that at the end of any chain of transactions waits someone who wants only to receive an item called "cash." Any economy must then define what cash is and how it is to be created. Much of the banking system and the organization of financial markets in an economy is set up to make it easy for people who want cash to get it.

With this principle constantly in mind, we will study the organization of securities markets, the choice of a monetary standard under which cash is created, the regulation of banking systems, the efforts of banks to escape regulation, and central banking.

Institutional arrangements evolve rapidly. Yet we believe it is crucial to develop a firm understanding of the details of current institutional arrangements. This is the way to become skilled at analyzing how institutions and their innovations work within the system to deliver cash or to economize on cash.

We have provided numerous exercises to help you explore the ways in which financial institutions and markets mesh to move cash and claims among different hands. Working these exercises and studying the applications of principles to recent events are the means by which the concepts will come alive for you.

P. M. G.
S. R. W.

Brief

Contents

Contents

5 Interest Rates

6 Market Makers, Dealers, Securities Exchanges, and Liquidity   129

PART FOUR The Role of Banks in the U.S. and World Economies　353

PART FIVE The Liquidity Requirements of Financial Innovation   449

17 Financial Innovation and the Creation of Bank-Like Deposits   451

20 Rogue Banks: Moral Hazard in the Banking System   572

21 Monetary Policy and Economic Activity   602

C H A P T E R

1

Trading with Strangers

In 1970, about 13 percent of the cars sold in the United States were imported. By 1990, this figure had increased to 30 percent. In the early 1970s, about 45 percent of the oil-field machinery produced in the United States was exported. By the late 1980s, this figure had risen to almost 65 percent. These numbers represent concrete evidence of what we all take for granted. Over the last 20 years, the economies of individual countries have become an integral part of one global economy.

Globalization of the marketplace has led to a high degree of specialization. Americans find that they are no longer very competitive in certain fields, such as clothing and consumer electronics, and very competitive in others, such as the production of aircraft, computers, and agricultural products.

However, increasing specialization is better described as a trend than as a startling, new phenomenon. In the United States, regional specialization has been a fact for a very long time. For example, heavy industry found its home in the Midwest, whereas light industry, such as textiles, migrated to the South. High-tech industries, such as computer software and hardware development, have grown up around universities in the West and Northeast.

Trade drives specialization, but on an individual level, specialization necessitates trade. For the overwhelming majority in the industrial economies, "work" means concentrating on a very narrow set of tasks that, by no stretch of the imagination, could even begin to supply anyone with the bare necessities of life.

In an economic sense, we must all interact with people from far and wide whom we will never meet and, much less, learn to trust. In our dealings, we need to have confidence that when someone pays us for doing something, we receive something that, in turn, people whom we must pay will accept as valuable.

A BARTER SYSTEM

One method of ensuring this confidence is to transact in commodities whose values are fairly familiar to both parties to the trade. A system of trade in which a commodity, such as apples, is exchanged for another commodity, such as oranges, is known as a **barter system.**

It is not hard to see that a barter system is a very cumbersome form of economic communication. The person with oranges to sell might meet an individual who would like to trade bananas for oranges rather than apples. Since bananas are just as likely as oranges to attract a potential apple seller, the banana seller may be able to convince the orange seller to swap those oranges for bananas.

The inducement might take the form of a small discount on the quantity of oranges required to purchase a given quantity of bananas. The banana dealer might be willing to make this price concession to avoid the time cost of finding an orange seller who wants bananas.

While such a modification to the barter system can reduce shopping time, it greatly complicates the pricing problem facing the orange seller. To make good deals while maximizing his trading possibilities, the orange seller must know the exchange rate both between oranges and apples and between oranges and bananas. Given these problems with barter, most societies soon recognize the value of improving on the system.

A Unit of Account

One improvement would be to adopt a common unit to express the relative values of oranges, bananas, apples, and everything else people need. Three bananas may be worth two oranges, and one orange may be worth two apples. However, if two traders meet to exchange bananas for apples, what should the exchange rate be? To come up with the result, the traders must do a little arithmetic. The trade would be much easier if relative value were expressed as follows: The price of a banana is 40 cents, the price of an orange is 60 cents, and the price of an apple is 30 cents.

In this example, a cent represents a measurement of relative value. Common units to describe relationships among things are quite prevalent in everyday life.

For example, an ounce is a common unit to express relative weight. We call the common unit to express relative value a **unit of account.**

Quoting prices in a unit of account gives everyone a better idea of what sellers think their product is worth relative to everything else. Thus even an economy that uses barter would find it beneficial to establish a unit of account.

Liquidity

Establishing a common unit of account is a giant step toward creating an efficient system to buy and sell goods and services. Without a common means to execute a transaction, though, trading would still be difficult. For example, the unit of account informs the person exchanging one orange for one banana that he should expect 20 cents in change. In a barter system, however, the change must be taken in a commodity. It may even require splitting an orange into thirds, a messy operation under the best of conditions.

An obvious solution is to create a common medium of exchange. To be useful, the medium of exchange must be widely accepted, and to be widely accepted, its value must be known to traders in terms of the unit of account. For example, in Japan, the U.S. dollar is not a useful medium of exchange because most people are not familiar with its value relative to the unit of account, the yen. We call the quality of having a well-known and stable value relative to the unit of account **liquidity.**

Cash

The best way to make the medium of exchange liquid, and therefore widely accepted, is to make it the physical representation of the unit of account. Thus, in the United States, the unit of account is dollars, and the medium of exchange is the dollar. By definition, the dollar maintains a fixed value relative to the unit of account. We call the physical representation of the unit of account **cash.**

SUBSTITUTES FOR CASH

Dollar bills are useful because they are liquid and easily portable, but they have several drawbacks that make them less useful for some transactions than for others. One major drawback is that they are expensive to hold in large quantities. When a person holds dollars, she sacrifices the pleasure she could have had by holding goods instead. This sacrifice may be well worth her while, if she is accumulating dollars for something she really wants, such as a new house. However, if someone else who wants to consume something immediately were willing to pay this person for the right to use her dollars now with a promise to return them later, her sacrifice for waiting would be less painful.

Loans and Securities

A mechanism exists for people who are accumulating dollars for later use to sell them to someone who wants to use them now. It is called the **loan.** The price of using dollars today is the **interest rate.** The individual who wants to buy a house in the future might consider placing, or investing, her dollars in the loan market, where she can earn interest until she is ready to withdraw them to buy her house. For example, let's say she lends $100,000 for 1 year at a 10 percent interest rate. At the end of 1 year, she expects to receive $100,000 plus interest of $10,000, which is 10 percent of the amount she lent.

However, before she does this, she must consider one important question: When she withdraws her investment, will she be able to receive the full amount of dollars she placed in the loan market plus accumulated interest? That is, is the value of the loan she made liquid in terms of the unit of account? If it is not, she may be quite willing to sacrifice the interest she could have earned from lending her dollars for the certainty that, in the future, she will have the cash to buy the house she wants.

One way the buyer might make a loan with her cash is to buy a security. Loans that are sold publicly and held directly by investors are called **securities.** The markets in which securities are bought and sold are called **securities markets** or **financial markets.** However, our security buyer has no guarantee that the price of her security will equal her original $100,000 plus interest when she is ready to buy her house. This is so because the value of her security is not determined by how much she invested, but by what the market is willing to pay for the security when she is ready to sell it.

Thus she has no guarantee that her security is liquid. However, she does not have to revert to holding cash. An institution has evolved whose business it is to make loans liquid for investors. It is called a **bank.** Instead of buying a security, the home buyer could place her cash in a bank.

The Role of Banks

When an individual places cash in a bank, he or she receives a bank deposit in exchange. A **bank deposit,** or **bank account,** is a contract between the bank and an investor. It states that the investor has the right to withdraw the same amount of cash he or she originally placed in the bank plus accumulated interest at a fixed point in time, called the **maturity date.** Thus the deposit is perfectly liquid in the unit of account at the maturity date of the deposit.

The bank invests the deposits that it collects in loans. The deposit is a **liability** of the bank because it represents an obligation of the bank to pay the depositor at maturity. The loan is an **asset** of the bank because it represents an obligation of the borrower to pay the bank at the date on which the loan matures.

The Banking System

Why does bank intermediation between a borrower and a lender make the loan market more liquid? The mechanics of this process are somewhat complicated and require several chapters of this book to explain fully. However, a simple, and basically correct, answer is that a single bank is part of a mutually supporting network of banks tied together by a central bank. A **central bank** is a bank that supplies liquid assets to the individual banks tied to it. In the United States, the central bank is called the **Federal Reserve System.** The central bank and the banks tied to it are known as a **banking system.** In modern-day industrial societies, central banks are owned by governments.

The liquid asset supplied by the central bank to individual banks is a deposit at the central bank.[1] In most banking systems, including the U.S. system, deposits held by banks at the central bank do not earn interest. However, they are perfectly liquid because they maintain their value in terms of the unit of account.

When our depositor withdraws her deposit to buy a house, she usually does not withdraw cash. Instead, she transfers ownership of her deposit to the seller of the house through the banking system. To execute the transaction, her bank directs the central bank to make a transfer from its account held at the central bank to the account of the bank of the current owner of the house. The current owner's bank accepts the transfer as a means of payment because deposits at the central bank are as liquid as cash.

The banking system has an important advantage over individuals in reducing the cost of exchange. If the buyer of the house, as an individual, wanted to be absolutely certain that she had $110,000 to buy a house, she would have held cash equal to that amount. In contrast, because banks engage in numerous transactions, the amount of the perfectly liquid asset they must hold to execute transactions is small relative to their total assets.

For example, let's say the buyer directs her bank to transfer $110,000 to the bank of the seller of the house. However, on that same day, in a completely unrelated transaction, the seller's bank also makes a payment of $100,000 to the buyer's bank. On net, the two banks must exchange deposits at the central bank equal only to $10,000, rather than $100,000. Thus, if the buyer's bank holds a $10,000 deposit at the central bank, it can meet its obligation without selling its loans. Therefore, it

---

1. At this point, we leave unanswered the important question of how banks obtain deposits at the central bank. The answer is that they sell assets to the central bank in return for deposits. We explain this transaction in detail in Chapter 9.

does not need to worry about the market price of its loans on any particular day. This is called **netting,** and it greatly reduces the amount of deposits banks must hold at the central bank, freeing up assets to be held in the form of interest-earning loans.

Money

The common attribute of bank deposits and cash is that both promise to maintain their value in terms of the unit of account. Because of this situation, both are collectively known as **money.** (See Box 1.1.)

INTERNATIONAL TRANSACTIONS

As indicated earlier, the dollar is not accepted as cash in Japan because most Japanese do not know its value relative to their unit of account, the yen. However, liquidity of the dollar could be transferred to yen if the rate at which yen could be exchanged for dollars were fixed. For example, if you could always trade 150 yen for 1 dollar, you could be perfectly certain of the value of the dollar relative to the Japanese unit of account. Thus, for you, the dollar would be perfectly liquid in Japan, after you had exchanged it for yen at the fixed exchange rate.

However, the exchange rate between yen and dollars is not fixed. Between 1985 and 1990, the value of the yen fluctuated between 240 and 120 to the dollar. It might seem that this fact would make it difficult for Japanese and Americans who wish to trade with each other to find a liquid medium of exchange.

Let's say an American retailer contracts with Sony to sell a shipment of Japanese compact disc players in the U.S. market. He expects to sell the entire shipment for $750,000. After the retailer sells the goods, he must pay Sony 100 million yen. When he signs the contract, the exchange rate is 140 yen to the dollar. Thus his expected dollar payment to the Japanese is approximately $714,000 (100 million yen divided by 140 yen to the dollar).

Assume that after the retailer sells the goods and converts his dollar receipts to yen, he discovers the exchange rate has fallen to 120 yen to the dollar. As a result, he finds that he must pay Sony the equivalent of approximately $833,000. Instead of making $36,000 on the deal, he loses $83,000. It would seem that the inability to fix the value of dollars relative to the Japanese unit of account increases the risk of trade.

Fortunately, a mechanism has arisen to make the dollar liquid relative to the Japanese unit of account. It is called the **futures market,** and it is a market in which an American dealer can contract to buy yen for dollars at a fixed price for delivery at a future date. Thus, if our American retailer expects to sell all the compact disc

Box 1.1

Bartering with Money

An article in the November 26, 1990, *Wall Street Journal* (pp. B1–B2) reported that small firms are returning to barter. Bob Meyer, publisher of *Barter News,* said that barter exchanges traded $750 million in 1990, double the amount of business they did in 1985. Trade officials say that the recent surge in bartering is due to the economic downturn, but that bartering has been growing in good times as well.

Bartering through an exchange works as follows: Assume that an automobile dealer who has trucks to sell wants to refurbish his showroom. He contacts the barter exchange to find out whether any member is in the refurbishing business. If the answer is yes, he agrees to sell the exchange a dollar volume of trucks equal to the contractor's asking price. The contractor, in return, receives trade credits equal to the dollar value of her work. She can use the trade credits for anything she wants—as long as it is provided by a member of the exchange. The automobile dealer must at some point make good his trade liability by delivering trucks to someone who wants to use trade credits.

Notice that this barter system has not abandoned the unit of account. Prices are still quoted in the unit of account. Also notice that the system is not really barter; in fact, it is a money system in which the barter exchange issues money. Why would such a system arise, especially in recessionary times?

Consider the alternative for the automobile dealer. He could take out a bank loan to pay for refurbishing his showroom. The contractor would then end up owning a bank deposit as an asset. The problem is that in a recession, bank credit is tight. Banks are reluctant to lend in a risky environment. In effect, therefore, the "barter" exchange creates its own loan. The contractor's trade credits are a liability of the automobile dealer; he must deliver trucks at some time in the future.

What is the cost of transacting through the exchange rather than taking out a bank loan? The contractor is free to use her trade credits as she pleases, but she is restricted to the goods and services available through the exchange. The exchange is also taking some risk. What if no one wants trucks at the price quoted to the contractor? If no one buys the trucks, the exchange could be left with an excess demand for some goods and services and an excess supply of trade credits. Trade credits are just not as liquid as real money.

players within 30 days, he can buy the right to exchange dollars for yen at a fixed price on that date. This permits him to lock in his dollar profits, as if he were dealing with a company that wanted to be paid in dollars rather than yen. In other words, he has fixed the value of the dollar in terms of the Japanese unit of account, making the dollar as liquid in the Sony transaction as yen.

THE VALUE AND COST OF LIQUIDITY

The international trade problem just described illustrates how the lack of a liquid medium of exchange increases the cost of transacting. However, creating a liquid medium of exchange is costly. We saw earlier that, in the domestic market, the liquidity of bank deposits depends on the willingness of banks to hold non-interest-bearing deposits at the central bank. When we study foreign exchange markets in some detail, we shall see that similar devices are necessary to make sure that dollars can, in fact, be exchanged for yen at a fixed price at a future date.

How liquidity is created and who bears the cost of providing it is a major theme of this book. Right now, based on our brief discussion of the loan market and the central bank, the answer might seem straightforward. Banks hold non-interest-bearing deposits at the central bank. Because these deposits are liquid, banks use them to transfer funds among themselves. The cost of liquidity is determined by the cost of holding non-interest-bearing deposits at the central bank. The individuals who use bank deposits—that is, those who demand the liquidity inherent in these accounts—pay for the cost of deposits at the central bank.

As we shall see, this straightforward answer is basically the right one, although we shall find that the cost of liquidity is borne by more than just bank depositors. However, discovering this answer among the workings of actual markets and actual institutions is not easy. As you might expect, people who depend on liquidity are constantly searching for ways to reduce or avoid the cost of obtaining liquidity while retaining its benefits. Because of their actions, tracing the sources and cost of liquidity in a real economy is often a tortuous procedure.

INNOVATIONS REDUCE THE COST OF LIQUIDITY

The past several decades have seen many market innovations to increase the liquidity of illiquid securities, permitting investors to hold fewer and fewer liquid assets, such as bank deposits. For example, in 1960, U.S. corporations held about 16 percent of their financial assets in cash and **demand deposits,** which are the most liquid form of bank deposit. Today that ratio is about 6 percent. If corporations today are in fact as liquid as they were in 1960, these figures suggest a major decline in the cost of achieving that liquidity.

A second theme of this book is that the attempt to reduce the cost of liquidity has been beneficial to the economy. This reduction has increased the availability and has reduced the cost of loans, creating a situation favorable to economic growth.

However, these innovations have not occurred without creating stress. As we shall see, these innovations are, at bottom, very similar to the "innovation" that gives liquidity to bank deposits, by economizing on the use of liquid deposits held at the central bank. The result is that liquidity is being supported by a shrinking base of liquid assets—deposits at the central bank.

In this book, we shall explain why some analysts consider this shrinkage a major potential weakness in the financial system. Central bankers and other government agencies that regulate bank and securities markets are among those who feel the system has become too risky. They have instituted policies to reduce the ability of markets to escape the cost of liquidity.

CONCLUSION

In this chapter we have provided an introduction to the basic themes of this book. A liquid asset maintains its value in terms of the unit of account, which is a measure of relative value. Cash is perfectly liquid in terms of the unit of account because it is the physical representation of the unit of account. Securities are less liquid than cash because their value in terms of the unit of account is uncertain.

On the other hand, bank deposits, like cash, are liquid in terms of the unit of account, because banks maintain deposits at the central bank that are also representations of the unit of account. Banks promise to settle transactions among each other for their deposit customers with payments to and from their deposit accounts at the central bank. Banks can make large numbers of payments while holding only a small fraction of the value of their deposits at the central bank, permitting them to provide liquidity at a lower cost than the household can provide by itself. However, the liquidity provided by banks is still expensive, creating incentives for the market to find ways to reduce its dependence on deposits at the central bank for liquidity, which is the major subject of this book.

KEY TERMS

barter system	bank account
unit of account	maturity date
liquidity	liability
cash	asset
loan	central bank
interest rate	Federal Reserve System
securities	banking system
securities markets	netting
financial markets	money
bank	futures market
bank deposit	demand deposit

EXERCISES

1. Will the prices offered by 10 bread sellers be more or less uniform in a barter economy compared with a money economy?

2. Explain how establishing a unit of account would make the quoted bread price more uniform in a barter economy.

3. What is the relationship between cash and the unit of account? What makes cash liquid?

4. How would the introduction of cash to a barter economy using a unit of account further increase the uniformity of the price of bread across sellers?

5. Why is cash costly to accumulate for making large payments?

6. What are the advantages of investing cash in a loan while accumulating resources to make a large payment? What are the disadvantages?

7. How does a bank reduce the disadvantages of making a loan?

8. What are the major attributes of money?

9. Explain how an importer can potentially lose in a world of floating exchange rates.

10. How can importers protect themselves from changes in exchange rates?

11. Why is it costly to create liquidity?

Financial Instruments and Markets

2

An Introduction to Capital Markets: Debt and Equity

Business firms that produce real goods and services need physical assets such as factories and machinery, and they usually finance these assets by borrowing from the public. They borrow for the same reason that a family might borrow to buy a car or provide for a college education. There is just not enough current income to cover the cost of a large outlay such as the price of a factory. When a firm, especially a large corporation like General Motors, borrows, it has a wide choice of liabilities it can issue. In this chapter we examine how a corporation chooses the liabilities it issues and how the market determines their relative prices.

OVERVIEW OF CAPITAL MARKETS

Stocks and Bonds

A firm can offer different securities to the investing public in order to raise financial capital, and these securities generally fit into two broad categories—stocks and bonds. **Stocks** are securities that represent ownership in the firm, although as Box

2.1 indicates, ownership does not always imply control. They represent what the owners of the firm owe to themselves and thus correspond to the net worth on a personal balance sheet. **Bonds** are securities issued to investors who have made a loan to the firm.

Stockholders receive income on their shares if the firm makes a profit. **Profit** is the income the firm earns after all other expenses, such as wages for labor, materials costs, and so forth, have been paid. However, not all profits are distributed to shareholders as cash payments. The board of directors, a group of decision makers elected by the shareholders, decides whether profits are to be paid in cash or retained by the firm. The payments from profits distributed as cash to shareholders are known as **dividends.**

Investors who purchase bonds are entitled to periodic interest payments from the revenue of the firm. A firm must meet its interest obligations before it can report profits. Thus, from the point of view of stockholders, the interest payments to bondholders are like labor and materials expenses. These expenses must be met before the stockholders are entitled to income.

Market Liquidity

In this chapter we examine the difference between bonds and stocks issued by an individual firm. We see how their prices must be linked and how market arbitrage works to ensure the linkage of prices. **Arbitrage** is the attempt to earn profits by buying a security in a low-priced market and immediately selling it in a high-priced market. The activity of arbitragers, that is, investors who engage in arbitrage, quickly eliminates the profit from buying in one market and selling in another. Thus arbitragers reduce price differentials between markets.

Arbitragers help create liquidity in financial markets. If a large investor places a large sell order for a security, the price of that security may temporarily fall because of the short-term increase in supply resulting from the sell order. If the arbitrager believes that this condition is truly temporary, she will buy the security and hold it for sale when the market "settles down." Her purchase helps maintain the price relative to the price that preceded the arrival of the large sell order. Thus her actions make a market more liquid.

By helping to maintain stability in the prices of securities, arbitragers benefit all investors. As we will see throughout this book, households and other buyers of financial assets strive to achieve stability in the value of the assets they hold. Liquid financial markets help them realize this goal.

We also will see that if arbitrage is successful, a business firm should be indifferent about whether it finances with bonds or equities. This theoretical indifference is known as the **Modigliani–Miller theorem.** In practice, however, firms are not indifferent about the choice of equity versus debt finance. What makes them choose one over the other? We will develop explanations in this chapter about why firms care about their financial structure. Their choices, as we will see throughout this book, sometimes lead to lack of liquidity in financial markets; special institutions are needed to create liquidity when financial markets are not themselves liquid. These special institutions include banks, which can mobilize liquidity quickly, and the central bank, which has the power to create liquidity by printing money.

DEBT VERSUS EQUITY FINANCE: AN EXTENDED CORPORATE EXAMPLE

Organizing a Corporation

Suppose that a group of people decide to form Whole Wheat Corporation to engage in bread making. The company purchases $100,000 worth of property, plant, and equipment (PPE), such as factories, ovens, and dough-making machinery. It also purchases labor, flour, and other inputs that it uses in conjunction with PPE to produce bread. Whole Wheat expects to sell 100,000 loaves of bread during the next year at $1 per loaf for revenues totaling $100,000. Labor, flour, and input expenses are $90,000.

The difference between the cost of labor and so forth and the revenue from selling bread is $10,000. This sum is not great enough to replace the $100,000 invested in PPE. However, PPE is durable; it will be around next year and into the future to produce more bread and more revenue. Therefore, its cost need not be covered out of 1 year's revenue. However, someone must come up with the money to buy the PPE in the first place, and that person is likely to expect some compensation for putting up the money.

Suppose the organizers of Whole Wheat put $100,000 of their savings into the company. They did this because they expect to earn a return for putting up the cash. This year the company made $10,000 above its expenses. As a result, the organizers have earned a $10,000 return on their investment.

Financial Liabilities

Suppose, however, that the organizers of Whole Wheat do not have the $100,000 required to buy the PPE to set up a bread-making business. They must find outside investors to fund their project, so they sell $100,000 of stock to a group of investors who naturally expect to earn income on the $100,000 paid to the firm's organizers in exchange for stock issued by the corporation. If all goes well, the stockholders will earn $10,000 the first year, or 10 percent of $100,000.

Stockholders Bear Risk

Because the $10,000 net income is not guaranteed, stockholders may receive more or less than expected, depending on the firm's actual income. For example, the price of a loaf of bread may fall to 90 cents, in which case the 100,000 loaves would bring in total revenue of only $90,000. If costs remain at $90,000, stockholders' dividends would fall to zero.

Stockholders can only receive net income—that is, whatever income remains after revenues have been collected and expenses have been paid, including taxes and any interest payments to bondholders. Because stockholders may receive income that is different from what they expect, they bear the risk that the firm's income may be lower than anticipated.

Whole Wheat Issues Bonds

As an alternative means of financing the $100,000, the organizers may issue a bond. For example, suppose that Whole Wheat decides to issue bonds to finance $90,000 of the $100,000 it requires for its business. The bond contract states that Whole Wheat agrees to pay the bondholders $8,100 annually.

Bonds have a maturity date. The **maturity date** is the date when the principal of a loan is due and payable, after which the borrower makes no further contractual payments. If a holder of one of Whole Wheat's bonds decides to sell it before it matures, the price she can receive for it will be affected by the current interest rate and the maturity date of the bond. In the next several sections we will see how a change in the interest rate affects the value of a bond.

Interest Rates and Securities Prices

An **interest rate** is the price of income today relative to income tomorrow. That is, it represents the amount of apples, oranges, or dollars that an individual must be promised for tomorrow as an inducement to give up a unit of apples, oranges, or dollars today. The act of saving, such as buying Whole Wheat's bond, entails giving up current resources to someone else to receive more resources tomorrow. Savings grow over time because they accumulate earnings at a rate determined by the interest rate.

For example, let's assume that you decide to put $100 into a bank account, and the interest rate is 10 percent. This means that you can expect to earn 10 percent of $100, or $10, for leaving your money in the account for a full year. This result can be described in equation form as follows:

$$FV = \$100 \times (1 + 0.10) = \$110$$

where the letters FV on the left-hand side of the equation stand for "future value." In this case, the future value (1 year hence) of $100 invested today at 10 percent is $110.

Now let's assume that instead of placing the money in your account for 1 year, you promise to keep it on deposit for 3 years. The bank promises to pay you the same interest rate as before, 10 percent per year. At the end of year 1, you receive $10, so you have $110 in the account. At the end of year 2, you receive 10 percent on $110, or $11, so you have $121 in the account. At the end of year 3, you receive 10 percent on $121, or $12.10. Thus the total value of the money in your account at the end of 3 years is $133.10. This result also can be written as an equation:

$$FV = \$100 \times (1 + 0.10) \times (1 + 0.10) \times (1 + 0.10) = \$133.10$$

Now let's suppose that the bank offers a 7-percent interest rate on a 3-year deposit. (We consider how the interest rate is determined in Chapter 5.) Assuming again a deposit of $100, at the end of the first year, the bank pays 7 percent of $100, making the account worth $107. At the end of year 2, it pays 7 percent on $107, or $7.49, making the account worth $114.49. At the end of year 3, it pays 7 percent on $114.49, or $8.01 to the nearest penny. At the end of 3 years, the value of the account is, to the nearest penny, $122.50. This result can be written as an equation as well:

$$FV = \$100 \times (1 + 0.07) \times (1 + 0.07) \times (1 + 0.07) = \$122.50$$

Note that the future value of $100 is less when the interest rate is low than when it is high.

The general formula for the future value of a sum of money is as follows:

$$FV = X \times (1 + i)^n \qquad (2.1)$$

where X is the sum to be invested, i is the prevailing annual interest rate, and n is the number of years.

Now let's assume that you decide to enter a savings plan at your place of work. You agree to have $100 deducted from your pay at the beginning of each year. You decide to participate in the program for 3 years. Your employer promises to pay 10-percent annual interest on the money in your account.

We can calculate the future value of your yearly payments into the savings plan as follows: At the end of the first year, the company pays 10-percent interest on the $100 you deposited at the beginning of the year, making your account balance $110. At the beginning of the second year, you deposit $100, increasing your account balance to $210. At the end of the second year, the company pays 10 percent of $210, or $21, so the account balance is $231. At the beginning of the third year, you deposit $100, making your balance $331. At the end of the third year, you receive 10 percent of $331, or $33.10. Thus your year-end balance is $364.10.

Let's suppose that the savings plan lasts for 5 years rather than 3. Calculating the future value as we did above would become quite laborious. Fortunately, we can obtain the result by using a formula. The end-of-year balance in the account for the first year is $100 multiplied by 1 plus the interest rate, or 1.10. At the beginning of the second year, you deposit $100. At the end of the second year, the first year's deposit has accumulated 2 years' worth of interest. From equation 2.1, we know that this is equal to $100(1.10)^2$. The second year's deposit has accumulated interest for only 1 year; thus its value is $100(1.10)$. The balance in your account is the sum of these two items. At the beginning of the third year, you make another deposit. At the end of the third year, the first year's deposit has accumulated 3 years' worth of interest, the second year's deposit has accumulated 2 years' worth of interest, and the third year's deposit has accumulated 1 year's worth of interest. The third-year value is the sum of these three items. The future value of $100 deposited every year for 5 year at 10-percent annual interest is

$$FV = \$100 \times (1 + 0.10) + \$100 \times (1 + 0.10)^2 + \$100 \times (1 + 0.10)^3$$
$$+ \$100 \times (1 + 0.10)^4 + \$100 \times (1 + 0.10)^5$$
$$= \$671.56$$

The general formula for the future of a stream of equal payments is

$$FV = \sum_{t=1}^{n} X \times (1 + i)^t \tag{2.2}$$

where the X is the sum to be invested, i is the prevailing annual interest rate, and n is the number of years.

Present Value

If we know the future value of a sum of money and the prevailing interest rate, we can determine the value of that sum of money today. For example, let's suppose that at the beginning of 1991, Jack promises to pay you $110 on December 31, 1991. The future value of your payment is $110. You are a little worried that Jack won't have the money to pay you, but he tells you not to worry because he has $100 in his bank account to cover the payment. You tell him that his promise is to pay $110, not $100. He responds that his bank will pay 10-percent interest on his money so that by year's end he will have $110. Thus the value today of $110 payable in a year is $100 if the interest rate is 10 percent. We call today's value of a sum of money payable in the future the **present value.**

Calculating the present value requires dividing the future value by 1 plus the interest rate. This process is known as **discounting.** For example, the equation for the present value of $110 payable 1 year hence is

$$PV = \frac{\$110}{(1 + 0.10)} = \$100$$

The general formula for the present value of a future payment is

$$PV = \frac{X}{(1 + i)^n} \tag{2.3}$$

where X is the sum to be received, i is the prevailing annual interest rate, and n is the number of years.

Now let's suppose Jack agrees to pay you $100 at the end of every year for the next 5 years. Again, he says he is good for his promise because he has money in his bank account, which we assume pays a 7-percent interest rate. How much does he need in the account today to make his promise to pay you believable? To determine this, we can calculate the present value of each payment separately. The present value of the first payment is $100/1.07, or $93.46. The present value of the second payment is $100/1.07², or $87.34. The present value of the entire stream of payments is the sum of the present value of each year's payment as follows:

$$PV = \frac{\$100}{(1.07)} + \frac{\$100}{1.07^2} + \frac{\$100}{1.07^3} + \frac{\$100}{1.07^4} + \frac{\$100}{1.07^5}$$
$$= \$93.46 + \$87.34 + \$81.63 + \$76.29 + \$71.30$$
$$= \$410.02$$

Thus Jack must have $410.02 in his account to make good on his promise.

The general formula for the present value of an equal stream of payments is

$$PV = \sum_{t=1}^{n} \frac{X}{(1 + i)^t} \tag{2.4}$$

where X is the sum to be received, i is the prevailing annual interest rate, and n is the number of years.

Calculating Loan Payments

A bank loan is often paid off with a series of equal payments of interest and principal. For example, assume that you borrow $10,000 at a 10-percent interest rate and you must pay it back in two equal annual installments. We can use the present value formula to determine how much you must pay. The present value of the stream is $10,000. We represent each equal installment by X, which must be discounted by the appropriate factor. Thus

$$\$10,000 = \frac{X}{1.10} + \frac{X}{1.10^2}$$
$$X = \$5,761.90$$

Valuing a Bond

A typical bond contract calls for interest payments to be made to the investor periodically. The **principal,** which is the face value of the bond, is paid in one lump sum at maturity. The last payment also includes an interest payment. For example, assume that a bond issued at the beginning of 1991 matures in 10 years, the end of 2000. It promises to pay $1,000 per year interest for the first 9 years and $1,000 interest plus $10,000, or $11,000, for the tenth year, 2000. This type of bond is known as a **coupon bond.** *Coupon interest* is the periodic interest payment on a bond. It is usually stated as a percentage of the face value, which in this case is $10,000. Thus the coupon rate is 10 percent.

If the interest rate is 10 percent, we can figure the 1991 price of the bond, which is the present value of the payments stream promised in the bond contract. To do this, we adjust equation 2.4 to reflect the fact that the last payment is not equal to the other nine. This is done as follows:

$$PV = \sum_{t=1}^{9} \frac{\$1000}{1.10^t} + \frac{\$11,000}{1.10^{10}} = \$10,000$$

Note that when the interest rate is 10 percent, which is the same as the coupon rate, the present value of the payments and the face value of the bond are both the same.

The Impact of an Increase in the Interest Rate

Recall that an increase in the interest rate raises the future value of current dollars. It therefore follows that an increase in the interest rate makes the present value of a given future payment less valuable. If the interest rate is 15 percent, the present value of the 10-year bond described above decreases from $10,000 to $7,490.62.

The longer the maturity of a bond, the greater will be the effect of an interest rate change on the price of the bond. For example, the British government used to issue perpetuities—bonds that never mature. These bonds do not have a maturity value; they pay interest forever, or as long as the British government does not default on the bond. When a payment stream becomes infinitely long, equation 2.4 simplifies to

$$PV = \frac{X}{i}$$

If the interest rate is 10 percent and the yearly payment on the perpetuity is $1,000, the present value is $10,000. If the interest rate is 15 percent, the present value decreases to $6,666.67. Compare this to the effect of an interest rate change on the 10-year bond described above.

WHOLE WHEAT'S BALANCE SHEET

Everything a corporation owns is obtained with funds raised in one way or another. Most simply, there are only two sources of funds—creditors who have lent money to the firm and investors who have invested in it. The liabilities of the firm (debt owed to creditors) and equity in the firm (money invested by owners) together equal a firm's assets. A firm's assets and liabilities and equity are listed on its **balance sheet.**

Whole Wheat's balance sheet is presented in Table 2.1 Because the balance sheet resembles a T, it is sometimes referred to as a *T account.* The left-hand side of the T is labeled "Assets," under which is listed the $100,000 in bread-making equipment and buildings that comprise the physical assets of the firm. On the right-hand side of the **T account,** under "Liabilities," is listed the $90,000 in bonds issued by the corporation. Bonds are considered liabilities because they represent an obligation to pay the investor back.

If Whole Wheat acquires $100,000 worth of equipment, it must raise $100,000 to pay for it. In Table 2.1, only $90,000 in bonds supports $100,000 in physical assets. The $10,000 difference supplied by the stockholders is the equity, or net worth, of the firm. If the corporation fails to meet its legal obligation to pay bondholders, it is in default, and the bondholders have the right to take possession of the company from the stockholders. If they do so, the company is said to be bankrupt. **Bankruptcy** is the legally declared condition of a company that cannot meet its obligations to creditors. In such a case, a borrower's assets are either distributed among its creditors or else administered for the creditors' sole benefit. However, as Box 2.2 suggests, owners sometimes declare bankruptcy to prevent bondholders from realizing value from the firm's assets.

The firm is under no contractual obligation to pay a return to its stockholders. Even if the firm pays no dividends and its stock price dropped precipitously, it owes its stockholders nothing. In an economic sense, the firm does owe the investors a return on their investment; in this sense, equity can be considered a liability of the firm. In a legal and accounting sense, however, equity is not a liability.

Table 2.1   BALANCE SHEET FOR WHOLE WHEAT, INC.

ASSETS	LIABILITIES
$100,000 plant and equipment	$90,000 bonds
	$10,000 equity

Box 2.2

Declaring Bankruptcy to Improve Your Position

Businesses sometimes use a declaration of bankruptcy as a negotiating tool to get what they want from their business associates. Take the example of a real estate partnership established for a building in Manhattan. The building had fallen drastically in market value and was running large losses. In early 1991, the general partner, Equitable Life Assurance Society, a very large insurance company, decided to file for bankruptcy of the partnership. Equitable had guaranteed to provide $95 million in credit for the partnership; if the partnership were declared bankrupt, it would be relieved of this obligation.

Manufacturers Hanover, a large New York bank, is the major lender to the partnership. It, of course, did not want to see Equitable relieved of this responsibility because the $95 million could have been used to pay principal and interest on Manufacturers' loan. Manufacturers sued Equitable, contending that Equitable was using the bankruptcy filing to renege on a promise to provide $95 million in credit to the partnership.

Equitable contended that the building was hopelessly insolvent and that filing for bankruptcy was a way to gain leverage with lenders. Equitable is hoping that a bankruptcy threat will force Manufacturers to renegotiate its loan on terms more favorable to the partnership.

When a lender commits itself to a partnership, it does so with a knowledge of how agreements have been interpreted by the courts in the past. If, historically, partners have found legal means to escape from commitments, this will be reflected in a high interest rate charged for the loan.

However, the financial arrangement also can affect the value of the real asset itself. For example, if the partners to a real estate venture believe there is a possibility that they cannot meet interest payments, they may fail to maintain the building properly, to the detriment of the long-term value of the building. By so doing, they can increase the loss to the bondholders while improving their own position by not spending money to repair the building. It is for this reason that a lender wants to be certain about the monetary commitments of a partner. In other words, if the owner has a large equity stake in the building, he may manage the building differently than if he had a small one.

The Modigliani-Miller theorem is based on the presumption that the value of the assets is unaffected by the liability structure. In the real world, financing decisions often affect how assets are managed and hence their value.

Returns

An asset is expected to generate income for its owner. For example, suppose someone you do not know asks to borrow your bicycle for the day. You agree, but because she is not a friend, you decide to charge her for the use. The money you receive is income from owning the bicycle. The **return** on owning an asset is the income generated by that asset. Returns refer both to dividends and interest paid on the asset and to any capital gains earned (or losses incurred) on it. A **capital gain** is an increase in an asset's value above its purchase price. When we discussed how interest rates affect bond prices, for example, we saw that when the interest rate falls, holders of securities promising to pay a stream of fixed dollar income have a capital gain that is added to interest payments in calculating the return. A simpler example would be a stock that you sell for $10 more than you paid for it; the $10 is a capital gain.

Leverage

Whole Wheat has decided to issue $90,000 in bonds, funding the remaining $10,000 needed for equipment by selling stock. The first year's expected net income is $10,000, which must be allocated between the bondholders and the stockholders. Of course, bondholders have a priority claim on $8,100 of net income. The stockholders, the residual income claimants, will receive the remaining $1,900 if the directors of the firm decide to distribute it as dividends rather than retain it for future growth.

Leverage is the use of credit, or borrowing, to build up a company's resources. An increase in a firm's debt-to-net worth ratio, say from 1 : 1 to 2 : 1, indicates that the firm is "leveraging up" or "leveraging." When the leverage ratio increases, it is a sign that bonds have increased relative to equity.

The decision of Whole Wheat to finance with 90 percent debt and 10 percent equity, a 9 : 1 leverage ratio, has a very interesting effect on the expected return on equity. Remember that the bondholders will be paid $8,100 interest out of the expected $10,000 net income. This leaves $1,900 for the stockholders, whose return therefore increases from 10 percent on $100,000 to 19 percent on $10,000 ($1,900 divided by $10,000). This happens because bondholders are paid a lower return than the stockholders. The expected return on Whole Wheat's equity plus bonds remains at 10 percent, however. Bondholders receive $8,100, and stockholders expect to receive $1,900. The sum of $10,000 is still 10 percent of $100,000.

On closer examination, however, stockholders pay a price for the increase in leverage and their own higher return. Because the firm has issued a promise to bondholders to pay them $8,100 before it pays a cent to stockholders, the risk has increased that stockholders will receive considerably less than $1,900.

For example, if the price of bread were to fall from $1 to 98.5 cents per loaf, the total revenue of the firm would decline to $98,500. Material and labor would consume $90,000 of the total, and the bondholders would have a priority claim on $8,100. This would leave only $400 for dividends to stockholders, for a 4-percent return on their $10,000 investment. If the firm had financed completely with equity, the same revenue shortfall would have left stockholders with $8,500, or an 8.5-percent return.

Leverage has increased the impact that possible price changes can have on the range of possible returns to the firm and on stockholders' income. The magnitude of the range of returns possible for stockholders provides a crude measure of risk.

Whether stockholders are content to hold the equity of Whole Wheat when it is leveraged 9 : 1 depends crucially, let us suppose, on their expectations about the price of bread. In our scenario, stockholders believe that the price of bread will be either 99.9 cents or 98.1 cents per loaf, and they view the two prices as equally likely.

In Table 2.2a and b, we compare the return to stockholders of an unleveraged Whole Wheat given the two possible prices, with that of a Whole Wheat leveraged

Table 2.2   WHOLE WHEAT, INC.

Price of Bread	Total Revenue	Income after Labor and Material
$0.999	$99,900	$9,900
$0.981	98,100	8,100

Funding Scenarios:

a. Equity Funding Only

Price	Payment/Return to Bondholders	Income/Return to Stockholders
$0.999	—	$9,900 or 9.9%
$0.981	—	$8,100 or 8.1%
	Avg. return	9.0%

b. Leveraged 9:1, 9% Bonds

Price	Payment/Return to Bondholders	Income/Return to Stockholders
$0.999	$8,100 or 9%	$1,800 or 18%
$0.981	$8,100 or 9%	$0 or 0%
	Avg. return	9.0%

c. Leveraged 9:1, 8% Bonds

Price	Payment/Return to Bondholders	Income/Return to Stockholders
$0.999	$7,200 or 8%	$2,700 or 27%
$0.981	$7,200 or 8%	$900 or 9.0%
	Avg. return	18%

in the ratio of 9 : 1. The stockholder of the unleveraged corporation earns 9.9 percent when the price is 99.9 cents and 8.1 percent when the price is 98.1 cents. Since the two prices are equally likely, he expects to earn a simple average of these two returns, or 9.0 percent. The stockholder of a leveraged Whole Wheat will earn 18 percent if bread prices are 99.9 cents and nothing if bread prices are 98.1 cents. The expected return is still 9.0 percent.

Stockholders therefore will be just as willing to hold the equities of either the leveraged or the unleveraged Whole Wheat if all they care about is expected rate of return. In Table 2.2a and b, the expected rate of return is 9 percent for all investors, including the bondholders. Investors who are indifferent among securities that have the same expected payoff are called **risk neutral.** Risk-neutral investors don't care whether they receive a sure 9-percent return or an expected 9 percent return whose realization can vary between 8.1 and 9.9 percent or between 0 and 18 percent.

Risk-averse investors, on the other hand, require a higher expected rate of return to hold a security that has an uncertain payoff than they would to hold a security paying a certain return, such as a bond. Risk-averse investors therefore will not hold an equity contract having an expected return of 9 percent when they can obtain a certain 9-percent return by holding a bond. We assume from here on that investors are risk averse unless otherwise indicated.

THE IMPORTANCE OF THE DECISION TO FINANCE WITH BONDS OR EQUITY

No matter whether the price of bread is 99.9 cents or 98.1 cents per load, the expected return on Whole Wheat's PPE is 9 percent. Regardless of how the firm finances itself, investors overall can expect to earn only 9 percent on their investment. Yet it is often believed that funding a firm's expansion with debt or issuing debt to replace equity raises a firm's stock price.

We frequently read in the business section of the daily newspaper that a company is undergoing a leveraged buyout. A **leveraged buyout** is a transaction in which a group of investors, often the management of the firm itself, borrows money to purchase shares from the firm's stockholders. This transaction increases the firm's leverage ratio because former stockholders are replaced by bondholders.

Effect of Leveraged Buyouts on Expected
Shareholder Return

An announcement of a leveraged buyout typically causes an immediate increase in the price of a firm's stock. In the Whole Wheat example, an increase in leverage causes the risk borne by the shareholders to rise. This should increase the required rate of return on the firm's stock. Yet, if expected dividends remain the same, an increase in share price implies that the expected return on the equity has declined. (Explain why.)

Since leverage increases stockholder risk, the stock price cannot rise if dividends are expected only to remain constant. A rise in share price thus indicates that the market must expect dividends to increase after the leveraged buyout. Many commentators have concluded that increasing leverage generally raises stockholder return by more than the amount required to compensate for the increased risk. We will examine the validity of this statement in a situation of well-functioning financial markets.

Can Stockholders Raise Their Return by Leveraging?

Can management issue debt and purchase equity to raise the price of its stock? Suppose that Whole Wheat is presently financed with equity only and that it pays an expected return of 9 percent to its stockholders, as in Table 2.2a. The managers decide to try to fund an expansion by selling bonds promising an 8-percent return. Let us presume that they can earn the same 9 percent on their investment in additional bread-making capacity as they make on their current investment.

If investors are risk neutral, management would find no one to buy bonds for 8 percent. Stockholders of the unleveraged corporation earn an expected return of 9 percent; in a risk-neutral situation, the certain return on bonds must equal the expected returns on equities.

More interesting possibilities arise if we assume that investors are risk averse. Suppose that after the bond-financed expansion, a firm is leveraged at a 9 : 1 ratio, as in Table 2.2c. If management can sell bonds promising an 8-percent return, then expected return on equity will increase to 18 percent—exactly twice the return expected when bonds paid 9 percent (Table 2.2b). If stockholders require less than an 18-percent expected return on their investment, then the price of the stock will rise, and current stockholders will gain from the increased leverage.

To determine the feasibility of the management's financing proposal, we must consider the current situation in the capital market. The **capital market** is the market for all financial securities collectively. Suppose that all the firms in existence make bread. These firms are in every way identical to Whole Wheat except for their leverage ratios. There is no possibility to default on bonds, so all bonds pay 8 percent regardless of the firm's leverage ratio. To have default-free bonds, no firm can finance only with bonds, and the price of bread cannot fall below the price at which the most leveraged firm would just be able to meet its payments to bondholders.

Suppose that risk-averse investors generally want to hold bonds and equity in a ratio of 4 : 1 and that bonds and equity are supplied in that desired ratio by all the other identical firms, taken as a group, except Whole Wheat.

Equity, on average, must have an expected return of 13 percent, given an overall leverage ratio of 4 : 1. As we saw in the case of Whole Wheat, not all equity pays

13 percent—returns for the individual firm depend on the leverage ratio of the firm. A particular firm's leverage does not matter to the household, however. Because all firms' securities are perfect substitutes and the economy-wide leverage ratio is 4 : 1, households can buy a few shares of equity of each of the firms in the economy and expect a 13-percent return on their entire investment.

Whole Wheat's Decision Upsets Equilibrium

Whole Wheat has upset this equilibrium by attempting to finance itself at a ratio of 9 : 1. This has created a surplus of bonds in the market and a scarcity of equity. The surplus of bonds should cause their price to fall (their interest rate yield to rise). Equity prices, on the other hand, should go up (their expected yield falls). Thus it is more expensive for firms to fund with bonds and cheaper to fund with stock. The only way Whole Wheat can gain from increasing its leverage ratio is to surprise the market. They must sell their bonds before bond prices fall—that is, before the market realizes that there are too many bonds.

Arbitragers, however, are quick to react to an expected change in the prices of stocks and bonds. As soon as they realize that Whole Wheat intends to sell bonds, they go into action. They sell bonds and buy stock to try to capture profits before bond prices fall and stock prices rise. Whole Wheat finds that it cannot make a profit for its stockholders because bond prices will have fallen before it comes to market with its new issue.

Suppose that Whole Wheat proceeds with its bond sale anyway. Now the economy has a higher overall leverage ratio than the desired one of 4 : 1. There are still too many bonds. Thus it appears cheaper to finance with stock than with bonds. Some bread firms will buy back their own bonds and sell stock, decreasing their leverage ratios. Of course, with active arbitragers, this process is also immediate, and no bread firm can gain from the lower bond prices.

The economy-wide leverage ratio of 4 : 1 will be restored. All this can happen because the market does not care which firm adjusts its position because all securities of all firms are perfect substitutes.

Note that we are using the term *arbitrage* here in an apparently different way from the definition at the beginning of the chapter. Arbitragers are selling bonds and buying stock rather than selling the same security in two different markets. However, the basic process is the same.

The underlying security in the transaction is the assets of the bread company. Any debt-to-equity ratio a firm chooses can be "undone" by an arbitrager by merely purchasing that combination of debt and equity issued by the firm. This pool of securities must trade at the same price as a pool of securities of any other bread company as long as the pool represents the leverage ratio of that firm. If Whole Wheat's securities sell at a higher price, an arbitrager will sell that pool and buy the pool of another identical firm: He buys where the price is low and simultaneously sells where it is high.

The Leverage Decision When Firms Have Different Assets

So far we have assumed that all firms are identical. This assumption has further permitted us to assume that all equities and all bonds, respectively, are perfect substitutes in investors' portfolios. A financial asset is a **perfect substitute** for another financial asset if an investor is indifferent between holding either one when the two are selling for the same price. If they are selling at different prices, investors will prefer the cheaper one, and no one will buy the more expensive one. Thus financial assets that are perfect substitutes must sell at the same price. If all firms have assets exactly identical to those of Whole Wheat, investors are indifferent about which firm's equity or bonds they hold.

Now, however, we relax the assumption of identical firms and replace it with the assumption that all investors have equal access to financial markets. This implies that any investors, even individuals, can buy all Whole Wheat's bonds and stocks by issuing liabilities of their own in any leverage ratio they choose. (The assumption that everyone has equal access is, of course, unrealistic, but later in this chapter we will describe some very real investors who most likely do have equal access.) Thus, whatever leverage ratio Whole Wheat chooses, individual investors can undo this leverage ratio by buying all the securities and financing the purchase with a different leverage ratio.

For example, suppose all firms issue only equity, but savers want to hold a ratio of bonds to equity of 4 : 1. Under the assumption of equal access, some investor can buy all the equities and finance this acquisition by selling bonds and equity to savers in the ratio of 4 : 1.

The assumption that all bonds or all equities are not perfect substitutes increases realism. For example, suppose that, in addition to Whole Wheat, the economy consists of the Ocelot Corporation, which manufactures cars, and the Lazidays Corporation, which arranges vacations to Florida. Most consumers will sacrifice new cars and vacations to eat. Thus, in a recession, a period of declining income, the demand for bread will not fall by as much as the demand for new cars and Florida vacations. When incomes decline, some consumers cut back on durables such as cars and refrigerators and luxuries such as vacations. They will cut back less on basic food items than on postponable purchases such as cars.

The net income of Whole Wheat is therefore likely to be more stable in a recession than are the incomes of Ocelot and Lazidays. Investors holding equity will certainly be interested in how a recession affects the net income of the companies whose equities they hold, because this determines the returns they can expect to receive. Shares in Whole Wheat are likely to pay a higher dividend during a recession than those of either Ocelot or Lazidays.

Whole Wheat's Expansion Under Equal Access

Under our previous assumption of identical firms and perfect substitution, one firm could upset the desired mix of equity and debt by increasing leverage in an expansion program. Now, however, because different companies produce different patterns of income, it is evident that one corporation may not be able to convert debt to equity to restore equilibrium as before.

If, however, we replace the perfect substitution assumption with the equal access assumption, we can restore equilibrium. The assumption of equal access means that anyone can buy the securities of any particular firm and finance the purchase by issuing a different combination of stocks and bonds than was issued by the original corporation. The market does not consider the risk of the actual seller of the securities but only the risk of the underlying firm whose securities are being reissued.

Suppose that Whole Wheat's managers again attempt to leverage the firm at a 9 : 1 ratio, which disturbs the market equilibrium of debt to equity. They issue bonds at 8 percent, the going rate on securities paying a definite rate of return. They also try to issue equity with an expected return of less than 18 percent, the expected rate that would absorb the expected net income of the firm (see Table 2.2c).

They believe that they can sell equity at a higher price than required to provide the investor with an 18-percent return because they have created a shortage of equity in the marketplace. Under the equal access assumption, any investor can step in and buy Whole Wheat's bonds and then partially reissue them as equity, earning a capital gain on the difference between the price paid for the bonds and the value of the securities the investor issues. Since everyone would try this game, no one could make a profit. Whole Wheat's very attempt to bring a bond issue to market will stimulate an immediate response to undo the change. In effect, Whole Wheat does not have control over its own leverage ratio.

THE NEED FOR A FINANCIAL INTERMEDIARY

We have made two different assumptions to arrive at the conclusion that leverage ratios do not matter in the overall funding cost of a firm. Both assumptions, however, appear unrealistic. All firms are not identical. Also, most people cannot issue equity in the market to finance the securities they buy.

We can overcome the latter difficulty by introducing a financial intermediary that buys stocks and bonds and reissues them in the ratio desired by investors. A **financial intermediary** is a firm that buys liabilities and/or equities issued by many firms and reissues new liabilities to investors based on the pool of financial assets that it has purchased. These new liabilities are the obligations of the financial intermediary and not of the individual firms whose liabilities and equities make up the assets of the asset pool.

An example of a financial intermediary that purchases the bonds and equities of corporations and issues it own liabilities is a pension fund. Pension funds create liabilities that guarantee investors a fixed income when they retire. This promise is similar to promises made on bonds, but pension payments only begin when the owner retires. The promise of the fixed income is a liability of the pension fund, not of the corporations whose securities it holds as assets. Another example of a financial intermediary that buys corporate stocks and bonds is a life insurance company. Life insurance companies issue liabilities that promise to pay a fixed sum in the event the insured individual dies. Again, the promise of a death benefit is not the liability of the corporations whose securities are held by the life insurance company; it is the liability of the insurance company.

We can consider a financial intermediary called Fairhope that buys securities of a large number of firms in the economy. Based on this pool of assets, it issues its own bonds and equity in the ratios demanded by investors. Fairhope has assets of $100 billion and has existed for over 100 years. It has earned enough credibility that it has equal access to financial markets. That is, it can buy the securities of individual firms and reissue them in proportion to the demands of individual investors. Individual investors cannot do this because they do not have the credibility of Fairhope.

Fairhope buys all the securities issued by each of the firms in which it invests, so its total return on that firm's securities is unaffected by the leverage ratio that the firm chooses. For example, recall that when the price of bread is $1, Whole Wheat earns a total return of 10 percent on its $100,000 of assets. If the investor buys all its securities, it does not matter in which proportion Whole Wheat issues debt or equity. The total return must be 10 percent. Thus the investor—whether an individual or a financial intermediary—will never pay more for Whole Wheat's liabilities and equity than would be needed to earn an expected return of 10 percent.

Of course, if Fairhope could buy a combination of Whole Wheat's debt and equity at a price with a greater expected return than 10 percent, it would quickly do so. Competition among financial intermediaries would ensure that a return of greater than 10 percent would be very short-lived.

Financial intermediaries thus are positioned to act as arbitragers if the prices of bonds and equities get out of line. If Fairhope buys Whole Wheat's securities for a low price so that they have an expected return of more than 10 percent and then turns around and sells them to investors at a higher price to yield an expected return of only 10 percent, it is acting as an arbitrager. It buys cheap in one market and sells dear in another.

Financial intermediaries would never have to decide on Whole Wheat's appropriate leverage ratio. They produce the public's preferred debt-to-equity ratio on the liability side of their balance sheets, and this ratio is independent of the form in which any corporation chooses to issue its liabilities. *Thus the leverage ratio of the firm does not affect the firm's overall funding costs.* As mentioned earlier, the proposition that the financing costs of an individual firm are independent of its leverage ratio

is known as the *Modigliani-Miller theorem,* named for the two economists who first
presented the arbitrage argument using the equal access assumption as proof.[1]

LIQUIDITY AND THE PRESERVATION
OF CAPITAL VALUE

Liquid markets are those in which investors can sell at close to the last transaction
price. Market arbitrage prevents the price of bonds and equities from changing
dramatically when an individual firm increases or decreases its leverage ratio. Therefore, the activities of arbitragers make markets more liquid.

Cash, of course, is the most liquid instrument in terms of the unit of account
because it is the physical representation of the unit of account, and its price never
varies in terms of the unit of account. Assets such as stocks may trade in liquid
markets, but they cannot be as liquid as cash because their price changes in terms
of the unit of account. We refer to the price of a financial asset as its **capital value.**
As we saw earlier, the price of a financial asset is determined by discounting the
income stream associated with it at a given interest rate. This process is called
capitalizing the income stream. The resultant price is an asset's **capital value.**

The liquidity of a financial asset depends on the extent to which it maintains
its capital value relative to the unit of account.

The Maturity of a Bond and Liquidity

An investor who buys a perpetuity for $1,000 must give up an equivalent amount
of potential consumption. If the interest rate is 9 percent, the investor receives an
income of $90 per year as compensation. Suppose that the investor believes that the
interest rate has an equal probability of rising to 10 percent, declining to 8 percent,
or remaining the same.

Earlier in this chapter we showed that if interest rates rise, the price of a long-
term bond goes down by more than the price of a short-term bond. Thus, if interest
rates rise, the investor will experience a **capital loss** on his bond, which is a fall in
the market value of an asset from the price an investor paid for it. The investor
could reduce the risk of a capital loss on his investment by buying a bond with a
very short maturity rather than a perpetuity. Since liquidity is defined as the pres-
ervation of capital value, an investor can improve the liquidity of his portfolio by
holding short-term assets.

---

1. They published their proof in 1958. In a 1978
article on the Modigliani-Miller theorem, Eugene
Fama showed that the equal access assumption could
be replaced with the assumption that the securities
of all firms are perfect substitutes.

Commercial Paper

Firms can choose to issue long-term bonds or short-term bills, just as they choose to issue equity or debt. Thus firms can and do directly create liquid securities. The short-term debt issued by corporations is known as **commercial paper.** Typically, commercial paper has a maturity of 3 months, although some companies issue paper with a maturity of only a few days. The interest rate on commercial paper is fixed for the length of the bill, but because the instrument is short term, the effect of interest rate changes on its value is minimal. Again, their choice of a funding strategy will not affect their funding costs.

Risk Aversion and Liquidity

The behavior of the investor concerned with the capital value of his securities is similar to the behavior of the risk-averse investor concerned with returns. Although the expected value of his investment remains $1,000, no matter whether he buys a bill or a perpetuity, the risk-averse investor whose objective is to maintain capital value prefers to hold short-term assets.

The situation is different for the risk-averse investor concerned with income. If this investor buys a short-term bill, she subjects herself to interest rate risk. If the interest rate rises to 10 percent, she receives $100 on a bill purchased for $1,000. If the interest rate falls to 8 percent, she receives only $80. The risk-averse investor concerned with income should prefer the long-term bond that "locks in" a fixed return of $90. If she "locks in" income, however, she takes the risk of uncertain capital value.

From our discussion we can conclude that one aspect of liquidity is the maintenance of capital value certainty rather than income certainty. Thus a bill is a more liquid instrument than a bond. An investor must decide whether capital value or income is more important to him or her. In the next chapter we consider why some investors prefer capital value certainty to income certainty.

EXPLANATIONS OF LEVERAGE

Arbitrage, as we have seen, has the effect of making the firm indifferent about its capital structure, and it increases the liquidity of financial markets. Yet leveraged buyouts have been popular in recent years, and they generally result in an increase in the stock price of the firm bought out. Does this mean that arbitrage does not work and that financial markets are not liquid?

The answer lies elsewhere. Investors can benefit from changes in the financial structure of a firm for reasons different from those considered in our discussion of the Modigliani-Miller theorem. These benefits cannot be eliminated through arbitrage, so gains from changes in leverage cannot be attributed to the failure of arbitrage. Economists have begun to think about the benefits of different financial structures in terms of a body of theory known as the **principal-agent problem.**

The Principal-Agent Problem and Leverage

A principal-agent problem arises whenever one individual acts on behalf of another. The person hiring an individual to act on his or her behalf is the principal, and the agent is the person hired. When you sell a house through a real estate agent, you are the principal and the realtor is the agent.

If Whole Wheat is a large corporation, it is likely that its stockholders do not work for the firm. The day-to-day decision-making functions are in the hands of managers, and major decisions are in the hands of the board of directors. These individuals act as agents for the stockholders.

Because stockholders have their own lives to worry about, they cannot monitor the activities of managers and boards of directors carefully. Thus managers and boards have some leeway to act on their own private behalf rather than on behalf of the stockholders. For example, suppose the firm has a very good year financially. The managers may claim that this performance is due to their astuteness, and they pay themselves a large bonus. However, casual scrutiny of the evidence indicates that, in fact, success was caused by a general upturn in the economy. The stockholders do not know this, so the managers have paid themselves more than they are worth.

In a bad year, the management loudly proclaims that the generally dim economic environment has negatively affected the firm's performance. Since the downturn is economy wide, the managers cannot be blamed for the problem—so they declare themselves a large bonus anyway.

Leverage Control

In our example, investors can reduce the risk that managers will pay themselves too much by demanding that Whole Wheat finance itself with a high leverage ratio. Whole Wheat must pay bondholders their contracted rate of return or go into bankruptcy. Even in a bad year, the firm must make its usual payment to bondholders. Managers will not be able to declare themselves a large bonus because a large portion of the revenues are already committed to making interest payments.

Such a strategy will not reduce bonuses in good years, but it will ensure that the managers cannot overpay themselves in bad years. If they do, the firm will go into bankruptcy, and the bondholders or, more likely, their court-appointed representatives can prevent the bonuses from being paid.

Of course, there is a cost to this strategy. Suppose that management actually

Box 2.3

The Impact of Leverage on Management Control

The impact of leverage in controlling management behavior is illustrated by an announcement in early January 1991 by Occidental Petroleum to narrow the focus of its business through sales of assets and elimination of debt that had financed the assets to be sold.

Over the years, Occidental Petroleum had entered a number of businesses far from its original petroleum base that were collectively losing $53 million per year. These included a beef and pork packer, a petrochemical joint venture with the Soviet Union, Arabian horse breeding, a Black Angus cattle ranch, and a film production company. These businesses had been financed with debt, a sure sign that the market was not convinced that they represented a profitable expansion. The sum total of the assets announced for sale equaled $3 billion.

The stock market greeted the announcement with a 25-cent increase in the price of Occidental's stock, to $17.625. This indicates that the market does not always welcome an increase in leverage; sometimes it prefers the reverse. In this case, leverage served its purpose—it had forced a sale of unprofitable assets. If Occidental is serious about narrowing the focus of its business, it will be welcomed back into the equity market.

did perform very well in a bad year. If it had not performed so superlatively, the firm would have lost much more than it did. If these good managers cannot receive compensation for their efforts, they might quit and join a less leveraged firm. Such possibilities lead to differing leverage ratios across firms. For example, management teams that are trusted by investors will manage firms with low leverage ratios. See Box 2.3.

Leverage in Japanese Corporations

In a recent book, James C. Abegglen and George Stalk, Jr., attempted to account for the fact that some Japanese corporations have outperformed their American counterparts.[2] As one explanation, they argue that the willingness of Japanese corporations to use debt increases the amount of funds available for expansion. They term this strategy "aggressive financial policy" and contend that it is a cheaper way to fund growth than the alternative of equity financing and retained earnings. We

2. James C. Abegglen and George Stalk, Jr., *Kaisha, The Japanese Corporation,* Basic Books, New York, 1985.

will consider an example, drawn from this book, of how a small competitor can use leverage to gain on the dominant firm in its industry. We will show, however, that agency theory readily explains the paradox that the authors perceive in Japanese financial structure.

Aggressive financial policies are often an important element of the strategy used by one competitor to outperform another. Such companies as Amerada Hess, Georgia Pacific, and Dow Chemical all changed and improved their competitive positions in large part because of aggressive financial strategies. The effect of differences in financial policies on the ability to grow aggressively can be appreciated from a study of the example in Table 2.3. Call one company "Leader." Call the smaller competitor "Follower." Leader is much larger in total sales than Follower. However, Follower is growing twice as fast as Leader.

The two companies have very different financial policies. Leader seeks high profit margins, pays healthy dividends, and scorns debt. Follower is a price cutter, with low margins, no dividends, and high leverage. Leader is very strong financially and has no debt on its balance sheet. Follower, having a debt-to-equity ratio of 2 : 1, is highly leveraged. To maintain growth, Leader must increase its asset base 15 percent per year and Follower must increase it 30 percent per year. Like all other companies, Leader and Follower must pay for the increase in assets using funds generated internally or obtained from outside the corporation.

Leader finances its growth entirely with retained earnings. Leader sets prices high enough to achieve after-tax profits of 15 billion yen. Half these profits are earmarked for dividends, leaving 7.5 billion yen, the amount required for the asset base of Leader to grow by 15 percent. Because of Leader's no-debt policy, no additional funds are borrowed to expand the asset base faster than 15 percent per year.

Follower practices much more aggressive financial policies. The combination of deep price discounts and slightly higher manufacturing costs yields a pre-tax operating margin of 37 percent for Follower compared with 60 percent for Leader. The operating margin of Follower is reduced by interest charges on its debt, and the resulting after-tax profit margin is 14 percent compared with 30 percent for Leader. The 1 billion yen of after-tax profits that Follower earns is not enough to increase the asset base by 30 percent, so the company elects to pay no dividend and to borrow 2 billion yen so that its asset base can be expanded at the desired rate of 30 percent per year. Follower's debt-to-equity ratio remains at 2 : 1.

The aggressive financial policies of Follower have created significant competitive advantages. Follower is discounting prices 28 percent off those of Leader despite a 13-percent manufacturing cost disadvantage. Of course, Follower cannot pay dividends and must borrow heavily, but it is growing twice as fast as Leader. If unchecked, it could eventually emerge as the real leader, with lower costs and potentially higher profits.

In the late 1970s and early 1980s, the average Japanese company pursued financial policies that made possible a sustained growth rate almost 25 percent higher than its U.S. counterpart, despite the lower profitability of the Japanese economy. The average rate of return on net assets for a U.S. manufacturer is about 12 percent.

Table 2.3 GROWTH STRATEGIES FOR LEADER VERSUS FOLLOWER

	Leader	Follower
Market share (%)	50	10
Growth rate per year (%)	15	30
Debt-to-equity ratio	0:1	2:1
Debt (¥ billions)	0	6.7
Equity (¥ billions)	50	3.3
Total assets (¥ billions)	50	10.0
Required reinvestment (¥ billions)	7.50	3.00
Sales (¥ billions)	50.00	7.17
Cost of goods sold (¥ billions)	20.00	4.50
Operating margin (¥ billions)	30.00	2.67
Less interest (¥ billions)	0	0.67
Less tax (¥ billions)	15.00	1.00
Profit (¥ billions)	15.00	1.00
Dividends (¥ billions)	7.50	0
Retained earnings	7.50	1.00
New debt (¥ billions)	0	2.00
Available for growth (¥ billions)	7.50	3.00

Source: Adapted from James C. Abegglen and George Stalk, Jr., *Kaisha, The Japanese Corporation,* Basic Books, New York, 1985, p. 155.

This compares with an 8-percent average for a Japanese manufacturer. The average debt-to-equity ratio for a U.S. manufacturer is 0.6 : 1, but for a Japanese manufacturer, it is 1.6 : 1. On average, U.S. and Japanese manufacturers pay out about the same percentage of their profits in dividends, and the U.S. company pays an average 6.5 percent after-tax interest rate, compared with 3.5 percent for the Japanese company. The combined effect of these differences is that the average Japanese manufacturer can grow about 10 percent per year without changing its financial structure, whereas the average U.S. manufacturer can grow at only 8 percent per year.

The authors draw the following conclusion: We cannot ignore the paradox in the application of aggressive financial policies. Although successful companies are most able to assume debt, it is usually the marginal competitor that uses the greatest leverage and incurs the highest financial risk. The marginal competitor often sets debt and dividend policies to compensate for an underlying and uncorrected cost disadvantage so as to defend its marginally competitive position.

Under principal-agent theory, however, the behavior of the weak competitor is not a paradox at all. Weak firms must use the debt market because they have no track record to provide investors with confidence that their managements can be

Table 2.4 EQUITY TO ASSET RATIO OF JAPANESE MANUFACTURING FIRMS

Year End	
1981	22.7%
1982	24.1
1983	26.2
1984	27.6
1985	29.6
1986	31.5
1987	33.1
1988	34.7

Source: Bank of Japan, *Economic Statistics Annual,* various issues.

trusted. Since they cannot sell stock, they sell bonds. Then, if the weak competitor fails, its bondholders can always force the company to reorganize under the bankruptcy laws or sell the firm's assets to the strong firms in the industry.

If Japanese corporations as a whole have historically performed well enough to instill confidence in investors, we should observe a decline in their leverage ratios (which would be the same as an increase in the ratio of net worth to total assets). In Table 2.4 we consider the ratio of net worth to total assets of Japanese manufacturing firms, as reported by the Bank of Japan, for an 8-year period. Since this ratio shows a steady increase, we can reasonably conclude that the leverage of Japanese companies is declining.

Thus, assuming that the popular notion that Japanese corporations are formidable competitors is correct, it appears that as firms become strong, they eschew high leverage. Leverage is not regarded as a "cheap" source of finance; the Japanese record suggests that leverage decisions instead are based on investor willingness (or unwillingness) to give management freedom to make its own decisions.

If leverage were a "cheap" source of funding for Japanese corporations, the Modigliani-Miller theorem that financial structure does not matter for the cost of capital would be inconsistent with the evidence. However, principal-agent theory provides us with an alternative explanation that is consistent with the facts. See Box 2.4.

Principal-Agent Theory and Market Liquidity

Effective market arbitrage is an important condition for establishing liquidity in financial markets. We have seen that effective arbitrage makes the leverage ratio of

Box 2.4

The Risk of Aggressive Use of Debt

In the late 1980s, the largest banks in the United States supported the market for leveraged buyouts by making loans to purchasers of companies. These loans became known as highly leveraged transactions, or HLTs. By 1990, bank shareholders and federal agencies responsible for the safety and soundness of banks, such as the Federal Reserve, became wary of the large bank exposure to clients with lots of debt and very little equity. Banks with particularly high exposure included Security Pacific in Los Angeles, Bank of New York, Bank of Boston, and Continental Bank in Chicago.

During 1990, these banks and others with high exposure, responding to shareholder and regulatory pressure, began reducing their HLTs relative to their total assets. As a result, the market funding for leveraged buyouts shrank markedly. According to the Loan Pricing Corporation, new issues of HLTs shrank from $25 billion in 1989 to $15 billion in 1990. This, of course, reduced the number of leveraged buyout deals, indicating that the market sees risk as well as rewards in debt finance.

Source: Adapted from *American Banker,* December 5, 1990, pp. 1 and 19.

a firm inconsequential for its cost of capital. Yet we observe that the leverage ratio is an important method by which investors can control the behavior of managers.

Just as investors concern themselves with the trustworthiness of managers, our fictional financial intermediary that buys all the securities issued by a firm is concerned about the financial structure of the firms whose securities it purchases. Does this concern hamper market liquidity?

The financial intermediary can no longer perform the way we assumed in a perfect Modigliani-Miller world of no transactions costs. A firm's financial leverage does make a difference in its funding costs. This fact reduces the ability of arbitragers to buy equities when a firm such as Whole Wheat disturbs market equilibrium by increasing its leverage ratio. Arbitragers must now determine whether Whole Wheat's managers are responding to investor demand to reduce their decision-making freedom.

Thus the shadow of principal-agent theory falls across financial markets, increasing uncertainty and reducing liquidity. However, the economy receives something in return for the reduction in liquidity. It receives better management of corporate assets. It also designs additional institutions to bring liquidity back into the marketplace. These institutions are banks.

CONCLUSION

We have begun to develop a framework for understanding how capital markets function and how financial intermediaries might improve the efficiency of capital markets. We began by describing a world in which the financial decisions of a corporation are of no concern to its investors and in which financial intermediaries are unnecessary. This is the world of the Modigliani–Miller theorem. We then created a need for a financial intermediary to maintain the conditions under which the financial structure of a firm is of no consequence to its investors.

Next, we defined liquidity and discussed how the financial intermediary we created increases market liquidity. Investors who want to remain liquid will try to preserve the capital value of their investments, but doing this requires the risk-averse investor to accept income risk. We consider the choice between risky capital value and risky income in the next chapter.

Finally, we indicated that financial intermediaries should make it impossible to predict the capital structure of individual firms. In fact, however, many observers have noted that market leaders primarily issue stock and followers issue bonds. We introduced principal-agent theory to account for this apparent anomaly. We shall see principal-agent theory again when we consider the role of financial intermediaries in policing the performance of the firms to which they lend.

KEY TERMS

stocks	return
bonds	capital gain
profit	leverage
dividends	risk neutral
arbitrage	risk aversion
Modigliani-Miller theorem	leveraged buyout
maturity date	capital market
interest rate	perfect substitutes
present value	financial intermediary
discounting	capital value
principal	capitalizing
coupon bond	capital loss
balance sheet	commercial paper
T account	principal-agent problem
bankruptcy	

EXERCISES

1. The Modigliani-Miller theorem makes an assertion about how the world operates. The assertion is that the value of a firm's assets is independent of how the assets are financed. Show with an arbitrage argument how this assertion makes the firm's financial decisions irrelevant for the value of the firm.

2. Professor Eugene Fama has shown that if firms can go bankrupt, current bondholders and stockholders have an interest in how the firm finances its expansion. That is, the marginal finance decision can lead to capital gains for one group or the other. Why do you suppose this is so? (*Hint:* Unlike the example in the chapter, the price of bonds is now affected by the leverage ratio.)

3. Does the possibility that one group of investors can gain relative to another from marginal funding decisions disprove the assertion that the firm's financial decisions are irrelevant for the value of the firm?

4. Why do you suppose bond issues sometimes have covenants prohibiting the issuer to increase the leverage ratio of the firm?

5. As of this writing, New York City is in (another) fiscal crisis. It faces a $300 million deficit in the current fiscal year. If its deficit exceeds $100 million, the state must take control of its finances. This requirement is a state law, and it is also written into an agreement with the city's bondholders. Why do you suppose the bondholders insisted in writing this covenant into the bond agreement when it was already a state law?

6. It is often argued that taxes are a major reason why the Modigliani-Miller theorem does not hold in the real world. Corporate profits are subject to a corporate income tax, and interest expense is not. Both interest and dividends are subject to personal income taxes. Currently, in the United States, the corporate tax rate and the marginal personal income tax rate are almost equal (34 versus 33 percent). Thus, if a firm funds with equity and pays some of its income in dividends, it is possible that its investors are taxed more heavily than if it had funded with debt. Explain why, if stock returns are taxed more heavily than bond returns, the value of the assets is no longer independent of the funding decision of the firm.

7. In a Modigliani-Miller world, how would firms fund themselves if, in fact, equity were subject to a higher tax rate than debt?

8. If a risky bond and a safe bond have the same market value and the same face value, what must be the relationship between the yearly payment that each bond promises to the investor? If market interest rates rise leaving risk premiums unchanged (that is, the spread between the yield on the risky and safe bond), which bond will suffer the largest decline in market value and why?

9. In late 1990, the interest rate on long-term, mildly risky corporate bonds was 10.43 percent, whereas the interest rate on high-quality corporate bonds was 9.05 percent. At year-end 1989, these two types of bonds yielded 9.39 and 8.86 percent, respectively. Thus in 1990 the spread was 1.4 percentage points, and in 1989 it was 0.96 percentage points. Why do you suppose the spread increased between 1989 and 1990?

10. Explain why, in a world of principal-agent problems, the value of the firm is not independent of how it is financed.

11. It is often argued that a corporation's long bonds are riskier than its commercial paper. Explain why this assertion is consistent with principal-agent theory.

12. If forcing a firm into the debt market is a way to control the behavior of unreliable or untested management, why do you suppose it is difficult for new firms to get a loan?

13. Suppose a firm that currently has $500 million in equity and $500 million in bonds outstanding decides to issue an additional $100 million in equity. The Fama argument in exercise 2 implies that the bondholders would obtain a capital gain. Under principal-agent theory, is it possible for them to experience a capital loss as a result of the new issue?

14. Under the equal access assumption, a firm's debt and equity are perfect substitutes. The financial intermediary having equal access simply does not care which security the firm issues. As long as it buys a firm's debt and equity in the same proportion that it is issued, it can even protect itself from Fama's redistribution problem. (Why?) Why can this intermediary not play the same role if there is a principal-agent issue?

15. Why does the existence of principal-agent problems reduce the liquidity of securities markets? (Why can't the arbitrager trade to keep the prices of debt and equity from affecting the value of the firm?)

FURTHER READING

Coase, Ronald H., "The Nature of the Firm," *Economica* (Nov. 1937), pp. 386–405.

Easterbrook, Frank H., "Two Agency-Cost Explanations of Dividends," *American Economic Review*, Vol. 74, No. 4 (Sept. 1984), pp. 650–658.

Fama, Eugene F., "The Effects of a Firm's Investment Decisions on the Welfare of its Security Holders," *American Economic Review*, Vol. 68 (June 1978), pp. 272–284.

Fama, Eugene F., "Agency Problems and the Theory of the Firm," *Journal of Political Economy*, Vol. 88 (April 1980), pp. 288–307.

Miller, Merton H., "Debt and Taxes," *Journal of Finance,* Vol. 32, No. 2 (May 1977), pp. 261–275.

Modigliani, Franco, and Merton H. Miller, "The Cost of Capital, Corporate Finance, and the Theory of Investment," *American Economic Review,* Vol. 74, No. 4 (Sept. 1984), pp. 288–307.

C H A P T E R

3

The Demand for Liquid Assets

In Chapter 2 we defined a liquid market as one that can handle a relatively large buy or sell order with a small change in price. We discussed how the interrelationship among prices of different financial instruments contributes to the liquidity of the market for any particular financial instrument.

A liquid asset maintains its value in terms of the unit of account. Therefore, it must trade in a liquid market because no matter what the size of the buy or sell order, the price of the liquid asset measured in terms of the unit of account does not change. However, not all assets that trade in liquid markets are liquid.

For example, the market for General Motors stock may be quite liquid—that is, trading volume can be quite high and the price may not change at all. Nevertheless, the owner of General Motors stock does not own a liquid asset. Over the year extending from August 1989 through August 1990, the price of this stock ranged from $50.50 to $35.50. The high price was over 42 percent above the low price. The price of General Motors stock is not driven by volume alone. It is affected by real events in the economy, such as oil crises, and factors specific to the firm, such as release of the movie *Roger and Me*.

In this chapter we discuss household demand for liquid financial assets. We begin by cataloging which assets in the economy are liquid. Next, we present a "lifecycle" view of why households invest in liquid assets and discuss empirical evidence of household asset holdings. We find that households hold most of their liquid and nonliquid financial assets in the form of liabilities of financial institutions.

Financial institutions can hold the securities of a wider variety of issuers than most individual households could hold separately because they pool the resources of many households. This permits them to achieve gains through diversification. **Diversification** is the holding of securities of many firms to reduce the risk that a decline in the fortunes of any one firm will significantly reduce the value of one's portfolio.

WHAT ARE LIQUID ASSETS?

Liquid assets must be able to weather any economic storm and maintain their value in terms of the unit of account. A particular event that affects asset prices is the rise or fall in interest rates. As we saw in the preceding chapter, the impact of a change in the interest rate on the price of a long-term bond is greater than its impact on the price of a short-term bond.

A long-term bond cannot be considered a liquid asset if there is a possibility that the market interest rate for this bond might fluctuate widely. In the recent past, interest rates on long-term bonds have been somewhat unstable. For example, in 1981, the interest rate on long-term U.S. government bonds was over 13 percent. In 1986, the interest rate on the same bond had fallen to less than 8 percent. In this kind of environment, a long-term bond cannot be a liquid asset because it does not maintain its value in terms of the unit of account.

Money Market Instruments

Short-term debt instruments issued by high-quality borrowers, known as *money market instruments,* are a major source of liquid assets for investors. For example, a 3-month U.S. Treasury bill, which is an obligation of the U.S. government that matures in 3 months, tends to maintain its value when the interest rate changes. This is so because on the date of maturity, the bill returns its face value to the investor. Since that date is relatively close, the bill's value is less affected by changes in the interest rate than is a perpetuity.

For example, assume that a Treasury bill has a face value of $10,000 and has 2 months until maturity. Interest on a Treasury bill is paid by the difference between its price at issuance or when it is purchased and its price at maturity or when it is sold. If the bill were sold with 2 months remaining until maturity, its price would be its value in 2 months discounted back to today. This means that the value of the bill today must reflect the amount of money an individual must invest to obtain $10,000 in 2 months time.

To find the answer to this problem, we call the money to be invested X. It must grow by the current rate of interest for 60 days (2 months) and equal $10,000 at the end of that period. Thus $FV = X(1 + r)^{60/360} = \$10,000$. (Treasury bill prices are based on a 360-day year.) If the interest rate today is 5 percent, the investor must invest $\$10,000/(1.05)^{60/360}$. The value of the bill today is $9,919. If the interest rate were to rise to 10 percent, the value of the bill would be $9,842. The difference in price caused by the rise in interest rates is $77, or a decline of 0.77 percent. Thus, in an uncertain interest rate environment, short-term assets tend to hold their value when interest rates change.

In addition, safe assets are more liquid than risky ones. For example, a U.S. government bond is considered safe because the government is not likely to *default* (fail to pay) on interest and principal. The promises of some corporations to pay interest and principal, on the other hand, are viewed quite skeptically by investors. When the economy faces a good deal of uncertainty, there is a "flight to quality." In these circumstances, the interest rate on risky corporate bonds tends to rise relative to the interest rate on government bonds.

For example, in 1981 when the interest rate on long-term government securities was 13.44 percent, the interest rate on risky corporate bonds was 16.04 percent. In 1987 when the long-term government interest rate was 8.59 percent, the interest rate on risky corporate bonds was 10.58 percent. The government bond experienced an interest rate decrease of 4.85 percentage points, whereas the typical risky corporate bond experienced a decrease of 5.46 percentage points. Larger swings in interest rates imply larger swings in capital value, which make the asset less liquid.

Because stockholders are residual income recipients, the price of a company's stock is more volatile than the price of its bonds. (Recall our discussion in Chapter 2.) In general, stocks are less liquid than bonds, holding the quality of the issuer constant.

Our list of money market instruments includes short-term bills issued by high-quality borrowers other than the U.S. government, such as commercial paper issued by corporations with strong historical records of paying interest and principal on time.

Bank and Thrift Deposits

The deposits issued by bank and thrift institutions are a major source of liquid assets for both businesses and households. They are liquid because they maintain their value in terms of the unit of account and are easily convertible into cash. We begin our discussion of bank and thrift deposits with transaction accounts, the most liquid of all bank and thrift deposits. **Transaction accounts** are deposits that permit the depositor to engage in third-party payments. The most common example of a depositor making use of third-party payment privileges is the writing of a check.

Every month, households receive bills to pay for such services as electricity, telephone, and so on. Typically, they pay these bills by drafting a note indicating that they wish to withdraw funds from their transaction account and transfer those funds to the bank account of the payee, say, the telephone or electric company. This note, usually sent to the payee by mail, is called a **check.** This form of payment is called a **third-party payment** because the household can direct its bank to send funds directly from its account to the bank account of another party.

There are possible alternatives to third-party payment services provided by banks. For example, the household could withdraw funds from its bank in the form of cash to take to the telephone or electric company to settle the monthly bill. Using transaction accounts rather than cash increases the convenience of settling debts in many circumstances.

One measure of the convenience value of transaction accounts is the dollar amount of transaction accounts outstanding in the economy compared with the amount of cash outstanding. In mid-1990, approximately $566 billion was deposited in transaction accounts of individuals, corporations, and partnerships at commercial banks and thrifts in the United States as opposed to $237 billion in currency.

Two major types of transaction accounts exist in the United States—demand deposits and NOW (negotiable order of withdrawal) accounts. The difference between these two types of accounts is primarily a matter of law rather than economic function. By law, banks cannot pay interest on demand deposits, but they are permitted to pay interest on NOW accounts. At midyear 1990, NOW accounts at commercial banks and thrifts equaled $291 billion, whereas demand deposits at commercial banks equaled $274 billion.

You may wonder why anyone would hold a demand deposit when he or she could earn interest by holding a NOW account. The answer, again, lies partly in the law—only households and nonprofit organizations are permitted to hold NOW accounts—but economics also plays a role. As you may expect, banks invest part of the funds placed in transaction deposits in interest-earning assets. The revenues so produced can defray the cost of providing third-party transfers.

If an organization has a large number of transfers relative to the funds in its account, all the revenues produced by investing these funds may be required just to cover the cost of the third-party payments. In fact, large corporations minimize the balances they keep in their demand deposits so that the revenues earned by the bank on these funds just offset the cost of providing third-party payment services to the corporation. This process is part of prudent cash management.

The rest of the deposits in banks and thrifts are known as **nontransaction accounts,** because third-party payments from them are severely restricted or prohibited. The types of nontransaction accounts and their amounts outstanding at commercial banks and thrifts as of midyear 1990 were as follows: money market deposits, $503 billion; savings deposits, $417 billion; small time deposits, $1,150 billion; and large time deposits, $531 billion.

Money market deposits and savings accounts can be converted to cash immediately, either by entering the bank and withdrawing the funds or by withdrawing the funds electronically through an automatic teller machine (ATM). In addition, by federal law, money market deposits permit only six third-party transfers per month, of which only three can be checks.

Savings and money market deposit accounts (MMDA) can be converted to cash at any time, and the depositor can recover full principal and interest earned. Interest rates paid on these accounts fluctuate with other short-term rates in the economy.

Small time deposits, also known as **certificates of deposit (CDs),** are accounts of less than $100,000. They have a specific maturity in contrast to money market and savings deposits, which can be withdrawn at any time. The *maturity,* or time after which the depositor can withdraw principal and interest in full, generally ranges from a period of 6 months to as much as 10 years. However, most small time deposits have a maturity range of 6 months to 1 year. Penalties are attached to early withdrawal, usually in the form of forfeiture of interest.

The long maturities and penalties attached to early withdrawals of some time deposits indicate that banks are in the business of producing assets (from the point of view of investors) that are not liquid because they cannot be immediately converted to cash. The penalty for early withdrawal of a time deposit is stated at the time the depositor purchases the contract. This is in contrast to the uncertainty attached to a bond, in which the penalty for early withdrawal is high if interest rates rise. The depositor knows in advance exactly what return he or she will have on a time deposit.

A depositor can borrow from his or her bank using the time deposit as collateral against the loan. **Collateral** is an asset held by a borrower that a lender can seize if the borrower should default on a loan. Because the time deposit maintains its value despite interest rate movements, it is very secure collateral. The household with such a deposit can borrow at favorable rates if it needs funds.

Large time deposits (also known as CDs) are sold in denominations of $100,000 or more. They are typically purchased by businesses as a short-term investment, and their maturity is generally shorter than that for small time deposits—typically 3 to 6 months. The denomination distinction between large and small time deposits is partially due to law. The federal government insures the principal and interest of deposits up to $100,000 issued by most banks in the United States. (There are a few banks that are not members of the federal insurance system.) We shall provide a detailed description of how deposit insurance affects the banking system in Chapter 19.

Large CDs are often **negotiable**—investors can sell them to third parties as if they were a bond. This does not imply that they are like transaction or savings accounts, because the ability of the seller to recover his or her principal depends on the level of interest rates at the time of sale compared with those at the time of purchase. Large, negotiable CDs are also considered money market instruments.

Small time deposits are not negotiable because transfer of ownership of a CD, whether large or small, places some cost on the investor. The cost of sale is independent of the size of the deposit, so small time deposits would be very expensive to sell relative to the principal in the account. In fact, the cost would be greater than the penalties charged by banks for early withdrawal. Therefore, it is cheaper for a household to bear the penalty for early withdrawal than to attempt to find a buyer for its time deposit.

Money Market Mutual Funds

Money market mutual funds are also liquid assets. They promise to maintain the value of your investment plus accrued interest. If you place $1,000 in a money market account, you can be very certain that your investment will be worth $1,000 plus interest earned, regardless of the performance of the stock and bond markets. To keep this promise, money market mutual funds invest only in liquid assets issued by the government or high-quality corporations. See Box 3.1.

HOUSEHOLD DEMAND FOR LIQUID ASSETS

Households demand liquid assets because the things they buy are denominated in the unit of account. For example, if Emily and Jack Chang decide to buy a car, they know that they must pay for that car in dollars. Since a car represents a relatively large expenditure, it is likely that the Changs will not have enough money from their current salaries to pay for it. Therefore, they will have to save some money before they can buy it. Even if they intend to borrow to buy the car, the lender will demand that they "put up some cash." That is, they must pay for part of the car with their own money.

We will assume that the Changs save some money to buy the car. It is likely that they do not want to forego purchasing the car if the stock market declines or interest rates rise. This is exactly what might happen if they save for the down payment by buying stocks and long-term bonds. (Of course, if they intend to borrow to buy the car, a rise in interest rates may cause them to forgo the car anyway because borrowing becomes more expensive.)

The Changs also may save to meet contingencies such as possible unemployment of one of the family members. Or someone in the family may get sick, creating unexpected expenditures and temporary loss of income during recovery. Or one of the breadwinners might die. The Changs do not want to have to worry about whether the stock and bond markets are up if one of these events should occur.

Inflation Risk

The Changs accumulate liquid assets because they want to maintain their planned lifestyle in the face of contingencies such as sickness or temporary unemployment. The material goods they must purchase to maintain that lifestyle are denominated in units of account, dollars in the United States. Thus, if they hold a bank account, they know that it will maintain a value of whatever they placed in the account plus accrued interest.

Box 3.1

Interest Rate Regulation and the Demand for Deposits

Until April 1986, deposits available to consumers at banks and thrift institutions were subject to interest rate regulation, known as Regulation Q, or Reg Q, by the federal regulatory authorities. For example, in 1982, the permissible interest rate on savings accounts offered by banks was 5.25 percent, and the permissible rate on the same account at thrifts was 5.5 percent. At the same time, Treasury bill rates exceeded 13 percent. Thus consumers who placed their money in a regulated deposit suffered a high opportunity cost—that is, they sacrificed potential income equal to the difference in the two rates multiplied by the size of their deposit.

In the mid-1970s, the marketplace responded to the demands of consumers to hold their liquid assets in a form that paid market interest rates by creating money market mutual funds. These funds hold liquid assets—primarily Treasury bills and commercial paper. They had no minimum maturity and a relatively small minimum balance, usually $2,500.

The regulators responded by creating a deposit that paid an interest rate tied to the 6-month Treasury bill. It had a minimum balance of $10,000 and a minimum maturity of 6 months. Despite this new account, money market funds achieved great popularity. By 1982, they equaled 27 percent of NOW and savings accounts.

In 1983, the regulators again responded by permitting banks to offer money market deposits. It originally had a minimum required balance of $2,500 and was not subject to an interest rate ceiling. The account caught on very quickly, and money market mutual funds fell drastically relative to consumer NOW, MMDA, and savings accounts in 1983, as you can see in the accompanying figure.

In 1986, all interest rate ceilings were removed, but by this time deregulation was a nonevent. As you can see from the figure, the final end to Reg Q had no impact on the market share of money market mutual funds. In fact, by 1989, money market mutual funds were regaining

However, if there is **inflation,** which is a general increase in the prices of all goods and services, it appears that the Changs cannot depend on a liquid asset to preserve their ability to purchase goods in the face of economic uncertainty. For example, if the price level is rising at 5 percent per year, the price of a $10,000 car will rise to $10,500 in that period of time. If the Changs need a 10-percent down payment to purchase the car, having $1,000 in a bank account will leave them $50 short. Thus inflation will have caused their liquid asset to depreciate by $50.

Does this imply that liquid assets do not provide protection in an inflationary period? Fortunately, as we will see in Chapter 5, the interest rate includes an inflation premium. If everyone had known that inflation would be 5 percent, the interest rate would incorporate this expectation. For example, if the interest rate with zero inflation is 5 percent, the Changs would know that to have $1,000 in the bank at

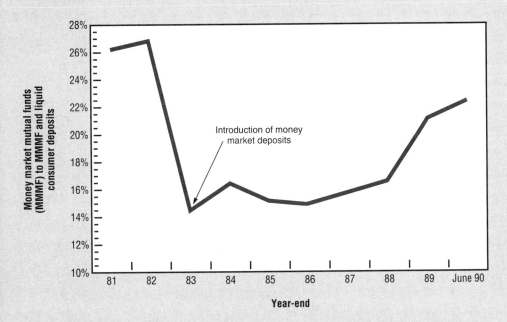

MONEY MARKET MUTUAL FUNDS VS. LIQUID CONSUMER DEPOSITS AT THRIFTS AND BANKS Liquid deposits = NOW, MMDA, savings, and DDAs at thrifts and credit union share draft balances

Source: Federal Reserve Bulletin, Table 1.21 of various issues.

popularity as banks reduced the interest paid on liquid accounts relative to open-market interest rates.

year end, they must place $952.38 in the bank at the beginning of the year. With inflation of 5 percent, they must have $1,050 in the bank in a year's time. Placing the same $952.38 in the bank, they will have $1,050 at year's end if the interest rate rises to 10.25 percent. The additional 5.25 percent is the *inflation premium,* which we derive in Chapter 5.

If the inflation rate is uncertain, an inflation premium cannot guarantee that an asset denominated in dollars will maintain its value. However, because liquid assets have a short maturity, investors can be fairly certain that unexpected inflation will not greatly reduce their buying power. If inflation is greater than expected, a short-term asset can soon be invested at the new interest rate, which includes a larger premium for inflation. Thus only in extremely high and uncertain inflations, called **hyperinflations,** is there large decline in the demand for liquid assets.

Insurance

Many of the contingencies that the Changs would hold liquid assets to provide for can be covered through the purchase of insurance rather than accumulating liquid assets. For example, the Changs can buy health and disability insurance to cover the contingency of sickness of a major breadwinner in the family. Health insurance can cover the doctor bills, and disability insurance can cover the lost income while the family member is sick. The Changs can buy life insurance to protect against the contingency of death. Insurance can substantially reduce the cost of meeting contingencies compared with accumulating liquid assets.

For example, suppose that both Emily and Jack earn $30,000 per year. To meet the remote contingency that one of the breadwinners may die would require a good deal of saving. The faster the family accumulates assets to protect itself against a death, the closer its current standard of living will fall toward the level that would occur if one of the spouses had died already.

Suppose, however, that the family tentatively decides to save $9,000 per year. Then, if a spouse were to die, say 4 years later, savings would have accumulated to $36,000 (plus interest earned), little more than 1 year's income from one of the breadwinners. This certainly would not permit the family to meet future expenditures such as college tuition.

Suppose that the death rate for people in the Changs' age group is only 1 in 1,000. Thus the probability of either one of them dying over the next year is $^1/_{10}$ of 1 percent. Furthermore, their chance of survival each additional year is very high over the next 20 years. Suppose that for people their age, 95 percent are expected to survive through age 55.

Given the small chance that one spouse might die, the price of income in the "death state" is too high if they must sacrifice a dollar now for every dollar of income in case of death. The family would, however, probably be willing to increase savings to some extent to meet the contingency of death. Insurance is the mechanism by which the cost of meeting the contingency of death (or sickness, and so on) can be reduced.

The Insurance Pool

The probability of death occurring to a reasonably healthy 35-year-old is $^1/_{10}$ of 1 percent. By pooling their individual risks of death, the 35-year-olds in the economy could substantially reduce the cost of purchasing income in the death state.

The cost of buying $1 of income in the "death state," or "insured state," should be $^1/_{10}$ of 1 cent plus any administrative costs. To see this, presume that 1,000 people, age 35, each place $1 in a pool. The proceeds will be paid to the survivors of the one individual from the group expected to die during the year. The survivors of that individual will receive $1,000 or 1,000 times more than he or she placed in the pool. Since the cost of purchasing $1,000 in the event of death is $1, the cost of a single dollar after death is $1 divided by 1,000, or $1/10$ of 1 cent.

The household's cost of a dollar's worth of income after a breadwinner's death has fallen from $1 in sacrificed consumption in case of no death to $1/10$ of 1 cent. This difference will raise the amount of insured-state income that the household is willing to purchase considerably above that which it would have provided for through the savings mechanism.

In practice, the insurance decision is more complicated, because insurance must cover both the current year's income if a spouse dies today and income for many years following death. Insurance is therefore likely to be obtained not just in the amount of $30,000—the sum needed to replace one spouse's income for 1 year— but in the amount of $300,000, a sum that would enable the family to make a gradual transition to a different consumption pattern.

The Need for Liquid Assets

Insurance can provide for the same sorts of events for which the household might otherwise accumulate liquid assets. However, there are practical reasons why insurance cannot completely replace the need for liquid assets. Some events are not insurable because of **moral hazard** problems. For example, the Changs cannot buy insurance that would permanently replace their expected future earnings if one of them should lose his or her job. The existence of such insurance would tempt many to try to get fired to enjoy their income without having to work. (States provide unemployment insurance, but it is only for a short period of transition to a new job.)

The problem of moral hazard is often solved by writing insurance contracts with large *deductibles*. That is, the insurance purchaser must pay a specified amount before the insurance company makes a payment on a claim. For example, it is not uncommon for health insurance policies to have a $5,000 deductible.

The fact that insurance does not exist for all contingencies, coupled with the fact that many policies carry large deductibles, implies that households must meet some unexpected expenditures through savings. Since the purpose of savings to meet contingencies is to preserve consumption levels in adverse situations, these savings are likely to be held in the form of liquid assets.

THE DEMAND FOR LIQUID ASSETS OVER THE LIFECYCLE

Liquid assets maintain their value in terms of the unit of account, whereas illiquid assets, such as long-term bonds, experience a price change when the interest rate changes. However, the long-term bond has an advantage over the liquid asset if the investor chooses to fix income in terms of the unit of account rather than capital value. For example, a long-term bond promising to pay $1,000 per year will pay that amount regardless of what happens to interest rates. On the other hand, a $10,000 investment in a money market mutual fund will yield $1,000 if the interest rate is 10 percent but only $500 if the interest rate should fall to 5 percent. We now examine why some households prefer to hold liquid assets rather than fixed-income assets and why most households have at least some demand for liquidity.

During the working years of its life, a family meets its expenses primarily from its wage and salary income. The family typically has not accumulated enough financial wealth with interest and dividends to replace wage and salary income. It holds financial assets and insurance to meet temporary contingencies, such as illness or unemployment, during which it cannot earn wage and salary income. Maintaining the capital value of its assets in order to meet contingencies is more important than maintaining income from its assets. In addition, a family periodically faces large cash demands, such as when it finances a college education or buys a car. To avoid this risk, the family holds liquid assets.

However, as the breadwinners approach retirement, the family's savings goals change somewhat. With the prospect of lower wage and salary income, the family will become more interested in assets that maintain their income value relative to their capital value. The retirement years themselves, of course, are a time when families depend on pension funds and annuities.

Empirical Evidence of Asset Holdings Based on Age of Householder

Table 3.1 shows Federal Reserve survey figures for household financial asset holdings in 1983 by age of householder. (These data are somewhat old because they were obtained from a survey of consumer behavior. However, because the consumer responses correspond to a well-developed body of economic theory, the lifecycle hypothesis, we believe that they are useful.) The Federal Reserve's definition of liquid assets includes bank accounts and U.S. Savings Bonds, a small-denomination bond issued by the U.S. government whose principal does not vary with interest rates. The survey excludes assets not controlled directly by the household, such as claims to a pension or Social Security payments.

In Table 3.1 we see two ratios for liquid assets to total financial assets across age groups. The first is the mean holding of liquid assets relative to the mean holding of total financial assets. The **mean** is merely the arithmetic average of all the responses to the survey. The second measure is the median holding of liquid assets to the median holding of financial assets. The **median** is the value such that half the responses are above it and half below it.

As we see from the table, the ratio of the mean of liquid assets to the mean of

Table 3.1 PERCENT OF FINANCIAL ASSETS HELD AS LIQUID ASSETS BY AGE

Age	Mean	Median
Under 25	74.5%	80.4%
25–34	53.7	79.5
35–44	61.8	80.0
45–54	64.4	80.1
55–64	46.3	79.5
65–74	46.9	84.9
75 and over	71.4	76.2

Source: *Federal Reserve Bulletin,* Sept. 1984, p. 686.

total financial assets generally declines after age 54 and then rises again after age 75. These results are consistent with the normal life pattern. In earlier years, labor income is high relative to financial assets, and the household must protect the capital value of its relatively meager holdings for use in emergencies. Householders older than 75 are likely to face major health uncertainties and other situations that raise the demand for liquid assets. A decline in liquid assets occurs for the 25- to 34-year age group. This occurs because young householders deplete their liquid assets to buy houses.

The ratio of the median of liquid assets to the median of financial assets tells a different story. By this measure, there is no age pattern to asset holding. The reason can be explained by examining the difference between the mean and median as measures of group behavior. The mean, as an arithmetic average, weights large values more heavily than small values. The mean explains more about the behavior of high-wealth individuals. The median treats all values equally.

The difference in the two ratios indicates that many households with relatively low financial wealth do not have many income-producing assets. Later in life, such households depend much more heavily on pensions and Social Security for retirement income than do relatively high-wealth individuals.

Liquid Asset Holdings Across Time.   Table 3.2 describes the historical holdings of illiquid and liquid assets of households. These data include the holdings of pension reserves and insurance reserves as well as the financial assets we have considered, such as stocks, bonds, and bank deposits.

Pension and Insurance Reserves.   Pension and insurance reserves are liabilities of the financial institutions that provide pensions and life insurance. The

Table 3.2 HOUSEHOLD BALANCE SHEET (IN BILLIONS OF DOLLARS)

	Year					
	1965	1970	1975	1980	1985	6/1990
Deposits and money market mutual funds	378.2	543.9	923.4	1577.7	2531.2	3365.8
U.S. govt. securities	78.9	102.1	131.7	259.1	551.9	1026.0
Tax-exempt obligations	36.4	46	68.1	86.9	223.2	345.1
Corporate equities						
Mutual fund shares	34.4	44.5	38.7	52.1	203	587.9
Other corp. equities	600.5	682.7	598.6	1111.3	1685.3	2011.3
Life insurance reserves	105.9	130.7	166.5	216.4	256.7	370.4
Pension fund reserves	155.5	240.8	444.1	916.1	1801.6	2966.5
Other	19.5	30.7	45.1	88.6	159.2	256.2
Corp. and foreign bonds	9	35.6	67.1	59.3	47.6	157.6
Mortgages	42.2	51.5	55.3	107	127.5	233.0
Open-market paper	5.8	11.8	5.7	40.3	58.7	207.7
Total financial assets	1466.3	1920.3	2544.3	4514.8	7645.9	11527.5
Equity in non-corp. bus.	438.8	560.4	935.4	2033.5	2196.3	2371.5

	Percentage Breakdown					
	1965	1970	1975	1980	1985	6/1990
Deposits	25.79%	28.32%	36.29%	34.95%	33.11%	29.20%
U.S. govt. securities	5.38	5.32	5.18	5.74	7.22	8.90
State and local obligations	2.48	2.40	2.68	1.92	2.92	2.99
Corporate equities						
Mutual fund shares	2.35	2.32	1.52	1.15	2.66	5.10
Other corp. equities	40.95	35.55	23.53	24.61	22.04	17.45
Life insurance reserves	7.22	6.81	6.54	4.79	3.36	3.21
Pension fund reserves	10.60	12.54	17.45	20.29	23.56	25.73
Other	1.33	1.60	1.77	1.96	2.08	2.22
Corporate and foreign bonds	0.61	1.85	2.64	1.31	0.62	1.37
Mortgages	2.88	2.68	2.17	2.37	1.67	2.02
Open-market paper	0.40	0.61	0.22	0.89	0.77	1.80
Total	100.0%	100.0%	100.0%	100.0%	100.0%	100.0%

Source: Federal Reserve Flow of Funds as reported through Data Resources, Inc.

Note: Totals do not sum because of rounding.

pension reserve is the present value of the pension income that a pension fund promises to pay to individual employees at their retirement. The **insurance reserve** is the liability an insurance company has accumulated to pay off its expected death claims. The pension and insurance reserves are financial assets for householders because they represent payments to households in the event of death or retirement. Insurance companies and pension funds themselves hold the securities of corporations and the U.S. government as assets against their reserves. Thus, through insurance and pension reserves, households indirectly hold the securities of corporations.

Time-Series Changes in Asset Demand.   According to Table 3.2, there was a major increase in the demand for liquid assets relative to illiquid ones between 1970 and 1975, and after that date, liquid and illiquid asset demand grew at about the same rate. Illiquid assets include U.S. government bonds, state and local bonds, corporate bonds, corporate equities, mortgages, and pension and life insurance reserves.

The major illiquid assets that households directly hold on their balance sheets are corporate equities and mutual funds. **Mutual funds** are pools of securities of many different companies. These pools can be either stocks or bonds. Through mutual funds, households can invest in the stock market and hold the securities of a large number of companies even though their investment is small. A mutual fund does this by pooling the investments of many small investors to buy stocks, bonds, and other assets. Small investors then hold shares in the mutual fund rather than in the securities held by the fund.

The percentage of household assets invested in equities has declined dramatically over the last 20 years, and pension funds have grown rapidly to become the major method of holding illiquid assets. It appears that in the early 1970s households withdrew funds from the stock market and have not returned as direct purchasers.

The large increase in demand for liquid assets in the form of bank deposits as a percentage of financial assets between 1970 and 1975 appears to offset the increase in very illiquid holdings in privately owned businesses over the same period. See Box 3.2.

Investing Through Financial Institutions.   Over 64 percent of household financial investment is held in a financial institution. Bank and thrift deposits are by far the major liquid asset on the household balance sheet, and pension and insurance reserves and mutual funds are now the majority of illiquid assets. One reason households hold their financial assets in the form of the liabilities of financial institutions is that financial institutions can bring the benefits of diversification to the household. For example, a bank can make loans to corporations and individuals that are not liquid because they are risky. However, by holding a large number of loans to different borrowers, banks are able to make these illiquid assets liquid. We now explain how diversification works.

Box 3.2

An Historical Decline in Bank Share of Consumer Assets?

The cover article of the April 22, 1991, issue of *BusinessWeek* was on banks as a dying industry. The article referred to banks' declining share of household assets held at financial institutions, which fell from 34.2 percent in 1960 to 26.6 percent in 1989, as one of the signs of trouble (p. 75). The largest gainers on the list were pension and mutual funds.

BusinessWeek's table overstates the loss of banks' share of financial assets because it includes only assets held with financial intermediaries. As we saw in Table 3.2, the largest decline in share occurred among corporate equities, which fell from 41 to 17 percent of household assets between 1965 and 1990. Recalculating their numbers based on total financial assets (including corporate equities), we find that deposits at commercial banks accounted for 16 percent of household assets in 1960 and 17 percent in June 1990. This indicates that the commercial banks' share of household financial assets has not changed at all over the last 30 years.

In this text we will see that the role of banks in the economy is becoming narrower as new financial institutions and products are developed. Yet we will also see that the basic business of banks is still vital to the economy. Those who claim banks are dying are overstating the case.

THE ROLE OF DIVERSIFICATION IN REDUCING RISK

Financial institutions hold a broad range, or portfolio, of the securities available in the economy. A **securities portfolio** is a group of securities held by one investor. The purpose of holding a broad range of securities is to reduce risk through diversification. When a particular security performs differently from what was expected (especially when it performs badly), diversification reduces the impact on the total portfolio.

Suppose an investor owns stock in a company on which he expects to earn a return of 10 percent per year. The president of the company, however, embezzles the company's assets, resulting in zero earnings for the shareholders and a 100-percent loss in their capital. The shareholder could have reduced the impact of this event by diversifying. Instead of holding one security, he could have held securities from two or more different firms. Suppose he had placed half his funds in a second security on which he expected to earn 8 percent per year. Given that the second company is unaffected by the losses of the first and earns as expected, the investor now receives interest earnings of 4 percent on his entire portfolio and a capital loss of 50 percent, an improvement on holding only the first security.

An investor holding more than one security in his or her portfolio reduces the risk that the serious underperformance of one security relative to expectations will substantially reduce his or her return. This is the benefit of diversification. If the Smiths had invested all their retirement money in the company whose assets were embezzled by the president, they would have spent the rest of their days getting by on Social Security. We now explain more formally how diversification reduces risk.

Calculation of the Mean Return on a Portfolio

First, diversification affects the **mean return** of investment, the portfolio's average return over all possible outcomes. Table 3.3 lists two events that affect security A: a low-income event denoted by 1 and a high-income event denoted by 2. (Security B will be discussed later.) The probability of event 1 is .4 and of event 2 is .6. The returns on security A vary from $R_1 = -8$ percent in event 1 to $R_2 = +12$ percent in event 2. The products of the probability and the return for each event are listed in column (c).

For example, let's suppose the security is shares in a gold mine. The possible events are a low or a high price of gold; if the price of gold turns out to be low, the returns will be low. The **mean,** or **expected, return (ER)** is the return in each

Table 3.3   EVENT IMPACTS ON SECURITIES A AND B

Security A

Event	(a) Probability	(b) Return	(c) Probability × Return
1	.4	−8.0%	−3.2%
2	.6	12.0%	+7.2%
		Expected return	4.0%

Security B

Event	(a) Probability	(b) Return	(c) Probability × Return
3	.5	−5.8%	−2.9%
4	.5	13.8%	+6.9%
		Expected return	4.0%

event multiplied by the probability that the event will occur and summed over all possible events. Formally, the mean return is

$$ER_A = P_1R_1 + P_2R_2$$

The mean, or expected, return on security A is 4 percent.

The Risk of a Security

Security A has an expected return of 4 percent, but in event 1, it would have an actual return of -8 percent. A risk-averse household would not hold this security if, for the same price, it could purchase another security paying 4 percent with certainty.

We might measure the risk of a security by the magnitude of the probability that it will pay less than its expected return. This interpretation of risk as the "downside" potential of a security is the way the term is commonly used. For example, we speak of the risk of a plane crash rather than the risk that the plane will arrive at its destination ahead of schedule. The risk-averse household is as much concerned with "upside" potential as with "downside" potential, however. It would prefer to hold a security that produces income in both recessions and booms than to hold one that pays off handsomely only in boom times.

Deviation as a Measure of Risk

The household is interested in the **deviation** of the return of a particular security from its expected value. For example, security A in Table 3.4 has a deviation from expected return of -12 percent in event 1 because the expected return on this security is 4 percent and the actual return in event 1 is -8 percent. That is, in calculating the deviation, we ask the question, How much does the return on each event deviate from the mean or expected return? We have already seen that security A in event 1 will have a return of -8 percent. This is 12 percent less than the security's mean, or expected, return of 4 percent. In statistical terms, event 1 has a -12 percent deviation from the mean. (The deviation from the mean is calculated by subtracting the mean from the observed value.) The deviation from expected return for event 2 is 8 percent, as shown in column (c) of Table 3.4. In comparing security A with other securities, households would not place equal value on each of the deviations from expected return. Rather, they would weight these deviations by their likelihood, or probability, of occurring.

To produce a summary statistic of risk for the two possible events, we might sum the two deviations from the mean weighted by their probability of occurrence. When this is done, however, the sum of the weighted deviations is zero. Mathe-

Table 3.4 CALCULATING STANDARD DEVIATION

Security A

Event	(a) Probability	(b) Return	(c) Deviation from Expectation	(d) Deviation of Return Squared	(e) Column (d) × Probability
1	.4	−8.00%	−8.00% − 4.00% = −12.00%	1.44%	0.576%
2	.6	12.00%	12.00% − 4.00% = 8.00%	0.64%	0.384%
				Variance	0.96%
				Standard deviation	9.80%

Security B

Event	(a) Probability	(b) Return	(c) Deviation from Expectation	(d) Deviation of Return Squared	(e) Column (d) × Probability
3	.5	−5.8%	−9.8%	0.96%	0.48%
4	.5	13.8%	+9.8%	0.96%	0.48%
				Variance	0.96%
				Standard deviation	9.80%

matically, this occurs because we have merely calculated the expected deviation from the mean return of security A, which, by definition, is zero.

For example, consider security A. Event 1 has a probability of occurrence of .4, and its deviation from the mean is -12 percent. The weighted deviation is -4.8 percent. Event 2 has a probability of .6, and its deviation from the mean is 8 percent. The weighted deviation is 4.8 percent. The sum of -4.8 percent and 4.8 percent is zero. Clearly, we must find another way of measuring risk.

Variance and Standard Deviation as Measures of Risk

An alternative risk measure that avoids this problem is called the **variance.** To compute the variance, we square each of the deviations from the expected value, weight them by the probability of occurrence, and sum the results. Formally, this can be written as

$$\text{var } R_A = P_1(R_1 - ER_A)^2 + P_2(R_2 - ER_A)^2$$

The calculation is shown in Table 3.4. The variance has the drawback that it is in squared units. To eliminate this problem, we take the positive square root of the variance, called the **standard deviation,** and use it as a measure of risk.

The standard deviation is very useful concept for making many kinds of business decisions as well as for investing. For example, a farmer might observe that the mean low temperature during early April is 35°F. However, the temperature in early April may fall to 20 degrees, in which case the farmer's seedlings will be killed by frost. By knowing the standard deviation around the mean low temperature, the farmer can more accurately predict the seedlings' chances of survival.

PORTFOLIO DIVERSIFICATION AND RISK REDUCTION

We assume that households are risk averse because they care about surviving under favorable as well as unfavorable circumstances. That is, if Emily Chang dies, the Chang household wants to still be able to send the children to college. Since a risk-averse household prefers to hold safe assets rather than risky ones, it is important to discover what happens to risk when two securities are combined into a portfolio. If risk can actually be reduced by diversification while return remains the weighted sum of the mean returns of the securities in the portfolio, then a real gain emerges from holding a combination of securities. Let's investigate this possibility when an investor combines security A with a new security B into one portfolio.

In Table 3.5, securities A and B are affected by different events. Only events

Table 3.5 IMPACT OF JOINT EVENTS ON RETURNS: EQUAL INVESTMENTS IN SECURITIES A AND B

Event	(a) Probability	(b) Return	(c) Probability × Return	
1 and 3	$P_1 \times P_3 = .2$	$-8 \times .5 + (-5.8) \times .5 = -6.9$	$-6.9 \times .2 =$	-1.38
1 and 4	$P_1 \times P_4 = .2$	$-8 \times .5 + 13.8 \times .5 = 2.9$	$2.9 \times .2 =$	0.58
2 and 3	$P_2 \times P_3 = .3$	$12 \times .5 + (-5.8) \times .5 = 3.1$	$3.1 \times .3 =$	0.93
2 and 4	$P_2 \times P_4 = .3$	$12 \times .5 + 13.8 \times .5 = 12.9$	$12.9 \times .3 =$	$\underline{3.87}$
			Expected return	4.00%

1 and 2 generate returns for security A; only events 3 and 4 generate returns for security B. Suppose that security A is issued by a company that exports computer software to Japan. Event 1 is a recession in Japan, and event 2 is a boom in Japan. Suppose that security B is the stock of an ice cream company. Event 3 is the occurrence of cold weather. This occurs with probability .5 and causes returns on security B to be -5.8 percent because of poor sales. Hot weather, which is event 4, also occurs with probability .5 and causes returns to be 13.8 percent.

The expected return on security B is therefore 4 percent, and its risk, measured by its standard deviation, is 9.8 percent. These results are presented in Tables 3.3 and 3.4. Note that we have chosen the returns on security B so that the expected return and the risk of holding the security are identical to those of security A.

The expected return on a portfolio is determined by summing the returns of the two securities for each situation. There are four possible situations for the portfolio. The two bad events, 1 and 3, may occur; the two good events, 2 and 4, may occur; or a low-payoff event for one security may coincide with a high-payoff event for the other. These are events 1 and 4 and events 2 and 3.

Events affecting the return on security A occur independently of events affecting the return of security B because economic conditions in Japan and the weather in the United States are unrelated. Therefore, the probability of each combination is found by taking the product of the probabilities of the events in the combination. For instance, the probability of events 1 and 3 occurring is $.4 \times .5 = .2$. The probabilities for the four possible outcomes are listed in column (a) of Table 3.5.

The sums in each situation are a weighted average of the returns on the two securities in that situation, the weights equaling the proportion of the portfolio invested in each of the securities. Suppose that the portfolio consists of $50 of security A and $50 of security B. The value share, or weight, of each security in the portfolio is .5.

The return on the portfolio in each state is represented by entries in column (b) of Table 3.5, calculated by multiplying the return on securities A and B by their weights in the portfolio, .5 and .5, respectively, and summing the results. The return in each outcome is then multiplied by the probability of the outcome, and the results are summed to compute the expected, or mean, return on the entire portfolio, as for the individual securities in Table 3.3.

We have deliberately chosen our example so that the mean return on the portfolio is the same as the mean return on each individual security. We did this to emphasize that diversification improves the position of the investor without reducing his or her expected return. In the real world, mean returns on portfolios will be the weighted sums of expected returns on individual securities, which will likely differ. Thus the portfolio will have a lower expected return than some of the securities that comprise it. However, a risk-averse investor will still view diversification as favorable because the reduction in risk is more valuable than the reduction in expected return.

Variance and Standard Deviation on a Portfolio of Securities

Treating each weighted combination of the two securities in Table 3.6 as a distinct, new security, we can calculate a variance and standard deviation, as we did in Table 3.3.

First, the squared deviation from the mean for each outcome is multiplied by the probability of the outcome. The results are summed to obtain the variance. Note—and this is the beauty of diversification—that the variance of the return on the new security is less than the variances of each of the old securities individually. Because the standard deviation is the square root of the variance, the new security is less risky than either security A or security B. Holding a portfolio of securities A and B is less risky than holding either A or B separately, and this kind of analysis permits us to measure the **gains from diversification.** See Box 3.3.

Table 3.6 IMPACT OF JOINT EVENTS ON STANDARD DEVIATION: EQUAL INVESTMENTS IN SECURITIES A AND B

Event	(a) Probability	(b) Deviation from Expectation	(c) Deviation of Return Squared	(d) Column (c) × Probability
1 and 3	.2	−10.9%	1.19%	0.238%
1 and 4	.2	−1.1%	0.01%	0.002%
2 and 3	.3	−0.9%	0.01%	0.002%
2 and 4	.3	8.9%	0.79%	0.240%
			Variance	0.482%
			Standard Deviation	6.940%

Achieving a Portfolio with No Risk Through Diversification

If risk can be reduced by investing in two securities rather than one, it might seem possible to invest in a large number of securities and reduce the risk of the portfolio to a very small standard deviation. We now show under what conditions this can happen.

Formally, the variance is the expected value of the squared deviation of a return from its mean. That is, it is the square of the probability of the occurrence of each event times the return on the portfolio if that event should occur minus the expected return on the portfolio summed across all events. In the case of the portfolio with equal shares invested in securities A and B, the variance can be written as

$$\text{var} (R_A + R_B) = E \left(\frac{R_A - ER_A}{2} + \frac{R_B - ER_B}{2} \right)^2$$

where E is used to represent the sum across all events of the deviations from the mean for each event times the probability of each event. Computing out this square, we can derive

$$\text{var} (R_A + R_B) = \frac{\text{var } R_A}{4} + \frac{\text{var } R_B}{4} + \frac{E(R_A - ER_A)(R_B - ER_B)}{2}$$

The first two terms—that is, var $R_A/4$ and var $R_B/4$—are the variances of the individual securities multiplied by their square weights ($1/4$) in the portfolio. The numerator of the last term is called the **covariance** between the returns R_A and R_B. It is the expected value of the deviation of each asset's return from its mean multiplied by the deviation of every other asset in the portfolio. You can verify that in this example the covariance is zero.

If the covariance between securities A and B were positive, diversification would be less effective in reducing risk. For example, let's assume that cold weather in the United States usually occurs simultaneously with a recession in Japan. Thus, when security A experiences a low return (recession in Japan), security B is also highly likely to experience a low return. In this case, a low return on one security is unlikely to be offset by a high return on the other, and diversification will lead to very little reduction in risk.

Because of the individual variances of R_A and R_B are the same, the variance of the equally weighted portfolio is

$$\text{var} (R_A + R_B) = \text{var } R_A/2 = 0.48 \text{ percent}$$

Extending this result, if three securities A, B, and C with equal variances and zero covariances are combined with equal weights in a portfolio, the variance of the portfolio's return would be

$$\text{var} (R_A + R_B + R_C) = \text{var } R_A/3$$

Box 3.3

Regional Diversification in the U.S. Banking Industry

Until the mid-1980s, U.S. banks were effectively restricted by law to operate in only one state. This prevented them from diversifying risks by holding loans to borrowers from outside their home state. That this was a handicap is evident from the impact of the 50-percent drop in oil prices that occurred in 1985 and 1986. The Texas economy was devastated and the major banks, which had lent heavily to the oil industry, were on the verge of bankruptcy. Texas had to change its banking laws to permit out-of-state banks to purchase Texas banks.

In the mid-1980s, the New England states changed their banking laws to permit any bank in a New England state to own a bank in any other New England state. Large banks in Massachusetts and Rhode Island quickly bought up banks in other states. However, in 1989, the entire New England region was hit by a severe recession, resulting in the failure of a large New England bank. As of this writing, it appears that this bank will have to be purchased by a bank from outside the New England region. The other New England banks are in such bad shape that they cannot afford to bid.

In the accompanying figure we display the returns on assets of banks by Federal Reserve district. The Federal Reserve System is divided into 12 districts. Each Federal Reserve bank supervises the banks within its district. As you can see, on a nationwide scale, bank returns are rather stable, but there are years when bank returns in particular districts are hard hit. Many commentators argue that the regulators should encourage more interregional mergers so that banks can have the benefit of diversification—that is, so that individual bank earnings can achieve the stability of the nationwide average of bank returns.

Diversification alone, however, does not ensure stable profits. The New York City banks diversified overseas by making large loans to Latin America. These loans turned sour, and their earnings suffered as a consequence, as indicated in the figure.

If n such securities were combined, then the resulting portfolio's return variance would be var R_A/n. As n gets large and many securities are combined, the portfolio's variance and risk can be driven down close to zero.

ZERO AND NONZERO COVARIANCES

In our original example, we assumed that cold weather in the United States and recessions in Japan are unrelated, or independent, events. If this is the case, we say that the events, and therefore the returns on the securities, have **zero correlation.**

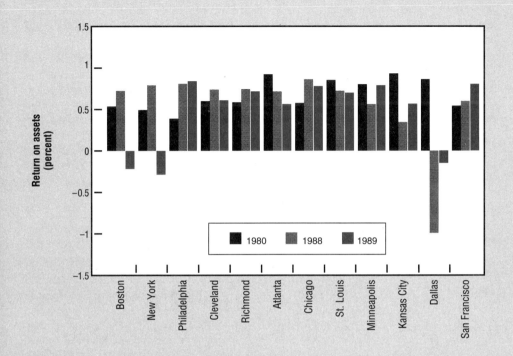

RETURN ON ASSETS BY FEDERAL RESERVE DISTRICT

Source: Federal Reserve Bulletin, July 1990, page 486.

For securities whose correlation is zero, the cross-relationship drops out of the portfolio variance. For example, event 3 does not affect the return of security A, so its occurrence creates no deviation from the expected return. As a result, the cross-product of the deviations from the mean of securities A and B in the case of event 3 is zero. The portfolio variance is then the sum of the variances of the returns of each of the securities weighted by the square of each security's share in the portfolio.

As the number of securities with zero covariance in a portfolio increases, each individual security's weight can move closer to zero, and the variance of the portfolio can approach zero. This is known as the **insurance principle.** The insurance principle—sometimes known as the *law of large numbers*—is the basis for the success of the insurance industry. An insurance company presumes that accidents or deaths are unrelated risks across individuals in an insurance pool. By forming a large enough pool, the company can push the variance around the expected cost of accidents or deaths down toward zero. This is crucial because an insurance company that cannot accurately predict its losses is clearly vulnerable to bankruptcy.

The insurance principle also has important ramifications for securities with nonzero covariances. The importance of the variance terms of individual securities declines as the number of securities in the portfolio rises, just as when the correlations are zero. The covariance terms in general do not approach zero because they are not divided by n, however; rather, they become for all practical purposes the sole determinant of portfolio risk.

THE CONSEQUENCES OF DIVERSIFICATION FOR MARKET LIQUIDITY

In creating diversified portfolios, investors monitor the relative prices of equities issued by different firms. Comparing risk and return, they buy or sell, depending on whether one security is priced too low or too high relative to others. Because investors make decisions about the appropriate prices of individual securities based on their risk and expected return, all securities become close substitutes for one another.

For example, suppose an investor places a large order to purchase the stock of General Motors. Such an order could cause the price of the stock to rise because current holders must sell to fulfill the order. However, let's assume that the order occurred without any change in the market's view of the risk of the stock. An increase in the price implies a decline in the expected return. Astute portfolio managers will quickly realize that the return is now too low for the risk assumed, compared with other stocks in their portfolios. They will sell the stock. This causes the supply available to fill the order to rise, preventing the price from rising. Thus diversification increases the liquidity of the market for individual stocks.

Portfolio Liquidity

Diversified portfolios are more liquid than the individual securities that make up that portfolio. If an individual security performs badly, its price will fall. If it is risky, this makes it illiquid. However, if the security is part of a well-diversified portfolio, some securities in that portfolio will perform well to offset the bad performance of others. Thus the price of the entire portfolio will change less than the price of some individual securities, implying that the portfolio is more liquid.

Financial intermediaries, such as banks, use diversification to create liquid liabilities in the form of deposits that are held as assets by households. Banks lend money to risky corporations and individuals in the form of loans. None of these individual borrowers can issue liquid securities on their own. However, by pooling many risky borrowers, banks are able to create liquid liabilities. However, as we shall see in later chapters, it takes more than diversification to create liquid deposits from illiquid loans.

CONCLUSION

In this chapter we have defined the role of liquid assets in household portfolios. The demand for liquid assets arises out of the desire to maintain a lifestyle in the face of economic and personal adversity. Thus the demand for liquidity in assets is based on the same needs as the demand for insurance. However, because insurance cannot exist to meet every contingency, households demand liquid assets. As householders approach retirement, the changing nature of their security needs causes them to increase their demand for income-preserving assets relative to liquid assets.

Householders satisfy their demands for financial assets primarily by holding the liabilities of financial institutions. A major reason for this is that financial institutions can provide them with the benefits of diversification, which reduces risk. Because investors hold portfolios of securities through financial intermediaries rather than individual securities, the securities of many issuers become substitutes. This improves the liquidity of the market for individual securities.

We next turn to the problem of how two major financial institutions that provide for household income-preserving savings needs are organized. These are life insurance companies and pension funds. We will see that these institutions must do more than hold a diversified portfolio to supply households with the assets they demand from them. We will also see that they have a demand for liquid assets as well as liquidity in financial markets, even though their main purpose is not to provide households with liquid assets.

KEY TERMS

diversification

transaction account

check

third-party payment

nontransaction account

certificate of deposit

collateral

negotiable

inflation

hyperinflation

moral hazard

mean

median

pension reserves

insurance reserves

mutual fund

securities portfolio

mean return

expected return

deviation

variance

standard deviation

gains from diversification

covariance

zero correlation

insurance principle

EXERCISES

1. Would the willingness of a risk-averse household to sacrifice yield to hold a liquid asset decline with an increase in age? With an increase in income? With an increase in wealth? How would a declining willingness to sacrifice yield for liquidity show up in actual data on household asset holdings?

2. The price of life insurance includes a "loading factor," the administrative cost of producing a policy. This cost is largely independent of the dollar size of the insurance policy. If all households have the same degree of risk aversion, why would we expect lower-income households to buy less life insurance relative to their income than higher-income households?

3. Why don't life insurance policies have a deductible, like automobile insurance or fire insurance?

4. Why do you suppose that retirement insurance is mandatory in the United States? (Workers must contribute to Social Security.)

5. If the inflation rate is high and certain, would there be less demand for liquid assets than if it were high and uncertain?

6. Would a risk-neutral household sacrifice yield to hold a liquid asset? Would it pay for the administrative costs of an insurance company?

7. In a Modigliani-Miller world, will investors' degree of risk aversion affect the types of securities issued by a firm? (Assume that financial institutions of the type introduced in Chapter 2 exist.) In a world of principal-agent problems, will the degree of risk aversion affect the types of securities issued by a firm?

8. If investors place no value on liquidity, would we still observe that some firms issue liquid liabilities? (Analyze the problem using principal-agent theory.)

9. Why do risk-averse holders prefer to hold a diversified portfolio of assets?

10. Assume that General Motors' stock is affected by two kinds of risk. One is of the *Roger and Me* variety—that is, occasionally it makes a mistake or is subject to bad press. The second is due to general movements in the economy. During

recessions, people buy fewer cars. Which type of risk can be most easily eliminated through diversification, and why?

11. Despite the benefits of diversification, households, in fact, do not diversify as much as Table 3.2 would suggest. A major asset that does not show up in the table is the family house. Explain why risk-averse households own houses.

12. Does principal-agent theory imply that diversification has a cost?

13. Explain why markets for individual securities are more liquid if investors hold portfolios of securities rather than individual securities.

FURTHER READING

Elliehausen, Gregory E., and Glenn B. Conner, "Survey of Consumer Finances, 1983," *Federal Reserve Bulletin,* Sept. 1984, pp. 679–692.

Markowitz, Harry, *Portfolio Selection,* Wiley, 1959.

Sharp, William F., *Investments,* 3rd Ed., Prentice-Hall, 1985, pp. 93–181.

4

Life Insurance Companies and Pension Plans

I n Chapter 3 we saw that households save primarily through holding the liabilities of financial institutions. An important reason for this is that financial institutions can provide the household with the benefits of diversification that they cannot provide for themselves because their financial asset holdings are too small. However, diversification cannot be the entire reason that households save through financial institutions. Otherwise, we would find that they invested in mutual funds, which pool investors' funds to achieve the advantages of diversification.

In fact, as we saw in Table 3.2, life insurance reserves make up a larger percentage of household financial assets than do mutual funds. Also, households use pension funds to save for retirement far more than they use mutual funds. It may seem peculiar to say that households "use" pension funds as a savings vehicle because pensions are usually provided by employers for employees. On an individual level, this is a condition of employment rather than something that is freely chosen. However, in labor negotiations, pension benefits are usually a point of contention between labor and management. The labor side bargains for greater benefits. In this sense, it appears that employees as a group demand pension benefits, and employers provide them in response.

Households prefer pension funds to mutual funds as vehicles for saving for retirement because pension funds promise a specific level of benefits to the retiree. On the other hand, the value of a mutual fund is determined by the performance of the assets held in the pool. A mutual fund makes no attempt to guarantee a specific level of benefits to the investor. Like a pension plan, life insurance policies provide for a specific level of benefits. The household usually buys a policy on a breadwinner that promises to pay a specific sum in the event of death.

Making good on a promise to pay a specific level of benefits cannot be achieved by diversification alone. We indicated in the preceding chapter that a portfolio containing a large number of securities with uncorrelated returns can generate a return with zero risk. A mutual fund holding a portfolio with zero risk could promise a specific level of benefits. However, in practice, the returns on most securities are positively correlated. Most firms in the economy are affected to some degree by the performance of the economy as a whole. For example, when interest rates rise, the prices of long-term securities decline. If a financial institution must occasionally sell assets to meet its obligations to pay benefits, it cannot guarantee a fixed level of benefits by diversification alone.

In this chapter we consider the problem of how life insurance companies and pension funds provide for a fixed benefit in an uncertain world. We will see that this requires diversification, but it also requires that financial institutions find ways to protect themselves from the risk of falling asset values. They could do this by holding liquid assets, but if they only held liquid assets, they would face income risk. Thus they are forced to seek other methods of securing the value of their assets relative to their liabilities.

LIFE INSURANCE COMPANIES AS FINANCIAL INSTITUTIONS

Based on Table 3.2, it may seem peculiar to begin our discussion with life insurance companies. After all, life insurance reserves are a declining percentage of total household savings. So why bother discussing them?

The traditional life insurance policy offered in the American market was a whole life policy—that is, one that protects the policyholder throughout his or her entire lifetime. It promised a fixed dollar payout in the event of death. The lack of success of this product is the reason for the decline in life insurance reserves. In many ways, this product declined because the insurance companies tried to promise too much for one product. They tried to offer a liquid savings account and a fixed-benefit long-term savings plan. By examining why insurance companies could not satisfy both savings demands, we can appreciate the problems in creating liquidity and long-term security in an uncertain economy.

Ordinary and Group Contracts

There are two basic types of insurance contracts—ordinary and group. **Group contracts** cover a group of people, such as employees in a large company. Each individual pays the cost of insurance based on his or her age. Older employees pay more because they face a higher probability of dying. **Ordinary contracts** are purchased by individuals for a specified period of time, ranging from 5 years to life. Ordinary policies accumulate reserves, and the decline in reserves in household assets indicates that the demand for these policies is declining. There are two basic types of ordinary life insurance contracts available, term insurance and whole-life insurance. The major difference between these two contracts is in the period covered. **Term insurance** is a contract that typically agrees to pay a death benefit during a specified number of years, usually 5 to 10 years. After the specified period, the insured may usually renew the contract at a higher premium rate. **Whole life policies** agree to pay a death benefit when the insured party dies, regardless of when death occurs as long as premiums are up to date.

Reserve Accumulation on Ordinary Contracts

Ordinary life policies are generally written on a level premium basis under which the payment due on the policy is the same every year. Since the probability of death rises with age, insurance should rise in price as the policyholder gets older, and this is why term insurance rates increase when they are renewed. To maintain a level premium, the policy price exceeds the cost of insurance in early years, and this difference represents the accumulation of reserves. In a whole life policy, as the probability of death approaches 1, reserves must equal the face value of this policy, because the payment of that face value is a certainty.

Reserves accumulate to cover the higher cost of insurance as the policyholder ages. Thus contributions to reserves are a high percentage of the premium in the early years of the contract. The reserve element in the premium of a life policy is greater than in a term policy because the difference in the cost of insurance between the early and later years of the contract is greater in whole-life policies. The rate at which reserves accumulate and the price of the insurance contract depend on the interest rate that the insurance company assumes it will earn when it invests these funds.

From the household's point of view, these reserves are an asset. Most whole life policies permit the policyholder to borrow against the policy reserves while the contract is in force. A household cannot just withdraw these reserves; it must borrow them at a specified rate of interest. Why? The reason is that the insurance company normally lends the money (through the purchase of bonds or other securities) and uses the income to partially cover the higher cost of insurance when the policyholder is older. If the household withdraws the reserves, the insurance company loses the interest it would otherwise earn on the bonds. Therefore, the household must reimburse the company for its forgone income. In short, the policy owner must borrow against his or her reserves, instead of withdrawing them, and must pay interest on the loan.

If the household should decide to terminate its policy, it usually receives its accumulated reserves as a surrender value. Thus whole-life policies can represent a form of long-term savings. For example, a household may surrender its life policies when the breadwinners reach retirement. The accumulated reserves can supplement other savings to provide for a secure retirement.

How Life Insurance Companies Invest Their Reserves

In Table 4.1, life insurance companies appear as the largest holders of corporate and foreign bonds in the U.S. economy. In 1989, life insurance companies held assets of $1.3 trillion and had life insurance policies outstanding of $10 trillion. Thirty-eight percent of life insurance company assets were invested in U.S. corporate bonds, the largest single category of investment on their balance sheet. Another 34 percent of life insurance company assets were invested in other fixed nominal income contracts such as U.S. government bonds and mortgages.

It may seem that the problem of providing a whole-life policy can be solved by holding a portfolio of bonds. After all, bonds pay interest and reserves accumulate interest. If the payments received from the bonds equal the interest received by policyholders on their reserves, there should be no problem in providing a whole life policy. We will see that complications arise, however.

Promising a Fixed Payoff

To promise a fixed payoff, the insurance company must make sure that reserves accumulate as specified in the contract. If the insurance company's interest rate assumption is too high relative to actual market rates, the reserves will be inadequate in the end to pay the death benefits. If it is too low, the price of the contract will be too high.

Two problems arise, even if the life insurance company only invests in fixed-income securities. The first is that the interest rate may, at any point in time, be different from that assumed in the calculation of reserves. The insurance company faces the risk that cash earned as interest on bonds held cannot be reinvested at the interest rate available when the cash is received. **Investment risk** is the risk that cash flow from a security must be reinvested at a lower return than that available on the original security.

For example, during the first year that the policy is in force, the insurance company may buy a long-term bond with a coupon yield of $10 per year. When the interest rate is 10 percent, this bond will have an approximate value of $100. Since the interest received becomes part of the reserve fund, the firm must reinvest

Table 4.1 CORPORATE AND FOREIGN BONDS, 1987 ($ BILLIONS)

Nonfinancial corporate business	764.1
Foreign	81.6
Commercial banking	77.0
Savings & loan associations	15.8
Finance companies	137.1
REITs	2.1
CMO issuers	103.1
Total Liabilities	**1180.9**
Households	92.2
Foreign	157.6
Commercial banking	71.3
Savings & loan associations	37.6
Mutual savings banks	14.5
Insurance	734.7
Life insurance companies	388.3
Private pension funds	157.4
State and local govt. RTR funds	135.2
Other insurance companies	53.9
Mutual funds	54.2
Brokers and dealers	18.8
Total Assets	**1180.9**

Source: Flow of Funds.

Note: Items may not sum to totals because of rounding.

the $10 annual interest at 10 percent if the reserves are to continue growing at 10 percent per year. If, in any year, the interest rate is less than 10 percent, the company will not be able to reinvest to achieve this growth rate.

To avoid the reinvestment risk, the insurance company could buy a zero-coupon bond rather than a $100 bond that pays $10 per year. A zero-coupon bond eliminates the reinvestment risk because it pays no interest until maturity and sells at a large discount relative to its face value. The relationship between the face value and the current price is such that the bond earns a steady return of 10 percent every year until maturity. Since there is no cash flow to reinvest, there is no reinvestment risk.

By purchasing a zero-coupon bond, the insurance company attempts to match the cash flows of its liabilities with the cash flows of its assets. Reserves accumulate at a constant interest rate, and zero-coupon bonds yield a constant interest rate because the income from the bond is always invested at the original rate. Thus cash inflow and outflow are perfectly matched or correlated. **Duration matching** is holding assets and liabilities whose cash flows are perfectly correlated.

Duration matching does not solve all the problems of the insurance company with regard to interest rate risk, even if it invests in zero-coupon bonds. Every year the policyholder must pay a premium to the insurance company, and part of these funds must be invested as reserves. If interest rates are less than those assumed in the policy, the firm will not be able to accumulate reserves at the specified rate.

To solve this problem, the company could engage in the following strategy: In year 1 of the policy it could borrow an amount equal to the entire face value of the policy at a fixed rate of interest. It could then invest the proceeds in a zero-coupon bond with the same maturity. Then the reserve payments coming due from the policyholder year by year could be used to pay off portions of the loan.

There are risks to this strategy as well. What if a policyholder ceases to pay premiums on his or her policy? Policyholders in the United States have the right to surrender their policies and receive a cash surrender value based on the reserves held on the policy. If they do so, premium payments will cease. The insurance company would have to sell the bond to meet the surrender benefits and pay off the remainder of the loan. If interest rates have risen since the bond was purchased, the price the insurance company could obtain on the bond would be inadequate to cover surrender benefits and pay off the loan.

This discussion indicates some of the many obstacles the insurance company must overcome to provide policyholders with a completely hedged contract. The only feasible alternative for the policyholders, who naturally want to protect their claims on reserves, may be to permit the insurance company to make rather conservative assumptions about the interest rate that reserves will earn. This leads to a higher level of reserves that must be funded at any point in time.

This solution leads to a bargaining problem between the insurance company manager and the policyholder. If the interest rate assumption is too low, the cost of the policy will be high, and the company will be in a good position to capture the difference between the actual investment yield and the cash flow required for the reserves to accumulate at the required rate.

Competition among insurance companies will not necessarily make the problem disappear. Policyholders cannot judge whether a firm that accumulates reserves at a relatively low interest rate is protecting them from default or stealing their money.

Reserves as a Liquid Asset

Until the early to mid-1970s, policyholders generally had the right to borrow their reserves at a fixed, and low, rate of interest. The amount of reserves that could be borrowed was stated in the insurance contract. It increased with the years the policy was in force. This benefit effectively made reserves a liquid asset as well as a long-term savings plan because their value remained fixed in terms of the unit of account.

Table 4.2   PERCENT OF ASSETS OF U.S. LIFE INSURANCE COMPANIES INVESTED IN POLICY LOANS VS. THE INTEREST RATE ON LONG-TERM GOVERNMENT BONDS

Year	Policy Loans (%)	Interest Rates (%)
1955	3.6	2.82
1960	4.4	4.12
1965	4.8	4.28
1970	7.8	7.35
1975	8.5	7.99
1981	9.3	13.91
1985	6.6	10.62
1989	4.4	8.58

Source: American Council of Life Insurance, *1990 Life Insurance Fact Book,* p. 83, and *Federal Reserve Bulletin,* Table 1.35, various issues.

Predictable problems arose from this. As indicated in Table 4.2, when interest rates rose, borrowing activity increased. Policyholders borrowed reserves at a low fixed rate and invested the money at current high yields. This caused a double problem for life insurance companies. They earned a substantially below market rate of return on a large portion of their assets, and they had to sell assets at depressed values to meet the demand for policy loans. They found that it was impossible to promise a liquid asset funded by long-term securities.

Life insurance companies ceased writing ordinary policies promising the right to borrow at a fixed interest rate. Consequently, by the late 1980s, as indicated in Table 4.2, policy loans as a percent of assets were less responsive to high interest rates. This, of course, did nothing to make the product more attractive. Therefore, life insurance companies invented new types of contracts. One of these is called **universal life.** Universal life has a fixed death benefit, just like ordinary policies. However, the insurance element and the savings element of the policy are separated. The insurance company establishes a savings account for the policyholder, who has the right to place funds into or withdraw funds from the account at any time. The investment performance of the savings account is determined by the market.

A second product innovation is **variable life.** In this product, premiums are fixed and a minimum death benefit is guaranteed. However, if investment experience is good, the death benefit is increased. The new policies have outpaced the demand for ordinary policies, but insurance reserves continue to decline as a percent of household assets.

The decline in the popularity of whole life insurance policies that require the accumulation of reserves is illustrated in the distribution of life insurance companies'

Table 4.3 LIFE INSURANCE COMPANIES' DISTRIBUTION OF LIABILITIES

Type of Liability	1960 $	1960 %	1970 $	1970 %	1980 $	1980 %	1989 $	1989 %
Life insurance	70.8	59.2	115.4	55.7	197.9	41.3	324.2	24.9
Annuities	26.9	22.4	48.9	23.6	181.4	37.8	729.5	56.1
Heath insurance	0.9	0.7	3.5	1.7	11.0	2.3	29.9	2.3
Total Policy Reserves	98.6	82.4	167.8	81.0	390.3	81.4	1083.7	83.4
Other Obligations and unassigned surplus*	21.1	17.6	39.5	19.0	88.9	18.6	216.1	16.6
Total Liabilities	119.6	100.0	207.3	100.0	479.2	100.0	1299.8	100.0

Source: Compiled from two tables from FACT BOOK (1990: pp. 78, 81) "American Council of Life Insurance, 1990 *Life Insurance Fact Book*."

Note: Items may not add to totals because of rounding.

*Includes policy dividend accumulations and funds set aside for such dividends, securities valuation reserves, special surplus funds, unassigned surplus, capital and retained earnings of stock companies, and other items.

liabilities by type in Table 4.3. Reserves on life policies declined from 59.2 percent of liabilities in 1960 to 24.9 percent in 1989. Reserves against annuities, which include reserves held against universal life policies and pension plans sponsored by life insurance companies, increased from 22.4 to 56.1 percent of total liabilities. An **annuity** is a contract that promises to pay the owner a fixed amount at specified intervals after a certain date. For example, a pension plan that promises to pay $25,000 per year upon the retirement of an employee is an annuity.

Life Companies' Demand for Liquidity

Table 4.3 indicates that in 1989 "other obligations and unassigned surplus" (securities valuation reserves, special surplus funds, and unassigned surplus and capital) compromised 16.6 percent of liabilities. These items are the capital account of insurance companies, which is the amount that the value of assets exceeds the value of policy reserves. This account ensures that if a company must sell an asset at a loss, policy reserve obligations will not be impaired.

Life insurance companies also can protect the value of policy reserves by investing in liquid assets. In Table 4.4 we see that life insurance companies' investment strategy has changed in recent years. They have moved out of mortgages and into

Table 4.4 DISTRIBUTION OF ASSETS OF LIFE INSURANCE COMPANIES

Type of Asset	Percent of Total Assets				
	1970	1975	1980	1985	1989
Short term					
Cash and other	1	1	1	1	0
Corporate securities	1	2	2	4	3
Long term					
Corporate bonds	34	35	35	32	38
Government securities					
U.S.	2	2	3	9	12
State, local, and foreign	3	3	3	4	2
Corporate stock*	8	10	10	9	10
Mortgages	36	31	27	22	20
Real Estate	3	3	3	3	3
Policy loans	8	8	9	8	4
Other†	4	5	6	8	8
Total	100	100	100	100	100
Total Assets (in $billions)	207.3	289.3	479.2	816.2	1299.8

Source: Compiled from two tables from FACT BOOK (1990: pp. 83, 86) "American Council of Life Insurance, 1990 *Life Insurance Fact Book.*"

*Market value.

†Includes due and deferred premiums and other investment income due and accrued and oil, mineral, timber, and other equity investments.

U.S. government securities. Because of their quality, U.S. government securities are more liquid than corporate bonds or mortgages. Also, the demand for short-term corporate assets has more than doubled since 1970. (The data do not permit us to distinguish between long- and short-term government securities.) The change in investment strategy reflects an increased demand for liquidity. The companies realized that they must maintain more liquidity to meet the policyholders' demands to withdraw their reserves. Thus they found that they cannot provide liquid reserves if they do not hold some liquid assets. As indicated in Box 4.1, however, some companies did not follow the trend toward investment in more liquid assets. In later chapters we will discuss other means by which insurance companies attempt to maintain the value of their assets.

The Regulation of Life Insurance Companies

In the United States, to protect policyholders from the risk that reserves will be inadequate to meet promised benefits, the various states have the power to regulate life insurance companies. States establish interest rates that are permissible to calculate reserves on ordinary policies. They also establish rules governing investments and how these investments must be valued to determine whether the value of assets equals the value of reserves. The permissible interest rates and valuation rules are meant to be conservative so that the asset values usually exceed the value of reserves.

In 1991, the insurance regulatory system came under a great deal of pressure as declining asset values threatened the solvency of several major insurance companies. Executive Life was seized by the insurance departments of the states of California and New York. Because the company had invested heavily in junk bonds, policyholders, who were concerned about the value of their reserves, surrendered their policies in droves. The regulators feared that if too many policyholders surrendered their policies, there would not be enough remaining assets to pay death benefits. On seizure of the company, the regulators prohibited further surrenders but guaranteed death benefits. Of course this action did not please those who wanted to get their money out of the hands of Executive Life. Events such as this contributed to the suspicion that state regulation is inadequate, which has led to cries for reform. (See Box 4.2.)

The regulatory solution has political overtones as well. For example, the older, established companies dominate the whole life market. They also write relatively conservative policies. They might attempt to use regulation to keep other firms from issuing policies based on more liberal interest rate assumptions that would sell for a lower premium. The deep skepticism that consumers feel about the whole issue of reserve accumulation is evidenced by their refusal to buy the whole life product. Thus it appears that no institution, government or private, has satisfactorily solved the problem of providing a fixed savings plan through the vehicle of individual ordinary life insurance.

PENSION FUNDS

Pension funds have proved to be a much more attractive method of providing for long-term security than life insurance. How have they avoided some of the pitfalls that made life insurance unattractive, and what problems do they face? We pursue these questions by first considering how pension funds are organized to make good on the benefits they promise.

Before we begin, we note that we are only discussing pension plans provided by employers. We do not discuss individual retirement accounts (IRAs) or employer-provided savings plans that employees can voluntarily fund.

Pension plans are devices to provide retirement income to households. In 1989, the assets of pension funds amounted to over $1.9 trillion. Of this figure, $640 billion was held in plans sponsored by life insurance companies and $1.2 trillion was held in plans directly sponsored by employers.

Box 4.1

Competition Can Lead to Insolvency

Table 4.4 indicates that the life insurance industry has increased holdings of "safe" assets such as government bonds. However, some companies have bucked the trend. They tried to attract customers by promising high yields. To fulfill these promises, they have taken on more risk. Inevitably, this has led to fears that a major insurance company may be headed for bankruptcy.

In 1990, the Traveler's Insurance Company set aside $650 million to cover possible losses on real estate and mortgage loans. Another insurance company, Executive Life Corp., recognized an $859 million loss on its portfolio of high-risk, or junk, corporate bonds. Among the large insurance companies, perhaps the one regarded most susceptible to economic hard times is the Equitable, which has some $250 billion in insurance in force. Equitable is in a particularly vulnerable position because its balance sheet is weak relative to other large companies.

Equitable's weak position is illustrated in the accompanying table. Its ratio of stock and loss reserves (a liability and net worth item) relative to assets is the lowest among the major U.S. life insurance companies. In addition, its assets appear to be more risky than the average. Based on data from the Townsend and Schupp Company, Equitable has invested a higher percentage of its assets in high-risk corporate bonds (junk bonds) than the industry average. The Equitable's ratio is 5.5 percent, compared with an industry average of 4.6 percent. Note also that its investment in junk bonds exceeds its loss reserve-to-asset ratio.

In addition, Equitable has invested a higher percentage of its assets in real estate and mortgages than the industry average. This is of concern because real estate markets are a particularly distressed segment of the American economy. Again, according to Townsend

Calculation of Pension Fund Reserves

Assets held in pension funds back up reserves analogous to the reserves held by life insurance companies on the policies they issue. These reserves equal the present value of a fund's liability to provide retirement income to the participants in the plan. A survey of pension programs sponsored by large corporations in the United States provides an example of how this liability is calculated.

In general, the present value of the benefits currently promised to present and former employees determines a fund's liabilities. When an individual joins a firm,

EQUITY AND SECURITIES LOSS RESERVES TO ASSETS: LARGEST U.S. INSURERS AS OF SEPTEMBER 30, 1990

Northwestern Mutual	7.54%
Prudential Insurance	7.44
New York Life Insurance	7.33
Connecticut General	6.90
Travelers	6.39
Metropolitan Life	6.17
Teachers Insurance & Annuity	6.10
John Hancock Mutual	6.08
Aetna Life Insurance	5.33
Equitable Life	5.32

and Schupp, Equitable's real estate and mortgage investments represent 33.7 percent of its assets, compared with 22.4 percent as an industry average.

The troubles of this large insurer have forced its president to resign. The new management team is trying to clean up the asset portfolio, cut expenses, and reduce the promise of high benefits that led to a large, and risky, growth in assets during the 1980s.

Loss reserves = reserves for stock and bond losses.

Source: Townsend & Schupp Company, company reports.

he or she begins to accumulate pension benefits. Employees with higher pay are entitled to higher benefits. Seventy-one percent of the corporations surveyed base employee benefits on their salary at the time they leave the company. The pension liability must then be calculated on assumptions about how salaries will increase over the years and about how long the average individual is likely to remain with the company.

In addition, an assumption must be made about how long the average employee will remain alive after he or she retires. Most pension plans also include survivors' benefits (payments to the family after the employee dies), so the pension managers also must form an expectation about how long spouses will live.

Box 4.2

A Change in How Insurance Companies are Regulated?

There is a growing concern about the financial health of America's insurance industry. The potential $500 billion cost of the savings and loan crisis is on the taxpayer's mind. (See Chapter 20.) Congress is concerned that another huge bailout bill will be forthcoming to protect Americans' insurance benefits. Unlike the savings and loan deposits, life insurance benefits are not guaranteed by a federal government agency. However, 47 states operate guarantee funds that are supported by the insurance companies to protect policyholders in the several states from the consequences of a bankruptcy.

To protect the integrity of these guarantee funds, states attempt to prevent insurance companies from investing in risky assets. With problems cropping up in insurance asset quality, many people wonder whether the states are doing an adequate job. According to the American Council of Life Insurance, between January 1985 and September 1989, 62 companies have gone bankrupt. This has created a call for federal regulation of insurance and the establishment of a federal guarantee fund.

IDS Financial Services has estimated that in a severe economic downturn, the life insurance industry could experience $11.5 billion in losses, a figure disputed by the American Council of Life Insurance. This is small potatoes relative to the $1.3 trillion in assets held by life insurance companies. It is certainly small relative to the projected losses of $500 billion in the savings and loan crisis, which was federally insured. Given the track record of the states versus the federal government in protecting the taxpayer from potential losses, we can expect the debate on who should regulate insurance safety and soundness to be a lively one.

Vesting Provisions

Pension funds sponsored by private employers also have vesting provisions. Typically, when an employee first joins a firm, he or she lacks the right to collect fully on pension benefits even though the employer incurs a pension liability for the employee's service. At some point after joining the firm, usually within 5 years, an employee will become vested in his or her claims against the pension fund. This gives the employee the right to receive pension benefits after he or she reaches a certain age whether or not he or she is still an employee of the firm. As an alternative, some firms allow vested employees to take a lump-sum pension distribution when they leave the firm, even before retirement. (See Box 4.3.)

Box 4.3

An Employee's Right to Pension Benefits

An employee's pension benefits are never secure until he or she is actually vested. A company can, and sometimes does, dismiss an employee shortly before he becomes vested, which makes him ineligible for pension benefits. However, if a company dismisses an employee shortly before he is scheduled to become vested, it can face a lawsuit on "wrongful discharge" to avoid paying retirement benefits. The company invariably argues dismissal for just cause, while the employee argues dismissal to avoid payment of benefits.

Dismissal to avoid paying benefits is illegal under federal law as well as under the laws of many states. Federal and state laws do not conflict in terms of the degree of protection offered workers, but they do conflict in the remedies offered. Suits under federal law permit workers to win compensation for lost benefits, whereas state laws often permit punitive damages for suffering, which can greatly exceed the value of the benefits lost.

In a decision in late 1990, the U.S. Supreme Court held that federal law preempts state law on this issue. The U.S. Chamber of Commerce, a business lobbying organization, argued for the federal preemption, whereas a coalition of local government groups opposed it. The state and local governments claimed that preemption "would make dramatic inroads into the states' authority" to shape their own laws on the subject of employee rights. The business groups argued that federal preemption would prevent employers from being subject to "multiple and potentially conflicting regulations" (*New York Times,* Dec. 4, 1990).

Because pension benefits have become such a large portion of Americans' financial assets, the rights to these benefits have become important legal and political issues. On the right to sue for "wrongful dismissal," the business community has successfully transferred the legal question to the federal level where it expects to receive less onerous penalties than at the state level.

Interest Rate and Security Price Assumptions

To compute the present value of the pension liability, the sponsor must include an assumption about the appropriate interest rate to use for discounting. There is some arbitrariness in setting this assumption. In 1982, a survey found that the most commonly used interest rate assumption was between 7 and 8 percent. In 1982, the long-term U.S. corporate bond interest rate was close to 13 percent. Since pension plan managers chose interest rates of 7 or 8 percent, it is clear that they were being very conservative in the calculation of their reserve liabilities.

Because pension liabilities are long term and economic conditions change over time, many companies change the assumptions on which their presumed pen-

Table 4.5 ASSETS OF PRIVATE PENSION FUNDS, 1989

Type of Assets	$Billions	Percent of Total
Cash and deposits	$ 72.8	6.0
Corporate equities	699.7	57.3
U.S. government securities	147.2	12.0
Corporate and foreign bonds	172.1	14.1
Mortgages	6.7	.5
Open-market paper	80.9	6.6
Miscellaneous assets	42.4	3.5
Total Financial Assets of Private Pension Funds	1221.8	100.0

Source: Board of Governors of the Federal Reserve System, Annual Statistical Digest, 1989.

sion liabilities are based from time to time. For example, in 1981, 37 percent of the companies changed the assumptions underlying their plan. Most companies change the benefits offered to participants from time to time as well. Only 26 percent of the companies surveyed in 1981 had never changed their benefits.

Changes in interest rates can have a major impact on the size of a pension liability. For example, let's assume that a pension plan promises to pay $100,000 to an employee when she retires at age 65. She is currently 45. If the interest rate is 10 percent, the present value of that liability is $14,864. If it is 5 percent, the present value is $37,689.

Usually an increase in the pension liability due to a decline in the interest rate is offset by an increase in the value of assets in response to the same decline. If interest rates should fall, bond prices will rise. However, as we will see, the government restricts the ability of pension funds to recognize capital gains on bonds due to a decline in interest rates. Thus a decline in the assumed interest rate can lead to an unfunded liability.

Table 4.5 indicates that common stocks make up a high proportion of pension fund assets. Pension funds must adjust the value of stocks they hold to current market prices. Stock prices do not always move in the opposite direction of interest rates. In the October 1987 stock market crash, stock prices fell with no appreciable change in interest rates. A decline in stock prices that occurs independently of a decline in interest rates causes a decline in the value of reserves without a corresponding decline in required reserves. This leads to an unfunded liability.

Trust Management of Pension Funds

Employer-sponsored pension funds are generally managed by a trustee, usually the trust department of a bank. The trustee invests the assets of the pension fund, but the responsibility for the actual liability to present and former employees remains with the sponsoring company. In the event of bankruptcy of the company, the unfunded liability of a pension plan has a claim on company assets.

Investors who consider investing in the equities of corporations sponsoring pension plans therefore are concerned about the unfunded portion of the pension liability, the assumptions made in determining the liability, and the quality of the assets in the fund. Employees also have a stake in the degree to which a pension liability is unfunded in the event of bankruptcy.

Employee Retirement Income and Security Act

In the early 1970s, the fate of workers' pensions in employer bankruptcy situations became a political issue. Since unfunded pension liabilities were claims on the company in bankruptcy proceedings, pension recipients had to stand in line with other creditors to obtain their claim to a pension annuity. In bankruptcy, a company's assets are generally insufficient to satisfy the claims of all the creditors. Thus, unless a third party has insured the unfunded pension liabilities, potential pension fund recipients could find that their benefits are not paid.

To remedy this situation, in 1974 the **Employee Retirement Income and Security Act (ERISA)** was passed. This act established the government as partial insurer of unfunded pension liabilities of employer-sponsored pension plans in the event of bankruptcy of an employer. The government thus has an interest in how pension funds are managed. As a consequence, it has set rules, which we will examine in a moment, for the investment of funds. The U.S. Labor Department became the administrator of the law. A corporation, known as the Pension Benefit Guaranty Corporation, was established to oversee pension plans. (See Box 4.4.)

Moral Hazard in Pension Fund Insurance

To insure pensions, the government had to eliminate the moral hazard problems typical in other insurance. Employers offering pension funds may have incentives to engage in highly risky investments. For example, employers may use the pension fund to buy large amounts of the company's own stock. This would provide current management with a means of obtaining cash at a favorable price. The management of a company with a high probability of bankruptcy may find this a particularly attractive means of finance.

Box 4.4

Pension Rights in Bankruptcy

In 1990, Eastern Airlines was attempting to reorganize under bankruptcy laws. One of Eastern's liabilities was its pension obligations to its employees. Since the Pension Benefit Guaranty Corporation must ultimately provide for the benefits of the employees, it took an active role in the reorganization plan.

As part of the reorganization plan, the Pension Benefit Guaranty Corporation agreed to take over payment of the retirement benefits of Eastern employees. It agreed that benefits would be paid in full as specified in the company pension plan. In return, the assets of the pension fund were turned over to the Guaranty Corporation.

However, as part of the deal, Continental Holdings, Inc., the parent company of Eastern Airlines, had to secure the payment with its assets. This means that if the pension fund assets assumed by the Guaranty Corporation are inadequate to pay the promised benefits, Continental Holdings must make up the difference.

It was estimated that Eastern's pension fund was underfunded by some $640 million. Under the agreement, Continental paid $80.5 million to the Guaranty Corporation and Eastern paid $30 million. Thus over $500 million in unfunded liability remains, which becomes a potential liability to Continental Holdings.

Continental Holdings is also the parent company for another airline, Continental, which also filed for reorganization under the bankruptcy laws in 1990. The claim of the Guaranty Corporation is only as good as the value of the assets held by the parent company. The pension benefits of Eastern employees are secure, but the Guaranty Corporation, which is funded by contributions from all private pension funds, might have to make up the difference if the security provided by Continental Holdings turns out to be worthless.

To forestall such activity, the government as insurer must police the investment decisions of the pension fund and establish rules to determine the extent to which a pension fund has an unfunded liability.

ERISA Requires That Funds Diversify

Section 404 of ERISA requires that fund managers diversify their portfolios "so as to minimize the risk of large loss." In the 1970s many investment managers assumed that minimizing the risk of large loss meant investing only in the relatively safe "blue chip" stocks. Blue chip stocks are the stocks of large American corporations.

In 1977, the administrator of the Pension and Welfare Benefits Programs in the U. S. Department of Labor claimed that section 404 does not require an investment manager to consider the risk of an individual security but only the risk of the portfolio. Since administrators of the law recognize the lessons of portfolio theory, investment in non-blue-chip stocks is not discouraged by the law.

Policing the Value of the Unfunded Liability

The law further requires each fund to report the value of its unfunded liability annually and places a 5 percent tax on that amount as a means of encouraging full funding. If the unfunded liability is not corrected within 90 days, a 100 percent tax is applied.

We have already seen that the liability is calculated on the basis of interest rate, salary, and mortality assumptions. To make the law meaningful, the government must also establish some rules for asset evaluation. These rules state that bonds not in default can be reported at their amortized value. Let's see how this works.

Amortization Value

A pension fund may buy a bond with a $1,000 value at maturity for less than face value. Since the bond will pay $1,000 at maturity, the holder will receive both interest and an expected capital gain, the difference between the purchase price and the maturity value.

For example, if a $1,000 bond paying 5 percent sells for $955 one year before maturity, it earns a total of $95 for that year, $50 in interest and $45 in capital gains. This is a return of nearly 10 percent.

Suppose the pension fund bought this bond two years before maturity when interest rates were 10 percent. The approximate price of the bond would be $914 to yield a capital gain of $41 during the year and $50 in interest. The total return is $91, or approximately 10 percent of the purchase price. In the year before maturity, if the interest rate is still 10 percent, the bond would sell for $955.

At the start of the year before maturity, the amortization value of the bond is $955. This is the value of the bond recorded on the asset side of the pension fund's balance sheet, regardless of what happens to interest rates during the year. If interest rates rise, the market value of the bond will be less than $955, but for accounting purposes, this does not affect the value of the pension fund asset.

In permitting pension funds to hold bonds on the books at amortized value, the government assumes that they hold bonds to maturity. The value of a bond at maturity is fixed *regardless of what happens to interest rates*. Amortization permits the pension fund to write the value of the bond progressively upward to its value at maturity.

Stocks Must Be Held at Market Value

In contrast to bonds, stocks must be held at market value. Thus large declines in the stock market can lead to large unfunded liabilities in pension funds. We can expect pension fund managers to attempt to reduce this risk. As we will see later, these attempts have grave consequences for the liquidity of the stock market.

Why does the government provide different valuation rules for stocks and bonds? Bonds pay a fixed income stream. Thus, when a pension fund buys a bond, its cash flow is certain (unless the issuer defaults). Likewise, the maturity value of a bond is certain. Thus the capital gain (or loss) that a pension fund will experience on a bond between the purchase date and the maturity date is certain (again, assuming away defaults). Amortization provides a standard method of recognizing this fact.

Stocks, on the other hand, have no maturity value and no certain cash flow. Thus a share of stock never reaches a point where it has a certain value. The only criterion for evaluation is its market value. (See Box 4.5.)

PENSION PLANS VERSUS LIFE INSURANCE

Why have pension plans gained on insurance as a long-term savings vehicle? A large part of the reason is that employers have more effective means of solving the dilemma we identified in the insurance market. Recall that consumers cannot really tell whether an insurance company that charges a high price for its policies is being conservative or is earning high profits at their expense. Regulation has apparently not allayed their fears.

Employers make contributions to pension funds based on the value of the assets held in the fund compared with the liability for future benefits. If the fund is overfunded, it does not contribute; if it is underfunded, it makes up the difference. Thus pension fund "premiums" are variable—they are based on the market performance of the fund relative to its liability.

Since employers have a direct stake in the performance of the pension fund, they often monitor the performance of the trustee of their plan. If the fund falls behind competitors, they will change trustees. Buyers of individual life insurance plans cannot do this so easily.

Employers also have an incentive to hire a trustee who invests in a very risky portfolio to try to obtain high returns to reduce the yearly contributions the employer must make to the plan. However, if the risky strategy fails, ERISA requires that the employer make up the unfunded liability or be subject to a tax on that unfunded liability, as we indicated earlier. When a company that is near bankruptcy engages in this strategy, the power to tax to recover the unfunded liability may be meaningless. To protect itself, the government does have priority over other liability holders.

Box 4.5

The Overfunded Liability

Between year end 1984 and the stock market crash of 1987, the stock market appreciated by over 90 percent. Consequently, the rise in prices resulted in an increase in the value of many firms' pension assets relative to their liabilities, thus creating an overfunded liability. Those firms whose pension funds were overfunded could then cease making payments to their pension funds until the value of the liabilities increased or until the market value of assets fell.

In 1987, before the stock market crash, Citicorp decided to cash in on its overfunded pension liability. It did this by selling the fund's assets and liabilities to an insurance company. The insurance company paid Citicorp the difference between the value of the assets and the value of the liabilities. It thereby assumed the risk of fluctuations in the value of Citicorp's pension assets.

One reason a company might want to sell its pension fund is to "lock in" its gain on the fund's stock portfolio. However, by selling, it also forgoes the opportunity to benefit from any future appreciation in stocks. Citicorp, however, had a different reason in mind. Bank regulators set standards for bank capital-to-asset ratios, and Citicorp needed capital to meet the standard.

The regulators do not recognize capital gains on pension assets as capital. That is, regulators do not include the appreciation in pension assets relative liabilities when valuing a bank's assets. Since capital is the difference between the value of assets and the value of liabilities, this implies that the appreciation in pension assets does not increase capital for regulatory purposes. However, the cash obtained from the sale is treated as an asset by the regulators. Thus the sale created an increase in the value of assets relative to liabilities, increasing regulatory capital.

Several other large New York banks also were under the capital gun and planned to sell their pension assets and liabilities. However, their timing was a little off. Their sales were completed after the crash, which reduced their gain over precrash stock prices by about 25 percent.

Thus pension funds have more effective methods of promoting competition among providers than holders of individual life policies. The competition to preserve asset values so that the size of contributions does not have to increase when the stock market declines in value has created a demand for methods to protect stock portfolios from declines in the market. This had led to the development of an investing technique called *portfolio insurance,* which, we shall see in a later chapter, has placed heavy demands on liquidity in the stock market.

CONCLUSION

In this chapter we have discussed how life insurance companies and pension funds create policies and savings plans that promise to provide a fixed level of benefits. Because the performance of the economy is uncertain, these financial institutions must develop procedures to protect the value of their assets from market fluctuations. They do this partly by evaluating their liabilities at interest rates that are low relative to the market. A low interest rate implies a large liability that must be funded. If the interest rate assumed is conservative, they end up funding a liability that is larger than the one they will probably have.

However, making conservative assumptions about the size of their liabilities has a cost. It raises the price to the individual or company that is paying for the plan or policy. Consumers have a difficult time determining whether insurance companies are playing fair, so they have decreased their demand for whole life policies. The behavior of pension fund managers is more easily policed because the buyer of the service is usually a large company.

Pension fund managers have incentives to hold risky assets and preserve the value of these assets in falling markets. Pension fund trustees who show good investment performance can reduce the contributions that employers must make to pension funds. This has led to a demand to give liquidity to risky assets, which are not usually considered liquid. We will see in later chapters that not everyone can have the liquidity that he or she demands.

KEY TERMS

group insurance policy

ordinary insurance policy

term insurance policy

whole life insurance policy

investment risk

duration matching

universal life insurance policy

variable life insurance policy

annuity

Employment Retirement Income and
  Security Act

EXERCISES

1. Consider a life annuity of the sort offered by pension funds or insurance companies. The annuity will pay its owner $10,000 per year from age 65 until the owner's death. Suppose that $1.00 payable i periods in the future exchanges for pi dollars currently in the bond markets. How would you determine the price that a 35-year-old woman would have to pay currently to acquire such

an annuity? How does the insurance company or pension fund avoid the risk inherent in the duration of payments being contingent on the time of death?

2. In Chapter 2 we introduced an ideal financial intermediary that has equal access to securities markets. This means that it can buy the securities issued by firms and reissue its own securities. The market only considers the risk of the underlying securities in pricing the securities issued by the financial intermediary.

In April 1991, Executive Life Insurance Company was seized by the insurance departments of the states of California and New York. It had invested heavily in junk bonds, and policyholders, fearful that assets were inadequate relative to reserves, began surrendering their policies for their cash value. The state insurance departments prohibited surrenders so that the company would have enough assets to pay its death claims.

Does this episode imply that Executive Life did not have equal access to financial markets? Would this episode reduce the possibility that other insurance companies can achieve equal access?

3. Let's assume that there are two insurance companies. One, Old Faithful, has been around since the Revolutionary War. It has kept its promises through every turbulent episode in the financial history of the United States. The other, Take Your Chances, is a brand new firm. The two companies hold identical asset portfolios. Will they offer identical prices on their policies? If they do not, who makes the profit or takes the loss?

4. If the main role of financial institutions is to recreate the Modigliani–Miller conditions by obtaining equal access to financial markets, would pension funds and life insurance companies be organized as separate entities?

5. Let's assume that the percentage of American workers employed by large corporations is declining. This would imply that a rising percentage of workers are building their own retirement plans. Let's also assume that they build these plans by buying annuities from life insurance companies. As we indicated in this chapter, compared with life insurance companies, employers can more easily smooth out variations in income in their pension plans because they can effectively vary the premium. Thus a decline in corporate employment decreases the number of investors that have a relatively low cost of absorbing risk. In a Modigliani–Miller world what happens to risk premiums as a result of the decline in corporate employment? What would happen to the types of projects undertaken by corporations?

6. In a Modigliani–Miller world, would a shift away from corporate employment lead to a change in the relative returns on stocks and bonds? Would it lead to a change in the liability structure of corporations?

7. As we have seen, in the real world, insurance companies hold more bonds than employer-sponsored pension funds because insurance companies are less able to absorb risk. This implies that a shift in savings toward insurance companies would increase the amount of bonds and decrease the amount of equity issued

by corporations. Explain why this shift in corporate liability structure results from principal-agent problems between the financial institution and its customers.

8. In a world of principal-agent problems, would a shift in savings toward life insurance affect the liability structure of firms? Would this have different consequences for real investment than in a Modigliani-Miller world?

9. If investors increase their demand for liquid assets, what happens to the types of projects undertaken by corporations? Is your answer the same whether Modigliani-Miller holds or not?

10. As the seizure of the Executive Life Insurance Company demonstrates, policyholders suffer the consequences if an insurance company goes bankrupt. Bank depositors do not have this worry; their deposits are insured up to $100,000 by an agency of the federal government. Why do you suppose we have not created such an agency for life insurance companies?

11. As we have seen, regulations prohibit insurance companies from acting as the ideal financial institution we introduced in Chapter 2. Does this mean that regulators increase the cost of creating liquidity in financial markets?

FURTHER READING

Curry, Timothy, and Mark Warshawsky, "Life Insurance in a Changing Environment," *Federal Reserve Bulletin,* July 1986, pp. 449–462.

Warshawsky, Mark J., "Pension Plans: Funding, Assets, and Regulatory Environment," *Federal Reserve Bulletin,* November 1988, pp. 717–730.

5

Interest Rates

We all have constant contact with interest rates. Our banks pay interest on deposit accounts; our credit card companies charge interest on our unpaid balances; and homeowners pay interest on their mortgage loans. In fact, we are faced with so many different types of interest rates on various securities that it is often difficult to compare one with another.

Cutting through the complex array of interest rates, economists often refer to "the interest rate" as a benchmark or underlying rate upon which all other observable interest rates are based. The underlying rate of return, or interest rate, that materializes in a society is the price for exchanging goods or money available currently for goods or money available at some future time. Expressed as the number of future goods or money paid per unit of current goods or money, it is a pure percentage. As a price in a market economy, it arises in an equilibrium between (1) the current and future goods that people want to consume and (2) those which it is possible for a society to produce, as you may expect. Thus it simultaneously represents the rate at which households are willing to substitute future for present consumption and the rate, imposed by technological and resource constraints, at which a postponement of current consumption can be transformed into future consumption goods.

Although we will depict the determination of the rate of return fairly readily on an abstract level in this chapter, it is difficult for us to measure "the rate of interest" in actual economies because of their complexity. We can try to infer the interest rate on loans from the prices observable in the markets for actual securities. Unfortunately, we have observations of the prices of existing securities that promise a wide range of different money payoffs and are complicated by many different conditions. We wish to use these observations to extract somehow a measurement of *the* rate of interest, the price at which current and future goods exchange.

We begin by examining some of the common methods used to measure interest rates. Then we consider the meaning of the *real interest rate.* Finally, we consider why securities of different maturities offer different yields, and we analyze an example of how short- and long-term interest rates would be determined in an economy subject to fluctuations in consumption.

MEASURING INTEREST RATES AND YIELDS

We have already considered how to calculate the present value of a stream of dollar payments when a given, constant interest rate can be used to discount future payments. Now we wish to reverse the problem and ask how we should measure the return, or yield, on an asset when we are given its price and its promised stream of dollar payments. We pose the problem in this manner because in *The Wall Street Journal, The Financial Times,* and elsewhere we observe the market prices of a wide array of assets that promise different payment streams. To make comparisons among such assets, we need a convenient statistic to summarize each asset's return, and such summary statistics are what we commonly use to characterize a particular security's interest rate. We may express the return on a single security by each of several numbers of varying usefulness. We survey four of these measures in the following sections.

Coupon Yield

The simplest measure of a security's interest rate is known as **coupon yield.** Certain types of longer-maturity bonds promise a payment stream of a constant dollar amount annually or semiannually, with a final large principal payment when the bond matures. For example, a bond may promise a payment of $10 per year in each of 10 years, as well as a payment of $100 after the tenth year. Such bonds are known as **coupon bonds** because the holder might apply for the periodic payment by clipping a coupon from the bond and sending it to the issuer. This would be the means of triggering payment for bonds represented by a paper certificate. The ownership of many bonds is now simply registered by computers, with the payments automatically made through the electronic payments system. Such a system of accounting for securities ownership is known as a **book-entry system.** The periodic payment is known as the **coupon,** and the final payment is called the **par value** of the bond. We compute the coupon yield by dividing the coupon payment by the par value. In our example, the coupon yield equals 10 percent.

Unfortunately, although simple to compute, the coupon yield ignores the current market price of the bond, an important piece of information about potential payoffs. If the current market price is less than the par value of the bond, someone purchasing the bond at that price would earn a return on investment exceeding 10 percent per year over the life of the bond. Thus the coupon yield is a misleading indicator of return.

Current Yield

A second statistic, the **current yield,** does make use of some of the information contained in the market price and is frequently included in newspaper reports of bond prices. The current yield is defined as the coupon payment divided by the security's market price. In the preceding example, if the market price of the bond is $90, the current yield is $(10/90) \times 100 = 11.1$ percent. The current yield, however, is misleading as a summary statistic of bond return because it does not include potential capital gains—that is, earnings from changes in the price of the security.

Yield to Maturity

A third statistic, the **yield to maturity,** incorporates information on the asset price, the payment stream of the bond, and those capital gains which will *certainly* accrue to the security holder if the security is held to maturity. Recall the formula derived in Chapter 3 for computing the present value PV of a stream of payments A_1, A_2, A_3, . . . , A_n when the constant one-period interest rate is r:

$$PV = \frac{A_1}{(1 + r)} + \frac{A_2}{(1 + r)^2} + \frac{A_3}{(1 + r)^3} + \cdots + \frac{A_n}{(1 + r)^n}$$

The yield to maturity is defined as that constant value r that equates the present value with the current market price of the bond. The idea behind the yield to maturity is that in pricing the security, the market must have in mind some appropriate constant period-by-period yields to discount the promised payments stream. Assuming that those yields are all the identical yield r, we can solve the preceding equation, with some effort, to produce a unique yield to maturity.

The issuer of the security effectively buys back the security at the maturity date by paying the principal to the lender. If, at the time of purchase, the current market

Box 5.1

Bond Tables

Bond tables (or bond price programs on electronic spreadsheets) have been prepared to provide ready solutions for the present value of a bond. An example of a bond table is presented below. For a given market yield to maturity, coupon, and maturity, the table provides the bond's price. This particular table is for a bond with a 10-percent coupon payable semiannually—that is, a $100 bond will pay a coupon of $5 every 6 months. A complete bond table would contain a similar page for every potential coupon yield, starting at 0 percent, and for a much longer range of maturities.

As an example of how to use the table to find the market yield to maturity, suppose that a 10-year bond with a 10-percent coupon payable semiannually has a current market price of $113.59. To find the associated yield to maturity, search down the column for 10 years to maturity until you find the price closest to the market price. Then determine the yield to maturity associated with the row in which you find the price. In this case, the yield is exactly 8 percent.

BOND PRICE TABLE 10-PERCENT COUPON PAYABLE SEMIANNUALLY

Years to Maturity

Yield	1	2	3	4	5	6	7	8	9	10
0.0	110.00	120.00	130.00	140.00	150.00	160.00	170.00	180.00	190.00	200.00
1.00	108.93	117.78	126.53	135.20	143.79	152.29	160.70	169.03	177.28	185.44
2.00	107.88	115.61	123.18	130.61	137.89	145.02	152.01	158.87	165.59	172.18
3.00	106.85	113.49	119.94	126.20	132.28	138.18	143.90	149.46	154.85	160.09
4.00	105.82	111.42	116.80	121.98	126.95	131.73	136.32	140.73	144.98	149.05
4.25	105.57	110.91	116.04	120.95	125.66	130.17	134.50	138.65	142.63	146.45
4.50	105.32	110.41	115.27	119.93	124.38	128.64	132.71	136.61	140.34	143.90
4.75	105.07	109.90	114.52	118.92	123.12	127.13	130.96	134.61	138.09	141.41
5.00	104.82	109.40	113.77	117.93	121.88	125.64	129.23	132.64	135.88	138.97
5.25	104.57	108.91	113.03	116.94	120.65	124.18	127.53	130.71	133.72	136.59
5.50	104.32	108.41	112.29	115.96	119.44	122.73	125.85	128.81	131.61	134.26
5.75	104.07	107.92	111.56	115.00	118.24	121.31	124.21	126.95	129.54	131.98

price of the security differs from the par value, a capital gain or loss automatically accrues to the investor holding the bond to maturity. The computation of the yield to maturity includes this certain capital gain or loss as part of the yield. For coupon bonds, we need not perform the tedious algebra required to solve this equation; rather, we can use bond tables, as discussed in Box 5.1.

Years to Maturity

Yield	1	2	3	4	5	6	7	8	9	10
6.00	103.83	107.43	110.83	114.04	117.06	119.91	122.59	125.12	127.51	129.75
6.25	103.58	106.95	110.12	113.09	115.89	118.53	121.00	123.33	125.52	127.58
6.50	103.34	106.47	109.40	112.16	114.74	117.16	119.44	121.57	123.57	125.44
6.75	103.09	105.99	108.69	111.23	113.60	115.82	117.90	119.84	121.66	123.36
7.00	102.85	105.51	107.99	110.31	112.47	114.50	116.38	118.14	119.78	121.32
7.25	102.61	105.04	107.30	109.40	111.36	113.19	114.89	116.47	117.95	119.32
7.50	102.37	104.56	106.61	108.50	110.27	111.90	113.42	114.84	116.15	117.37
7.75	102.13	104.10	105.92	107.61	109.18	110.64	111.98	113.23	114.39	115.46
8.00	101.89	103.63	105.24	106.73	108.11	109.39	110.56	111.65	112.66	113.59
8.25	101.65	103.17	104.57	105.86	107.05	108.15	109.17	110.10	110.97	111.76
8.50	101.41	102.71	103.90	105.00	106.01	106.94	107.79	108.58	109.30	109.97
8.75	101.17	102.25	103.24	104.14	104.98	105.74	106.44	107.09	107.68	108.22
9.00	100.94	101.79	102.58	103.30	103.96	104.56	105.11	105.62	106.08	106.50
9.25	100.70	101.34	101.93	102.46	102.95	103.40	103.80	104.17	104.51	104.83
9.50	100.47	100.89	101.28	101.63	101.95	102.25	102.51	102.76	102.98	103.18
9.75	100.23	100.44	100.64	100.81	100.97	101.12	101.25	101.37	101.48	101.57
10.00	100.00	100.00	100.00	100.00	100.00	100.00	100.00	100.00	100.00	100.00
10.25	99.77	99.56	99.37	99.20	99.04	98.90	98.77	98.66	98.55	98.46
10.50	99.54	99.12	98.74	98.40	98.09	97.82	97.56	97.34	97.13	96.95
10.75	99.31	99.68	98.12	97.61	97.16	96.75	96.38	96.04	95.74	95.47
11.00	99.08	98.25	97.50	96.83	96.23	95.69	95.21	94.77	94.38	94.02
11.25	98.85	97.82	96.89	96.06	95.32	94.65	94.05	93.52	93.04	92.61
11.50	98.62	97.39	96.28	95.30	94.41	93.63	92.92	92.29	91.72	91.22
11.75	98.39	96.96	95.68	94.54	93.52	92.61	91.80	91.08	90.44	89.86
12.00	98.17	96.53	95.08	93.79	92.64	91.62	90.71	89.89	89.17	88.53
12.25	97.94	96.11	94.49	93.05	91.77	90.63	89.62	88.73	87.93	87.23
12.50	97.72	95.69	93.90	92.31	90.91	89.66	88.56	87.58	86.72	85.95
12.75	97.49	95.28	93.32	91.59	90.06	88.71	87.51	86.46	85.52	84.70
13.00	97.27	94.86	92.74	90.87	89.22	87.76	86.48	85.35	84.35	83.47
13.25	97.05	94.45	92.16	90.15	88.39	86.83	85.46	84.26	83.20	82.27
13.50	96.82	94.04	91.59	89.45	87.57	85.91	84.46	83.19	82.07	81.09
13.75	96.60	93.63	91.03	88.75	86.75	85.01	83.48	82.14	80.97	79.94
14.00	96.38	93.23	90.47	88.06	85.95	84.11	82.51	81.11	79.88	78.81
14.25	96.16	92.82	89.91	87.37	85.16	83.23	81.55	80.09	78.82	77.70
14.50	95.95	92.42	89.36	86.69	84.38	82.36	80.61	79.09	77.77	76.62
14.75	95.73	92.02	88.81	86.02	83.60	81.51	79.69	78.11	76.74	75.56

A security's yield to maturity is the most frequently reported summary statistic indicating its payoff. The yield to maturity, however, also has a drawback. As the average annual yield over the security's lifespan, its computation assumes that the maturity date is known. Many kinds of securities, however, have an uncertain maturity because the borrower has the right to repay the loan prior to the stated maturity date. Examples of such loans are mortgage loans, consumer loans such as automobile loans, industrial bonds, municipal bonds, and even long-term U.S. government bonds.[1] Even certain very long maturities may not be as rock solid as the investor might desire. See Box 5.2.

If a security is paid off prior to its official maturity date, the yield to maturity may seriously misstate the average yield over the security's true maturity. For example, consider the 10-year, $100 bond discussed in Box 5.1. If an investor buys the bond at below par, say $80, the yield to maturity would be approximately 13.75 percent. You can verify this in the bond table. If the $100 face value of the security is prepaid after the first year, the investor earns the coupon payment of $10 plus a capital gain of $20 for a yield of $(30/80) \times 100 = 37.5$ percent during the true life of the loan. The yield to maturity understates this yield because, in effect, it averages the capital gain over 10 years of the bond's life rather than assigning it to just 1 year.

Holding Period Yield

A fourth summary payoff statistic, the **holding period yield,** considers the payoff from holding a bond for an arbitrary duration, usually different from the maturity of the bond. A lender always has the option of purchasing a security one year and selling it the next, providing that there is a ready market for the security. In such a case, the holding period is 1 year. The payoff during the holding period is the coupon payment plus any capital gain between the time of purchase and the time of sale of the security. Dividing this payoff by the initial market price produces the holding period yield. Again, suppose that in the example in Box 5.1, the security is purchased for $90 and sold after 1 year for $80. The holder has suffered a capital loss of $10 and has received a coupon payment of $10, for a zero payoff. The holding period yield is 0 percent. If the investor has sold after 1 year for $105, the payoff would have equaled $25—$10 in coupon payment and $15 in capital gain. The holding period yield would be $(25/90) \times 100 = 27.8$ percent.

If when we purchase a security we always know with certainty its future price at the end of any holding period, then the holding period yield would provide an ideal summary statistic to measure the yield. We would embrace this number as reflecting what we mean by "the rate of interest." Unfortunately, future security prices are almost always uncertain, and expectations of their value vary widely. Therefore, since expected capital gains are highly conjectural, the financial press does not report them. The yield to maturity is used as a compromise statistic

---

1. In the case of government bonds, the Treasury usually agrees contractually not to call (prepay) the bond prior to a specific date. For calculating yields to maturity, the earliest possible call date is con- sidered the maturity date of the bond even though the bond may not be paid off until several years afterwards.

to represent "the interest rate" because at least the capital gain built into holding a security to maturity is relatively certain and not subject to a divergence of opinion.

NOMINAL VERSUS REAL INTEREST RATES

Economists distinguish between two kinds of interest rates—nominal and real. **Nominal interest rates** are the percentage payoffs on loans denominated in the unit of account. For example, a person borrowing $100 for 1 year may agree to repay $110, the principal of $100 plus $10 interest. The interest is the price the borrower must pay to use the principal for 1 year. For ease of calculating the interest charge regardless of the size of the loan, interest is always quoted as a percentage of the principal on an annual basis. In this case, the interest rate is 10 percent per year.

Although the financial markets report only nominal interest rates, economic decisions on the allocation of resources are guided by **real interest rates.** People who lend funds are giving up access to currently available goods. Their willingness to lend depends on the amount of goods they can command with the funds received when the loan is repaid. The real interest, therefore, is the price in terms of goods that the borrower must pay to use the goods effectively loaned to him or her. For example, a person borrowing 100 units of goods may agree to repay 105 units next year; in this case, the real interest charge is 5 units, or 5 percent, per year.

When repayment is made in money, however, rather than goods, we must distinguish between real and nominal rates of return. Nominally, $1 is $1. But will $1 a year from now have the same real purchasing power as $1 today? Nominal interest rates can be associated with an implied real interest rate if we know the changes in the price level anticipated by lenders and borrowers. The **price level** is the price of goods in terms of the unit of account. For example, a unit of goods may cost $1.00 when a nominal loan is undertaken and $1.05 when it is repaid in 1 year. We would say that an inflation of 5 percent has occurred or, equivalently, that the unit of account has depreciated 5 percent relative to goods. If this inflation was expected when the nominal loan of $100 was made, the lender anticipated that the repayment of $110 would be worth $110/$1.05 = 104.8 units of goods. Put another way, since the $100 principal was worth 100 units of goods at the time of the loan and the lender expected 5 percent inflation, then she anticipated that the nominal interest rate of 10 percent would mean a real interest rate of only 4.8 percent.

More generally, if the nominal interest rate on a loan is i percent per year, the anticipated inflation rate is c percent per year, and the real interest rate is r percent per year, the nominal interest rate can be expressed as

$$i = r + c$$

This expression is known as **Fisher's equation** after Irving Fisher. The ideas in Fisher's *The Theory of Interest* (1930) underpin most current theories of the determination of interest rates.

Fisher's equation can be interpreted as a definition of the real and nominal interest rates, in which case it must always be true. The observable nominal interest rate would then always be the sum of an unobservable real interest rate and expected rate of inflation, by definition.

Alternatively, Fisher's equation can be interpreted as a proposed theory of behavior under which nominal and real loans are perfect substitutes. Under such a theory, holders of nominal loans would demand no premium for bearing the risk of inflation, requiring only that securities denominated in money pay some real interest rate demanded by their holders. To determine the nominal interest rate that they require to hold the security, lenders simply add their anticipated inflation rate to the real interest rate they demand.

To form expectations of the inflation rate requires a theory of the determination of the price level, which we will study in Chapters 7, 8, and 21. For now, we will assume that households have formed anticipations of the inflation rate for various future periods, and we will consider the impact of these anticipations on nominal interest rates.

DETERMINATION OF THE TERM STRUCTURE
OF INTEREST RATES

We now turn to the issue of what determines equilibrium yields on securities that mature at different future times. For future times, sometimes stretching out for 50 years, financial markets offer bonds promising to make payments at that time. Associated with the price of these bonds are their yields to maturity. At any given time, yields can differ greatly with maturity.

The **term structure of interest rates** is the name given to a plot of yields to maturity against remaining time to maturity for bonds unlikely to be defaulted. Bonds of the same maturity offered by different institutions carry different risks of default and therefore have different yields to maturity. Construction of the term structure of interest rates avoids this problem by plotting only yields on riskless securities, such as obligations of the U.S. Treasury.

Figure 5.1 plots yield against maturity for U.S. government bonds on three different dates. In part (A), we see that the slope on July 31, 1981 was negative; yields on short-term securities were higher than those on long-term securities. In part (B), we see that by 1985 the picture changed and the plot slopes upward; in part (C), the third curve, representing yields to maturity in 1989, is relatively flat.

The lines depicting the term structure of interest rates connect points that represent bonds with approximately identical features other than maturity. In particular, the lines connect only points representing highly liquid issues. These usually are fairly recently issued securities that are still traded heavily by securities dealers. Typically, the yields on numerous government issues lie off the curve, although we do not indicate such issues in Figure 5.1. These generally are issues with tax advantages or that are much less liquid than the issues on the curve.

Even issues on the curve may differ in liquidity. For example, newly issued 30-year bonds are highly liquid because many dealers trade them before they find their way to the portfolios of final investors. On the other hand, 29-year bonds (the 30-year bonds sold last year) are not as liquid. Because of their added liquidity, 30-year bonds typically have yields 25 basis points ($\frac{1}{4}$ of 1 percentage point) lower than 29-year bonds. This represents a premium price paid for access to greater liquidity. We will focus a great deal of attention on the liquidity characteristics of securities in Chapters 6 and 13.

We now explore why term structures of interest rates are shaped as they are and why their shapes change over time.

An Example: The Sandunian Term Structure
of Interest Rates in Peace

To come to grips with how an economy generates an equilibrium term structure, let's consider an example of the previously peaceful country of Sandunia that now

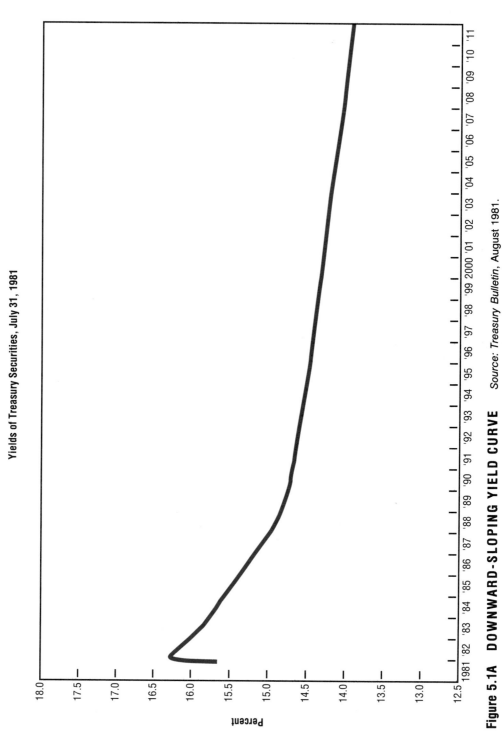

Figure 5.1A DOWNWARD-SLOPING YIELD CURVE *Source: Treasury Bulletin,* August 1981.

Note: The curve is fitted by eye and based only on the most actively traded issues. Market yields on coupon issues due in less than 3 months are excluded.

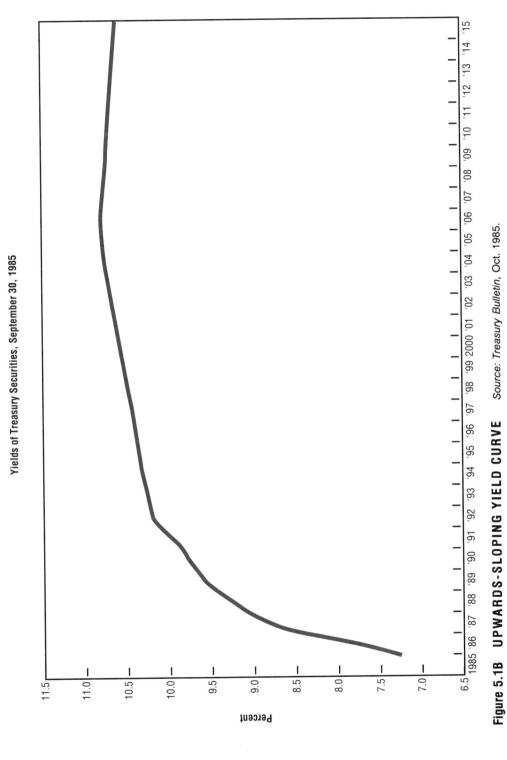

Figure 5.1B **UPWARDS-SLOPING YIELD CURVE** *Source: Treasury Bulletin,* Oct. 1985.

Note: Callable issues are plotted to the earliest call date when prices are above par and to maturity when prices are at par or below.

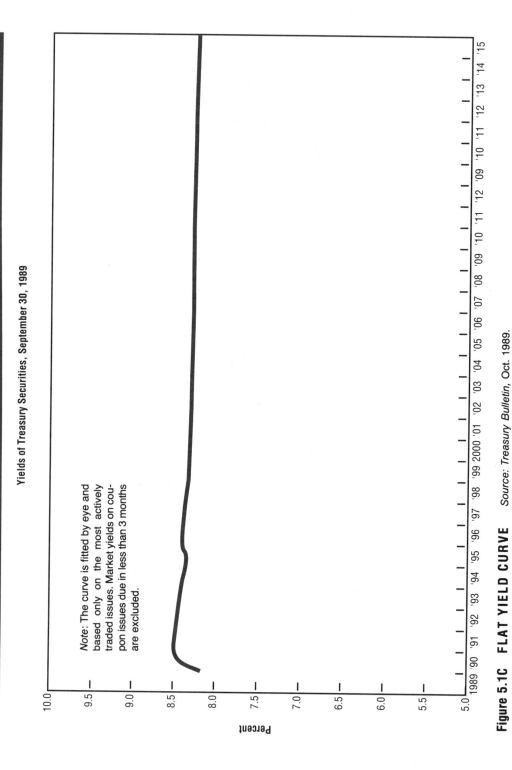

Yields of Treasury Securities, September 30, 1989

Note: The curve is fitted by eye and based only on the most actively traded issues. Market yields on coupon issues due in less than 3 months are excluded.

Figure 5.1C FLAT YIELD CURVE   *Source: Treasury Bulletin,* Oct. 1989.

Note: Callable issues are plotted to the earliest call date when prices are above par and to maturity when prices are at par or below.

unexpectedly enters a war. First, we will examine the term structure when everyone in Sandunia is certain that no war is possible in the foreseeable future.

Our analysis begins in 1992. We presume for now that households anticipate zero inflation in the future, so the interest rates we derive are both nominal and real. Later, we will see how nominal interest rates are determined when the anticipated inflation rate differs from zero. To avoid worrying about the production sector, we assume that Sandunia receives 100 units of perishable goods per household as a constant annual endowment paid in equal quantities to every household. By *perishable,* we mean that the goods cannot be saved for later consumption.

All Sandunian households have the same tastes between consuming in time t and in time $t + 1$, represented by the indifference curves in Figure 5.2A. Each indifference curve represents all those combinations of time t and time $t + 1$ consumption levels that will make the household equally well off. They are drawn with downward slopes to indicate that a household will not mind a loss of consumption in time t if it is compensated with a sufficient gain in time $t + 1$ consumption. In this case, the household is indifferent between the two possible consumption combinations. The slopes of the indifference curves are steep when the household has relatively small amounts of time t consumption and relatively large amounts of time $t + 1$ consumption. This means that the household would be willing to sacrifice a unit of relatively scarce time t consumption only if it were compensated with a large amount of time $t + 1$ consumption. Alternatively, the slopes of the indifference

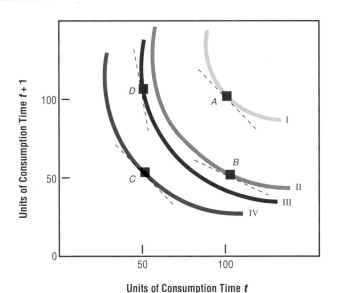

Figure 5.2A   SANDUNIAN INDIFFERENCE CURVES AND CONSUMPTION OPPORTUNITIES

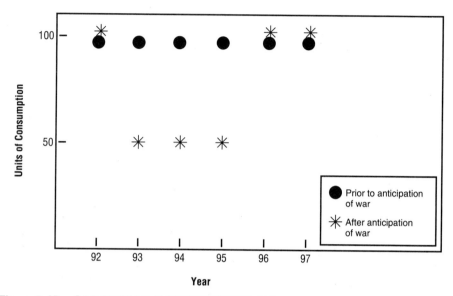

Figure 5.2B SANDUNIAN CONSUMPTION LEVELS

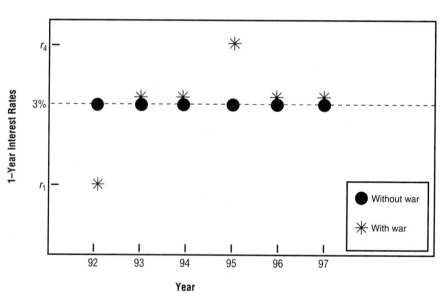

Figure 5.2C INTEREST RATES ON 1-YEAR LOANS

curves are flat when the household has relatively large amounts of time t consumption and relatively small amounts of time $t + 1$ consumption. The household would then be willing to sacrifice a unit of time t consumption for a relatively small compensation of time $t + 1$ consumption. Finally, the higher the indifference curve in Figure 5.2A, the better off is the household. In this way, we indicate that the household always prefers to have more of both goods. For example, any point on indifference curve I represents a consumption combination preferred to any combination on indifference curves II, III, or IV.

In this example, Sandunia's opportunity for consumption in times t and $t + 1$ is the single point A on indifference curve I, representing an endowment of 100 units of goods per household now and 100 units next period. Assuming that households have no means of transforming currently available goods into future goods, they must consume the bundle A. Market interest rates adjust to make them want to consume at A, and the only such rate is that given by the slope of the line tangent to indifference curve I at point A. Supposing that this interest rate equals 3 percent, the slope of the tangent line is -1.03. At this market rate, each household is content with its consumption bundle, so no loans will actually be undertaken, but any other rate will lead to an excess supply or demand for loans. For example, at an interest rate lower than 3 percent, households will want to borrow to increase current consumption at the price of a reduction in future consumption. Since all households now want to borrow, the increased demand for funds will drive up the interest rate.

If people are certain that no war will break out to change the situation, the 3-percent equilibrium interest rate will remain unchanged. Every period people will consume 100 units of goods, and the market interest rate on one-period loans will be 3 percent. In Figure 5.2B, we plot this constant consumption path against time. The sequence of circles represents the constant level of 100 units of consumption year after year. In Figure 5.2C, we depict the unchanging interest rate on one-period loans for the year in which the loan is originated with a sequence of circles at 3 percent.

Finally, in Figure 5.3A, against the time to maturity, we plot the yields to maturity for loans of one period, two periods, three periods, and so on. These are yields on **discount loans** or zero-coupon loans that promise to pay a given amount at maturity but nothing before maturity. We have depicted the yields as invariant to the maturity of the loan. How do we know that the term structure of interest rates is 3 percent regardless of maturity?

Arbitrage Between One- and Two-Period Bonds

To show how knowledge of interest rates of future one-period loans can shape the term structure of interest rates, we consider first the relation between yields on one-period and on two-period loans. We can then generalize this relationship to determine yields on longer maturities.

Suppose that a two-period bond has a yield to maturity of 2 percent. Then a

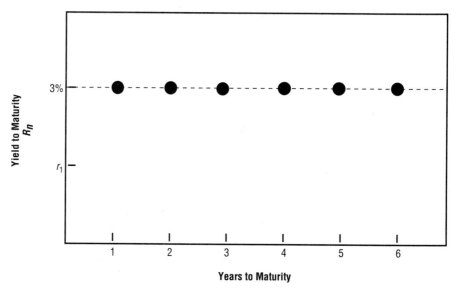

Figure 5.3A   SANDUNIAN TERM STRUCTURE IN PEACE

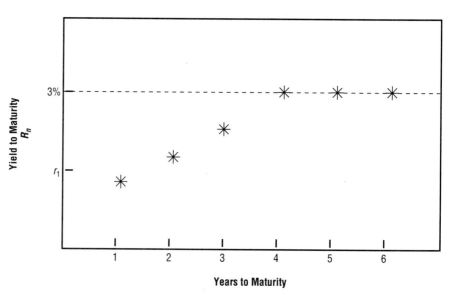

Figure 5.3B   1992 SANDUNIAN TERM STRUCTURE IN WAR

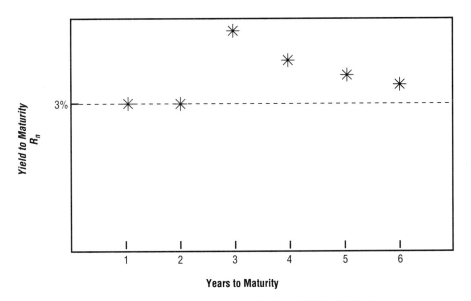

Figure 5.3C   1993 SANDUNIAN TERM STRUCTURE IN WAR

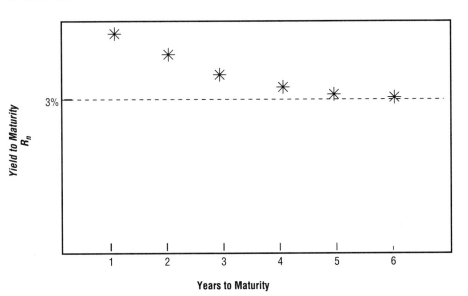

Figure 5.3D   1995 SANDUNIAN TERM STRUCTURE IN WAR

loan of $1 now will repay $(1.02)^2$, which is about $1.04 after two periods. A one-period loan of $1, however, will pay off $1.03 dollars after one period. That is, it pays 3 percent. If this payoff can be rolled over into a new one-period loan at the same 3-percent yield, the sequence of transactions will have a total payoff of $(1.03)^2$, which is about $1.06 after two periods. With a yield to maturity of 2 percent on two-period loans and a certain yield of 3 percent on the sequence of one-period loans, households would recognize that they could gain by borrowing $1 for two periods at 2 percent and lending the $1 in a sequence of two one-period loans at 3 percent. With no current commitment of its own resources, a household would have a pure profit of $1.06 − $1.04 = $0.02. Since all households would presumably try to take advantage of this great opportunity, there would be an excess demand for two-period loans, thereby bidding the yield to maturity on such loans up to 3 percent. We will now see that the same argument is applicable to yields on loans of longer maturity.

The Expectations Hypothesis of the Term Structure

The preceding development of the two-period structure of interest rates is an example of an argument known as the **expectations theory of the term structure.** This hypothesis supposes that the yield to maturity on n-period loans is simply the average of the expected yields on one-period loans occurring in sequence during the life of the n-period loan.

If the future one-period yields are *certain*, then the expectations hypothesis must hold to prevent unusual arbitrage profits. To see this, suppose that $i_1, i_2, \ldots , i_n$ are the certain yields on future 1-year loans. i_j is the yield on loans originating in period j and paid off in period $j + 1$. Let I_n be the annualized yield to maturity on a loan originating in period 1 and terminating in period $n + 1$. To preclude riskless arbitrate profits, it must be true that

$$(1 + I_n)^n = (1 + i_1) \times (1 + i_2) \times \cdots \times (1 + i_n)$$

Suppose that, on the contrary, the right-hand side exceeds the left-hand side of this equation. An arbitrager could risklessly profit by borrowing $1 for n periods at a yield to maturity of I_n and by lending the $1 in a sequence of loans at the short-term rates $i_1, i_2, \ldots , i_n$. In period $n + 1$, when he must deliver to pay off the n-period loan, he will have more than enough from his sequence of short-term loans, pocketing the difference as pure profit. Since there is no risk in such an operation, everyone would want to perform the same operation, and they would demand n-period loans. This would create an excess demand for such loans and drive up the yield to maturity I_n until the equality is reestablished. A similar argument can be employed to demonstrate the impossibility of the left side of the equation exceeding the right side.

The expectations hypothesis of the term structure follows from the preceding equation. If we actually carry out the multiplications across the n terms on both sides of equation, we will find that

$$1 + nI_n + \text{second-order terms} = 1 + i_1 + i_2 + i_3 + \cdots$$
$$+ i_n + \text{second-order terms}$$

For example, when $n = 2$, we have $(1 + I_2)^2 = 1 + 2I_2 + I_2^2$. The second-order terms consist of numerous products of two interest rates. Since interest rates are small, their product is much smaller, so the second-order terms can be dropped to produce the approximation

$$1 + nI_n = 1 + i_1 + i_2 + i_3 + \cdots + i_n$$

Rearranging, we find that

$$I_n = \frac{i_1 + i_2 + i_3 + \cdots + i_n}{n}$$

The annualized yield to maturity on an n-period loan is the average of the anticipated yields to maturity, $i_1, \ldots, i_n$, on a sequence of one-period loans spanning the life of the n-period loan.

The expectations hypothesis provides a ready explanation of the term structure of interest rates. If short-term interest rates are currently low but expected to rise in the future, the term structure will be upward sloping; if short-term rates are expected to remain roughly constant, the term structure will be flat; and if they are expected to fall in the future, the term structure will be downward sloping. Also, interest rates for longer maturities will tend to fluctuate less than short-term interest rates, because temporary movements in short-term rates are averaged out over longer periods.

Nevertheless, while the expectations hypothesis moves us a long way in explaining the term structure of interest rates, it is not the whole story. It presumes, for example, that households are indifferent between holding long maturities and short maturities with the same expected payoffs, even though future short-term rates are uncertain. Thus it assumes risk neutrality. If households are risk averse, then a risk premium will emerge either in long-term or short-term interest rates, and the expectations hypothesis will not fully explain the term structure. We examine the impact of risk aversion on the term structure in the Appendix to this chapter.

Example Continued: The Sandunian Term Structure with Anticipated War

Earlier we determined that in a peaceful environment, the Sandunian term structure of interest rates would be flat. To illustrate why observable term structures are not static, we now consider a disturbance that will shift the term structure over time. Suppose that at the start of 1992 the government and households in Sandunia suddenly realize that they will surely engage in a war starting in 1993. They know with certainty that the war will terminate in a stalemate at the end of 1995, to be followed by everlasting peace.

To fight the war, the government will tax each household 50 units of goods from its endowment in 1993, 1994, and 1995. After 1995, households will have 100 units of goods to consume once more. Households will maintain their anticipation that future inflation rates will be zero.

What effect will the war have on the term structure of interest rates in 1992, 1993, 1994, and so on? Again, we can find the term structure by remembering that it must be related to the future pattern of short-term (1-year) interest rates. The short-term rates can be found by considering the future pattern of consumption, depicted by the asterisks in Figure 5.2B. In 1992, consumption remains unchanged at 100 units. From 1993 to 1995, it falls to 50 units per year and returns permanently to 100 starting in 1996.

In Figure 5.2A, the change in 1993 consumption appears as a shift in endowment from point A on indifference curve I to point B on curve II. The slope of indifference curve II at point B is less than the slope on indifference curve I at point A, so interest rates on 1-year loans must decline in 1992 to reconcile goods supplies and demands. This occurs because of the desire of households to smooth consumption across periods. Faced with a 50-percent cut in consumption in 1 year, households would attempt to save (buy 1-year bonds) in 1992 to have more goods available in 1993 when the war starts. At the original interest rate of 3 percent, investors flock to buy bonds. Indeed, there is an excess demand for bonds, so the interest rate must fall to stifle that demand and satisfy households with the given consumption bundle at point B. Thus, for 1-year loans originated in 1992, the interest rate will be $r_1 <$ 3 percent.

When the war is waged in 1993, 1994, and 1995, households have 50 units of goods available for consumption, indicated by point C on indifference curve III in Figure 5.2A. At point C, the ratio of one-period-ahead consumption to current-period consumption is 1 : 1, as it is at point A. Unless the slopes of the indifference curves shift dramatically with the level of consumption, there should be little difference between the slope of indifference curve III at point C and that of indifference curve I at point A.[2] Hence the interest rates r_2 for 1-year loans from 1993 to 1994 and r_3 for 1-year loans from 1994 to 1995 should be the same as for the peacetime consumption level, 3 percent.

2. At any point along a positively sloped line drawn from the origin in Figure 5.2A, the ratio of next-period consumption goods to current-period consumption goods is constant. As an operational assumption, economists often presume that indifference curves intersecting such a ray have identical slopes at the point of intersection. Then indifference curve III at the point (50, 50) would have the same slope as indifference curve I at the point (100, 100), since both points lie on a single straight line through the origin.

Since 1995 is the last year of the war, consumption will return to the peacetime norm of 100 in 1996. Hence the consumption bundle for 1995–1996 will be point D on indifference curve IV in Figure 5.2A. In this case, the slope of curve IV at point D must exceed the slopes at points A and C so that the interest rate on one-period loans originated in 1994 will exceed 3 percent. Households, foreseeing a large amount of consumption in 1996, would like to borrow against it to augment 1995 consumption. Since goods cannot move across periods, this leads to an excess demand for loans, and a rise in the one-period interest rate results that effectively chokes off the excess demand.

After peace is restored in 1996, the situation returns to that which we originally analyzed for peaceful Sandunia. The interest rates on 1-year loans originating in 1996, 1997, and so on are then $r_5 = r_6 = \cdots = 3$ percent. The foreseeable sequence of 1-year interest rates, given a war, is summarized by the asterisks in Figure 5.2C, starting in 1992.

How will the advent of war affect the Sandunian term structure of interest rates in 1992, 1993, and so on? Recall that the term structure was flat prior to the anticipation of war. When war suddenly is anticipated, households can foresee the shift in future short-term loan rates. Immediately, the interest rate r_1 for 1-year loans originating in 1992 falls below 3 percent, as in Figure 5.2C. The yield to maturity for 2-year loans is the average between r_1 and r_2. Since $r_2 = 3$ percent, the yield to maturity on 2-year loans exceeds r_1 but is less than 3 percent, as in Figure 5.3B. As the average of r_1, $r_2 = 3$ percent, and $r_3 = 3$ percent, the yield to maturity on 3-year loans exceeds that on 2-year loans but is also less than 3 percent. The yield to maturity on 4-year loans is the average of r_1, r_2, r_3, and r_4. As the yield on 1-year loans between the last war year and the first year of peace, r_4 exceeds 3 percent. If r_4 exceeds 3 percent by the same quantity that r_1 falls short of 3 percent, then the yield to maturity on 4-year loans exactly equals 3 percent. For 5-year loans and beyond, the additional 1-year interest rates in the average always equal 3 percent, so these loans also have yields to maturity of 3 percent.

We conclude that the sudden awareness that a war will start in a year leads to a shift from a flat term structure to a rising term structure, with the greatest shifts in yield at the short end of the yield curve. Little or no shifts in yield to maturity occur for bonds at the long end of the spectrum because the fall in the short-term rates in 1992 is effectively canceled by the jump up in a short-term rates in 1995.

Shifting to 1993 with the war now begun, how does the term structure of interest rates change? The 1993 term structure is depicted in Figure 5.3C. The yield on both 1- and 2-year loans is 3 percent during the war. The yield on 3-year loans must exceed 3 percent, since we now average the high 1-year interest rate in 1995 with the 3-percent 1-year rates in 1993 and 1994. The rates on loans with maturities of 4 or more years exceed 3 percent but decline steadily toward 3 percent. Thus, in 1993, we observe a humped yield curve.

Finally, in 1995, the term structure will be downward sloping, as depicted in Figure 5.3D. In 1996 and afterward, the term structure will once again be as described in Figure 5.3A.

ACCOUNTING FOR ANTICIPATED INFLATION

We have assumed until now that the anticipated inflation rates were zero in Sandunia so that nominal and real interest rates coincided. In periods of great wars or large shifts in income, however, price levels can change significantly. How would the term structure of nominal interest rates change if Sandunians expected nonzero inflation rates during the war? Specifically, suppose that people in 1992 anticipate the following inflation rates once they realize that war will occur:

Year	Inflation Rate
1992–3	0%
1993–4	4%
1994–5	8%
1995–6	8%
1996–7	−3%
After 1997	0%

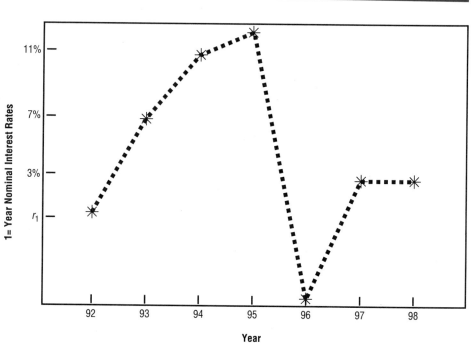

Figure 5.4 NOMINAL INTEREST RATES ON 1-YEAR LOANS

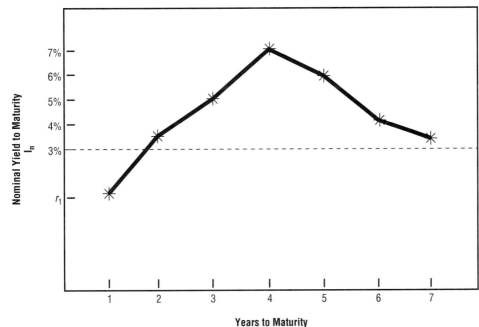

Figure 5.5   1992 TERM STRUCTURE OF NOMINAL INTEREST RATES

Using the same reasoning as before, we can determine the term structure of nominal interest rates once we know the pattern of nominal interest rates on future 1-year loans. This pattern can be constructed by using Fisher's equation, adding these anticipated inflation rates to the pattern of real yields on future 1-year loans constructed earlier.

Figure 5.4 depicts the path of nominal yields on one-period loans starting in 1992. The yield on 1-year loans originating in 1992 is simply r_1 from Figure 5.2C, since the anticipated inflation for this year is zero. For 1-year loans originating in 1993, however, the nominal yield is 7 percent—made up of the 3-percent real interest rate plus the 4-percent anticipated inflation. The yields for future years are constructed in a similar manner.

The term structure of nominal interest rates implied by this pattern is depicted in Figure 5.5.

The Gulf Crisis and the Term Structure

The Gulf War of January 1991 presents an example of how an anticipated conflict has an impact on the term structure of interest rates. The Iraqi invasion of Kuwait, which occurred on August 2, 1990, came as a surprise. Prior to the invasion, bond prices had been determined on the presumption of a long-term era of peace, given that the Cold War had ended.

Figure 5.6 depicts the term structure determined in the bond markets for U.S. government securities on dates before and after the invasion. We can interpret the term structure of July 31, 1990 as the peacetime term structure. The August 3, 1991 term structure reflects the market's response to the information that a war might become likely in the near term. Note that the term structure became steeper and that the short-term interest rate fell, as you might expect in a period just before a fall in consumption goods availability. Such a fall might have been anticipated because of the potentially impending cutoff of the supply of oil. Of course, neither the timing of the outbreak of war nor its magnitude were certain on August 3,

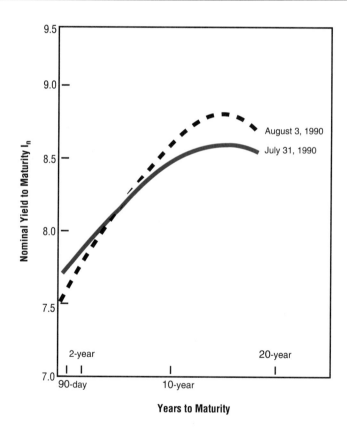

Figure 5.6 TERM STRUCTURE SHIFTS IN THE GULF CRISIS

1990, and these uncertainties would greatly complicate the shape of the term structure, as would changes in expected inflation. In the Appendix to this chapter, we consider the effects of uncertainty on the term structure.

CONCLUSION

The interest rate, or yield, on a particular security can be measured in various ways, such as the coupon yield, the current yield, the yield to maturity, or the holding period yield. The most common method is the yield to maturity, which includes capital gains that will be realized if the security is held to maturity. The holding period yield incorporates a recognition that securities may be sold before maturity, but it can be measured only after the sale.

The interest rates that we normally observe are nominal; that is, they are in terms of money. Borrowers and lenders, however, generally are concerned with the real interest rates that they pay or receive. Real interest rates are the amount of goods that must be paid later for a unit of goods borrowed now. The relation between the nominal and real interest rate is defined by the Fisher equation—the nominal interest rate is the sum of the real interest rate and the expected inflation rate.

Numerous bond maturities are available on securities markets. The term structure of interest rates plots yield to maturity against maturity for government bonds. The term structure may be upward sloping, flat, or downward sloping. The expectations hypothesis of the term structure seeks to explain the relation between yields on short-term securities and yields on long-term securities. Under this hypothesis, yield on a long-term security is the average of the expected yields on a sequence of one-period securities ending when the long-term security matures.

Short-term real interest rates are determined by household tastes over current versus future consumption and by current versus future availability of goods. Disturbances in the amount of goods available shift short-term real interest rates along with the term structure.

Appendix: THE TERM STRUCTURE IN A RISKY ENVIRONMENT

We have developed the expectations hypothesis of the term structure in a situation in which households are certain about future events. We demonstrated that a potential purchaser of a security would be indifferent between buying an n-period bond or a sequence of n one-period bonds. The market price of the n-period bond should adjust to deliver the same payoff on a given investment as the one-period bonds. Since there is no risk, the two investment strategies are perfect substitutes. Under this hypothesis, households will not pay premium prices to acquire bonds of a particular maturity.

In this Appendix we will consider how the term structure of interest rates is determined in a risky environment, and we will show that the term structure can diverge from the predictions of the expectations hypothesis if households are risk averse.

An Uncertain War

Specifically, we will extend the war example to an uncertain environment. We will assume that although people in 1992 realize that a war will occur, they are uncertain about its magnitude. If the war is small, the government will require only 25 units of goods from each household in 1993 and 1994 and 50 units in 1995. This means that the consumption pattern will be as in the column labeled "Small War" in Table 5.A1. If the war is large, the government will require 50 units of goods in 1993, 75 units in 1994, and 50 in 1995. People attach probability b to a small war and $(1 - b)$ to a large war, but they will not find out what the magnitude of the war will be until the beginning of 1993.

From our analysis of the certainty war model in Figure 5.2A, recall that in equilibrium the indifference curve's slope at a point of actual consumption equals the payoff on any asset that delivers goods next period in exchange for a unit of current goods. Let's denote the slope of the indifference curve through the 1992–1993 consumption point (C_{92}, C_{93}) as $S(C_{92}, C_{93})$. Also, let A_{93} represent the actual 1993 payoff from any asset bought in 1992 for one unit of goods. It does not matter if the assets are bonds, equities, or something else, since in a world of certainty, their payoffs will all be identical. Then, according to the preceding equilibrium condition,

$$\frac{S(C_{92}, C_{93})}{A_{93}} = 1$$

A similar condition also holds in an uncertain world, one in which, for example, c_{93} and A_{93} are random. In this case, the condition holds in an expected-value sense:

$$E\left[\frac{S(C_{92}, C_{93})}{A_{93}}\right] = 1$$

where expectations are formed before C_{93} and A_{93} are known. According to this condition, any asset must have a one-period payoff such that the expected value of the ratio of the indifference curve slope to the asset payoff equals unity.

Table 5.A1   CONSUMPTION IN LARGE AND SMALL WARS

Year	Small War	Large War
1992	100	100
1993	75	50
1994	75	25
1995	50	50
1996	100	100

To determine the meaning of an uncertain environment for the term structure, we consider the yields to maturity on one- and two-period bonds as of 1991, after people realize that a war will occur.

The Yield on One-Period, Fixed-Payment Loans

Suppose that a household wants to borrow one unit of goods in 1992 in return for a guaranteed payment of $(1 + r_1)$ goods in 1993. What must the value of r_1 be in equilibrium? The payoff $(1 + r_1)$ can be substituted for A_{93} in the preceding formula. Also, $C_{92} = 100$ and C_{93} can be either 75 or 50. Since the payoff is not random, it is known in 1992 and can be taken from the expectations formula to provide the solution:

$$(1 + r_1) = E[S(100, C_{93})]$$

The yield on one-period, fixed-payment securities then must equal the expected slope of the indifference curve.

The Yield on Two-Period, Fixed-Payment Loans

Suppose that a household wants to borrow one unit of goods in 1992 in return for a guaranteed payment of $(1 + R_2)^2$ goods in 1994. What must R_2 be to satisfy the expectations formula introduced above?

Notice that although the borrower does not pay off until 1994, this security still has a 1-year holding period yield between 1992 and 1993 because it can be sold at a capital gain or loss in 1993. To find the security's holding period yield, we must calculate its price in 1993. This price is $(1 + R_2)^2/(1 + r_2)$, the 1994 payoff discounted by 1 plus the interest rate on 1-year loans originating in 1993. Since, according to the preceding section, $(1 + r_2)$ will depend on whether consumption in 1993 turns out to be 75 or 50 units, r_2 is random and unknown as of 1992. Hence the return on the two-period, fixed-payment loan that is held for only one period is random, and the security may be a risky asset.

Substituting in place of A_{93} the payoff of the two-period loan in the expectations formula, the yield to maturity R_2 on the two-period loan must satisfy

$$E \left[\frac{S(100, C_{93}) \times (1 + r_2)}{(1 + R_2)^2} \right] = 1$$

Since R_2 is known in 1992, it can be taken out of the expectations operation to generate

$$(1 + R_2)^2 = E[S(100, C_{93}) \times (1 + r_2)]$$

Remember that both C_{93} and therefore the slope $S(100, C_{93})$ are random. Also, r_2 is random. Recall also that the covariance between two random variables, y and z, is $E(y \times z) - Ey \times Ez$. Now add and subtract the product $E[S(100, C_{93})] \times E(1 + r_2)$ to the right side of the preceding equation. The right side of the equation is then the covariance between the slope of the 1992–1993 indifference curve and the payoff on 1-year loans originating in 1993 *plus* $E[S(100, C_{93})] \times E(1 + r_2)$. The equation can be written as

$$(1 + R_2)^2 = \text{cov}[S(100, C_{93}), (1 + r_2)] + E[S(100, C_{93})] \times E(1 + r_2)$$

or substituting $(1 + r_1)$ for $E[S(100, C_{93})]$, we have

$$(1 + R_2)^2 = \text{cov}\,[S(100, C_{93}), (1 + r_2)] + (1 + r_1) \times (1 + Er_2)$$

Notice that the product on the right side is exactly the expectations hypothesis of the term structure. The yield to maturity on longer securities, however, must be adjusted by the covariance between the indifference curve slope and the payoff on future 1-year loans to determine the equilibrium yield on 2-year loans. Thus 2-year loans pay higher or lower yields than predicted by the expectations hypothesis, depending on whether the covariance is positive or negative, respectively.

What is the sign of the covariance in this example? In Figure 5.A1, draw the two possible 1992–1993 consumption points, A and B. If the war is relatively small, consumption will occur at point A, and the slope of the indifference curve will turn out to be higher than its expected value. In Figure 5.A2, we draw the two possible 1993–1994 consumption points, C and D. If the small war occurs, consumption is at point C, and the slope of the indifference curve also turns out to be higher than its expected value. However, the realized slope of the 1993–1994 indifference curve is also the payoff on 1-year bonds originating in 1993, so $(1 + r_2)$, which equals this realized slope, is also higher than its expected value. Thus, in a small war, the deviations from the mean of $S(100, C_{93})$ and $(1 + r_2)$ are both positive, so the product of the deviations is also positive. A similar argument can be made to show

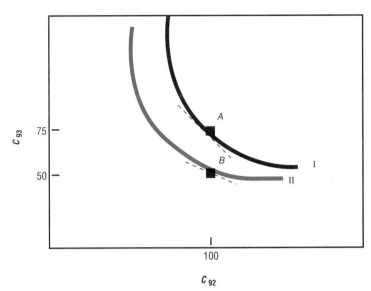

Figure 5.A1   1992–1993 SANDUNIAN CONSUMPTION

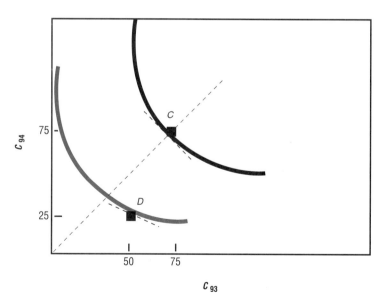

Figure 5.A2   1993–1994 SANDUNIAN CONSUMPTION

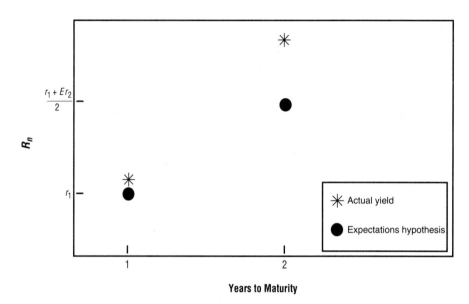

Figure 5.A3   1992 TERM STRUCTURE WITH UNCERTAIN WAR

that in a large war, both deviations are negative, so the product of the deviations is also positive. Since the covariance is the probability-weighted average of two positive numbers, it must be positive.

Thus, in our example, two-period bonds require a premium yield above the prediction of the expectations hypothesis. The yield curve for 1- and 2-year loans would appear as in Figure 5.A3.

KEY TERMS

coupon yield

coupon bonds

book-entry system

coupon

par value

current yield

yield to maturity

bond tables

consol

perpetuity

holding period yield

nominal interest rate

real interest rate

price level

Fisher's equation

term structure of interest rates

discount loans

expectations theory of the term structure

EXERCISES

1. A bond with a par value of $100 and a coupon rate of 5 percent has a price of $90. What is the current yield of the bond?

2. Use Table 5.1 to find the price of a bond with a 10-percent coupon payable semiannually maturing in 8 years if the market interest rate is 12.5 percent.

3. Use Table 5.1 to determine the market interest rate if the price of a 10-percent coupon bond payable semiannually and maturing in 6 years is $122.73.

4. Suppose that a 14-percent coupon bond is purchased for $50, held for 1 year, and then sold for $80. What is the holding period yield?

5. Suppose that you buy a 1-year $100 par bond with a 40-percent coupon for $100 in 1993. By the time the bond pays off in 1994, the price level doubles from its value in 1993. What is the bond's yield in terms of 1993 dollars?

6. Figure 5.1A depicts a downward-sloping term structure, except for securities of the shortest maturity. Why might the term structure have been upward sloping for only the last 5 months of 1981?

7. Suppose that 1-year loans currently yield 9 percent annually and that you know that next year you will be able to borrow or lend for 1 year at a yield of 5 percent. Two-year loans currently pay an annualized yield of 8 percent. Show that you have an opportunity to earn an arbitrage profit.

8. The term structure of interest rates for August 3, 1990 is depicted in Figure 5.6. The short-term rate fell from its level on July 31, 1990, and the long-term rate rose. Can the uncertain magnitude and duration of the war explain the long-term rate increase?

9. For the Sandunian economy described in the text in a war whose magnitude is a certainty, derive the term structure of nominal interest rates in 1994.

10. Suppose that in the random war described in the Appendix, the consumption pattern in a large war is $(C_{92}, C_{93}) = (50, 75)$. Show that 1-year securities will trade at a discount relative to 2-year securities—that is, the predictions of the expectations hypothesis will exceed the yields to maturity on 2-year loans.

11. Suppose that $1 payable n periods in the future exchanges for x dollars currently in the bond markets.

a. How would you determine the annualized interest rate r_n on n-period, pure discount loans?

b. Suppose that a coupon bond promises to pay $10 per year for 10 years plus the par value of $100 in the tenth year. Alternatively, consider some individual discount bonds of up to 10 years in maturity, each of which pays $10 at maturity. Present an arbitrage argument for why the coupon bond should sell at the same price as a specific bundle of the discount bonds.

FURTHER READING

Barro, Robert, "Government Spending, Interest Rates, Prices, and Budget Deficits in the United Kingdom, 1701–1918," *Journal of Monetary Economics,* Vol. 20 (1987), pp. 221–247.

Benjamin, Daniel, and Levis Kochin, "War, Prices, and Interest Rates: A Martial Solution to Gibson's Paradox," in Michael Bordo and Anna Schwartz (Eds.), *A Retrospective on the Classical Gold Standard, 1821–1931,* University of Chicago Press, 1984, pp. 587–612.

Campbell, John, "Bond and Stock Returns in a Simple Exchange Model," *Quarterly Journal of Economics,* Nov. 1986, Vol. 101, pp. 785–803.

Cecchetti, Stephen, "The Case of the Negative Nominal Interest Rates: New Estimates of the Term Structure of Interest Rates during the Great Depression," *Journal of Political Economy* (December 1988), pp. 1111–1141.

Fisher, Irving, *The Theory of Interest,* The Macmillan Company, 1930.

C H A P T E R

6

Market Makers, Dealers, Securities Exchanges, and Liquidity

In Chapters 2 and 3 we discussed the importance of arbitrage and portfolio pricing in creating liquidity in financial markets. If investors view a single security as only one part of a portfolio, it will be relatively easy for a seller to find a market. Investors will absorb the offering by making small adjustments in their portfolios. They will price the security based on the required rate of return given their perceptions of its market risk. The degree of liquidity in a securities market can be measured by how large a buy or sell order can be absorbed without a change in the price of the security. An investor who holds a security that trades in a liquid market can confidently expect to sell or buy a large amount of the security without materially affecting the price of the security. We can call this characteristic of a liquid market its **immediacy.**

Many securities, such as the securities of closely held companies, do not enter into most investors' portfolios. And for good reason. Suppose that John needs to sell the stock he holds in his uncle's firm because he must meet a payment deadline to someone who has performed a service for him. If he cannot find a market for the security, he must borrow from a bank or some other liquid lender to make his payment. Alternatively, he could sell other, more liquid assets if he holds them. We saw in Chapter 3 that an increase in households' holding of the stock of closely held companies leads to an increase in the demand for liquid bank deposits.

Liquidity in a market for a particular security does not mean that a potential seller can expect to obtain the price he or she originally paid for the instrument immediately. For example, if an investor wants to sell a long-term government bond that was purchased when interest rates were 5 percent, and they are now 10 percent, she cannot expect to receive the same price she paid for the bond.

The market for the bond is liquid as long as someone quotes a price for the bond that is continuously available to potential sellers. If an investor can sell a bond with the expectation that he can receive a price close to the last quoted price, we say the market has immediacy and is therefore liquid. In other words, a market for a security is liquid if a potential seller can be assured that a decision to sell will not affect the price at which the security trades. If such a buyer is not immediately available, the seller must wait to place his security, financing his immediate cash requirements with a bank loan.

Of course, we need to distinguish between a liquid market and a liquid security. A **liquid security** is one that maintains its value in terms of the unit of account. Thus money is the most liquid of all securities. A **liquid market** is one in which an individual transaction does not disrupt the continuity of the market.

Liquidity in financial markets helps all investors make better decisions in adjusting their portfolios. For example, suppose that Ellen decides to sell her portfolio of stocks to buy a refrigerator. In so doing, she makes a decision about the relative value of refrigerators and of the market portfolio—according to her calculations, she values refrigerators more highly relative to her portfolio of stocks than does the market.

Ellen bases her calculation on the last reported price of transactions in her portfolio. How reliable is her calculation, though? That depends on the accuracy of the last reported prices for securities in her portfolio. If the market is liquid, then trades are frequent, either in the securities being sold or in securities very similar to them, and prices are reliable. Because the prices are reliable—that is, because Ellen thinks that prices on Monday will be close to those she reads in the paper on Saturday—Ellen decides to go ahead and sell enough stock to purchase the refrigerator, rather than take out a bank loan.

Who sets these prices, however? What mechanism keeps them relatively stable? It is market makers, dealers, and securities exchanges that provide continuity in the pricing of securities. We now turn to a study of these players in the financial market place.

SECURITIES EXCHANGES

A **securities exchange** is an organized market where financial securities are bought and sold in an organized manner. By bringing together buyers and sellers, the exchange increases the liquidity of the market because it reduces the need to call on a bank line instead of a securities sale to provide good funds. It does this by providing a stock of buyers.

The best-known securities exchange in the United States is the **New York Stock Exchange,** but other exchanges exist in the United States and throughout the world—the most famous being the Tokyo and London exchanges.

An Exchange Centralizes Trading

To begin a detailed discussion of securities exchanges, we return briefly to the barter problem and review how a monetary system improves the welfare of a society. Recall that our shopper in Chapter 1 had apples that she wanted to exchange for oranges, but she was forced by circumstances to accept a trade of apples for bananas as an intermediate transaction. In our barter example, the existence of a monetary system increases the number of acceptable buyers for apples. Our shopper need not look for an orange seller who wants apples. She can sell apples to anyone willing to pay her money.

Even within a monetary system, the apple seller will probably find it in her interest to spend some time searching for the best price, defined in units of money (dollars, yen, or whatever), for her apples. Her search costs could be reduced substantially if a centralized location existed where most apple trades take place. Trading in this location would permit the seller of apples to find buyers whose bids represent the highest price available, given supply and demand conditions in the market. She would then reap the benefits of trading her apples in a liquid market. That is, she would have continuously quoted prices representing the best estimate of current market conditions. As a result, she would be able to use the last-quoted price as a reliable guide to the value of her apples.

In real life, we do not observe apple exchanges where traders meet to buy and sell apples at continuously quoted prices—at least at the retail level. This statement implies that there are costs are well as benefits to running an institution that creates liquidity. Let's turn now to an extended example of how an exchange increases liquidity, noting both the costs and the benefits of the process.

A Stock Exchange Transaction

If Bryan Hope, an investor in the stock of Ocelot Automotive Company, decides to sell 100 shares of stock, he will try to obtain the highest net price he can, where *net price* is the money he actually receives for the sale less the cost of finding a buyer and executing the trade. To do this, he will usually try to find a buyer who believes that Ocelot's stock is at least as valuable as the last transaction price. We will assume that the Ocelot Corporation trades on (or is listed on) the New York Stock Exchange, so a seller would go to the exchange to look for a buyer.

To execute a transaction on the New York Stock Exchange, Mr. Hope must find a broker who is a member of, or holds a seat on, the exchange. A **broker** is an individual who buys and sells securities for someone else. That is, he or she executes a transaction for a buyer who wants to own a particular stock or for a holder of that stock who wants to sell. An individual broker often works for a firm known as a *brokerage house*. A seat on the exchange gives the holder the right to trade listed securities on the exchange floor. **Listed securities** are the securities of those companies which have qualified to trade on the New York Stock Exchange. Members may be either individuals or firms.

Buying Stock

When you buy a stock listed on the New York Stock Exchange, you typically pick up the phone and call a local broker. The broker works for a firm or has a contact at a firm that has a seat on the New York Stock Exchange. The exchange member places your order on the exchange floor electronically, and you receive the price prevailing at the time. The whole process takes place within minutes, and you receive confirmation of your buy order and its price while you are still on the phone. However, we will explain the process step by step, as if it were handled physically rather than electronically, to demonstrate the role of the exchange and all its participants in creating liquid markets.

Specialists

Suppose that our investor finds a broker, Ms. Lillian Brown, a member of the New York Stock Exchange (NYSE), to handle the transaction. He informs her that he desires to sell a round lot (100 shares) of Ocelot at the prevailing market price. The broker takes the order to the exchange and presents it to the specialist "at the post" where trades in Ocelot Corporation must take place. A **specialist** is a member of the exchange who is designated to "make a market" in the securities assigned to him or her. "At the post" refers to the physical place where the specialist stands on the floor of the exchange and where all trades in the stocks of the specialist's assigned company or companies must occur.

A specialist is a dealer. A **dealer** is a firm that buys and sells securities for its own account. This means that it buys stocks purchased with its own or borrowed money and sells stocks that it holds. As we shall see, a specialist acts as both a dealer and a broker in stock transactions.

Making a Market

The specialist carries out his assignment to "make a market" in Ocelot's stock by receiving orders to buy and sell shares and matching buy and sell orders through several alternatives. These include the following: his own inventory (as a dealer), his limit book, and the floor of the exchange (as a broker).

The specialist maintains a **bid–offer spread** that represents the prices at which he will buy or sell for his inventory. He bids to buy at one price; he offers to sell at another. Naturally, the *offer price* will always exceed the *bid price* because he can profit only by buying at a low price and selling at a high price.

The specialist compiles all buy and sell *limit orders* that he has received in a *limit book,* which is, in fact, a computer screen. A *limit order* is an order to buy or sell a share of stock at a specific price. For example, suppose another broker has a client who wants to sell Ocelot's stock, but only if the price is $100 or more. However, assume that the most recent transaction price is $99\frac{3}{4}$. The broker will relay the limit order to sell at $100 to the specialist, who will place it in the limit book for execution when and if the price of Ocelot's stock rises to $100. Of course, there are also limit orders to buy, but they are always less than the prevailing market price, or they would have (logically) already been executed.

When Mr. Hope's market order to sell 100 shares of Ocelot comes to the post, the specialist, in his role as market maker, will attempt to get the best price for him. The specialist does this by checking all his sources for prices, his bid–offer spread, the limit book, and the floor, which is, in fact, an electronic board listing bid prices from members. Suppose that he is willing to buy 100 shares at $99\frac{5}{8}$ and sell at 100 on his own account. (These prices all refer to dollars and are quoted in minimum units of $\frac{1}{8}$ of a dollar.) In Figure 6.1 we present a schematic of the following discussion.

The specialist then checks his limit book. It contains orders to buy 100 shares at $99\frac{1}{2}$ and sell 200 shares at $99\frac{7}{8}$, which would not be as advantageous for Mr. Hope. The transaction for Ms. Brown's client will therefore take place at the specialist's bid of $99\frac{5}{8}$ unless he can find a better offer for her from a broker on the floor.

Suppose that another broker wants to buy 300 shares of Ocelot's stock. The arrival of a buyer for 300 shares causes the specialist to reevaluate the demand for Ocelot's stock. He knows that there is a seller of 200 shares in the limit book at $99\frac{7}{8}$ and that, with the order to sell 100 shares at the prevailing price from Ms. Brown's client, he can find 300 shares to satisfy the order from the floor.

To find the 300 shares necessary to satisfy the buy order from the floor, the specialist must go to two sources. The buyer will pay $99\frac{7}{8}$ for the 200 shares sold from the limit book and $99\frac{7}{8}$ for the 100 shares sold by Ms. Brown's client.

In this process, the specialist has found the best price for both buyer and seller. Finding the best price for the opposite sides of a transaction may may sound like a contradiction, but in this situation, the specialist has improved the position of both buyer and seller.

By checking the floor before executing the sale at his bid price at $99\frac{5}{8}$, the specialist has permitted Ms. Brown's client to earn $\frac{1}{4}$ point more per share of stock than he would have if the specialist had bought for his inventory. By checking the floor, he also has saved the buyer of 300 shares from having to purchase at the specialist's offer price of 100. The specialist has made the market in Ocelot's stock

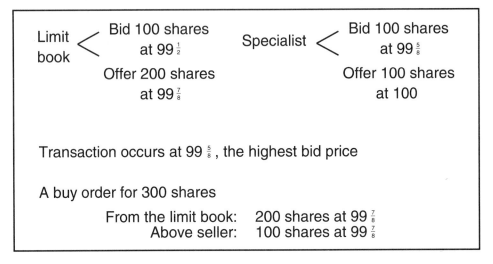

Figure 6.1   A SELL ORDER FOR 100 SHARES

because he has compared the prices of all participants, including himself, to get the best price for both buyer and seller. The specialist, who is also called a *market maker,* is compensated for his services by a brokerage fee and by trading from his inventory with a potential for earning capital gains. However, a market maker need not be a specialist standing at the post on the New York Stock Exchange. He or she can be any dealer in a stock. See Box 6.1.

A MODEL OF MARKET MAKER BEHAVIOR

A market maker is always willing to quote a bid or offer price for the security in which he makes a market. This certainly implies that any buyer or seller can obtain immediacy. Immediacy, however, comes at the potential cost of buying at a substantially higher price or selling at a substantially lower price than if the buyer or seller had waited. If the market is liquid, the cost of immediacy is low, which means that the risk of paying too much or receiving too little in an immediate transaction is low. This is more likely if someone is willing to continuously quote prices in a security. How does this come about, however? In this section we turn to the problem of how market makers ensure frequent price quotes.

First, to help you better understand the role of the market maker in supplying liquidity to a securities market, we will develop a model of market maker behavior.

Box 6.1

The Citicorp Specialist

1990 was a difficult year for bank stocks, and Citicorp, the nation's largest bank, suffered a decline in price from $27 to $11 over the course of the year. A declining market is a tough environment for a specialist, who holds inventory in the stock he or she deals in and tries to make a profit from trading that inventory. A declining market, of course, means that the specialist's inventory tends to depreciate in value. It is hard to make money when the asset you hold is falling in value.

Nevertheless, James McMullin, Citicorp specialist on the New York Stock Exchange, made money in 1990 because "stocks [for the most part] do not go straight down or straight up. In any kind of major move, there are [contrary] moves, and if you're astute, you can do O.K. on those," he said. Mr. McMullin describes his role as follows: "Buyers and sellers converge on my area, and what I try to do is pair them off at a price I think is rational."

Mr. McMullin, who works for M. J. Meehan & Company, had a particularly hectic day in the fall of 1990, when Citicorp announced that it was cutting its dividend at the same time that the Federal Reserve announced its intention to lower a key interest rate. Recall that a decline in interest rates tends to increase asset values. A cut in the dividend, on the other hand, is bearish because it signals a decline in a company's future earnings. Thus, on that particular day, Citicorp stock was buffeted by two countervailing forces.

Mr. McMullin opened trading in the stock 10 minutes after the opening bell on the exchange at $14, the same price at which it closed at the end of the previous day. Most stocks opened substantially higher on the news of the interest rate decline, but Citicorp dropped 62.5 cents almost immediately. Volume (the number of trades) was heavy, 1.17 million shares in a little over an hour. Typical daily volume in Citicorp stock is about 2 million shares. Mr. McMullin was in a frenzy. He had to announce the market price to hordes of buyers and sellers, fill orders that brokers had left with him, and try to make money by trading his own inventory.

Around noon, the trading volume in Citicorp's stock subsided. The stock rallied to within 12.5 cents of its opening price. However, in the last hour of trading, the stock took a pounding, falling to $13.125. "It just broke down," Mr. McMullin said.

Source: Adapted from *The American Banker,* January 10, 1991.

We start with the assumption that to maintain a bid-offer spread, the market maker must be able to make credible promises. That is, the market maker must be able to promise delivery of a security he agrees to sell and payment for a security he is buying.

One sure way to make such promises credible is to hold inventories of that security and cash. An alternative to inventories of cash and securities would be to have lines to a bank to borrow cash and lines to other market makers to borrow securities. A *line* gives the holder of the line the right to borrow. For example, if a broker holds a bank line for $500,000, he has the right to borrow that amount from the bank. Holding a securities inventory, cash, and lines is a signal to buyers that a security can be delivered, and it is a signal to sellers that the market maker can deliver cash.

Financing Inventory

If the market maker is going to hold an inventory, he must purchase and hold the security for which he is making a market. This implies that he must find someone or some financial institution to provide him with good funds to buy the security he wants to hold as inventory. Let's assume for simplicity that he is able to provide his own cash.

What return can the market maker expect on his capital, which is the cash he puts up to finance his inventory? We assume that the security the market maker holds in inventory is also held by many other investors as part of a market portfolio. This implies that the expected return on the market maker's portfolio will not include an expected return for bearing risks that most investors can diversify away.

The market maker holds an undiversified position because he typically specializes in observing price movements in a particular security. It is difficult to be a market maker in many securities because such a market maker would have to watch too many prices. On the New York Stock Exchange, specialists are designed market makers who are generally restricted by the exchange to trading in a few securities. We will see later that this tendency exists throughout securities markets.

Since the market maker holds only a few of the securities in the market portfolio, he absorbs more risk than he gets paid to absorb based on the expected return on the securities. Thus the expected return on the market maker's capital is less than he could expect if he held a diversified position of comparable risk in the market portfolio.

If this were the end of the story, there would be no market makers at all, because every one of them could do better by holding the market portfolio. What causes market makers willingly to take an undiversified position?

The Market Maker's Return on Inventory

Recall that the market maker maintains a bid-offer spread. He quotes a buying price (bid) that is lower than his selling price (offer). He is able to do this only if potential buyers cannot find a price below his offer price and potential sellers cannot find a buyer who is willing to pay above his bid price.

On an organized exchange, we would not expect to find a situation in which a market maker simultaneously buys at his bid price and sells at his offer price. The reason is that a simultaneous buy-sell transaction does not involve the market maker's inventory. The buyer and the seller can find some mutually agreeable price between the market maker's bid-offer spread.

The market maker's spread becomes important when someone wants to buy or sell and there is no one else currently in the market at prices better than the market maker's. It is at these times that the market maker will buy at a price below that at which he could have bought if there were a simultaneous buyer. An analogous result holds for a sale by the market maker. In these situations, the market maker can supplement the expected return on his portfolio by buying lower or selling higher than if there were other active players. Thus he achieves a sufficient return on his equity for the risk he bears.

The market maker earns his return by supplying immediacy to the market. Let's assume that a seller comes into the market and there is no buyer that immediately comes forward. The seller could wait until a buyer appears, and the two could split the market maker's bid-offer spread. However, if the seller wants to sell her security immediately, she will have to sell at the market maker's bid price.

The Skill of the Market Maker

Providing the service of immediacy requires some skill on the part of the market maker. The expected return on his security is positive, but it can fluctuate. It is in light of this fact that he must interpret the arrival of a seller without the simultaneous arrival of a buyer. Could the seller's appearance signal that the price of the security is expected to fall? Or is this merely a timing mismatch in the supply of buyers and sellers at close to the current market price?

To evaluate the possibilities, the market maker needs to have a good "feel" for the market. This does not imply that he must have a better idea of what the "real" expected return on the security will be, but he must be able to interpret price signals from potential buyers and sellers.

For example, the specialist on the New York Stock Exchange has ongoing knowledge of buyers' limit orders. If he finds there are a lot of willing buyers at a price just slightly below his bid price and a lot of limit orders to sell at just above his offering price, he may interpret the arrival of a seller without a buyer as a pause in the market rather than a fall in the price of the security.

Summary of Costs Facing the Market Maker

The return to the market maker, as we have seen, is dependent on his ability to "buy low and sell high." This return must cover his cost of doing business. He has an inventory cost. His undiversified position has risk that could be partially eliminated through diversification. The expected return he could achieve by holding a diversified portfolio would, of course, be greater than the expected return on an undiversified portfolio that is similarly affected by overall movements in the economy. We call the latter risk **market risk.** In addition, he has his "labor" costs— the costs of learning the market and operating in it.

The Market Maker's Costs per Transaction

We would expect that as the market maker's inventory holdings rise, the absolute costs of holding an undiversified portfolio also rise. For example, assume that the market maker holds an inventory of $100,000 of a security with an expected return of 8 percent, whereas the expected return on a diversified portfolio with similar market risk is 10 percent. Thus the market maker could earn 2 percent more on the cash he puts up if he held the diversified portfolio. On the $100,000 investment, he sacrifices an expected $2,000 to be a market maker. If he were to increase his inventory to $1 million, he would sacrifice $20,000 in expected income to be a market maker.

We assume that a market maker needs a large inventory if he plans to use it for a large number of buy-sell transactions. Since the absolute amount of money at risk increases as his inventory grows, he must find some way of being compensated for this extra risk. (We assume he is risk averse.) Where will he make the extra money? On transactions, of course. In this way, he will be able to finance his costs and compensate himself for the risk of his position.

We also make the assumption that the market maker's labor costs do not rise as his number of transactions rises. Thus his labor costs per transaction decline the more transactions he makes. This implies that over a certain range of transactions, his costs of providing market making services decline.

Revenues from Market Making

Every time a market maker buys at his bid price or sells at his offer price, he expects to earn revenue. This is so because the "market price" to buyers and sellers arriving on the scene simultaneously is somewhere between these two prices. Thus the market maker sells at a higher price than the usual investor and buys at a lower price. This represents his return for providing immediacy.

As the market maker's bid-offer spread increases, his revenue will rise as well because the higher spread increases the difference between the price at which he buys or sells and the price at which the usual investor buys or sells. Also, as the bid-offer spread widens the market maker engages in fewer transactions. Why is this? Investors who are sellers realize that selling at the market maker's bid price is the cost of immediacy. If they wait for a buyer, the two can split the bid-offer price between them. Thus the higher the spread, the more likely investors will wait for simultaneous sell and buy orders, and market makers therefore engage in fewer transactions.

A Diagram of the "Market Maker" Market

Under the assumption of competition, our description of an individual market maker's behavior is summarized in Figure 6.2. The bid-offer spread is on the vertical axis, and the number of transactions is on the horizontal axis. The market maker's average and marginal costs per transaction first decline as he amortizes his skill and then rise as the cost of bearing inventory risk takes over. The demand curve for an individual market maker's transactions is horizontal because of competition from other market makers.

The market maker will supply his services in the long run as long as the bid-offer spread and the number of transactions cover his average costs, as they do in Figure 6.2. If the demand curve crosses the cost curve at a higher point than the minimum of the average cost curve, then more market makers will enter the market until the bid-offer spread declines to the competitive level.

If the demand curve cuts below the minimum point of the average cost curve of the most efficient market makers, no one will bother to make a market for that security. The greater the risk of inventory holding, the higher is the market maker's

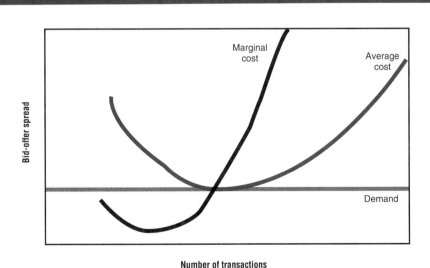

Figure 6.2   MARKET MAKER UNDER COMPETITION

cost and the higher is the cost of immediacy. The model predicts that market makers will not exist for extremely risky securities because the cost of holding inventory is too high. Of course, if no one wants to be a market maker, it does not pay the firm issuing the security to list it on an exchange.

The demand curve also can cut below the minimum average cost position for the most efficient market maker if there are so many buyers and sellers that having a specialized inventory holder is uneconomical. In this case, the market will be liquid, but it will be a broker market. Such securities also will not be listed on an exchange.

A Securities Exchange Clearing House

Our model of market maker behavior is based on the cost of financing an undiversified securities portfolio. This limits the ability of market makers to buy for their own portfolio, which, under some circumstances, can greatly handicap the creation of market liquidity. Suppose that a large sell order for General Motors stock is placed on the floor of the exchange one morning. There are not, at that particular moment, enough buy orders to prevent the price from falling drastically without the intervention of market makers.

Suppose that there has been no bad news that should reflect negatively on the price of General Motors stock and the stock market as a whole is rising. In these circumstances, market makers are very confident that by the end of the day sufficient buy orders will arrive to absorb the shares placed on the market without a decline in price. However, if market makers must actually fund the large block of stock, they would incur huge financing costs. It appears that liquidity cannot be maintained in the market, and the price of General Motors stock must fall that morning, only to (probably) rise again at the end of the day.

Is there any way to maintain market liquidity under these circumstances? The answer is yes. Market liquidity can be sustained because market makers do not actually have to finance their intraday inventory. The reason is that trades are settled periodically rather than continuously. This means that when a market maker buys a security for his portfolio, he does not need to come up with the cash immediately. He may have until the end of the day or as long as 5 days, depending on the settlement rules for that particular market.

How does this benefit market liquidity? Market makers can buy a large amount of General Motors stock in the morning without financing the transaction. When the expected buy orders materialize later in the day, those who purchased General Motors stock earlier in the day can sell the stock to other dealers or other investors. They can net their buy orders against their sell orders at settlement time. They must only finance their net position—that is, the difference between what they have bought and what they have sold. The netting arrangement among dealers is commonly referred to as a **clearing house.** It is an arrangement that applies not to just one stock, as in the preceding example, but to all trades among all dealers in a given market. For example, assume that Mr. Hope, who works for a large insurance company, sells $10 million of Procter and Gamble stock to a dealer, Ms. Wu, early in the trading day. Later that morning, Ms. Wu sells $5 million of General Electric stock to Mr. Gonzales, another dealer. That afternoon, Mr. Gonzales sells $15 million of Merrill Lynch stock to the insurance company represented by Mr. Hope.

We will assume that settlement takes place at the end of the day. At settlement, the insurance company and the two dealers net out their trades. This determines how much additional inventory the two dealers must carry overnight at considerable cost owing to the fact that their portfolios are undiversified. Ms. Wu has purchased $10 million of stock from the insurance company and has sold $5 million; thus her inventory also has increased by $5 million. Mr. Gonzales has purchased $5 million in stock and has sold $15 million to the insurance company; his inventory has declined by $10 million.

The clearing house is a significant advantage to the dealers because it reduces the likelihood that they must finance a large, undiversified inventory. In effect, this permits them to take advantage of the lower funding costs of a diversified investor, represented by Mr. Hope, until enough trades have taken place to reduce each dealer's net position. Mr. Hope's insurance company also gains from this arrangement because it has been able to sell a large block of stock in a market that maintained its liquidity as a result of dealers not having to incur funding costs.

There are, of course, risks in this clearing house arrangement. What if General Electric stock declines rapidly from the time that Mr. Gonzales purchases it in late morning and settlement at the end of the day? He might then default on the trade. Ms. Wu might then not be able to pay the insurance company for the Procter and Gamble stock she purchased. If the price of this stock also had declined from its morning level, the insurance company would end up a loser as well. If Ms. Wu had been required to pay the insurance company for the Procter and Gamble stock at the instant the trade had occurred, the insurance company would not have been held hostage to the inability of Mr. Gonzales to deliver funds. To reduce the possibility of such defaults, clearing houses generally have provisions for all members to cover the defaulted trades of one member. See Box 6.2.

The Market Maker Supply Curve and the Cost of Liquidity

In a "crisis," which we define as a sudden surge in sell orders, individual market makers will see an upward shift in the (horizontal) demand curve for their services. They will not be able to find same-day buyers for the securities they purchase, and this will greatly increase the net position they must finance after settlement.

In such a situation, the funding cost of carrying an undiversified position rises dramatically. In the short run, we cannot expect new market makers to enter to

Box 6.2

Clearing Trades in Stocks and Corporate Bonds

The certificate of ownership of a share of stock or a corporate bond traded in the United States is a piece of paper. This is in contrast to U.S. government securities, which are book-entry securities—that is, they are an electronic blip rather than a piece of paper.

The problem with paper is that it is expensive to trade. Every time a dealer buys stock from another dealer or a customer, a piece of paper must trade hands. This would normally imply that someone must pick the paper up from the seller and deliver it to the buyer. To avoid this expense, the New York Stock Exchange, the American Stock Exchange, and the National Association of Securities Dealers have established the Depository Trust Company (DTC). The DTC keeps 2.4 trillion certificates in its vaults. It then keeps electronic records of who owns these securities. For example, if Merrill Lynch buys 1,000 shares of Procter and Gamble from Morgan Stanley, DTC will deduct 1,000 shares from Morgan Stanley's account and credit the same to Merrill's account.

Before the DTC will transfer the securities, Merrill must pay Morgan Stanley. They pay each other through the National Securities Clearing Corporation (NSCC), which was formed in 1977 by the same three organizations that formed the DTC. Suppose Merrill and Morgan Stanley make their trade on Monday for $100 a share. That night, Merrill's computer informs the NSCC computer that it has bought 1,000 shares from Morgan Stanley, and Morgan Stanley's computer sends a similar "we sold" order. They both agree to settlement 5 business days hence, the following Monday, which is standard in the equities market. If Morgan Stanley's and Merrill's messages do not agree, the NSCC computer so informs them; there is plenty of time to straighten out mistakes.

spread the burden of carrying an undiversified inventory over more investors. Thus the short-run supply curve of transactions must be upward sloping, even with competition among market makers. (If there is free entry into market making and all potential entrants have the same skill, the industry supply curve must be horizontal in the long run.) As demand by sellers increases, market makers' spreads rise. In a crisis, the supply curve of market making may become almost vertical. Spreads will become very wide.

If we change the assumption and acknowledge that market makers of various skills exist, then the long-run market supply curve is upward sloping. Skill differentials across market makers affect the supply curve because less skillful operators

On the Friday before settlement, the NSCC places itself in the middle of this trade. It sends a message to Morgan Stanley stating that on Monday you have an obligation to deliver 1,000 shares of Procter and Gamble stock for which the NSCC will pay $100 per share. It sends a message to Merrill that it has an obligation to accept 1,000 shares at the same price. Thus the NSCC guarantees the trade.

That night, the NSCC computer contacts the computer at the DTC, stating that Morgan Stanley owes the NSCC 1,000 shares of Procter and Gamble and that the NSCC owes Merrill 1,000 shares of the same stock. The book entries at the DTC are so made. On settlement day, Merrill pays the NSCC and the NSCC pays Morgan Stanley.

Of course, Merrill and Morgan Stanley make a lot of trades in a lot of different securities, between themselves and with others. Since the NSCC is a clearing house, participants settle their net positions with the NSCC (not with each other) across all securities they have traded.

The whole system could break down if a member firm failed to settle—that is, could not make payment to cover the securities it purchased or could not deliver the securities it had sold. If the failed party was obligated to purchase securities, the NSCC is forced to buy them. If it was supposed to sell securities, the NSCC must go into the market and buy the securities to sell to the buying party to the order. If the market has moved against the NSCC's position, it must take a loss. To cover such contingencies, member firms must keep a deposit of cash and U.S. government guaranteed securities on deposit. In the event of bankruptcy, the NSCC has first claim on the deposit to cover losses. If the deposit is insufficient, it uses the deposits of other members to cover the loss.

Source: Adapted from Martha Stigum, *After the Trade*, Dow Jones Irwin, 1988, pp. 245–262.

require a higher spread to enter the market. The supply and demand curves under these conditions are depicted in Figure 6.3. The demand curve is downward sloping because as the cost of immediacy rises, less is demanded.

Market Making and Price Continuity

We said that price continuity is a beneficial side effect of liquid markets. We can now see why this is so in the context of the market making model. The process of setting a bid–offer spread for a security requires a continuous reassessment of market

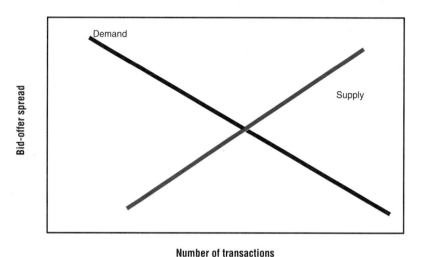

Figure 6.3 MARKET MAKER INDUSTRY

conditions. When there is a temporary imbalance in buy and sell orders, market makers must determine whether a price is changing.

THE STRUCTURE OF SECURITIES EXCHANGES: NYSE

The New York Stock Exchange (NYSE)

The New York Stock Exchange, as the leading exchange in the United States, is an excellent example of how securities exchanges are organized. Like all other organized exchanges, the NYSE presents a means for all buyers and sellers to transact in the same place. This reduces the search costs of a buyer looking for a seller, or vice versa. Low search costs imply, for example, that a buyer can coax a seller into the market quickly by offering the buyer a price somewhat lower than the midway point between a market maker's bid and offer spread.

The effect of the exchange should be to reduce the number of transactions market makers make from their own inventory for any given bid-offer spread. This implies a leftward shift in the demand curve for market makers. This, in turn, will force less efficient market makers out of the market, and spreads will narrow.

NYSE Controls the Number of Market Makers

The NYSE determines how many specialists there will be for each stock traded. Recall that a specialist is a market maker who holds an assigned position at a post on the exchange. Since any member of the exchange can buy and sell stock for his or her inventory, the specialist is not the only one making a market on the floor of the exchange. In 1989, 23.7 percent of the volume on the NYSE represented members of the exchange buying or selling for their own accounts. Less than half this volume represented members acting as specialists. However, the specialist is given one advantage over other market makers. He is the only person who has access to the limit order book. Thus the specialist knows what prices are "waiting in the wings," knowledge that is not available to other market makers.

Thus exchange rules give the specialist a protected position in trading the stock he is assigned. Assuming that this protected position gives him an advantage over other market makers, he has some degree of monopoly power. The bid–offer spread is therefore not determined by the downward-sloping demand curve in Figure 6.3, but by the marginal revenue curve associated with it. This would lead to a higher price, as Figure 6.4 illustrates. Does this protected position provide a benefit to investors?

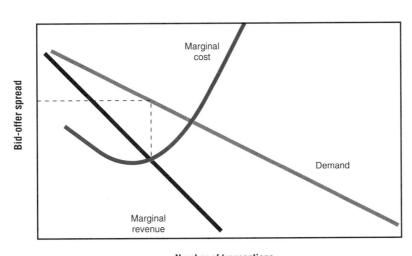

Figure 6.4   MARKET MAKER AS A MONOPOLIST

The Value of a Specialist's "Monopoly"

The one advantage that the specialist has over other traders on the floor of the exchange is that he is the only person with access to the limit book in the stock for which he is the specialist. This permits him to be a better judge of price trends for the smaller orders executed on the floor of the exchange. Other members have a higher price of holding inventory because, without access to the limit book, their risk is greater. Thus the specialist can behave as a partial monopolist. The monopolist's position is depicted in Figure 6.4.

If the demand curve for the specialist's services is very elastic, as depicted in Figure 6.4, the value of the specialist's monopoly is very limited. An elastic demand curve implies that as the specialist's spread narrows, the number of transactions he is party to increases dramatically. What would cause such a situation?

If the specialist existed in a market with free entry, his revenue curve would be very elastic because a small rise in his spread relative to competitive market makers would cause a large decline in his volume. Also, if immediacy were not terribly important to investors, the "industry" demand curve, that is, the aggregate demand curve facing all specialists, would be very elastic. A small rise in the cost would cause many to forgo immediacy.

For stocks traded on the NYSE with fairly heavy volume, the demand curve for immediacy is likely to be fairly elastic because the waiting time for a simultaneous trade is short. Thus the cost to the investing public and securities issuers of permitting a specialist monopoly is fairly low.

Why Should the Specialist Have a Monopoly?

If the price of a security begins to fall very rapidly, the number of sell orders *at the last transaction price* is likely to overwhelm the number of buy orders. In such a situation, the risk facing a market maker will increase dramatically because he will be forced to accumulate inventory at precisely the time when there is great uncertainty about the expected return on his security. He will attempt to cover this risk by increasing his expected profits.

According to the model, the market maker can increase his profits only by increasing the spread—without decreasing the number of transactions he participates in enough to offset the revenues gained. In a falling market, the number of transactions he participates in as a buyer is likely to increase dramatically. His normal strategy would be to increase his spreads dramatically.

Under certain circumstances, such as a stock market crash, the market maker may believe that there is no spread that would allow him to earn sufficient profit for the risk he incurs, and he may want to withdraw from the market by refusing to provide a bid price. NYSE rules, however, require that a market maker always provide a bid price. Thus the market maker must stay in the market; in return for this cruel risk, he is given a monopoly on the floor of the exchange in his security.

On December 28, 1990, the Securities and Exchange Commission (SEC) issued a report on the performance of specialists during the volatile market of October 1989. It found that specialists "generally acted in a manner consistent with their obligation to maintain fair and orderly markets and to protect investors and the public interest." It urged the New York Stock Exchange to "continue developing relative, objective standards for performance for evaluating specialists."

The Value of Liquidity

The corporations that issue securities naturally have an incentive to encourage someone to make a market for their securities as long as investors value liquidity. They can sell their securities at a higher price (lower interest cost) if the market is liquid. Of course, liquidity has its costs; after all, the market maker must be paid.

When a corporation lists on an exchange, it does so because it believes that listing will increase the liquidity of its securities. As we have seen, the exchange should serve to reduce the bid-offer spread.

Investors show their preferences for liquidity by buying and selling securities through brokers who are members of the NYSE. New York–listed stocks, however, need not be traded on the New York Stock Exchange. They also may be listed on, and traded on, several regional exchanges in the United States. In addition, there is a nationwide electronic dealer market, known as the **National Association of Securities Dealers Automated Quote System (NASDAQ)**, that lists many of the stocks traded on the New York Stock Exchange. Despite these other exchanges, in 1989, 69.2 percent of the trade in New York–listed shares occurred on the NYSE. However, this figure was 85.4 percent in 1980.

Why are investors and issuers so willing to trade on an exchange in which the specialist is given a monopoly? The answer has to be that providing liquidity under extreme circumstances must be more valuable than the cost of having a slightly higher bid-offer spread under normal circumstances.

The NYSE measures the liquidity of the exchange by the number of transactions that occurs within an eighth of a point or less of the previous trade. In 1989, for trades of 3,000 shares or less, 87 percent occurred with a price change of an eighth or less. See Box 6.3.

Trades That Originate Off the Floor

As you can see from Table 6.1, most of the NYSE trades that nonspecialist members make for their own accounts originate "off the floor." This means that a dealer arranges to buy or sell shares outside the bidding system described earlier in this chapter. Much of this activity has to do with block positioning.

Large institutions buy and sell individual company stocks in very large quantities. If they present such large orders on the floor, the price of the stock would

Box 6.3

An Electronic Market

Stocks listed on the New York Stock Exchange can be traded off the floor, and they are, sometimes through faxes and telephone calls between investors. There are also electronic trading systems through which investors can buy or sell. The competition has affected trading volume on the exchange, as we indicated in the text. The incentive to move off the floor is to save money. It costs from 3 to 7 cents to trade on the floor—a fee must be paid to the exchange—and from $1/2$ cent to 2 cents off the floor.

Even though trades are made off the floor, they take place at prices that are quoted on the floor. For example, electronic screens flash current NYSE prices, and investors agree to make the trade at that last-quoted price.

This may change if Steve Wunsch has his way. He is establishing an electronic board that actually makes a market. A computer will receive buy and sell orders. Three times a week, it will establish a price, independent of the exchange, and execute the transactions. The computer will take the place of the market maker.

The disadvantage of this system is that price quotes, at three times a week, will be infrequent. Thus investors who use this system must not have a demand for immediacy. For this they must go to the exchange. It seems sensible that those investors who do not have a demand for immediacy should not have to pay for it. Specialists exist to make markets liquid; if someone does not want liquidity, he or she should not have to pay for it.

The major stock exchanges in the United States are fighting Mr. Wunsch's proposal. The SEC must still determine whether it will be allowed. Mr. Wunsch also must find enough participants to be able to generate a market. Even illiquid markets must have some degree of liquidity.

Source: Adapted from *The New York Times,* January 24, 1991, pp. D1 and D10.

temporarily soar or plummet, depending on whether they were buyers or sellers. Since specialist inventory is limited (risk is a rising function of inventory), the specialist would not be able to maintain a smooth market with the arrival of a large seller or buyer.

Thus large institutional trades are arranged off the floor. However, after the price is negotiated, the transaction occurs on the floor, and thus the price becomes available to all market participants. (This is in contrast with an off the floor trade described in the preceding section in which the trade does not take place on the NYSE.) In 1989, 51.1 percent of total NYSE trades were block trades arranged off the floor. As you can see from Table 6.2, the percentage of total volume accounted for by block trades has been rising steadily since 1970.

When member dealers originate deals for their own accounts off the floor, they are **block positioning**—that is, they are helping a large institutional investor buy

Table 6.1 NYSE MEMBER PURCHASES AND SALES IN ROUND LOTS (IN MILLIONS OF SHARES)

Year	As Specialists	Originating on Floor	Originating off Floor
1940	44	30	14
1950	110	36	50
1960	237	39	78
1970	868	32	447
1975	1,205	77	856
1980	2,829	4	3,215
1983	4,800	4	7,606
1985	5,872	2	8,656
1987	11,647	3	13,869
1988	7,536	2	11,190
1989	7,964	2	11,921

Source: NYSE Fact Book, 1990, p. 83.

or sell a block of shares. Why would a nonspecialist member be willing to take the inventory risk that a specialist will not take? The answer is that the dealer only takes a large position in a block of stocks when he has commitments from other customers to purchase the stocks he accumulates. Thus he need only hold the inventory until his buying customers have arranged the funds to purchase the shares they have committed to purchase.

This activity by dealers is quite consistent with our view of the role of market makers. Market makers do not have superior information about the value of a

Table 6.2 NYSE LARGE BLOCK TRANSACTIONS

Year	Transactions (Thousands)	Shares (Millions)	Percent of Volume
1965	2	48	3.1
1970	17	451	15.4
1975	34	7,791	6.6
1980	134	3,311	29.2
1983	363	9,842	45.6
1985	539	17,811	51.7
1987	921	24,497	51.2
1988	768	22,271	54.5
1989	873	21,316	51.1

Source: NYSE Fact Book, 1990, p. 81.

security, but they do know the prices that others are willing to pay. Dealers have better knowledge of institutional investors than do specialists on the floor because institutions usually trade off the floor.

DEALER MARKETS

NASDAQ

The National Association of Securities Dealers Automated Quote (NASDAQ) system is an electronic exchange in which NASD member dealers provide bid-offer spreads on listed securities electronically to other dealers nationwide. Dealers who quote bid-offer spreads are required to buy or sell a specific number of shares at the quoted price. The number varies with the security. However, competition among dealers as market makers is fairly open.

Why would securities issuers and investors desire to trade in an environment of free competition among market makers rather than in the NYSE's monopoly system, in which specialists must stay in the market under all circumstances? The model implies that the decision must depend on the elasticity of demand for market maker services, as shown in Figure 6.3. The demand curve for stocks listed on the NYSE must be more elastic than that for NASDAQ stocks, so we conclude that the cost of permitting monopoly is low.

The frequent appearance of buyers and sellers is likely to make investors less willing to pay a high price for immediacy—that is, the demand curve for market maker services is more elastic. Thus we would expect to find more frequent trades in NYSE stocks than in NASDAQ stocks.

In 1990, on a high-volume day on the NYSE, more than 200 million shares changed hands. Since there are about 2,000 stock issues traded on the exchange, about 100,000 shares are traded per issue on a high-volume day. About 150 million shares traded on a high-volume day on the NASDAQ in 1990. On this exchange, there are about 4,000 stock issues listed. Thus there are about 37,500 trades per issue on the NASDAQ, about three-eighths the average volume per issue on the NYSE.

Securities That Do Not Trade on Formal Exchanges

U.S. government securities are usually traded "over the counter." This means that they do not trade on a formal exchange; instead, the market consists of "dealers" trading privately among themselves and with the public. As you can see by checking the papers, bid-offer spreads exist in this market, so there are market makers. There just is no formal, organized way in which buyers and sellers meet.

In the U.S. government market, the risk of holding inventory is quite small. Interest rate risk can be hedged to a large extent, and there is very little nonmarket risk that the unhedged investor must absorb. This implies that the cost of holding inventory is low, and the bid–offer spread will be low as well. The supply curve of transactions for an individual dealer will be very elastic, so it is unnecessary to have rules requiring dealers to engage in a certain number of transactions.

Some stocks are also traded "over the counter." The National Association of Securities Dealers reports trades in these stocks, but they are not part of the NASDAQ national market systems. That is, there are no rules that bind dealers to agree to buy a certain number of shares at a given bid price. Trades in these shares are so infrequent that the demand curve for market maker services is probably highly inelastic. However, the risk of taking a position in lightly traded stocks is so high that market makers cannot afford to hold enough inventory to provide price continuity.

Thus we see two extremes in markets not organized as exchanges. One represents the case where there is no benefit to having a market maker with some monopoly power, and the other is the situation in which no market maker can afford to guarantee continuity.

INVESTMENT BANKS

Investment banks are financial institutions whose major function in secondary markets for securities is to act as brokers and dealers. They buy and sell securities for their customers and make markets in securities, which provides liquidity and price continuity for their customers. In the new issues, or primary, markets, investment banks act as underwriters of securities. An **underwriter** is a firm that buys new security issues from the firm that issues those securities and sells them to the investment public and other investment banks.

Investment Bank Revenues

Table 6.3 presents the revenue statement for all NYSE member firms for the first 9 months of 1988 and 1989. Member NYSE firms include the largest investment banks in the country, such as Salomon Brothers, Merrill Lynch, Shearson, Goldman Sachs, and so on. As you can see from Table 6.3, about 40 percent of investment bank revenues are derived from securities commissions, which result from buying and selling securities for others, and from trading and investment income, which results from buying and selling securities for their own accounts. The two other major sources of revenue for investment banks are "other income related to securities" and underwriting fees. Other security-related income come from custodial fees and fees for investment advice and counsel.

Fees for investment advice and counsel include such things as arranging mergers and acquisitions among corporate clients. In 1990, these fees were reported to be

Table 6.3 REVENUE STATEMENT FOR NYSE MEMBER FIRMS

	Full Year		Jan. to Sept. 1989	
	$ Billions	Percent of Total	$ Billions	Percent of Total
Securities commissions	$ 8.8	16.9%	$ 7.6	16.9%
Trading and investment	12.7	24.5	10.3	23.0
Interest on debt balances	3.0	5.8	2.8	6.2
Underwriting	5.2	10.0	2.9	6.5
Mutual fund sales	1.4	2.7	1.2	2.6
Commodity revenues	1.4	2.7	1.1	2.4
Other income				
Related to securities	16.6	32.0	16.7	37.1
Unrelated to securities	2.8	5.3	2.4	5.3
Total	51.8	100.0%	45.1	100.0%

Source: NYSE Fact Book, 1990, p. 69.

Note: Items may not sum to total because of rounding.

down by at least 50 percent from 1989 across the industry. This was due to the decline in corporate mergers and acquisitions during the year, as we shall discuss in Chapter 14. However, 1990 was reported to have been a good year for trading stocks and bonds, which offset losses in investment advisory activities.

Custodial fees arise because some investors permit their brokers to maintain custody of the securities they have purchased, sending them dividend and interest checks periodically. Brokerage firms will sometimes borrow the securities on deposit with them to sell to other clients. This practice can cause losses to the investor if the firm should go bankrupt while it has borrowed the investor's securities, for the investor then becomes a creditor of the brokerage firm. See Box 6.4.

Fees from underwriting arise in making markets in new securities. We shall discuss this item further below.

Investment Bank Balance Sheets: Assets

How investment banks carry out their role as market makers can be observed in the composition of their balance sheet, which we present in Table 6.4. On the asset side, the largest single item is a long position in securities. An investor has a **long position** in a security when she would make a profit if that security were to increase in price. A simple example of a long position is owning a long-term bond outright—that is, not borrowing money to finance the purchase. If interest rates fall, the bond price rises, and the holder gains.

Insuring Brokerage Accounts

There is an agency of the federal government to protect investors from failure of their brokerage firm. It is known as the Securities Investors Protection Corporation, widely known as SIPC. Each customer account is covered for up to $500,000, including $100,000 in cash. Between 1971 and 1990, SIPC paid out $221 million to 260,000 customers of 220 liquidated brokerage firms.

When a firm that is a member of SIPC is about to fail, SIPC applies to a federal court for the appointment of a trustee to liquidate the firm. Investors' accounts are insured while the trustee goes through the process of transfering accounts to another broker.

SIPC obtains the resources to insure accounts from assessments made on member firms. If the fund available is inadequate for the losses insured, SIPC has the right to borrow from the U.S. Treasury, but it is not backed by the full faith and credit of the United States.

A major problem faced by investors who are insured by SIPC is that while their accounts are tied up in court proceedings, the accounts are frozen, which means that an investor cannot sell the securities that are in his or her account. If the stock market is falling, such an investor can incur substantial losses. SIPC only insures that such an investor will receive his or her securities; it does not guarantee the price as of the day the brokerage firm was placed in receivorship.

For many large investment banks, about half the securities they own are actually reverse repurchase agreements. A **reverse repurchase agreement** exists when an investment bank buys a security under an agreement to resell that security to the original holder for a specific price at a specific time.

Does a security purchased under a reverse repurchase agreement represent a long position—that is, does the current holder gain from an increase in price? Our answer must be no. Since the current holder gets the same cash price for the security regardless of what happens to its market price, it is not a long position in the security. It is classified as such on the balance sheet in Table 6.4, however. We will explain why when we discuss the liability side of the balance sheet.

The other two major items on the asset side of the balance sheet are receivables from other brokers, dealers, customers, and partners.[1] These receivables arise from cash loans to these parties, who then authorize the investment bank to purchase and carry securities.

---

1. A partner is a part owner of an investment bank. Many investment banks are organized as partnerships.

Table 6.4 BALANCE SHEET FOR NYSE MEMBER FIRMS, SEPTEMBER 30, 1989

ASSETS	$ BILLIONS	PERCENT OF TOTAL
Cash and bank balances	6.9	1.3
Receivables	124.9	23.0
Long positions in securities	390.1	71.7
Exchange memberships	0.3	0.1
Fixed and other assets	21.9	4.0
Total Assets	$544.1	100.0
LIABILITIES AND CAPITAL	$ BILLIONS	PERCENT OF TOTAL
Money borrowed	296.9	54.6
Payables	89.0	16.4
Short position in securities	81.0	14.9
Other	38.0	7.0
Total Liabilities	504.8	92.8
Total Capital	39.3	7.2
Total Liabilities and Capital	544.1	100.0

Source: NYSE Fact Book, 1990, p. 71.

Note: Items may not sum to total because of rounding.

Loans to Carry Securities and Margin Requirements

Loans to carry securities subject the investment bank to credit risk. Suppose you call up your broker and place an order to purchase 100 shares of General Motors stock. To pay for the securities, you request credit from the broker. Your credit request is granted. You now own 100 shares of General Motor stock, and the brokerage firm has an equivalent receivable equal to the value of the loan to you. Your loan is secured by the stock you purchased; if you default on the loan, the brokerage company takes your 100 shares of General Motors stock.

If the price of the stock you purchased should fall, the loan to carry securities rises in value compared with the value of the security. If the price of the security is too low relative to the loan, you might consider **defaulting,** or refusing to pay your loan. You would have to surrender your stock to the brokerage firm, but this is cheaper than paying back a loan equal to the price you originally paid for the stock.

To prevent defaults, loans on securities carry **margin requirements.** Currently, an investor in the United States can borrow only up to 50 percent of the value of his or her security. Thus the security price would have to decline by 50 percent before the value of the loan equals the value of the security.

The Liability Side

Referring again to Table 6.4, we see that the major item on the liability side of the balance sheet is "money borrowed." Although the table does not show the breakdown, a small percentage of this item is loans from commercial banks, which lend money to brokers and dealers at an interest rate called the *broker dealer rate*. The broker dealer rate tends to reflect short-term interest rates. On March 31, 1990, bank security credit to *all* securities brokers and dealers totaled $17.4 billion, less than 10 percent of borrowings at New York Stock Exchange firms only.

A major item included in borrowed money is **repurchase agreements,** or sales of securities with an agreement to repurchase later for a given price. A repurchase agreement generates the same security price movements as if the dealer had not sold the security, because the value at which it must be repurchased is fixed by agreement and cannot fluctuate with market conditions.

An investment bank will engage in a repurchase agreement using the securities it has acquired through reverse repurchase agreements on the asset side of the balance sheet. This is how it makes markets. The bank acquires securities by borrowing them, and it finances the inventory by lending the securities in a repurchase transaction.

Since the investment bank holds inventory to make markets, it must have this inventory available for sale. Hence the repurchase transaction is generally of shorter maturity than the original reverse repurchase transaction. If interest rates should rise before the reverse repurchase agreement matures, investment bank funding costs will rise. It is for this reason that reverse repurchase agreements are classified as long positions in securities.

Table 6.5 illustrates how an investment bank can engage in a repurchase agreement with a security that it owns outright in order to finance an increase in its securities inventory.

The next major item on the liability side of the balance sheet in Table 6.4 is "payables." Suppose that an investment bank buys a security from another investment bank and has not yet paid for it. As a result, the security shows up as an asset; it is financed by a payable item.

The next item on the liability side in Table 6.4 is "short positions in securities." A **short position** is the opposite of a long position: The investment bank owes the security to someone else. It benefits from a fall in the price of the security, which implies gaining from a rise in interest rates.

A short position in securities occurs when an investment bank borrows a security from an investor to sell to another client. If the price of the security goes down when the agreement to borrow matures, the investment bank gains because it sold a security at a higher price than it ended up owing to the lender.

Table 6.5 REPURCHASE TRANSACTIONS (REPOS)

Balance Sheet before Repo Transaction

ASSETS	LIABILITIES
$1,000 Securities owned	$900 Bank loans
	$100 Equity

Balance Sheet Just after Repo Transaction

ASSETS	LIABILITIES
$1,000 Securities owned	$900 Bank loans
$100 Cash	$100 Repo
	$100 Equity

Balance Sheet after Divesting Cash

ASSETS	LIABILITIES
$1,100 Securities owned	$900 Bank loans
	$100 Repo
	$100 Equity

Organization of Securities Trading at Investment Banks

Investment banks act as market makers, but there is no apparent specialization among them in terms of the securities they make markets in. The major investment banks are rather large—some have assets of $40 billion or more. These banks are not specialists in the sense that the market maker on the NYSE floor is a specialist in a small number of securities.

Table 6.6 lists the capital of the five largest investment banks as of January 1, 1990. Capital is used as the primary measure of size because total assets fluctuate according to market conditions. If these firms, on average, have a 5-percent capital-to-asset ratio, which is common among large investment banks, their average asset size would range from $35 to $65 billion.

We built our market maker model on the assumption that the market maker does not hold a diversified portfolio, however. How does this square with the fact that some investment banks are large enough to be diversified?

Investment banks are organized so that classes of securities, such as government bonds, corporate bonds, and corporate equities, are traded in separate departments, each with its own profit and loss statements. Within these departments, individual **traders,** people who buy and sell securities, are responsible for trading in a very limited number of securities. They, too, have their own profit and loss statements, just like the departments in which they work.

Table 6.6 LARGEST U.S. INVESTMENT BANKS RANKED BY CAPITAL, JANUARY 1, 1990

	$ Billions
1. Shearson Lehman	$6.60
2. Salomon Brothers	3.11
3. Merrill Lynch	2.87
4. Goldman Sachs	2.77
5. Drexel Burnham (bankrupt as of 2/90)	1.97
6. The First Boston Corporation	1.65
7. PaineWebber Group, Inc.	1.46
8. Bear Stearns Companies, Inc.	1.42
9. Dean Witter Reynolds, Inc.	1.34
10. Morgan Stanley & Co., Inc.	1.33

Source: *Securities Industry Yearbook,* 1989–1990, published by the Securities Industry Association.

The investment bank supplies capital to departments and individual traders. Each department and trader must show a profit on that capital, which is equivalent to what the firm could earn on a diversified investment of similar risk. If the trader does not earn this return over a certain period, he or she is generally looking for another job. Whole departments that do not perform well are often disbanded.

Why are there big investment banks? The existence of block positions is one major reason. To hold a large amount of inventory temporarily for institutional clients requires an ability to mass a large amount of capital quickly. Large firms are more easily able to do this than small ones because they have access to a large number of lenders.

Underwriting

Underwriting is the process by which new securities issues are brought to market. When borrowers—especially large corporations that rely on publicly traded securities to raise funds—desire to raise additional cash either by issuing bonds or equities, they contact an investment banker. The investment banker agrees to bring the issue to market. This involves a good deal of paperwork, preparing legal documents, fulfilling all the regulatory requirements of the Securities and Exchange Commission (the regulatory agency for public securities markets in the United States), and so on. For these services, the investment bank earns an underwriting fee.

From an economic perspective, however, the most important function of the investment bank in the underwriting process is guaranteeing a price to the issuer at which the security will be sold. As this text has emphasized before, securities represent claims to income streams. Although a corporation may issue a bond at a stated interest rate, its actual cost of debt depends on the price at which it can actually sell the bond in the marketplace. In the case of stock, the owner's claim is to future dividends and retained earnings available to shareholders. A higher price for the new stock issues means that current shareholders and managers receive more money in return for the same (from their perspective) profit commitment.

In 1990, according to Securities Data, underwriting fees for corporate stocks and bonds plunged to a 6-year low, to $1.39 billion from $3.09 billion in 1989. This was due to a contraction in new issues, an estimated decline of 16 percent for common stocks, and keen competition among investment banks for the smaller market.

Underwriting and Bid-Offer Spreads

As underwriter of a new issue, an investment bank guarantees a specific price to its issuing client. In effect, this represents the investment bank's bid price (the price at which it would buy for its inventory) in its role as market maker. Its offer price is the price at which it is willing to sell the issue in the market.

The underwriter's behavior is affected by two incentives: the desire to promise its client a higher (bid) price than competing investment banks might offer and the desire to maximize the (offer) price at which it sells the issue relative to its bid price. The investment bank makes its profit on the spread between the bid and offer prices. The offer price determines the expected yield of the ultimate investor. In investment banking parlance, the expected yield of the ultimate investor is known as the **reoffering yield.** Of course, a higher offer price implies a lower reoffering yield.

Syndicates

To maximize the spread, the underwriter forms a **syndicate** to sell the particular issue. A syndicate represents a group of investment banks, each of which agrees to purchase a portion of the new issue at the bid price. The underwriter who originally assembled the deal is known as the **lead manager.**

Syndicates form because each investment bank has a list of investors to which it usually sells securities. Assuming that each investor attempts to maintain a diversified portfolio, an investment bank's demand for a particular security at the bid price is likely to be limited. Forming a syndicate permits a lead manager to reach a larger pool of investors, reducing the likelihood that he or she will have to cut the offer price to sell the issue. This maximizes the underwriter's spread between the bid and offer price.

Liquidity Guarantees in Underwriting

Because investors view liquidity as desirable, they are willing to purchase securities at higher prices from investment bankers who have been willing to maintain markets in the securities underwritten in the past. Providing liquidity, however, costs the investment bank money. The offer price, therefore, must be high enough to offset the cost of this liquidity.

Many sales of new issues are accompanied by a guarantee that the underwriter will stand ready to quote a price in the issue being underwritten. This does not mean that the investment bank guarantees a specific price. It only guarantees that it will always be a buyer when no one else is in the market. Thus it only promises market continuity. This is strong evidence that the investment bank plays an important market making role and that the market values liquidity.

CONCLUSION

In this chapter we studied the institutional arrangements that securities markets have evolved to increase liquidity. These include securities exchanges, which provide a central forum for buyers and sellers to meet, and market makers, who buy and sell securities for their own accounts. The market maker stands ready to buy a security at a bid price and sell it at an offer price. However, the services of market makers come at a price, because they must finance an undiversified portfolio.

The New York Stock Exchange, the largest exchange in the United States, assigns some market makers, called specialists, the task of maintaining liquid markets in the stocks they trade. In return for this assignment, a specialist has the privilege of access to the limit order book, which helps him or her defray the cost of providing liquidity. NASDAQ is an exchange that operates without designated specialists. However, market makers still provide bid and offer quotes for the stocks traded on this exchange.

A market maker is not necessary to maintain a liquid market for a security that is traded frequently. For very infrequently traded securities, the cost of maintaining a market maker is so prohibitive that investors sacrifice liquidity. During crises, everyone wants to sell to the marker maker, and the marginal cost of funding the market maker's undiversified portfolio greatly increases, thus pushing up liquidity premiums.

Investment banks increase the liquidity of financial markets by underwriting new security issues and making markets in securities. When an investment bank brings a new issue to market, it often guarantees the issuer a specific price for all or part of the issue it sells. Thus it absorbs the risk for the issuer. The investment bank often promises to maintain a market in the securities it underwrites. To do this, it must buy and sell securities, like the specialist on the NYSE. It finances its securities inventory primarily with repurchase agreements.

KEY TERMS

immediacy

liquid security

liquidity market

securities exchange

New York Stock Exchange

broker

listed securities

specialist

dealer

bid-offer spread

market risk

clearing house

NASDAQ

block positioning

underwriter

long position

repurchase agreement

default

margin requirement

reverse repurchase agreement

short position

traders

reoffering yield

syndicate

lead manager

EXERCISES

1. Describe how the specialist makes money.

2. Why does a market maker rarely participate in the trade of a liquid security?

3. All else equal, what can we say about the expected return on a NYSE security that market makers actively trade versus one that they do not actively trade? If we make the same comparison between a NYSE security with active market maker participation and a NASDAQ-listed security with inactive dealer participation, can we draw the same conclusion?

4. As a trader in securities, would you prefer a securities market with a specialist like the NYSE or with multiple dealers posting bid-offer spreads as in the over-the-counter market?

5. If the cost of market maker financing rises (relative to other interest rates in the economy), what happens to the relative rate of return on liquid versus

illiquid securities? What could cause a relative increase in the market maker's financing costs?

6. Commentators on the nightly business report point to stock exchange volume as an important indicator of whether a price movement is significant. For example, they point to high volume on an up day as an indication that the sentiment for rising prices is widely shared among investors. For every buyer, however, there is a seller who holds the opposite opinion, so how do you justify this comment? (Are prices in liquid markets more dependable guides to value than prices in illiquid markets?)

7. Do market makers make more money on high-volume or low-volume days?

8. We indicated that large stock trades are often negotiated off the floor of the NYSE. Why is it not in the seller's interest to take his or her offering to the floor of the exchange? After all, where there are many buyers, the seller might find a better price.

9. We noted that a growing percentage of the trades in NYSE–listed stocks takes place off the exchange. Why might this be happening?

10. Sometimes the NYSE suspends trade in a particular stock when especially bad news about that company is announced. Does trade suspension aid or hinder liquidity?

11. The theory of finance stresses that investors do not hold individual securities. They hold portfolios. If investors invest in portfolios, why are individual securities traded?

12. Which investor, an individual or a large financial institution, would be more likely to buy and sell portfolios rather than individual securities?

13. What is the role of an investment bank?

14. When an investment banker guarantees the price of a security she underwrites, she acts as a market maker. (Why?) Assume that an investment banker presents a corporation issuing a security with a choice as to whether she will guarantee the price of the issue or not. In which case do you think the expected funding cost to the corporation is lower? In which case is the expected return to the investor higher?

15. During the first quarter of 1991, Security Pacific, a large California-based banking company, issued some bonds. At the end of the first quarter, it announced that its loan portfolio had suffered greater losses than the market had anticipated. Its bond prices fell. Many investors argued that the company should buy the bonds back because it sold them under false pretenses. Under what circumstances would this be a profitable solution for the company?

16. Investment bankers are said to make more money than usual when interest rates fall. What does this tell us about their funding position?

FURTHER READING

Amihud, Yakov, Thomas S. Y. Ho, and Robert A. Schwartz (Eds.), *Market Making and the Changing Structure of the Securities Industry,* Lexington Books, 1985.

Grossman, Sanford J., and Mertin H. Miller, "Liquidity and Market Structure," *Journal of Finance,* Vol. 93 (July 1988), pp. 617–636.

Stigum, Marcia, *After the Trade,* Dow Jones Irwin, 1988, pp. 49–64 and 243–263.

PART TWO

Money Demand and Supply

C H A P T E R

7

Money Demand and the Price Level

T he concept of money is at the same time obvious and elusive. Everyone has daily contact with money in the form of currency or bank checks, and we all refer to money in many different contexts. For instance, when we consider "how much money we make" or "how much money we have," we are referring to the cash value of our annual income or of our wealth, respectively.

When economists and policymakers talk about "money," they are referring to a subset of all the nominally denominated assets held by individuals and institutions that they think has an important impact on movements in the price level, levels of nominal income, and interest rates. From such a viewpoint, the definition of money should be based on an observably close relationship with the price level and interest rates. We begin this chapter by introducing several classes of assets that enter into the definition of the money supply. Next we introduce the concept of money demand. The combination of money demand and money supply provides a crucial building block for any examination of price level and interest rate movements. The achievement of equilibrium in the **money market** is a key element in determining nominal quantities such as the price level, inflation rates, and nominal interest rates.

Alternatively, money may be defined functionally according to the services that it provides. First, it can be interpreted as that group of assets which provide the **service of facilitating transactions:** cash, deposits of banks at the central bank, and checking deposits at private financial intermediaries. Aside from any impact of these assets on the price level, we would like to understand what determines the supply and demand for assets with such properties because checking deposits comprise a major portion of bank liabilities. In this chapter we will also show what determines the demand for assets used in transactions.

To serve as a medium of exchange, an asset must itself have value. A second function provided by money, therefore, is to serve as a **store of value.** Since stores of value can include all forms of wealth, this function gives us a wide latitude in defining money. Generally, however, we include only those liquid assets which are readily exchangeable for a certain amount of cash on short notice.

Money also serves as a **unit of account,** the unit in which all prices or accounts are generally expressed. For instance, balance sheet values are typically written in terms of numbers of dollars rather than bushels of wheat. While it is a convenience, the use of money as a unit of account does not require actually holding quantities of money.

Another important service of money is to provide a **standard of deferred payment,** a standard unit in which contractual prices for payment in the future can be written. Courts more readily enforce contracts written in terms of monetary units rather than barter contracts. Again, contracting parties need hold no money to contract in monetary units, although when the contracted date of delivery arrives, they must acquire some means of payment.

CLASSIFYING MONETARY ASSETS

There are many potential measures of money supply, two of which are described in Table 7.1. These measures start with a group of assets used mostly in transactions, known as **M1,** and broaden to a group that adds to M1 savings deposits and small time deposits, known as **M2.** Table 7.1 indicates that growth in M1 and M2 is roughly similar. Even broader money definitions are available with ever-expanding types of assets included. We examined most of the components of these definitions in Chapter 3.

ASSETS USED FOR TRANSACTIONS—M1

Households and businesses constantly purchase and sell goods, services, and assets. The buyer in almost every transaction delivers either cash or claims on deposits at banks promising to pay a fixed amount of cash on demand. Such assets are called **media of exchange** because they facilitate transactions. Table 7.2 indicates the importance of different media in the U.S. economy.

Table 7.1 VARIOUS DEFINITIONS OF MONEY ($Billion)

Definition	12/84	12/86	12/88
1. M1	558	731	790
Currency	159	184	212
Traveler's checks	5	6	8
Demand deposits	248	308	289
Other checkable deposits	146	232	282
2. M2	2369	2801	3069
Including M1 plus			
Savings deposits	289	366	430
Small time deposits	885	853	1025
MMMFs	230	292	327

Source: From *Federal Reserve Bulletin,* January 1988 and January 1990.

Cash

In a list of items usually considered as money, we must include **cash,** the paper currency and coin used in transactions. Cash generally circulates in small transactions when it is legally used or in large transactions when it is used illegally.

Currently in the United States, paper currency is provided almost exclusively by the Federal Reserve, and it comprises the major part of the liabilities of the Federal Reserve.[1] Historically, other institutions have created cash; for example, prior to

Table 7.2 IMPORTANCE OF MAJOR PAYMENTS MEDIA

Medium of Exchange	Percent of Transactions	Dollar Value of Average Transaction	Percent of Total Value of Transactions
Cash	87.7	$1.50	0.6
Checks	10.5	$500.	22.7
Credit cards	1.8	$25.	0.2
Wire transfers	Negligible	$1.7 million	76.5

Source: From R. Kimball, "Wire Transfer and the Demand for Money," *New England Economic Review,* March/April 1980, Table 1.

1.   About $300 million of U.S. notes (the original "greenbacks"), liabilities of the U.S. Treasury, still circulate. In addition, about $1 billion of Treasury currency no longer issued remains in circulation.

1935, national banks circulated bank notes.[2] Also, the Treasury has circulated high-value gold and silver coins and paper currency.

Cash now in circulation is **legal tender;** its delivery legally satisfies contracts calling for payment in dollars. Legally, it is the physical manifestation of the concept "dollar."

Checking Deposits

The demand deposits and NOW accounts described in Chapter 3 provide the second form of "money" used by the public because checks are usually readily accepted in day-to-day transactions. Most small transactions in modern economies involve either cash or demand deposits, as indicated in Table 7.2. Banks guarantee one-to-one convertibility of such transactions deposits (checking deposits) with cash, so little risk is involved with checks, except when banks are threatened with bankruptcy.[3]

Cash and business transactions deposits in the United States pay zero yields, and individual deposits pay a relatively low yield. Most personal accounts are now held in the form of NOW (negotiable order of withdrawal) accounts. These pay interest rates near those of noncheckable savings accounts, but they generally have minimum balance requirements.

TRANSACTIONS MEDIA NOT INCLUDED IN MONETARY MEASURES

Credit Cards

One item not generally included in measures of the money supply is the use of credit cards. This exclusion, however, does not distort greatly the measure of transactions media, since households that use them, on average, transacted only 8 percent of their expenditures with credit cards in 1986. A person who uses a credit card is

2. Such notes were authorized under the National Banking Act of 1863, which established the system of national banks. The notes had to be backed by a certain amount of U.S. government bonds. In 1935, the last of the U.S. bonds for which this "circulation privilege" was not prohibited were redeemed, leaving the Federal Reserve notes and Treasury currency as the only paper money. Nevertheless, the entire legal machinery that authorized bank note circulation remains in the statutes of the United States. If the U.S. Treasury were ever to issue a bond for which the circulation privilege is not prohibited, i.e., outside the authority of the Second Liberty Loan Act of 1917, national banks would once again be free to circulate their own bank notes.

3. Individuals, of course, may write bad checks, so the recipient does have to expend some effort at verification. This is not generally a problem with cashier's checks, which are promises by banks to pay on demand.

writing a general IOU, exchanging a promissory note for goods. The promissory note is a negotiable security. The seller of the good will then sell the note on the market to a buyer, generally the bank that issued the credit card. The total amount of such IOUs outstanding is generally not included in measures of the money stock.

Bank Deposits at the Federal Reserve

Although carried out only by banks serving as agents for customers, the vast bulk of transactions in the United States by value are effected by deliveries of deposits at the Federal Reserve. These deposits, called **fed funds,** turn over rapidly through electronic accounting transfers among individual accounts. The Federal Reserve also converts such deposits one-for-one into currency on demand.

Most transactions in fed funds are effected through wire transfers. While not usually counted directly in monetary definitions such as M1, fed funds do represent an important part of the payments system that we will address in Chapters 9, 11, 12, and 13. Fed funds *plus* currency issued by the Fed are defined as a monetary aggregate called the **monetary base.**

M 2

A much wider range of bank liabilities is not checkable, but these liabilities are close substitutes for checking accounts. Added to M1, these liabilities comprise a broad category known as **M2.**

Savings Accounts

Savings accounts can be converted to cash at any time. Such claims, however, cannot be transferred by check, so they cannot be used directly for transactions. Rather, the depositor must order the bank to transfer funds from a savings to a checking account. Since this can be done nearly costlessly, savings accounts are easily substitutable for checking accounts.

Time Deposits

Small time deposits of less than $100,000 also are included in M2. These deposits have a specific maturity and pay relatively high interest rates. Penalties for early withdrawal, however, generally make ready conversion to cash unattractive.

Money Market Mutual Funds

Also included in M2, money market mutual funds allow their shareholders to make demand-type deposits. These funds hold only short-term money market instruments, such as T-bills, that are guaranteed to pay off in a short time. Each shareholder owns a prorated claim against the value of the assets of the fund. The claims against these funds are secure in nominal terms, and the claims can be redeemed at any time with a phone call and can be quickly moved into a bank deposit. Even limited check writing is permitted against the accounts.

DEVICES FOR AVOIDING INTEREST RESTRICTIONS

Businesses can use other instruments, not included in the money stock as transactions balances, as devices to avoid restrictions against interest on demand deposits. Banks are prohibited from paying interest on deposits held by corporate entities. Yet businesses, which comprise the largest users of demand-type deposits, are adept at avoiding this type of restriction. The most important devices are repurchase agreements and Eurodollar deposits.

Repurchase Agreements

Repurchase agreements consist of either a purchase or sale, usually of a Treasury security, together with a promise to repurchase the security at some specific time in the future at a prearranged price. For example, in a typical transaction, a business may receive a payment in the morning. It wishes to hold it in a demand-type deposit during the day to cover potential cash outflows. Toward the end of the day, realizing that it will carry the funds overnight, the business purchases a T-bill from the bank. The bank agrees to repurchase the T-bill the next day. Overnight, the business holds no demand deposits in the bank, holding a T-bill instead. The next morning it resells the T-bill to the bank at a somewhat higher price than it paid. In this way, the bank effectively pays interest to the business for holding its cash overnight.

Eurodollar Deposits

Another device to avoid interest restrictions is a **Eurodollar deposit.** A Eurodollar is simply a liability of a bank denominated in dollars when the bank is situated outside the United States. The market for this sort of deposit began in Europe, but the term is now much more general, applying to bank deposits located in the Caribbean or in Asia.

How does a bank avoid interest restrictions through Eurodollar deposits? As an example, a business with a deposit in a New York bank at the end of the day tells the bank to shift the deposit to the bank's subsidiary in the Bahamas. This converts the deposit in the U.S. bank into a Eurodollar deposit in the Bahamian bank. Since it is outside the jurisdiction of the United States, the Bahamian bank is not affected by the U.S. interest rate restrictions. The Bahamian bank pays overnight interest on the deposit, and the next morning, it wires all the funds back to the business's account in New York to make them available for the next day's transactions. The difference between this transaction and a repurchase agreement is that instead of a T-bill, the bank sells overnight a deposit outside the United States. We will see in our detailed discussion of Eurodollars in Chapter 15 that the different payment mechanisms associated with Eurodollar deposits and repurchase agreements give them a different degree of liquidity.

THE ARBITRARINESS OF MONEY STOCK DEFINITIONS

It is hard to maintain a tightly defined concept of "the money supply," even if we define the supply as that subset of assets engaged principally in transactions. They all have close substitutes that can be converted almost immediately into transactions-type assets. It is difficult to start our formal definition of the money supply with transactions media because we can only arbitrarily cut off the definition of which assets are used for transactions. For instance, money market securities such as T-bills are such liquid assets, salable almost instantly to many buyers with ready access to cash, that they are often held only in anticipation of a transaction. Holding them reduces costs; it also shifts demand away from transactions media. Nevertheless, we will now use an explicit money demand function based on a transactions approach to money demand to explain the demand for cash by households.

A SPECIFIC FORM OF HOUSEHOLD MONEY DEMAND

Some securities, such as cash or checkable deposits, are generally acceptable in exchange for goods. These are clearly identifiable and distinct from other kinds of securities that exist only for holding wealth. The other types of securities have a payoff in the form of an interest yield that we can label R. We will assume that money itself pays a yield of zero in the simplest case.[4] The interest cost of holding money is then $R \times M$, where M is the *average* amount of money held.

Money is useful in that it allows you to buy or sell goods. The amount of money you want depends on the value of the goods you wish to buy or sell. We assume that the amount of goods you want to buy per year is y. The nominal price per unit of goods is P, so in nominal terms, you make $P \times y$ dollars of nominal expenditures per year. Expenditure occurs at a constant rate. If $P \times y$ is $20,000 per year, this means that you spend about $55.00 every day.[5]

You can get money by making a trip to the bank and drawing down a savings account. Alternatively, if you are relatively wealthy, you can call your broker and tell him or her to sell one of your securities. It is costly in terms of time to make a trip to the bank, and a fee is involved in selling securities to cover the labor costs of brokerage. For every transaction converting high-yield securities into cash, we assume that a fixed amount b of real resources is used, independent of the nominal amount converted in the transaction. In nominal terms, this cost of transacting has a dollar value of $P \times b$ for which you must pay.

By withdrawing funds more frequently from interest-bearing deposits, you can reduce your costs in terms of foregone interest because the amount of cash you keep on hand is smaller on average, leaving more deposits in your account to earn interest. More frequent withdrawals increase transactions costs, however. Resolving the tension between these conflicting means of reducing costs will determine your total cost-minimizing cash holdings. Let's see how this works.

When you withdraw funds from the bank, you convert a certain amount of deposits into cash. The money will be expended gradually, and once it runs out, you must withdraw cash once again. Letting C represent the amount of cash that you acquire each time you withdraw funds, we can plot your money holdings against time as in Figure 7.1.

In this figure, the *average* amount of money M that you hold is $0.5 \times C$. We arrive at this result by examining the amount of money on hand each day between withdrawals and adding across days. This total is simply the area under one of the sawteeth in Figure 7.1. This area is $0.5 \times C \times$ (time between withdrawals), or one-half times the base times the height of the triangle. We find the average daily cash on hand between withdrawals by dividing the time between withdrawals—that is, $M = 0.5 \times C$.

The number of times per year that you make withdrawals is Py/C, the total cash expenditure on goods in a year divided by the amount withdrawn on each visit

---

4. This is true of cash. Demand deposits held by businesses pay no explicit interest. However, in lieu of interest, banks often provide free services. Checking deposits held by households currently pay some interest. To the extent that money yields interest, R can be interpreted as the difference between interest paid on other assets and interest paid on money.

5. Of course, this is not the normal expenditure pattern for a household. A household has to spend a big lump in rent at the beginning of the month and several smaller lumps over the course of the month. We make this simple assumption to produce a simple form for the money demand function of the household.

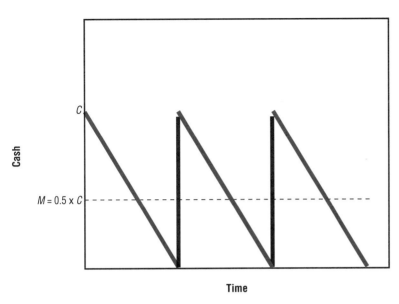

Figure 7.1   PATTERN OF HOUSEHOLD CASH HOLDING

to the bank. The days that elapse between withdrawals are then C/Py. For example, if $Py = \$100$ per year and $C = \$20$, the number of withdrawals per year is 5, and the time elapsed between withdrawals is $\frac{1}{5}$ of a year.

What costs do you face in holding $M = 0.5 \times C$ on average? You will forego interest income of $R \times M$ on average. Your transactions costs will be $Pb \times Py/2M$, the dollar cost per withdrawal multiplied by the number of withdrawals. Your total costs will therefore be

$$R \times M + Pb \times \frac{Py}{2M}$$

To find the minimum cost of the average money holding, we plot both sources of cost in Figure 7.2 against the average M. The straight line 1 represents the interest cost, which increases at a constant rate as money holding increases. The curved line 2 is the total transactions cost, which declines as money holding rises. The curved line 3 is the sum of the individual costs for each level of money holding. Notice that this curve reaches a minimum at that level of money M^d in Figure 7.2 for which the two sources of cost are equal. That is,

$$R \times M^d = Pb \times \frac{Py}{2M^d} \tag{7.1}$$

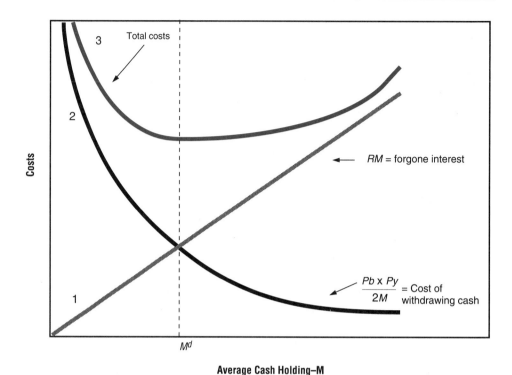

Figure 7.2   COSTS OF AVERAGE CASH HOLDINGS

To convince yourself that this is the right condition for a minimum cost, increase M slightly to the right of M^d. Costs of withdrawal fall, but interest costs rise by more, so an increase in M above M^d increases costs. Reducing M below M^d reduces interest cost but increases withdrawal costs by more. M^d is therefore the cost-minimizing money holding.

Solving equation 7.1 for M^d, we find

$$M^d = \sqrt{Pb \times \frac{Py}{2R}} = \sqrt{\frac{P^2 by}{2R}} \tag{7.2}$$

Notice that P^2 is in the numerator of equation 7.2, so by dividing both sides by P, we have an expression for a real quantity of money:

$$\frac{M^d}{P} = \sqrt{\frac{by}{2R}} \tag{7.3}$$

This is a demand for a real stock of money, the value of the average money holding in terms of goods, so a higher price level implies a proportionally higher nominal money demand. The demand for money also depends inversely on the yield on other types of securities; a rise in R implies a fall in real money demand. The demand for money also depends on the real expenditure pattern y. If y rises, real money demand rises. Finally, real money demand depends on the transactions technology reflected in the withdrawal cost b. For example, suppose that an automatic teller system reduces the cost of withdrawal b. You would then make withdrawals more frequently and demand less cash on average.

EXAMPLE: USING THE MODEL TO EXPLAIN HOUSEHOLD DEMAND FOR CASH

In a survey of households in 1986, the Federal Reserve elicited data on cash acquisitions and expenditures undertaken with cash on a monthly basis.[6] We report these data by income class in Table 7.3. Note that higher-income families do not have a remarkably higher *cash* expenditure than lower-income families. Higher-income

Table 7.3 MONTHLY HOUSEHOLD CASH MANAGEMENT, 1986*

(1) Income ($1,000)	(2) Cash Acquired per Withdrawal	(3) Cash Expenditure	(4) Average Cash on Hand	(5) $M/\sqrt{Py}$
<10	194	331	97	5.3
10–20	139	440	69	3.3
20–30	153	433	76	3.6
30–50	140	514	70	3.1
<50	130	473	66	3.0

Source: From Robert Avery, Gregory Elliehausen, Arthur Kennickell, and Paul Spindt, "Changes in the Use of Transaction Accounts and Cash from 1984 to 1986," *Federal Reserve Bulletin,* March 1987, pp. 179–192.

*All data are means across all households in an income category.

6. For details of this survey, see Robert Avery, Gregory Elliehausen, Arthur Kennickell, and Paul Spindt, "Changes in the Use of Transaction Accounts and Cash from 1984 to 1986," *Federal Reserve Bulletin,* March 1987, pp. 179–92.

families make most expenditures with checks or credit cards and use relatively little cash.

The mean amount of cash required at each withdrawal is reported in column 2.[7] Column 3 contains data on cash expenditure per month. The average holding of cash, one-half the amount acquired, is reported in column 4. Finally, in column 5 we report the ratio of average money holdings to the square root of cash expenditure, or $M/\sqrt{Py}$. According to equation 7.2, this ratio should equal $\sqrt{Pb/2R}$. If transaction costs Pb and forgone interest R are the same across income categories, entries in column 5 should be identical. Evidently, while this equality holds approximately for higher-income categories, it does not hold for the lowest. Lower-income families, however, generally face lower earning opportunities on investments. For example, they may lack the minimum amounts necessary to buy bank certificates of deposit that pay high yields, leaving as their only alternative a lower-yielding passbook deposit. For such families, R will be relatively low, and their demands for cash will be relatively high.

CURRENCY IN ILLEGAL ACTIVITIES

Although we all use cash regularly, household and business holdings do not account for the bulk of the dollar currency in circulation. The Federal Reserve survey of cash holdings cited earlier concluded that households in the United States held only $20 billion of cash in 1986, only 11 percent of the $177 billion in currency outside of banks at the time of the survey. Holdings of legitimate businesses should be substantial, but they probably would not exceed those of households, since businesses find it worthwhile to convert cash acquisitions from households into bank deposits as rapidly as possible. They normally hold cash only to make change for cash-using customers. Even if legitimate businesses account for another 11 percent of the cash, this still leaves $138 billion unaccounted for.

While a considerable amount of dollar currency circulates abroad, one possible conclusion is that much of the outstanding currency is held for use in illegal transactions. In fact, the dollar is the international currency of choice for drug deals, gambling, political corruption, tax evasion, and the evasion of currency and capital controls. These would generally include many large-scale transactions requiring large bills. Table 7.4 contains a breakdown by denominations of the currency in circulation. Note that 65 percent of the total value of currency is in $100 and $50 notes, denominations not commonly used by households.

To account for this source of demand for currency, we can slightly modify the model for legal cash demand to derive a demand function for illegal cash holding of the same form as equation 7.3. Now we interpret Py as the cash *inflow* to the typical drug dealer from sales. Since holding cash yields no interest, the dealer would

---

7. Households typically hold a positive amount of cash on hand at the time of a withdrawal to avoid the risk of being caught short of cash. We have ignored this minimum holding, assuming that it is not used for ongoing transactions.

Table 7.4 U.S. CURRENCY IN CIRCULATION BY DENOMINATION, SEPTEMBER 30, 1990

Denomination	Quantity ($Billion)
$1	4.7
$2	0.8
$5	5.8
$10	11.7
$20	64.9
$50	32.1
$100	132.6
>$100	0.3
Total	253.3

Source: From Department of the Treasury, *Treasury Bulletin,* December 1990, p. 127.

like to convert his receipts into securities or bank deposits yielding an interest rate R. This is called **money laundering.** Laundering cash through the banking system into legal investments costs the fixed nominal amount Pb. For a drug dealer, the cost Pb of getting cash into a bank is probably much higher than the cost to a household of getting cash out of a bank. Given this cost, the dealer accumulates a

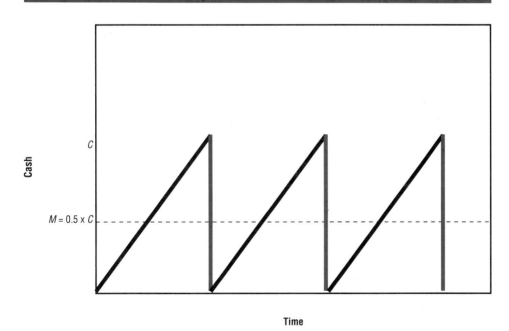

Figure 7.3 MONEY LAUNDERING DEMAND FOR CASH

fair amount of cash and launders it only periodically. This creates the sawtooth pattern of cash holding depicted in Figure 7.3, where C is the maximum cash holding attained before laundering. Again, the average cash holding is $M = 0.5 \times C$. The dealer selects M to satisfy the condition in Figure 7.1, producing a currency demand function of the same form as in Figure 7.3.

If the real magnitude of drug sales increases, so does the demand for currency. If laundering of funds becomes more costly—that is, b rises—the demand for currency also increases. See Box 7.1.

THE PRICE LEVEL AND MONEY MARKET EQUILIBRIUM

The price level is the exchange rate—the relative price—between money (nominal units) and goods (real units). Economists explain how the price level is determined by constructing a theory of **money demand** and finding the price level and interest rate that equates money demand and money supply. Finding the forces that drive the price level allows us to determine how the price level changes and how such changes are anticipated. In Chapter 5 we learned that anticipated changes in the price level or inflation affect the nominal interest rate. We can now begin to explore the relation between movements in the money supply and the rate of inflation.

We have already derived a particular form of money demand based purely on transactions. Since there are other reasons for holding money that would generate other functional relationships, economists usually feel free to use other formulas for money demand that are convenient for developing important concepts. To determine an equilibrium price level, we will assume that the demand for money is of a particularly simple linear form:

$$\frac{M}{P} = ay - bR \tag{7.4}$$

This form still specifies the demand for real money as related positively to real income y and negatively to the nominal interest rate R.[8] We will treat a and b as constants. We will assume for now that the real interest rate and real income are constant.[9]

If c is the expected inflation rate, recall that Fisher's equation (see Chapter 5) allows us to write the nominal interest rate as $R = r + c$, where r is the real interest rate.

8. To guarantee a positive money demand, we assume that $ay - bR > 0$ for all relevant values of real income and nominal interest rate.

where we will concentrate on the interactions among the price level, inflation, real income, and the real interest rate.

9. We will relax this assumption in Chapter 21,

Box 7.1

How to Launder Money

"Bank investigators estimate that as much as $100 billion from selling cocaine in the United States is being sent from the country annually through the electronic transfer of money from American banks to accounts in foreign countries. The money is believed to end up in the hands of the violent and powerful Medellin drug cartel in Colombia. . . .

"In the type of modern electronic, or wire, money transfer that has become so difficult to monitor, a customer may instruct his personal computer to tell his bank's computer to take money out of his account and send it to another account in a foreign bank. The bank's computer then tells a banking clearing house—a kind of automated middleman that assists banks in switching funds from one to another—to send the customer's funds to the account abroad. . . .

"Federal investigators did succeed last week in obtaining the first agreement of a foreign bank to plead guilty to taking part in a drug-money conspiracy. The criminal plea, to be entered in federal court Monday in Atlanta against Banco de Occidente, comes as part of a $1.2 billion money laundering case known as Operation Polar Cap. . . .

"It was a tip-off by the Wells Fargo Bank in Los Angeles that led federal investigators to the money laundering ring. Wells Fargo tellers reported to federal authorities that the Andonian Brothers Manufacturing Company, known to the Los Angeles business community as Nazareth Jewelers, had been making unusually high deposits, $25 million in three months.

"Wells Fargo and other banks in the area are frequently used by legitimate jewelry businesses that traditionally deal in cash. Jewelry, being physically small, is easily transferred from hand to hand in jewelry exchanges, often in return for large sums of cash. Other businesses that deal in large amounts of cash and have been used in money laundering schemes include casinos, groceries, and parking garages. Taking advantage of this tradition, drug dealers set up fictitious jewelry operations in Los Angeles, New York, Houston, and Miami so they could deposit large amounts of cash and transfer it without causing suspicion.

"The Polar Cap laundry began in midtown and downtown Manhattan and in business districts of Miami, Houston, and Los Angeles. Drug dealers took hundreds of millions of dollars in cash from cocaine sales and hauled them off in cartons and briefcases to the jewelers in Los Angeles that deposited the cash there and ordered it to be transferred electronically to accounts in New York, where some of it originated, and then transferred abroad. . . . "

For a detailed discussion of electronic payments systems, see Chapter 12.

Source: From Stephen Labaton, "Banking's Technology Helps Drug Dealers Export Cash," *New York Times,* August 14, 1989, p. A1. Copyright © 1989 by The New York Times Company. Reprinted by permission.

As an example of how the price level depends on the money supply, we assume that the quantity of money grows at a constant percentage rate c. One requirement of equilibrium is that money demand always equals money supply. The second requirement is that expected inflation rates coincide with actual inflation rates. Since there is no uncertainty about the future in our simple example, there should be no surprises for people in the money market. We will show that a price level change at a constant percentage rate c is the *constant* inflation rate consistent with equilibrium.

If the inflation rate actually is always c, the nominal interest rate R must always equal $r + c$ through Fisher's equation. Otherwise, people would mispredict an inflation rate that they can perfectly foresee. From equation 7.4 we infer that the demand for real money must always equal $ay - b(r + c)$, so the equilibrium price level must initially equal $P = M/[ay - b(r + c)]$ to equate money supply to money demand.

The money supply is M in period 1, as indicated by vertical line 1 in Figure 7.4. It is $M(1 + c)$ in the next period, as indicated by line 2. The initial demand for nominal money, represented by line 3, can be found by multiplying equation 7.4 by P, the current price level. This line slopes downward because increases in the interest rate reduce the demand for money. The position of the money demand curve depends on the current price level. For instance, an increase in price level

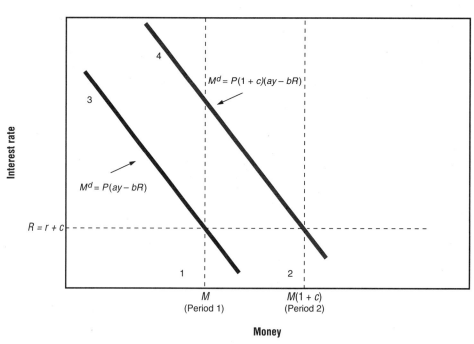

Figure 7.4 EQUILIBRIUM PRICE LEVELS

from P to $P(1 + c)$ would shift the money demand curve uniformly rightward by c percent to line 4.

By the second period, the money supply has shifted rightward by c percent to line 2. A c-percent rise in the price level would produce an equilibrium at the same nominal interest rate, $r + c$. The equilibrium inflation rate c would then replicate itself as we add more future periods.

The equilibrium $P = M/[ay - b(r + c)]$ is of interest to us because it implies a proportional relationship between the price level and the quantity of money. If we imposed an experiment in which we suddenly doubled the money supply, the price level would instantly double, but inflation would thereafter remain constant at rate c if money continued to grow at rate c. Alternatively, even with no increase in the current supply, an increase in the expected growth rate of money also would immediately increase the current price *level* because it would increase the expected inflation rate.

CONCLUSION

Money is that group of nominally denominated securities whose change in quantity is most closely linked to movements in the price level. Money is an empirically defined concept, and there is a constant dispute over which securities should be counted as money. These definitions start from currency in circulation and deposits at central banks, a total called the monetary base. A broader definition, known as M1, extends to all generally acceptable transactions media. Other definitions can include most short-term nominally denominated securities.

Concentrating on items yielding transactions services provides an uncomplicated form for the demand for money that depends proportionally on the price level, positively on real expenditure, and inversely on the nominal interest rate. Data for household currency management tend to follow this form of money demand. Determination of equilibrium in the supply and demand for money is the means by which we can explain movements in the price level.

KEY TERMS

money market

service of facilitating transactions
  (transactions medium)

store of value

unit of account

standard of deferred payment

M1

M2

media of exchange

cash

legal tender

fed funds

monetary base

repurchase agreements

Eurodollar deposit

money laundering

money demand

EXERCISES

1. Suppose that it costs $2 to make a trip to your bank to withdraw cash and that your annual cash expenditure is $12,000. If the interest rate on bank deposits is 5 percent per year, how much cash will you have on average during the year?

2. If the cost of withdrawing cash from your bank falls to $1 because of the installation of automatic teller machines around town, how much cash will you have on average during the year?

3. In exercise 3, suppose that the interest rate on bank deposits falls to 3 percent. How much cash will you have on average during the year?

4. In Table 7.3, can the higher cash holdings of the lowest-income groups be explained by its receiving a lower interest rate on deposits? Relatively, how much smaller would you presume the rate available to the lowest-income group to be than that available to the next income group?

5. Prior to 1935, national banks could circulate bank notes that looked almost like Federal Reserve notes. The U.S. Treasury guaranteed the notes, so people readily accepted them. The notes paid zero interest, but banks had to back the notes by holding U.S. government securities with a market value of 110 percent of the face value of the notes in circulation. There was also an annual cost per dollar issued to keep the notes in circulation. Under what circumstances was it profitable for banks to issue bank notes?

6. Suppose that half the U.S. currency supply is either held in foreign countries or used as a means of payment in the illegal drug trade. Suppose that the fall of communism in Eastern Europe and success in the war on drugs reduce the demand for currency for such uses to zero. What will happen to the price level in the United States?

7. Suppose that the government starts to enforce currency laws more strictly, thereby making it more costly for drug dealers to launder their money. What will happen to the demand for currency? What will happen to the U.S. price level?

8. Suppose that the development of electronic funds transfers reduces the cost of a money laundering transaction by 50 percent. By what percentage will the drug cartel's holding of dollar currency fall?

9. If the money supply grows steadily at 5 percent per year, at what rate will the price level grow?

10. Suppose that real income and the nominal interest rate both double. If there is no change in the nominal money supply, what will be the effect on the price level?

11. If the rate of growth of the money supply suddenly increases from 5 to 10 percent, what will be the immediate effect on the price level?

FURTHER READING

Avery, Robert, Gregory Elliehausen, Arthur Kennickell, and Paul Spindt, "Changes in the Use of Transaction Accounts and Cash from 1984 to 1986," *Federal Reserve Bulletin,* March 1987.

Baumol, William J., "The Transaction Demand for Cash: An Inventory Theoretic Approach," *Quarterly Journal of Economics,* November 1952, pp. 545–66.

Tobin, James, "The Interest Elasticity of the Transactions Demand for Cash," *Review of Economics and Statistics,* August 1956, pp. 241–47.

C H A P T E R

8

The Monetary Standard

Economic history is filled with a sequence of different **monetary standards,** rules that define the item serving as money and determine how money is created. Such standards have ranged from various metals, such as copper, iron, silver, and gold, to commodities such as tobacco. In this chapter we will study various monetary standards that have evolved over time. Each standard determines the forces that influence the currency supply and thus the behavior of prices and inflation. We will examine the different qualities that these systems impart to a promissory note that will deliver one unit of money and show that the same note can have markedly different values depending on the monetary standard.

THE RELATION OF THE LEGAL DEFINITION OF MONEY TO ECONOMIC BEHAVIOR

People usually post prices or write payment contracts in terms of the unit of account, such as the yen or the dollar. Some item must be delivered to satisfy the terms of the contract. We have seen that delivery of the asset defined as **legal tender** is acceptable as good funds and legally extinguishes the obligation of the party who has previously agreed to deliver the unit of account. Other assets, such as checks, are also traditionally acceptable by the party receiving payment, but they are themselves merely credit instruments, promises to pay legal tender. If such assets provide a means of reducing the need for holding legal tender, changes in their supply will strongly affect the demand for legal tender and determine how changes in the amount of legal tender affect the price level and interest rates. These monetary assets are normally the liabilities of a banking system, and in Chapters 11, 12, and 13 we will consider how the bank liabilities come to be close substitutes for good funds. In Chapter 9 we will study how the supply of bank liabilities is determined relative to the supply of good funds. Now, however, we will work with the simplifying assumption that the nature of the item chosen as the monetary standard determines the movements of nominal values.

How is legal tender defined? Certain physical or financial assets are given legal tender status by passing a law that requires everyone to accept them in payment of contracts specifying payment in the unit of account. These assets are known as "legal tender." Since laws can be changed on short notice, so can the items defined as legal tender. For example, in the United States, legal tender was defined in the Mint Act of 1792 as U.S. coins containing a certain weight of gold or silver, and legal tender silver dollars containing the quantity of silver defined in 1792 still circulated at face value until the mid-1960s. During the Civil War, U.S. notes, a paper currency also known as greenbacks, were given legal tender status as well. The U.S. notes were given the status of claims on equally denominated gold or silver coins in 1879. Silver certificates, claims on silver coin or bullion, circulated as legal tender until 1968. Federal Reserve notes, currently the only legal tender in circulation other than minor coins, originally were claims on gold coin held by the Federal Reserve; since 1933, they have been claims on nothing in particular. Instead, they must be accepted by fiat—that is, by government decree—so they are known as **fiat money.** Bank deposits at the Federal Reserve also are acceptable in payments among banks, although they are not themselves legal tender.

Example: A Shift in Legal Tender

Since legal tender can be defined with the stroke of a pen, its quantity can be changed instantly. For example, suppose a government defines legal tender as gold coin alone. Suppose that $100 million in gold coin circulates in the economy. Contracts written in dollars envision payment in gold coin, so dollar prices and future payments are arranged accordingly. If the government suddenly adds a new paper currency to the list of legal tender and circulates $400 million in that paper currency to purchase goods, everyone who posts prices in dollars must now accept both the paper currency and the gold coins in payment. From our analysis in Chapter 7, we can conclude that the increase in supply of legal tender will lead to an increase in the price level.

Sellers of goods must accept the new currency, but they can post whatever dollar prices they want.

Gresham's Law

Suppose that the dollar prices of goods rise by 400 percent with the introduction of the paper currency. In a foreign country, however, the relative price between gold and goods remains unchanged. What will happen to the gold dollars that originally circulated? If the government insists on enforcing the legal tender law, the gold dollars, exchanged for goods at nominal face value, will buy only one-fourth as many goods as before. Holders of gold dollars will have an incentive to ship them abroad, where they still purchase as much as before. Gold dollars will thus be removed from circulation, and the legal tender supply, now consisting only of paper currency, will be four times greater than it was before the paper currency was introduced.

That "bad money" drives out "good money" is known as **Gresham's law,** named for Sir Thomas Gresham, financial agent and adviser of Queen Elizabeth I of England. Gresham's law operates when two different forms of legal tender are circulated simultaneously and one—the "good" money—has a market value that exceeds its officially denominated face value. A strict enforcement of legal tender laws will drive the "good" money out of circulation. In Queen Elizabeth's day, the government circulated light-weight coins containing less precious metal than older, heavy-weight coins but bearing the same denomination, and a legal tender law required that the light-weight coins be accepted at face value. Violation of the law was a treasonous insult to the crown, so only "bad" money circulated, in the form of light-weight coin, and the heavier coin was shipped abroad. If the legal tender law is not strictly enforced, the two moneys can circulate simultaneously, either with the "good" money exchanging at a premium above quoted prices or the "bad" money exchanging at a discount.[1]

Long-Term Contracts

Anyone who has previously contracted for future receipts of dollars may be harmed by a shift in what comprises legal tender. For example, suppose that a bond promises to pay $1 in 1 year. The real value of the $1 on delivery will fall as the price level rises. Since the price of the bond is $P_B = \$1/(1 + R)$, where R is the interest rate

---

1. Arthur J. Rolnick and Warren E. Weber, "Gresham's Law or Gresham's Fallacy," *Journal of Political Economy*, February 1986, pp. 185–199, show that Gresham's law was apparently suspended in California during the U.S. Civil War, when greenbacks should have driven out gold coins, because of lack of strict enforcement.

for contracts promising to pay in nominal dollars, a lower bond price reflects a higher R. If the expected rate of inflation increases, R rises to offset an anticipated real depreciation of the dollar. If the real interest r is 5 percent, a bond would sell initially for $P_B = 1/1.05 = \$0.952$ if a noninflationary monetary standard were in effect. If a switch in standard will cause a likely 5-percent price level increase during the year of the loan, a price of $P_B = \$1/(1 + r + 0.05) = \$1/1.10 = \$0.91$ would be paid by a lender who wants the same real return. For a bond contract signed prior to the shift in monetary standard, the shift in the definition of legal tender causes a real transfer from creditor to debtor; the debtor now must repay a smaller real amount than both had anticipated.

The ability to redefine legal tender arbitrarily or to change its quantity can have a powerful redistributive effect on those who contract in dollars. If bond purchasers believe that a shift in the definition of legal tender will occur in the future, they may write clauses in the loan contract to protect themselves against such shifts. For instance, they may insist that the contract specify the delivery of "gold dollars" rather than "dollars." Then a shift to a paper legal tender would not affect them.

For example, consider the behavior of creditors of dollar-denominated bonds from mid-1860s through 1933. Harmed by the introduction of greenbacks as legal tender during the Civil War and the subsequent inflation, lenders began to write long-term bonds in terms of "gold dollars" after the Civil War—that is, the bonds had to be repaid in U.S. gold coins of a particular gold content or their equivalent value. These contracts were upheld as valid by the Supreme Court in a series of rulings in the 1860s and 1870s known as the "**legal tender cases.**" By the 1920s, although the United States had been officially on a gold standard since the passage of the Gold Standard Act of 1900, most private and government bonds in the United States promised to pay in gold dollars. A joint resolution of Congress in June 1933 abrogated all contractual obligations to pay in gold, so the word "dollars" was suddenly substituted for "gold dollars" in all debt contracts. In a series of rulings known as the "**gold clause cases**" in 1935, the Supreme Court explicitly upheld the abrogations for private contracts and effectively upheld them for government bonds, so such protective devices proved illusory.

Alternatively, in the absence of such devices, bond purchasers will offer a low price for the bond; the bond will then earn a yield high enough to offset anticipated losses resulting from changes in legal tender definitions. The price paid for a bond promising a given stream of dollar payments thus depends on the purchaser's expectation of a stable or unstable monetary standard.

To emphasize the importance of the monetary standard, we now turn to the determination of securities prices under several possible monetary standards: a monometallic or gold coin standard, a bimetallic standard, and a paper money backed by gold bullion standard. In Chapter 7 we have already studied a pure fiat paper currency standard in which currency is not backed by promises of convertibility to other assets or commodities. Under each standard, we will determine the current dollar price of a security promising to pay $1 in 1 year, assuming that the real interest rate is constant at r percent per year.

A GOLD COIN STANDARD

Suppose that legal tender consists only of gold coins of standard weight produced by the government. Coins containing 1 ounce of gold are given a denomination of P_g dollars, so the official price of gold is P_g dollars per ounce. For the pre-1933 U.S. gold standard, for example, 1 ounce of gold had an official value of about $20. If anyone delivers lumps of gold with a weight of 1 ounce, the government will convert it on demand into coins with a face value of P_g.

We depict the gold market in Figure 8.1. The total world stock in ounces of gold is represented by the length of the horizontal axis. The vertical axis represents the relative price of gold in terms of goods. The relative price of gold—that is, the amount of goods that exchanges for 1 ounce of gold—can be expressed as the dollar value of 1 ounce of gold, P_g, divided by the dollar value of a unit of goods, P. Defined legally by the government, the P_g per ounce nominal gold price is unchanging in this example. P is simply the price level, and only through movement in P can the relative price of gold, P_g/P, change.

The curve labeled D is the demand for gold used for jewelry and for industrial and decorative purposes. The demand for gold declines when its price (in terms of other goods) rises. As the price rises, people start to buy less pure alloys of gold or to substitute other metals for decorative purposes.

Equilibrium combinations of the money supply and the price level are depicted by the curve labeled M/P. For this curve, the origin labelled O' represents a zero quantity of gold used for monetary purposes. On the horizontal axis to the left of origin O', we plot the weight of gold M/P_g used in the nominal money stock M. Recall from Chapter 7 that the demand for real money, M/P, depends on real income y and on the nominal interest rate R. In deriving our solution for the price level in Chapter 7, we used a simple linear relation between money demand, real income, and the interest rate:

$$\frac{M}{P} = ay - bR$$

where a and b were constants. We will assume for this example that money demand is of the same form and that anticipated inflation is zero so that the nominal interest rate R coincides with the real rate r. For now we will assume that real income and the real interest rate are constant. The demand for real money is then constant, so the product

$$\frac{M}{P} = \frac{M}{P_g} \times \frac{P_g}{P} = ay - br$$

remains unchanged, a relationship depicted by the hyperbola in Figure 8.1. Any point on the hyperbola represents the same ratio of the money stock to the price level.

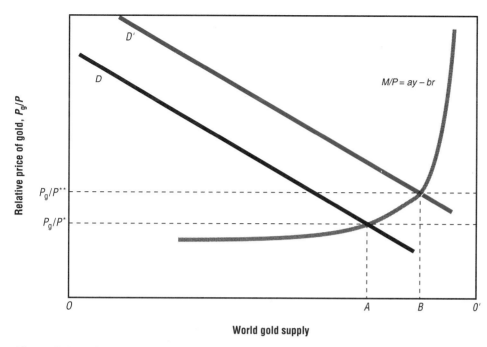

Figure 8.1   EQUILIBRIUM PRICE LEVEL IN A GOLD STANDARD

To see how disturbances in the gold market can affect the price level, we begin with an equilibrium price level $P\star$ such that the relative price $P_g/P\star$ clears the gold market—the total stock of gold is then equal to the amount demanded for decorative and industrial purposes OA and the amount used for money AO'. At price level $P\star$, the nominal money supply $M\star = P\star(ay - br)$ clears the money market, so the weight of gold AO' circulating as money equals $M\star/P_g$. If this situation is expected to continue, there is an anticipation of a static monetary gold stock, and in an absence of changes in the real interest rate and real income, the price level $P\star$ will continue to clear the money market. Hence the price level $P\star$ will clear both the gold and money markets indefinitely.

A Shift in the Demand for Jewelry

Now suppose that gold jewelry becomes more fashionable, so the demand curve shifts upward—at any specific relative price, people want more gold for such jewelry.

In Figure 8.1 this shift is drawn as a new demand curve labeled D'. The new equilibrium occurs at a lower price level—that is, at a higher relative price $P_g/P\star\star$.

Gold moves from monetary to nonmonetary uses. At the original relative price $P_g/P\star$, people now value the gold in coins more highly as jewelry, so coins are melted. This shrinks the nominal money stock and therefore proportionally lowers the price level because real money demand is constant. In the new equilibrium, OB ounces of gold will be used for jewelry and BO' will circulate as coins.

A Gold Discovery

Suppose now that a major gold discovery increases the stock of gold available. This shift is drawn as a lengthening of the horizontal axis in Figure 8.2. Since both nonmonetary demand for gold and the money market equilibrium curve are downward sloping, their intersection will occur at a lower relative price of gold—that is, at $P_g/P\star\star$ in Figure 8.2. A lower relative price can occur only with a higher price level. A higher price level raises the demand for gold coins to keep the real money

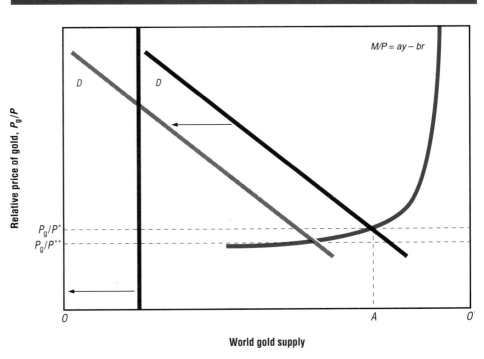

Figure 8.2 IMPACT OF A GOLD DISCOVERY

supply constant. The reduction of the relative price of gold also raises nonmonetary demand for gold. Both sources of demand increase to absorb the increased supply if the price level rises.

An Increase in Real Output

Suppose now that real income rises from y to y', through either improved technology or the use of additional resources input into the production process. The increase in real income shifts the money market equilibrium locus in Figure 8.3 upward and to the left from the curve labeled 1 to the curve labeled 2. At the old relative price of gold, there is now an excess demand for gold for monetary use. The relative price of gold must rise—that is, the price level must fall. A rise in the relative price of gold reduces the demand for nonmonetary uses. BA ounces of gold are delivered to the mint and converted to coin, so the total coinage of gold increases by the same amount. The increased demand for real money is met partly with a deflated price level and partly with an increase in monetary gold.

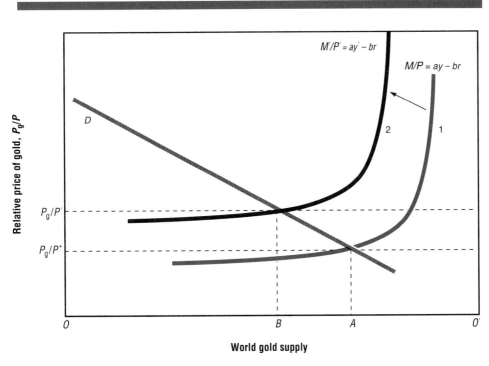

Figure 8.3 AN INCREASE IN REAL OUTPUT

The Vagaries of the Gold Market

Disturbances that affect the demand for money also will affect the price level, as we should expect. In a gold standard, however, disturbances in the market for gold, a small market relative to the markets for all other goods, also have major impacts on the price level. We have seen that increases in the gold supply tend to raise the price level but that real income increases tend to reduce it.

In some periods, real income increases may be just matched by increases in the world gold supply, so the price level is stable. Such an event would be coincidental, however. More often, there should be periods when the gold supply grows faster than real incomes or when real incomes grow faster than the gold supply.

In Figure 8.4 we depict two such periods in a chart of the U.S. wholesale price index from 1879 to 1913. This period was the heyday of the world gold standard to which the United States adhered starting in 1879. From 1879 to 1896, worldwide real incomes grew rapidly and the world gold supply grew slowly. This resulted in a steady deflation. Exploitation of the newly discovered South African gold and improved refining processes caused the rate of increase of the gold stock to jump

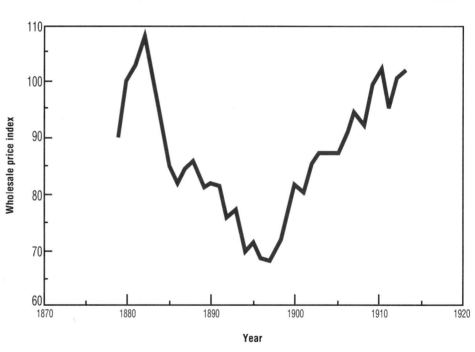

Figure 8.4   WHOLESALE PRICES DURING THE U.S. GOLD STANDARD

CHAPTER 8 THE MONETARY STANDARD

relative to the rate of increase of real incomes starting in 1896. These changes left their tracks in the form of a steadily increasing price level after 1896.

What will drive the price of a nominal bond in such a system? Anyone considering the purchase of a note promising to deliver $1 in 1 year would have to understand the gold market to determine an appropriate price to pay. For instance, suppose that in our demand shift example, the deflation rate is 3 percent for 1 year and the real interest rate is 5 percent per year. A note buyer anticipates earning a 5-percent real return while receiving a nominal rate of 2 percent. He or she would therefore pay about $0.98 to buy the $1 note. Alternatively, if lenders anticipate a rapidly growing gold supply, they will forecast inflation and insist on nominal yields higher than 5 percent.

We conclude that under a gold coin standard, the price level, the nominal interest rate, and the supply of legal tender are all driven by the vagaries of the gold market. When the gold supply or nonmonetary demand is disturbed, the nominal prices of all other goods must adjust to move the relative price of gold back to a point where the supply of gold equals the demand for gold for monetary and nonmonetary uses. Indeed, this feature provides the primary criticism of any type of gold standard: Arbitrary movements in the supply of legal tender may occur without regard to their impact on the economy as a whole.

A BIMETALLIC STANDARD

For five centuries prior to 1900, many European countries simultaneously circulated both gold and silver legal tender coins. When the unit of account is defined in terms of both gold and silver coins containing precisely defined weights of metal, the monetary standard is known as a **bimetallic standard.** When it began centuries ago, use of the bimetallic standard arose partly as a result of a technical problem. It was difficult to make small-denomination coins from gold because gold is relatively valuable per unit of weight. Either the gold coins would have to be impracticably small in physical size or the gold would have to be heavily alloyed with base metals, which made detection of counterfeits difficult. The answer was to use silver in lower-denomination coins and gold in higher-denomination coins.

Indeed, in the United States the dollar was connected to both gold and silver for almost 180 years until 1968, when the U.S. Treasury stopped converting silver certificates into silver dollars. Until 1933, the United States used silver for small coins such as dimes, quarters, and dollars and gold for more valuable coins such as the $20 "double eagle." When it explicitly operated a bimetallic standard through 1873, the U.S. mint guaranteed **free coinage** of both metals. If a given metal were delivered to the mint, the mint would in exchange deliver coins containing the same weight of the metal.

Defining the unit of account in terms of either of two metals *and* permitting free coinage of both metals generally produce a monetary standard in which only one of the metals actually circulates as money. To see this, let us define *one unit of silver* as the weight of pure silver legally contained in the silver dollar. (In the United States, the amount of silver in the silver dollar was 371.25 grains from 1792 to 1968, so one unit of silver would weigh 371.25 grains.) Similarly, *one unit of gold* is the weight of pure gold legally contained in the gold dollar. (From 1834 through 1933, the gold dollar contained 23.2 grains of gold. From 1934 until 1971, it was 13.71 grains, or $35 per ounce. Since 1973, it has been 11.37 grains, or $42.22 per ounce.) Officially, one unit of gold seems to exchange for one unit of silver, since both are defined as "one dollar." This is not an exchange that the government will actually make under a bimetallic standard, however. Specifically, governments under such a standard did not maintain a silver coin reserve for exchange on demand with bearers of gold coins.

On the private metal markets, however, nothing fixes the relative price between a unit of gold and a unit of silver at one unit of gold per one unit of silver. In fact, this price can fluctuate freely depending on supplies and demands for gold and silver bullion. We define P_s as the number of units of gold exchanged on the market for one unit of silver.

Table 8.1 indicates what would happen to gold and silver coins when P_s exceeds or is less than 1. If $P_s < 1$, silver is officially overvalued in terms of gold; the market offers less than one unit of gold for one unit of silver. Anyone faced with the need to deliver $1 to satisfy a dollar obligation would deliver a silver dollar. Rather than delivering a gold dollar, the debtor would profit by melting it down to extract the unit of gold, using part of it to buy a unit of silver, and delivering the silver to the mint for a silver dollar. The debtor could make the dollar delivery and still retain part of a unit of gold. In this case, the silver dollar is a "cheap" money that drives out the more expensive gold dollar, yet another example of Gresham's law. Alternatively, if $P_s > 1$, gold would circulate and silver coins would disappear.

Figure 8.5 indicates that P_s moved significantly during the nineteenth century. From 1792 to 1834, P_s was less than 1, and only silver coins circulated in the United States. A reduction of the gold content of the dollar in 1834 drove P_s above 1. This happened because the new "units" of gold contained a smaller weight of pure gold, so it took more of them to buy a unit of silver. Therefore, from 1835 to 1861, only gold coins circulated, although the bimetallic standard was still in effect. From 1862 to 1878, the greenback, inconvertible into coin, circulated as legal tender, so neither gold nor silver coin circulated at face value. Gresham's law had struck again as the "bad" paper money drove out the "good" coins.

Table 8.1 DISPOSITION OF BIMETALLIC COINS

	$P_s < 1$	$P_s > 1$
1. Gold coins	Melt	Deliver
2. Silver coins	Deliver	Melt

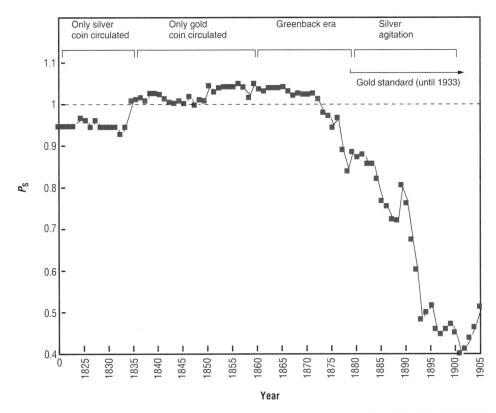

Figure 8.5 MARKET RATIO OF VALUE OF SILVER DOLLAR TO VALUE OF GOLD DOLLAR

The true bimetallic era ended in 1873 when, in a new law governing coinage, free coinage of silver dollars was terminated and their legal tender status was withdrawn. Later, this law became known as the "**Crime of '73.**" The subsequent collapse in the relative price of silver indicated in Figure 8.5 and the deflation depicted in Figure 8.4 brought about by relatively small supplies of monetary gold in the world led to the Populist agitation to restore free coinage of silver dollars. With silver at so low a value, free coinage in the 1890s would have meant that only silver coins would have circulated, as in the period before 1833, and that a large amount of silver would have been delivered to the mint for coinage. The increase in the now silver-based money supply would have raised the price level and ended the deflation. The silver agitation climaxed in 1896 when the presidential nominee of the Democratic party, William Jennings Bryan, gave his famous "Cross of Gold" speech in favor of the free coinage of silver. In Box 8.1, we describe one of the

Box 8.1

The "Wizard of Oz" and Free Coinage

Although the agitation to return to free coinage of silver during the 1890s seems alien to us now, it has left its traces in anyone who has read L. Frank Baum's *The Wonderful Wizard of Oz* or seen the movie *The Wizard of Oz*. Baum was a supporter of the Populist movement's drive to restore the bimetallic standard, personified in William Jennings Bryan's campaign for the presidency in 1896. The movement's strength lay in western and midwestern farmers who suffered real losses on their fixed-value mortgages during the deflation in the 1880s and 1890s brought about by adherence to the gold standard.

Thus Dorothy comes from a poor Kansas farm. The tornado that carries her to the land of Oz is the Populist movement itself. Oz is an allusion to America, a land ruled especially in the East by the gold standard (Oz. is the abbreviation for ounces of gold). Dorothy's landing kills the "wicked witch of the East"—that is, Grover Cleveland, the Democratic president through 1896, who defended the gold standard and whose wing of the party was defeated by the Populists in the 1896 convention. The witch wears silver (not ruby) shoes with magical powers. Dorothy follows the yellow (gold) brick road to the Emerald City (Washington, D.C.), picking up along the way the scarecrow (a farmer), the tin woodmen (a worker left unemployed by the deflation and depression of the 1890s), and the cowardly lion (Bryan himself, who wavered in his support of bimetallism after 1896). The "Wizard of Oz" is Marcus Alonzo Hanna, the chief power broker and string puller in Washington at the time. Hanna ran McKinley's campaign of 1896 that defeated Bryan. The "wicked witch of the West" is McKinley, who campaigned in favor of the gold standard. When the witch is killed, the woodman is given a bimetal axe, made of gold and silver, just the thing to keep him employed. Dorothy finally can return to Kansas and solve her problems by invoking the magic of her silver slippers, clicking her heels three times.

Other allusions to the bimetallic controversy that abound in Baum's story can be found in Hugh Rockoff, "The *Wizard of Oz* as a Monetary Allegory," *Journal of Political Economy*, August 1990, pp. 739–760.

permanent impacts of the silver agitation. The silver dollar was, in fact, restored as legal tender in the 1870s, but it was coined only in limited quantities. Since free coinage was never restored, both gold and silver dollars circulated simultaneously from 1879 to 1933, although P_s fell substantially below 1. During this period, the United States officially operated a gold standard in which most paper currency was exchangeable for gold coin on demand at the Treasury or the Federal Reserve.

Determination of the Price Level Under Bimetallism

How is the price level determined under a bimetallic standard? To answer this question, we will consider an example in which the world operates on a bimetallic standard. The official prices of a unit of silver and a unit of gold are both $1. In Figure 8.6 we examine first the case that only gold coins circulate. The horizontal axis in the left panel of the figure is the world silver supply, an amount represented by the length O_sA. The price in terms of goods of a unit of silver is represented by the vertical axis. The downward-sloping nonmonetary demand for silver is the curve labeled D_s.

The horizontal axis in the right panel of Figure 8.6 is the world gold supply, an amount represented by the length AO_g. The nonmonetary demand for gold is depicted by the curve labeled D_g. It is upward sloping in the panel because the origin for gold demand is O_g, so we move leftward from O_g to find the nonmonetary demand for gold. The goods price of a unit of gold is represented by the vertical axis originating at O_g.

The origin for the hyperbola representing money market equilibrium is at O_M. The hyperbola is to the left of this origin, the same as we drew it for our earlier analysis of the gold standard. Under bimetallism, however, either silver coins, gold coins, or both may satisfy the demand for metallic money.

To find the equilibrium price level, we slide the money market equilibrium origin O_M either to the right or to the left. When the sum of the metallic money

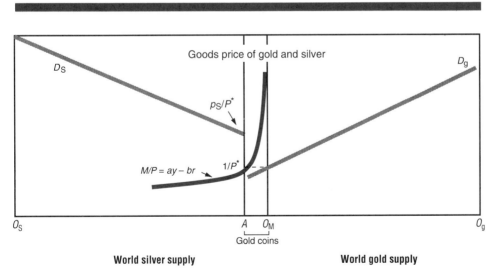

Figure 8.6 PRICE LEVEL UNDER BIMETALLISM WHEN ONLY GOLD COINS CIRCULATE

forthcoming from the two metals markets at a particular price level has a real value equal to real money demand, that price level is an equilibrium. We have drawn Figure 8.6 so that the equilibrium price level is $P\star$. At $P\star$, the goods price of gold is $1/P\star$, and AO_M units of gold circulate as gold coins. Indeed, gold coins satisfy the entire demand for money.

No silver coins circulate in this equilibrium because silver has a high value in nonmonetary uses. Even when the entire silver supply is used for nonmonetary purposes, the goods price of silver exceeds $1/P\star$, as you can see in the figure. The nominal market price of a unit of silver p_s must then exceed the official price of \$1 per unit of silver. In other words, silver is undervalued at the mint, so Gresham's law ensures that it will not circulate as money.

In these circumstances, the steady-state price level will be determined in the gold market. The situation is similar to how the U.S. bimetallic standard operated in the pre-Civil War period.

To find a case in which silver circulates as money, let's consider in Figure 8.7 a shift downward in the demand for silver from D_s to D_s'. This shift lowers the goods price per unit of silver that people are willing to pay for any given amount of silver. To find the equilibrium price level, we slide the money market equilibrium origin O_M to the left of the position that it had in Figure 8.6. The equilibrium price level is such that the sum of the metallic money forthcoming from the two metals markets has a real value equal to real money demand.

In Figure 8.7, the equilibrium price level is $P\star\star$, and the goods price of both a unit of gold and a unit of silver is $1/P\star\star$. The nominal market price of both gold

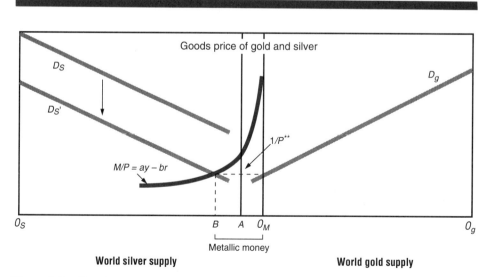

Figure 8.7   PRICE LEVEL UNDER BIMETALLISM WHEN GOLD AND SILVER COINS CIRCULATE

and silver is $1 per unit, the same as the mint price. Neither metal is undervalued, so both circulate as money. In Figure 8.7, BA units of silver and AO_M units of gold circulate as coins. Since the price level $P\star\star$ is higher than the equilibrium price $P\star$ that emerged in Figure 8.6, the goods price of gold is lower, so less gold is used as money.

Further downward shifts in the demand curve for silver would draw more silver into coinage and lead to the melting of more gold coins. If these shifts were to continue, the demand curve for silver would move down far enough that the goods price of gold evaluated at the mint price, $1/P$, would be less than the market goods price of gold when all gold is used for nonmonetary purposes. At this point, the nominal market price of a unit of gold would exceed the mint price, and gold, undervalued at the mint, would cease to circulate as money. This would be the beginning of a silver era.[2]

Pricing Securities Under Bimetallism

Because the metal in circulation could shift whenever there was sufficient movement in the relative price between gold and silver, the bimetallic standard was also known as the **alternating standard.** The potential for payment of dollar obligations in coins containing one or other metal affects the pricing of dollar securities, because debtors have an option or choice of which metal to use in repayment. They will naturally use the cheaper metal when dollar obligations come due.

An option in the hands of the debtor will reduce the price that a lender would be willing to pay for a security compared with a monometallic standard because options always have a positive value to their buyer and a negative value on the accounts of their seller.[3] A bond under a bimetallic standard will therefore pay a higher yield to maturity than the same bond under a gold standard.

To convince yourself of this, consider once again a bond promising to pay $1 in 1 year. *We will determine the market price of the bond by finding the value of a portfolio of other assets whose payoff exactly mimics the payoff of the bond.* The first line in Table 8.2 indicates the value, in terms of gold, of the payoff on the dollar bond. When $P_s < 1$, the silver dollar is worth less than the gold dollar; our debtor in the dollar loan—call him Bryan—will then pay one silver dollar with a value of P_s units of gold. When $P_s > 1$, he will pay one gold dollar with a value of 1 unit of gold.

To mimic these payoffs, we will construct a portfolio for Bryan consisting of positions in a gold bond and a gold option. The gold bond promises to pay one gold dollar in 1 year. The gold option gives its holder the right to purchase one unit of gold in exchange for one unit of silver from the person who sold the option.

2. For estimates of the nonmonetary demand curve for silver and the impact that maintaining bimetallism might have had on the U.S. price level in the late 1800s, see Milton Friedman, "The Crime of 1873," *Journal of Political Economy,* December 1990, pp. 1159–1194.

3. We will examine options in more detail in Chapter 17.

Table 8.2 PAYOFFS FROM DOLLAR BOND, GOLD BOND, AND GOLD OPTION

Asset	$P_s < 1$	$P_s > 1$
1. Dollar bond	P_s	1
2. Gold bond	1	1
3. Gold option	$P_s - 1$	0

Bryan has the choice of whether to *exercise* the option or not. Such a right is referred to as a **call option on gold** with an **exercise price** of one (unit of silver) and an **exercise date** of 1 year.

We can verify that a portfolio that contains one gold bond and has sold off one call option exactly mimics the dollar bond payoffs. One gold bond will pay off one gold dollar in any circumstance, so we enter 1 in both payoff columns for the gold bond. If $P_s < 1$, Bryan will exercise the option because he can deliver a unit of silver worth P_s to get a unit of gold worth 1. Since this portfolio has sold off one gold option, it must then deliver a unit of gold for a unit of silver, so the portfolio will receive a negative payoff of $P_s - 1$. Adding to this the payoff of the gold bond, we find that the gold bond–gold option portfolio pays P_s if $P_s < 1$, exactly the payoff from the dollar bond. However, if $P_s > 1$, a unit of silver is worth more than a unit of gold. The option then will not be exercised and will have a payoff of 0 for the portfolio. The payoff from the gold bond–gold option portfolio is 1, again identical to the payoff from the gold bond.

Since the payoff from the gold bond–gold option portfolio mimics the payoff from the dollar bond, the portfolio should sell at the same price as the bond to preclude arbitrage profits. If R_g is the payoff on a \$1 gold loan (as before, R indicates the nominal rate of return) that will be repaid in gold and G is the value of the gold option, the dollar bond should have a price

$$\frac{1}{R_g} - G$$

The first term is just the discounted present value of the payoff from the gold bond, that is, the price that the gold bond will fetch on the market. The value of the option is subtracted from the value of the gold bond because the portfolio is short one gold option; that is, the option is a liability of the portfolio. If the price of the bimetallic bond exceeds $1/R_g - G$, anyone can profit by selling bimetallic bonds at a high price and buying the mimicking portfolio at a lower price, taking the difference as a profit. In the next period, the payoff from the portfolio will exactly cover the obligations of the bimetallic bond, with no further commitment

Box 8.2

The Computation of Bimetallic Bond Value

Suppose the payoff R_g on a gold loan is 1.05, so a gold bond is worth $1/R_g$ = $0.95 gold dollars. The payoff on loans denominated in silver is R_s = 1.06. Suppose that the current price of a unit of silver in terms of gold is P_s = 1; that is, one unit of gold buys one unit of silver—and one year from now the price P_s^* may either be 0.8 or 1.2.

What is the value G of the gold option? We can price the gold option by mimicking the option payoffs with positions in gold bonds and in silver bonds in the same way that we priced the bimetallic bond. The holder of the option will deliver silver if the option is exercised. The exercise price in the option is 1, since one unit of silver can be delivered to get one unit of gold.

The payoffs from the gold option can be mimicked by a combination of x gold loans and y silver loans, where x and y are to be determined (see the accompanying table).

PAYOFFS IN TERMS OF GOLD

Asset	$P_s^* = 0.8$	$P_s^* = 1.2$
1. Gold option	0.2	0
2. x Gold bonds	$xR_g = 1.05x$	$1.05x$
3. y Silver bonds	$yR_sP_s^* = 0.848y$	$1.272y$

If P_s^* = 0.8, gold is relatively valuable. By exercising the option, the holder will receive one unit of gold for a unit of silver worth only 0.8 units of gold on the market—that is, a payoff of 0.2 units of gold. If P_s^* = 1.2, the option will not be exercised. A gold loan pays the same 1.05 units of gold in either event. Similarly, a silver loan will pay off R_s = 1.06 units of silver in either case, but for comparability, these payoffs must be converted to gold units by multiplying by the prevailing price P_s^*.

We choose x and y so that the payoffs on the portfolio of gold bonds and silver bonds exactly mimic the payoffs on the gold option. You should verify that the portfolio of x = 0.57 gold bonds and y = − 0.47 silver bonds mimics the gold option. Since the current relative price between gold and silver P_s equals 1, the current gold value of this portfolio and the value of the gold option is G = 0.57 − 0.47P_s = 0.1 units of gold. The price of a bimetallic bond is then P_B = $1/$R_g$ − G = 0.85 gold dollars. The yield to maturity on the bimetallic bond would be about 17 percent. Compare this to the yields on bonds promising to deliver only gold dollars or only silver dollars.

Box 8.3

Currency Option Bonds

The modern equivalent of bimetallic bonds are bonds that give the debtor the option of paying in one of two currencies. The currency chosen depends on exchange rates at the time of repayment. For example, suppose that the debtor in a 1-year loan can deliver either $1 or ¥150 to pay off the loan. The contracted exchange rate is ¥150/$1. If the market rate in 1 year exceeds ¥150, the debtor will deliver ¥150. If it is less than ¥150, the debtor will deliver $1. By the logic used in pricing bimetallic bonds, the dollar price of the currency option bond would be $P_B = \$1/R - G$, where R is the payoff on dollar loans and G is the dollar value of an option to exchange ¥150 for $1. The yield on the currency option bond would then exceed the yield on dollar loans.

---

from the person who put the deal together. Market arbitrage will eliminate this profit opportunity.

Since the dollar bond under a bimetallic standard sells for a lower price than an otherwise identical bond under a gold standard, bond yields to maturity computed in the standard way will be greater under bimetallism. See Box 8.2 for an explicit computation of the value of a bimetallic bond and Box 8.3 for an application to modern currency option bonds.

FIAT MONETARY STANDARDS

If the primary goal of governments or central banks were to maintain a fixed nominal price of gold or a stable price level, they could do so. Gold standards have existed in the past, but the policy of maintaining a fixed nominal price of gold did not receive top priority. Such a policy prevents governments from using their discretion to determine the supply of money, as we saw in several examples. Other, more pressing goals led to currency creation or steady inflation that was inconsistent with maintaining the gold standard.

Traditionally, the need of using money creation to finance government expenditures in times of crisis such as war has caused temporary suspensions of the gold standard. The gold previously used as money could be sold abroad to help pay for the war. In recent times, however, governments have turned to money creation as a source of revenue on an ongoing basis; government finance obviously has a higher priority than the stability of the price of gold. We will examine how governments gain revenue from money creation in more detail when we discuss inflation tax revenues in Chapter 21. Central banks also have created currency during times of financial crisis to bail out or protect key financial institutions to ensure the stability of the financial system. As the number of institutions that central banks attempt to protect has expanded, so has the number of situations in which monetary expansion will occur. We consider the reasons for this objective when we study financial crises in Chapter 18. Finally, central banks aim to influence real interest rates, real income, and exchange rates by using monetary policy, as we discuss in Chapters 16 and 21.

Depending on the state of the economy and on which of the policy goals currently has priority, there are many events that may cause a central bank to step up or reduce the growth rate of money. The political importance of these variables has made a permanent gold standard untenable in recent years. The current money system provides flexibility for continual shifting among policy goals. It recognizes the impossibility of defining a monetary standard in an environment of constantly shifting goals, so it leaves the standard undefined. Rather than frequent shifts from one well-defined standard to another, fiat money facilitates the rapid shifting of policy goals by more or less rapid increases in central bank liabilities. To price our $1 bond in a fiat system requires, once again, that buyers form an anticipation of inflation. With all the conflicting policy goals, however, this is a more difficult problem than under a well-defined standard with only one or two monetary policy goals. To form an expectation of future money creation by the government, a buyer must now consider all the policy goals, form anticipations of all future developments in the economy that might drive monetary policy toward a particular goal, and understand the personalities of the officials who have discretion to implement monetary policy. This is obviously a more difficult problem than understanding what drives the supply and demand for gold or silver. In succeeding chapters we will explore how various policy goals can influence money creation.

CONCLUSION

Many contracts arrange for payments to be made among the contracting parties. Generally, such payment agreements specify a given amount of units of account, such as the dollar. The unit of account is like a blank space in the contract whose explicit meaning is filled in when a government sets the monetary standard—that is, the government defines those items whose delivery satisfies the contract. Since the monetary standard is a legal definition, it can be changed without notice, effectively placing a new item in the blank space. Such changes historically have brought a large variety of physical objects into use as money—tobacco, gold, silver, and paper currency. The markets for those physical items which have been defined as the monetary standard are made perfectly liquid because their prices are usually legally fixed.

Under different monetary standards, the price level and inflation rate will behave differently. For example, under a gold standard, the price level will be driven by events in the gold mining industry and in the industrial uses of gold. A bimetallic standard will be more inflationary than a monometallic standard such as a gold standard, and this is reflected in higher interest rates on bimetallic bonds. In a pure fiat standard, money creation is independent of particular commodity markets; rather, it is driven by the discretion of those in control in the central bank, who shift the provision of liquidity across many markets. Under different monetary standards, lenders will insist on different bond yields to protect themselves against inflation.

KEY TERMS

monetary standards

legal tender

fiat money

Gresham's law

legal tender cases

gold clause cases

bimetallic standard

free coinage

Crime of '73

alternating standard

call option on gold

exercise price

exercise date

EXERCISES

1. "Since silver supplies increased rapidly in the last quarter of the nineteenth century, the termination of bimetallism in the United States avoided a large inflation in the dollar price level." Comment on this statement.

2. Diagramatically, show how the steady-state price level is determined under a bimetallic standard. The diagram should include the nonmonetary demands for gold and silver, the demand for monetary metal, and the global supplies of silver and gold.

3. With reference to your diagram, under what circumstances will only one of the metals circulate as money?

4. With reference to your diagram, under what circumstances will both metals circulate as money?

5. Suppose that the nonmonetary demands for both gold and silver depend negatively on the real interest rate. With reference to your diagram, show that a rise in the real interest rate in a bimetallic world will raise the price level.

6. Suppose that Mexico sells a bond promising to deliver one "unit" next year, where a "unit" is defined as either one U.S. dollar or one British pound. Mexico

can choose which currency to deliver. Show that the market value of this bond in dollars equals the market value of a bond promising to deliver one dollar next year minus the market value of an option to deliver one pound in exchange for one dollar next year.

7. Show that in a bimetallic monetary standard, a bond promising to pay a given stream of dollars through time will have a lower market price than a bond promising to pay the same stream of silver dollars.

8. Explain graphically how the discovery of the South African gold mines generated the world inflation of 1896–1914.

9. Explain why Gresham's law will not hold if "good" money is allowed to circulate at a premium to "bad" money.

10. In the 1850s, only gold coins circulated in the United States, although the United States was on a bimetallic standard. The British operated a pure gold standard at the time, and the Prussians operated a pure silver standard. Explain why both British and Prussian bonds paid lower yields than U.S. dollar bonds.

11. **a.** Suppose that under a gold coin standard, a major deposit of high-grade ore suddenly plays out. Explain what will happen to the price level.

    b. Suppose that the demand for industrial gold suddenly falls. Explain what will happen to the price level.

12. Suppose that under a gold standard, the demand for money suddenly falls because of an increase in expected inflation. Explain what will happen to the price level and to the allocation of the gold supply among monetary and nonmonetary uses.

13. Under bimetallism, why would silver coins disappear if $P_s > 1$?

14. Suppose that the gold bond–gold option portfolio has a higher price than the dollar bond. How can you make an arbitrage profit?

15. Suppose that the yield on yen loans is 3 percent, the yield on dollar loans is 7 percent, and the current exchange rate is ¥150/$1. In one period, the exchange rate may be either ¥180/$1 or ¥120/$1. What is the yield to maturity on a currency option bond?

FURTHER READING

Friedman, Milton, "The Crime of 1873," *Journal of Political Economy,* December 1990, pp. 1159–1194.

Barsky, Robert, and Lawrence H. Summers, "Gibson's Paradox and the Gold Standard," *Journal of Political Economy,* June 1988, pp. 528–550.

Garber, Peter, "Nominal Contracts in a Bimetallic Standard," *American Economic Review,* December 1986, pp. 1012–1030.

Rockoff, Hugh, "The *Wizard of Oz* as a Monetary Allegory," *Journal of Political Economy,* August 1990, pp. 739–760.

Rolnick, Arthur J., and Warren E. Weber, "Gresham's Law or Gresham's Fallacy," *Journal of Political Economy,* February 1986, pp. 185–199.

9

The Fed Funds Market
and Supply and Demand
for Reserves

In making our payments, we all use currency, and most people use checking accounts in banks. To satisfy their demand for liquid savings, many people use savings deposits and time deposits at financial institutions. We take for granted that when we want a particular kind of deposit, our local bank will supply it, perhaps thereby expanding itself and its total deposits. We also take for granted that when we want to dispose of funds in a deposit, our bank will buy the deposit back for cash, perhaps thereby contracting itself.

Now we begin a detailed consideration of how banks manage the transactions among themselves and the public that create the supply of deposits that we demand. We will examine the supply of M1, the sum of currency in circulation and transactions deposits. We will study how the money supply is determined through shifts in the size and composition of central bank balance sheets, regulation of the behavior of private banks and of their ability to deliver liquidity, and demands for bank services. We will develop a rather mechanical method of determining the money supply using a highly simplified interpretation of regulations and market behavior. In later chapters we will extend our analysis to a more realistic view of the banking regulatory environment and bank behavior.

THE FEDERAL RESERVE SYSTEM

The modern central bank is a nationalized banker's bank. Its operational role is to provide currency, payment clearing, and settlement services, and to provide credit to banks, governments, and individuals. It serves as a fiduciary agent and investment banker for the national treasury and as a regulator of banks and other financial institutions. Typically, to finance itself, it possesses a monopoly power to create legal tender currency and an unlimited ability to create its own deposit liabilities held by other banks. The central bank of the United States is the **Federal Reserve,** often called the **Fed.** In this chapter we will be concerned mainly with the impact on the money supply of the balance sheet operations of the Fed. In later chapters we will examine the Fed's organization, regulatory activities, clearing operations, and policy objectives.

The Central Bank Balance Sheet and the Monetary Base

One of the roles of a modern central bank is to provide currency to the economy. Paper currency is demanded by households and nonfinancial businesses for purposes that we explored in Chapter 7. It is also held by financial institutions. At any time, depositors in a bank may ask for a withdrawal in currency. The bank cannot count on an inflow of new currency that will exactly meet these outflows, so it always maintains a supply of **vault cash** to cover itself in those cases where it must settle payments in cash.

For institutions making numerous large payments, the physical delivery of paper currency is very inconvenient. For larger payments among banks themselves, banks' cash reserves take the form of deposits by the banks in their own accounts in the central bank. These deposits are not themselves cash or legal tender; rather, they are promises by the central bank to deliver legal tender to the banks making the deposits on demand.

The Fed maintains a policy of exchanging deposits at the Fed for currency at a rate of $1 of deposits for $1 of currency. Since the central bank can create practically unlimited amounts of currency, banks never doubt the conversion promise. Therefore, banks consider deposits at the Fed as **good funds**—that is, they are always willing to receive them from other banks as representing final payment of dollar claims. The sum of Federal Reserve currency and the deposits at the Fed by private financial institutions is called the **monetary base.**[1]

Table 9.1 provides a simple version of the Federal Reserve's balance sheet. As a bank, the Federal Reserve keeps books that look like those of commercial banks,

---

1. Coinage and Treasury currency remaining in circulation are also a part of the monetary base. However, they are relatively unimportant.

Table 9.1 FEDERAL RESERVE BALANCE SHEET

ASSETS		LIABILITIES	
1. U.S. securities	230	1. Federal Reserve notes	200
2. Loans to depository institutions	10	2. Deposits by banks	40

except for its ability to circulate legal tender currency notes. In liabilities, the Fed has $200 billion in Federal Reserve notes in circulation and $40 billion in bank deposits. In assets, it has $230 billion in U.S. Treasury bills, notes, and bonds. It also has $10 billion in loans to depository institutions. These are loans made directly to banks, called **discounts** and **advances.** A discount consists of an outright Fed purchase from a bank of a promissory note made by a private borrower or of a U.S. Treasury or agency security. An advance is a loan that is made directly to the bank collateralized by promissory notes held by the bank, usually U.S. Treasury securities.

THE MAGNITUDE OF THE FED

What determines the magnitude of the Fed's balance sheet? In this example, the total assets and liabilities of the Fed are $240 billion, but the Fed has complete discretion over this quantity. Suppose it wishes to hold $10 billion more in U.S. securities. In a process known as an **open-market operation,** it approaches a securities dealer willing to sell securities worth that amount and buys the securities for its own account. It pays $10 billion for the securities by making a bookkeeping entry adding $10 billion to the deposit account that it maintains for the dealer's bank. The transaction also adds $10 billion of U.S. securities to the Fed's asset column. With a simple peck at a terminal keyboard, both the assets and the liabilities of the Fed have increased by $10 billion. If the Fed does not reverse this expansion through a subsequent sale of securities, the expansion is permanent because the private banking system and currency holders have no means of getting rid of their expanded claims on the Fed. The Fed currently makes no commitment to exchange its assets for its liabilities on demand.

Alternatively, the Fed could have expanded its balance sheet by lending $10 billion more to a bank through a credit line known as the **discount window.** It would simultaneously credit the deposit account of the bank with $10 billion. The Fed's asset mix would be different in this case, but its liabilities would be the same as in the case of a security purchase. In both cases, reserves increase by $10 billion.

The Liabilities of the Fed

The Fed finances itself by creating liabilities that pay zero interest: Federal Reserve notes and deposits of member banks. Why would anyone hold such liabilities? First, the Fed has a legal monopoly on the circulation of paper currency, and it prescribes the features of the currency without fear of competition. If people wish to buy and sell goods, services, or securities with paper money, they must use whatever currency the Fed supplies. Second, the Fed legally requires banks to make reserve deposits at the Fed as a fixed percentage of the quantity of transactions accounts they provide their customers. Currently, the **reserve requirement** stipulates that banks make deposits at the Fed worth 3 percent of the value of transactions deposits of less than $41 million and 12 percent of the value of transactions deposits exceeding $41 million. Before December 27, 1990, the Fed also required reserves of 3 percent of nonpersonal time deposits, usually certificates of deposit held by institutions, that matured in less than $1\frac{1}{2}$ years and 3 percent of all net **Eurocurrency deposits** (the amount of dollars borrowed from foreign banks less the amount of dollars loaned to foreign banks). Although the Fed pays zero interest on deposits from banks that are part of required reserves, any financial institution wishing to offer unlimited checking accounts must hold deposits at the Fed. Otherwise, it would be impossible to transmit large payments or to clear checks. Even if reserves were not legally required, banks would still maintain deposits at the Fed to participate in the business of providing payment services. Some banks regularly hold deposits at the Fed in excess of required reserves. These excess reserves are called **clearing balances,** and the Fed pays interest approximately equal to the Fed funds rate for such deposits. Such interest, however, can be used by banks only to pay the fees that the Fed charges for the various services, such as check clearing, that it provides banks.

Effectively, bank reserve holdings at the Fed and their associated zero-interest income are the price that banks pay for access to the liquidity that the Fed provides to the banking system.

THE MULTIPLE EXPANSION OF BANK DEPOSITS

Bank reserve holdings combine with the amount of liabilities that the Fed is willing to supply to restrict the quantity of private bank deposits. An example can illuminate this restriction. We will assume at first that the nonbanking public does not change the $200 billion of currency that it holds (as in Table 9.1). Then all changes in Fed liabilities take the form of changes in member bank deposits. To ease the arithmetic, we will also assume that the reserve requirement is 20 percent of the transactions deposits in a bank at the *end* of each day's business.

A Banking Day Without Federal Reserve
Security Purchases

As a benchmark, it is useful to consider how a simple banking system operates during a day when deposits at the Fed remain constant. Our banking system will consist only of two banks, Citibank and the U.S. subsidiary of Daigin Bank of Tokyo, and the transactions will be exaggerated in magnitude.

In Table 9.2, column 1 indicates the balance sheets of the banks at the beginning of the day. Citibank has decided to supply $100 billion of deposit liabilities to its customers. As assets, it holds $20 billion on deposit at the Federal Reserve to satisfy its required reserves. It also holds $80 billion in interest-earning loans or securities. Daigin has an identical balance sheet. By deciding on the amount of deposits that they supply, the banks can tailor their required reserves to the amount of reserves they want to hold. The banks earn no interest on deposits at the Fed, but they can earn interest on loans. Therefore, holding reserves is costly in forgone income. On the other hand, reserves are useful to banks in providing an immediate source of liquidity. To make sure they will hold no **excess reserves**—that is, more reserves than they want—banks establish a "fed funds desk" to manage their deposits at the Fed. The purpose of the fed funds desk is to minimize the cost of a given level of access to the liquidity of the banking system.

During the day's transactions, the banks send out and receive a large number of payments. For example, Citibank's depositors may order it to send funds to Daigin for dispersal to Daigin depositors in payment for goods or assets. Citibank may itself purchase securities for its own account or make loans by sending funds to securities dealers or borrowers who deposit the funds in their accounts at Daigin. Daigin will make similar payments to Citibank.

For the large payments typical of securities markets, this transfer of funds is not accomplished through shipments of cash. Rather, each payment is effected by sending an electronic computer message to the Fed to transfer funds from the sending bank's deposit account at the Fed to the receiving bank's account. The electronic system is known as **Fedwire.** The Fed's computer will immediately make this transfer, crediting the receiving bank's account and debiting the sending bank's account. During the day, the sending bank may even experience an **overdraft** at the Fed; that is, it may have a negative balance in its deposit account. Nevertheless, payment messages sent over Fedwire are guaranteed by the Fed as good funds to the recipients. The Fed thus provides ready liquidity during the day to banks making heavy use of the payment system.

For example, to pay for securities bought by one of its customers, Citibank may start the day by sending $25 billion to a customer of Daigin. This gives Citibank a deposit of *minus* $5 billion at the Fed. This also brings Citibank below its $15 billion required reserve (= 0.2 × $75 billion in remaining deposits). The daylight shortfall of reserves does not matter, however, because reserve requirements are enforced only at the end of the day. Also, Daigin now potentially has deposits at

Table 9.2 BALANCE SHEETS OF SYSTEM BANKS ($BILLIONS)

1 Start of Day

Citibank

ASSETS		LIABILITIES	
Reserves	20	Deposits	100
Loans	80		

Daigin

ASSETS		LIABILITIES	
Reserves	20	Deposits	100
Loans	80		

2 Near End of Day
400 Paid to Daigin
350 Paid to Citibank

Citibank

ASSETS		LIABILITIES	
Reserves	0	Deposits	50
Loans	80	Due to Fed	30

Daigin

ASSETS		LIABILITIES	
Reserves	70	Deposits	150
Loans	80		

3 End of Day
Fed Funds Operations Completed

Citibank

ASSETS		LIABILITIES	
Reserves	10	Deposits	50
Loans	80	Fed funds purchased	40

Daigin

ASSETS		LIABILITIES	
Reserves	30	Deposits	150
Loans	80		
Fed funds sold	40		

4 Near End of Day
Citibank Buys Securities

Citibank

ASSETS		LIABILITIES	
Reserves	10	Deposits	60
Loans	80	Fed funds purchased	40
U.S. bonds	10		

Daigin

ASSETS		LIABILITIES	
Reserves	30	Deposits	150
Loans	80		
Fed funds sold	40		

the Fed in excess of its reserve requirement, since the payment brings its deposits at the Fed to $45 billion against deposits at Daigin that have increased to $145 billion.

As the flurry of payments orders passes through the Fed during the course of the day, the banks cumulate **net credit** or **debit positions** on their payments. Let's assume that near the day's end, payments due to Citibank from Daigin amount to $350 billion and payments due to Daigin from Citibank amount to $400 billion. Citibank's net debit position is then $50 billion. All funds are sent from and received into customers' deposit accounts in each bank.

Column 2 in Table 9.2 indicates each bank's balance sheet near the end of the day. Deposits have fallen to $50 billion in Citibank and risen to $150 billion in Daigin because of the transfers of funds. Loans held as assets in each bank remain constant at $80 billion, since we have assumed that all payments have been from customers' deposit accounts. Citibank's deposits at the Fed are zero, and Citibank owes a "due to" of $30 billion to the Fed, the amount of its overdraft. Daigin holds *plus* $70 billion at the Fed. Momentarily, the Fed is a liability holder of Citibank because Citibank has overdrawn its Fed account. The $30 billion "due to" must be paid because the Fed does not permit overdrafts to be carried on its books. The end-of-day deposits at the Fed will remain constant at $40 billion $[= 70 + (-30)]$ because the Fed has neither bought nor sold securities for its own portfolio.

This situation cannot persist at the close of business because Citibank would not satisfy its end-of-day reserve requirement, and the Fed would not readily lend to Citibank overnight. Citibank has several methods to bring its reserve requirement in line with the reserves it desires to hold. We will suppose that Citibank actually wants to have reserves required for maintaining the $50 billion of deposits on its books.

First, Citibank can attempt to market some of its securities and loans quickly to generate a further inflow into its Fed account, but this process may be costly if the assets are illiquid. It may have to accept a very low price for the assets if it sells them immediately, only to pay a high price if it wants to reacquire them in the near future if net payments flow into the bank.

Rather than contract its balance sheet because of what may be a temporary outflow of deposits, Citibank can use the alternative of borrowing from Daigin. That is, it can use the banking network to buy good funds. Citibank can acquire additional reserves at the Fed by borrowing from other banks on the **fed funds market,** a loan market for bank deposits at the Fed. The manager of Citibank's fed funds desk, who is responsible for bringing the bank's desired deposits at the Fed and required reserves into equality, would have tracked customer deposits at Citibank and Citibank's deposits at the Fed throughout the day. Recognizing the shortfall in reserves from their desired level near the day's end, the fed funds manager can enter the fed funds market as an overnight borrower, attempting to make a deal before business closes. Once a deal is closed at an agreed interest rate between Citibank and a bank that wants to lend fed funds, the lending bank sends a message to the Fed to move funds from its account to Citibank's account.

In this case, Citibank wants to borrow $40 billion on the fed funds market: It needs reserves of *plus* $10 billion against the $50 billion of customer deposits that it *wants* to hold on its books, and it has a "due to" of $30 billion at the Fed. If it wished, Citibank could avoid holding the customer deposits on its books overnight by arranging overnight repurchase agreements with its deposit customers, as we will see in Chapter 13. This would eliminate both the customer deposits *and* the need to hold reserves at the Fed. That this does not occur in our example indicates that Citibank *wants* to have $10 billion in reserves overnight at the Fed. To settle with the Fed, it must move $40 billion into its Fed account.

Daigin's fed funds manager then finds that Daigin will end the day with excess reserves of $40 billion if she does not quickly lend them in the fed funds market. Daigin's required reserve is only $30 billion (= 0.2 × $150 billion in deposits), but it has $70 billion deposited at the Fed. Supposing that Daigin wants to have no more than the $150 billion in deposits on its books, it also wants to have only $30 billion in reserves.

The two managers will find each other through a fed funds broker and agree on an overnight loan of $40 billion from Daigin to Citibank at some mutually agreeable interest rate. Daigin sends a message to the Fed to pay $40 billion into Citibank's account and enters the deal on its balance sheet as $40 billion in fed funds "sold" (actually loaned). Citibank enter it as $40 billion in fed funds "purchased" (or borrowed).

With this last payment message, the day's business closes, leaving the banks with the balance sheets in column 3 of Table 9.2. Although deposits have been shifted from one bank to another, total deposits in the banking system are $200 billion at the close of the day, the same as at the start. The amount of bank deposits at the Fed is $40 billion (or 0.2 × $200 billion). Alternatively, bank customer deposits can be computed by dividing bank deposits at the Fed by the required ratio:

$$\text{Bank customer deposits} = \frac{\text{bank reserves at the Fed}}{\text{required reserve ratio}}$$

An Overexpansion of Bank Deposits

In our example, total banking system deposits were always constant at $200 billion throughout the day because we assumed that all payments were to the order of the bank's deposit customers and that banks wanted the reserves required for $200 billion in deposits. We will now add another kind of transaction. Toward the end of the day, Citibank's U.S. securities dealers, perhaps sensing a favorable low price, buy $10 billion worth of bonds from a dealer whose account is also at Citibank. Consequently, Citibank adds $10 billion to the selling dealer's deposit account and adds the bonds to its own assets.

Suppose that this order is executed just as Citibank's fed funds manager finishes the transaction that produce the balance sheets in column 3 of Table 9.2. The balance sheets of the banks then instantly change to those in column 4.

Now the fed funds manager at Citibank has a problem. Deposits at Citibank have expanded by $10 billion, and the banking system's deposits are $210 billion. However, now Citibank needs $2 billion more on deposit at the Fed to meet its reserve requirement before business closes. Daigin (the only other bank in this banking system) has exactly the level of deposits at the Fed and associated customer deposits that it wants, however. The Citibank manager can find no additional funds in the fed funds market. He informs the bank's bond dealers that they have to sell off $10 billion in securities to a Citibank depositor. The bank contacts a bond dealer depositor to engage in a $10 billion overnight repurchase agreement for the securities. This will contract the bank's deposits back to the $50 billion for which the required $10 billion of reserves are on deposit at the Fed. Total bank deposits are still $200 billion. This expansion of Citibank's deposit liability will be undone by the reserve requirement and the lack of available reserves in the market. Note, however, that the bank still effectively controls the securities; it has simply found an alternative means to finance them. This transaction would be entered as an expansion of Citibank's liabilities with an entry of $10 billion in the category "securities sold under agreement to repurchase," as discussed in Chapter 6.

Of course, Citibank's adjustment to its own deposit overexpansion is only one of many possible outcomes. We have assumed that Daigin is uninterested in reducing its reserve holdings regardless of how high Citibank may bid up interest rates on fed funds. However, if the rate goes high enough, Daigin may find it profitable to reduce its own holdings of securities by a repurchase sale to one of its depositors. The reduction in Daigin deposits thus releases reserves for sale in the fed funds market. Daigin would then be the institution whose balance sheet size is reduced as a result of Citibank's aggressive purchases. We stress, however, that Daigin *voluntarily* shrinks itself because it can increase its income by selling its reserves. The interest rate on fed funds is sufficiently high that Daigin reduces its demand for reserve deposits at the Fed, and it finds a way to shrink its customer deposits to match its desired reserves to its required reserves.

A Banking Day with a Federal Reserve Security Purchase

In the preceding section, we derived end-of-day balance sheets for Citibank and Daigin based on a certain pattern of payments during the day. Now let's consider how an open-market purchase of securities by the Federal Reserve on the same day will affect the balance sheets of the banks. We presume at first that except for the end-of-day transfers attributable to fed funds lending, all other payments during the day remain the same as before, and we derive the end-of-day bank balance sheets. Then we consider additional payment orders that will arise subsequent to the Fed's action.

Following our earlier example, suppose that at 11:00 A.M. the Fed buys $10 billion in securities from a bond dealer who banks at Citibank. The Fed deposits the funds with Citibank's account at the Fed, and Citibank credits the payment to the dealer's Citibank account. This expands the total reserves in the banking system by $10 billion. *If all other payments remain unchanged*—that is, the $350 billion in payments from Daigin to Citibank and the $400 billion in payments from Citibank to Daigin—the end-of-day balance sheets of Citibank and Daigin will be like column 1 of Table 9.3. These balance sheets should be compared with those in column 3 of Table 9.2. Customer deposits at Citibank have now increased to $60 billion, because the $10 billion payment by the Fed was to the account of a Citibank depositor.

A second change in the balance sheets of the banks is the reduction in fed funds purchased and sold from $40 billion to $32 billion. To understand this change, consider the position of Citibank's fed funds manager at the end of the day. Previously, he had to make up a shortfall of $40 billion in deposits at the Fed. The Fed's purchase of securities, however, has added $10 billion to Citibank's Fed account while increasing the reserve requirement by $2 billion because of the customer's deposit increase, a net improvement in Citibank's reserve position of $8 billion over the situation with no Fed security purchases. Citibank's fed funds desk must raise only $32 billion prior to the close of business, which accounts for the new balance sheet entry for fed funds purchased.

Reserves for Citibank have increased to $12 billion, the amount required against $60 billion in deposits. Note that total reserves held by the banking system are now $50 billion, and total deposits are $210 billion. These balance sheets reflect excess reserves in the banking system (since $0.2 \times \$210$ billion < $50 billion). This should tip you off that the balance sheets do not provide a complete description of how the banks behave during the day.

To see this, consider the position of Daigin's fed funds manager. She finds that Daigin will close the day with reserves of $38 billion but required reserves of only $30 billion. Since these excess reserves of $8 billion carried overnight will cost Daigin a great deal of forgone interest, the fed funds manager immediately starts generating further payments among banks to avoid holding the excess reserves.

Therefore, the balance sheets in column 1 of Table 9.3 cannot represent the end-of-day balance sheet of the banks because they ignore these further transactions. The Fed's security purchase will generate a flurry of further purchases and payments during the day so that the additional reserves will be absorbed. Like the soft tissues of a creature that falls to the floor of a tropical rainforest at noon, no trace of the excess reserves will remain by nightfall.

The process by which excess reserves disappear can take on innumerable forms, and which banks will finally demand the existing reserves cannot be determined in advance. In the preceding example, we assumed that a bank's fed funds desk acted to even out reserves only at the end of the day. In fact, the fed funds desk tracks the bank's reserve position and makes sales and purchases of fed funds throughout the day at varying interest rates to prepare for the end-of-day settlement with the Fed. After the Fed's 11:00 A.M. purchase, Citibank's fed funds manager will suddenly find that his reserve problem has eased, with reserve holdings much closer to his demanded level, and immediately reduce the scale of fed funds purchases. Daigin's

Table 9.3 BALANCE SHEETS OF SYSTEM BANKS

	1	2
	Fed Bond Purchase with Other Payments Unchanged	End of Day After 1. Citibank Buys $10 Billion in T-Bills 2. Daigin Buys $30 Billion in T-Bills 3. Final Fed Funds Adjustments

Citibank

ASSETS		LIABILITIES	
Reserves	12	Deposits	60
Loans	80	Fed funds purchased	32

Citibank

ASSETS		LIABILITIES	
Reserves	18	Deposits	90
Loans	80	Fed funds purchased	32
T-bills	10		
Fed funds sold	14		

Daigin

ASSETS		LIABILITIES	
Reserves	38	Deposits	150
Loans	80		
Fed funds sold	32		

Diagin

ASSETS		LIABILITIES	
Reserves	32	Deposits	160
Loans	80	Fed funds purchased	14
Fed funds sold	32		
T-bills	30		

manager will notice that she can sell fewer reserves than before and will begin to sell them at a lower interest rate *relative* to rates on alternative assets available on the market.

Both managers will immediately signal other departments in their banks that they sense that overnight funds can be obtained relatively cheaply. Managers of the banks' security portfolios, bond trading, and loan departments will immediately begin to make deals to purchase bonds either outright or on repurchase agreements and to make overnight loans to securities dealers and nonfinancial corporations. All these deals will expand bank balance sheets and generate many new rounds of payment orders. The banks' departments make their deals independently, and the fed funds desk does *not* orchestrate their actions. Its job is the residual task of cleaning up the banks reserve position *after* the deals are all made.

To complete the example, we consider one of the many possible outcomes at the end of the day, any of which may materialize subsequent to the Fed's action. In *all* outcomes, however, keep in mind that the amount of the deposit liability for the entire banking system will be identical.

Suppose that the security departments in the two banks are run by aggressive managers who begin buying T-bills immediately after realizing that the fed funds market has eased. Specifically, suppose that Daigin's manager buys $30 billion in

T-bills from a securities dealer whose deposit account is in Citibank, generating an order to the Fed to move $30 billion from Daigin's account to Citibank's account. Citibank's manager buys $10 billion in T-bills from a Daigin depositor, generating an order to the Fed to move $10 billion from Citibank's account to Daigin's account.

Column 1 of Table 9.3 is the situation prior to the advent of the T-bill purchases. If these are the only two additional transactions with bank customers that occur, the balance sheets of the banks at the end of the day will look like column 2 of Table 9.3.

Let's go back and trace the changes one by one. Deposits in Citibank have increased by $30 billion to $90 billion as a result of Daigin purchase of T-bills. The $32 billion in fed funds purchased by Citibank were accumulated by its fed funds manager prior to this new inflow of funds into its depositor's account.

As assets, Citibank holds required reserves of $18 billion (that is, 0.2 × $90 billion in deposits). Citibank had previously arranged to have $12 billion of reserves through dealings in the fed funds market. Daigin's T-bill acquisition caused $30 billion in additional reserves to flow into Citibank's Fed account, topping reserves up to $42 billion. Citibank's purchase of $10 billion in T-bills brought reserves back down to $32 billion. Since only $18 billion is required, Citibank's fed funds manager immediately sold off $14 billion in the fed funds market, a sum that is entered as an asset. Citibank's original loans are unchanged at $80 billion, but it has acquired $10 billion in T-bills, which is also entered under assets.

Deposits at Daigin have grown from $150 billion to $160 billion because of Citibank's T-bill purchase from a Daigin depositor. As assets, Daigin has acquired $30 billion in T-bills. Loans are unchanged at $80 billion. Prior to the T-bill purchases, Daigin had reserves of $38 billion and had sold $32 billion in fed funds. The outflow of $30 billion resulting from Daigin's T-bill purchase and the inflow of $10 billion resulting from Citibank's acquisition leave actual reserves at $18 billion against required reserves of $32 billion (which is 0.2 × $160 billion in deposits). The shortfall galvanizes Daigin's fed funds manager into buying $14 billion of fed funds, which appears as a liability on the balance sheet.

The T-bill purchases and the additional deals on the fed funds market close out the day's business. Both banks have settled their required reserves with the Fed, and neither holds excess reserves. Total reserves have grown by $10 billion to $60 billion. The banks have converted this increment from excess reserves to required reserves with a near-instantaneous ballooning of their balance sheets. They accomplish this by unleashing their asset managers into a round of acquisitions financed by a simultaneous expansion in the banking system's deposits. Total deposits in the banking system have grown by $50 billion to $250 billion, that is, $90 billion in Citibank plus $160 billion in Daigin.

The ratio of expansion of bank deposits to reserves is $50 billion/$10 billion = 5/1. An additional dollar of reserves allows a **multiple expansion of bank deposits** amounting to $5. Stated more generally,

$$\text{Change in bank customer deposits} = \frac{\text{change in reserves}}{\text{required reserve ratio}}$$

Finally, you should convince yourself that the final balance sheets for the individual banks are arbitrary. In this example, the final outcome depends on which bank's portfolio manger is more aggressive in T-bill acquisition and on which bank's customers sell the bonds. We have assumed that Daigin acquires far more T-bills than does Citibank and that Daigin buys from Citibank customers. Citibank therefore looks as if it has expanded its deposits more than Daigin because of the Fed's reserve expansion. The initial Fed purchase of $10 billion in securities was indeed from a Citibank customer, so it first appeared as a Citibank deposit expansion. Where the first deposit initially falls, however, does *not* determine the amount by which deposits in one bank expand relative to those in the other. If Citibank's portfolio manager had acquired all $40 billion in T-bills from a Daigin customer, most of the deposit expansion would have occurred in Daigin.

THE CONVERTIBILITY OF RESERVES TO CURRENCY: AN EXTENSION

We have produced a simple expression for the way in which bank deposits are determined. Letting D represent the dollar quantity of such deposits, R represent the amount of reserves, and r represent the required ratio of reserves to deposits, we have found that $D = R/r$. Since we usually consider currency a close substitute for transactions deposits, we typically add currency in the hands of the nonbank public C to deposits to form an expression for the money supply called **M1,** which combines those assets used for transactions:

$$M1 = C + D$$

In our example, M1 = $200 billion in currency + $200 billion in deposits = $400 billion at the start of the day and M1 = $200 billion + $250 billion = $450 billion at the end of the day after a Fed bond purchase.

As you have learned by now, any idea that looks this simple will soon be modified into one that is more complicated—and the money supply concept is no exception. In developing the money supply formula, we have assumed that the public's currency holdings are constant. This may be true on the day of an increase in deposits at the Fed as a result of a Fed bond purchase, but from Figure 9.1 it is evident that currency holdings are not constant over time. Eventually, the public alters its demands for currency as the Fed changes the monetary base.

How does the public get the currency it wants? The public can obtain paper currency from banks in exchange for deposits in banks. Since the Fed's policy is to convert its deposits—that is, the banks' reserves—dollar for dollar for Federal Reserve notes, banks can obtain paper currency from the Fed at any time. Therefore, each $1 increase in currency holdings by the public generates a $1 decline in reserves deposited at the Fed or held as cash by banks.

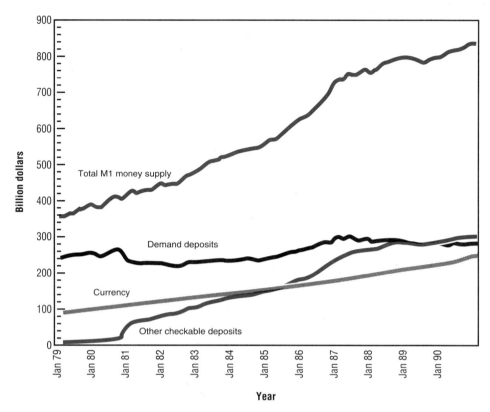

Figure 9.1   COMPONENTS OF M1 MONEY SUPPLY

We have already shown that an increase in reserves will spur a multiple expansion of deposits on the banking system's books. Similarly, a fall in reserves, in this case due to a conversion to currency, causes a multiple contraction. Let us continue the example of Tables 9.2 and 9.3 to understand how this would happen. At the start of the day, the public holds $200 billion in currency and $200 billion in bank deposits. Let's assume that the public finds it convenient to maintain this one-to-one ratio of currency to deposits. By the end of the day of the Fed's open-market purchase, however, the banks' balance sheets appear as in column 2 of Table 9.3. Deposits have increased to $250 billion while currency in circulation remains at $200 billion, a ratio of currency to deposits of 0.8.

This lack of immediate adjustment of currency is understandable. The open-market operation and the consequent balance sheet adjustments occur nearly instantly, because they involve electronic transfers of funds and active market operations by aggressive participants in the wholesale money markets. Adjustments to currency will occur more slowly. They involve a physical medium; to increase holdings of currency, the public must visit a bank and withdraw funds. Also, the market for currency is essentially a retail market; the quantities involved for any one currency user would probably be so small that immediate adjustment would not be worthwhile. Rather, the public will adjust its currency holdings in the normal course of business over the weeks and months after the open-market operation.

Once the public tops up its currency holdings, what will be the value of M1? To answer this question, it is convenient to write out explicitly the ratio of M1 to the monetary base B:

$$\frac{M1}{B} = \frac{C + D}{R + C}$$

The quantity $C + D$ is M1, and $R + C$ is the monetary base. If the public has a preferred ratio of currency to deposits, which we denote as c, then $C = cD$. The reserves held are required, so $R = rD$. Substituting these values into the ratio, we now have

$$\frac{M1}{B} = \frac{cD + D}{rD + cD} = \frac{c + 1}{r + c}$$

We have divided out the D in the middle expression to produce the final expression of the ratio.

Since $r = 0.2$ and $c = 1$ in our example, the ratio $M1/B = 1\frac{2}{3}$ when the public is holding its desired ratio of currency to deposits. At the start of the day, the monetary base is $240 billion ($40 billion in reserves as in Table 9.2 and $200 billion in currency). Multiplying the base by the M1 multiplier, we find that M1 = $240 billion $\times 1\frac{2}{3}$ = $400 billion. M1 consists of $200 billion in currency and $200 billion in deposits, which satisfies the public's desired currency/deposit ratio of one to one.

During the day the Fed increases the monetary base by $10 billion to $250 billion. If the Fed takes no further action in subsequent weeks, M1 will eventually adjust to a higher level. The new M1 will equal $250 billion $\times 1\frac{2}{3}$ = $416.67 billion after the public tops up its currency holdings to desired levels. Thus the leakage of monetary base into currency will contract bank deposits in the days after the Fed's open-market purchase. Since the public wants to hold as much currency as deposits, both currency holdings and deposits in banks will expand over time to $208.33 billion from their original level of $200 billion. Of the $10 billion increase in monetary base, $8.33 billion is held as currency and only $1.67 billion is held as reserves.

What Determines the Currency/Deposit Ratio?

Although the currency/deposit ratio is determined by the choice of the public, we have treated the ratio c as if it were unchanging. In fact, the ratio fluctuates, but it has changed relatively little in recent times.

One important determinant of c is the public's perception of the riskiness of deposits. If depositors sense a serious risk that the banks may not pay off their deposits, they will hold less in deposit accounts and more in currency for transactions and even for portfolio purposes. This is reflected in the high values of c during the early 1930s when many banks failed. Since deposits are now credibly insured, depositors do not fear default risk anymore, so banking instability is no longer a major factor in determining c.

Recall from Chapter 7 that currency is used by middle-income households principally for small transactions. Poorer households use cash for most transactions because access to bank deposits is not worth the cost to them. Also, currency is used for transactions in illegal markets, such as drugs, and in otherwise legal markets to avoid leaving a trail of records for the Internal Revenue Service. If these types of transactions remain constant as a proportion of overall transactions, then c will tend to remain constant also.

Finally, currency pays no interest, whereas bank deposits pay interest either directly or in services. When market interest rates are low, the forgone income involved in holding currency will be small, so people will hold relatively more currency. When interest rates are high, they will tend to shift from currency to deposits, driving down c.

THE FED'S BALANCE SHEET OPERATION IN DETAIL

We described the multiple expansion of bank deposits by using a highly simplified version of the Federal Reserve's balance sheet. We now explore the Fed's balance sheet in more detail to gain an appreciation of the variety of activities of the Fed.

Table 9.4 is a snapshot of the Fed's assets and liabilities on October 31, 1990.

Table 9.4 BALANCE SHEET OF FEDERAL RESERVE BANKS, OCTOBER 31, 1990 ($BILLIONS)

ASSETS		LIABILITIES	
1. Gold certificate account	11.1	1. Federal Reserve notes	256
2. Loans to depository institutions	0.6	2. Deposits	
3. Federal agency obligations	6.3	a. Depository institutions	34.5
4. U.S. Treasury securities	237.7	b. U.S. Treasury	7.3
5. Items in process of collection	5.9	3. Deferred credit items	5.0
6. Assets denominated in foreign currency	35.6	4. Other	5.6
7. Other	17.8	5. Capital account	6.3
Total	315	Total	315

The Fed had $315 billion in assets on that date. We have already seen how the Fed acquires U.S. Treasury and federal agency obligations, which totaled $244 billion at that time. Thus 77 percent of the Fed's assets consisted of loans to the U.S. Treasury or other government entities. Similarly, we have examined the liability categories of Federal Reserve notes and deposits of depository institutions at the Fed. The remaining items reflect one or another aspect of Federal Reserve operations.

The Gold Certificate Account

The gold certificate account is a remnant of a now defunct requirement that the deposit and currency liabilities of the Fed be backed by claims on gold. In the United States, the government entity holding actual gold is the U.S. Treasury, not the Fed. The Treasury can create gold certificates, which are claims against its gold stock, and exchange them for credits to its deposit account at the Fed. The gold certificates now held by the Fed are claims on $11.1 billion worth of gold. Since the Treasury officially still defines the price of gold as $42.22 per ounce (versus a market price of around $400 per ounce) the Fed's gold certificates theoretically represent a claim against 262 million ounces of Treasury gold ($104 billion worth of gold at market prices). In practice, however, the gold certificate account category hardly changes on the Fed's books. Any change that does occur arises at the instigation of the Treasury, asking for a dollar-for-dollar exchange of Treasury deposits at the Fed for certificates, not from an exchange of certificates for bullion.

Loans to Depository Institutions

To price its loans to member banks, the Fed establishes a **discount rate** to reflect the interest that it will charge banks. The discount rate can be set arbitrarily by the Fed. Prior to the 1920s, central bank operating principles prescribed setting the discount rate somewhat higher than market interbank rates and permitting banks free access to loans. Therefore, except in unusual situations, banks had little incentive to borrow from the central bank. When the central bank wished to expand bank system credit, it would reduce the discount rate. In modern times, the Fed has followed a policy of relying primarily on open-market operations to expand and contract reserves and to provide liquidity to markets. It has pushed the discount operation into a secondary role, as is evident from the relatively small value of these loans to depository institutions on its balance sheet.

Since banks can borrow either from each other or from the Fed, the comparison of the Fed funds rate with the discount rate presented in Figure 9.2 is relevant. Note that the Fed seldom changes the discount rate and that it is typically exceeded by the fed funds rate. This presents an obvious profit opportunity to banks, which could borrow at the Fed's discount window and lend to other banks at the higher fed funds rate.

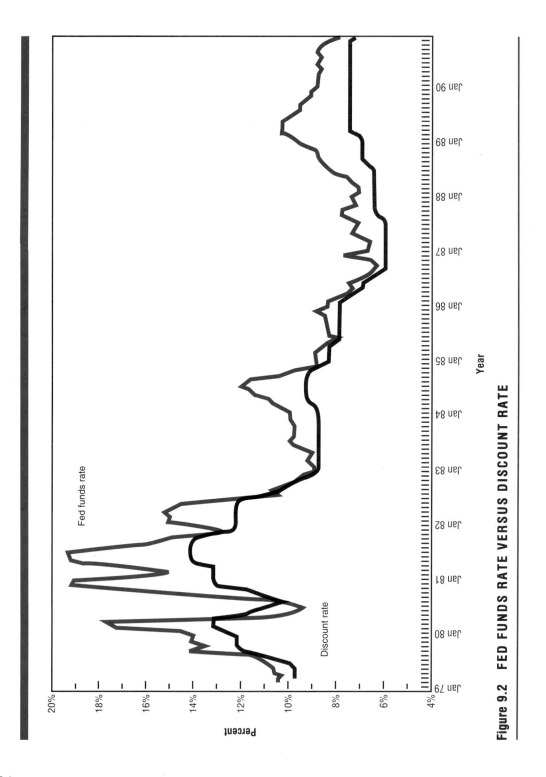

Figure 9.2   FED FUNDS RATE VERSUS DISCOUNT RATE

If the Fed permitted unlimited borrowing by member banks, the fed funds rate would never exceed the discount rate. If it did, member banks in need of reserves would simply borrow directly from the Fed. Lack of demand for fed funds would then drive down the fed funds rate until it equaled the discount rate.

That the fed funds rate exceeds the discount rate signals that the Fed must be limiting bank access to its loans at the discount window. The Fed maintains a set of general principles for lending to banks and then decides whether a bank applying for an advance is borrowing for a purpose that the Fed deems appropriate. The principles serve as a device to ration loans to banks.

Specifically, the Fed will lend, usually for no more than 90 days, to institutions that experience seasonal withdrawals of funds and that lack ready access to money market credit. Such institutions tend to be small banks serving agricultural areas. It also extends **adjustment credit** on a short-term basis to institutions with temporary requirements for funds. To restrict access to such credit, the Fed maintains rules for how often during a given time period it will permit a bank to borrow. Eventually, any bank that the Fed believes borrows too frequently will find that its requests for loans are rejected. The Fed also grants **emergency credit** to banks and nonbank institutions and individuals to meet unusual national, regional, or local credit problems. The power to provide emergency credit permits the Fed to carry out its role as the **lender of last resort.**

By analogy with the private banking system, we may interpret access to the discount window as a line of credit available from the Fed to its members. More typically, however, the Fed provides liquidity to its members collectively through open-market operations rather than individually through direct loans.

Items in Process of Collection and Deferred Credit Items

Items in process of collection and deferred credit items reflect the activities of the Fed in the check-clearing process that we will examine in Chapter 11. When a bank presents the Fed with a check for clearing, the Fed does not immediately credit the deposit account of the bank with the amount of the check. Rather, it adds the bank's claim to the Fed liability category, **deferred credit items,** until the bank on which the check is drawn authorizes payment. The offsetting asset category for the Fed is **items in process of collection,** since the Fed wants to reflect its claim for payment against the bank on which the check is drawn. The difference between these two items is called **Federal Reserve float.**

Assets Denominated in Foreign Currency

As we will see in Chapter 16, the Fed often intervenes in foreign exchange markets— that is, in markets where dollar-denominated commercial bank deposits are exchanged for bank deposits denominated in foreign units of account such as deutsche-marks or yen. Frequently, the intervention takes the form of a sale by the Fed of foreign securities. To satisfy itself that it can make such interventions, the Fed maintains as an asset a substantial quantity of foreign-denominated securities.

The Fed as the Treasury's Commercial Banker

When you receive a check from the U.S. Treasury, it is not drawn on a private bank. Rather, it is drawn on the Treasury's account at the Federal Reserve. The Fed thus serves as the Treasury's commercial bank. This role of the Fed is evident in the liability side of the Fed's balance sheet, where the deposit account of the U.S. Treasury is listed separately.

The Treasury also maintains special deposit accounts, known as **tax and loan accounts,** in private banks. The Treasury keeps revenue received from taxes or bond sales in these accounts until it is ready to spend it. This policy prevents fluctuations in Treasury revenues from having an impact on the amount of deposits in banks. For example, suppose a corporation orders its bank to pay $1 billion to the Treasury for taxes. If the Treasury simply put the funds into its account at the Fed, reserves available to the banking system would decline by $1 billion until the Treasury spends the funds from its Fed account. The contraction of reserves would generate a contraction in deposits in banks. To prevent this situation, the Treasury deposits the $1 billion in a tax and loan account in a private bank. Since reserves in the banking system remain unchanged, no deposit contraction occurs. When the Treasury is ready to spend the $1 billion, it moves the funds to its Fed account. The Treasury then writes a check drawn on its Fed account, which moves the funds quickly back to the private banking system.

Capital Account

The Federal Reserve is officially a private financial intermediary, although it is controlled by the U.S. government. The member institutions formally own the Fed, and it carries in the capital account entry of its balance sheet the paid-in capital of its member institutions plus undistributed surpluses. The Fed's holdings of interest-bearing securities and loans generate its revenues, along with profits earned in trading assets. Federal Reserve profits are taxed away by the Treasury with a special 100-percent tax, however, so the Treasury actually pockets all the Fed's profits.

DETAILS OF RESERVE ACCOUNTING PERIOD

In our studies of bank behavior in the presence of reserve requirements, we assumed for simplicity that the banks must *settle* their reserve obligations with the Fed at the end of each day. Under the current reserve regulations, however, reserve requirements need not be satisfied that often, so banks can be more flexible in accumulating reserves. Instead, the Fed computes the average reserves held by a bank during a 2-week **reserve maintenance period.** During this period, the average of the daily reserves must be greater than or equal to required reserves.

Reserves required against transactions deposits are computed against the average end-of-day transactions deposits at the bank during a 2-week **computation period.** The transactions deposit computation period ends 2 days before the end of the reserve maintenance period. The calendar in Figure 9.3 indicates the timing of these periods.

To determine a bank's average reserves on hand, the Fed computes the average of daily vault cash on hand during a 14-day computation period that begins 30 days before the start of the reserve maintenance period, as indicated in Figure 9.3. In addition, it computes the average of the bank's deposits at the Fed during the reserve maintenance period. The sum of these two items is defined as the average daily reserves on hand during the maintenance period. This sum must not be less than required reserves.

As an example of how this computation would occur, suppose that Daigin Bank has liabilities of $80 billion in transactions deposits each day during the week from October 11 to October 17, 1988 and $100 billion in transactions deposits each day during the week from October 18 to October 24. During the 2 weeks from September 13 to September 26, it has vault cash holdings averaging $3 billion.

Suppose that the required reserve ratio against transactions deposits is $r = 0.2$. Required reserves during the reserve maintenance period against transactions deposits are then $0.2 \times (80 + 100)/2 = \$18$ billion.

During the maintenance period, the average of actual reserves must exceed or equal this amount. Actual average reserves consist of the $3 billion in vault cash plus the average of Daigin's deposits at the Fed during the maintenance period. Remember that this can only be an average. On any one day during the maintenance period, Daigin can hold no reserves at all. For instance, suppose that during the first week of the maintenance period, Daigin holds zero deposits at the Fed. This is permissible if it then holds an average of $30 billion during the second week. That is, required reserve = $18 billion = $3 billion in vault cash + (0 + $30 billion)/2 = average reserves during maintenance period.

Under this "contemporaneous reserve accounting," the job of a bank's fed funds desk is much more complicated than in our example earlier in the chapter. Daigin's fed funds manager can now act much more flexibly on her anticipation of movements in the fed funds rates. If during the first week of the maintenance period the market interest rate on fed funds is much higher than she thinks it will be in

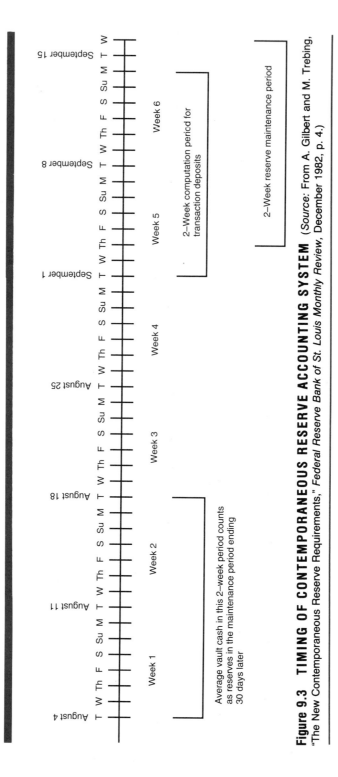

Figure 9.3 TIMING OF CONTEMPORANEOUS RESERVE ACCOUNTING SYSTEM (*Source:* From A. Gilbert and M. Trebing, "The New Contemporaneous Reserve Requirements," *Federal Reserve Bank of St. Louis Monthly Review*, December 1982, p. 4.)

the second week, she can earn income for the bank by lending all its reserves to other banks. She can then retain the bank's reserves in the second week and borrow the rest of Daigin's required reserves at a lower fed funds rate. Of course, if she is wrong and interest rates are higher in the second week, she will lose income for the bank.

Finally, the Fed's reserve accounting policy has a carryover feature that permits a bank to count excess reserves of up to 2 percent of its required reserves in one computation period against its required reserves for the next computation period. Thus, if Daigin's fed funds manager finds that she will have excess reserves on the last day of a computation period, she may prefer to hold them, even at the cost of a day's lost interest. Why should she do this? If she believes that the fed funds rate will be substantially higher in the next computation period, she can recoup the lost interest by greater lending in the fed funds market.

CONCLUSION

A central bank's liabilities supply the most basic forms of money: paper currency that the public can use in small transactions and reserve deposit accounts that banks can use to make payments to each other. The Federal Reserve, the central bank of the United States, controls its liabilities by controlling the assets that it acquires. Its most important assets are securities of the U.S. government or its agencies, and it generally acquires these assets through open-market purchases. The Federal Reserve also can lend directly to banks through the discount window.

When they supply transactions or checking deposits to customers, banks are required by the Fed to maintain a minimum amount of assets in the form of reserves, either vault cash or reserve deposits at the Fed. This minimum reserve places a maximum on the amount of transactions deposits that the banking system can supply because the total of cash and reserve deposits is limited by the Fed. Nevertheless, it does not place a limit on the overall balance sheet of the banking system, since banks can enter repurchase agreements to finance their acquisition of securities.

KEY TERMS

Federal Reserve (Fed)	discount window
vault cash	reserve requirement
good funds	Eurocurrency deposits
monetary base	clearing balances
discounts	excess reserves
advances	Fedwire
open-market operation	overdraft

net credit (or debit) position	lender of last resort
Fed funds market	deferred credit items
multiple expansion of bank deposits	items in process of collection
M1	Federal Reserve float
discount rate	tax and loan accounts
adjustment credit	reserve maintenance period
emergency credit	computation period

EXERCISES

1. With a constant amount of base money, what will happen to M1 if the public reduces its desired holdings of currency?

2. If the Fed funds market were eliminated, what would happen to reserves held by commercial banks?

3. Starting with the initial balance sheets in Table 9.2, suppose that after a Fed bond purchase of $10 billion, Citibank's portfolio manager acquires $40 billion in T-bills. Derive the final balance sheets of both banks in the system.

4. Suppose that the desired currency/deposit ratio c is 0.5 and that the required reserve ratio r is 0.1. By how much does M1 increase with a $10 billion open-market purchase by the Fed?

5. Starting with the Fed's balance sheet in Table 9.1, suppose that a bank borrows $5 billion from the Fed in the form of cash to pay its depositors. What is the Fed's new balance sheet?

6. The Treasury also maintains deposit accounts with the Fed from which it makes its payments. Suppose that initially the Treasury's account has a zero balance and that a depositor in a bank orders the bank to pay $1 billion to the Treasury to cover fines. In the context of Table 9.1, by how much does this change the amount of base money.

7. Describe how it is possible for banks to overdraw their accounts at the Fed.

8. Why do open-market operations show up immediately as an expansion of reserves and bank balance sheets and only gradually as an expansion of currency?

9. Who owns the Fed? Who controls the Fed?

10. The Fed requires banks to hold reserves that average a certain ratio of average deposits over a 2-week period. Alternatively, the Fed could require a fixed reserve ratio against deposits every day. Show that the former convention is equivalent to the latter convention combined with interest-free Fed loans to

banks (a) that are equal to the shortfall from required reserves and (b) whose cumulated total must be repaid at the end of the 2-week period.

FURTHER READING

Goodfriend, Marvin, *Monetary Policy in Practice,* Richmond, Va., Federal Reserve Bank of Richmond, 1987.

Stigum, Marcia, *The Money Market,* Homewood, Ill., Dow Jones–Irwin, 1990, Chap. 12.

P A R T   T H R E E

Banks and the Banking System

CHAPTER

10

Banks as Financial Institutions

e begin our study of the banking system by analyzing bank balance sheets and income statements. We first study bank balance sheets to learn the types of liabilities and assets held by banks. In earlier chapters we described in some detail the types of deposit liabilities issued by banks and the role of the liability item, fed funds. Thus our description of this side of the balance sheet will be brief.

Next we consider bank income statements. Like all business enterprises, banks earn revenues and generate expenses. Because banks are in the business of borrowing and lending, they earn interest revenues and incur interest expenses. In addition, they must incur noninterest expenses in attracting lenders or depositors and finding suitable borrowers. Besides issuing deposits and making loans, banks provide many services to their customers that do not have a direct impact on their balance sheets. These services entail noninterest expenses as well.

In performing their functions, banks are exposed to two major types of risks—credit risk and interest risk. We discuss how banks evaluate the risks to which they are exposed, how they attempt to reduce these risks, and how they protect themselves from any residual risk that has not been eliminated.

We also briefly consider the balance sheets of thrift institutions.

LIABILITIES

The consolidated balance sheet of U.S. commercial banks' domestic and foreign offices for March 31, 1990 is presented in Table 10.1. On this balance sheet, you will find the dollar volume of the various deposit liabilities of banks. On that date, total liabilities and net worth of insured commercial banks in the United States totaled $3.3 trillion. Deposits represented $2.5 trillion of this total, and equity capital represented $210 billion. The remaining $562 billion in liabilities (assets less deposit and equity capital) included various types of borrowed funds.

The largest single item in the "borrowed funds" category is fed funds purchased and securities sold under agreement to repurchase, totaling $280 billion. Fed funds represented $179 billion.

Table 10.1   INSURED COMMERCIAL BANK ASSETS AND LIABILITIES: CONSOLIDATED REPORT OF CONDITION, MARCH 31, 1990

Assets	$Millions
Cash and balances due from depository institutions	318,977
Total securities, loans, and lease financing receivables, net	2,722,917
Total securities, book value	581,868
U.S. Treasury securities and government agency and corporations obligations	395,583
Securities issued by states and political subdivisions in the United States	90,727
All other securities	95,558
Fed funds sold and securities purchased under agreements to resell	145,416
Total loans and lease financing receivables, gross	2,062,310
Total loans by category	
Loans secured by real estate	774,478
Commercial and industrial loans (C&I)	620,231
Loans to individuals for household, family, and other personal expenditures	387,539
All other loans	280,062
Total loans and leases net of unearned income, allowance for loan and lease loss, and transfer risk	1,995,687
Fed funds sold and securities purchased under agreement to resell	145,416
Lease financing receivables	36,729
Assets held in trading accounts	47,725
Premises and fixed assets (including capitalized leases)	48,465
Other real estate owned	14,173
Investments in unconsolidated subsidiaries and associated companies	3,276
Customers' liability on acceptances outstanding	25,714
Intangible assets	7,182
Other assets	112,066
Total Assets	3,300,548

Table 10.1 continued

Liabilities	$Millions
Total deposits	2,528,630
Total transaction accounts (domestic only)	616,710
Demand deposits (included in transaction accounts)	411,003
Nontransaction accounts (domestic only)	1,585,185
Fed funds purchased and securities sold under agreement to repurchase	279,586
Fed funds purchased	179,326
Securities sold under agreements to repurchase	100,260
Other borrowed money	130,204
Bank liability on acceptances executed and outstanding	25,820
Notes and debentures subordinated to deposits	19,559
All other liabilities	92,470
Limited-life preferred stock	83
Total liabilities	3,089,976
Total equity capital	210,448
Total Liabilities, Limited-Life Preferred Stock, and Equity Capital	3,300,548

Source: From *Federal Reserve Bulletin*, January 1991, Table 4.20, p. A72.

Securities sold under agreement to repurchase also represent borrowings from banks as well as from other financial and nonfinancial institutions. We explained this transaction for investment banks in Chapter 6. A bank repurchase agreement works in exactly the same way.

Sometimes banks convert a corporate demand deposit into a repurchase agreement to avoid the legal restrictions against paying interest on demand deposits. For example, for large corporate clients, the amount of overnight funds left in the bank exceeds the amount necessary to pay for payments services associated with demand deposits, as we discussed in Chapter 3. Competition forces banks to offer compensation in addition to payments services to retain large corporate accounts. They do this by an overnight sale of a bond to a corporation in exchange for the demand deposit. The demand deposit is replaced by a repurchase agreement ("repo") on the liability side of the bank's balance sheet, and the corporation earns the interest paid on the bond while it owns it. Thus the transaction does not change total liabilities; it only exchanges one liability for another. Because liabilities do not change, assets cannot change either. Equality between assets and liabilities (and net worth) is maintained because the bond itself remains on the asset side of the bank's balance sheet. Since the bank has agreed to repurchase it at a fixed price in the morning, it continues to absorb the risk of ownership, for example, a change in value resulting from a change in interest rates.

Overnight repurchase agreements with corporations are relatively small compared to demand deposits. In March 1990, total repurchase agreements equaled $100 billion, and about half of these were for maturities of more than one night. Domestic demand deposits totaled $411 billion. (Foreign branches of U.S. banks are not required to report specific deposit items. Table 10.1 reports domestic figures only for types of deposits offered by banks.) Total transactions deposits, which also include interbank and government deposits, were $617 billion.

The additional major item on the liability side of a bank's balance sheet is the "capital account," which includes equity (stock) issued by the bank. Bank equity performs the same role that equity plays on the balance sheet of any corporation— it protects other liability holders. We will have more to say about equity when we discuss the risks faced by banks.

BANK ASSETS

Now we turn to the asset side of the aggregate balance sheet for insured commercial banks in the United States as of March 1990. This is the first part of Table 10.1. Total assets (which always, by definition, equal total liabilities and the capital account) equaled about $3.3 trillion.

Cash Assets

Approximately 9.7 percent, or $319 billion, of total assets was held in the form of cash and balances due from depository institutions. Cash and "due froms" consist of the following items:

1. Cash items in process of collection

2. Currency and coin

3. Balances due from depository institutions in the United States and overseas

4. Balances due from Federal Reserve banks

An example of a **cash item in the process of collection** is a check that a bank customer has deposited in her account that has not yet been collected from the check writer's bank. We will explain the process of collection in detail in the next chapter. A "**due from**" balance represents a payment owed to one bank by another. The bank owed money has an asset, a "due from." On end-of-day balance sheets, a "due from" is usually a deposit held at another bank. We will discuss intraday "due froms" in Chapter 12.

All these items are related to the role that banks play in providing (1) third-party payments services and (2) holding deposits that are immediately convertible into cash. We will spend the next several chapters discussing these items in detail.

The holding of cash and balances at other banks is a necessary part of providing transactions services. It is apparent from Table 10.1 that these assets equal a substantial portion of the $617 billion in transactions deposits that are a liability of commercial banks.

Loans

The most common asset on banks' balance sheets are loans. On March 31, 1990, loans at commercial banks totaled $2.1 trillion, which amounted to about 60 percent of total assets (see Table 10.1). Major loan categories on commercial banks' balance sheets include the following items: loans secured by real estate, commercial and industrial loans (C&I), and loans to individuals for personal expenditures.

On March 31, 1990, loans secured by real estate at commercial banks totaled about $774 billion, the largest single loan category. **Secured by real estate** means that the real estate serves as collateral for the loan. There are three major categories of loans secured by real estate. They are loans for construction and land development, one- to four-family residential properties, and nonfarm residential properties.

The one- to four-family residential property category mainly consists of consumer home mortgages. These are loans of very long maturity—up to 30 years. Of total real estate loans, about $357 billion was lent to finance home mortgages on one- to four-family properties. (These loans are not shown as a separate item in Table 10.1.)

Home equity loans are an increasingly popular form of loan secured by one- to four-family properties. In March 1990 these loans, not shown separately in Table 10.1, equaled about $50 billion. When a household buys a house, it must usually make a down payment—that is, the family must pay for part of the house with its own savings. It takes out a mortgage to cover the rest. The portion of the house financed with savings represents the **owner's equity** in the house. In addition, if the price should appreciate above the purchase price, the increase in value represents additional equity of the owner. **Home equity loans** are secured by the owner's equity in the house. They are junior to the original mortgage. By this we mean that if the borrower should default on his or her payments and the house must be sold to pay off the loan, the original mortgage gets paid off first.

Thrift institutions are also important sources of home mortgage funding—with more than $640 billion in one- to four-family mortgage loans outstanding as of June 1990. This figure includes home equity loans.

Businesses that borrow long term from banks often secure their loans with real estate. Another important use for real estate loans is for construction. A builder borrows from a bank to finance the acquisition of land and the building process. Often the bank provides financing in stages so that it can stop throwing good money after bad if the market for the project turns downward. These loans are generally of short maturity—they mature when the project is completed. The loan is paid off when a buyer is found for the project. The buyer takes out a mortgage and uses the proceeds to pay the builder, who in turn repays the bank.

Commercial and industrial (C&I) loans, which totaled $620 billion at commercial banks on March 31, 1990, represent loans to business enterprises. They are often of very short maturity, usually due in less than 3 months and often due on the business day following the day on which they were made. We describe these loans in some detail in Chapter 14.

Personal loans are typically made to purchase a car, finance an education, make home improvements, and so on. On the date of the balance sheet we are discussing, personal loans totaled about $388 billion at commercial banks. They are typically of longer maturity than commercial and industrial loans—a 4-year maturity is not uncommon for car and home improvement loans.

Some consumer loans are directly related to the payments functions of banks. These are the credit card loan and check overdraft facilities. These loans have no stated maturity, but they are generally taken out for short periods of time to cover short-term cash needs without selling longer-term assets. As of March 31, 1990, these loans totaled $123 billion at commercial banks. We discuss credit card loans in detail in the next chapter.

Loans to carry securities, while a small item on banks' balance sheets at $16 billion on March 31, 1990, play an important role in providing liquidity to securities markets. When a market maker or dealer borrows from a bank to support his or her securities inventory, the loan shows up in this category. Thus these loans help provide the financing that market makers and dealers need to buy securities to maintain liquid markets.

Other Assets

Among the other assets on commercial banks balance sheets, we find fed funds sold and securities purchased under agreement to resell ("repos"), customers liability on acceptances outstanding, and securities.

Securities purchased under agreements to resell is the asset counterpart of securities sold under agreement to repurchase. A financial institution that purchases a security with agreement to resell is in effect making a cash loan to the institution from which it purchased the security. The loan is secured or collateralized by the security purchased, much as a mortgage is secured by real estate. On March 31, 1990, fed funds sold and "repos" totaled $145 billion. (The "securities sold" item on the liability side of the balance is often called a "reverse repo" to distinguish it from the asset item.)

On March 31, 1990, commercial banks held $582 billion in securities. About $91 billion of these represented bonds issued by state and local governments in the United States. These **municipal bonds,** as they are known, are exempt from federal income taxes in the United States. It is commonly accepted that banks hold these bonds to reduce their federal tax burden. Most of the remainder of the securities held by commercial banks represent obligations of the U.S. government and agencies of the U.S. government.

Customers' liability on acceptances outstanding are loans primarily made to facilitate international trade. Acceptances arise in the following manner: An importer requests a letter of credit from his bank. The letter of credit is a guarantee by the importer's bank that he will faithfully pay his bill to the exporter from whom he is purchasing the imported goods. In effect, the letter substitutes the bank's credit reputation for the importer's reputation. This is necessary because the exporter often has no experience in dealing with a particular importer, and she does not know whether he can be trusted.

The importer sends the letter of credit to the exporter. The exporter takes the letter of credit to her bank for evaluation because she probably does not know anything more about the creditworthiness of the importer's bank than she does about the importer himself. The exporter's bank will forward the letter of credit and the shipping documents for the exported goods back to the importer's bank, indicating that the exporter's bank has assured the exporter that she will be paid for her goods. As a consequence, the goods are released to the importer.

At the same time, the importer's bank sends funds to the exporter's bank for payment to the exporter. From the bank's point of view, this is a loan, but it is a rather peculiar loan compared with the ordinary loan that a bank makes. This is so because the importer's bank sends funds to the exporter's bank to be lent to the exporter, but the liability for repayment rests with the importer. When the importer's bank lends money based on its letter of credit, it "accepts" its obligation under the letter of credit, and the letter of credit becomes a **banker's acceptance.** However, because the importer is responsible for repayment of the loan, he, not the exporter who received payment, has a liability to his (the importer's) bank. This item appears on the asset side of the bank's balance sheet as a "customers' liability for acceptances outstanding." In March 1990, acceptances outstanding represented $26 billion.

The importer's bank could fund its loan (the customer's liability item) by issuing deposits as it does with any other loan. However, a common practice in the acceptance market is for banks to sell the acceptance directly in the marketplace to raise the cash to fund the loan. The bank, not the importer, is responsible to the purchaser of the acceptance for its repayment. Thus sale of the acceptance does not relieve the bank of a liability. The liability item appears on the balance sheet as "bank's liability on acceptances executed and outstanding." As of March 31, 1990, this item equaled $26 billion.

Off Balance Sheet Items

The focus of our discussion up to this point has been on assets and liabilities that represent actual funds borrowed and lent. When a bank receives a deposit, it must receive funds, for example, cash or deposits at another bank or at the Federal Reserve. When it creates a loan, it provides funds to its borrowing customer that the customer will use to pay other parties for goods and services. Both deposits and loans appear on the balance sheet because they represent actual funds received and paid by the bank.

In addition, a bank often agrees to lend money under specific circumstances. There are three major types of agreements to lend—lines of credit, commitments, and standby letters of credit. **Lines of credit** are the weakest form of an agreement to lend. They state that a corporation (or any other borrower) has access to a certain amount of funds for a specified period of time—say, access to $1 million for 6 months. The line can be canceled by the bank at any time. The conditions under which the line will be canceled are specified in a general way by "material change" clauses, which state that if the financial condition of the company should change, the line will be canceled.

Commitments to lend are more stringent promises to provide funds. "Material change" conditions are still invoked, but they are specified in detail. If a bank backs out of a commitment to lend, it will usually find itself in a lawsuit to defend its actions.

Standby letters of credit are irrevocable commitments to lend. They are usually issued when a corporation floats publicly traded obligations such as commercial paper. The bank states that if the corporation fails to meet its interest and principal payments, it will step in and make the payments for the corporation. This obligation is meant to be drawn upon if the corporation goes bankrupt. Therefore, for it to have meaning, it must be legally binding under all circumstances. At year end 1988, standby letters of credit at large U.S. banks totaled over $150 billion.

Because these three items only commit banks to lend and are not actual loans, their issuance does not require banks to raise a deposit to fund a loan. Therefore, these promises do not appear on the balance sheet. Nevertheless, because they represent an obligation to raise funds to provide a loan the bank has committed to make, such promises are called **off balance sheet items.**

Another example of an off balance sheet item is the letter of credit used by importers, which we discussed earlier. Such a letter of credit represents a liability because it is a commitment to provide funds. In our preceding example, the letter of credit, like standby letters of credit, represents a commitment to send funds to the exporter's bank. Until the letter of credit is delivered to the importer's bank, however, no funds flow from the bank, so it does not affect the balance sheet.

Interest rate and currency swaps also represent off balance sheet items. Let's assume that a corporation in Germany has borrowed deutschemarks to set up a factory in the United States. The cash flow from this investment will be in dollars, but the interest payments will be in deutschemarks. The corporation will therefore be subject to "currency risk." If the dollar should depreciate relative to the deutschemark, the corporation will receive fewer deutschemarks for a given dollar of cash flow, and the corporation may not have enough deutschemark revenue to cover its interest payments.

To avoid this risk, the corporation can find a bank to arrange a currency **swap** of its deutschemark liability for a dollar-denominated liability. The bank finds another party that receives deutschemark revenues and faces dollar interest rate commitments. The two parties then swap liabilities. The pricing and purpose of this transaction will be considered in Chapter 17.

The bank arranging the transaction has created an off balance sheet risk for itself because if either party should fail to provide the currency demanded by the other, the bank must step in. For example, suppose corporation A receives dollar revenues and has borrowed deutschemarks, whereas corporation B is in the opposite circumstance. Corporation A swaps dollars for deutschemarks with corporation B. If corporation B falls into bankruptcy, it will not deliver deutschemarks to corporation A. Corporation A still earns dollar revenues to pay its interest commitments, but it again has a currency risk.

The bank that arranged the swap must now step in and buy dollars from corporation A, providing it with deutschemarks at the exchange rate stipulated in the original contract. Thus the bank creates a potential exchange rate exposure when it arranges a currency swap transaction.

Interest rate swaps operate in a similar fashion. One party to the swap has a short-term liability or a long-term liability that has an interest rate that floats with short-term rates. Another party has a long-term, fixed interest rate liability. The two parties swap debt so that the first one pays a fixed rate and the second one pays a floating rate. A bank stands in between to guarantee the performance of both parties. We discuss the function of interest rate swaps in more detail in Chapter 17. Interest rate and currency swap markets combined totaled some $1.5 trillion in 1989.

THE INCOME STATEMENT

Banks, like other business enterprises, incur expenses and receive revenues in providing services to their customers. Also, as in other business enterprises, bank stockholders receive the difference between revenues and expenses for bearing the risks associated with the enterprise in which they have invested. In this section we analyze the income statements of commercial banks over the period 1985 through 1989.

An Overview of the Income Statement

In Table 10.2 we have a combined income statement for all commercial banks in the United States based on year-end data for the years 1985 through 1989. Unlike the balance sheet, which represents the status of an entity at a certain moment in time, much like a snapshot, an **income statement** represents change over a period of time, such as a year. The revenue and expense items in this income statement are expressed as a percentage of total average assets of the banking system in each particular year. It is customary to compare bank income statistics across individual banks and across time by dividing the absolute numbers by average assets. This

Table 10.2 INCOME STATEMENT FOR ALL COMMERCIAL BANKS FROM 1985 TO 1989: INCOME AND EXPENSES AS A PERCENT OF AVERAGE NET CONSOLIDATED ASSETS (%)

	1985	1986	1987	1988	1989
Gross interest income	9.45	8.38	8.21	8.95	9.92
Gross interest expense	6.06	5.10	4.94	5.42	6.41
Net interest margin	3.38	3.27	3.27	3.53	3.51
Taxable equivalent	3.77	3.68	3.50	3.61	3.70
Noninterest income	1.33	1.40	1.55	1.47	1.55
Loss provisions	0.68	0.78	1.27	0.54	0.93
Other noninterest expense	3.18	3.23	3.31	3.33	3.37
Securities gains	0.06	0.14	0.05	0.01	0.02
Income before tax	0.90	0.80	0.29	1.14	0.80
Taxes	0.21	0.19	0.18	0.33	0.31
Extraordinary items	0.01	0.01	0.01	0.03	0.01
Net income	0.70	0.62	0.11	0.84	0.51
Cash dividends declared	0.33	0.33	0.36	0.44	0.44
Net retained earnings	0.37	0.29	−0.25	0.40	0.07
Memo					
Return on assets	0.70	0.62	0.11	0.84	0.51
Return on equity (% equity)	11.18	9.97	1.80	13.52	7.94
Average assets ($billions)	2,559	2,753	2,883	2,959	3,112
Number of banks	13,898	13,733	13,273	12,691	12,323

Source: From *Federal Reserve Bulletin,* July 1990, pp. 483 and 491.

removes the problem of scale differences in the numbers. For example, between 1985 and 1989, bank average assets (averaged over each year) grew from $2.6 trillion to $3.1 trillion. The absolute revenue and expense items, as reported on a conventional income statement, would tend to increase along with the growth in assets. It is much easier to compare the composition of expenses and revenues across time, however, if we standardize for this difference.

The first line of the income statement is entitled "gross interest income." As we indicated in the previous section, banks hold assets that have many of the characteristics of a bond contract. These assets earn interest income, which is stated in the first line as a percentage of average assets. It is interesting to note that gross interest income declined steadily between 1985 and 1987 but rose again in 1988 and 1989.

This is primarily due to the decline and then rise in interest rates in the U.S. economy (see Figure 10.1). The decline in interest income was less than the decline in interest rates, indicating that bank assets have longer maturities than Treasury bills.

The second line in Table 10.2 is "gross interest expense," again measured as a

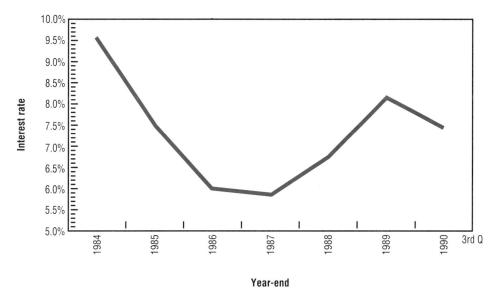

Figure 10.1 THREE-MONTH TREASURY BILL AUCTION RATE *Source:* From
Federal Reserve Bulletin, Statistical Table A24 of various issues.

percentage of average assets. Recall from our discussion of bank liabilities that, with
the exception of demand deposits, banks pay interest on the liabilities they borrow
from households and businesses. By measuring interest expense relative to assets,
we understate the interest expense of interest-bearing liabilities because demand
deposits make up a substantial portion of bank liabilities and therefore of assets as
well. Also, assets equal capital plus liabilities, and equity capital has no interest
expense associated with it because payment to equity holders is a residual.

We note that interest revenue earned on assets is affected by the same phenomenon, but less drastically. Cash items in the process of collection do not earn interest.

Some liabilities, such as time deposits issued to households, can have fairly long
maturities, and the cost of these liabilities should change rather slowly relative to
the change in short-term interest rates in the economy. In addition, demand deposits,
which do not have interest expense, should reduce the impact of changes in interest
rates on the gross interest expense of commercial banks. Despite these two effects,
gross interest expense appears to decline as interest rates fall, along with the decline
in gross interest revenue. However, the decline was less dramatic during the period
than the decline in the T-bill rate (again, see Figure 10.1).

The next line on the income statement is "net interest margin." The **net interest
margin** is the difference between the gross interest income line and the gross interest

expense line. As you can see, on a taxable equivalent basis, the net interest margin fluctuated from between 3.50 and 3.77 percent of average assets.

The fluctuation in net interest margin taxable equivalent occurred independent of movements in the Treasury bill rate. Over the period 1985 through 1989, the spread between its high and low was 27 basis points. Its impact on pre-tax return on equity would be about 16 times this level, because the bank equity-to-asset ratio is about 6 percent.

The next item on the income statement is "noninterest income." This item has been increasing steadily as a percentage of average assets over the years. Banks generate noninterest income from fees on deposits, credit cards issued, cash management services, trust management, trading securities, trading foreign exchange, and off balance sheet items.

Fees are typically charged on transactions deposits when the costs of providing transactions services exceed the interest revenues earned on the assets in which the deposit funds are invested. This situation is most likely to arise for small account holders, such as consumers, because the number of their third-party payments is likely to be high relative to balances held in the account. As we indicated earlier, banks provide cash management services for their business customers to minimize their customers' holdings of cash and noninterest-bearing demand deposits. The fees charged for these services (although some are provided as compensation for holding demand deposits with the bank) show up in the noninterest revenue line. Banks manage more than cash for their customers. They also manage long-term investment portfolios. This service is called **trust fund management,** and the fees charged for it also show up in the noninterest revenue line.

Large banks earn noninterest income because they are active traders of U.S. government securities and foreign currency. Their role in these markets is similar to the role of the market maker we discussed in Chapter 6. There is no organized exchange for U.S. government bonds, so dealers like banks play the role of market makers. They play the same role in foreign exchange markets, where they stand ready to make markets between the U.S. dollar and major foreign currencies such as the yen, the pound sterling, and the deutschemark. The large banks in New York, and sometimes those in Chicago and California as well, are known as **money center banks.** This title is partly due to their role as market makers in currencies and government securities. The money center banks earn noninterest income from trading currencies and government securities through the bid-offer spread we described in Chapter 6. That is, they bid for a currency or security at a low price and offer it at a higher price. Of course, sometimes the market turns against them, and they suffer a loss.

Banks also obtain fees for issuing off balance sheet guarantees, such as lines and letters of credit, and for arranging corporate mergers and acquisitions.

The increase in noninterest income has occurred primarily at large banks, which are more heavily engaged in securities and foreign exchange trading, trust activities, and off balance sheet items.

The next two items on the income statement are noninterest expense items. The first is entitled "loss provisions." We will discuss **loss provisions** in some

Box 10.1

Recession Hits the Northeast Regionals

The impact of the recession of 1990 was more severe on some areas of the country than on others. The Northeast was particularly hard hit, and this was reflected in past due and nonaccrual loans at the major regional banks in the Northeast. For example, at six large Northeast regionals, nonaccruals and past dues to loans rose from 3.47 percent of loans in December 1989 to 6.19 percent of loans in June 1990. This compares with an increase from 3.47 to 3.98 percent at the 28 largest banks nationwide over the same period.

The large increase in nonperforming loans at the Northeast regionals brought on fears that loan troubles would spread nationwide, and consequently, 1990 was a terrible year for bank stocks. In a year when the Dow Jones Industrial Average, an index of the stock prices of major U.S. industrial companies, declined about 4 percent, bank stock prices fell about 25 percent.

---

detail below, but simply put, they are the bank's contribution to a reserve to cover losses resulting from defaults on loans. Notice that this item increased substantially in 1987 and again in 1989. This does not mean that banks made particularly bad loans in those years. These provisions were taken to offset losses on Latin American loans made in the 1970s and early 1980s. In 1990, banks were forced to increase provisions again, this time for domestic commercial real estate loans. See Box 10.1.

"Other noninterest expense" items include wage and salary expenses, real estate expenses for the offices banks occupy, and so forth. These noninterest expenses are the cost of producing noninterest income. Notice, too, that this item has risen steadily in recent years. See Box 10.2.

"Securities gains or losses" represent the profit or loss on the sale of investment securities. If a bank sells a security when interest rates are higher than when it purchased the security, it will experience a loss. Banks hold securities for both investment and trading purposes. The gains and losses from trading account securities show up as noninterest income, whereas the gains and losses on the sale of investment securities are a separate item. Notice that in the low interest rate year of 1986, banks experienced relatively large gains on their securities sales.

An additional item representing gains or losses on the sale of assets is the item called "extraordinary items." For example, if a bank sells an office building for more than it paid for it, it is considered "extraordinary" because it stems from a nonrecurring event. Citicorp sold its New York headquarters in 1987 to produce an extraordinary gain to help offset an increase in its loan loss provisions on its foreign debt.

The remaining items on the income statement are all calculations of net income or profits. "Income before taxes" is the sum of the revenue items appearing above this line less the sum of the expense items appearing above this line. "Net income"

Box 10.2

Money Market Mutual Funds and Bank Deposits

BusinessWeek's cover article of April 22, 1991 was about banks. The article argued that money market mutual funds are an attractive alternative to the bank transactions account. The customer has access to the account through checks, and the account pays higher interest than a NOW account. Money market mutual funds can pay higher rates because their noninterest expenses are a lot lower than those of banks. As we indicated in the figure in Box 3.1, mutual funds have grown relatively rapidly, representing 22 percent of NOW, MMDA, and savings accounts at midyear 1990.

One of the services that money market mutual funds do not offer is immediate access to cash, but the article says that providing access to accounts through an ATM is a possibility. If money market mutual funds are going to get into the business of supplying small amounts of cash to their customers, they will have to absorb the costs. We would not be surprised if these costs come pretty close to banks' costs. After all, running an ATM network and keeping the ATMs filled with cash is expensive. Higher costs mean lower interest rates.

Another cost faced by banks that money market mutual funds do not absorb is the cost of handling small checks. Money market funds place a minimum size on checks, usually $500. Processing checks is expensive; the smaller the denomination, the higher is the cost per dollar of check. Lots of small checks can push costs way up. Again, this would reduce the interest rate money market accounts could pay.

is the "income before taxes" item adjusted for taxes and extraordinary items. As you can see, it took a plunge in 1987, primarily due to the large increase in loss provisions.

As a memo item to Table 10.2, we show "return on equity." Return on equity can be calculated from return on assets by multiplying return on assets by the asset-to-equity ratio. Notice the low return in 1987. This was due to the large loan loss provisions taken in that year. See Box 10.3.

Interest Expense and Revenues

Table 10.3 provides a detailed breakdown of various interest revenue and expense items that make up the totals presented in Table 10.2. One important point in this

Box 10.3

The 1990 Earnings of Large Banks

The cover article on banking in the April 22, 1991 issue of *BusinessWeek,* which focused on banks as a dying industry, declared that "whatever the obstacles, there is little doubt that a massive wave of mergers and buyouts is necessary if the banking industry is to become competitive again" (p. 78). The argument is made that there are tremendous unexploited economies of scale in banking, which means that big banks should have lower costs and higher returns.

However, when you look at the 1990 earnings results across banks, it is hard to find evidence that bigger banks are more profitable. For example, Citicorp, by far the largest bank in New York and in the country, earned 3.7 percent on equity in 1990. Chemical and Manufacturers, two other large New York banks, earned 7.45 and 3.04 percent, respectively. There is much talk that these two banks will merge, partly to give Citicorp a run for its money in the New York retail market. However, since Citicorp is not doing better than the other two, it is difficult to see how creating another very large bank out of two somewhat large ones will improve profitability.

Among the 100 largest banks in the country, banks with less than $5 billion in assets, the smallest banks in the group, outperformed their larger competitors. The median return on equity for these banks was 15.04 percent, and the range of returns extended from over 35 to 10.5 percent. For "superregionals," non-money-center banks with more than $20 billion in assets, the median return was 14.95 percent, and the range extended from 25 to 2.5 percent. Money centers, the largest banks in the country, performed worse than any other set of banks in the top 100. Thus there is no evidence that massive consolidation among the 100 largest banks will improve the profit picture for banks.

table is that large time deposits (in U.S. offices) and deposits in foreign offices are much more sensitive to changes in interest rates than are other interest-bearing deposits, which are primarily the time and savings deposits of consumers. Thus banks that depend on large domestic time deposits and deposits in foreign offices can be expected to have more highly interest sensitive liabilities than other banks.

Table 10.3 also provides a breakdown of interest revenues. Note that taxable equivalent yield on securities fell much more rapidly than the unadjusted yield on securities. As we indicated earlier, banks hold state and local government securities because they are exempt from federal taxation. The before-tax yield on these securities is generally lower than alternative securities investments, which are U.S. Treasury and U.S. guaranteed bonds. However, the after-tax yield on tax-exempt securities is generally higher than the alternatives.

To calculate the after-tax yield on a tax-exempt security, its yield must be divided by 1 minus the tax rate. For example, if the tax rate is 40 percent, the taxable

Table 10.3 EFFECTIVE INTEREST RATES ON PORTFOLIO COMPOSITION: ALL COMMERCIAL BANKS FROM 1985 TO 1989

	Effective Interest Rates (%)				
	1985	1986	1987	1988	1989
Rates earned:					
Securities	9.27	8.34	7.89	8.06	8.58
State and local governments	7.42	7.20	7.28	7.38	7.46
Loans, gross	12.07	10.84	10.44	10.80	11.97
Net of loss provisions	10.87	9.46	8.24	9.92	10.48
Taxable equivalent					
Securities	11.45	10.52	9.11	8.06	9.32
Securities and gross loans	11.93	10.77	10.12	10.31	11.48
Rates paid:					
Interest-bearing deposits	8.20	6.98	5.82	6.81	7.84
In foreign offices	9.48	7.78	7.90	8.92	10.89
In domestic offices	7.66	6.67	5.10	5.34	6.88
Large time deposits	8.72	7.31	6.86	7.39	8.63
All interest-bearing liabilities	8.29	7.01	6.11	7.26	8.52

Source: From *Federal Reserve Bulletin,* July 1990, pp. 483 and 491.

equivalent yield on a tax-exempt security paying 10 percent is 16.67 percent. A security subject to a 40-percent tax rate must earn 16.67 percent to earn an after-tax return of 10 percent because the investor keeps only 60 percent of the income.

In 1986, Congress changed the tax laws to make it less attractive for banks to hold tax-exempt securities. Investments in these securities fell from 7.5 percent of bank assets in 1986 to 2.75 percent of bank assets by 1989. The disinvestment in relatively high after-tax yielding municipal bonds caused the taxable equivalent yield on securities to decline relative to the before-tax yield.

MANAGING THE RISKS BANKS FACE

Banks and other financial institutions are subject to two major kinds of risk—credit risk and interest rate risk. Both must be carefully managed.

Credit Risk

Credit risk is the most substantial risk most commercial banks face. **Credit risk** is the risk that borrowers may not be able to meet their contractual obligations to the bank. For example, a borrower may face temporary cash flow problems and stop paying interest and principal on his loan. If the temporary cash flow problems are only temporary, he will eventually begin making payments again. Sometimes, however, temporary cash flow problems become permanent, and the borrower goes bankrupt. Banks are unable to regain their asset, and the borrower is in default.

Banks have established rules concerning when a borrower who has ceased making scheduled payments is declared in default. In this section we describe the process of declaring a borrower in default and the effect of such a declaration on the bank's balance sheet and income statement.

Banks risk large amounts (the principal of a loan) to make small amounts (the net interest revenue). A default implies that a bank loses, or "writes off," the entire principal of a loan, even though it must still pay its depositors the full amount of the funds it obtained from them to make the loan. Thus the bank must cover the cost of defaults out of its capital and current income. As we have seen from our previous discussion, both these items are small percentages of the entire balance sheet of the bank. Thus it is easy to see how a few defaults can force a bank itself into bankruptcy.

The portions of bank capital and income that are set aside to cover possible defaults on loans are given special accounting status, primarily because they are accorded favorable tax treatment. The income statement item, as we indicated earlier, is known as "provisions for loan loss." The balance sheet item is known as the **loan loss reserve.** We did not mention the balance sheet item in the liability section because it does not appear on the liability side of the balance sheet like equity capital. Instead, it appears on the asset side of the balance sheet as a contrary item, or contra-asset. This means that loan loss reserves are subtracted from the asset side of the balance sheet, specifically from the loan account, rather than appearing on the liability side of the balance sheet. Of course, subtracting an item from the asset side of the balance sheet is equivalent to adding it to the liability side.

The following is a description of a typical scenario for dealing with a problem loan. When a loan customer fails to make a payment, the bank immediately considers the payment "past due." Interest income is accrued in anticipation of a late payment. When interest is accrued on an asset, there is an accounting presumption that interest is being paid by the borrower. Thus, even though the payment is past due, the bank still assumes it is being paid. The bank covers the interest revenue not actually received by increasing the principal of the loan outstanding. When the loan is past due 90 days or more and still accruing interest, it must be reported on the quarterly report that all banks must submit to the state and federal authorities that supervise banks.

At some point, a past due loan must be placed on nonaccrual status. *Nonaccrual status* means that the bank has ceased assuming that interest is being paid on the loan. This point involves some judgment on the part of the banker, who must decide how soon, if ever, the borrower can begin paying interest again. Bankers are sometimes reluctant to place loans on nonaccrual status because this action reduces reported net income. The bank generates its usual expenses on deposits, but it shows no income to cover them. As a result, net income falls. The bank must report nonaccrual loans on its quarterly report to bank supervisors.

At some point, a loan that is on nonaccrual status is considered in default, and the bank reduces its loan loss reserve by the amount of the loan. Bank supervisors apply pressure to declare loans in default if they think bankers are being too optimistic about the chances that a problem loan will again accrue interest.

The accounting item by which this is accomplished is called a *charge-off*. The loan account also falls by the amount of the loan in default. Because the loan account and the loss reserve, which is a contrary item, are reduced by the same amount, a default has no immediate impact on the rest of the balance sheet. Thus, as long as the loan loss reserve is adequate to cover the default, reported equity capital or net worth is unaffected at the time the bank finally writes off the loan.

A bad loan has its impact on the balance sheet when a bank makes provisions for loan loss. Provisions, an income statement item, are placed in the loan loss reserve account, a contrary item on the asset side of the balance sheet. When provisons exceed net income, the accounting value of assets is reduced relative to liabilities. Since assets must always equal liabilities plus net worth, and since the value of liabilities is fixed as long as the bank remains solvent, an increase in the loan loss reserve causes a decline in the accounting value of net worth.

A bank can increase its loan loss reserve at any time during the life of a loan. It usually sets aside some loan loss reserve for each loan at the time it makes the loan. Under normal circumstances, the initial loan loss reserve is adequate to cover losses. However, during periods of recession or as a result of fraud and bad judgment, losses can rise significantly above normal levels, and banks must increase their loan loss reserves. It is these occurrences, rather than the normal level of losses, that cause major declines in the net worth of banks. For example, in 1987, when New York money center banks took large charge-offs, the capital-to-assets ratios of these banks declined to 4.33 from 4.78 percent in 1986.

Because banks sometimes recover income and principal from loans they had previously declared in default, they subtract charge-offs after recoveries, or net charge-offs, from their loan loss reserves. The net charge-off item is treated as a reconciliation item (also known as an *adjustment entry*). That is, at the end of the reporting period, banks reduce their reserves for loan loss by the amount of net charge-offs.

Although reported net worth is unaffected by default, it is obvious that stockholders have suffered from it. Loan loss reserves are established from provisions for loan losses, which represent income that could have been paid to stockholders in the form of dividends. Banks take provisions for loan losses out of income based on their anticipation of default because they attempt to keep their loss reserve adequate to meet potential losses. Thus we might expect banks to spend income to find ways to reduce loan losses so that they will not have to allocate so much of their income to provisions for losses. See Box 10.4.

Part of the money banks spend on loss prevention is used to fund an extensive credit review process. Loan officers are bank employees charged with evaluating the creditworthiness of potential loan customers. By analyzing the financial state-

Box 10.4

The Credit Crunch: Caused by Regulators?

The 1990 recession arrived with many commentators blaming the bad economic news on a credit crunch—that is, banks allegedly stopped lending to many creditworthy borrowers. The federal agencies that supervise banks came in for much of the blame. As we saw in Box 10.1, between year-end 1988 and June 1990, nonperforming loans at some banks rose sharply. The Bank of New England, a large regional bank, failed in early 1991. Many analysts charged that regulators overreacted to these figures, denying credit to many sound borrowers and deepening the recession.

The chairman of banking at the University of South Carolina's College of Business Administration, Timothy W. Koch, conducted a survey of real estate developers in that state to determine whether they felt a credit crunch existed and, if it did, who was to blame.

The South Carolina real estate market remained relatively strong during the recession. The ratio of nonaccrual real estate loans to total real estate loans was among the lowest in the country at the end of September 1990. Yet 88 percent of the developers responding to the survey indicated that borrowing had become more difficult during the preceding 6 months. Sixty percent of the developers blamed bank supervisors for the problem. They said that their bankers told them that making a new real estate loan would automatically trigger an audit by bank supervisors (*The American Banker,* February 1, 1991, p. 4).

Was the credit crunch of 1990 worse than in previous recessions? To answer this question, we looked at loan growth during the recession year 1982 compared with loan growth in 1990. We found that for the period March through October, commercial and industrial loan growth was substantially higher, at 6.2 percent, in 1982 compared with 1.3 percent in 1990. However, real estate lending growth was faster in 1990 (5.0 percent) than in 1982 (3.1 percent). Thus it appears that commercial borrowers suffered more than real estate developers from the credit crunch.

---

ments of a potential borrower, the quality of its management, the stability of its market, the diversity of its customer base, and so on, a loan officer evaluates the likelihood that a particular borrower will repay the loan. The loan officer then rates the quality of the credit after his or her evaluation. The interest rate charged to the loan customer will depend partly on the rating evaluation of the loan officer. (It also will be determined by the level of interest rates in general.) Recall from the rules of diversification presented in Chapter 3 that bankers could hold a portfolio of loans whose returns are uncorrelated. They could then reduce the risk of their portfolio to zero, and each loan would have a yield such that its expected return is the risk-free interest rate.

Realistically, this cannot be done because the returns on loans are not uncorrelated. Thus the portfolio will have some risk, and its expected return will be above the risk-free rate. Bankers set relative interest rates on loans to yield an expected premium for bearing risk, just as riskier securities carry a higher expected rate of return. Bankers also allocate a greater portion of the revenue from risky loans to loan loss reserves than they do for higher-quality loans.

Loan officers monitor their loan customers and adjust the quality ratings as changes in financial statements warrant or as market conditions change. If the quality of a loan deteriorates, the loan officer recommends that the bank allocate more of the revenues from that loan to reserves for loan loss.

Credit investigation is expensive. As long as there are some fixed costs to credit investigation, we can expect that the relative cost will rise as loan size declines. Unless banks can find ways to reduce this fixed cost, making small loans might become prohibitively expensive.

We would expect banks to find cheaper methods of credit investigation per dollar of loan as loan size declines. Evidence for this can be found in the methods banks use to control risk on consumer loans, which are very small loans when compared with large C&I loans at large banks. Loan officers play no role in the evaluation of individual consumer credits.

Instead, credit quality is viewed as a statistical problem called **credit scoring.** Key statistics such as income, indebtedness, financial and nonfinancial wealth, and so on are provided by potential borrowers. These data are then weighted by their ability to predict default in a large pool of borrowers. The individual borrower receives a credit score based on the weighted sum of his or her personal statistics that determines whether or not he or she can obtain a loan. When general economic conditions deteriorate, consumer loans as a group are often reclassified to reflect their greater risk in the new environment.

In addition, consumers are asked to put up collateral for loans on highly marketable items such as houses and cars. For example, when a consumer takes out a mortgage to buy a house, the house becomes collateral. In the event of default on the loan, the bank gains possession of the house. Collateral is only useful if it is highly marketable, because the bank must sell it to recover the principal on the loan.

Reducing the cost of making small or risky business loans is more complicated, because it is more difficult to predict the performance of small or risky businesses from standardized accounting ratios.

Credit policy at banks involves more than being careful about individual loan contracts. Banks also limit their loan exposure to individual companies. A **bank's exposure** to a customer is the amount the bank would lose if the individual or corporation becomes completely unable to repay. Exposure includes all the loans the bank has to a customer as well as the value of commitments to lend and letters of credit. By limiting exposure, banks reduce the impact one customer's bankruptcy can have on the bank that lends to it.

Similarly, these policies often involve limiting exposures to whole industries, countries, or geographic regions. The goal is the same as individual customer credit limits—to reduce the extent to which one event can damage bank returns. This process should be easily recognizable—banks are applying the rules of diversification to reduce risk to the bank portfolio.

Interest Rate Risk

Banks take on interest rate risk as well as credit risk. They offer investors deposits with mostly short-term maturities. They also offer credit with fixed terms and rates to borrowers. The risk created by the spread between asset maturities and liability maturities is called **interest rate risk.** In the preceding section we indicated that the primary risk faced by commercial banks is credit risk. In the late 1970s and early 1980s, the primary risk faced by thrift institutions was interest rate risk, but this is less true today. We discuss thrift risk in Chapter 20.

The important issue for a bank managing its interest rate position is the difference between how assets and liabilities are affected by changes in interest rates. If large proportions of both assets and liabilities have yields set by long-term contracts, the net interest margin, or spread, will not change much when interest rates change. If both assets and liabilities are largely short term, a rise in interest rates will increase both the interest expense and the interest revenue of the bank, but the spread will still be stable.

Table 10.4   BANK FINANCIAL STATEMENT

Balance Sheet (000s)

ASSETS		LIABILITIES	
Cash (reserves)	$10,000	Nontransaction savings account deposits @ 7%	$90,000
Fixed-rate, low-risk, long-term secured mortages @ 10%	90,000	Equity	10,000

Annual Income Statement (000s)

Revenues	$9,000	Interest from mortgage holders
Expenses	6,300	Interest expense on savings accounts
	1,000	Operations/payroll/miscellaneous
	$1,700	Annual profits

Return on equity = 1,700/10,000 = 17%

If interest rates rise by 5 percentage points, the bank's loan customers, with their long-term contracts, are protected. They still pay 10 percent. Savings account customers, however, are able to withdraw their funds. If a competing institution offers a 12-percent yield on deposits, the bank must compete with this rate — there isn't enough cash to allow the depositors to all leave. This results in the following annual income statement:

Revenues	9,000	Interest from mortgage holders remains unchanged
Expenses	10,800	Interest expense on savings accounts, up sharply
	1,000	Operations, etc.
	(2,800)	Loss

If these losses persist — interest rates do not decline — they will eventually wipe out the capital of the bank.

Table 10.4 presents an example of how interest rate risk can affect the net interest margin and, consequently, the net income of a bank. It is an extreme illustration of mismatched funding. The fictional bank had long-term assets—loans with yields that would not change for some time. These assets were funded with short-term liabilities—deposits with yields that change, as a result of market forces, in a very short time. This mismatch between the repricing schedules of the different sides of the balance sheet created an interest rate exposure. While the example is purely fictional, this is in fact what happened to many thrift institutions in the late 1970s and early 1980s.

To avoid this situation, bank managements try to limit interest rate risk. This process begins with calculating the repricing schedules of both assets and liabilities. A **repricing schedule** is merely a calculation of the maturity schedules of all assets and liabilities. A central group within the bank, usually called the asset and liability committee, attempts to equalize asset and liability repricing within certain time frames. What this means is that the committee attempts to have the interest received on bank assets and the interest paid on liabilities move together as interest rates change.

Excesses of assets (or liabilities) at a given repricing horizon (say an excess of 90-day assets over 90-day liabilities) are considered "mismatched." The magnitude of the mismatch for any one time period is called the **interest rate gap.** If more assets than liabilities come due within 90 days, the bank faces the risk that if interest rates decline, its revenue from its assets will be less than its interest commitments on its liabilities.

Duration matching, introduced in Chapter 4, is a more sophisticated version of matching. It involves comparing revenue cash flows and expense cash flows instead of asset and liability maturities. This method recognizes that if cash is received on an asset before it must be paid on a liability, the bank faces reinvestment risk on the cash received that it must reinvest until the liability payment is due.

For example, let's assume that the bank holds a 90-day asset and a 90-day liability. The liability requires the bank to pay principal and interest at the end of 90 days, whereas the asset pays interest monthly. The bank must reinvest the cash received from the asset to meet principal and interest payments on the liability at the end of 90 days. If interest rates should fall, the value of the asset, including accumulated interest, will be less than the liability at the maturity of both.

A bank's asset and liability committee concerns itself with interest rate gaps on its assets and liabilities, or its cash inflow and outflow if it uses duration matching. This group sorts out every asset and liability on the balance sheet (or cash inflow and outflow) into maturity categories. The maturity profile of a bank's assets and liabilities might look like the schedule presented in Figure 10.2a. The maturity schedule for liabilities might look like the plain columns in the same figure.

The point of this analysis is to find mismatches between the sides of the balance sheet. This involves taking the differences between assets and liabilities at each maturity. The sides of the balance sheet are always equal overall, but they can differ

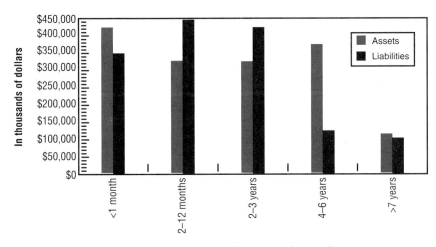

In thousands of dollars

Assets and liabilities groups by maturity

Figure 10.2a   REPRICING OF ASSETS AND LIABILITIES

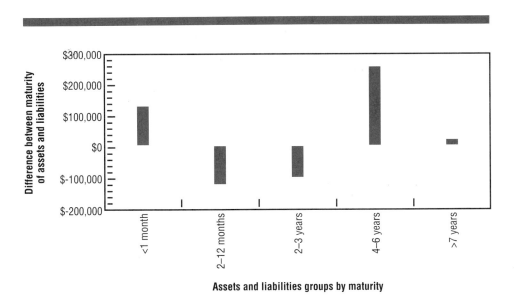

Difference between maturity of assets and liabilities

Assets and liabilities groups by maturity

Figure 10.2b   REPRICING GAPS

considerably at various maturities. Figure 10.2b shows the mismatches resulting from the assets and liabilities in Figure 10.2a.

Banks attempt to reduce their gaps by **match-funding,** which is the process of funding assets with liabilities that have similar repricing characteristics. For example, if a bank makes a 90-day fixed-rate loan, it will try to fund it by raising a 90-day CD (which also has a fixed interest rate). In fact, matching is difficult, because the actual maturity structure of many assets and liabilities is difficult to predict. For example, many home mortgages have 30-year maturities and require the borrower to pay fixed interest payments—that is, the interest rate on the mortgage is determined at the time it is written and does not vary when market interest rates change. (This type of mortgage is in contrast to an adjustment-rate mortgage, in which the interest payments rise or fall depending on whether interest rates rise or fall.)

Theoretically, this asset would be considered a long-term asset, but households have the right to pay off their mortgage at any time. If interest rates should fall, many mortgage holders will pay off mortgages written at high rates by taking out a new mortgage at a lower rate. This is called **refinancing.** It is events like this that make it difficult to estimate interest rate exposure.

THE CAPITAL ACCOUNT

It is economically infeasible for banks to eliminate all interest rate and credit risk from their balance sheets. Since most liabilities of banks are designed to preserve the depositors' principal and pay interest at specific intervals, banks must find equity investors willing to absorb the remaining risks so that depositors can have confidence that their investments are liquid. Bank equity includes several accounting subcategories, all of which are included under the single item "total equity capital" or capital account line on the liability side of the balance sheet in Table 10.1.

THE BALANCE SHEETS
OF THRIFT INSTITUTIONS

Thrift institutions are not close substitutes for banks for commercial businesses, and they supply different financial products to consumers. On the deposit side, banks focus on transactions accounts and liquid savings deposits, whereas thrifts focus on less liquid time deposits. Banks generally supply installment and credit card loans to households, whereas thrifts concentrate on supplying mortgage credit to households.

Thrift Portfolios versus Bank Portfolios

Table 10.5 compares the balance sheets of banks and thrifts for several basic asset and liability products. Note that thrifts have about $1\frac{1}{2}$ times as many one- to four-family mortgages as commercial banks, but banks have a dominant share in installment and revolving consumer credit. Car loans are an example of installment credit, and credit card loans are an example of revolving credit. Installment loans are paid off in installments of fixed payments, but revolving credit has no fixed schedule when the entire account must be paid off.

In 1982, thrifts were given the power to invest up to 20 percent of their assets in commercial loans. However, they have made little use of this power. Banks have an overwhelming share of the commercial loan market.

On the liability side, we have compared bank and thrift shares of consumer deposits only. Most thrifts are allowed to provide transactions accounts to businesses only if they make a loan to those businesses. They have less than a 1–percent share

Table 10.5   COMPARATIVE BALANCE SHEET: BANKS VS THRIFTS, JUNE 1990

	Banks	Thrift Institutions	Thrift Share of Commercial Bank and Thrift Total
Assets ($billions):			
Real estate loans*	$ 804	$ 868	51.9%
One- to four-family	388	640	62.2
Multifamily and commercial	398	226	36.2
Consumer installment and revolving credit	336	53	13.6
Commercial loans	519	29	5.3
Total Domestic Assets	$2,940	$1,396	28.6%
Liabilities ($billions):			
NOW accounts	$ 201†	$ 87‡	30.1%
Money market	368	133	26.5
Savings	195	221	53.1
Small time deposits (less than $100,000)	559	588	51.3

Sources: From *Federal Reserve Bulletin,* December 1990 and January 1991, pp. A13 and A26; special table from *Federal Reserve Bulletin,* January 1991, p. A74, and *FDIC Call Reports,* June 1990.

*Excludes mortgage-backed securities.   ‡Includes share drafts at credit unions.
†As of March 31, 1990.

of demand deposits nationwide. The exception is a type of thrift institution called *savings banks,* which operate primarily in the Northeast and are allowed to take deposits from businesses in some states. Even in this region of the country, thrift share of business demand deposits is very small.

As you can see from Table 10.5, banks dominate the consumer transactions accounts (NOWs). They are also dominant in money market accounts. Thrifts dominate the market in the less liquid savings and small time deposits.

CONCLUSION

In this chapter we described the balance sheets and income statements of banks. We explained how the two measured risks that banks face—credit risk and interest rate risk—arise in the ordinary course of bank business and how banks manage them. We also described how these risks affect the income statement and balance sheet. We compared the balance sheets of banks and thrift institutions.

Over the next five chapters we will use the basic information presented here as we develop models of the role of banks in an industrial economy with well-developed financial markets.

KEY TERMS

cash item in the process of collection	swap
"due from"	income statement
loan secured by real estate	net interest margin
owner's equity	trust fund management
home equity loan	money center banks
commercial and industrial (C&I) loan	loss provision
personal loan	credit risk
loan to carry securities	loan loss reserve
municipal bonds	credit scoring
letter of credit	bank exposure
banker's acceptance	interest rate risk
line of credit	repricing schedule
commitment to lend	interest rate gap
standby letter of credit	match-funding
off balance sheet items	refinancing

EXERCISES

1. What is the balance sheet impact when a bank customer deposits a check into his account and the bank has not yet collected the funds?

2. Show the impact on a bank balance sheet on a conversion of a demand deposit to a security sold under agreement to repurchase item (a "reverse repo").

3. When a bank reduces demand deposits and increases repurchase agreements, what happens to fed funds purchased?

4. Trace the impact of the issuance of a banker's acceptance on a bank balance sheet from an off balance sheet item (letter of credit) to a customer liability and a bank liability on acceptances outstanding. Identify the parties holding an asset and the parties holding a liability.

5. Retail bank deposits were deregulated between 1983 and 1986. It was widely predicted that this would cause a major deterioration in banks' net interest margin. Yet, between 1981 and 1986 (taxable equivalent) net interest margin at large, non–money-center banks actually increased. Why do you suppose that deregulation was a nonevent for banks? (Refer to Box 3.1 for help with the answer.)

6. Show how placing a loan on accrual status affects net income.

7. Trace the impact on the capital account of an increase in loss provisions that exceeds net income.

8. Describe the balance sheet impact when a company to which a bank has issued a standby letter of credit goes bankrupt.

9. Assume that two banks report identical earnings per share, but one bank is known for its conservatism in providing for future loan losses and the other is not. Which one will have a higher stock price?

10. In the first quarter of 1991, J. P. Morgan earned record bond trading profits. During the quarter, the fed funds rate fell from 7.3 to 5.5 percent. Describe Morgan's probable funding position.

11. Assume that two banks hold identical assets, but one funds its assets on a matched basis and the other funds with liabilities that have shorter maturities than the assets. Will the expected rate of return on equity that investors require from the two banks be the same?

FURTHER READING

Duca, John V., and Mary M. McLaughlin, "Developments Affecting the Profitability of Commercial Banks," *Federal Reserve Bulletin,* July 1990, pp. 477–499.

11

The **U.S.** **R**etail **P**ayments **S**ystem

When you purchase an item in a store, you must be prepared to pay for the item or suffer the possibility and consequences of a shoplifting conviction. In the United States, payment can take the form of a transfer of legal U.S. currency from you to the merchant for the value of the article you have purchased. This is the most straightforward way of satisfying your obligation to the merchant, but it is not the only way. You can give the merchant a check, which gives him or her the right to collect your debt by deducting the payment from your checking account. You can also give many merchants a credit card, such as VISA or MasterCard, to cover your obligation. The credit card signals to the merchant that a third party, usually a bank, will guarantee your obligation to pay and take the responsibility of collecting from you.

The merchant from whom you have purchased the item is designed the **payee** and you, the purchaser, are designated the **payor.** The payee goes to considerable trouble to determine whether the payor is offering "good funds"—that is, funds which people to whom the merchant owes debts will accept as payment. U.S. legal tender is the simplest way to handle most transactions in the United States because there is no doubt about its acceptance. For large transactions, however, it is not the simplest way. Delivering U.S. currency for large payments, such as for the purchase of a car, also subjects the payor to the risk of either robbery before the transaction is completed or, in these days, investigation as a possible drug dealer.

THE PAYMENTS SYSTEM
AS A CREDIT SYSTEM

If a merchant in the United States does not receive U.S. currency for her product, she takes some risk in handing the item over to her customer. If the customer writes a check to cover his purchase, the **payee,** the merchant, must take the check to her bank to receive cash or to deposit the check into her account. Her bank will accept the check on condition that it can collect the funds from the **payor's** bank. If the merchant accepts payment by credit card, she also must take the credit card receipt to her bank to receive cash or an equivalent credit to her checking account.

The merchant must take the credit card receipt or the check to her bank to convert it to cash because she cannot use these items to satisfy her debts. For example, suppose you enter a drug store to purchase a tube of toothpaste costing $3. You hand the merchant a $20 bill. Would you take a $17 check given to the merchant by a previous customer as change, or would you take a credit card receipt of the same value? If your answer to both these questions is not no, you risk losing $17. You will not accept these items as change because you are uncertain about whether they are really worth $17. Also, you cannot use them as payment for a purchase at the bookstore next door.

A Payment as a Loan

When a payee accepts a credit card or a check as payment for a product or service, she actually extends a loan to her customer until she can convert the check or credit card slip into currency or a credit to her bank account. These forms of payment represent loans because the payee cannot use them to satisfy her debts. Because they are of no use to her until they are converted to a more generally accepted form of payment, it is almost as if *she had not yet been paid.* The merchant must take care that she can collect her loan in a more universally accepted form of payment. She must determine whether she can convert her credit card receipts and checks into cash or into a deposit at her bank.

In this way, the merchant accepts a certain risk—the credit risk that she will not be able to collect cash for a check or a credit card sale. The merchant must take steps to be assured that her customers have written checks convertible into "good funds." If the customer does not have enough funds in his checking account, the merchant will not be paid. Also, if the merchant accepts a stolen credit card, she may not be paid. In these cases, the merchant would suffer the same consequences as a bank that experiences a credit loss on a loan—she would not receive payment to cover the costs of her merchandise, just as a bank would not be paid to cover the costs of the funds it had borrowed to make a loan.

Thus *the payment system is also a credit system*. For it to function smoothly, the cost of verifying the quality of the debts presented as payments must be low. Banks play a very important role in making the credit-based payments system function at low cost. The payee takes her non-currency receipts to her local bank to receive "good funds."

The Role of Banks in the Credit-Based Payments System

In March 1990, there were 12,572 commercial banks in the United States that offered demand deposits and NOW accounts to consumers. As we mentioned in the preceding chapter, both kinds of accounts permit consumers to write checks. In addition, at year end 1988, there were 3,441 savings and loan and mutual savings banks offering NOW accounts. There were also about 14,000 federally insured credit unions that offer checking-type accounts to consumers. A **credit union** is a consumer bank whose customers jointly own the bank. The "members" all have something in common, such as belonging to the same labor union. With such a large number of institutions on which a check can be drawn, it is obvious that merchants will often deposit checks written by payors who do not use the same bank as the merchant.

A merchant's bank cannot give the merchant cash or credit her account for a deposited check unless it is certain that it can collect the funds from the payor's bank. Thus the merchant faces two possible sources of credit risk in accepting a check from her customer—that the customer's account is empty or that the customer's bank will go bankrupt before the merchant's bank is able to collect the funds. If the merchant accepts a credit card for a purchase, she must be certain that her bank will give her cash or credit her account when she presents the credit card receipt. Her bank will do this only if it is certain that it can collect payment on the receipt from the bank that issued the credit card to the merchant's customer.

The role of banks in the credit-based payments system extends beyond the point at which the merchant receives "good funds" as payment from her customer. The customer's bank may offer him credit to finance his purchase after it has sent "good funds" to the merchant's bank to cover the customer's obligation to the merchant. For example, a customer who purchases an item with a credit card may not pay his credit card bill until weeks or months after his bank reimburses the merchant's bank. Since the customer's bank must ultimately be paid by the customer, it has extended the customer a loan until the credit card bill is paid. A customer who pays by check may have arrangements with his bank to cover the value of the check with a loan rather than with funds in the account.

In addition, even if the customer covers his credit card and check obligations immediately with funds deposited in his account, it is almost certain that the bank has invested the customer's funds in a loan to someone else. It is to the depositor's advantage that his funds are so invested, because loans earn interest that can help defray the bank's cost of making payments. However, if the default rate on the bank's loans is high, it will not be able to make good its promise to transfer "good funds" to the merchant's bank.

PROCESSING CHECKS INTO "GOOD FUNDS"

Suppose that you have entered a store and selected an item to purchase for $100 and that you ask the merchant to accept your check as payment. As we indicated earlier, the merchant is taking some risk if she says yes. In this section we describe what those risks are and how they are handled in the U.S. banking system as we trace the process by which your check becomes "good funds."

Accepting a Check as Payment

You might have trouble getting some merchants to accept your check under any circumstances because they wish to avoid entirely the risk that they will not be able to convert checks into "good funds." Of course, if a merchant makes it too difficult for her customers to pay her, she will make fewer sales. Thus she has some incentive to be accommodating and accept the risk that she will not be able to collect on a certain percentage of her checks.

If she accepts the check, the merchant will probably insist on one or more pieces of identification, such as a driver's license or student identification card. The purpose of the identity check is to determine whether you are who you say you are. By checking your identity, the merchant attempts to verify that the name you are signing is your real name. Of course, as we all know, identifications can be forged, so this procedure is not foolproof.

When you write a check, you are actually writing a draft on your checking account at your bank. Your **draft** is an order for your bank to pay the merchant the amount specified on the check from your account. The name of your bank usually appears on the lower left-hand corner of your check. The merchant will probably insist that your check be written on a local bank. She does this because even though you may be who you say you are, you may be writing a check on a bank that does not exist.

Even if you meet all the preceding criteria (you are who you say you are and your bank is local), the merchant still accepts the risk that you actually have an account at the bank with funds in it and that the bank is solvent. Generally, however, the merchant is not overly concerned about the quality of your bank.

When the Merchant Accepts a Check, Is She Paid?

Suppose that the merchant takes your check and gives you the goods. Has she been paid? From her point of view, the transaction is not yet complete. The merchant cannot give your check to another customer as change, nor can she give it to her suppliers as payment for goods that she purchases from them to sell to you and other customers.

To complete the transaction, she must deliver your check to her bank for deposit in her account. After she does this, her account is provisionally credited with your $100 check, but her bank must still collect the item from your account. Her bank has a "cash item in the process of collection" on the asset side of its balance sheet for the $100 check the merchant placed in her account. The provisional crediting of the merchant's account is a liability item for her bank. The funds in the merchant's account will not be released until her bank can collect the funds from your bank. The asset "cash items" is in fact a non-interest-bearing loan to your bank—and ultimately to you.

To see this, let us return to your view of the transaction. You have received your purchase and have taken it home to enjoy it. If you have a NOW account, you will earn interest on your account until the merchant's bank actually collects the money from your account. Thus you earn interest on your deposit *and* the "income" derived from the enjoyment of your purchase, because the merchant gave you the product before she actually received "good funds" from you.

Float in the Check-Clearing System

The non-interest-bearing loan the payor obtains from the merchant is called **float.** Float arises even when either or both of the parties to the transaction do not have NOW accounts. In fact, the merchant is not permitted, by law, to have a NOW account. Since she cannot receive interest on her demand deposit, she will have an incentive to keep only a small balance in her account by frequently transferring funds into an interest-bearing account. The sooner the merchant can receive the funds on checks she deposits, the sooner she can invest the money in an interest-bearing deposit overnight.

Not surprisingly, since the payor benefits from float, frequent writers of large-denomination checks spend time and money to find ways to increase the time it takes for a payee's bank to collect the funds due the payee. Payors are able to do this because checks are pieces of paper that, in the U.S. banking system, must be presented before they can be paid. This means that when the merchant takes your check to her bank, the bank must physically deliver your check to your bank before it can collect the funds. As you might imagine, the process of delivery can be quite expensive and can take a good deal of time.

The payee's and payor's banks must find a bank at which they both keep accounts in order for the payee's bank to collect the funds from the payor. The paper check must travel through this system in order for the payee to receive her money. This complex process can add considerably to float time by the judicious use of what has become known as the **remote dispersal and lock box system.**

Businesses that frequently pay by check have maintained checking accounts at banks with remote, out of the way addresses. These addresses are known as remote dispersal points. A business issues a check from a remote dispersal point to the payee, who takes it to her bank for collection. If the payee's bank does not have an account at the account payor's bank or vice versa, the payee's bank must find a third bank that has the accounts of both. If no such third bank exists, a bank must be found that holds the accounts of two banks, one of which has an account from the payee's bank and the other of which has an account from the payor's bank. Since the object is to find a remote place from which to issue checks, this has often meant that the check must travel a tortuous route to be collected.

You might expect that with such a complicated bank collection network, the payee's bank could speed up the process by sending the payor's check directly to the payor's bank. Then the tortuous route of payment would start more quickly because only the funds, rather than the check and the funds, would have to travel through the bank network until a point is reached where the two banks have an account in common or where their correspondents have an account in common. Typically, however, the payee's bank will send the payor's check through the bank network for collection. It is cheaper to ship checks in bundles than individually, and a bank generally forwards many checks to its major correspondents every business day. This means that a check must sometimes travel a long way before it is received by the payor's bank.

Of course, two can play this game, and payees have reacted by using bank accounts in many locations so that they can deposit their checks at banks that are close to the bank on which the payor has written a check. They request payors to send their checks to lock boxes in locations that vary depending on where the payor's bank is located.

Is Float a Free Loan?

The problem of float arises in the United States because the payor typically receives the goods before funds are actually collected by the payee from the payor's bank. Under normal circumstances, we would not consider the cost of float to the payee to be a real cost because she should have figured her interest expenses into her costs. Her interest cost is reflected in a higher price for goods, so she effectively charges you—and all her other customers—interest on the loan she is making you.

If a merchant buys goods (for resale) from her suppliers, she must pay interest until she pays for the goods. A merchant accepts checks because it makes her goods more salable. Since selling goods faster speeds up her inventory turnover and thus reduces interest costs on debts to suppliers, the merchant accepts the interest cost on check float. When the system is abused, however, the lost interest due to float

Box 11.1

Shortening Check Availability Schedules

The Expedited Funds Availability Act of 1987 mandated a reduction in the time it takes to make funds available on checks. It began with a 3-day availability requirement for local checks and a 7-day availability for nonlocal checks. On September 1, 1990, the availability schedule was reduced to 2 days for local checks and 5 days for nonlocal checks.

As the deadline approached for the shorter availability schedule, bankers began to complain that they do not have enough time to verify whether a check writer had sufficient funds in his or her account before they paid the check. Bankers have reported a significant increase in fraudulent checks over the past several years, and they blame tighter availability schedules as one of the causes.

While complaining, however, bankers are taking steps to reduce fraud and still meet the availability schedules. One such step is the introduction of electronic check presentment. Banks will send each other electronic files containing check information so that payor banks can begin processing check transactions before the paper checks are presented. The checks will not actually be paid until they are physically presented, but the new system should permit them to be paid immediately upon presentment rather than after they have been presented and processed.

is an unexpected loss to the payee because she did not figure it as part of her costs of accepting checks.

If the buyer had to wait until the check clears through the system to receive goods, he would have to make a second trip to the store. These trips are costly and would discourage the use of checks. Merchants would also suffer if the cost of transacting were increased in this manner. Under current law, attempts are being made to reduce the uncertainty about how long it takes to clear a check. However, banks are reluctant to speed up check clearing because they say it increases fraud (see Box 11.1). It appears that the current system has unavoidable costs that must be borne by all its users. The question then arises: Are there feasible alternatives that might have lower costs?

Alternative Assignment of Collection Risk

Let's consider the possible benefits and costs of assigning the risks of collection to the payee's bank. Under such a system, the payee's bank might discount the payor's check by the amount of the expected float and give her immediate credit for "good funds." The payee's bank would be responsible for making sure that the float costs are minimal and that the funds can be collected. If it accepts the credit risk of the check, the payee's bank will insist on being consulted before the payee takes the check.

If the payor's bank, rather than the payor, were responsible for checks written by its depositors, the payee's bank would have a lower cost of evaluating the collectibility of the check because it has more information about the soundness of other banks than it does about the payor. Under this system, the payee's bank would discount the value of the check by the interest cost of the loan during collection period, plus a premium for the risk that the payor's bank might go bankrupt.

The system does not work this way because the payor's bank would not generally want to guarantee all checks written on its accounts.[1] For example, a bank could not prevent a customer from writing a check on an account with insufficient funds. The payor's bank would want to be consulted before a merchant accepted that customer's check. The bank would want to be assured that the merchant took the same care that she would take if she were accepting the risk that the check might be uncollectible. It is more efficient to force the risk of collection onto the party that makes the credit decision. This party is the merchant.

Banks have evolved several mechanisms to reduce the risk that merchants face when accepting a check. One familiar item is the **cashier's check.** When you purchase a car, you generally will not be able to write the dealer a check as if you were buying a $100 item. The dealer would face a risk that such a large check could not be collected. He accepts your check only if your bank certifies that you have the required amount of money in your account. The check is a liability of your bank. You purchase the cashier's check by telling the bank to withdraw the required sum of money from your account and to write a bank-guaranteed check to the dealer. The dealer will probably insist that the check be drawn on a local bank.

The checking system in the United States places responsibility for payment and collection on you and the merchant, respectively. This responsibility is assigned in the Universal Commercial Code of the United States. It is an efficient assignment of liability in that it places responsibility on the parties that benefit from the system and are in the best position to judge the credit risk.

The Risk of Bank Insolvency

If the payor's bank is unsound, his bank may go bankrupt before the funds are collected. In this case, the system still holds the payor responsible for payment. The payee's responsibility for judging the quality of your bank, however, is assigned to a U.S. government agency. The overwhelming majority of U.S. depositors have

---

1. European banking systems do guarantee the checks written by payors. Access to checking accounts, however, is severely limited to the most creditworthy customers. All other deposit customers make payments through Giro accounts. In a Giro account, a depositor (the payor) orders his bank to make a transfer of funds to the payee's account in another bank. Since the payor's bank knows whether the funds are actually in the payor's account, it bears no credit risk.

their deposits insured up to $100,000 by a federal agency. Thus, if the payor's bank goes bankrupt, the payor's deposit will be safe (at least to $100,000), and the payee will be paid, as long as the payor has sufficient funds in his account. We discuss the insurance system in some detail in Chapter 19.

THE FEDERAL RESERVE IN THE CHECK-CLEARING SYSTEM

As the central banking system of the United States, the Federal Reserve provides essential services with regard to check processing. In fact, the Fed has legal responsibility for maintaining an efficient payments system. In this role, it provides check-clearing services for banks and thrifts, just like a private correspondent bank.

Banks hold balances in the form of reserves, as we discussed in Chapter 9, with the local Federal Reserve bank. (The Federal Reserve System is made up of 12 regional bank districts and a board in Washington. The local Federal Reserve bank maintains the reserve accounts of banks in its district. We describe the organization of the Federal Reserve System in detail in Chapter 19.) When bank A receives a check written on bank B, it can take that check to the Federal Reserve bank, where bank A's account will be credited for the amount of the check and bank B's account will be debited.

If a depositor at a bank in Los Angeles issues a check to a customer of a New York bank, the New Yorker deposits his check in his account, and his bank presents it to the Federal Reserve. Based on an availability schedule mandated by the Federal Reserve, the New York bank may have had its reserve account credited in 2 days, but the check may not have been presented to the bank in Los Angeles for 3 or more days. Thus the New York bank will have the funds, but the Los Angeles bank will not yet have paid the funds. In this way, the Federal Reserve creates float. (If, however, the Los Angeles bank does not honor the check, the Fed reclaims the funds from the New York bank.)

As mandated in the Monetary Control Act of 1980, the Fed must price the check-processing services it provides to banks to reflect costs and must charge interest on any float generated when collections are made later than indicated by the availability schedule. The Monetary Control Act sought to encourage competition in providing payments services. Thus it sought to have the Fed behave like a private correspondent bank in the check-clearing process.

The Fed clears about 40 percent of the checks written in the United States. Its advantage lies in its ability to handle nationwide check transactions between large cities promptly. As the preceding example indicates, if the New York bank clears through the Fed, it knows when funds will be credited to its reserve account. (It will probably not make them available to the customer, however, until the Los Angeles bank actually honors the check.) If it sent the check through a private correspondent network, it would not have this certainty.

On the other hand, banks in small cities and towns do not have easy access to a Federal Reserve bank or branch. Presentment at the Fed is expensive, so they are likely to use a private correspondent. Also, local checks can often be cleared through local clearing houses with the same availability certainty as the Fed provides.

A Diagram of the Check-Clearing Process

In Figure 11.1 we can follow the check-clearing process. The top line illustrates the paper flow *P,* and the bottom line the funds flow *F.* The process begins when the payor writes a check in step *P*1. He gives the check to the payee, who deposits it in her account (*P*2). Simultaneously, "uncollected funds" are credited to the payee's account for the amount of the check (*F*1).

The payee's bank then sends the check out for collection (*P*3). The check may go directly to the payor's bank, which "posts" it, or agrees to make payment on the check (*P*5). Often, however, the payee's bank will have sent the check through another bank acting as a clearing agent. A **clearing agent** is a bank in which both the payee bank and the payor bank have accounts so that the payor bank can pay the payee bank. The clearing agent may be the Federal Reserve or a correspondent bank. If the check goes through a clearing agent, the clearing agent forwards the check to the payor bank (*P*4).

Flow	Payor	Payee	Payee Bank	Clearing Agent	Payor Bank
Paper flow	*P*1. Prepares check	*P*2. Deposits check	*P*3. Sends check for collection	*P*4. Forwards check	*P*5. Posts check and files
Funds flow		*F*6. Can use funds	*F*1. Uncollected funds credited to payee account *F*5. Credits payee account with collected funds	*F*4. Forwards collected funds	*F*2. Debits Payor's account *F*3. Forwards collected funds

Figure 11.1 TYPICAL CHECK PAYMENT: PAPER AND FUND FLOW
Source: From *Report on Payments System,* Association of Reserve City Bankers, Washington D.C., 1982, p. 113.

When the check is posted, the payor bank debits the payor's account ($F2$). The payor bank then forwards collected funds ($F3$), either directly, if the payee bank holds an account with the payor bank, or indirectly through an agent ($F4$). The clearing agent or the payor bank credits funds to the payee bank, and the payee bank credits the account of the payee ($F5$).

CREDIT CARDS

Credit Card Approval Procedures

As indicated in Chapter 5, about 8 percent of all transactions in the United States are carried out with credit cards. There are two major interbank credit card networks—VISA and MasterCard—and several other competing networks. All of them significantly alter the pattern of risk and float found in the checking system.[2]

Suppose that you make a $100 purchase by paying with a credit card. Several months ago, you applied to your bank for a card; it ran a credit screen on you and issued a VISA or MasterCard with a credit limit of $2,000. This gives you the right to borrow up to that amount from the bank by merely using your card.

You present your credit card to the merchant, and she electronically contacts the credit card interchange system (either VISA or MasterCard) to determine whether or not the credit card has been stolen and, if it has not, whether you have been paying your bills on time. If you survive this instant credit evaluation, the merchant accepts your card as payment. You sign a receipt that contains several carbon copies—one for you, one for the merchant, and one for the bank.

Procedures by Which the Merchant Receives "Good Funds"

At the end of the day, the merchant takes the bank's copy to her bank, where it is discounted, and the merchant's account is immediately credited with the funds. Because the bank discounts the receipt, the merchant receives less than the full $100 you must pay. Here we have the first difference between the credit card system and the check system. The merchant pays for the float with a discount on your payment rather than with the interest lost as a result of the time difference between your purchase and collection.

The merchant's bank then presents its copy to the VISA or MasterCard interchange (we assume a simplified world with only two kinds of credit cards), which

2. For a good discussion of the credit card system, see William F. Baxter, "Bank Interchange of Transactional Paper: Legal and Economic Perspectives," *Journal of Law and Economics,* Vol. 26 (October 1983), pp. 541–588.

presents the receipt to your bank for payment. Your bank "buys" the loan from the merchant's bank at a premium over the price paid by the merchant's bank to the merchant but at a discount from the $100 you originally paid.

The price at which your bank purchases the receipt is established by the credit card interchange rather than by your bank. If banks posted differing prices for the purchase of the receipts of their customers, which bank's credit card is used would become important to the merchant's bank and the merchant. Since the purpose of a credit card system is to create a universally accepted form of noncurrency payment, the credit card interchanges have imposed universal pricing standards to avoid this problem.[3]

The Bank Extends Credit to the Payor

Your bank purchases the paper for less than $100 because it effectively extends a loan to you until you pay the bill. This loan appears on its balance sheet as a "revolving credit" consumer loan. Since it bills you only for the $100, it must have some method of recouping the interest on the float. It could charge you directly, but recall that the merchant is willing to pay for float if it reduces her other costs of doing business.[4] When you are billed, however, you have the option of not paying your credit card bill in full, and if you do not, you must then pay interest on your balance. See Box 11.2.

The second major difference between the credit card and the check system is that the risk of noncollection from you is removed from the shoulders of the merchant. As long as the merchant contacts the credit card interchange for approval of your credit standing, she will receive cash from her bank. If you fail to pay your bill, the bank that issued your credit card suffers the loss. When the merchant's bank discounts your receipt, it enters the loan as a "cash item in the process of collection" because your bank is responsible for payment.

Pricing of Float and Liability Assignment:
Credit Cards versus Checks

Why do the check and credit card systems differ with regard to their pricing of float and their assignment of liability for noncollection? From the merchant's point of view, the superiority of the credit card over the check begins when she turns to a centralized credit file on credit card holders before she accepts payment. This disposes her to accept credit cards for payment from customers whom she would not permit to pay by check.

---

3. *Ibid.*, pp. 576–578.
4. Sometimes merchants do not believe that credit cards reduce their overall costs, and they charge lower prices for cash.

Box 11.2

Competition in Credit Cards

A common consumer complaint about bank credit cards is that the interest rate charged on loans is high, often 18 percent or more, and that these rates do not decline when market interest rates fall. There is also a perception that credit card loans are one of the most profitable products for banks.

The high profits have attracted nonbank entrants into the credit card market. Sears has entered the market with its Discover Card, and American Express has entered with its Optima Card. (The traditional American Express Card is not technically a credit card because cardholders must pay their bills in full each month. The gold card has a credit line attached to it, but that credit line is arranged through a bank.)

American Telephone and Telegraph entered the credit card market with its Universal Card, which is a VISA or MasterCard credit card with the AT&T logo on it. (This is known as an *affinity card.*) VISA, which is owned by participating banks, decided to write new rules, effective October 8, 1990, to block nonfinancial institutions, such as AT&T, from issuing affinity cards. The new rules do not apply retroactively, so AT&T's program was not immediately threatened. However, VISA said it is reviewing this decision.

AT&T described the new rules as "anticonsumer, anticompetitive, and outrageous" (*American Banker,* October 11, 1990, p. 11). The attorneys general of 14 states also plan to investigate the new rules for anticompetitive effects.

Enhancing the value of the central credit file (and giving it credibility) is the fact that the credit card system relieves the merchant of responsibility for nonpayment. The issuing bank guarantees the payment by screening the creditworthiness of the customer beforehand. See Box 11.3. The credit card interchange, in turn, guarantees that the receipt can be presented for discount regardless of which of its member banks issued the card. For the check system to operate this way, a credit check would have to be a part of opening a checking account, as in Europe, and a system similar to the credit card interchanges would be necessary to guarantee that all bank checks are alike.

The pricing of float follows from the assignment of liability. From the merchant's point of view, the responsibility for payment of the note no longer resides with an unknown party such as the writer of a check. It immediately provides "good funds" at a discount to the merchant because the bank is much more willing to make a loan to a member of the credit card system than it is to the check writer directly.

AUTOMATED CLEARINGHOUSES

The paper check system is expensive to operate because paper checks must be separated according to destination and returned to the bank of the customer who wrote the check. Many large organizations send and receive large numbers of paper checks from individuals. For example, the U.S. government sends Social Security checks to 18 million retired Americans every month. Large private employers pay their employees at least monthly, many of them twice a month or even weekly. It costs about $0.55 to process a check, whereas the cost of sending a payment directly to the recipient's bank through electronic means is only pennies. Thus substantial savings can be achieved if payments are automated.

The institutional arrangements for electronic transfers are known as **automated clearinghouses (ACH).** They clear electronic payments in a manner analogous to

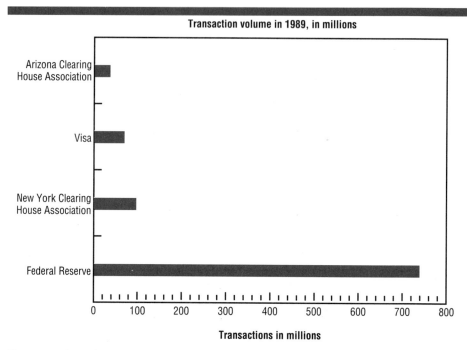

Figure 11.2 TOP COMPETITORS IN THE AUTOMATED CLEARINGHOUSE ARENA   *Source:* From *American Banker,* December 19, 1990, p. 1.

the check-clearing functions of correspondent bank networks. In 1989, about 1.3 billion transactions were completed through automated clearinghouses. Volume is growing at the rate of about 25 percent per year. Figure 11.2 presents the major providers of clearinghouse services. As you can see, the Federal Reserve is by far the largest player, with over half the market. See Box 11.4.

The Fed's share of the automated clearinghouse market is higher than its share of the check-processing market. Part of the reason for this is that the ACH market is more national in scope than the check-processing market. A large segment of the check market—consumers writing checks to pay bills—is a local market. Checks can be exchanged through a clearinghouse of local banks. ACH payments, on the other hand, are often payments by large, nationwide organizations to consumers, such as in the Social Security example. The Fed was, until recently, the only organization that provided automated clearinghouse services on a nationwide scale.

In the fall of 1990, the Fed liberalized its rules to permit VISA to become a nationwide automated clearinghouse. ACH transactions are settled among banks through reserve accounts held at Federal Reserve banks. Until this ruling, no organization could permit banks using its system to settle at any Federal Reserve bank.

For example, a bank receiving ACH payments through VISA could only receive funds through a reserve account at the Federal Reserve Bank of San Francisco, which effectively limited VISA to the West Coast market.

HOW HOUSEHOLDS MAKE PAYMENTS

It is estimated that over 85 percent of all transactions conducted in the United States are in cash. The reason is that cash transactions are the cheapest and lowest risk way for a merchant to get paid. Thus, most merchants discourage use of credit cards and checks for small transactions. A much discussed alternative to cash is the **debit card.** Will this card change the way small payments are made in the future?

A debit card can take one of two forms. One type, issued by VISA or MasterCard, looks like a credit card. When the customer buys something with a debit card, the procedures for making payment are also the same as those used for a credit card. The merchant fills out a slip and contacts a central file to verify that the card is

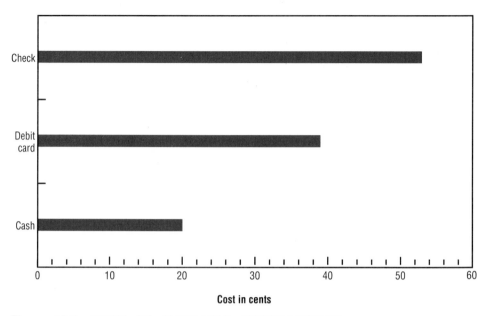

Cost in cents

Figure 11.3 COST OF HANDLING TRANSACTIONS *Source:* Adapted from "D'Agostino to Accept Debit Cards for Purchases" from *New York Times,* Saturday, May 19, 1990, p. 43.

good. However, when the merchant takes the debit card slip to the merchant's bank, the bank sends the slip to the payor's bank, just as if the payor had written a check. Upon receipt of the debit card slip, the payor's bank deducts the amount of the purchase from the payor's account. In this transaction, the customer pays for the goods as soon as the transaction is cleared rather than at the next cycle in the customer's credit card billing. Since payment is more immediate than in the case of the credit card, the loan extended to the merchant is of short duration. It only lasts as long as it takes the merchant's bank to collect funds from the payor's account.

Bank ATM cards can also be used as debit cards. The merchant has a device, similar to an ATM machine, in which the customer inserts his card. However, instead of receiving cash when he inserts his card, the customer transfers funds directly from his checking account to the merchant's checking account. The customer's account is debited at the time of the sale. Unlike the VISA and MasterCard system, no paper flow is created, and, as a result, costs are much lower.

Figure 11.3 indicates the estimated cost per transaction at a New York supermarket chain of paying by check (ATM-type), debit card, and cash. Credit card cost is missing from the data, but we can surmise that even excluding the interest cost to the merchant, it is somewhat more expensive than handling a check. Unlike

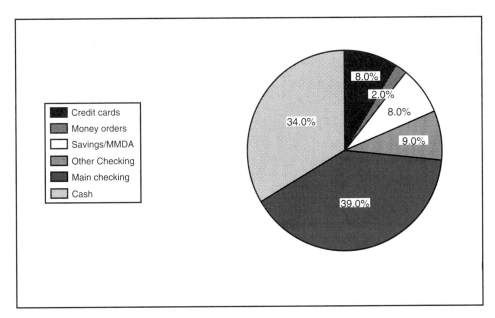

Figure 11.4   METHOD OF PAYMENT: PERCENT OF AGGREGATE HOUSEHOLD EXPENDITURES IN 1986   *Source:* From *Federal Reserve Bulletin*, Vol. 73, p. 180.

a check transaction, a credit card transaction must be verified electronically. Like a check transaction, a credit card transaction creates a piece of paper that must be processed. The merchant must take the credit card receipt to the bank to be discounted, just as she must deliver a check to a bank for processing.

Because the cost of handling cash is relatively low, merchants often discourage consumers from using noncash forms of payments for small transactions. It appears that the debit card will not change this fact. Hence the large dominance of cash in the number of transactions data is likely to continue.

In terms of the dollar volume of household transactions, cash plays a much smaller role. We base this statement on the economics of payments transactions described earlier and on some relatively old data (1986) provided in a survey of consumer payments behavior sponsored by the Federal Reserve. (Because these kinds of data must be provided by surveys, which are expensive to conduct, they cannot be as current as other data reported in this text.) The results of this survey are presented in Figure 11.4. As you can see, cash makes up only 34 percent of the total dollar volume of transactions. Note that as of 1986, debit cards were not significant enough to show up in the survey. Since then, anecdotal evidence indicates that their use has increased, but their share of the payments market is still extremely small.

CONCLUSION

In this chapter we have described the retail payments system in the United States. We have seen that for noncash transactions, payments generate loans from the payor to the payee. Thus there is credit risk in the retail payments system that is borne by banks in the case of credit cards and by payees in the case of checks. Banks and the Federal Reserve System play important roles in settling these debts.

In the next chapter we will see that the system for large payments has a very different liability structure. The Federal Reserve bears the risk for failure to settle a payment. In later chapters we will see that this has important implications for the liquidity of the U.S. financial markets.

KEY TERMS

payee

payor

credit union

draft

float

remote dispersal and lock box system

cashier's check

clearing agent

automated clearinghouses (ACH)

debit card

EXERCISES

1. What is the difference between the assignment of liability when a merchant accepts a check versus when she accepts a credit card?

2. Why do merchants accept checks rather than insisting on credit cards or cash?

3. How is the cost of float covered?

4. Describe the flow of funds and the paper flow in the check-clearing process. Assume that the payor's bank settles with the payee's bank through a correspondent.

5. Why do the banks argue that speeding up the check-clearing process will result in a greater incidence of fraud?

6. If fraud does increase with the speedup in clearing, who do you suppose will bear the cost?

7. What advantages does the Fed have over private banks in providing check-clearing services to banks?

8. American Express forces merchants to take a deeper discount on charges than VISA or MasterCard. Why do you suppose merchants accept American Express? (See Box 11.3.)

9. Should merchants be required to give a discount to cash customers?

10. Suppose credit card fraud increases. Who pays? Suppose counterfeiting increases. Who pays?

11. Organizations that routinely issue a large number of checks to the same individuals are the major users of automatic clearinghouses. What does this tell you about the relationship between fixed and variable costs in using this system?

FURTHER READING

Association of Reserve City Bankers, *Report on the Payments System,* Cambridge, Mass., Arthur D. Little, Inc., April 1982.

Baxter, William F., "Bank Interchange of Transactional Paper: Legal and Economic Perspectives," *Journal of Law and Economics,* Vol. 26 (October 1983), pp. 541–589.

Wood, John C., and Dolores S. Smith, "Electronic Transfer of Government Benefits," *Federal Reserve Bulletin,* April 1991, pp. 203–217.

CHAPTER

12

Electronic Payments Systems and the Demand for Reserves

Most payments by dollar volume are made through electronic networks. In the United States, paper checks account for 95 percent of the noncurrency payments but only 14 percent of the dollar volume. Payments on the electronic systems account for only 0.1 percent of the number of transactions but for 80 percent of the dollar volume.[1] As in the check clearing system, the Federal Reserve clears electronic payments. Unlike the check clearing system, however, the Fed's electronic system provides a guarantee on the delivery of funds sent by payors to avoid any hindrance to payment flows. That is, it assumes the risks of nonpayment. In the next several chapters we will see that the major economic impact of this policy is to increase the liquidity of the money market.

In this chapter we examine how the electronic payments systems currently operate and how different Fed policies may affect credit risk on these systems. We will also develop an example of a hypothetical private clearing system to analyze

1. See Association of Reserve City Bankers, *Report on the Payments System,* Cambridge, Mass., Arthur D. Little, Inc., 1982, p. 12.

how credit is extended and risk is managed. We then discuss how the existence of the Federal Reserve System produces different credit and risk management conventions from a private system. From this analysis, we consider the effects of various policies for controlling risk and pricing credit in Federal Reserve guaranteed systems.

LARGE DOLLAR TRANSFER NETWORKS

Large domestic payments are made electronically over **fedwire,** a system operated by the Federal Reserve. **CHIPS,** the Clearing House Interbank Payments System, a private clearing network among major international banks, is the primary international system for clearing large dollar payments. Estimated daily average transactions in 1986 were $460 billion on Fedwire, $400 billion on CHIPS, and $225 billion through the book-entry U.S. government security transfer system, which also uses Fedwire. These figures compare with a daily average of $200 billion in check transactions in 1986.[2] By 1990, the average daily volume had risen to $890 billion on CHIPS, $790 billion on fedwire, and $400 billion through the book-entry system.[3]

Payments on Fedwire

Unlike the check cashing system, little time lapses between the instant a signal is sent to execute a payment on Fedwire and the moment at which "good" funds arrive in the payee's account. Fedwire is used for such transfers as fed funds transactions, interbank settlement payments, and large corporate payments.

For example, suppose a large corporation receives a major shipment of equipment and directs its bank to pay the supplier. The bank sends an electronic signal to the supplier's bank notifying it of the payment. It also sends a message to the Federal Reserve ordering payment into the account of the payee's bank and a debiting of its own account. The Fed makes these accounting transactions immediately; at the same time, it notifies the receiving bank that a payment has been credited to its account.

A major difference between the fedwire transaction and check payment is in the assignment of credit risk. In the check cashing system, the liability for payment falls only on the payor. If the payor has insufficient funds in his account to cover the check, the payee will not be paid, and she must sue the payor to collect the funds. In the Fedwire transaction, the Federal Reserve guarantees the supplier's bank

2. See T. Belton, M. Gelfand, D. Humphrey, and J. Marquardt, "Daylight Overdrafts and Payments System Risk," *Federal Reserve Bulletin,* November 1987, p. 846.

3. See Bruce J. Summers, "Clearing and Payments Systems: The Role of the Central Bank," *Federal Reserve Bulletin,* February 1991, pp. 81–91.

that it will have good funds in its Fed account, even if the corporation's bank fails to provide good funds.

Payments over CHIPS

CHIPS, a private clearing system comprising about 150 international banks, is operated by the New York Clearing House Association. Payments on CHIPS consist mostly of foreign exchange transactions involving dollars and Eurodollar payments. (Eurodollars are dollars held in banks overseas. We will discuss them in Chapter 15.) Payments messages are sent to a central CHIPS computer, and settlement occurs at the end of the day. On CHIPS, good funds do not arrive in the payee's account until all payment orders are cleared at the end of each day. Thus payments on CHIPS are less final than payments on Fedwire. Since 1990, member banks on CHIPS have collectively guaranteed that payment orders will be settled, so payments orders are now effectively treated as if they were good funds.

RISK BEARING IN ELECTRONIC PAYMENTS

The Bank of New York Computer Crash

The payments problems of the Bank of New York (BONY) on November 21, 1985 demonstrate the scope of the risk that the Fed takes in operating the electronic payments system. Although BONY is a member of the New York Clearing House Association and does a major payments business clearing transactions for the securities markets, it had assets at that time of only $15 billion. This factor helped trigger what could have been a major financial crisis because of a computer software malfunction.

To understand BONY's problems, we must understand how securities transactions are cleared on Fedwire. Fedwire is used to transfer U.S. government securities from one owner's account to another. Most U.S. government securities do not assume the form of paper certificates. Rather, they are simply electronic bookkeeping entries on a computer that have no physical manifestation.

This is known as the **book-entry system.** For example, a person who buys a T-bill may receive a receipt indicating the purchase, but the receipt cannot be traded—only the electronic entry can be transferred across accounts.

How do these entries change when a transaction occurs? Figure 12.1 illustrates the process. If dealer B, who banks at the Bank of New York, buys a T-bill from dealer A for $900,000, dealer A sends a message to clearing bank X ordering it to deliver a T-bill to dealer B.

Bank X has a securities account at the New York Federal Reserve Bank, where most securities transactions take place. Bank X tells the Fed to move a T-bill from

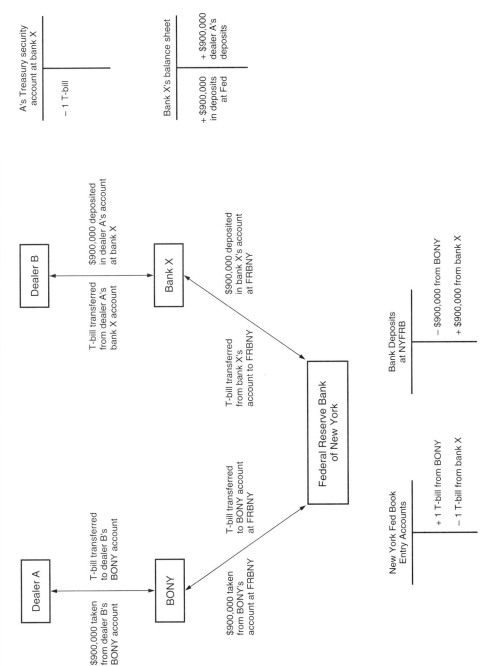

Figure 12.1 FEDWIRE MESSAGES AND BALANCE SHEET ENTRIES FOR A TREASURY SECURITY TRANSACTION

bank X's securities account to the securities account of the Bank of New York. The order to transfer securities goes out over Fedwire. The New York Fed then places a credit for a T-bill in the Bank of New York's securities account.

Simultaneously, the New York Fed reduces BONY's reserve account (BONY's deposits at the Fed) by $900,000 and increases bank X's reserve account at the Fed by the same amount. Bank X will then credit dealer A's deposit account. This is the typical sort of book-entry security transaction that takes place every day.[4]

On the day of BONY's crisis, there were 36,000 such transactions, and these overwhelmed the computer software that BONY had established to clear its securities transactions. Somehow the program did not keep track of which of BONY's customers were supposed to receive the securities that the bank was receiving in transfer. The Fed had transferred securities in and transferred cash out of BONY's accounts. Since the payments from the customers' accounts at BONY or from other banks for the securities they purchased could be made only after the securities were delivered to the customer's account at BONY and other banks, BONY was accumulating a huge net debit position relative to the Fed. In essence, it was buying securities and effecting payment by making huge overdrafts on its account at the Fed. An **overdraft** is a payment in excess of the amount on deposit.

Normally, such overdrafts would clear out by the end of the day as the bank received payments from its customers after BONY delivered the securities. By the end of November 21, 1985, however, the malfunction was still not corrected. At 1 A.M., the Fed decided that it was unable to straighten out the overdraft problem. The Fed was forced to make an overnight loan from the discount window of $22.6 billion to BONY. The next day BONY finally solved the computer problem, completed the transactions, and paid off the loan. In the meantime, the Fed had made a loan exceeding 10 percent of the monetary base, far larger than any other loan in its history. In this case, the Fed did not hesitate to undertake the loan because it knew that BONY was sound and that the problem arose from a computer problem. Also, the loan was collateralized by $36 billion in securities.[5]

Nevertheless, this computer problem cost BONY several million dollars for the overnight loan. More important, it signalled that serious problems could materialize in the payments system.

Controlling the Fed's Credit Risk and Intraday Lending on Fedwire

Before 1986, the Federal Reserve did not control the extent of daylight overdrafts by its member banks. Starting in 1992, the Federal Reserve will explicitly charge

---

4. For details of these actions, see Marcia Stigum, *After the Trade* (Homewood, Ill.: Dow Jones–Irwin, 1988).

5. The legality of the Fed's claim on the securities as collateral was not clear.

banks for the credit risk it bears in fedwire transactions. The BONY example should convince you that this credit risk can be substantial; because of rapid growth of system use, the daylight overdrafts of all banks now reach peaks of $50 billion at some period during each day, which amounts to about 20 percent of the assets on the Fed's overnight balance sheet.

The Fed has attempted to control the amount of credit risk it assumes for individual users of the system by limiting the size of a bank's overdraft on CHIPS and on Fedwire. Known as a participant's **sender net debit cap,** this limit depends on a bank's capital.[6] A participant that reaches the overdraft limit is not permitted to make further payments until incoming receipts reduce the overdraft.

A PRIVATE CLEARING SYSTEM

Before the Federal Reserve came into existence in 1914, clearinghouses were privately owned by groups of banks. The largest and most powerful clearinghouse was the New York Clearing House Association. This association of New York banks still exists, but it is a pale copy of its former self, at least domestically; the Federal Reserve has replaced it as the major force in large domestic payments. Nevertheless, to understand the current system of electronic payments, it is helpful to consider a hypothetical example of how a private electronic clearing system operates.

Private clearing systems exist in many securities markets, as well as in banking. These include stock markets, options and futures markets, and foreign exchange markets. In these markets, well-defined groups of participants undertake numerous, mostly offsetting trades during any given day. End-of-day clearing and settlement procedures are established, eliminating the need for cash payment with every deal. Only the net payments need then be sent over electronic payment systems.[7]

Our model system consists of three banks, A, B, and C, whose balance sheet is given in Table 12.1. They each have assets that consist of $9.5 billion in loans and $500 million in an item called *reserves*. Reserves are good funds; they are a

Table 12.1 BALANCE SHEET FOR BANKS A, B, AND C* ($MILLIONS)

ASSETS		LIABILITIES	
Reserves	500	Deposits	9,500
Loans	9,500	Capital	500

*Each bank has the same balance sheet.

6. Formally, it depends on a bank's risk-based primary capital, which we discuss in detail in Chapter 19.

7. For a description of clearing and settlement systems in stock, options, and futures markets, see Securities and Exchange Commission, *The October 1987 Market Break* (Washington, D.C.: U.S. Government Printing Office, 1988).

mutually agreed upon means of making payments among the group. We will assume that these reserves are in the form of currency. The liability side consists of $9.5 billion in deposits at each bank, and $500 million in bank capital provides the balancing item.

A Feasible Sequence of Payments with Continuous Settlement

Now let's assume that a sequence of payment orders is sent and received among the three banks for their customers as follows: Bank B sends $1 billion to bank A, bank C sends $900 million to bank B, and bank A sends $500 million to bank C. The payments are depicted in Figure 12.2a.

Settlement for these payments is made continuously. By **continuous settlement,** we mean that each payment message for a given amount is physically accompanied by an identical amount of actual reserves. However, bank B clearly cannot execute the first payment signal by delivery of actual reserves because it holds only $500 million in reserves, just half the $1 billion it needs to transfer to bank A. It can execute the payment by borrowing $500 million in reserves from another bank, however. We assume that bank A lends the funds and physically delivers them to bank B. Now bank B can execute its payment order by delivery of good funds.

The new balance sheets of banks A and B at the moment after the transaction are presented in Table 12.2. Notice that deposits at bank B have fallen by $1 billion, the value of the funds transferred. On the asset side, reserves have fallen to zero,

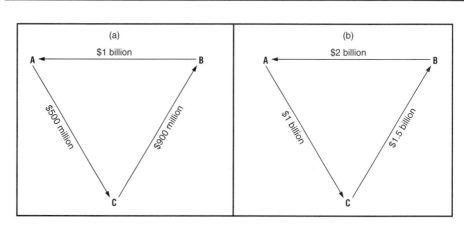

Figure 12.2 TRANSACTIONS AMONG CLEARING SYSTEM MEMBERS

Table 12.2 BALANCE SHEETS FOR BANKS A AND B ($MILLIONS)

Bank A				Bank B			
ASSETS		**LIABILITIES**		**ASSETS**		**LIABILITIES**	
Reserves	1,000	Deposits	10,500	Reserves	0	Deposits	8,500
Loans	9,500	Capital	500	Loans	9,500	Due to A	500
Due from B	500					Capital	500

but this has reduced assets by only $500 million, less than the decline in deposits. The difference is made up by a liability item for $500 million called a "due to bank A." Bank A now has an additional $1 billion in deposits, but only $500 million in additional reserves. The remaining assets are accounted for as a "due from" item that represents bank A's loan to bank B.

We assume that the remaining payments go through in sequence. Bank B's receipt of $900 million in reserves from bank C permits it to pay off its loan from bank A by the end of the day. The end-of-day balance sheets of the three banks are presented in Table 12.3. Notice that the amount of loans has not fallen from what it was in the morning—$9.5 billion at each bank. Also, the amount of capital at each bank is the same as it was. The distribution of deposits is different, however. Bank A has grown by $500 million in deposits and has increased its reserves by the same amount. The other two banks have gotten smaller by $500 million each. Total reserves in the system are still the same, but they have been redistributed across the three banks.

An Infeasible Sequence of Payments with Continuous Settlement

Starting with the balance sheet of the three banks represented in Table 12.1, a different sequence of payment orders arrives as follows: Bank B sends $2 billion to bank A, bank C sends bank B $1.5 billion, and bank A sends bank C $1 billion. These payments are depicted in Figure 12.2b.

Bank B sends its payment message to bank A along with the $500 million it holds in reserves. To effect a continuous settlement, however, it must send along an additional $1.5 billion in reserves. It asks to borrow the additional $1.5 billion in reserves from bank A. Bank A replies that it has insufficient reserves to cover the whole loan and suggests that if bank B wants the payment to go through, it should borrow the additional reserves from bank C. Bank C has only $500 million in reserves, however. The system holds insufficient reserves to effect settlement of all three payments messages. In such a situation, the payments system is said to be **gridlocked.**

Table 12.3 BALANCE SHEETS FOR BANKS A, B, AND C ($MILLIONS)

Bank A

ASSETS		LIABILITIES	
Reserves	1,000	Deposits	10,000
Loans	9,500	Capital	500

Bank B

ASSETS		LIABILITIES	
Reserves	400	Deposits	9,400
Loans	9,500	Capital	500

Bank C

ASSETS		LIABILITIES	
Reserves	100	Deposits	9,100
Loans	9,500	Capital	500

Consequences of a Switch to Continuous Net Settlement

The three banks can avoid this problem by increasing the amount of reserves each holds. This would involve selling loans to other banks or to investors in return for reserves. Of course, by doing this the banks would sacrifice some of their interest income, and the return on deposits or capital would fall. To avoid the necessity of increasing reserves, the three banks might instead decide to engage in **continuous net settlement** with each other. They would simply pay the difference between total payments and total receipts.

As a more binding arrangement, they can form a clearinghouse for the purpose of executing the net settlement. All reserves might be transferred to the clearinghouse.

The net reserve positions of the three banks after the last sequence of payments messages is as follows: Bank B owes $500 million, bank C owes $500 million, and bank A is owed $1 billion. The amount of reserves is sufficient to cover the transfers, and there is no need for interbank borrowing of reserves. Bank A has grown by $1 billion in deposits and reserves. Banks B and C have shrunk by the sum of this amount and hold no reserves. The banks gain from continuous net settlement in that they avoid holding additional reserves while processing these much larger payments.

Periodic Net Settlement

Even with continuous net settlement, however, reserve holdings may be inadequate to effect all payments. In the preceding example, we have assumed that payment orders are sent out simultaneously. If the customer of bank B directed his bank to pay $2 billion to bank A before bank B was notified that it would receive a payment, the system would not have enough reserves to make the payment because there would be no incoming payment to net against this transfer. Bank B would then be forced to delay its payment.

To solve this problem, the banks could move to **periodic net settlement.** They might choose to make net settlement at the end of the day. Then bank B would be able to net its $2 billion payment against a receipt of $1.5 billion sent later in the day.

What is sacrificed by the decision to settle net at the end of the day rather than to net continuously? To answer this question, let's look at the early morning balance sheets of banks A and B, just after bank B has sent its morning message that it intends to pay $2 billion to bank A. The balance sheets of banks A and B are depicted in Table 12.4. Bank B still technically has $9.5 billion in deposits because no payment has been made. Likewise, it still holds $500 million in reserves. It has a "due to" item on the liability side equal to the $2 billion it has agreed to deliver to bank A

Table 12.4   BALANCE SHEETS FOR BANKS A AND B ($MILLIONS)

Bank A				Bank B			
ASSETS		**LIABILITIES**		**ASSETS**		**LIABILITIES**	
Reserves	500	Deposits	9,500	Reserves	500	Deposits	9,500
Loans	9,500	Due to		Loans	9,500	Due to A	2,000
Due from B	2,000	customer	2,000	Due from		Capital	500
		Capital	500	customer	2,000		

at the end of the day. Thus it has $12 billion in combined liabilities and net worth. On the asset side, it has an item we will call "due from own customer" of $2 billion, indicating that the customer will lose $2 billion of his deposits upon settlement. Bank A also has increased in size by $2 billion. It has a $2 billion "due to" its own customer on the liability side and a $2 billion "due from" bank B on the asset side. As further payment messages are processed, the daytime balance sheets of the banks all expand in a similar manner.

Length of the Settlement Period

Banks do not choose continuous settlement because it requires more reserves than an end-of-day settlement scheme. If this is so, however, why not choose a settlement period equal to 1 year or even a decade?

The reason is that a bank with net "due to's" may change its behavior between settlement periods, thereby presenting the payee banks with a riskier position than they had originally anticipated when they agreed to participate in a payments system with the payor. This is the same moral hazard issue raised in Chapter 3 in connection with insurance. A payee bank can reduce this problem in dealing with payor banks by shortening the time between settlements. Thus a tension between the speed of the payments system and the extent of settlement risk determines the settlement time.

This is illustrated in Figure 12.3. Time is represented on the horizontal axis. The opportunity cost of settling sooner rather than later is represented on the vertical axis. As the period between settlements increases, the opportunity cost of holding reserves declines because fewer reserves must be held to effect settlement. On the other hand, the chances of a member failing to settle increase with time. Thus the expected loss from member failure is an increasing function of time. The vertical axis, therefore, also represents the expected loss from settling later rather than sooner. The length of the settlement period is determined where the marginal cost of failure equals the marginal opportunity cost of reserve holdings.

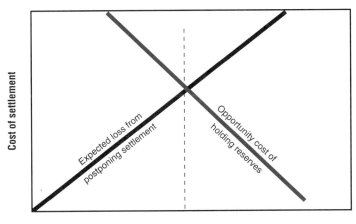

Length of settlement period (time)

Figure 12.3   DETERMINING THE LENGTH OF THE SETTLEMENT PERIOD

Settlement When Reserves Are Inadequate

Consider the occasional situation in which reserves in the clearinghouse are inadequate to cover the net "due to's" at settlement time. The members must establish rules to determine how net positions are to be settled. One method of doing this is to force net debtors into the open market to purchase additional reserves. Another method would be to increase the length of the settlement period when reserves are inadequate.

The latter method might be executed as follows: Members of the clearinghouse might be required to hold low–risk commercial paper as secondary reserves. When their regular reserves are inadequate, members could satisfy their net "due to" positions by selling the commercial paper to members with net "due from" positions. This commercial paper would be redeemed by the seller for reserves at the end of the next settlement period.

Reserve Requirements and the Pricing of Guarantees

We have assumed throughout that the clearinghouse, not the individual banks, credibly guarantees delivery of reserves at the end of the day. As one way to carry out this pledge, the clearinghouse can impose reserve requirements against net

Table 12.5 BALANCE SHEETS FOR BANKS A, B, AND C ($MILLIONS)

(a) Start of Day

Bank A

ASSETS		LIABILITIES	
Reserves	500	Deposits	5,000
Loans	4,595		

Bank B

ASSETS		LIABILITIES	
Reserves	300	Deposits	3,000
Loans	2,700		

Bank C

ASSETS		LIABILITIES	
Reserves	200	Deposits	2,000
Loans	1,800		

(b) End of Day

Bank A

ASSETS		LIABILITIES	
Reserves	600	Deposits	6,000
Loans	4,500		
Due from B and C	900		

Bank B

ASSETS		LIABILITIES	
Reserves	250	Deposits	2,500
Loans	2,700	Due to A	450

Bank C

ASSETS		LIABILITIES	
Reserves	150	Deposits	1,500
Loans	1,800	Due to A	450

positive "due to's" summed across banks, with the reserves physically held at the clearinghouse.

There can be no failure to deliver reserves at the next settlement as long as positive net "due to" positions summed across banks do not exceed the total amount of reserves in the system because the reserves act as collateral to guarantee delivery of good funds against "due to" positions. *The cost of this guarantee is the forgone interest on the reserves.* The higher the reserve requirement, the more secure is the promise to deliver reserves, but the higher too is the cost of the guarantee.

A Bank Failure in a Clearinghouse System with Reserve Requirements

How does the clearinghouse system guarantee delivery of payments in the event of a bank failure, and how is the cost of failure allocated? Table 12.5 presents the start-of-day balance sheets of three banks that are part of a clearinghouse. The clearinghouse imposes a 10-percent reserve requirement on deposit liabilities. Payments orders are sent and received during the day, as they were in Figure 12.2b.

If there were no bank failure, the end-of-day balance sheets would look as they do in Table 12.5b. Each would hold reserves equal to 10 percent of deposits, and bank A, holding excess reserves as a result of the payments sequence, would supply the reserves to the other two banks through the interbank market.

Now assume that bank C is bankrupt at settlement. The clearinghouse has $1,000 million in reserves, so all payments are feasible (see Table 12.6). At settlement, however, bank A refuses to lend the $450 million that bank C needs to settle the day's payments. Does this imply that payments messages cannot go through? First, bank C does not need the full $450 million to satisfy its net "due to" position. It needs only $300 million (its net "due to" less the reserves held at the clearinghouse).

The clearinghouse delivers the $300 million from its reserve account. To see how this happens, consider the clearinghouse's balance sheet after settlement (Table 12.6). Banks A and B settle as before. Bank B pays $50 million in reserves to bank A and covers the rest of its obligation with a "due to." In effect, it borrows $450 million in reserves from bank A and then returns the reserves as payment. The

Table 12.6 CLEARINGHOUSE'S BALANCE SHEETS ($MILLIONS)

Clearinghouse Before Settlement				Clearinghouse After Settlement			
ASSETS		LIABILITIES		ASSETS		LIABILITIES	
Good funds	1,000	Due to A	500	Good funds	1,000	Due to A	750
		Due to B	300			Due to B	250
		Due to C	200				

Table 12.7 BALANCE SHEETS FOR BANKS A AND B ($MILLIONS)

Bank A				Bank B			
ASSETS		LIABILITIES		ASSETS		LIABILITIES	
Reserves	750	Deposits	6,000	Reserves	250	Deposits	2,500
Loans	4,500			Loans	2,700	Due to A	600
Due from B	600	Capital	−150			Capital	−150

clearinghouse transfers bank C's $200 million to bank A's account, but it still owes bank A $300 million.

To pay the additional $300 million, the clearinghouse assesses the two remaining member banks for the funds. Assuming that the two banks own equal shares in the clearinghouse, they each pay $150 million. Bank B borrows an additional $150 million from bank A and delivers these funds back to bank A's account. This implies that bank B has acquired a liability without creating an asset. It has negative net worth and must raise $150 million in equity (see Table 12.7).

Bank A's balance sheet is also displayed in Table 12.7. It now has a due from bank B of $600 million, but this is not sufficient to make up for its loss from the failure of bank C to deliver funds. Therefore, bank A's liabilities also exceed its assets, and it must raise equity as well.

The clearinghouse system ensured that all payments went through, but it could not prevent a loss to other banks because the net "due to" position of bank C exceeded bank C's reserves. Nevertheless, the clearinghouse and its members finished in a better position than other creditors for two reasons. First, the clearinghouse could seize the reserves that were an asset of bank C and deny them to other creditors. Second, members were able to net their "due from's" against their "due to's." Thus members were, in effect, given prior claim on their claims on bank C over other creditors. For example, depositors had no claim on bank A's $1,000 liability to bank C. See Box 12.1.

THE ROLE OF BANK CAPITAL AND THE PRICING OF DEPOSITS

Bank capital, or net worth, need not play any direct role in the liquidity guarantee at settlement time. If banks lend reserves to each other by discounting certain assets on the borrower's balance sheet, the lending bank will be indifferent to the size of the net worth of the borrowing bank. The depositors of the borrowing bank will

Box 12.1

The Panamanian Banking Crisis:
Putting a Squeeze on Clearing*

In early 1988, the U.S. government attempted to press the overthrow of the Panamanian regime controlled by General Manuel Noriega by attacking the Panamanian banking system. Panama was particularly vulnerable to U.S. financial attack because its banking system and, indeed, its currency are based on the use of dollars. Thus payments of good funds must take the form either of a delivery of U.S. dollar currency or an electronic funds transfer that must ultimately pass through the U.S. banking system. Private Panamanian banks maintained dollar reserve deposit accounts for settlement purposes with the Banco Nacional de Panama (BNP), the central bank under the control of Noriega. The BNP did not hold these deposits in the form of dollar bills. Rather, it held them as interest-bearing deposits in several large New York banks.

To take advantage of this situation, the U.S. House of Representatives on March 2, 1988, in Concurrent Resolution No. 257, stated that "the Board of Governors of the Federal Reserve System should take such steps as may be necessary to prevent electronic funds transfers between financial institutions in the Republic of Panama and financial institutions in the United States. . . ." The Federal Reserve froze $54 million in BNP funds in the United States on March 3, 1988. The BNP and the entire Panamanian banking system then lacked the good funds necessary for settlement of payments. The Panamanian banking system closed down unofficially on March 2, 1988 and officially on March 5, 1988. The banking system was severely disrupted for many months. Only in November of 1988 were clearing and settlement reestablished through the use of BNP dollar deposits made in a German bank willing to defy the Federal Reserve blockade.

*Source: Details of the Panamanian banking crisis can be found in Laura Flores and Anamae Maduro, *The Panamanian Banking System Under Crisis: Causes and Effects,* unpublished Ph.D. thesis, Brown University, April 1989.

care, however, because the discounted liquid assets will be unavailable to them in the event of bankruptcy. In fact, if the interbank payment market requires discounting of high-quality assets, bank lenders effectively have priority over depositors in bankruptcy.

This brings us to the impact of the value of clearinghouse membership on the pricing of deposits of member banks. The clearinghouse system is a guarantee of credit arising only in payments transactions among members. It has nothing to do with the riskiness of deposits at member banks; it affects only the reliability of promises to deliver funds into those accounts.

Thus a bank may hold a very risky loan portfolio, have a low capital-to-asset ratio, and still meet the reserve and asset requirements of the clearinghouse. Payments to and from the depositors of other clearinghouse banks will be made without differentiation because they are guaranteed by the collateral of the clearinghouse. In the event of bankruptcy, however, the depositors of the risky bank are in danger of losing their funds. The clearinghouse will take the good assets to satisfy any net "due to's" owed the clearinghouse, and the depositors will take the remainder. In addition, transactions between the depositors of the risky bank and nonclearinghouse members are not collateralized, so risk premiums will be very large.

Caps and Pricing of Net "Due To's"

The clearinghouse can require that its members deposit sufficient reserves to cover nominal overdrafts. Since the reserve deposits must occur *before* payments messages are sent, they do not limit the total net "due to" position of an individual bank on any given day, as we saw with the failure of bank C. Thus individual banks are unconstrained in the amount of risk they may impose on the payment system. To limit this risk, the clearinghouse may place a **cap**, or ceiling, on the amount of net "due to's" outstanding at any time. To discourage overdrafts within the cap, it may also charge a fee on overdraft use and pay out the fee to creditor banks with net "due from's." The fee compensates the creditor banks for bearing disproportional credit risks in the payment system.

THE FEDERAL RESERVE AS A CLEARINGHOUSE

The most obvious difference between the powers of the Federal Reserve and those of a private clearinghouse is that the Federal Reserve creates reserves while the clearinghouse must buy them. In addition, the member banks of a private clearinghouse bear the burden of individual bank failure, whereas in the Federal Reserve system the consequences of failure are borne by the Federal Reserve. Do these differences affect our conclusions about the operation of the payments system? See Box 12.2.

The Equivalence of Fed Practice to End-of-Day Settlement

In accounting for a payments system transaction during the day, the Fed deducts the amount of the payment from the payor bank's deposit account at the Federal Reserve and credits it to the payee bank's account. Since any overdrafts in a bank's account must be extinguished at the end of the day, any additions to bank deposits

Box 12.2

Clearing in the European Currency Unit

The European currency unit, or ecu, is an imaginary currency created from a basket of European currencies. It is imaginary because no physical representation, or ecu cash, exists, and there is no ecu central bank to supply ecu reserves to banks. Yet payments are made in ecu bank deposits, and these payments are settled through a clearinghouse with 45 member banks in 10 European countries, known as MESA (Mutual Ecu Settlement Account). The Bank for International Settlement (BIS) acts as the settlement bank for the group, but it does not guarantee settlement.

The BIS keeps track of each member bank's "due to" and "due from" positions during the day. At settlement, banks with a net "due to" position borrow from those with a net "due from" position to settle their accounts. "Due to's" must equal "due from's" because it is a closed system—that is, settlement is only effected among the member banks.

To effect settlement, banks with net "due from" positions must lend to those with net "due to" positions. Banks with a surplus of ecu payments are, in reality, merely holding the deficits of other members as assets. To see why this is so, compare the ecu settlement to the alternative available in a private clearinghouse that holds reserves. If no bank wants to lend reserves to a bank with a net "due to" position, the clearinghouse makes good that bank's net "due to's" by delivering reserves from the clearinghouse's reserve account. Thus the banks with a net "due from" position have a choice as to which asset they want to hold— the "due from's" of the deficit banks or the reserves held by the clearinghouse.

In a clearing system run by a central bank that guarantees settlement, such as Fedwire, the members have, in effect, the option of forcing the central bank to make good the "due to's" of any member. The central bank can do this by creating reserves and lending them through the discount window.

In the ecu clearing system, member banks with net "due from" positions cannot demand ecu reserves because there are no ecu reserves. Nevertheless, they can force a deficit member to deliver reserves of the basic European currencies that make up the ecu. However, doing this would be so time-consuming that settlement could not be effected at the end of the day. Therefore, provisions in the rules state that the position of a bank that cannot find a lender will be "unwound." This means that the offending bank would have all its payments sent and all its payments received canceled. The remaining banks would settle as if the offending member were not a member.

at the Fed arising through payments operations disappear at settlement. Hence they are not reserves of the banking system and are not counted as satisfying the Fed's reserve requirement. Only the amount of deposits in a bank's account at the end of the day are counted as part of the bank's required reserves against its own deposit liabilities. Therefore, the Fed mixes together two different types of "deposits" in tracking daytime deposit accounts: those with a transitory daytime existence and those permanent entries which survive settlement. The standard term for the latter is *reserves*. The former are a particular accounting treatment of net "due to's."

Let's consider an alternative Fed accounting convention. Suppose that the Fed does not adjust entries in member bank deposit accounts during the day. Instead, it keeps track of every payment and receipt of the member banks, labeling them "due to's" and "due from's," respectively. In this accounting convention, the Fed guarantees that it will pay each bank's "due from's" by crediting its Fed deposit account with an equal amount of reserves at the end of the day. It will also debit each bank's deposit account by the amount of its "due to's" at the end of the day. Any bank with negative deposits at the end of the day must immediately extinguish them by acquiring reserves from other banks in the overnight market.

The behavior of the member banks would be identical under both accounting conventions. Their accumulating receipts are now called "due from's" and not credits to deposits, but since payment in reserves is guaranteed, banks accept them as if they were reserves. Their accumulating payments are called "due to's" rather than debits from deposits. Their obligations and end-of-day balance sheets, however, are identical under both accounting conventions. Similarly, the end-of-day balance sheets and the risk position of the Fed are identical under the two accounting methods. The only difference in the two methods arises in the accounting names that are given to the payments transactions.

The alternative accounting convention is identical to the accounting method for end-of-day settlement used by the clearinghouse we studied in the preceding section, except that transaction records are now continuously recorded and centralized in the Federal Reserve. The Federal Reserve payments system under current practice therefore is an end-of-day settlement system.

The Reliability and Cost of the Fed's Guarantee

How reliable are the guarantees under the Federal Reserve and the private clearinghouse, and how should they be valued? With the private clearinghouse, the guarantee is only as good as the reserves on hand. The price of the guarantee then equals the forgone interest on the reserves held to fulfill the requirement. Introducing an institution like the Federal Reserve, which can create reserves, removes the limitation on the guarantee. The unlimited guarantee is clearly more valuable to the banks and their customers than the limited one, but how can we measure this difference? One way is to consider a transaction in the government securities market as an example. Under a private clearinghouse regime, a dealer who sells securities to a bank early in the morning cannot be absolutely certain that he will receive good funds into his bank account at the end of the day. Since he incurs some risk of not receiving good funds, he will sell securities at a higher price before settlement than at settlement as compensation for bearing the risk. The difference in price will be smaller, the higher the reserve requirements are at the clearinghouse.[8] The difference in price does not reflect the presence of an interest rate on "due from's" but only a premium for bearing the risk that the bank buying the security may not be able to deliver good funds. In fact, the risk premium has the opposite effect on the price demanded by the seller than the existence of an interest rate would have, since an interest rate would require a discounted price, whereas the risk adds a premium to the price.

With introduction of the Federal Reserve, the delivery of good funds to the dealer's bank account is not in doubt, so the security price will be the same at the beginning of the day as its expected price at settlement. The gain accrues to the bank or its customers, because they can buy the security at a lower price than they would otherwise.

Pricing the Fed's Guarantee

One way to make the bank pay for this benefit, as we have seen, lies in imposing reserve requirements. The private clearinghouse could provide a risk-free guarantee only by increasing the level of reserve requirements to 100 percent on net "due to" positions. The Fed can follow a similar policy. Another way would be to charge a risk premium for overdraft use. This would compensate the Fed if it ever took a loss from overdrafts.

In the private clearinghouse example, a risk premium is incorporated into securities prices because no one can be certain of settlement. If the clearinghouse cannot make good a delivery of reserves on a net "due to" position, the receiving bank is under no obligation to make good the payment due its customer. No Federal Reserve risk pricing scheme, short of charging the same price as the private clearinghouse, would charge for an absolute guarantee (that is, 100-percent reserve coverage of net "due to's"), can duplicate this outcome as long as the Federal Reserve absolutely guarantees payments.

In 1992, the Federal Reserve will impose a policy of charging the buyer's bank for an intraday overdraft, but it will not permit banks with excess reserves (that is, a large accumulation of "due from's") to earn the premium paid by the banks incurring overdrafts. As a price for imposing risk on the system, this seems appropriate because the Fed bears the risk of failure, not the banks with excess reserves. Eventually, the Fed will charge 25 basis points (0.25 percent) on a bank's average daily overdraft, not giving credit for periods with excess reserves. In Chapter 13, we comment on the question of whether the Fed needs to charge for risk at all, beyond the current level of reserve requirements.

At this writing, Fed policy has yet to be implemented. However, the imposition

---

8. Whether the price actually is higher in the morning than in the afternoon just before settlement depends on whether the marketplace can perceive any intraday deterioration in the quality of the clearinghouse guarantee.

The Fed will implement its charge for intraday overdrafts in the spring of 1992. To get ready for this policy, banks must make a decision as to when and how to charge their customers for the use of overdrafts. The issue hinges partly on posting times—that is, on when the Fed credits banks for incoming checks cleared through the Fed and ACH (automated clearinghouse; see Chapter 11) payments. Retail banks tend to accumulate relatively large "due from" positions with the Fed from incoming checks and ACH payments. The Fed intends to post these items to bank reserve accounts early in the day. These payments are usually large enough to offset "due to" positions accumulated over fedwire in the afternoon. Thus retail banks, usually the smaller banks, will probably be unaffected by the policy.

However, the story is entirely different for money-center banks. The Fed will allow a net "due to" position of up to 10 percent of capital before it charges for overdrafts. However, these money-center banks often have net "due to" positions equal to their capital, and they must decide if and how they will charge their customers. As the bankers see it, the main problem is how to identify which customer is responsible for the overdraft.

An economist sees the problem somewhat differently. If the Fed's policy is effective—that is, if banks do not postpone all payments to the last minute—it will have made overdraft space scarce. This creates a market price for that space. A two-price system should evolve—those who demand immediate execution of payments and those who are willing to wait. The customers demanding immediacy should pay the cost of the overdraft, regardless of the actual state of overdrafts when the payment is made. The price for immediate execution will depend on the probability of exceeding the cap at any time after the payment is made. Those not demanding immediacy should not be charged for the space.

Competition among banks will spread payments evenly across banks in proportion to their capital. Thus, in the end, the price for space will be the same at all banks.

of a risk surcharge is likely to generate several responses. First, transactions will be driven from fedwire onto other payments systems. Second, securities market participants will attempt to postpone any Fedwire payments until the end of the day, generating a queuing solution. Why? A securities dealer will be unwilling to pay the 25 basis points at the beginning of the day if he can buy a security at the end of the day without paying the Fed's overdraft premium. The bank will be unwilling to bear the cost of the premium either. Large numbers of transactions will thus pile up at settlement time, and the Federal Reserve might have to charge peak-load pricing on Fedwire to spread transactions more evenly across the day. See Box 12.3.

Besides charging for overdraft risk, the Federal Reserve limits the size of the net overdraft position of any one institution, since the credit quality of the recipient of the guarantee can deteriorate as the size of the net guarantee increases. In addition, an institution may take other actions during the day that increase the exposure of the Federal Reserve but that the Fed cannot monitor.

CREDIT RISK ON CHIPS

The Clearing House Interbank Payments System, or CHIPS, is primarily used for Eurodollar and foreign exchange transactions, dollar transactions not arising domestically between U.S. banks. Most foreign banks are not part of the Federal Reserve system and therefore lack access to Fedwire, which is used for domestic wire transfers. CHIPS processes about $890 billion in transactions a day in about 150,000 separate transactions. It is an appendage of the New York Clearing House Association, a private institution, unlike Fedwire, which is a public wire transfer system.

The Source of CHIPS Credit Risk

Banks participate as equal members in CHIPS even though they have varying credit ratings. For example, the major New York Clearing House Association banks, the Japanese banks, European banks, and Latin American banks all participate. As members of the system, they all extend credit to each other, so they are all at risk if one of the banks in the system is unable to make its payments during the day.

CHIPS operates like a private clearinghouse of the sort described at length earlier in the chapter. Participating banks' balance sheets balloon during the day with "due to's" and "due from's" as in Table 12.4. This ballooning puts the member banks at risk. First, some risk arises because many payments will go out before receipts start to flow in. By chance during the day, bank A's customers may pay out a lot of funds before they receive any. For instance, at 9 A.M. they could order bank A to pay out all $9.5 billion of their deposits. Immediately, bank A would find itself with an uncomfortable volume of funds due to other banks, although settlement would not be made until the end of the day.

Then suppose that at 9:30 A.M. messages to deposit $1 billion in bank A's customer accounts are received from another bank. Bank A knows that its customers will receive this $1 billion from another bank at the end of the day. The customers may then order bank A to send out more payments, although bank A has not yet determined if the expected $1 billion is good funds. Why does bank A commit itself to allow its customers to send out more funds than it currently has on hand?

The bank could adopt a policy of not allowing further payments from customers' accounts until it receives good funds at the end of the day. After all, this is the normal bank policy to small depositors in the normal paper check clearing

Box 12.4

Netting to Avoid Overdrafts

As we indicated in the text, banks can avoid overdrafts by withholding payments until immediately before settlement. An organized form of this already takes place on CHIPS for foreign exchange transactions. In this bilateral netting process, two banks agree to withhold transactions between them until debits and receipts approach a balance. Then they report their net position to CHIPS. This, of course, reduces one or the other bank's net "due to" position with the clearinghouse during the day.

The Bank for International Settlement, which is located in Basel, Switzerland, and functions as a semiofficial supervisor of international banking for the major industrial countries, has recommended that bilateral netting be used more frequently as a method to reduce daylight overdrafts.

However, does bilateral netting reduce risk or merely reshuffle it? When two banks agree to settle only the net amount between them, they are really placing themselves ahead of other creditors in the event of bankruptcy. For example, if bank A owes bank B $100 million and bank B owes bank A $75 million, the net position is $25 million due bank B. In the event of bank A's bankruptcy, bank B would face only a $25 million loss because it could offset the amount it owed bank A. However, if the two banks had reported their gross positions through a clearinghouse, all members would have benefited from bank B's offset. Thus it is quite likely that bank B would have sustained a larger loss, but other banks that owed bank A less and were owed more by bank A would have gained.

system. If a bank operated in this manner, however, a customer would simply take his or her account and business to a competing bank. Both the customer and bank A are in fact confident that the new deposit actually will be made good at the end of the day, and a refusal to allow the customer to make interim payments forces the customer to incur extra costs in making transactions. Competition thus forces the bank to act as if the new deposit were good funds.

After receiving a message informing it of a receipt at 9:30 A.M., the bank allows the customer to send out another $1 billion in payments at 10 A.M. The continuation of this process throughout the day permits the bank to turn over its deposits many times before clearing. The ballooning of the balance sheets of the banks involves the transfer among banks of a large number of electronic IOUs, accounting entries on the banks' and CHIPS' electronic bookkeeping system. The messages are cleared through CHIPS, so each time a payment is sent from one bank to another, CHIPS keeps a record of the payments due. At 4:30 P.M., CHIPS clears, netting out the positions of all the banks.

It does this by adding all orders from other banks to make payments to bank A and all orders from bank A to make payments to other banks. Subtracting one from the other, CHIPS then requires that banks with a net debit make up the net. Suppose that bank A has a net debit position: It has received only $9 billion and has paid out $10 billion. Once the accounting is complete, CHIPS will order bank A to make a deposit of $1 billion in the CHIPS account at the Fed. Bank A then orders the Fed to shift $1 billion from its reserve account to the CHIPS account.

Where does bank A get $1 billion dollars in reserves? Perhaps it borrows from the discount window. Or perhaps it goes to the fed funds market and buys reserves from other banks that have more reserves than they require. Perhaps it sells some T–bills in the repurchase market for cash. Perhaps it is a foreign bank with little access to the domestic funds market or to the discount window. In this case, it probably would have previously acquired a line of credit with one of the clearing-house banks to arrange for the funds. The clearinghouse bank must then provide the needed liquidity.

After the debit banks have made their deposits into the CHIPS account, CHIPS uses the funds to send out payments to the creditors, ordering the Fed to shift funds from its account into those of the creditor banks. With this, the CHIPS account has netted out to zero, thereby completing the clearing process. Settlement on CHIPS is supposed to occur by 6 P.M. in New York.

If a bank is not a member bank of the Fed, such as a foreign bank, it clears through a CHIPS member or clearinghouse bank that is a Fed member. CHIPS then sends a message to the clearinghouse bank giving the net position of the foreign bank for which it clears. The clearinghouse bank informs the foreign bank of its net position and requires payment if it is in a debit position. The clearinghouse bank then makes the deposit into the CHIPS account at the Fed. See Box 12.4.

Risk in the System

Where does the risk arise? Inherent in the system is the granting of credit among institutions subject to bankruptcy, just as in the benchmark private clearinghouse system that we studied earlier. In 1990, CHIPS implemented a system of **settlement finality** by which the net debit position of individual banks is guaranteed by all participants on CHIPS.[9] The participants pool collateral to back up this guarantee.

---

9. The details of how settlement finality is provided on CHIPS can be found in New York Clearing House Association, *CHIPS: Settlement Finality, Rules and Documents,* April 1990.

In addition, CHIPS has a formula for allocating losses among its members if the collateral is insufficient. Each day, each member specifies bilateral net credit ceilings—that is, it informs CHIPS of the size of the net debit position that it will allow each of the other members to accumulate with it. If a bank attempts to make a payment that causes it to exceed the credit ceiling imposed by another bank, the CHIPS network will not process the payment. If a bank fails to settle its net debit to CHIPS at the end of a day, the remaining banks are sent an **additional settlement obligation** (ASO). A remaining bank's additional obligation is calculated as

$$ASO = ND \times CL/TCL$$

where ND is the net debit of the failed bank to CHIPS, CL is the highest bilateral credit limit granted by the remaining bank to the failed bank during the day, and TCL is the total of the bilateral credit limits granted by all remaining banks to the failed bank. Thus, there is a pro-rata sharing of the loss on CHIPS.

To cover potential failures to settle, a member is required to deposit book entry U.S. Treasury securities with CHIPS with a value of 5 percent of its highest bilateral credit limit with other members. Of course, in the event of large failures to settle, this amount may provide CHIPS insufficient resources to settle, so its promised "settlement finality" is not foolproof.

Length of the CHIPS Settlement Period

Since CHIPS is an international payments system, it begins netting transactions among members at the beginning of the business day in Tokyo, say 9 A.M. Tokyo time, which is 7 P.M. Eastern Standard Time in New York. At the close of business in Tokyo, 6 P.M., it is 9 A.M. in London and 4 A.M. in New York. Thus, when Tokyo is closing, London is just opening. Payments transactions continue to occur among CHIPS participants.

When New York opens for business, Tokyo is asleep and London is at lunch. Meanwhile, CHIPS participants keep transacting. CHIPS transactions are settled at the New York Fed at 6 P.M. local time, which is 8 A.M. in Tokyo. Thus the length of the settlement period on CHIPS is almost 24 hours, compared with the 8-hour settlement period for Fedwire.

Why is the settlement period for CHIPS much longer than the settlement period for Fedwire? The easy answer is that CHIPS operates over the full global range of time zones. However, dollar settlement could occur in Tokyo or in London, providing CHIPS members were willing to hold reserves in these markets to affect settlement. However, holding reserves is expensive. If the same reserves held in New York can be used to effect settlement over both CHIPS and Fedwire, it pays to do so. In terms of Figure 12.3, the opportunity cost of holding dollar reserves in London or Tokyo exceeds the expected cost of losses resulting from an extended settlement period.

CONCLUSION

In this chapter we discussed how electronics payments are settled. We found that banks can form clearinghouses to increase their ability to make large payments among each other. Clearinghouses net payments among member banks and settle periodically with a transfer of good funds from members with net "due to" positions to members with net "due from" positions. Periodic settlement reduces the potential cost of transferring large amounts of good funds among banks because banks with large net "due to" positions early in the period are likely to receive funds by the end of the period.

The "due to" positions are covered by the collateral of member reserves held at the clearinghouse. If a member fails to settle, the clearinghouse makes good its liability by transferring reserves to the accounts of the banks with net "due from" positions with the failed bank. Also, permitting banks to offset their own liabilities to the failed bank prior to other creditors gives clearinghouse members a preferred position in case of bankruptcy.

The Federal Reserve acts as the electronics clearinghouse for domestic dollar payments. It follows a policy of settlement finality—that is, payments are guaranteed as good funds at settlement when they are made. To compensate for the risk, the Fed imposes reserve requirements on member banks, just as the private clearinghouse does. In addition, beginning in 1992, the Fed will charge for daylight net "due to" positions.

CHIPS is a major private clearinghouse. It has recently adopted settlement finality that is guaranteed by a system of collateral similar to reserves. CHIPS also has developed a mechanism for dealing with defaults when a failed bank's net "due to" position exceeds the available collateral.

In the next chapter we will see that the ability of the banking system to execute settlement with a minimal use of good funds represents its major advantage over other financial institutions in credit markets. Minimizing the use of good funds also decreases the cost of transacting in securities markets. Thus we will find that an efficient payments system is necessary to have liquid financial markets.

KEY TERMS

fedwire

CHIPS

book-entry system

overdraft

sender net debit cap

continuous settlement

gridlock   cap

continuous net settlement   settlement finality

periodic net settlement   additional settlement obligation

EXERCISES

1. Compare the Fedwire liability rules to check clearing liability rules. Are there efficiency reasons for these differences?

2. What do you suppose would have happened to the cost of trading in the government securities market if the Fed had not lent BONY the $23 million necessary for it to settle its liability to securities sellers on November 21, 1985?

3. Explain the difference between continuous and periodic net settlement. Which system provides better protection for depositors in the event of bankruptcy?

4. What would happen to the desired length of the settlement period if banks experience a rash of loan losses that reduce the public's confidence in the banking system?

5. Why is cash used more frequently to settle large payments in developing countries than in the industrialized world?

6. What happens to the desired length of the settlement period if interest rates fall? Would you expect to see the settlement period adjust over an interest rate cycle?

7. Explain how a fractional reserve banking system can guarantee payments but not deposits.

8. If reserves exist to guarantee delivery of payments, why would a clearinghouse consider placing a cap on a member's net "due to" position?

9. Under the old CHIPS rules, why do you suppose banks treated CHIPS payments as good funds before they were actually settled?

10. Why do you suppose the Fed placed pressure on CHIPS to devise a system for guaranteeing settlement finality?

11. Suppose that three banks form a clearinghouse as a depository for their reserves. The clearinghouse operates with settlement finality (that is, it guarantees all payment orders among the banks), and the banks settle with each other on a net basis at the end of each day. The clearinghouse insists that a bank maintain a ratio of reserves against deposits of 1 to 10; otherwise, the bank will not be permitted to make payments during the next business day. If a bank fails to settle at the end of the day, the clearinghouse will settle for it and assess each of the remaining banks equally to make up its loss.

The bank balance sheets (in millions of dollars) are as follows:

	ASSETS		LIABILITIES	
First National	Reserves	270	Deposits	2,700
	Loans	2,600	Capital	170
Daigin	Reserves	180	Deposits	1,800
	Loans	1,750	Capital	130
Midland	Reserves	90	Deposits	900
	Loans	900	Capital	90

Suppose that during one day the payment traffic is as follows:

—— First National pays Daigin   1,000
—— Daigin pays Midland   1,500
—— Midland pays First National   2,000

a. If all banks have ready access to the interbank market, describe the end-of-day balance sheet of each bank and of the clearinghouse.

b. Suppose that Midland defaults because it cannot raise funds in the interbank market. Describe the end-of-day balance sheets of First National, Daigin, and the clearinghouse.

c. Suppose that the three banks were the only members of CHIPS. First National places a net credit limit of $2 billion on Midland, and Daigin places a net credit limit of $1 billion on Midland. These are the highest net credit ceilings imposed on other members by these two banks. In addition, Midland's highest net credit ceiling is $2 billion on Daigin. First National and Daigin have credit ceilings of $1.5 billion for each other. The reserves of these banks are all held at the Fed.

If the loans can serve as collateral at CHIPS, how much of its loans does each bank have to deliver to CHIPS as collateral? If Midland fails to settle its CHIPS net debit, how will the loss be allocated between each of the remaining banks? If both the remaining banks settle their ASOs, depict the balance sheets of First National and Daigin at the start of the next day's business.

d. What advantages does a clearinghouse have in creating confidence among banks that payment messages will be settled? How do these advantages affect the positions of the remaining depositors in the failed Midland?

12. Suppose that in the middle of the day's transactions, Brazil, Argentina, Mexico, and Venezuela jointly announce a total repudiation of their foreign debt, more than wiping out the capital of the New York money-center banks. Holders of large CDs coming due at these banks refuse to roll them over and therefore demand payment. Large holders of demand deposits immediately order payments to regional banks unaffected by the default and redirect incoming payments to other banks. Describe what will happen to the net settlement position of the New York banks on CHIPS and on fedwire. If the banks cannot settle at the end of the day, what will be the impact on the positions of other international banks settling through CHIPS? What will be the impact on the Federal Reserve balance sheet that night?

13. How does replacing a private clearinghouse guarantee of payment delivery with a central bank guarantee increase the liquidity of securities markets? Who potentially pays for the increase in liquidity?

14. Why does CHIPS have a 24-hour settlement period?

FURTHER READING

Association of Reserve City Bankers. *Report on the Payments System.* Cambridge, Mass.: Arthur D. Little, Inc., April 1982.

Belton, T., M. Gelfand, D. Humphrey, and J. Marquardt. "Daylight Overdrafts and Payments System Risk," *Federal Reserve Bulletin,* November 1987, pp. 839–852.

Flannery, M. "Payments System Risk and Public Policy" (Occasional Paper). Washington: American Enterprise Institute for Public Policy, 1987.

Humphrey, D. "Payments Finality and Risk of Settlement Failure," in A. Saunders and L. White (Eds.), *Technology and Regulation of Financial Markets.* Lexington, Mass.: Lexington Books, 1986.

Large-Dollar Payments System Advisory Group. *A Strategic Plan for Managing Risk in the Payments System.* Washington: Board of Governors of the Federal Reserve, August 1988.

Mengle, D., D. Humphrey, and B. Summers. "Intraday Credit: Risk, Value, and Pricing," Federal Reserve Bank of Richmond, *Economic Review,* Vol. 73, No. 1 (January/February 1987), pp. 3–14.

Summers, Bruce J. "Clearing and Payments Systems: The Role of the Central Bank," *Federal Reserve Bulletin,* February 1991, pp. 83–91.

Task Force on Controlling Payments System Risk. *Controlling Risk in the Payments System.* Washington: Board of Governors of the Federal Reserve, August 1988.

CHAPTER

13

Banks in the Market for Liquidity

In Chapter 12 we saw that reserves play a crucial role in guaranteeing that interbank payments will be delivered. Thus they can be seen as a cost of being in the payments business. Nevertheless, market participants have an incentive to obtain the benefits of a safe payments system while avoiding the cost of guaranteeing such a system by creating securities that have the liquidity of bank deposits but are not subject to reserve requirements. An example of this is commercial paper, which has the maturity and liquidity characteristics of a bank certificate of deposit (CD) but is not subject to reserve requirements. The settlement of transactions in commercial paper depends on having an efficient payments system, but if everyone held commercial paper rather than reservable deposits, no one would pay for such a system.

Economists have long recognized the incentive to avoid reserve requirements, and they have expended some effort to determine who actually bears the burden of reserves. If everyone could escape the burden of reserve requirements, bank deposits subject to reserves would disappear, since no one would be willing to absorb the cost. As a result, no banks would exist to settle in good funds, even if everyone perceives the benefit of having this form of settlement available. In this chapter we consider the issue of who pays for reserves and consequently why the banking system exists even though everyone has an incentive to avoid the cost of reserves.

On January 1, 1991, the Fed suspended the reserve requirement on large CDs. As a result, we no longer have a bank instrument comparable with commercial paper (CP) that bears a reserve requirement. The issue of who bears the cost of reserves remains important, however, because it determines who shoulders the cost of providing liquidity to financial markets. Thus in this chapter we will examine the CD and CP markets as they operated at a time when the bank deposit carried a reserve requirement. This environment was well suited to analyze who bears the cost of reserves. We will also comment on the impact of the removal of reserve requirements on the cost of liquidity.

A CONVENTIONAL MODEL OF WHO PAYS FOR RESERVES

The existence of the commercial paper (CP) market has made economists skeptical that bank depositors, especially large depositors such as corporations and securities dealers, can bear the cost of reserves. If banks tried to offer a lower yield on CDs to cover the cost of holding non-interest-bearing reserves at the Fed, wholesale depositors would switch their funds into commercial paper.

Eugene Fama (1985) has formalized this argument. He begins by observing that a bank certificate of deposit (CD), which is subject to reserve requirements, trades at the same yield as two apparently identical financial instruments not subject to reserve requirements. (See Table 13.1.) These two identical instruments are commercial paper (CP) and bankers acceptance (BA). **Commercial paper** is similar to a CD in that it is a marketable, short-term liability. However, commercial paper is issued by corporations with strong credit ratings rather than by banks. A **bankers**

Table 13.1 INTEREST RATES ON RESERVABLE AND NONRESERVABLE ASSETS, JANUARY 1967 TO MAY 1983

Instrument	Average Interest Rate by Maturity		
	1 Month	3 Months	6 Months
Certificate of deposit	8.14	8.28	8.35
Bankers acceptance	8.13	8.25	8.36
Commercial paper	8.25	8.32	8.34

Note: Quotes are compounded yields to maturity on high grade issues from Part IV, Table 1, of the *Analytical Record of Yields and Yield Spreads,* various issues, published by Salomon Brothers.

Adapted from Fama, Eugene, "What's Special About Banks?" *Journal of Monetary Economics,* Vol. 15 (January 1985), p. 30.

acceptance is a bank liability similar in maturity to a CD but not subject to reserve requirements. We explained this instrument in detail in Chapter 10.

Fama reasoned that if a CD trades at the same yield as a CP or a BA, bank borrowers rather than depositors bear the burden of reserves. Bank loans must then be a unique source of credit, or borrowers would avoid paying for reserves as well by seeking alternative suppliers of credit.

Many economists have concluded that banks have special information about some borrowers not possessed by other financial intermediaries.[1] These borrowers are presumed to be small and middle-sized businesses that do not have easy access to public securities markets. The information advantage held by banks prevents these borrowers from easily seeking alternative sources of credit. Hence banks can charge a higher interest rate than warranted by the risk, and the difference covers the cost of reserve requirements. This is the conventional view of how the cost of reserves is covered.

A Graphical Representation of the Conventional Model

Figure 13.1 presents a graphical representation of the traditional view. The vertical axis represents the interest rate paid on bank deposits or earned on loans by banks, holding other interest rates in the economy constant. The supply of deposits to the banking system is perfectly elastic at interest rate r. The cost of reserve requirements, the forgone interest on reserve holdings at the central bank, is represented by the difference between the dashed line and the supply curve for deposits. The demand curve for bank loans is downward sloping.

The shape of the supply curve for deposits in Figure 13.1 indicates that investors' portfolios contain perfect substitutes for bank deposits. Investors are unwilling to earn a lower yield on bank deposits than on the perfect substitute, which is exempt from reserve requirements. As a result, depositors will not bear the cost of reserves, which is the interest forgone on the required reserves.

On the other side of the balance sheet, nonbank loans are not perfect substitutes for bank loans because of the informational advantage banks have over some borrowers. If the interest rate on bank loans rises relative to rates on other credit market instruments, bank borrowers will continue to demand bank loans, although in reduced amounts. The lack of perfect substitutes is the source of the downward slope in the demand curve. Thus borrowers bear the cost of reserves in Figure 13.1.

---

1. James (1987) developed evidence that capital markets regard banks as possessors of private information about borrowers. He found that the announcement of a bank line of credit causes the stock of the recipient company to exhibit excess returns immediately after the announcement. In contrast, he found that the announcement of a commitment to lend by an insurance company causes no such reaction in the stock market.

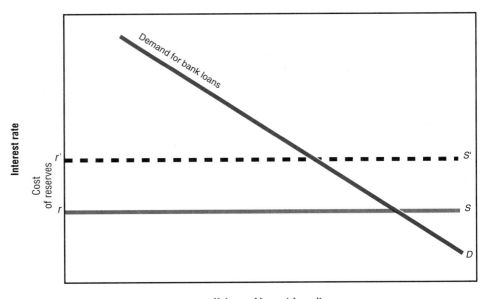

Figure 13.1 caption labels:

Interest rate

Cost of reserves

r' .... S'

r _____ S

D

Demand for bank loans

Volume of loans / deposits

S = Supply of funds (deposits) to banking system
S' = Supply of funds to banking system after accounting for cost of reserves

Figure 13.1 CONVENTIONAL ANALYSIS OF THE COST OF RESERVES

The intersection of the demand curve with the supply curve marked up for the cost of reserves determines the interest rate on loans, r'. See Box 13.1.

Are There Perfect Substitutes for Bank Deposits?

Commercial paper (CP) offers one alternative short-term investment to bank certificates of deposit (CDs). Like a bank deposit, commercial paper promises to deliver good funds at maturity, but since commercial paper is not a bank liability, it does not have a reserve requirement. Commercial paper issued by creditworthy corporations in the United States trades at the same yield as bank CDs. (See Table 13.1.) Bank CDs, like commercial paper, are negotiable, so both instruments can be sold to other parties before maturity. Alternatively, both can be used as collateral to obtain bank loans.

That commercial paper and certificates of deposits trade at the same yields indicates that the market views commercial paper as having the same liquidity and

Box 13.1

Nonbank Competition for Loans

During the week of April 22, 1991, *BusinessWeek* ran a cover story on the future of banking. The article suggested that banks have lost their unique place in the loan market as suppliers of credit to small businesses. The article opened with the case of an Atlanta restauranteur who could not obtain a loan from a local bank to expand his business, so he turned to a New York investment partnership that specialized in financing restaurants for equity funding. The partnership was dominated by Prudential Insurance, corporate pension funds, and foreign investors. The authors of the article took this as an example how the banking industry is dying.

However, principal-agent theory explains why the partnership was better able to manage the risk of the restaurant business than a bank, or any other lender. It was limited to a few investors and had a management that specialized in the restaurant business. You can bet that the partnership made its payments through a bank deposit and probably had large bank lines of credit to back up its position. If the prospects for the partnership deteriorated, the banks no doubt would have pulled their lines until the partners placed more equity into the business.

Many commentators have confused an observation of increasing financial specialization with an interpretation that the banking industry is dying. What we are really observing is that specialization affects banks like everyone else. Their business is narrowing to payments functions.

risk characteristics as certificates of deposit. From this evidence of substitutability and the graphical analysis of Figure 13.1, we might conclude that costs of reserves are paid by bank borrowers, not by bank depositors, as the traditional analysis argues.

This reasoning, however, ignores an important element in the commercial paper market that we discussed in Chapter 10: Corporations that issue commercial paper maintain revolving credit lines, representing the right to borrow good funds from a bank during a certain period. Credit lines give commercial paper issuers access to the liquidity of the banking system. Commercial paper issuers sometimes require bank loans to pay off their commercial paper; as occasional bank borrowers themselves, they also must pay for reserves according to the conventional view that bank borrowers pay for reserves.

AN ALTERNATIVE MODEL FOR WHO BEARS THE COST OF RESERVES

Pricing a Revolving Line of Credit: A Basic View

Commercial paper issuers "attach a line" because they must assure lenders that they can deliver good funds at maturity. Normally, issuers can obtain funds by simply reissuing or rolling over their commercial paper; as one series of notes matures, it is replaced by another series, usually at a slightly different interest rate, in response to the market. During times of liquidity stress in the money markets, however, it is difficult for even high-quality borrowers to issue short-term paper. Even in normal times, a CP issuer may face technical problems in rolling over its paper. Cash payoff to investors can be ensured only by buying a line of credit from a bank, which in turn has access to the banking system and to the liquidity services of the central bank.

We will see that commercial paper holders also must bear some of the issuer's cost of accessing bank liquidity and that the cost of using a line of credit is related to the cost of reserve requirements. To analyze these claims, we turn now to the banking transactions involved when CDs and CP mature.

A Certificate of Deposit Matures

In Table 13.2 we analyze the impact of a maturing deposit on the balance sheet of a banking system consisting of two banks. In Table 13.2a, bank A has $900 in loans and $100 in reserves on the asset side. It funds these loans with a $100 certificate of deposit and $900 in demand deposits (DD). Suppose that banks generally hold 3-percent reserves against CDs and 10-percent reserves against demand deposits, so bank A holds excess reserves of $7, which, as we will see, guarantees the liquidity of the CD. Bank B has loans of $540, reserves of $60, and demand deposits of $600.

Now assume that the CD on bank A's balance sheet matures. The holder of that deposit uses the funds to pay a customer of bank B, who, in turn, buys a demand deposit from bank B with the funds. The customers of the banking system as a whole, then, do not roll over the CD but require settlement in demand deposits. On the other hand, if they were always willing to roll over the CD, the existence of CDs would place no liquidity demands on the system. Occasional demands to settle CDs in the form of demand deposits make CDs somewhat illiquid.

If the system settles at the end of the day, the payment order appears on bank B's books as a "due from" bank A of $100 and an addition to demand deposits of $100. On the other hand, if this is a continuous settlement system, bank A would send $100 in reserves to bank B.

Bank A still has $900 in loans, which it funds with $900 in demand deposits.

Table 13.2   A CD MATURES

a. Opening Position

Bank A				Bank B			
ASSETS		**LIABILITIES**		**ASSETS**		**LIABILITIES**	
Loans	$900	CD	$100	Loans	$540	DD	$600
Reserves	$100	DD	$900	Reserves	$ 60		

b. Final Position

Bank A				Bank B			
ASSETS		**LIABILITIES**		**ASSETS**		**LIABILITIES**	
Loans	$900	Due to bank B $ 90		Loans	$540	DD	$700
Reserves	$ 90	DD	$900	Reserves	$ 70		
				Due from bank A	$ 90		

It settles its payment to bank B with the delivery of $100 in reserves; its reserves were sufficient to cover its end-of-day net "due to" position. Bank A may feel, however, that its position is not balanced because it does not have sufficient reserves to process further payments the next day. Therefore, it borrows $90 from bank B in the interbank market, so bank B now has a "due from" bank A on the asset side of its balance sheet and bank A has a "due to" bank B on the liability side of its balance sheet. The final positions of banks A and B are illustrated in Table 13.2b. The CD was liquid because bank A could guarantee the delivery of good funds through its reserve holdings and its ready access to interbank loans. Reserves on hand also guaranteed liquidity by eliminating bank B's risk in receiving the payment.

Commercial Paper Matures

Suppose now that the borrower from bank A issues commercial paper instead. The holder of the CP is a customer of bank B. Since commercial paper is the direct liability of the borrower, both loans and CD are initially $100 less than in the preceding example. The issuer of CP arranges a line of credit from bank A to ensure payment at maturity.

The initial positions of banks A and B are presented in Table 13.3a. Bank A has a credit line for $100 to the commercial paper issuer. Appearing as a memo item, this line represents a potential liability, because bank A must raise a liability if the line is used.

Suppose that the CP issuer cannot roll over the paper when the CP matures. Then the issuer of the CP, calling on his line of credit, takes a loan from bank A

Table 13.3 COMMERCIAL PAPER MATURES

a. Opening Position

Bank A				Bank B			
ASSETS		LIABILITIES		ASSETS		LIABILITIES	
Loans	$800	DD	$900	Loans	$540	DD	$600
Reserves	$100			Reserves	$ 60		
Memo: $100 credit line							

b. Position after Activation of Credit Line

Bank A				Bank B			
ASSETS		LIABILITIES		ASSETS		LIABILITIES	
Loans	$900	DD	$900	Loans	$540	DD	$700
				Reserves	$160		

c. Final Position

Bank A				Bank B			
ASSETS		LIABILITIES		ASSETS		LIABILITIES	
Loans	$900	DD	$900	Loans	$540	DD	$700
Reserves	$ 90	Due to bank B	$ 90	Reserves	$ 70		
				Due from bank A	$ 90		

to pay the customer of bank B. The customer of bank B again buys a demand deposit (DD) from her bank with the funds. The balance sheets of the two banks up to this point are illustrated in Table 13.3b. Bank A's assets consist of its original $800 in loans plus its new $100 loan to the CP issuer. The accounts of the two banks are balanced through the use of "due to's" and "due from's" if settlement is at the end of the day. If settlement is continuous, balancing takes place through a delivery of reserves. With a private clearinghouse or with a central bank bearing the risk for the entire payments system, bank A will have to restore its reserve position to cover the risk to the payments system for its next day transactions. Bank A borrows $90 in the interbank market to leave the end-of-day position of the banking system as in Table 13.3c. As an effect of these transactions, bank assets and liabilities have been substituted for the maturing commercial paper.

Holding Reserves Against a Line of Credit

As we have seen, raising the demand deposits in bank B requires additional reserves for settlement directly connected to providing liquidity for commercial paper. Bank

B cannot expand its demand deposits carried overnight without increasing its reserves by $10 because it must cover its greater potential next day net "due to" position. Bank A can satisfy its commitment to the CP issuer by holding sufficient good funds as reserves on its balance sheet to cover the increased reserve holdings on the demand deposits that will be required if the CP cannot be rolled over at maturity. Bank A knows that the delivery of $10 in good funds plus the $90 of "due to's" will satisfy its credit commitment to the CP issuer while still allowing it to serve the payments needs of its remaining demand deposit customers.[2] More generally, bank A need not hold the additional reserves directly, as long as they are available somewhere in the banking system.

The Price of the Line of Credit and the Cost of Holding Reserves

In our example, the reserves held against the CP and CD are equivalent. If bank A holds $10 in reserves to cover its liquidity commitment for the customer's line of credit, the opportunity cost will be covered in the price of the line on the commercial paper. In turn, the CP issuer will offer a lower yield to cover this cost of providing liquidity, so the CP holder indirectly bears the cost of reserves needed in the payments mechanism to provide liquidity. CP and CDs are perfect substitutes; they are both short term and liquid, and they should therefore pay the same yields. Both depend on the holding of good funds (or easy access to good funds) as reserves against demand deposits to ensure liquidity, so both pay for the cost of reserves.

This stark example is not a realistic view of the CP market, however. As members of a banking system, individual banks can provide lines of credit without actually holding reserves. They can provide liquidity for nonbank securities at a much lower cost than our example would imply. We will show below, however, that the banking system's ability to economize on reserve holdings does not really change the incidence of the cost of reserves.

BANKS AS MARKET MAKERS IN LIQUIDITY

Access to good funds makes banks suppliers of cash to commercial paper issuers. Since any financial institution can hold good funds, it is necessary to explore the organization of the banking system to understand why banks are the lowest-cost market maker in cash.

2. If settlement in bank claims alone were sufficient to operate the payments system, there would be no need for reserves. Reserve holdings, even in a private clearinghouse system, provide the most liquid collateral for participants.

Banks hold only a small percentage of their assets in good funds. Individual banks can make a credible statement about delivering good funds to their deposit customers and borrowers on demand because banks are part of a banking system, a group of banks tied together by the clearing and settlement mechanism of a clearinghouse where member banks hold good funds as reserves. Members of the system generally lend good funds to other members who experience a drain on their good funds on any particular day, that is, to members whose market-making activities in good funds cause them to be large sellers of good funds. Whenever a deposit is cashed or a loan is made, a bank becomes a buyer of good funds at a posted bid price, because it must make delivery of funds to a customer or another bank. Whenever a loan is repaid or a deposit is made, a bank becomes a seller of good funds at a posted offer price.

A Clearinghouse Conserves Good Funds

In Chapter 12 we studied the organization and operations of a clearinghouse to indicate the advantage that a clearing and settlement system gives to banks in the market for cash. Banks can deliver good funds while holding minimal reserves because the individual members of the clearinghouse (and their customers) have faith that net "due to" positions accumulating during the day will be covered by delivery of good funds at settlement. Members are justified in their belief if the clearinghouse guarantees "due to's" and holds reserves equal to the sum of its net "due to" exposures between settlement periods.

In the private clearinghouse system, reserves are the cost of providing assurance that good funds will be delivered to banks for their net "due to" positions. The clearinghouse does not ensure that all the deposits in an individual bank will be treated as cash by the marketplace, but it does guarantee that good funds will be delivered for payment orders among banks.[3] Thus bank payment orders to the account of a depositor can be treated as good funds by that depositor.

The Federal Reserve, as we have seen, is a clearinghouse with the power to create good funds by purchasing government or private securities. The Fed's power to create reserves freely does not obviate reserves as a source of liquidity. The Fed bears the same risk of settlement failure as the private clearinghouse: Reserves serve as a guarantee of the delivery of good funds against net "due to" positions.

In Fedwire payments, banks with net "due to" positions in their reserve accounts borrow fed funds from other members at settlement. The Federal Reserve guarantees

---

3. In settling net positions, the clearinghouse has a right if a member becomes bankrupt to offset payments due from that member with payments due to that member. The clearinghouse makes prior claim over all other creditors to the bankrupt member's liabilities to the clearinghouse to the extent that they are offset by that member's loans to the clearinghouse. Much of the security the clearinghouse adds to the payments mechanism is derived from these liability rules. Reserve requirements protect the payments mechanism in a similar fashion. They are assets of the several member banks, but the clearinghouse has prior claim to them in the event of bankruptcy.

unconditionally that a bank payment message sent over Fedwire will be honored as good funds at settlement. If a bank fails to deliver good funds, the Fed supplies them without assessing other banks. During the day, the Fed thus insures the whole market in wholesale payments. The revenue on reserves deposited with the Fed serves as a compensation for the risk it bears.

The interconnection among banks and their connection to the central bank permits the quick movement of good funds from banks with a surplus of good funds to deficit banks. This is the advantage that banks have as a source of liquidity to the economy. However, banks must be compensated for their cost of providing liquidity, which is the reserve burden, if they are to remain in business. We now turn to the question of how banks get compensated for holding reserves in a world in which reserves are not held against bank lines.

THE COST OF LIQUIDITY: A MORE REALISTIC COMMERCIAL PAPER MARKET

In our simplified commercial paper example, we concluded that both CP and CD holders pay for reserves. Now we consider again a commercial paper market in which issuers hold bank lines of credit to ensure the delivery of good funds to investors at maturity. If the line is used, the CP issuer has a bank loan as a liability. The issuer's bank has a loan as an asset and a "due to" position with the CP holder's bank as a liability. The CP holder's bank has a "due from" position with the issuer's bank and a "due to" position with the CP holder. At settlement, the CP issuer's bank must deliver reserves to the CP holder's bank to effect settlement. However, since the Fed guarantees that the "due to's" of the holder's bank will be converted to good funds at settlement, the issuer's bank does not need to hold reserves against the issuer's line to guarantee that good funds will be delivered. We will discuss in detail how this affects the split in the cost of reserves between the CP issuer and the CP holder.

The CP Holder's Cost of Bank Liquidity

Suppose that the commercial paper issuer faces a probability of .1 of borrowing from a bank at the maturity of the CP in 5 business days. The CP issuer then expects to use a bank loan only overnight, at maturity, if at all. As an alternative to issuing CP with a line, he can issue a liability of the same maturity without a liquidity guarantee. He would issue the less liquid liability if he could sell it at an interest expense less than the explicit interest expense on the CP plus the expected additional cost of the bank loan plus the up-front cost of the line of credit. That is, if $i_s < i_{CP} + E(i_{bl}) + L,$ where i_s is the interest expense on the illiquid security, i_{CP} is the interest expense on the CP, $E(i_{bl})$ is the expected additional cost of the bank loan, and L is the up-front cost of a bank line, the issuer will issue an illiquid security.

The cost of reserves plays a crucial role in determining whether the issuer funds with commercial paper or an illiquid security because it determines the expected additional cost of a bank loan. Assume that the interest rate in the interbank fed funds market is 10 percent and the reserves held as a percentage of demand deposits are also 10 percent. Since the bank can sell reserves in the fed funds market, its opportunity cost of reserves is an annualized 1 percent of the deposits that it creates to fund its loans.

The *CP issuer's* expected annualized cost of the reserve requirement is $\frac{1}{5} \times .1 \times 1$ percent, or 2 basis points. The issuer faces a 10-percent probability of using a bank loan once every 5 days. He will issue commercial paper backed by a credit line rather than a less liquid liability if he can obtain at least a 2-basis-point reduction in his annual interest rate for doing so, such as 8.76 percent instead of 8.78 percent.

The *CP buyer* in this case will accept the 2-basis-point reduction from the yield on less liquid paper, such as the same paper without a bank line, because she values the guaranteed liquidity. Thus, in this example, we can say that the CP buyer's cost of bank liquidity is 2 basis points.

The CD Buyer's Cost of Bank Liquidity

To compare the cost of reserves for the CD holder with that of the CP holder, we must consider whether a CD can substitute for CP in all illiquid market in which CP generally cannot be rolled over. The fact that the two instruments have the same liquidity characteristics implies that they are affected similarly when the market demands delivery of cash. However, if the delivery of a CD is accepted as settlement when the delivery of CP is not, a CD must be more liquid than CP and therefore must trade at a lower yield.

However, let's assume that a CD and commercial paper are equally liquid and that investors reluctant to hold CP also shun CDs.[4] In this case, a demand for cash payment requires settlement with a demand deposit, which always maintains its value in good funds. If holders of both CP and CDs require delivery of a demand deposit in a liquidity crunch, they must both pay for the reserve requirements on a demand deposit. In this case, holders of both instruments pay for the *expectation* that investors will require a demand deposit at settlement, and their yields are less than the yield of a less liquid instrument by the expected cost of holding reserves on demand deposits.

4. More generally, the CP of an individual firm may not roll over even though there is no general CP crisis. The bank loan may then be funded with a CD.

The CP Issuer's Cost of Bank Liquidity:
The Role of the Dealer

Our analysis of reserve requirement costs is not yet complete because the holder of CP or a CD may wish to sell the security before maturity. Assume that the investor sells to a dealer who in circumstances of illiquidity in CP and CD markets cannot sell the security under a repurchase agreement to finance his inventory. The dealer must then finance with a bank loan, which, in turn, must be financed by the issue of a demand deposit, given that the CP and CD markets are not then liquid.

Since the CP or CD has not matured, it must be sold at a discount today. The discount must be greater than normal by the cost of reserve requirements, which represents an additional funding cost for the dealer.[5] We assume again that the interest rate on fed funds is 10 percent and that the reserve ratio against demand deposits is also 10 percent, so the annualized cost of reserves will be 1 percent of demand deposit funding.

As before, we assume that there is a probability of .1 that the CP or CD cannot be sold before maturity without bank funding to the dealer and that 5 days remain until maturity. On issue, the investor must be compensated for the expected extra cost of illiquidity in the CP and CD markets; that is, she must receive a higher yield to cover the extra "haircut" administered by the dealer to cover the reserve cost of his bank loan. We assume an equal probability that the paper cannot be sold on any of the 4 days before maturity. On an annualized basis, then, the expected cost of liquidity of a sale before maturity is $\frac{4}{5} \times .1 \times 1$ percent, or 8 basis points. The investor is then paid 8 basis points above the rate of return on good funds, which in the United States are fed funds.

It is not necessary for all investors to sell their CP and CD for demand deposits in a liquidity crunch. As in all markets, the demands of the marginal investor determine the price. The 8 basis points is the incremental return required to make the marginal investor willing to bear the risk of a decline in the value of her security relative to good funds in a crunch, whether she sells her security or not.

The liquidity crunch requiring the raising of a demand deposit occurs with probability of .1 spread evenly over the time to maturity of the paper. The *total* expected cost of reserves for loans providing liquidity to CP is then 10 basis points (.1 × 1 percent). If the CP buyer were to pay this entire expected cost, the issuer would have to compensate her by offering a yield 10 basis points above fed funds. The issuer, however, achieves a 2-basis-point lower yield because the market is virtually certain that he can deliver cash in 5 days at the maturity of the paper. He expects to pay for his 2-basis-point reduction in the form of the cost of reserves.

---

5. This analysis presumes that there is an ample number of dealers with well-prepared bank lines. If not, there is even greater illiquidity owing to the limited capacity of individual dealers to bear risk. On this issue, see Sanford Grossman and Mertin Miller, "Liquidity and Market Structure," *The Journal of Finance,* Vol. 43, No. 3 (July 1988), pp. 617–634.

Prior to maturity, the buyer must be compensated for the possibility that she might have to sell to a dealer who must finance inventory with a bank loan. For this, the buyer must receive an interest rate that is 8 basis points higher than that for fed funds. The issuer pays four-fifths of the cost (the higher interest rate paid to the buyer) and the buyer pays one-fifth of the cost of constantly providing liquidity to the CP.

The expected cost of reserves can take the form of an up-front fee for a line or a premium over the overnight interbank rate. In practice, lines cost about 5 or 10 basis points up front, and users pay between 50 and 75 basis points over the fed funds rate.

Who Pays the Cost of Reserves on CDs? The Market for Less Liquid Securities

In the last few pages we have discussed a liquidity problem in which marginal investors wanted to convert their CP or CDs into a demand deposit. We now consider less severe liquidity problems that may affect financial instruments that are less liquid than CDs and CP. We will refer to the more severe crisis in which only demand deposits are acceptable as a **DD crisis** and to the less severe liquidity problem as a **CD/CP crisis.** During the milder liquidity crises, investors attempt to convert their less liquid financial instruments into CDs or CP rather than into demand deposits.

We assume, as before, that the fed funds rate is 10 percent and that the ratio of reserves to demand deposits is also 10 percent. In addition, the reserve ratio on bank CDs is 3 percent, and the less liquid security has the same 5-day maturity as the CP in our previous example. We assume that the probability of a CD/CP liquidity crisis in the five days before maturity is .2. The probability of a DD liquidity crisis through maturity is .1, as before. The occurrence of the two types of crises is mutually exclusive. Therefore, the probability of some kind of liquidity problem affecting a holder or issuer of the illiquid security is .3.

How does the cost of liquidity affect the market for the less liquid instrument? At maturity, the issuer of the less liquid instrument faces a probability of $\frac{1}{5} \times .3$ that he cannot roll over his security and must fund it with a bank loan. When this happens, the probability is .67 that the bank can fund the loan with a CD and .33 that it must issue a demand deposit.

By taking out a bank line to guarantee delivery of whichever kind of bank deposit is demanded in settlement, the issuer faces an expected cost for reserves. This expected cost consists of two components: $\frac{1}{5} \times .2 \times 30$ basis points is the expected cost of a mild liquidity crisis, and $\frac{1}{5} \times .1 \times 100$ basis points is the expected cost of a major liquidity crisis. The total expected cost of bank liquidity at maturity is then 3.2 basis points. The issuer is willing to sell a security backed by a line if he can achieve a 3.2-basis-point reduction in interest expense for doing so.

The holder of the security also faces an expected cost of reserves in selling to a dealer in a crisis. In a mild crisis, the dealer funds with a bank loan funded by a CD. The cost is .2 × 30, or 6 basis points. In a severe crisis, the bank loan is funded by a demand deposit, at a cost of .1 × 100, or 10 basis points. The total expected cost is absorbed between issuance and maturity—that is, for 4 out of 5 days. Thus the expected cost of reserves borne by the holder is $\frac{4}{5}$ × 16 basis points, or 12.8 basis points. The holder must be paid 12.8 basis points over the fed funds rate to be content to hold the less liquid security.

The cost of reserves on CDs will be split between the issuer of a security less liquid than a CD and the holder of that security. The expected cost of reserves on a CD is .2 × 30, or 6 basis points. The holder pays an expected 1.2 basis points by accepting a lower yield than on the same security without a bank line. The issuer pays an expected 4.8 basis points in terms of a higher yield to compensate the investor for the cost of selling in a mild crisis.

The Cost of Reserves for an Illiquid Security

Consider a potential issuer whose security is so illiquid that if it were sold, a dealer would always have to fund his purchase with a bank loan. The security is also so illiquid that it certainly cannot be rolled over at maturity—a bank loan is surely required to deliver cash at maturity. We will show that the potential holder and the issuer of this security face an expected cost of reserves equal to the actual cost of reserves against such a security held directly by a bank. No incentive then arises to hold this security off a bank balance sheet.

Suppose that the fed funds rate is 10 percent, the reserve ratio on a demand deposit is 10 percent, and the reserve ratio on a CD is 3 percent. For now we assume that the security is held by a nonbank lender, that it matures in 5 days, and that it would be affected by a DD crisis in the same way as all other securities. The probability is .1 that investors will attempt to sell these securities for demand deposits before maturity or that the issuer will have to deliver demand deposits at maturity. This security, however, is in a constant state of mild liquidity crisis. If an investor were to sell the security, it would always have to be bought by a dealer funded by a CD, except in a DD crisis. Similarly, the issuer must always borrow from a bank at maturity, again in the form of a CD, except in a DD crisis.

When he takes out a bank line, the issuer of the illiquid security knows he must borrow at maturity. His expected cost of reserves is .1 × 100 basis points to cover the expected cost of delivery of demand deposits. It is .9 × 30 basis points to cover the expected cost of delivery of a CD. Since the security matures every 5 days, his expected cost of reserves is $\frac{1}{5}$ × .1 × 100 basis points plus $\frac{1}{5}$ × .9 × 30 basis points, or 7.4 basis points. He will take out a bank line if he can issue his security for 7.4 basis points less than if had he not obtained a bank line.

The holder of the security must be compensated for the expected dealer financing costs. These costs are .1 × 100 basis points for the expected cost of the delivery of a demand deposit and .9 × 30 basis points for the expected cost of the delivery of the CD. The holder faces these costs over 4 days. Thus her total expected cost is $\frac{4}{5} \times .1 \times 100$ basis points plus $\frac{4}{5} \times .9 \times 30$ basis points, or 29.6 basis points. The holder will hold this security only if she can earn 29.6 basis points above the interest rate on a liquid security.

The total expected cost of reserves is thus $7.4 + 29.6 = 37$ basis points. Given the market's expectation of liquidity crises, a bank can expect to fund its loans with 90 percent CDs and 10 percent demand deposits. The expected cost of the reserve burden facing the bank is thus $.9 \times 30$ basis points plus $.1 \times 100$ basis points, or 37 basis points. The expected cost of reserves for this very illiquid security is exactly equal to the cost of reserves facing the bank.[6]

THE FED FUNDS MARKET AND THE BURDEN OF RESERVES

In the previous sections we showed how arbitrage ensures that everyone who demands liquidity pays for the cost of reserves, whether the party holds a liability that has a reserve requirement attached to it or not. This cost is borne by parties who have an expectation of using bank liquidity services as well as those who actually use the liquidity services of banks.

Earlier, we identified the overnight fed funds rate as the opportunity cost of holding reserves because banks can lend them in the fed funds market. Banks that borrow overnight fed funds view them as substitutes for demand deposits, creating another opportunity to reduce reserves to the desired level. Like the arbitrage between CD and CP markets described in the previous sections, bank efforts to reduce the reserve burden should equalize the interest rate paid on demand deposits and the interest rate paid on overnight fed funds. We now turn to the question of how this arbitrage takes place.

Why Demand Deposits and Overnight Fed Funds Are Substitutes

In Table 13.4a we present the balance sheet of a bank at the end of the business day. There are $1000 in demand deposits, $2000 in CDs, and $50 in capital funding, $950 of overnight fed funds loans, and $1940 of securities. Reserves are $160, which is the sum of 10 percent against DD and 3 percent against CD. The business day is

6. We note that depositor and borrower share the burden of reserves in the ratio of 4 to 1, which is determined by the maturity characteristics of the note. In a more complete model, the maturity characteristics would be endogenously determined. If borrowers bore the burden of more frequent cash verification, depositors would pay a higher percentage of the reserve burden.

Table 13.4 DEMAND DEPOSITS AND FED FUNDS

a. End-of-Day Bank Balance Sheet Hold DD

ASSETS		LIABILITIES	
Reserves	$ 160	DD	$1,000
Fed funds	$ 950	CDs	$2,000
Securities	$1,940	Capital	$ 50

b. Next Morning Balance Sheet Fed Funds Payoff

ASSETS		LIABILITIES	
Reserves	$1,110	DD	$1,000
		CDs	$2,000
Securities	$1,940	Capital	$ 50

over, and the customer with demand deposits has loaned the funds to the bank overnight; the customer will again have access to the funds at the start of the next business day. The bank thus has good funds overnight that it has loaned at the fed funds rate.[7]

Good funds will be returned by the borrower at the start of business next day. Hence, the characteristics of the fed funds loan are identical to those of the demand deposit held as an asset by the customer. Table 13.4b depicts the balance sheet at the start of business next day. Reserves have increased from $160 to $1110 as the fed funds loan for $950 is repaid immediately into the bank's reserve account at the Fed.

Alternatively, the DD holder can elect to hold a repurchase agreement overnight instead of a DD. In a repurchase agreement, the customer will purchase a government security from the bank at the end of the day, and the bank will buy it back the next morning for a predetermined price. The bank's end-of-day balance sheet will have fewer demand deposits by the purchase price of the security, and this will release reserves to lend on the fed funds market overnight. The next morning, the bank receives repayment on the fed funds and repurchases the security, making the funds available to the customer at the start of business.

Table 13.5a depicts the end-of-day bank balance sheet if demand deposits are all expended on a repurchase agreement. Demand deposits are now zero, so reserves are only $60 (which is 3 percent of $2000 in CDs). The bank makes an additional $100 in overnight fed funds loans. The $1000 in securities will be repurchased next morning; they remain on the asset side of the bank's balance sheet.

Table 13.5b depicts the start-of-day bank balance sheet after the fed funds overnight loans have been repaid on Fedwire and after the bank exchanges a demand deposit credit for its securities. For both the bank and the customer, the start-of-day position is identical to that of holding a demand deposit overnight.

We can conclude from all this that the repurchase agreement permits the customer to convert a demand deposit into a collateralized loan with liquidity properties

---

7. Alternatively, having the demand deposit allows the bank to avoid borrowing overnight fed funds.

Table 13.5 AN OVERNIGHT REPURCHASE AGREEMENT

a. End-of-Day Bank Balance Sheet Hold Repurchase Agreement				b. Next Morning Balance Sheet Fed Funds Payoff			
ASSETS		LIABILITIES		ASSETS		LIABILITIES	
Reserves	$ 60	CDs	$2,000	Reserves	$1,110	DD	$1,000
Fed funds	$1,050	Repo	$1,000	Securities	$1,940	CDs	$2,000
Securities	$1,940	Capital	$ 50			Capital	$ 50

identical to those of fed funds so both should trade at the same interest rate.[8] Neither the fed funds nor the repurchase agreement are subject to reserve requirements. Both demand deposits and repurchases entail delivery of good funds at the end of the day to the bank for resale on the fed funds market. Both require the receipt of funds available for expenditure the next morning. From the viewpoint of the customer, these are identical claims.

By the same logic we used in discussing the CD market, the customer will not sacrifice yield on a DD relative to a repo to help the bank cover the cost of the reserve requirement on the latter instrument. If the implicit yield on DD is less than the overnight fed funds rate (which is the same as the repurchase agreement rate), the customer will substitute entirely into repurchase agreements, leaving no demand deposits in the bank.

This discussion leads to a result analogous to the incidence of the cost of reserves for CD and CP. Banks must charge the same cost of reserves to fed funds lenders and demand deposit holders. Demand deposits and fed funds pay the same liquidity premium because they have the same liquidity characteristics.

If we could compare the interest rate on overnight fed funds with the interest rate on demand deposits, we could test this conclusion directly. Unfortunately, as we explained in Chapters 3 and 10, demand deposits pay interest in terms of payments services so no explicit interest rate is available. Fortunately, we can compare the explicit interest rate on 30-day fed funds and 30-day CDs to determine whether the arbitrage we described above in fact takes place. The same arbitrage can take place in the thirty-day market. The bank can offer its customer a 30-day repo instead of an overnight repo to arbitrage differences between the 30-day CD rate and the 30-day fed funds rate.

---

8. Since the repurchase agreement is collateralized while fed funds are not explicitly guaranteed, repurchase agreement rates are typically somewhat lower than the fed funds rate. To ease clerical problems, however, banks typically ask that the security be deposited with the bank itself. The extent of the guarantee of repayment therefore is questionable.

A Comparison Between the Thirty-Day CD and Fed Funds Rates

Even though we have explicit interest rate data on 30-day CDs and 30-day fed funds, we cannot directly compare their yields because the two instruments are not strictly comparable. Thirty-day CDs are negotiable, whereas 30-day fed funds are not. Thus the CD is a more liquid instrument, and it should have a lower yield as long as liquidity is costly to produce and has value. Fortunately, we can correct for this factor because the 3 percent reserve requirement was removed from the CD on January 1, 1991.

As you can see from Table 13.6, from January through mid-June 1991, the weekly average of the 30-day fed funds rate was, on average, 4 basis points above the weekly average of the 30-day CD rate. We take this as the cost a borrower must pay to issue a nonnegotiable liability. According to the same table, the spread between the fed funds rate and the CD rate was, on average, 10 basis points between January 1987 and November 1990. (We exclude December from the data because the reserve requirement change may have affected the spread on 30-day liabilities issued in December but maturing in January.) Thus, the spread was 6 basis points greater before the change in reserve requirements than after, and this difference is statistically significant.

According to Table 13.6, the average cost of the reserve burden on CDs between 1987 and 1990 was 25 basis points. Thus, if reserves had been a burden, banks would have been willing to pay 25 basis points more for fed funds, which far exceeds the actual differential of 6 basis points.

Why should the 6-basis-point differential exist? Freeing reserves for sale in the fed funds market must not be costless. That is, there must be some expense in exchanging a CD for a repurchase agreement; and, if a bank is to engage in this transaction, it must be compensated with a higher fed funds rate. Selling a security

---

Table 13.6 COMPARISON OF 30-DAY FED FUNDS AND 30-DAY CD RATES

Weekly Average of Daily Yields to Maturity

Period	a. Fed Funds Rate	b. CD Rate	c. a-b
Jan.–Jun. 1991	6.50%	6.45%	0.04%★
Jan. 1987–Nov. 1990	8.13	8.03	0.10
Jan. 1987–Nov. 1990 (Corrected for Reserve Requirements.)	NA	8.28	NA

Source: CD rates are secondary market offer rates as perceived by Bank of America. Fed funds rates are offer rates as perceived by Bank of America. Data obtained from Data Resources, Inc.

*Note: Difference does not equal due to rounding.

involves costs, and an agreement has to be written to ensure that it is returned as its appointed time. We conclude that, prior to the removal of reserve requirements on CDs, reserves were almost, but not completely, reduced to their desired levels in wholesale banking markets.

One further question needs to be addressed. If it was expensive to reduce the the reserve burden through the fed funds market, why did the commercial paper market not expand further to reduce reserves to the desired level? The answer is that all borrowers do not have access to the commercial paper market, a point we will address in the next chapter.

Reserves Are the Most Liquid Asset

The availability of perfect substitutes for reservable deposits from investors' points of view permits banks to reduce their level of reserves to any desired level (up to transactions costs) while still supplying liquid liabilities to the market. Since banks nevertheless do issue demand deposits, they must not view reserves as a cost from which they derive no benefit. Indeed, as we have seen, they hold approximately the level of reserves necessary to supply liquidity to the market. We now consider how banks choose the amount of reserves that they will hold and their structure of reservable liabilities.

Clearinghouses allow banks to conserve on the holding of reserves, thereby lowering the cost of delivering good funds. Settlement, however, is designed to transfer risk from the clearinghouse back to the individual members. Periodic settlement is needed because of a risk of material change in the creditworthiness of banks. If a member's position deteriorates so that it cannot deliver reserves for settlement of the day's payment orders, then the entire clearinghouse loses the reserves necessary to cover that bank's net "due to" position, which could weaken otherwise strong members of the clearinghouse.

To assure that bank deposits are liquid instruments, periodic settlements thus are necessary. Risk transfer cannot be accomplished unless reserves are held in the system, so reserves can be considered the most liquid instrument of all. Their presence makes credible the guarantee of liquidity to other securities.[9]

9. This basic interpretation of reserves has been held since the early days of the Federal Reserve. For example, in a book entitled *Contemporary Banking* (New York, Harper, 1933, p. 257), Willis, Chapman, and Robey state: "Thus, the reserve requirement under the Federal Reserve Act is really that there be maintained a net balance between claims upon the banks and those held by it against other banks equal to a given percentage of the claims (deposits) it has agreed to pay, and this balance is the outcome of the clearing which has been described. It represents the net live credit of the banks which make up the Federal Reserve System—the credit which has not become subject to draft as the result of checking by depositors. Reserves in the Federal Reserve sense are thus the proportion of unquestionably liquid claims to total outstanding claims against the members. The Federal Reserve System is thus, in its reserve aspect, a means of testing and assigning credit to those entitled to it."

Recall that the Federal Reserve absolutely guarantees delivery of reserves associated with daylight payments and consequently absorbs the risk of nonsettlement. In addition, because member banks can borrow overnight from the Fed to cover net "due to" positions, they themselves have no apparent incentive to hold reserves to effect risk transfer. To provide this incentive, the Fed must limit the use of its overnight loans.

The Fed's limit creates a shadow price for borrowing reserves from the Fed. A *shadow price* is an unstated price that is higher than the stated price. For example, the Fed posts the discount rate as the explicit cost of borrowing from the Fed. However, a bank that borrows too frequently from the Fed is subject to pressure to find other sources of funds. Because of this implicit penalty, the cost of borrowing from the Fed, the shadow price, is higher than the discount rate. To avoid incurring the shadow price at the Fed, a bank participating in the market will pay for fed funds lines instead. These lines represent a contract to borrow a specified amount in the fed funds market.

While the Fed guarantees delivery of net "due to" positions when payments messages are sent, it does not guarantee that fed funds are a risk-free asset to the lending bank. In fact, the overnight fed funds rate is usually between 50 and 75 basis points above the short-term Treasury bill rate, indicating there is some risk in this market. There must be risk in the settlement market; otherwise, no bank would care whether it receives good funds to settle a net "due to" position. A running account would merely be kept of who owes what to whom. To guarantee settlement in good funds, someone must hold reserves on his or her balance sheet. We now turn to the question of how banks get paid for holding reserves.

As an example, assume that a seller of overnight fed funds arranges two fed funds lines for $50 million each. It holds $90 million in reserves on its balance sheet to make sure it has fed funds available to meet its commitments. (Assume there is very little likelihood that both customers will simultaneously draw the maximum amounts on their lines.) Suppose on Day 1 the seller sells $35 million on one line and $40 million on the other. It frees these reserves for sale by engaging in repos with demand deposit customers. This leaves it with $15 million in reserves that it must potentially hold overnight, earning no interest.

Let's assume that the seller decides to engage in a few more repurchase agreements with its demand deposit customers to free its remaining reserves. It sells them on the spot market to banks that have not purchased lines from it. Such an act will make the two banks that purchased lines most unhappy. They depend on the seller for liquidity. If the seller cannot retrieve the $15 million in reserves the following morning because the bank that bought the funds has become illiquid overnight, its contract customers cannot be assured of having sufficient access to good funds the next day. The contract customers will pay the seller to have sufficient reserves available to meet their demands for good funds. For this reason, reserves are the most liquid of all assets in the banking system.

DETERMINATION OF THE FED FUNDS RATE: A DIAGRAMMATIC PRESENTATION

In the preceding section we indicated that banks would choose to hold a certain amount of reserves, even in the absence of reserve requirements, because reserves are necessary to settle transactions among banks. As we indicated in Chapter 9, however, the Fed is the sole supplier of reserves to the banking system. Thus the nominal quantity of reserves available to the banking system is whatever the Fed wants it to be. When we say that banks choose the nominal level of reserves, we really mean that they determine the fed funds rate at which they are willing to hold the nominal quantity of reserves supplied by the Fed. That is, the fed funds rate is not affected by the reserve requirement.

In this section we will see how Fed manipulation of the quantity of nominal reserves supplied and the penalty rate for borrowing from the discount window affect the fed funds rate. This is a short-run analysis; we assume that the price level remains fixed. Thus a change in the nominal quantity of reserves is also a change in the real quantity of reserves.

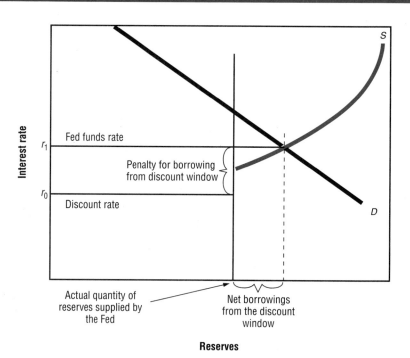

Figure 13.2 DETERMINING THE FED FUNDS RATE

We begin in Figure 13.2 with a graph that has the fed funds rate on the vertical axis and the quantity of reserves on the horizontal axis. The amount of reserves supplied by the Fed equals the vertical line labeled "Actual Quantity of Reserves Supplied." However, the supply of reserves can be greater than that initially supplied by the Fed because banks can borrow through the discount window. If the Fed charges a penalty over the discount rate for borrowing through the window, the supply curve of funds can be represented by a vertical line at the quantity of reserves supplied and an upward-sloping segment that diverges from the vertical line at a point above the discount rate representing the penalty for borrowing. The upward-sloping segment occurs if the penalty increases as the amount borrowed increases.

The Demand for Reserves

In our model of the banking system we have a downward-sloping demand curve for reserves against the fed funds rate that is independent of any reserve requirement that may be imposed by the Fed. The banking system demands reserves because they represent the means to effect settlement. Thus it would hold reserves whether the Fed imposed a requirement or not.

If reserve requirements are effective, demand for reserves at each fed funds rate will be higher than it would be if reserve holdings were determined by the free market. When the fed funds rate is low, it is cheaper to settle in good funds, and banks demand more reserves. The elasticity of the demand curve for reserves is determined by how liquid markets are on their own. If investors believe they can forgo the cost of settlement of securities transactions at relatively low cost, the demand curve for reserves will be very elastic. The more sophisticated an economy's financial markets, the more likely it is that the demand curve for reserves will be highly elastic. For example, in an economy with a well-functioning market for repurchase agreements among securities dealers, the demand curve for reserves will be highly elastic.

In Figure 13.2 we have drawn the demand curve so that it crosses the supply curve at a point where some reserves are borrowed from the Fed.

The Impact of an Increase in the Discount Window Penalty

In Figure 13.3 we analyze the impact of an increase in the penalty for borrowing from the discount window. An increase in the penalty for borrowing shifts the supply curve from S to S'. We have shifted the supply curve up, indicating that the base penalty increases, and we have also made it steeper, indicating that the penalty increases at a faster rate as borrowing increases. The higher penalty reduces borrowing and raises the fed funds rate.

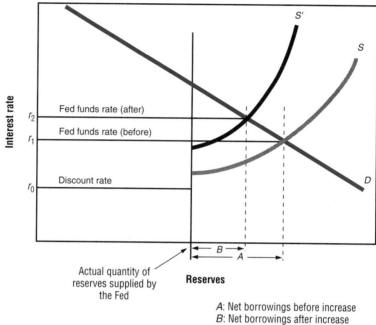

Figure 13.3   AN INCREASE IN THE DISCOUNT WINDOW PENALTY.   Supply
curve shifts from S to S'.

A Decrease in the Quantity of Reserves Supplied

If the Fed conducts an open-market operation by selling government securities, it decreases the quantity of reserves supplied to the banking system (see Chapter 9). We see how this operation affects the fed funds rate in Figure 13.4. We assume that the Fed withdraws reserves so that the quantity of reserves shifts from R to R'. This forces the supply curve to shift horizontally by the same amount from S to S'. The new equilibrium has fewer reserves and a higher fed funds rate. Figure 13.4 shows an increase in borrowing through the discount window after the decline in the quantity of reserves supplied. This occurs because the Fed does not increase the penalty for borrowing from the window. See Box 13.2 on page 340.

An Increase in a Binding Reserve Requirement

If reserve requirements are binding—that is, if they affect the quantity of reserves banks actually hold—a change in reserve requirements will affect the fed funds rate,

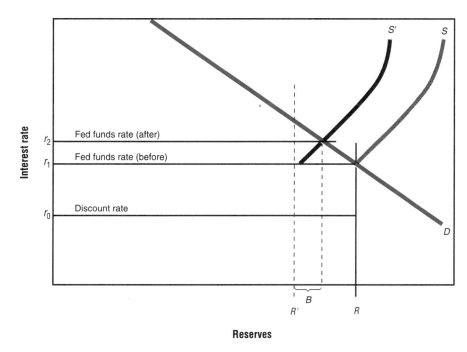

Figure 13.4 A DECREASE IN THE SUPPLY OF RESERVES.   Reserves supplied by the Fed shifts from R to R'.

Note: Initially, banks do not borrow from the discount window as the supply and demand curves (S and D) intersect at the point of actual supply of reserves. When the Fed decreases reserves, R shifts to R', forcing a horizontal shift in the supply curve by the same amount. At the new equilibrium, represented by fed funds rate r', banks borrow from the discount window represented by the amount B.

as indicated in Figure 13.5. An increase in reserve requirements shifts the demand curve to the right, increasing the fed funds rate. Assuming that the penalty for borrowing through the discount window remains unchanged, both the fed funds rate and borrowing through the window increase. See Box 13.3 on page 343.

WHEN ARE RESERVE REQUIREMENTS A TAX?

If banks and other securities issuers can freely create perfect substitutes for reservable deposits, banks can reduce reserve requirements against total liabilities to the level

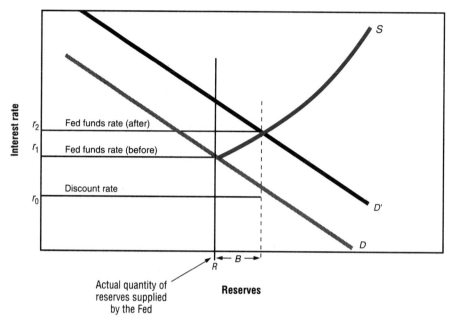

Figure 13.5   AN INCREASE IN A BINDING RESERVE REQUIREMENT   Demand curve shifts from *D* to *D'*.

desired to effect payments. The process of creating new instruments to reduce reserves to the desired level is known as **financial innovation.** See Box 13.4 on page 346.

However, as we indicated earlier, banks cannot reduce the quantity of reserves supplied by the Fed unless they can convert them to cash held by the public. If they cannot, in the short run, the nominal quantity supplied is adjusted to the nominal quantity demanded through adjustments in the fed funds rate.

If banks and other issuers cannot freely create substitutes for bank deposits, the Fed can force banks to hold more reserves than they would want to hold purely for the purpose of settling payments among themselves. In this situation, reserve requirements can become a tax if the quantity of reserves the Fed forces banks to hold is greater than the amount necessary to compensate the Fed for the risk it bears in the payments system. If banks can freely substitute out of reservable liabilities and the Fed ends up with fewer reserves than necessary to compensate it for the risk it bears, banks and financial markets receive a subsidy from the Fed.

If reserves really are a tax, the burden is then borne by all participants in financial markets and not just by depositors or borrowers from banks. This section discusses the circumstances under which reserves can be a tax.

Are Reserves a Tax in the Federal Reserve System?

Assuming that the Fed can impose an effective reserve requirement—that is, it can force the banks to hold more reserves than they would voluntarily hold—what is the appropriate level of reserve requirements in the Federal Reserve System? The Fed's guarantee of delivery of reserves at settlement is absolute. Ideally, the Fed should set the reserve requirement such that the income on its portfolio of securities financed by reserves plus income from other charges covers expected losses from the payments system.

The Fed can mimic the private clearinghouse that we discussed in Chapter 12. It can set reserves equal to expected net "due to's" and charge a fee for expected losses in reserves. Required reserves in the United States are currently about $49 billion, of which about $19 billion represents bank deposits held at the Fed. An additional $30 billion is vault cash held directly at banks for use in the banks' everyday operations. Net "due to" positions on fedwire, CHIPS, and U.S. government securities trading add up to about $100 billion at some time during the day. Total reserves are then less than the "due to" position. This is below the level that a private clearinghouse would set to provide an absolute payment guarantee.[10]

Reserve requirements are not necessarily too low, however. The Federal Reserve System is much larger than the stylized clearinghouse system in Chapter 12. It may not be necessary for reserves to equal the sum of net "due to's" to provide virtual certainty that payments will be delivered. In addition, unlike the private clearinghouse, the Fed earns interest on reserves. Since it can create good funds at will, it can invest the reserves without worrying about its ability to convert them to good funds to satisfy net "due to" positions. This income can be viewed as compensation for having to supply additional reserves in the event that an additional bank or group of banks cannot deliver good funds at settlement.

The question of whether the Fed's income is adequate to cover the risk it bears is a hotly debated topic. If its income is too high, reserves are a tax. However, it is very likely that reserves in the U.S. wholesale banking system cannot be a tax whatever the level of requirements set by the Fed because the market can too easily create securities with the characteristics of deposits that are not subject to reserves.

Because it is difficult for the Fed to collect additional revenue from an ineffective reserve requirement, it has turned to a charge on daylight overdrafts that we described in Chapter 12. Whether this charge is necessary depends on whether the Fed is extracting enough revenue from the marketplace already.

---

10.   The net "due to" position in the government securities market is $40 billion. If a bank fails to make payment on a government security it has received for its customer and the Fed delivers re- serves as payment to the seller's bank, it is not clear who has claim to the security—the purchaser or the Fed.

Box 13.2

The Supply of Reserves and the Fed Funds Rate

In Figure A we plot the fed funds rate and the reserve deposits held by banks with the Federal Reserve. As you can see, beginning in the third quarter of 1984, reserve balances began to increase, and by the time they peaked in the fourth quarter of 1986, they had increased by over 75 percent. At the same time, the fed funds rate fell from over 10 percent in the third quarter of 1984 to a low of less than 6 percent in the second quarter of 1986. When reserve growth ceased, the fed funds rate began to rise, again reaching 10 percent in the first quarter of 1989. These data are consistent with the model of the relationship between nominal reserves and the fed funds rate developed in Figures 13.2 through 13.4.

However, Figure A also indicates that the fed funds rate fell in periods when reserve balances were declining. For example, the fed funds rate fell from about 19 percent in the second quarter of 1981 to about 9 percent in the first quarter of 1983, while reserve balances fell by over 25 percent. The rate also fell from the first quarter of 1989 through the third quarter of 1990, while reserve balances declined slightly.

The long-run relationship between reserve growth and the fed funds rate is not consistent with our short-run model because real economic growth and the expected rate of inflation play major roles in determining the nominal interest rate, as we discussed in Chapter 5. In Figure B we plot the real quarterly growth rate for the U.S. gross national product (GNP) for the 1980s through the third quarter of 1990. The rapid fall in the fed funds rate in the early 1980s can be attributed at least partly to the decline in real income that occurred during that period. It also can be partially attributed to the deceleration in inflation that accompanied the recession. Likewise, the decline in the fed funds rate in the late 1980s can be attributed to the general slowing of the economy over that period.

Paying Interest on Reserves

Alan Greenspan, the Chairman of the Board of Governors of the Federal Reserve System, has publicly come out in favor of paying interest on reserves that banks hold with the Fed. We have calculated the liquidity premium based on the opportunity cost of holding reserves to make payments. If the Fed pays interest on reserves, what happens to the liquidity premium?

To analyze this problem, we must first remember that the revenue the Fed earns from issuing non-interest-bearing reserves is compensation for the risk it bears in guaranteeing interbank payments. The guarantee permits payees to use the anticipation of delivery of good funds to make payments themselves, which increases the liquidity of financial markets. For example, a payee can use anticipated good

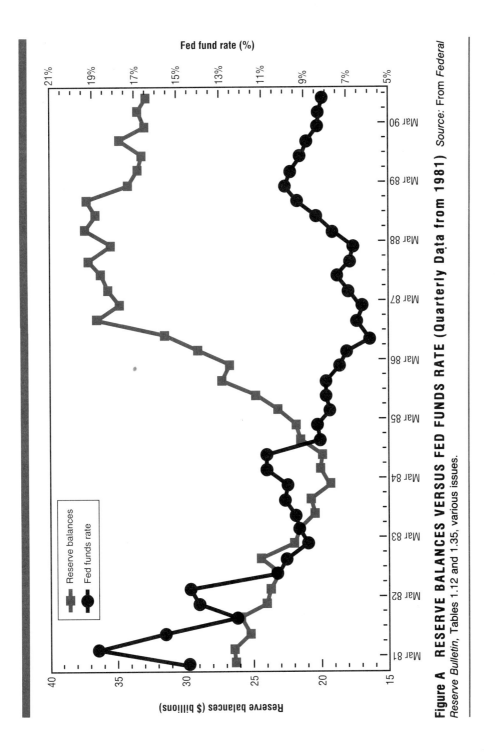

Figure A RESERVE BALANCES VERSUS FED FUNDS RATE (Quarterly Data from 1981) *Source: From Federal Reserve Bulletin*, Tables 1.12 and 1.35, various issues.

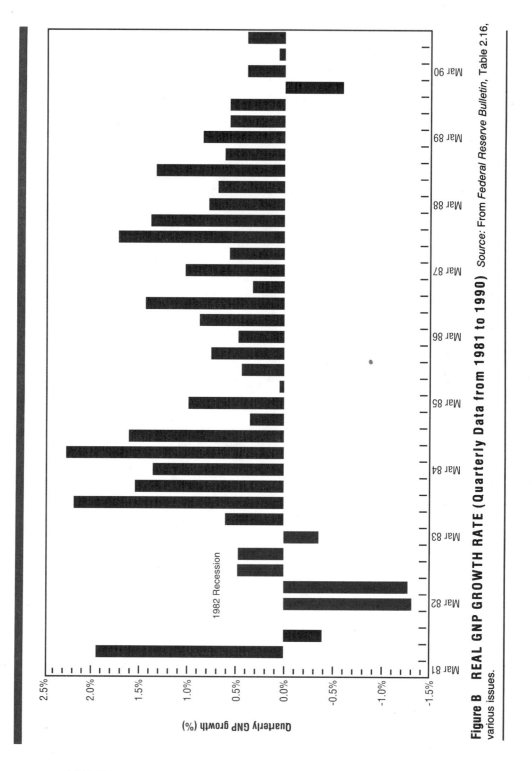

Figure B REAL GNP GROWTH RATE (Quarterly Data from 1981 to 1990) *Source:* From *Federal Reserve Bulletin*, Table 2.16, various issues.

Box 13.3

Fed Easing During the Recession of 1990–1991

The Fed took two actions to combat the recession that began in the fourth quarter of 1990. The first was to reduce, in two stages, reserve requirements on nonpersonal certificates of from 3 to 1.5 percent, and on January 1, 1991, they were suspended all together. The move was supposed to cut bank required reserves by over 20 percent, from about $61 billion before the reduction to less than $50 billion, since reserves on the affected deposits were $13.6 billion at the end of November 1990. On January 2, 1991, the Fed reduced the discount rate from 7 to 6.5 percent, and on February 2, it reduced it again to 6 percent.

In response to the announcement of the reserve requirement change in early December 1990, bank stock prices rallied. The accompanying table indicates that for the month ended December 13, bank stock prices rose 7.29 percent, while the Dow Jones Industrial Average increased by only 3.22 percent. Bank stocks rallied because the market assumed that the lower reserve requirements would improve bank earnings. This assumption was based on a simple calculation that banks would place the funds released from non-interest-bearing reserves accounts into interest-earning assets, improving earnings. This implies that the market believed that banks would hold fewer reserves if the Fed let them. In other words, the market believed that reserves are a tax and the tax was paid for by bank stockholders.

However, over the next month, as the table shows, bank stocks fell 6.43 percent, compared with a decline of 3.27 percent for the Dow Jones average. Thus the relative gains of bank stocks that occurred after the announcement of the reserve requirement reduction were almost wiped out.

PERCENTAGE CHANGE IN STOCK PRICE INDICES

Index	Month Ending			
	Dec. 12	Jan. 13	Feb. 4	Feb. 12
Dow Jones Industrial Average	3.22%	− 3.27%	8.04%	15.73%
American Banker Bank Index	7.29	− 6.43	16.05	29.33

Source: Adapted from *American Banker,* December 13, 1990, p. 23, January 14, 1991, p. 23, February 4, 1991, p. 15, and February 13, 1991, p. 23.

(continued)

funds to purchase commercial paper. If the payee had to wait until the actual delivery of good funds at settlement, the payee would not be able to purchase commercial paper until the next business day and consequently would have to hold a demand deposit overnight.

If the Fed pays interest on reserves *and* continues to guarantee delivery of good

Box 13.3 (continued)

Why did the market change its view of bank stocks relative to industrial stocks so soon after the decline in reserve requirements? After all, reserves declined about as predicted. Required reserves fell from about $60 billion to $48 billion, although actual reserves fell to about $49.5 billion. (The lower reserve requirements were accompanied by an increase in excess reserves.)

The change was partly due to the discovery that lower reserve requirements were not such a benefit to the largest banks after all, and the stock index is weighted toward the largest banks. Many large banks, such as Bankers Trust, Morgan Guaranty, and Republic New York Corporation, reported that they experienced no material decline in reserves at all. "It's marginal for us," Thomas Robards, executive vice president and treasurer of Republic, was quoted as saying in the January 7, 1991 *American Banker* (p. 12). The lack of impact on wholesale banks is further evidence that they were able to reduce reserve requirements to desired levels without a change in the requirements. Thus the liquidity premium in wholesale markets was probably not affected by reserve requirements.

However, because overall reserves fell, reserves at small banks before the change in requirements obviously were greater than the desired level. Thus they must have been a tax on someone. Who paid this tax? Our candidate is small business depositors who cannot easily substitute out of bank deposits for commercial paper.

According to the same *American Banker* article just mentioned, reduced required reserve holdings dramatically increased the volatility of the fed funds market. In the accompanying figure we plot the intraday range in the fed funds rate. As you can see, beginning in late December 1990, the range became very wide. The *American Banker* reported that many banks have found it difficult to manage their liquidity with reduced reserve balances. With the smaller reserve balances, a relatively small change in the demand for reserves can lead to large swings in the interest rate. That is, the market has greater difficulty handling increases in the demand for delivery of reserves.

This volatility will undoubtedly cause more banks to increase their reserve holdings despite the change in the reserve requirement. In January and February 1991, excess reserves, reserves held beyond required reserves, averaged about $1 billion more than they had averaged during the fall of 1990. However, total reserve holdings, including excess reserves, are likely to remain below their previous levels. Thus the fed funds rate is likely to remain more volatile.

The second reduction in the discount rate in early February again sent bank stocks soaring. According to the table, bank stocks rose by over 29 percent, while the market for industrial

---

funds, it must find some other means of compensation for the risk that it bears. An obvious choice would be a charge for intraday overdrafts similar to the one discussed in Chapter 12. Can this serve as the basis of a liquidity premium?

Assume a corporation issues a security. As before, the investor is concerned about its liquidity characteristics. For example, the investor might decide to sell the

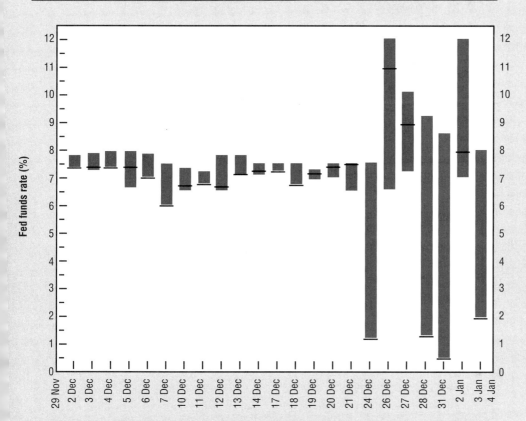

FED FUNDS VOLATILITY (HIGH, LOW, AND CLOSING RATES THROUGH 5 P.M. DAILY) *Source:* Adapted from *American Banker,* January 7, 1991, p. 12 (original source: Fulton Prebon).

stocks was up less than 16 percent. A decline in the discount rate is a signal of a more liberal reserve policy, which should lead to a lower liquidity premium and consequently more use of bank deposits for payments settlement. This is bullish for bank stocks, as long as the elasticity of demand for cash settlement is greater than 1.

security before it matures. Assume he sells it to a dealer who tries to finance it with a repo position. If the dealer successfully arranges the repo, no net "due to" position will be incurred. A payment to the investor will be offset by a receipt from the party that buys the security under the repurchase agreement. If the dealer cannot repo the security immediately, an overdraft is created and a charge is incurred. If

Box 13.4

Substituting Out of Reserve Requirements

During the summer of 1990, First Union Corporation, a large regional banking company headquartered in North Carolina, devised a scheme that the Fed charged evades reserve requirements. The bank sent notices to many of its NOW account and demand deposit customers stating that it would change its method of internally accounting for their deposits that would permit the customers to earn higher interest on their transactions balances.

First Union created a series of large time deposits with 7-day maturities. Each evening, NOW account and demand deposit balances were automatically "swept"—that is, transferred—into a new time account. During the day, customers could write checks on their accounts. These checks were paid from collections as well as from the balances in maturing CDs. The bank saved on reserve requirements because reserve requirements on CDs are less than those on transactions accounts. As an inducement to switch, the bank offered its transactions customers a higher interest rate than they could earn on a standard transactions account.

First Union said that it established the new account to compete with money market mutual funds, which have check-writing privileges and pay substantially higher interest than NOW accounts. Money market mutual funds, as we indicated earlier, invest in short-term obligations such as commercial paper. To provide their customers with checking privileges, they hold a demand deposit at a bank on which customer checks are drawn. Their customers pay for reserves in two ways. The securities that money market funds hold earn a low interest rate because they are liquid. In addition, a small portion of the funds is held in a demand deposit, or perhaps overnight repurchase agreements, to cover net checks written.

In effect, money market mutual funds permit smaller account holders to wholesale their transactions accounts to achieve the same returns that are available to large corporate customers. In return, these customers give up some liquidity. They cannot immediately access cash, and there is a minimum denomination placed on the checks they can write.

First Union claimed that it was trying to duplicate a service already available to its customers from nonbanks. In April of 1991, the Fed claimed that First Union was trying to evade

the security is illiquid, the dealer will have a difficult time finding a buyer; it will be likely that she must incur an overdraft charge. The liquidity premium is the overdraft charge times the probability that it will be used.

However, this is not the end of the story. If the dealer cannot find a buyer for the repo by the end of the day, she must finance her inventory with a bank loan.

reserve requirements and prohibited the practice. The Fed made its claim based on the presumption that reserve requirements are a tax on banks. Alan Greenspan, the chairman of the Federal Reserve Board, was quoted as saying that the problem of bank evasion will continue to crop up until Congress permits the Fed to pay interest on reserves, a policy position he supports.

Let's assume that First Union *thought* it found a way to reduce its reserve requirements and earn interest on the previously idle funds. If the banking system were holding its desired level of reserves before the First Union plan, how would it restore equilibrium? First Union's action would increase the amount of reserves it could sell in the fed funds market. The bank purchasing the funds could then expand deposits by the money multiplier formula introduced in Chapter 9. This would increase the amount of promises to deliver next-day funds relative to the amount of reserves in the system.

Since the amount of reserves relative to payments demand had fallen, there would be fewer reserves to effect payments. This would cause an increase in the variance in the fed funds rate as payments that used to be handled routinely now placed a strain on the availability of fed funds. Some banks would now see an opportunity to increase profits by increasing their reserve holdings, which would give them more fed funds to sell when the fed funds rate was inordinately high.

Another possibility is that First Union created an account that was less liquid than the usual NOW account or demand deposit. For example, let's assume that the new account has the same liquidity as money market mutual funds, which do not permit direct customer access to cash. If a customer wants cash, he or she must write a check on the fund and wait several days for it to clear. Since the new account is less liquid under this assumption, it places a lower demand for reserves on the banking system, and the banking system responded by substituting out of reserves.

The Fed's policy response to First Union is based on the notion that reserves are a tax. If this assumption is incorrect, as we believe the evidence on relative interest rates indicates, its response is bad policy.

Source: Facts were assembled from two articles in *The American Banker*, April 9, 1991, p. 1, and April 11, 1991, p. 2.

This implies a demand for reserves. Because reserves now pay interest, is there no longer an opportunity cost to holding reserves?

Consider the position of a bank selling fed funds. Its alternative is to hold interest-bearing reserves on its balance sheet. If the bank holds reserves overnight, it knows for certain that it will have reserves available the next morning to make payments. After all, reserves are a liability of the central bank and are therefore completely liquid. On the other hand, if it sells reserves in the fed funds market, the bank that buys them might become illiquid during the night. There is some possibility that the selling bank will not be able to retrieve the reserves in the morning. Thus, a bank selling fed funds will demand a spread between the rate it receives on fed funds and the interest rate it would earn if it held the reserves overnight. This spread is the opportunity cost of holding reserves. A dealer who must fund with a bank loan overnight must pay this opportunity cost.

Thus the liquidity premium must also include a charge for the expectation that an overdraft will become a bank loan. It will therefore have two parts: a charge for the expectation that an overdraft will be used and a charge for the expectation that the overdraft will become a bank loan. If Fed revenue remains unchanged with the institution of a policy to pay interest on reserves, the liquidity premium will be the same as before.

CONCLUSION

We have shown that the liquidity premium depends on the cost of reserves and that this cost must be reflected in the prices of all securities. Liquid securities carry a low liquidity premium because they are infrequently settled with the delivery of reservable deposits. Consequently, holders and issuers of these securities pay little of the cost of reserves. The cost of reserves cannot be a tax on liquidity as long as the market can create instruments that have no reserve requirements but have the same liquidity characteristics as reservable deposits.

KEY TERMS

commercial paper

bankers acceptance

DD crisis

CD/CP crisis

shadow price

Fed fund lines

financial innovation

EXERCISES

1. Reserve requirements are generally interpreted as a tax on the banking system. Also, along with controls on the supply of monetary base, reserve requirements limit the size of the banking system.

a. Describe the evidence that indicates that the incidence of the tax falls on bank borrowers. What is the role of the banking system in such a context?

b. Describe nonreservable substitutes for bank deposit liabilities that bear reserve requirements. If such substitutes are available, why does any bank hold reserves?

2. "Banks are different because they have an informational advantage about their borrowers compared with other, nonbank intermediaries." Comment.

3. Assume that the central bank raises reserve requirements on demand deposits from 10 to 20 percent. It supplies the additional reserves to keep the fed funds rate constant. What happens to the liquidity premium? (Base your answer on the probabilities and interest rates given in the text.)

4. Assume that there is an exogenous increase in the demand for demand deposits, as measured by an increase in the probability that investors will demand settlement in demand deposits. Assuming that the central bank supplies reserves to keep the fed funds rate constant, what happens to the liquidity premium? (Base your answer on the probabilities and interest rates given in the text.)

5. In Chapter 10 we observed that banks hold about 17 percent of their total assets in the form of securities. Securities, of course, are not uniquely held by the banking system. Also, banks issue deposits not subject to reserve requirements as well as those which are. Are these two facts consistent with Fama's model of who bears the cost of reserves?

6. Assume that investors consider CP and CDs, which are subject to reserve requirements, as identical investments. Banks try to cover the cost of reserve requirements by reducing the interest rate they offer on CDs. How will investors react to this? Using the Fama model, under what circumstances will banks continue to issue CDs, even if they must pay the same interest rate as is offered in the CP market?

7. In fact, we have seen that, unlike the assumption made in the Fama model, CP issuers and CP holders are also bank borrowers from time to time. Thus CP issuers and CP holders pay for the cost of reserves. Why does this imply that CD holders must pay for the cost of reserves?

8. Reserve requirements were removed from CDs on January 1, 1991. Is the CD market still affected by the cost of reserves?

9. If banks try to lower the interest rate on CDs to cover the cost of reserve requirements, what can we say about the reserves they have to hold relative to the reserves they desire to hold?

10. In this chapter we have assumed that all commercial paper is alike. In fact, the quality of commercial paper issuers varies widely. Assume that the paper issued by the riskier firms is less liquid than the paper issued by high-quality firms. Which issuer (and holder) bears the greater expected cost of reserves?

11. A few corporations have the privilege of issuing commercial paper without attaching a specific bank line to their paper. These companies hold enough liquid assets to cover emergencies in the commercial paper market, and they have general bank lines that can be used for any purpose. How do these companies pay for the cost of reserves?

12. When the fed funds rate rises, the cost of settling in good funds increases. Why?

13. An increase in the cost of settling in good funds with an increase in the fed funds rate should cause market participants to substitute out of settlement in good funds. Will the liquidity premium rise or fall with an increase in interest rates? (Or is the answer indeterminant?)

14. If the liquidity premium rises with an increase in the fed funds rate, what does this say about the elasticity of the demand curve for reserves? About substitutes for settlement in reserves?

15. Assume that a bank, thinking it can save money, substitutes out of reservable deposits. Holding the level of reserves constant, this increases the amount of immediately available funds relative to the reserve base. If the banking system actually holds the desired level of reserves, how is equilibrium restored?

16. If commercial banks were no longer able to count vault cash as a part of their required reserves, would there be any impact on the price level?

17. In the absence of labor and plant costs of servicing bank deposits, the rate of interest on deposits should tend to be equal to the rate of interest on loans made by the bank. Comment.

FURTHER READING

Calomiris, Charles. "The Motivations for Loan Commitments Backing Commercial Paper," *Journal of Banking and Finance,* Vol. 13 (1989), pp. 271–277.

Fama, Eugene. "What's Different About Banks?" *Journal of Monetary Economics,* Vol. 15 (January 1985), pp. 29–40.

Grossman, Sanford, and Mertin Miller. "Liquidity and Market Structure," *The Journal of Finance,* Vol. 43, no. 3 (July 1988), pp. 617–634.

James, Christopher. "Some Evidence on the Uniqueness of Bank Loans," *Journal of Financial Economics,* Vol. 19 (1987), pp. 217–236.

Parker, Willis H., John Chapman, and Ralph Robey. *Contemporary Banking.* New York: Harper, 1933.

The Role of Banks in the U.S. and World Economies

14

The Role of Bank Loans in the U.S. Economy

In the summer of 1990, Donald Trump turned to his bankers to avoid falling under the supervision of bankruptcy court. He was about to miss payments to bondholders of one of his casinos in Atlantic City. He called on his bankers to rescue him with a fresh infusion of cash. The bankers responded positively, but only after they extracted concessions over how his empire was to be managed and who was to manage it. In addition, they placed, what is for him, onerous restrictions on his lifestyle. He was required to confine his monthly expenditures to $325,000, and he was forced to sell his helicopters.

Providing loans to corporations in financial distress is a typical example of the role that banks play in the world of corporate finance. This often places them in a position of being lender of last resort for businesses struggling to find sources of credit.

In Chapter 13 we noted that the banking system is unique because it supplies liquidity to financial markets. In this chapter we discuss how banks' role in providing liquidity is related to their role as lender of last resort to corporations. We find that banks' special role in providing liquidity gives them an advantage in providing bank loans to risky corporate customers. In demonstrating this point, we compare bank loans to other types of corporate funding, such as finance company loans and corporate bonds. We also compare the role banks play in corporate finance in the United States with their role in another major industrial country, Japan.

Finally, we consider the role of banks in consumer finance in the United States. We conclude that banks play a major role in this market because they have large branch systems that provide consumers with easy access to their services. These branch systems have been established primarily to give consumers and small businesses easy access to cash withdrawals from their bank accounts. Thus the role of banks in consumer finance is also related to their role in providing liquidity.

THE ROLE OF BANK LOANS IN U.S. CORPORATE FINANCE

Terms of Lending Survey

Table 14.1 presents a survey of the terms of commercial and industrial loans made by U.S. banks conducted periodically by the Federal Reserve System. The data in this table provide information on loans made during the week of August 6–10, 1990. In the first column loans are broken into two broad categories—short- and long-term loans. Each of these categories is further subdivided. The second column provides an estimate of the total amount of loans during that particular week, by category. (It is an estimate because the data are based on a sample of banks blown up to represent the total banking system.) The third and fourth columns indicate the average size of loan and average maturity, respectively, by category. The fifth column indicates the percentage of loans made under commitment.

The sixth column, labeled "Most Common Base Pricing Rate," indicates which interest rate is used in pricing the typical loan in each category. For example, most overnight loans are priced from the fed funds rate, meaning that the lending bank charges an interest rate of, say, 50 basis points over the fed funds rate. A "domestic" pricing base means that the bank prices from a money market rate other than the fed funds rate, such as the interest rate on bank certificates of deposit. A "foreign" pricing base indicates that an overseas money market rate, such as the London interbank dollar market offer rate, is used. "Other" base pricing rates are those which do not fit into any of the specified categories.

The **prime rate** is a base interest rate set by banks for lending to business customers. Unlike the interest rates on money market instruments that are established continuously in the marketplace, the prime rate is set by banks on a periodic basis. Because it is changed relatively infrequently, it moves in large steps, compared with the continuous change of money market rates such as the fed funds rate. Notice that loans based on the prime rate carry higher interest rates than those based on money market interest rates. Figure 14.1 plots the historical relationship between the prime rate and the fed funds rate.

Table 14.1 COMMERCIAL AND INDUSTRIAL LOANS, SURVEY OF LOANS MADE, AUGUST 6 TO 10, 1990

Characteristic	Amount of Loans ($Million)	Average Size ($Thousand)	Weighted Average Maturity (Days)	Loan Rate (Weighted) (%)	Loans Made Under Commitment (%)	Most Common Base Interest Rate
Short term						
Overnight	14,105	6,834	*	9.03	55.7	Fed funds
1 month and under	8,880	1,131	17	9.44	88.2	Domestic
1 month to 1 year	11,147	168	135	10.14	82.8	Prime
Demand	11,352	195	*	10.40	80.2	Prime
Total Short Term	45,485	338	49	9.72	74.8	Fed funds
Long term		(Months)				
All fixed-rate loans over $1 million	1,283	160	42	10.31	66.1	Other
	956	5,135	41	9.86	76.4	Foreign
All floating-rate loans over $1 million	3,300	313	42	10.88	72.4	Prime
	2,284	3,483	43	10.46	72.9	Prime
Total Long Term	4,583	247	42	10.72	70.7	Prime

Source: Adapted from the *Federal Reserve Bulletin*, December 1990, Table 4.23, p. A77.

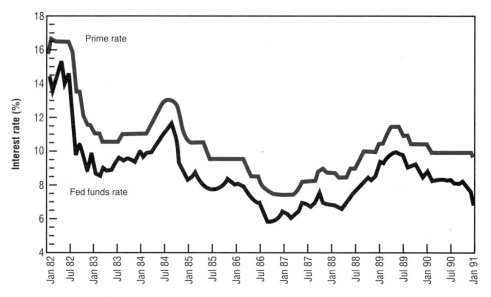

Figure 14.1 PRIME RATE VERSUS FEDERAL FUNDS RATE, JANUARY 1982 TO DECEMBER 1990   *Source:* Collected by DRI/McGraw-Hill from the Federal Reserve System.

Short-Term Commercial Loans

Table 14.1 indicates that the dollar volume of short-term loans made during the week of August 6, at $45.5 billion, was 10 times greater than the volume of long-term loans. This does not mean that the dollar volume of short-term loans outstanding is 10 times the dollar volume of long-term loans, however. Short-term loans outstanding disappear from the books much more quickly than long-term loans. Thus new short-term loans are a higher percentage of outstanding short-term loans than is the case for long-term loans.

Among short-term loans, overnight loans are somewhat unique. They are of very large average size compared with the other categories of short-term loans. Also, they are priced from the fed funds rate and have the lowest typical interest rate of any type of short-term loan. The high average size and the low interest rate indicate that these loans are made to large, low-risk customers. (We do not mean to imply that all large customers are low-risk customers, only that customers using overnight loans are both large and low risk.)

These are the liquidity loans used by large corporations that we described in Chapter 13. When a major corporation finds itself in a temporary liquidity squeeze, it borrows overnight from a bank. We have already discussed the commercial paper rollover crisis in Chapter 13. Liquidity squeezes also can arise as a result of a 1-day mismatch between payments and receipts. For example, a corporation may have a large payment due its bondholders on Monday. It holds Treasury bills that mature on Tuesday. Rather than sell the Treasury bills on Monday, the corporation may decide to borrow overnight from its bank.

Treasury bill rates in August 1990 were over 100 basis points lower than the 9.03 percent interest rate that was typically charged on overnight loans. Why wouldn't a corporation merely sell its Treasury bills rather than take out an overnight loan? The expense involved in selling the Treasury bills plus the interest sacrificed from selling them a day early is greater than the interest cost of borrowing from a bank overnight. Also, it is not economical to issue commercial paper to cover an overnight obligation. While the interest rate on commercial paper is lower than the overnight loan rate, issuing commercial paper involves a noninterest expense that adds to the cost, making the instrument too expensive for overnight funding.

A noteworthy aspect of the overnight loan market is that only 55.7 percent of the loans are made under commitment, compared with 74.8 percent for the short-term loan market as a whole. In Chapter 13 we indicated that because commercial paper issuers draw on bank credit lines (a form of commitment), they pay the expected cost of reserve requirements. These data indicate that many large corporate borrowers use bank loans not made under commitment. This does not mean they avoid the expected cost of using reserves, however. This cost is in the interest rate they face when they borrow from a bank.

Notice that as the maturity of the short-term loan increases, the average loan size declines and the average effective interest rate increases. Large, low-risk corporations use banks less frequently for loans extending beyond 1 night because, for longer maturities, it pays to sell Treasury bills or issue commercial paper rather than use bank loans.

The final category of short-term loan is demand loans. Demand loans have characteristics similar to consumer credit card loans. They have no fixed maturity and can be paid off at any time, in full or in part. These loans are used for liquidity purposes, just like overnight loans. If a business borrower must meet a payment but has insufficient funds available in her bank account, she can draw down a commitment for a demand loan.

The average demand loan size is substantially smaller than the average overnight loan size. The typical demand loan also has a higher interest rate than the typical overnight loan. Thus demand loans are used by smaller and riskier companies than overnight loans.

Why do small companies use demand loans while large companies that are also good credit risks use overnight loans? Large, safe companies have much better control over their cash flow. They know when payments to their investors must be made and when large receipts such as interest payments on financial investments come due. When mismatches between payments and receipts are expected to last several days, they make adjustments by issuing short-term securities or selling liquid assets rather than by borrowing from banks. Small companies cannot predict the mismatch of payments and receipts so accurately. Since they cannot predict when they can repay the bank loan, they use demand loans.

Long-Term Loans

Long-term loans (which we will refer to as *term loans,* following industry custom) are typically priced from the prime rate, indicating that they are, on average, made to riskier companies than are short-term loans. During this survey, term loans had an average maturity of $3\frac{1}{2}$ years, which is fairly typical of other surveys as well. Notice that some very large customers use the term loan market. Over 70 percent of the dollar volume of loans is accounted for by loans over $1 million. Most of these large loans are priced from the prime rate, indicating that they are made to relatively risky, large borrowers.

Corporations have several alternatives to raising funds by taking out a term loan from a commercial bank. These alternatives are illustrated in Table 14.2, which provides the aggregate balance sheet for American Corporations as of June 1990. The largest single liability item is corporate bonds. Bank loans are the next largest source. (We will explain other major liability items throughout the chapter.) Since large, safe borrowers shun the term *bank loan market,* we can infer that they use the bond market for long-term finance. Risky firms, as the terms of lending data demonstrate, use the term bank loan market. However, many of these firms also have access to and use the bond market, as the Trump example indicates. Can we make a distinction between how risky corporations use the term bank loan market and how they use the bond market?

Term Loans versus Bonds

Bank loans are apparently different from bonds. For example, Christopher James developed evidence indicating that the announcement of a bank commitment to lend causes the stock price of the recipient company to rise immediately after the announcement by more than general market movements and its risk would seem to warrant.[1] He found that an announcement of a commitment to lend by an insurance company causes no such reaction in the stock market. He inferred from this result that capital markets regard banks as possessors of valuable private information about borrowers, which other lenders, such as insurance companies, do not possess. James interpreted this evidence to mean that banks are uniquely reliable evaluators of creditworthiness. A bank line of credit is interpreted as a valuable stamp of approval.

1. *Source:* Christopher James, "Some Evidence on the Uniqueness of Bank Loans," *Journal of Financial Economics,* Vol. 19 (1987), pp. 217–236.

Table 14.2 NONFINANCIAL CORPORATE BALANCE SHEET, JUNE 1990 (FINANCIAL ASSETS AND LIABILITIES ONLY)

	($Billions)
Total Financial Assets	2043.4
Liquid assets	447.5
Demand deposits and currency	123.7
Time deposits	99.6
Money market fund shares	20.9
Security repurchase agreements	76.0
Foreign deposits	16.4
U.S. government securities	60.8
Tax-exempt obligations	10.0
Commercial paper	40.0
Consumer credit	32.5
Mutual fund shares	14.3
Trade credit	833.7
Miscellaneous assets	715.5
Foreign direct investment	378.3
Insurance receivables	131.6
Equity in spons. agencies	1.3
Other	204.3
Total Liabilities	3142.7
Credit market instruments	2124.8
Tax-exempt debt	115.5
Corporate bonds	953.3
Mortgages	113.6
Home mortgages	50.9
Multifamily	25.8
Commercial	82.7
Bank loans	543.1
Commercial paper	128.6
Nonbank finance company loans	138.5
U.S. government loans	9.6
Profit taxes payable	24.5
Trade debt	582.0
Foreign direct investments in United States	411.4

Source: From Board of Governors of the Federal Reserve, as reported by Data Resources, Inc.

Scott Lummer and John McConnell (1989) found that James's results hold only when bank lines are renewed, not when they are initiated.[2] That is, the market does not view banks' first credit evaluation as valuable, new information. Once a bank has observed a borrower's behavior, however, its subsequent evaluation is considered valuable.

2. Scott Lummer and John McConnell, "Further Evidence on the Bank Lending Process and the Capital Market Responses to Bank Loan Agreements," Working Paper Draft, June 1989.

Banks' renewal signal is more important than signals provided by original bank terms or by other borrowers because banks play a special role in monitoring borrowers' behavior. This special function is conferred on banks because of their role in the payments system.

To see how bank loans are special, we compare the contract terms offered by insurance companies when they buy bonds with the terms offered by banks when they make long-term loans. Insurance companies are active purchasers of private placement bonds. **Private placements** are bonds that are not issued publicly, nor are they allowed to be sold to the general public after issuance because they are not registered with the Securities and Exchange Commission (SEC). In 1989, $115 billion in private placement corporate bonds were issued in the United States, compared with $181 billion in domestic public offerings.

How do the terms of a private placement differ from the terms of a bank loan? In the sample of bank loans and private placements used by James (1987), bank loans have a shorter maturity (5 years on average) than a private placement (15 years on average). Because bank loans have a shorter maturity, they force corporations to meet larger cash demands than do private placements. For example, let's assume that both a bank loan and a private placement require periodic payment of principal as well as interest. Since the entire principal must be paid off by maturity, the shorter the maturity, the greater each installment payment of principal must be.

From principal-agent theory we can infer that this feature is used to control the behavior of the borrower more closely. A borrower who must produce large amounts of cash at specific intervals must invest in projects with a relatively certain cash flow. Thus banks provide loans that place more restrictions on borrower behavior than loans provided by insurance companies. As a result, banks pay closer attention to the short-term conditions of their clients than do insurance companies. We will see that banks end up with the role of monitoring customers more closely because they have the means at their disposal to immediately effect a change in borrowers' behavior. The means is control over the borrower's ability to make payments.

The Role of Banks in Monitoring Borrowers

Banks in the United States force risky corporate borrowers to maintain compensating balances as part of the loan agreement. **Compensating balances** are demand deposits that the borrower must hold with the bank. The loan agreement generally specifies what the level of these balances must be. Banks also charge for noncredit services through required demand deposit balances. These requirements are designed to force borrowers to maintain their major transaction accounts with the lending bank, which, we shall see, has important consequences for banks' role in the monitoring process.

The terms of the loan agreement are designed to take full advantage of the fact that banks provide payments services to their customers.[3] Two important clauses in loan agreements are associated with banks' role in the payments system. One is the acceleration clause, and the second is the right of setoff. The **acceleration clause** gives banks the right to demand full and immediate payment when they determine that a clause in the loan agreement has been violated. **Setoff** gives the lender the right to seize the debtor's assets in the lender's possession in the event of default.

The Universal Commercial Code (UCC) does not grant these rights exclusively to banks; however, the payments function of banks give them unique opportunities to exercise these rights. The important borrower asset the bank has to seize is the deposits the customer utilizes to receive and make payments.

This is an important asset to have in possession for two reasons. First, the size of the deposit can often be large relative to the loan outstanding. For example, as reported in the Bank for International Settlement (BIS) 1989 *Annual Report,* the dollar volume of bank loans to 14 heavily indebted countries was $265 billion at year-end 1988. The bank deposits of these countries totaled $97 billion.

The dollar volume of deposits in a borrower's account can vary widely depending on the timing of receipts and payments. Alert account officers keep a watchful eye on changes in balance levels. If a bank does invoke the acceleration clause, it is likely to do so when balances appear to be at relatively high levels.

This leads to the second advantage that banks have over other lenders. When they freeze an account, they prevent the borrower from making payments to other claimants. This effectively forces the borrower and other claimants to come to the bank to negotiate a solution to a perceived credit problem. See Box 14.1.

The authority to stop payments places banks in a better position to exploit new and detailed information about a borrower than other lenders. Banks have the means at their disposal to use recent information to constrain the behavior of the borrower, whereas other lenders do not. As a result, they accumulate more detailed and current information about borrowers than do other lenders. Because a bank constantly observes the behavior of a borrower, renewing a line of credit on favorable terms is positive information for the market. Banks' special position also gives them the leadership role among creditors in renegotiating terms with a borrower that has fallen into financial difficulty, as we shall see in the next several sections.

Bank Role in Leveraged Buyouts

We introduced leveraged buyouts in Chapter 2. Bank lending typically plays an important role in getting a leveraged buyout off the ground because banks provide temporary funding while the bond financing is being arranged. The bonds used to finance leveraged buyouts are often referred to as junk bonds. **Junk bonds** are high-

---

3. See Anthony C. Gooch and Linda B. Klein, *Loan Agreement Documentation: Sample Annotated Loan*   *Agreement for Syndicated Eurodollar Transaction* (London: Euromoney Financial Law Series, 1986).

Box 14.1

Seizing a Payment

In late September 1990, the stock price of Polly Peck International (PPI), an international conglomerate trading on the London stock exchange, collapsed. The firm, which has interests in Turkish businesses, Japanese electronics, and fruit distribution in North America, had been having liquidity problems, and the market believed that the firm would not survive. On October 3, PPI attempted to make a $15 million payment to a group of its creditor banks, led by Credit Suisse First Boston. One of the banks in the correspondent network, thought to be a British bank, that was forwarding the payment on to Credit Suisse was owed money by Del Monte Fresh Produce, a subsidiary of PPI formerly owned by Del Monte Corporation. The bank seized the payment under the right of setoff against its loan to Del Monte Fresh Produce.

Both U.K. and U.S. law recognizes the right of setoff. However, the right only applies in cases of mutuality, which is when the party that owes and the party that has its deposits seized are one and the same. In this case, Del Monte Fresh Produce was the party that owed, and PPI was the party that had its deposits seized. Thus, technically, there was no mutuality. However, lawyers familiar with the case were quoted in the *Financial Times* (October 4, 1990) as saying that in situations such as this, banks take the view that possession is nine-tenths of the law.

Thus PPI was placed in a position where it could not use the payments system without fear that a bank would intercept the payment before it arrived at its intended destination.

risk, high–yield securities. They are called "junk" because of the presumed high risk of the companies that issue them. Banks' evaluation of a deal is an important signal to bond buyers that a prospective buyout has potential.

In leveraged buyouts, the size of the deal often runs into the billions of dollars. The largest leveraged buyout, RJR Nabisco, required $25 billion in funding, $5 billion of which was provided by bank loans. Because it would be too risky for one bank to absorb a large exposure to a single borrower, banks form syndicates to handle large loans to a single borrower. A **syndicate** is a group of banks formed to divide a loan among themselves to reduce the exposure that each faces. In form, a bank syndicate is similar to the underwriting syndicate we introduced in Chapter 6. The difference is that members of a bank syndicate retain a portion of the loan for their balance sheets, whereas investment banks usually sell the entire issue to investors. See Box 14.2.

Members of the syndicate are each bound by a single loan agreement. All parties share in the information collected by the lead bank in the syndicate, called an *agent*. Any collateral that is held by any member of the syndicate is shared by all in the event of default. This includes deposits subject to the right of setoff.

In leveraged buyouts, banks are usually senior creditors to bondholders—that is, their claims have precedence in bankruptcy court. Before the bond market is willing to commit itself to a deal, it wants to see how large a stake banks are willing to take in a deal. This determines how active a role the banks will play in seeing a borrower through a difficult financial bind. There is an old adage in banking that says if a borrower owes you $100,000, you control him; if he owes you $100 million, he controls you. See Box 14.3.

The Leveraged Buyout Market in Distress

In 1990, the market for junk bonds, which had been wracked by several spectacular corporate bankruptcies as well as the bankruptcy of the leading junk bond dealer, dried up, reducing considerably the dollar volume of mergers and acquisitions. According to the Loan Pricing Corporation, in February 1990, the dollar volume of deal flow was $18.3 billion. By April it had fallen to $11.9 billion. See Box 14.4.

Deals in place also began to suffer because cash flow at many companies heavily burdened with debt proved insufficient to cover interest payments. The bonds issued in many leveraged buyouts were called *PIKs—payment-in-kind securities*. PIKs pay interest in more bonds. For example, let's assume that an investor buys a $10,000 PIK with a coupon payment of $1,500 per year. The coupon payment is not paid in dollars; it is paid in more bonds issued by the same corporation that issued the original PIK. PIKs are usually subject to a time limit. After a certain number of years, the issuing corporation must begin to pay interest in cash. The deadline for many PIKs issued in the late 1980s occurs sometime between 1991 and 1995. Analysts predict that many firms will not have the cash flow to meet the additional expenses. Thus they will be forced to restructure their debt or face bankruptcy. Banks are bound to play a major role in the restructuring.

Bank Lending in Recession

In the fall of 1990, the U.S. economy slid into a recession. Bank stock prices had been falling for about a year before the recession occurred as the market became concerned about the quality of bank loans. For example, major banking companies which were the lenders that had invested the most effort in evaluating the deal, believed that it could be successful.

The high-yield junk bonds that financed most of the buyout were a tremendous strain on the cash flow of RJR. In June, KKR began the process of restructuring the massive debt to reduce borrowing costs. KKR wanted to redeem $6 billion in junk bonds with a combination of $1.7 billion in equity supplied by them and a package of bank loans and preferred stock. Banks were to supply an additional $2.5 billion in loans.

In addition, KKR wanted RJR to pay off its $500 million subordinated loan to KKR with a new bank loan. The banks balked at this for two reasons. First, they said that with over $5 billion in RJR bank debt floating around the syndicated bank market, it was difficult to place the additional loan. Second, the banks were not enthused about KKR, which is an equity investor, withdrawing funds from the deal.

The banks agreed to refund the subordinated loan, but only after several conditions were met. First, RJR's income had to exceed its budget projections, and second, all amortization schedules had to be met.

The remaining bond investors, however, were unhappy with this agreement. The $500 million loan had originally been subordinated to other bondholder claims. The banks negotiated the new loan so that it would mature before the bonds. Thus the banks would be able to pull their money out before the bondholders could. If bankruptcy occurred after the maturity of the bank loan, the bondholders would, in effect, be junior to the new loan.

such as Citicorp and Chase saw their stock prices fall by 65 percent or more. The weak financial condition of banks led to a general reluctance of banks to extend new loans, creating fears that a credit crunch would prolong the recession. See Box 14.5. However, at the same time, the press reported that many corporations that were habitual commercial paper issuers, such as MCI, began turning instead to banks for credit.

The immediate reason for the shift was the increase in perceived risk of the securities of many corporations. Publicly offered debt is evaluated by credit rating agencies such as Moody's and Standard & Poors. These agencies rate the riskiness of the issue based on a corporation's equity-to-assets ratio, its stability of cash flow, its quality of management, and the long-term prospects for the industry. A low-risk corporation's bond offering receives a AAA rating. The equivalent low-risk commercial paper rating is A-1. Corporations often receive a higher commercial paper rating than a bond rating, indicating that their short-term prospects are better than their long-term prospects.

When the recession hit, the credit quality of many corporations declined, and consequently, their cost of issuing debt increased. The rating agencies responded to the greater risk by downgrading many corporate ratings. These same corporations had bank lines that included a fixed cost of borrowing relative to the prime rate or a market interest rate. For example, a corporation might have a bank line that states

Box 14.4

The Junk Bond Market in Chaos

The investment banking house that pioneered the junk bond market, Drexel Burnham Lambert, filed for bankruptcy in February 1990. The event that triggered the bankruptcy was a missed payment on commercial paper the firm had issued, but, of course, the missed payment was merely a symptom of a more fundamental problem. That fundamental problem was the condition of the junk bond market.

Junk bonds are an extremely expensive source of debt that place great strains on a company's cash flow. By early 1990, it was clear that many firms could not handle the pressure. For example, in January, Campeau, which had used junk bonds to purchase the Federated (the owner of Bloomingdale's) and Allied department store chains, filed for bankruptcy. In November, Days Inns failed to meet payments on its junk bonds and began negotiations with its bondholders to restructure terms.

As the leading investment bank in junk bonds, Drexel Burnham held an inventory of junk bonds as well as equity positions in the deals it had generated. When the bonds and equity ceased generating cash flow, Drexel had no funds to pay its liability holders. Hence it missed a payment on its commercial paper and was forced to file for bankruptcy.

The failure of Drexel Burnham signified the end of the junk bond boom and reduced the financing available for leveraged buyouts. This appears to have changed significantly the structure of the funding for leveraged buyouts. In the 1980s it was common for the equity stake in leveraged buyouts to be as little as 10 to 15 percent of assets. However, many bankers say that the terms of two proposed acquisitions in 1990 may represent the future trend.

A proposed acquisition of Maybelline carried a price tag of $300 million, with $160 million in equity and $140 million in bank loans. Another proposal, Prime Motor Inns, Inc., carried a price tag of $170 million, with $90 million in equity and $115 million in bank loans. Junk bonds were totally absent as a source of funds.

the bank will lend for 75 basis points over the domestic CD rate. As a result of the higher cost of accessing the credit market, many companies turned to bank financing, even though, at this writing, it is not clear that they can get it.

This pattern was typical of the 1982 recession as well. During that year, bank commercial and industrial loans to U.S. borrowers increased 9.6 percent from $358 billion to $392 billion, whereas commercial paper of nonfinancial corporations out-

Box 14.5

The Credit Crunch and Foreign Banks in the U.S. Market

Foreign banks play a substantial role in the domestic U.S. banking market. At the end of September 1990, domestic commercial banks that were more than 50-percent owned by foreign banks held commercial and industrial (C&I) loans to U.S. businesses equal to $51.1 billion. Foreign banks made an additional $72.7 billion in commercial and industrial loans through their American branches. At the end of the third quarter of 1990, total C&I loans made by subsidiaries of foreign banks and branches of foreign banks equaled more than 17 percent of all C&I loans made to U.S. businesses.

Some Americans are quite concerned about the scale of foreign bank presence in the United States. They argue that banks are too important to the well-being of U.S. financial markets and the economy to be placed in the hands of foreigners, who might not have as strong a commitment to the United States as Americans. In addition, they argue that American banks are effectively excluded from competing in the home markets of many of the foreign banks that compete actively in the United States.

Despite these fears, it seems that the American economy has benefited from the participation of foreign banks. In late 1990 and early 1991, many commentators argued that a credit crunch was the major problem preventing recovery of theU.S. economy. For example, the Fed periodically surveys senior loan officers on bank lending practices. The surveys for late 1990 and early 1991 showed that almost half the banks surveyed reduced credit lines to large commercial borrowers and increased loan interest rates to all commercial customers.

These policies are reflected in the fact that commercial and industrial loans made by U.S. banks did not grow at all during 1990. However, domestic commercial and industrial loans at foreign banks rose by more than 15 percent over the same period, providing a needed supply of cash to credit-hungry businesses.

standing declined 11 percent from $54 billion to $48 billion. In contrast, in the prosperous year of 1989, bank loans grew at a much slower rate than commercial paper. They rose 5.9 percent from $592 billion to $629 billion; commercial paper of nonfinancial firms, on the other hand, rose 26.5 percent from $103 billion to $129 billion.

Figure 14.2 plots the ratio of commercial paper issued by nonfinancial firms to commercial and industrial loans. As you can see, this ratio has been rising over time, but it declined steeply in 1982. If borrower behavior is similar during the 1990–1991 recession, this ratio should, at least, cease its upward trend.

Why are banks willing to step in to provide funding when the public market is not? One possibility is that banks make mistakes in pricing loans. That is, they set their interest rates too low for the risk of lending in a recession and too high for the risk of lending during a boom. However, this has been the pattern of loan

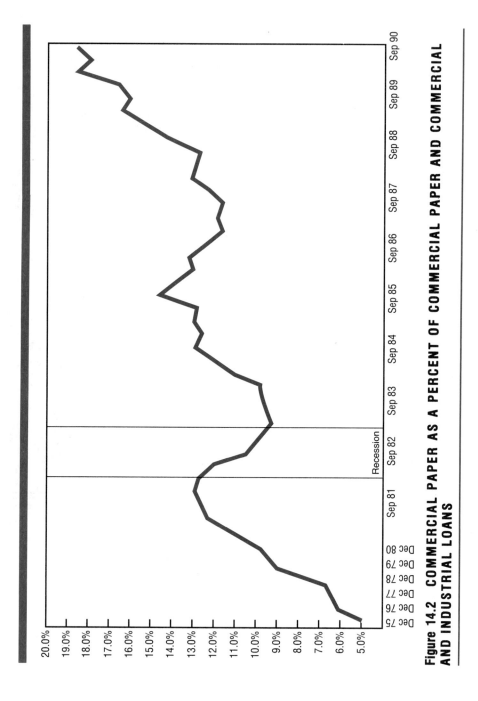

Figure 14.2 COMMERCIAL PAPER AS A PERCENT OF COMMERCIAL PAPER AND COMMERCIAL AND INDUSTRIAL LOANS

pricing over at least two recessions. A persistent pricing pattern is a signal that something more fundamental is determining the price of bank credit relative to open-market paper than mistakes.

In addition to risk of the borrower, the cost of a bank loan relative to open-market paper is determined by the cost of monitoring. Banks must use real resources to watch borrowers' accounts and monitor their behavior closely. Monitoring activities are risk reducing, but this comes at a cost. The cost of other forms of credit is determined by lenders' perceptions of the risk of lending to a borrower who is relatively free to behave as he or she pleases.

During periods of economic stability, the risk premium in the open market makes bank loans relatively unattractive for moderately low-risk corporations. When a recession arrives, this changes. Lenders become worried and raise their risk premiums. At such times, some borrowers find that by subjecting themselves to the monitoring straightjacket, they can reduce their cost of borrowing. Borrowers' risk changes with a bank loan because their behavior changes.

A Model of Bank Lending

The market conditions that determine the amount of bank loans relative to open-market borrowing are illustrated in Figure 14.3. The minimum cost of a bank loan is determined by the cost of monitoring. Figure 14.3a presents the supply and demand conditions for open-market paper for a moderately risky borrower. In prosperity, the supply curve of credit is lower than it is during a recession, indicating that investors are more cautious in a downturn and demand a higher risk premium.

Figure 14.3b presents the supply and demand conditions for bank loans for the same borrower. The supply curve of bank loans is upward sloping in the short run because limited resources are available for monitoring. It crosses the vertical axis at a fairly high interest rate. That is, the minimum cost of a bank loan is determined by the cost of providing monitoring services in a period of slack demand, such as a period of economic stability.

As long as the open-market interest rate displayed in Figure 14.3a is below the interest rate necessary to cover the basic cost of monitoring, the firm will only issue open-market paper. When the supply curve in the open market shifts upward as a result of recession, the cost in the open market exceeds that necessary to cover bank costs. This increases the demand for bank loans, as illustrated by the shift in the demand curve in Figure 14.3b.

In addition to the specialized role just described, banks can, in principle, act like any other investor during periods of prosperity. That is, they could make loans that have the same characteristics as commercial paper and provide no monitoring services.

Banks do not invest in loans that have the characteristics of commercial paper to avoid conflicts of interest. A **conflict of interest** is created when a person or corporation is in a position to benefit from a decision (or advice) made by the person

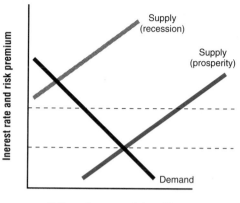

Figure 14.3a SUPPLY AND DEMAND CONDITIONS FOR OPEN-MARKET PAPER

or corporation for another party. For example, a Defense Department official that has a cousin in the defense industry has a conflict of interest when she decides which company will receive a lucrative defense contract.

The bank receives a fee for the line of credit it arranges with its customer. The terms of the line send a signal to the market about the borrower's cost of accessing

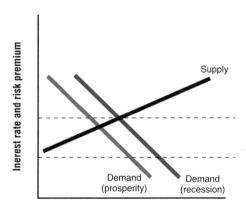

Figure 14.3b SUPPLY AND DEMAND CONDITIONS FOR BANK LOANS

credit under adverse economic conditions. The market uses this information to make judgments about the appropriate interest rate to charge the borrower in good times.

If a bank bought the borrower's commercial paper in addition to providing the line of credit, it would have a stake in the market price of the paper. The market would be skeptical of the signal conveyed by the price of a line of a bank holding the borrower's commercial paper because the bank might try to send a false signal to raise the price of the paper. The market prefers a bank to send a signal that is untainted by its own self-interest. Hence banks avoid holding loans that are equivalent to commercial paper and supplying lines of credit. See Box 14.6.

Loan Sales

In recent years, commercial banks have increasingly engaged in the practice of selling loans. This is not an entirely new practice; however, the form and extent of the practice have undergone some change.

Loan sales, representing 4.4 percent of total loans at commercial banks in 1986, rose to 12.5 percent of loans by 1989. In 1990, loan sales stood at 7.8 percent of total loans. Loans sales have traditionally been made through the syndication contracts we discussed earlier, but based on the Fed's Senior Loan Officer Opinion Surveys, much of the expansion in loan sales has taken place under a different contract form. Under this contract, the bank selling the loan retains all rights over the borrower in case of bankruptcy, but it has no obligation to buy the loan back in the event that the borrower defaults. The separation of rights from obligations in these new contracts is somewhat puzzling to many analysts.[4]

What types of loans are sold? Many are consumer loans, which we will discuss later in this chapter. The information on the commercial and industrial loans sold is derived from the Senior Loan Officer Surveys as analyzed by Gary Gorton and Joseph Haubrich (1987). These surveys indicate that about 80 percent of these loans have maturities of less than 90 days. This evidence is consistent with the data obtained from the survey of terms of lending at commercial banks discussed earlier, which indicate that a much higher percentage of short-term loans are participated out (sold) than are long-term loans. The loans that are sold are generally made to borrowers that have access to the commercial paper market. Since 1985, the majority of buyers have been foreign banks. The domestic bank purchasers of these loans have generally been the smaller banks. Nonbanks also participate as buyers.

Loan sales under the new type of contract appear to be primarily liquidity loans. Why are the large banks selling them rather than funding them through the fed funds market or with repurchase agreements? We think that a major explanation is that bank regulators have been placing pressure on large American banks to decrease

---

4. Gary B. Gorton and Joseph G. Haubrich, "Loan Sales, Recourse, and Reputation: An Analysis of Secondary Loan Participations," 23rd Annual Conference on Bank Structure and Competition, Federal Reserve Bank of Chicago, May 6–7, 1987.

Box 14.6

Conflicts of Interest in Banking

Since 1934, banks have been prohibited from underwriting and dealing in publicly traded corporate stocks and bonds by the Glass Steagall Act. In 1989, the Federal Reserve suggested a reinterpretation of this law, which was approved by the courts, that gave banks limited power to underwrite and deal in corporate bonds. Citicorp, along with other money-center banks, received permission from the Fed to engage in this activity.

Banks have traditionally argued that they should be permitted to underwrite corporate securities because this activity utilizes many of the same skills and information they have accumulated as their business clients' commercial bankers. To take advantage of the complementarity between the two businesses, Citicorp thought it would be a good idea to place the junk bond trading department next to the loan sales department. Citicorp had made bank loans to many of the same companies that issued junk bonds traded by the bank. Since the two departments dealt with the same set of borrowers, Citicorp felt that it could save on research expenses if the two departments shared the analysis.

Citicorp shelved its plan to share resources between the two departments when questions arose about conflicts of interest. When a bank makes a loan, it is privy to information that cannot legally be shared with the public, including buyers of junk bonds. Borrowers give information to their bankers in confidence. The possibility that this confidence might be breached to make money trading public securities places the bank in a potential conflict of interest position. In addition, if the nonpublic information were used, it would place the bank in potential violation of insider trading laws. That is, holders of nonpublic information are prohibited from trading on their knowledge.

The problem of conflicts of interest is not limited to banks' exercise of securities underwriting powers. The large size of leveraged buyout deals has created a demand to form larger and larger syndicates that often include lenders other than banks. All members of a syndicate share the confidential information about a borrower. As this information becomes dispersed to a large number of parties that engage in public securities trading, concern is rising about whether the confidential information is indeed remaining confidential.

---

their leverage ratios. In Chapter 19 we will explain why regulators have been concerned about bank leverage ratios (under Modigliani-Miller assumptions, they should not matter) and why such a policy might drive banks to consider selling loans.

The decline in loan sales in 1990 provides support for the hypothesis that capital regulation has driven loan sales. Japanese banks, which were major purchasers of liquid loans, were not constrained by leverage regulation until 1990, which was when the boom in loan sales was halted.

If banks are necessary suppliers of liquidity, how can we explain the sale of liquid loans? The answer is that the banking system usually guarantees the liquidity of the loans sold. For example, the selling bank usually backs the loan sold with a line established with a third-party bank that guarantees the timeliness of the cash payments. We define this arrangement in some detail when we discuss the sale of consumer loans.

BANK LENDING TO CORPORATIONS IN JAPAN

Throughout the preceding section we have stressed that American banks' special ability to control borrower behavior is due to their role in the payments system. In Japan, banks play a similar role, but their enforcement powers are derived from a different source. When a corporation is threatened by bankruptcy in Japan, the firm's main bank replaces some or all of the management with its own people. The bank takes a very direct role in managing the company.

In the United States, a lender must be more circumspect. If he acts like an equity holder, he will be treated like an equity owner in bankruptcy court. That is, he will become the last creditor to be paid. This rule is established to prevent a conflict of interest. For example, if a bank were on the board of a company, it might direct the company to sell assets to swell its bank account right before declaring bankruptcy. Just before the announcement, the bank could announce that the company is in trouble and declare the right of setoff.

Why are the Japanese not concerned that creditors who are also insiders will behave in their own interests at the expense of creditors who are not insiders? One major reason is that banks play a much larger role relative to other creditors than they do in the United States. For example, at year-end 1989, the ratio of domestic bank loans to gross national product in Japan was 105 percent, whereas in the United States it was 38 percent. Since consumers make up a larger portion of bank borrowers in the United States than in Japan, this understates the dependence of Japanese business on banks relative to U.S. business. (The best comparison would be commercial and industrial loans in Japan versus the United States, but because the data in the two countries are collected differently, this is not possible.)

In contrast, the bond market in Japan is a much smaller source of funding than in the United States. At year-end 1989, bonds (those issued both domestically and overseas) represented 8.5 percent of Japanese corporate liabilities and 30.8 percent of U.S. corporate liabilities. One major reason for this difference is that issuing restrictions on domestic bonds in Japan are quite onerous. Before a corporation can issue a bond that is not collateralized by a specific physical asset, it must pass a stringent financial test. There is no junk bond market in Japan.

The predominant role of banks as lenders to corporations implies that other investors have little to lose if banks become insiders in a corporate financial crisis. Banks' share of the debt is generally so large that it is difficult for them to behave in their own interest without acting in other creditors' interests as well. And for good measure, many bondholders have claims on specific assets.

Why Japanese Banks Are Large by U.S. Standards

Table 14.3 lists the 25 largest banking companies in the world as of year-end 1989. Seventeen of them are Japanese. Part of the reason that there are so many large Japanese banks is that the Japanese economy is very large. At year-end 1989, the

Table 14.3 TOP 25 BANKING COMPANIES IN THE WORLD (RANKED BY ASSETS ON DECEMBER 31, 1989 OR NEAREST FISCAL YEAR END)*

Bank	Country of Origin	Assets ($US Billions)
1. Dai-ichi Kangyo Bank, Ltd., Tokyo	Japan	403.4
2. Sumitomo Bank, Ltd., Osaka	Japan	368.2
3. Fuji Bank, Ltd., Tokyo	Japan	362.6
4. Mitsubishi Bank, Ltd., Tokyo	Japan	360.0
5. Sanwa Bank, Ltd., Osaka	Japan	353.7
6. Industrial Bank of Japan, Ltd., Tokyo	Japan	256.9
7. Credit Agricole Mutuel, Paris	France	242.3
8. Banque Nationale de Paris	France	231.8
9. Tokai Bank, Ltd., Nagoya	Japan	227.7
10. Citicorp, New York	U.S.	227.0
11. Norinchukin Bank, Tokyo	Japan	220.0
12. Mitsubishi Trust & Banking Corp., Tokyo	Japan	213.5
13. Credit Lyonnais, Paris	France	211.0
14. Barclays Bank Plc., London	U.K.	205.5
15. Mitsui Bank, Tokyo	Japan	203.3
16. Deutsche Bank, Frankfurt	Germany	202.6
17. Bank of Tokyo, Ltd.	Japan	200.5
18. Sumitomo Trust & Banking Co., Ltd., Osaka	Japan	190.9
19. National Westminster Bank Plc., London	U.K.	187.1
20. Mitsui Trust & Banking Co., Ltd., Tokyo	Japan	182.6
21. Societe Generale, Paris	France	176.0
22. Long Term Credit Bank of Japan, Ltd., Tokyo	Japan	174.2
23. Taiyo Kobe Bank, Ltd., Tokyo	Japan	173.0
24. Yasuda Trust & Banking Co., Ltd., Tokyo	Japan	157.8
25. Daiwa Bank, Ltd., Osaka	Japan	155.5

Source: From American Banker, *Top Numbers: Part Two, 1990 Update*, p. 130.

*Excludes contra accounts and contingent liabilities.

GNP of Japan was almost $3 trillion, making it the second largest non-Communist world GNP after the United States, whose GNP was $5 trillion at year-end 1989. In contrast, there was only one U.S. bank, Citicorp, among the top 25.

One reason there are so many large banks in Japan is that, unlike in the United States, large, low-risk Japanese corporations use bank loans as a major source of funding. Referring again to the terms of lending survey in Table 14.1, notice that while the average size of a U.S. commercial loan is small, most of the dollar volume of loans is accounted for by large borrowers. If large borrowers do not use banks, banks, measured in terms of dollar assets, will not be very large.

If bank lending in the United States were 105 percent of GNP, U.S. bank loans would equal $5 trillion, 2½ times the actual level. Citicorp, the largest U.S. bank, has assets of about $230 billion, counting all its subsidiaries. If it were 2½ times larger, it would have assets of $560 billion, which would make it the largest bank in the world.

The Future of the Large Japanese Banks

The Japanese main bank system is coming apart. Many Japanese corporations attempt to get around the controls on the domestic bond market by issuing overseas.

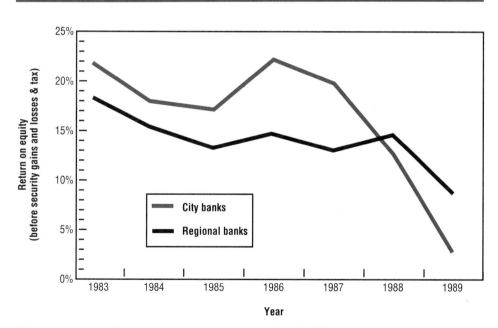

Figure 14.4   PROFITABILITY OF JAPANESE BANKS   *Source:* From Federation of Bankers Associations of Japan, *Analysis of Financial Statements of All Banks,* various years.

The popularity of overseas issues is growing rapidly. In March 1986, overseas bonds issued by Japanese corporations equaled 40 percent of those issued domestically. By year-end 1989, overseas bonds represented over 60 percent of domestic bonds. In addition, as we saw in Chapter 2, the leverage ratio of Japanese corporations is declining.

These factors are making large Japanese corporations less dependent on bank credit. As this occurs, the profitability of the large Japanese banks, collectively known as "city banks," has nosedived. Figure 14.4 presents the before-tax return on equity of Japanese banks, excluding securities gains and losses. We divide the banks into two groups—the city banks, which are the large ones mentioned in Table 14.3, and the smaller regional banks. As you can see, returns have fallen dramatically, from 22 percent for the city banks in 1983 to 2 percent in 1989.

FINANCE COMPANIES AS LENDERS TO BUSINESSES

Finance companies are probably most well known for their role in providing credit to consumers to purchase automobiles. The largest finance company in the United States is owned by General Motors. It is the largest for two very obvious reasons. Car loans are big business, and General Motors sells more cars in the United States than anyone else. Thus General Motors has access to more potential borrowers than any other company. In this section we focus on a less well-known segment of the finance company business—providing credit to businesses.

Table 14.4 presents the aggregate balance sheet of finance companies in the United States for the second quarter of 1990. More than half of finance company assets are invested in business loans. Note that the asset side of finance company balance sheets also has "contra" items, just as bank balance sheets do. These are reserves for unearned income and for loan losses. Reserves for unearned income are reserves for late payments on loans. Loan loss reserves play the same role they play at banks.

Moving ahead, we look to Table 14.5 for a breakdown of business credit. Most loans, which are called "financings" in this table, are made to finance automobiles. Wholesale automobile financings represent loans to dealers to carry inventory. They are typically made by the finance company subsidiaries of the automobile companies.

Notice that, excluding wholesale finance, most equipment receivables are leases, whereas a majority of automobile receivables are loans. Leasing is a special kind of financing arrangement in which the lessor (the finance company) owns the equipment rather than merely financing the equipment.

Leasing is attractive for some companies for tax reasons. Under a lease, all payments are immediately tax deductible as a business expense. Under a loan, the value of the equipment must be depreciated for tax purposes. Business and industrial equipment suffers a loss in value, or **depreciation,** from the wear and tear of use.

Table 14.4

Table 14.4 DOMESTIC FINANCE COMPANIES, ASSETS AND LIABILITIES ($BILLIONS)

Account	Second Quarter, 1990	Percent of Total
Accounts receivable, gross*	468.8	93.41
Consumer	138.6	27.62
Business	274.8	54.75
Real estate	55.4	11.04
Less:		
Reserves for unearned income	54.3	10.82
Reserves for losses	8.2	1.63
Accounts receivable, net	406.3	80.95
All other	95.5	19.03
Total Assets	501.9	100.00
Bank loans	15.8	3.15
Commercial paper	152.4	30.36
Debt		
Due to parent	72.8	14.50
Not elsewhere classified	153.0	30.48
All other liabilities	66.1	13.17
Capital, surplus, and undivided profits	41.8	8.33
Total Liabilities and Capital	501.9	100.00

Source: From *Federal Reserve Bulletin*, December 1990, Table 1.51.

Note: Items may not sum to total because of rounding.   *Excludes pools of securitized assets.

The government recognizes this as a business expense that is tax deductible. A commonly recognized method of depreciation is "straight line" depreciation over 5 years. One-fifth of the original cost of the equipment is tax deductible each year for 5 years.

In a lease, therefore, all cash outflows are immediately tax deductible, whereas in a purchase, the deductibility of the cash outflow is delayed. Of course, the **lessor,** who is the party that lets property under a lease, must pay taxes on the income received from the **lessee,** who is the party holding the lease. Depreciation is a business expense for the lessor and, therefore, is tax deductible. Thus the cost of the delay is transferred from the lessee to the lessor. Whether this is a profitable arrangement for both parties depends on their relative value of immediate cash.

Because the lessee does not own the equipment, she does not need to come up with a down payment to purchase it. However, because she has no equity interest in it, she has more of an incentive to misuse the equipment than she would if she owned it. This is a risk to the finance company that is reflected in a higher interest

Table 14.5 DOMESTIC FINANCE COMPANIES, BUSINESS CREDIT OUTSTANDING ($MILLIONS, SEASONALLY ADJUSTED)

Type	August 1990	Percent of Total
Retail financing of installment sales		
Automotive	38,610	13.64
Equipment	30,707	10.85
Pools of securitized assets*	987	0.35
Wholesale		
Automotive	34,429	12.16
Equipment	9,812	3.47
All other	9,707	3.43
Pools of securitized assets*	650	0.23
Leasing		
Automotive	30,942	10.93
Equipment	78,714	27.81
Pools of securitized assets*	1,703	0.60
Loans on commercial accounts receivable and factored commercial accounts receivable	19,974	7.06
All other business credit	26,809	9.47
Total	283,043	100.00

Source: From *Federal Reserve Bulletin*, December 1990, Table 1.52.

Note: Items may not sum to total because of rounding.   *Pools of securitized assets are not seasonally adjusted.

rate charged on the lease compared with a loan. The government subsidizes the greater risk through the tax system because interest expenses are tax deductible, even though part of the "interest payment" is also a fee for bearing risk.

The other major item of business credit is loans on accounts receivable and factored accounts receivable. When a business sells goods to its customers on credit, it records the amount it is owed as an asset item known as **accounts receivable.** Accounts receivable are also known as **trade credit,** which is the term utilized on the asset side of the aggregate corporate balance sheet presented in Table 14.2. The corresponding liability item is **accounts payable,** or **trade debt,** as it is labeled in Table 14.2. Finance companies extend credit based on accounts receivable as collateral, or they purchase the accounts receivable outright. The latter is known as **factoring.** When a finance company purchases accounts receivable from a company extending trade credit to its customers, it becomes a creditor of that company's customer rather than of the company extending the trade credit. Accounts receivable and factoring loans are short term compared with leasing contracts, which extend over 5 years or more.

Notice in Table 14.4 that commercial paper makes up the single largest specifically identified liability. However, finance companies also maintain credit lines with banks, as illustrated by the small percentage of liabilities that are bank loans. Thus banks play their typical role in maintaining liquidity at finance companies.

BANKS' ROLE IN CONSUMER LENDING

In Chapter 10 we described various categories of consumer loans as they appear in bank balance sheets. In this section we describe the role banks play in these markets relative to other lenders.

Installment Loans

Table 14.6 presents a breakdown of consumer installment loans by type of loan and by type of holder for year-end 1988 through 1989 and for the end of August 1990. The largest single category of consumer installment credit is loans to purchase automobiles. Revolving credit, the second largest item, is mainly made up of credit card loans. Commercial banks are the largest suppliers of consumer credit, with over 46 percent of the total. The second largest supplier is finance companies, with about 19 percent of the total.

Among the consumer loan categories, banks dominate the revolving credit market, where, at year-end 1989, they had almost 63 percent of the market. The most popular credit cards, VISA and MasterCard, were pioneered by banks. Originally, applications were taken through bank branch networks. As the market matured, large banks purchased the portfolios of smaller banks.

They did this to take advantage of economies of scale in processing credit card loans and payments. When a consumer makes a purchase with his credit card, the transaction must be recorded and money must be transferred from the bank that discounts the paper to the merchant. This procedure is called *processing,* and it is a "back office" activity that is computer intensive. It is also an activity subject to economies of scale. At year-end 1988, Citicorp was the largest single issuer of credit cards, with $22 billion in credit card loans. Chase was second, with $7 billion. Bank dominance in the field has recently been challenged by Sears with the Discover card and AT&T with the Universal Card.

Securitized Consumer Loans

Pools of securitized consumer loans are a recent phenomenon in the market. These are packages of consumer loans that are grouped and sold in the marketplace as securities. The packages are usually made up of loans originated by banks that are

Table 14.6 CONSUMER INSTALLMENT CREDIT: AMOUNTS OUTSTANDING, END OF PERIOD (NOT SEASONALLY ADJUSTED) ($BILLIONS)

Holder and Type of Credit	1988	1989	1990 (Aug.)
Total	674.7	727.6	733.5
By major holder			
Commercial banks	324.8	343.9	342.6
Finance companies	146.2	140.8	139.5
Credit unions	88.3	90.9	91.3
Retailers	48.3	42.6	37.2
Savings institutions	63.4	57.2	52.4
Gasoline companies	3.7	3.9	4.7
Pools of securitized assets	N.A.	48.2	65.7
By major type of credit (including estimates for certain holders for which consumer credit totals are available)			
Automobile	284.3	290.4	N.A.
Commercial banks	123.4	126.6	127.9
Finance companies	97.2	82.7	77.2
Pools of securitized assets	N.A.	18.2	21.5
Revolving	183.9	208.2	N.A.
Commercial banks	123.0	131.0	126.0
Finance companies	43.7	38.0	32.7
Gasoline companies	3.7	3.9	4.7
Pools of securitized assets	N.A.	23.0	37.6
Mobile home	25.1	22.3	N.A.
Commercial banks	9.0	9.2	9.6
Finance companies	7.2	4.7	5.4
Other	181.3	206.7	N.A.
Commercial banks	69.4	77.1	79.2
Finance companies	41.8	53.4	56.9
Retailers	4.6	4.7	4.5
Pools of securitized assets	N.A.	7.0	6.6

Source: Adapted from *Federal Reserve Bulletin,* December 1990, Table 1.55, p. A39.

N.A. = not available.

Note: Items may not sum to total because of rounding.

sold to investors, such as pension funds and life insurance companies. As part of the procedure for creating a security, banks set up an **escrow account,** which is an account that one party holds for the sole benefit of another. Monthly payments of principal and interest from consumers whose loans are part of the pool are placed in the escrow account. Payments from consumers are due by a certain date each month. Several days later the bank creating the security promises to pay the security holders from the escrow account. The bank collects more than it pays out because it holds reserves against potential late payments and defaults.

Thus, even if payments by consumers are somewhat irregular, the bondholders will not notice, unless the irregularity exceeds the reserves set aside by the issuing bank. The issuing bank often reduces this risk further by buying a line of credit from another bank to cover temporary shortfalls in the escrow account.

Mortgage Loans and Mortgage-Backed Securities

Table 14.7 provides a breakdown of the mortgage market by type of borrower and type of lender for year-end 1987 and the end of the second quarter of 1990. Mortgages on one- to four-family homes, which are consumer mortgages, make up more than two-thirds of the mortgage market. Notice that the dollar volume of consumer mortgages is more than triple the dollar volume of consumer installment loans. (For the consumer installment loan number, see Table 14.6.)

Commercial mortgages are the second largest loan category. These are mortgage loans taken out by businesses. They are typically used to finance such projects as office buildings and shopping centers. Defaults on commercial mortgages were a major cause of bank and savings and loan failures in the United States in the late 1980s and 1990. For example, the Bank of New England, a major regional bank, failed for this reason.

Savings institutions are the largest single holder of one- to four-family mortgages. However, their holdings declined by over $30 billion between year-end 1987 and the end of the second quarter of 1990. This occurred at a time when the entire market grew by more than $300 million. Savings institutions are losing their share of mortgages because they are losing their share of deposits. The public is worried about the safety of thrifts. With a shrinking deposit base, savings institutions have not had the funds to hold new mortgages.

Commercial banks are the second largest holders of one- to four-family mortgages. Their dollar volume expanded by over $70 billion between 1987 and second quarter of 1990. Banks and savings institutions are the leading players in consumer mortgages because they have branch networks to collect deposits that provide them with local offices to originate mortgages as well. In consumer lending, the lender that has developed low-cost distribution networks for customer contact always ends up with a large share of the business.

As Table 14.7 indicates, more than a quarter of all mortgage holdings is held in mortgage pools and trusts. These are most often held in the form of securities, like the pools of securitized installment loans discussed earlier. Most of these mortgage pools are for one- to four-family mortgages, and most are insured by a government agency, such as the Government National Mortgage Association (GNMA). Government-insured mortgages are easy to securitize because the credit risk is borne by the government. However, these securities are subject to peculiar interest rate risks. See Box 14.7.

Table 14.7 MORTGAGE DEBT OUTSTANDING ($BILLIONS, END OF PERIOD)

Type of Holder and Type of Property	1987	1990 Second Quarter
All Holders	2,971.0	3,657.7
1 to 4 family	1,958.4	2,492.8
Multifamily	272.5	314.4
Commercial	651.3	765.5
Farm	88.8	85.1
Selected Financial Institutions*	1,657.9	1,924.6
Commercial banks	592.4	803.7
1 to 4 family	275.6	388.0
Commercial	269.6	358.4
Savings institutions	860.5	867.6
1 to 4 family	602.4	640.0
Commercial	150.9	125.9
Life insurance companies	205.0	253.3
1 to 4 family	12.7	14.5
Commercial	160.9	200.1
Finance companies	29.7	47.1
Federal and related agencies	192.7	230.5
Mortgage pools or trusts†	718.3	1,012.0
Government National Mortgage Association	317.6	384.3
1 to 4 family	309.8	372.1
Federal Home Loan Mortgage Corporation	212.6	291.9
1 to 4 family	206.0	283.8
Federal National Mortgage Association	140.0	259.7
1 to 4 family	138.0	250.7
Individuals and others	402.1	490.6
1 to 4 family	242.1	310.7

Source: Adapted from *Federal Reserve Bulletin,* December 1990, Table 1.55, p. A39.

*Subcategories do not sum to total because of missing subcategories.
†Includes private pools and trusts as well as pools and trusts insured or guaranteed by the government agencies indicated.

Note: Items may not sum to total because of rounding.

Mortgage Bankers and Brokers

A **mortgage banker** is anyone who is involved in the origination or servicing of a mortgage loan. Servicing a mortgage loan requires accepting payment from the consumer and sending it along to the holder of the mortgage. It is the same as the loan processing function discussed earlier. Until the mid-1970s, these functions were

Box 14.7

The Risks of Trading Mortgage-Backed Securities

In the first half of 1987, Merrill Lynch lost $275 million in trading mortgage-backed securities. It blamed the loss on unauthorized trades by one of its employees, but part of the loss was due to a risky trading strategy intentionally pursued by the firm. Merrill was engaged in trading two modified versions of the mortgage-backed security—principal-only and interest-only securities.

Holders of mortgage-backed securities face a risk that when interest rates decline, many borrowers choose to pay off the mortgage contracted at a high interest rate by taking out a new mortgage funded at the lower rate. The investor in the mortgage-backed security receives the principal when the borrower pays off his mortgage early, but the investor must reinvest this payment at a lower interest rate than he would have received had the borrower not paid off the mortgage.

To reduce this risk to the investor, investment banks created a principal-only mortgage-backed security and an interest-only mortgage-backed security. The principal-only security pays off when interest rates unexpectedly fall because principal payments are made faster than expected. The interest-only security pays off when interest rates unexpectedly rise because borrowers refinance at a slower rate than anticipated.

In the spring of 1987, Merrill had issued principal-only and interest-only securities based on a pool of government-insured mortgages. It sold the interest-only securities and held the principal-only securities. Between February and May of that year, the interest rate on 1-year Treasury notes rose from 5.96 to 7.00 percent. The principal-only securities plummeted in value—hence the $275 million loss at Merrill.

all performed by one player—the local savings institution, which also held the loan. The development of the market for securitized mortgages has forced a separation in these functions. Mortgage servicers purchase the servicing rights for mortgages held by third parties. These mortgages are most often ones that are placed in government-insured pools. For example, in June 1989, Citicorp Mortgage, the largest mortgage servicer in the United States, serviced mortgages with a total value of $55 billion. Its customer base included 8,070 GNMA pools and 335 others.

Mortgage brokers originate loans through real estate agents and advertisements in telephone books and sell these loans to savings institutions and other investors. Because mortgage brokers do not have the benefit of lots of local branches to originate loans, they are best able to compete with banks and thrifts in booming real estate markets. Mortgage brokers account for about 30 percent of mortgage originations during periods when mortgage demand is very strong. When it is weak, their share falls to less than 20 percent. Also, they tend to do most of their business in large metropolitan areas so that they can achieve enough volume to cover the costs of offices dedicated to one purpose—mortgage origination.

CONCLUSION

In this chapter we have considered the role that banks play in lending to corporations and consumers. We have found that banks play a special role in corporate finance. They specialize in lending to risky corporations and taking the lead among lenders in restructuring the liabilities of financially troubled borrowers. They play this role because of their position in the payments system. Banks' control over their customers' bank deposits places them in a position to monitor and control who gets paid. As a result, banks have an incentive, relative to other lenders, to maintain current, detailed information about borrowers. When a problem develops, a bank can prevent other lenders from being paid by seizing the deposit. Banks do not hold the publicly offered securities of their loan customers, such as commercial paper, because of potential conflicts of interest.

Banks play a large role in the origination and holding of consumer loans. This role is largely due to the retail distribution networks banks have in the form of branch offices. Many other lenders, however, hold the same consumer loan portfolio as banks. Banks play no special negotiation role in this market because the average loan is too small to apply the resources to restructuring that exists in the corporate market.

KEY TERMS

prime rate	lessor
private placement	lessee
compensating balance	accounts receivable
acceleration clause	trade credit
setoff	accounts payable (trade debt)
junk bonds	factoring
syndicate	escrow account
conflict of interest	mortgage banker
depreciation	

EXERCISES

1. Explain how a loan with a short maturity gives the lender greater control over a borrower than a long-term loan.

2. Why do banks make long-term loans to relatively high-risk corporations and short-term loans to low-risk corporations?

3. In what way are payment-in-kind bonds (PIKs) similar to stocks?

4. Why would we expect commercial and industrial loans to rise relative to commercial paper during a recession?

5. During the 1990–1991 recession, commercial and industrial loans did not increase as rapidly as they did during the 1982 recession. Many policymakers and analysts worried about the credit crunch—that is, a lack of availability of bank credit. Evaluate the legitimacy of their concern.

6. Describe a conflict of interest situation.

7. Describe how banks can be exposed to conflicts of interest. Explain how potential conflicts affect the scope of bank business.

8. If banks have special information about borrowers, would they sell loans? Describe a set of contractual arrangements between the selling bank and the loan buyer that might emerge if the selling bank had special information about the borrower.

9. If banks have special means to control borrower behavior (such as seizing a deposit), would they sell loans? Describe the appropriate set of contractual arrangements between the selling bank and the loan buyer.

10. Banks have found it difficult to sell long-term loans. To solve this problem, they sell "strips," which are short-term claims to payment streams from long-term loans. For example, assume that a loan has a 12-month maturity. A buyer purchases a 1-month claim to the payments. At the end of the month, the principal is returned to the buyer, and the selling bank must find a new buyer or hold the loan itself. In this arrangement, does the selling bank retain an incentive to monitor the borrower?

11. Explain how selling liquid loans might be another way to reduce reserve holdings to the desired level.

12. Why do we observe a different role for Japanese bankers in corporate finance than their American counterparts?

13. Why do some borrowers find leases preferable to loans?

14. Describe the functions of a mortgage banker.

15. What has led to separation of the various functions of making and holding a mortgage?

FURTHER READING

Canner, Glenn B., and Charles A. Luckett. "Home Equity Loans," *Federal Reserve Bulletin,* May 1989, pp. 333–344.

Elliehausen, Gregory E., and John D. Wolken. "Banking Markets and the Use of Financial Services by Small and Medium Size Businesses," *Federal Reserve Bulletin,* October 1990, pp. 801–817.

Gooch, Anthony C., and Linda B. Klein. *Loan Agreement Documentation: Sample Annotated Loan Agreement for Syndicated Eurodollar Transaction.* London: Euromoney Financial Law Series, 1986.

Gorton, Gary B., and Joseph G. Haubrich. "Loan Sales, Recourse, and Reputation: An Analysis of Secondary Loan Participations," 23rd Annual Conference on Bank Structure and Competition, Federal Reserve Bank of Chicago, May 6–7, 1987.

Grabbe, Leland E., Margaret H. Pickering, and Stephen D. Prowse. "Recent Developments in Corporate Finance," *Federal Reserve Bulletin,* August 1990, pp. 593–603.

CHAPTER

15

The Dollar in the International Marketplace

When a dealer must take out a bank loan to finance a security that he buys, he generates a demand for reserves. We say that the market for this security is illiquid. The liquidity premium on a security is determined by the probability that a dealer will have to resort to a bank loan and the amount of reserves that the banking system chooses to hold relative to bank deposits to ensure the liquidity of securities markets.

As we have seen before, the Federal Reserve imposes reserve requirements on banks in the United States, which, under certain conditions, could force banks to hold more reserves than they otherwise would desire. We have seen that reserve requirements provide incentives to create securities not subject to these requirements that have the same characteristics as bank deposits. If this can be done easily, financial markets in general can reduce reserves relative to all deposit-like instruments to the ratio they would desire to hold in the absence of reserve requirements.

Over the last several decades, a large overseas dollar banking market has developed. American bank regulatory authorities exercise much less control over this market than over the domestic market. For example, overseas dollar deposits are not subject to reserve requirements. Consequently, many analysts argue that the overseas market has evolved to avoid domestic bank regulation.

In this chapter we look at the size and growth of the overseas dollar banking market as well as other overseas financial markets to determine the role that regulation has played in their evolution.

THE EURODOLLAR MARKET

The large dollar market outside the United States is known as the **Eurodollar market** because it is centered in London. In this section we describe the size of this market and the mechanics of how it developed.

Size of Offshore Banking Markets

We begin by describing the Eurocurrency assets and liabilities of banks. Table 15.1 lists the 1989 cross-border positions of banks of the major industrial countries of the world, as calculated by the **Bank for International Settlements (BIS).** The BIS is an organization jointly owned by the central banks of the major industrial countries. Its purpose is to facilitate coordination of the policies of these central banks.

A **cross-border position** is an asset (called a "claim" in Table 15.1) or a liability in a bank of one country owned or owed by an entity from another country. For example, if an American bank lends dollars to an Italian corporation or if that corporation places a dollar deposit with an American bank, a cross-border dollar asset or liability is created. The overseas assets and liabilities of banks are often referred to as *Eurodollars, Euroyen,* and so on.

Table 15.1 indicates that the total cross-border positions of banks in the industrial countries summed to $6.2 trillion in assets and $6.1 trillion in liabilities at year-end 1989. About 55 percent of the Eurocurrency assets and liabilities were in U.S. dollars. About half the remaining 45 percent were distributed evenly between deutschemarks and yen. The table presents the values of cross-border exposures in U.S. dollars.[1]

For comparison, at year-end 1989, the assets booked in U.S. offices of banks

---

1. The BIS calculates on the basis of "exchange rate adjusted" flows. Between 1985 and 1989, the U.S. dollar depreciated from ¥238 to ¥140. Translating the yen flows into dollars at current exchange rates would have caused a substantial increase in yen flows just for evaluation reasons. The BIS eliminates evaluation increases from this table by translating other currency holdings into dollar terms by using an average exchange rate.

It is not readily apparent that this adjustment should be made because we want to measure the relative buying power of cross-border assets and liabilities by currency. Thus the role of the U.S. dollar will be somewhat underestimated in years when the dollar rises and somewhat overestimated when it falls.

Table 15.1   MAIN FEATURES OF INTERNATIONAL BANKING ACTIVITY FOR BANKS IN MAJOR INDUSTRIAL COUNTRIES IN 1989*

Balance Sheet ($US Billions)	Stock at Year End
1. Claims on outside-area countries	719.3
2. International claims on entities within the reporting area, of which	5,318.7
2a. Cross-border claims within the reporting area	4,185.8
2b. Reporting banks' domestic claims in foreign currency, of which	1,132.9
2c. Claim on nonbanks	1,255.3
2d. Banks' own use of international funds for domestic lending	539.8
2e. Double counting of interbank operations	3,523.6
3. Unallocated	125.6
4. Total gross international bank assets (1 + 2 + 3)	6,163.6
5. Estimated Net International Bank Credit (1 + 2 + 3 − 2e)	2,640.4
6. Liabilities to outside-area countries	565.6
7. International liabilities to entities within the reporting area, of which	5,230.3
7a. Cross-border liabilities within the reporting area	4,350.6
7b. Reporting banks' domestic liabilities in foreign currency, of which	879.7
7c. Liabilities to nonbanks	787.7
7d. Banks' own supply of domestic funds for international lending†	1,022.0
7e. Double counting of interbank operations	3,420.6
8. Unallocated	264.7
9. Total gross international bank liabilities (6 + 7 + 8)	6,060.6
Estimated Net International Bank Funds (6 + 7 + 8 − 7e)	2,640.0

Source: Bank for International Settlements, *Annual Report, 1990,* p. 125.

*OECD countries.

†Including trustee funds channeled into the market via banks in Switzerland and deposits by official monetary institutions.

Note: Claims are assets on banks' balance sheets. These include loans and securities.

totaled some $3 trillion. Since about half the Eurocurrency assets and liabilities are dollar denominated, we can assume that the U.S. dollar overseas banking system is about 10 percent larger than the domestic U.S. banking system. Where do these dollars held abroad come from?

Dollars Flowing from U.S. Banks to Overseas Offices

The $3.4 trillion in dollar liabilities of overseas bank offices could have been borrowed from banks in the United States. At the end of 1989, however, banks in the

United States had claims on overseas banking offices (both their own and offices of other banks) equal to $432 billion. Between 1988 and 1989, U.S. banks increased their lending to banking offices overseas by $45 billion. In the same period, Eurodollar liabilities increased by approximately $385 billion. Thus funds from U.S. banking offices cannot account for a large portion of either the stock or the flow of Eurodollar liabilities.

Trade Deficits as a Source of Overseas Dollars

If foreigners are not borrowing dollars from banking offices in the United States, where are they getting them? A major source of dollars for foreigners over the last several years has been the deficit in the U.S. trade position vis-à-vis other countries. The United States has had a trade deficit because U.S. residents have bought more goods and services from foreigners than they have sold to them.

To measure the extent to which the trade deficit has contributed to a source of dollars for foreigners, we use the "balance on current account." The **current account** is compiled by the U.S. Department of Commerce. It is a record of the dollar value of goods and services purchased from foreigners less how much foreigners purchase from Americans. It also includes how much investment income Americans receive from foreigners (and vice versa), as well as net gifts and grants.

In 1985, the U.S. current account was in deficit by $116 billion; in 1987, by $143 billion; and in 1989, by $106 billion. This obviously represents a major source of dollar supply to foreigners. For example, if a Yugoslav exports tapestries to the United States, she receives dollars sent to her bank by the American importer.

Foreigners, of course, accumulate dollars because they want to do something with them. As a group, they can reduce their holdings only by selling them to Americans—that is, by purchasing U.S.-held assets (both financial and real) or U.S. goods and services. As individuals, they can lend them to each other to trade them among themselves for goods and services.

Foreigners could return the entire amount of the current account deficit to the United States through the Eurodollar market. For example, a Japanese steel company that sells steel in the United States could deposit its dollars in the London branch of a Japanese bank. The Japanese bank could then lend dollars to another customer to purchase a U.S. corporate bond. The dollars would then end up in the U.S. bank account of the corporation that issued the bond. Eurodollar deposits would have expanded in this operation.

Nevertheless, even if the cash payments generated by the current account deficit had returned entirely to the United States through the overseas dollar banking market, only part of the expansion of dollar bank assets and liabilities held abroad would be explained. Let us therefore consider a more likely avenue of expansion—the interbank market.

How Dollars Are Created in the Interbank Market

Suppose that a Japanese steel company sells steel in the American market and receives US$1 million as payment. The steel company deposits the dollars in the New York office of its bank, which is also Japanese. The Japanese bank now has a liability item worth $1 million and an asset item of cash for an equal amount. Of course, the bank is not going to hold cash for long, because the lost interest would reduce profits.

The Japanese bank could sell the funds for yen, or it could find a customer who wants to borrow dollars. The bank probably has many large Japanese corporations for clients. These corporations buy raw materials worldwide, for which they are likely to pay in dollars because the dollar is the most widely accepted means of international payment. They also have subsidiaries in the United States that have occasional needs for large amounts of dollars.

In Chapter 14 we saw that U.S. corporations use bank loans when they experience a sudden demand for cash because they cannot roll over their commercial paper. Assuming that bank finance plays a similar role for Japanese corporations, we might expect that major Japanese banks would try to be certain that they can get their hands on large amounts of dollars quickly. In the United States, the fed funds market plays a crucial role in transferring liquidity to where it is needed. In the Eurodollar market, the interbank market plays the same role.

Table 15.2 EURODOLLAR DEPOSIT EXPANSION ($THOUSANDS)

Bank A: New York

ASSETS		LIABILITIES	
Interbank loan to bank B	1,000	Deposit from Japanese steel company	1,000

Bank B: London

ASSETS		LIABILITIES	
Loan to customer of bank B	1,000	Interbank deposit from bank A	1,000

Bank C: London

ASSETS		LIABILITIES	
Interbank loan to bank D	1,000	Deposit from customer of bank C, who received payment from customer of bank B	1,000

Bank D: London

ASSETS		LIABILITIES	
U.S. Treasury bill	1,000	Interbank deposit from bank C	1,000

In the United States, the fed funds and repurchase market equaled $190 billion outstanding at the end of 1989. As Table 15.1 indicates, the size of the interbank Eurocurrency market is nearly $3.4 trillion. We can easily see that interbank assets and liabilities make up a substantial portion of the total Eurocurrency market. Without interbank borrowing, the market would sum only to $2.6 trillion. Thus 57 percent of the Eurocurrency bank market is an interbank market, far from the 8 percent share of total assets represented by interbank loans in the U.S. domestic market.

Table 15.2 indicates how the $1 million received by the Japanese steel company and deposited with its bank can easily expand to $4 million in Eurocurrency assets through the interbank market. Assume that the steel company's bank, bank A, places the funds in the interbank Eurodollar market, and these funds are bought by London bank B. Bank B then makes an overnight loan to its corporate customer, who uses the funds to pay a corporate customer of London bank C. Bank C's customer deposits the funds in an account in bank C.

Bank C again places the funds in the interbank market. These funds are bought by London bank D, which uses them to buy U.S. Treasury securities to be held for delivery to a customer later in the day. Let's assume that it buys the Treasury securities from a U.S. resident so that the funds return to the U.S. banking system at this point, and the expansion of the Eurocurrency market ceases. This set of transactions, however, has generated an increase of $3 million in the Eurocurrency market, that is, in the liabilities of banks outside the United States.

Why the Interbank Market Is So Large Relative to the Eurodollar Market

There are several possible explanations for why banks play such a large role in dollar markets overseas compared with their role in the domestic market. One is that reserve requirements in the United States have restricted the size of the banking system compared with the overseas banking system.

We saw in Chapter 13 that a reserve requirement can be made nonbinding through the expansion of nonbank liabilities, such as commercial paper, that have the same liquidity characteristics of deposits subject to reserve requirements. This, of course, would reduce the relative volume of bank deposits that investors hold as financial assets.

Another possibility is that dollar markets overseas are less liquid than their U.S. counterpart, requiring a greater role for settlement in bank deposits. If banks play a larger role in overseas dollar markets because they are less liquid than domestic markets, we should see higher liquidity premiums in overseas markets than we see in the domestic market. Recall from Chapter 13 that liquidity premiums are driven by the probability that a security must be financed with a bank loan. If this probability is high, liquidity premiums will be high. In the next section we will consider this reason for the existence of a large overseas dollar banking market. We will return to the regulatory question later in the chapter.

LIQUIDITY IN THE EURODOLLAR MARKET

The Historic Cost of Eurodollar Liabilities

One method of measuring differences in liquidity premiums across two markets is to compare interest rates on securities issued in each market, which should be similar if liquidity premiums are the same in the two markets. For example, banks issue CDs in the domestic and overseas dollar markets. Holding maturities constant, domestic and Eurodollar CDs should trade at the same interest rate, assuming the two markets are equally liquid.

Figure 15.1 compares Eurodollar CD rates with domestic CD rates from 1980 through June 1989. In the early 1980s, the spread between these two rates was large. Spreads declined almost continuously in the 1980s. By 1989, the spread between them fell to an average of about 4 basis points. These data indicate that the cost of raising short-term money in Europe declined dramatically relative to raising short-term money in the United States. Thus it appears that the Eurodollar market was very illiquid relative to the domestic market in the early 1980s but that it became increasingly liquid.

A high dollar liquidity premium in Europe in the early 1980s also should be reflected in a high interest spread between liquid and illiquid securities issued in that market. Thus this spread should have been higher in 1980 than it was in 1989. Again, this result follows from the model developed in Chapter 13. When market liquidity increases, bank deposits need not be delivered as frequently against illiquid securities. This reduces the spread that investors demand for holding illiquid securities relative to liquid ones.

Table 15.3 presents the average interest rate paid on Eurodollar CDs and

Table 15.3   LIQUIDITY PREMIUMS IN EURODOLLAR MARKET (AVERAGE WEEKLY WEDNESDAY CLOSING RATES)

	Percent	
	June 1980 to June 1981	June 1988 to June 1989
1. Average 1-month Eurodollar certificates of deposit offer rate (bond equivalent)	14.663	8.929
2. Average 1-month Eurodollar deposit offer rate, London close	14.825	8.952
Liquidity Premium (2 − 1)	0.161	0.022

Sources: From Reuters Information Services, Inc., and Bank of America, San Francisco, as reported through Data Resources Incorporated.

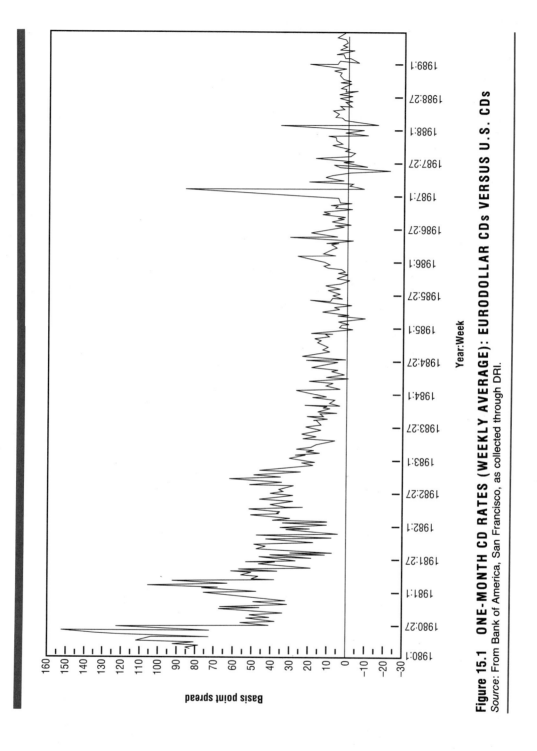

Figure 15.1 ONE-MONTH CD RATES (WEEKLY AVERAGE): EURODOLLAR CDs VERSUS U.S. CDs
Source: From Bank of America, San Francisco, as collected through DRI.

Eurodollar bank deposits, both of 1-month maturity, for June 1980 through June 1981 and for the same period in 1988 and 1989. Eurodollar deposits are issued overseas by the same banks that issue CDs. However, CDs are negotiable—that is, they can be sold before maturity—whereas deposits are not. Thus deposits are a less liquid instrument than CDs.

As Table 15.3 indicates, the spread between the deposit rate, known as the *London interbank offer rate (LIBOR),* and the Eurodollar CD rate was substantially greater in the early 1980s than at the end of the decade. This is further evidence that in the early 1980s the European dollar market was much less liquid than the domestic market. However, by the end of the decade, the difference in liquidity almost disappeared. Before determining why it disappeared, we must understand why the overseas market was so illiquid in the first place.

Why the Cost of Liquidity Was High in Europe

To show why the European money market was less liquid than the U.S. market, we must first demonstrate that the two markets were separate—that is, a domestic CD was not a perfect substitute for a Eurodollar CD. The differences in the settlement system across the two markets ensure that the two instruments cannot be perfect substitutes for the investor.

The Eurodollar CD settlement system is based on 2-day delivery (of the security) and payment. As illustrated in Figure 15.2, the trade of a Eurodollar CD requires delivery of the CD to the buyer in London and delivery of cash to the seller in New York. Two days elapse between the day of the trade (T) and the day of delivery of cash and security $(T + 2)$. In addition, on $(T + 2)$, perhaps 6 hours can elapse between delivery of the security in London and delivery of cash in New York. Part of this delay has to do with the 5-hour time difference between the two markets. In contrast, in New York there is a cash market for domestic CDs and CP. A seller can make a trade and receive cash the same day.

Suppose an American corporation buys a Eurodollar CD on Monday. As assets, it holds the Eurodollar CD and plant and equipment. Its liabilities include an obligation to its suppliers, known as *trade debt,* and equity. On Tuesday, the company requests additional supplies from its suppliers. The suppliers indicate that they will not deliver unless the corporation pays its current outstanding bill.

The corporation decides to sell the CD to deliver cash. However, it discovers that it must wait 2 days for the money, because of the 2-day delivery system in the European market. To cover the liability to its suppliers, the corporation must take out a bank loan, calling on reserves. Had it bought a U.S. CD, it would not have had to borrow from the bank because a cash CD market would have been available. Thus, from the American perspective, the Eurodollar CD is a less liquid instrument than a domestic CD. The American investor must be compensated for the difference in liquidity.

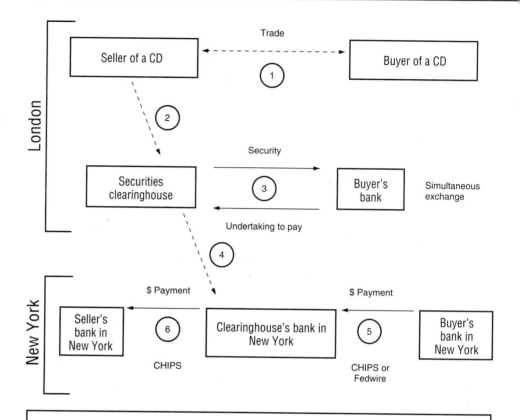

1. Trade executed over telephone on trade date T.

2. Instructions must be received by 9:30 A.M. on $T+2$. Instructions are to deliver CDs to buyer's bank, to expect payment of dollars from buyer's bank in New York, and to pay the proceeds to the seller's bank in New York.

3. A messenger delivers the CD to the seller's bank in exchange for an undertaking to pay dollars to the clearinghouse's bank in New York that same afternoon London time.

4. In mid and late afternoon London time, instructions are sent to the clearinghouse's bank in New York to pay to the seller's account and expect funds from buyer's bank in New York.

5. Buyer's bank pays the clearinghouse's bank dollars in fulfillment of the undertaking to pay over CHIPS or Fedwire. If this is in the late afternoon, the clearinghouse bank may have an intraday exposure to the buyer's bank.

6. Clearinghouse's bank pays proceeds to seller's bank in New York over CHIPS in accordance with its overall risk management.

Figure 15.2   EXECUTING A EURODOLLAR CD TRANSACTION   *Source:* Adapted from Federal Reserve Bank of New York, "The International Money Markets in London and First Chicago's Role in Clearing and Settling for Dealer Instruments," May 1989, p. 32.

Why the Rate Differential Declined

The large rate differential between the domestic and Eurodollar CD markets in the early 1980s implies that Eurodollar CDs were thinly traded at that time. That is, sales frequently required dealers to finance inventories with bank loans. Given the fact that payment for Eurodollar CDs is settled in New York, every sale of a CD that is not offset by a purchase of a CD should result in the creation of a net "due to" position for the foreign bank relative to its New York office or for the foreign branch of a U.S. bank relative to its home (New York) office.

While we do not have actual numbers on CD trades in the early 1980s, we do have volume of payments made over CHIPS. Recall from Figure 15.2 that trade in a Eurodollar CD generates a CHIPS payment. In 1980, average daily CHIPS volume was $37 billion per day. By 1990 it had risen to $890 billion. Thus the number of trades in Eurodollar CDs (and other Eurodollar transactions) accelerated sharply in the 1980s.

The amount of net borrowing of overseas offices from their New York offices (net "due to's") relative to the amount of daily CHIPS volume should give us some idea of what percentage of trades (again, in all kinds of instruments) had to be settled with a transfer of reserves—that is, the creation of a bank loan in New York. As you can see from Table 15.4, the ratio of net "due to's" to CHIPS volume declined from more than 22 percent in 1980 to 4.5 percent in 1986. By 1990, New York was a net receiver of funds from overseas offices.

These data demonstrate that fewer Eurodollar securities transactions are now settled with delivery of reserves in New York, which, based on our model in Chapter 13, is reason enough for the liquidity premium to decline. However, for a more

Table 15.4 FOREIGN BRANCHES OF U.S. BANKS' AND NON-U.S. OFFICES OF FOREIGN BANKS' NET "DUE TO'S" RELATIVE TO THEIR NEW YORK OFFICES

Year	Net "Due To's" Owed New York Office ($Billions)	CHIPS Volume ($Billions)	Net "Due To's" Divided by Volume (%)
1980	8.2	37	22.2
1985	26.6	300	8.8
1986	19.0	425	4.5
October 1990	−27.8	890	N.M.

Source: From Federal Reserve Bulletin, Table 1.24; Terrence M. Belton, Matthew D. Gelfand, David B. Humphrey, Jeffrey C. Marquardt, Nancy E. Bowen, Oscar B. Barnhardt, and Elaine J. Peterson, "Daylight Overdrafts and Payments System Risk," *Federal Reserve Bulletin,* November 1987, pp. 839–852; Association of Reserve City Bankers, *Report on the Payments System,* Cambridge, Mass., Arthur D. Little, Inc., 1982, p. 12.

N.M. = not meaningful.

complete explanation, we must turn to the question of why trading increased and borrowing in New York declined.

The Eurocurrency Commercial Paper and Eurobond Markets

One reason why fewer bank loans in New York had to be issued to settle European dollar transactions is that the scope of Eurocurrency securities markets broadened throughout the decade. **Eurocurrency securities** are securities issued outside the issuer's home country. They are issued in countries, such as Luxembourg and the United Kingdom, that have relatively liberal securities laws. A Eurocurrency commercial paper market developed in the mid-1980s. In 1986, total Eurocurrency commercial paper outstanding equaled $4.5 billion. By September 1989, it totaled $58.5 billion (85 percent of which was dollar denominated), compared with $130 billion of non-financial firm commercial paper outstanding in the United States in 1989. Eurocurrency commercial paper outstanding in 1989 was essentially unchanged from 1988.

The **Eurobond market**, which is a market for securities that are not registered for sale in the United States, also expanded in the 1980s. One reason for this is government regulation of domestic bond markets. For example, bonds sold in the United States must be registered with the Securities Exchange Commission (SEC). The SEC imposes certain reporting requirements on traded securities. These are avoided if an issue is floated in the Eurobond market. As we saw in Chapter 14, Japan also regulates its domestic bond market. Many of the issues in the Eurobond market were Japanese corporate bonds. See Box 15.1.

In 1982, gross new issues of dollar-denominated Eurobonds totaled $40.9 billion. In 1985, the total reached $98.6 billion. In 1988, gross new issues totaled $83 billion. This compares with public offerings of domestic corporate bond issues of $202 billion in 1988. Gross Eurobonds outstanding, which represents the pool of possible securities trades, rose from $145 billion in 1982 to $470 billion in 1988.

Increased trades among dealers in these securities strengthened the possibility that net positions among dealers could be settled without resorting to bank lines of credit. For example, assume that an investor holding a CD decides to sell it and buy a Eurobond. If the holder of the Eurobond is willing to buy a CD rather than hold a demand deposit, the two transactions will net, and no reserves will change hands.

International Currency Transactions and Dollar Liquidity

As Table 15.5 indicates, currency trading (buying and selling foreign currency for dollars) appears to have grown very rapidly in the 1980s. Foreign currency trades,

Table 15.5 AVERAGE DAILY FOREIGN EXCHANGE TRADING VOLUME BY LOCATION AND CURRENCY, MARCH 1986

	Tokyo	London	New York	New York (1977)
Volume of Trading				
U.S. ($billions)	$48	$90	$50	$5
Percentage Share				
Sterling		30	19	17
Deutschemarks		28	34	27
Yen	82	14	23	5
Swiss francs		9	10	14
French francs		4	4	6
Italian lires		2		1
Canadian dollars		2	6	19
Cross-currency and ecus		4		
Dutch guilders			1	6
Others	18	7	3	5
Total	100	100	100	100

Sources: From Richard M. Levich, *Financial Innovations in International Finance Markets,* NBER Reprint No. 1090, p. 219. Data adapted from press releases of the Bank of Tokyo, Bank of England, and the Federal Reserve Bank of New York.

as well as securities transactions, are settled over CHIPS. A major part of the growth in volume on CHIPS was the result of an increase in foreign currency trades. The settlement/delivery system is very similar to that outlined for Eurodollar CDs—it takes 2 days to complete a trade.

Did the growth in these transactions generate more liquidity on CHIPS and permit settlement of fewer transactions through U.S. bank lines? In an active foreign currency market, dollar-denominated securities become substitutes for foreign currency–denominated securities. This increases the potential buyers for dollar-denominated securities issued abroad, implying that Eurodollar securities are more likely to be able to be bought and sold without settling in bank deposits.

The **interest rate parity theorem** states that if, for example, nominal interest rates on deutschemark securities are lower than nominal interest rates on dollar securities, the future price of the dollar in terms of deutschemarks will be lower than the spot price. (The *spot price* is the price for immediate delivery.) That is, dollars will exchange for fewer deutschemarks per dollar for delivery 3 months from now than for current delivery.

Why should this be so? The interest rate parity theorem states that an investor with dollars can purchase a deutschemark security and receive the same return in dollars that he would have earned had he purchased a dollar security. He does this by buying deutschemarks in the spot market and purchasing a futures contract to sell deutschemarks and buy dollars.

Assume that he buys a deutschemark (DM) security maturing in 1 year and receives an annual interest rate of 5 percent in deutschemarks, while the dollar interest rate for the same maturity is 10 percent. The interest rate parity theorem states that

$$\frac{\text{Spot DM/\$}}{(\text{Future DM/\$})} = \frac{1 + r\$}{1 + r\text{DM}}$$

If the spot price of deutschemarks per dollar is 2 deutschemarks per dollar, the future price 1 year hence must be 1.9 deutschemarks per dollar. If the investor holds a deutschemark security paying 5 percent and contracts to buy dollars at 1.9 deutschemarks per dollar 1 year hence, he will earn the equivalent of 10 percent in dollar terms.

For example, a German bank operating in the United States cannot engage in underwriting securities in the United States, even though this activity is legal for banks in Germany.

Before 1978, foreign banks that entered the U.S. market were exempt from many U.S. banking laws and regulations. This was so because these laws and rules were written to apply to banks incorporated in the United States. Thus branches of foreign banks were exempt from reserve requirements, and their parent bank could establish companies in the United States to underwrite corporate securities. Even if the foreign bank chartered a bank in the United States, domestic rules applied only to the chartered bank, not to the U.S. activities of the foreign parent bank. Swiss banking companies were particularly active in entering the securities business in the United States.

In 1978, Congress passed the International Banking Act to remedy what domestic banks saw as an unfair advantage for foreign banks. Congress established the doctrine of "national treatment" for foreign banks. That is, they were treated as if they were American banks. Thus the rules were applied to all U.S. activities of the foreign parent, regardless of the vehicle the banking company chose to use to operate in the United States.

A competing doctrine for treating foreign banks in the U.S. market is reciprocity. This doctrine says that the U.S. activities of banks from a given country ought to be determined by what U.S. banks can do in that country. For example, if U.S. banks are not allowed to buy banks in Japan, Japanese banks ought not to be permitted to buy banks in the United States. (This example is hypothetical. It is probably the case that an American bank can buy a commercial bank in Japan, although none have tried. American banks do own specialized banks, known as trust banks, in Japan.)

The supporters of reciprocity claim that adoption of this policy would give the United States leverage to open up banking markets overseas to more competition.

The Role of the Eurocurrency Dealer

Assume that a holder of a dollar CD wishes to sell that security to make a deutsche-mark payment. She sells the CD to a dealer and receives dollars, which she must then convert to deutschemarks. The dealer could finance the purchase with a bank loan, but given an active foreign exchange market, he could instead enter into a repurchase agreement with a holder of deutschemarks.

The holder of a deutschemark security sells his security to obtain deutschemarks, with which he buys dollars to lend to the dealer through the repurchase agreement. At the same time, he purchases a futures contract to sell dollars for deutschemarks at the time the repurchase agreement expires. In so doing, he is assured of receiving the same deutschemarks return that he would have received had he held a deutschemark security.

The dealer received dollars from the repurchase transaction. He delivers the dollars to the seller of the U.S. security, who then purchases the deutschemarks sold by the deutschemark security holder when he engaged in the repurchase agreement. She then delivers deutschemarks to make her payment. The receiver of the deutschemark payment then buys the security that the holder of the deutschemark security had sold to purchase the dollar security under the repurchase agreement.

The transactions arising among the banks of the preceding parties is somewhat complicated, but they net out in both dollar and deutschemark terms. The process is illustrated in Figure 15.3.

To execute these transactions, no bank loans are necessary because all these transactions are completed on the same 2-day delivery and settlement system described for Eurodollar CDs. That is, even though the participants think that dollars and deutschemarks are trading hands on settlement day, no actual dollars or deutschemarks are used. The trades are settled in New York at the end of the day. Since they net out, no good funds change hands. Therefore, no net "due to" positions need be created to be settled in New York. The dealer's position with his bank is even. His dollar payments are matched by dollar receipts from the repurchase agreement. The holder of the deutschemark security has a ready market for his security as well as a ready market for his deutschemarks.

In Figure 15.3 there is one contract that is unsettled at the end of the day, with no identified counterparty. This is the futures contract to buy deutschemarks. However, this is the next day's settlement problem; it does not affect the demand for good funds on the day described in Figure 15.3.

A liquid market involves so many potential transactors that no one has to worry about lining up matched transactions as we have in the preceding example. The existence of an active futures market in foreign exchange implies that dealers can finance their inventory without resorting to bank loans under most circumstances. See Boxes 15.2 and 15.3.

REGULATION AND THE EXISTENCE OF OFFSHORE MARKETS

The Eurodollar Banking Market
versus the Eurosecurities Market

We have shown that Eurodollar securities markets have grown to the point where they are almost as liquid as the domestic market. Yet the Eurodollar banking market, which is about 110 percent of the size of the domestic banking market, is still large relative to open-market financial instruments compared with the domestic market.

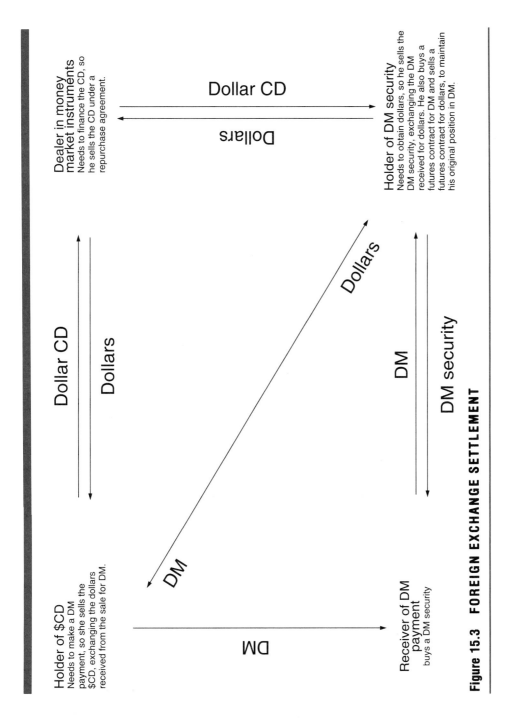

Figure 15.3 FOREIGN EXCHANGE SETTLEMENT

Box 15.2

The Importance of Bank Lines in Foreign Exchange Trading

Currency trading has become an important part of the profit picture for U.S. money-center banks. Banks earn profits by playing the role of market maker in foreign exchange. That is, they take positions in dollars versus major foreign currencies. When markets are particularly volatile, banks have been known to reap large profits by making markets between dollars and deutschemarks, or yen, or sterling, and so on.

In the third quarter of 1990, foreign exchange markets were extremely volatile because of the uncertainties in the Persian Gulf. It was reported that revenues from foreign exchange trading for eight money-center banks hit an all-time high of $748 million.

An important element in being able to trade foreign exchange is to have access to the foreign currency to deliver against dollar trades. American banks obtain access by arranging lines of credit with foreign banks to borrow the currency of a bank's home country. Of course, the foreign banks make the same arrangements in dollars with U.S. banks.

In liquid markets it is unlikely that large amounts of dollar or, say, deutschemark good funds trade hands at settlement because the net position of one bank relative to the entire clearinghouse is likely to be small. However, individual banks can still have relatively large exposures to each other after clearinghouse positions are settled. (These large exposures will not necessarily generate a large demand for reserves, however, because reserves are only delivered against net "due to" positions with the clearinghouse.)

Banks providing currency lines are thus concerned about the credit quality of the borrowing bank. With the worsening of the economic climate in the United States in 1990, many foreign banks became concerned about the financial strength of some of the American players in the foreign exchange markets. These banks found their lines reduced, which prevented them from participating in the lucrative activity of making markets in foreign exchange.

For example, we have already seen that the overseas commercial paper market is about half the size of the domestic market. The Eurobond market is about 60 percent of the size of the domestic corporate bond market.

Since the Eurodollar market has become fairly liquid and banks still play a very large role, illiquidity alone is an inadequate explanation for the existence of the Eurodollar banking market. An additional explanation is regulation. We have seen in Chapter 13 that the existence of reserve requirements is a major reason liabilities are driven off the balance sheets of banks. This happens because it is one way that financial markets can reduce the level of reserves required to the desired level of reserve holdings. Since there are no reserve requirements in the Eurodollar market, there is no reason for liabilities to move off bank balance sheets.

Box 15.3

The Market For Foreign Cash

When you travel outside the United States, you usually must convert your U.S. dollars into the local currency to have locally accepted money to spend. In the accompanying table we present buy and sell rates for conversion of U.S. dollars and Japanese yen in Tokyo on June 16, 1988. The table presents buy and sell rates for round trips into yen and back for various other currencies as well, such as the deutschemark and pound sterling. The relative costs of round trips in the various currencies are typical of what you might have expected on any day over the last 5 years or so.

YEN BUY-SELL SPREADS AT THE BANK OF TOKYO, JUNE 16, 1988

Currency	Buy	Sell	Spread	Spread as Percent of Buy
U.S. dollar	129.55	123.55	6.00	4.63
Pound sterling	283.83	212.83	26.00	10.89
Deutschemark	76.08	68.68	7.40	9.73
Swiss franc	91.38	82.58	8.80	9.63
French franc	24.88	18.08	6.80	27.33
Australian dollar	115.49	86.49	29.00	25.11
Hong Kong dollar	18.65	13.79	4.86	26.06
Singapore dollar	68.40	52.74	15.66	22.89

Source: From Bank of Tokyo.

The most interesting feature of the table is that the cost of a round trip from dollars to yen and back is less than the cost of a round trip in any of the other currencies listed. The Swiss franc "spread" is the second lowest on the table, but it is almost twice the size of the dollar spread. The spreads for such currencies as the Hong Kong dollar and the Malaysian dollar are positively huge—exceeding 25 percent.

The cost of holding dollar cash and the cost of holding another currency's cash is the same, because differences in interest rates are arbitraged according to the spot forward formula we presented earlier. Thus the dollar can be cheaper for Japanese banks in Tokyo to hold than other currencies only because the market for cash in dollars is more liquid than the market for the other currencies. Earlier in the chapter we described the historical increase in the liquidity of the U.S. dollar. This has been a major benefit to the U.S. tourist.

The Relative Size of the Eurodollar and Domestic Financial Markets

Many commentators have argued that the size of the Eurodollar banking market relative to the domestic market is driven by domestic forces as well. That is, the whole reason for the development of the overseas banking market was to avoid regulation, specifically reserve requirements, that exist in the domestic market. In this view, the Eurodollar banking market developed to reduce the reserve burden on domestic financial markets, just like the domestic commercial paper or repurchase agreement markets.

In showing how commercial paper or repurchase agreements could reduce the reserve burden, we made one crucial assumption that, until recently, could not be assumed about the overseas banking market. That is, commercial paper and repurchase agreements are perfect substitutes for CDs and for demand deposits, respectively.

In the early 1980s, the Eurodollar market was unable to reduce the domestic reserve burden because it could not produce perfect substitutes for domestic bank deposits. In fact, we saw that the overseas market generated, until the mid-1980s, an increase in the demand for reserves. Therefore, it is unlikely that the market developed to avoid domestic reserve requirements.

The Eurodollar banking market did provide investors who were willing to forgo liquidity the opportunity to earn a few extra basis points on their investments. Thus we might say that the Eurodollar market developed to provide a greater supply of illiquid money market instruments than was available in the United States. It was a market tailored to the preferences of those who do not place a high value on immediacy.

The Future of the Eurodollar Banking Market

In Chapter 14 we explained that when financial markets become liquid, there are very good reasons for banks to assume a relatively narrow role in the world of corporate finance. Their special function is to act as suppliers of liquidity of last resort, both in times of general crises and when an individual borrower faces difficulty. They avoid a more general role to remove themselves from potential conflicts of interest.

We have seen that the Eurodollar market has become liquid, but that securities markets, as measured by Eurocurrency issues, remain small relative to the bank assets and liabilities. In their 1990 *Annual Report,* the BIS commented that the reason that growth in the Eurocurrency commercial paper market stalled in 1989 was that many industrial countries have liberalized domestic rules for issuing commercial paper so that their corporations need no longer issue in Eurocurrency markets.

Industrial countries' securities markets will surely liberalize further. The European Economic Community (EEC) has targeted 1992 as the year in which domestic security and banking regulations are to be standardized throughout the European market. This will undoubtedly mean a great deal of liberalization for the securities and banking markets in major markets that have traditionally been restrictive, such as Germany. If this comes to pass, we can expect slow growth in Eurocurrency issues. See Box 15.4.

Box 15.4

Europe after 1992

The European Economic Community (EEC) has the goal of building unified financial and money markets after 1992. This means that financial institutions of member countries would be free to operate in any other member country. Presumably, borrowers would be free to raise capital in any market they might choose as well.

If financial institutions and their potential customers can do business wherever they like (within the EEC), they will naturally choose the market with the least regulation, because this is likely where the cost of doing business will be lowest. However, as we saw in Chapter 12, bank regulators absorb risk that would, in their absence, be absorbed by private participants. If regulators are not compensated for their efforts or they do not have the means to control the risk of private players, taxpayers may have to shoulder the burden of bailing out a failed institution. For example, if a German bank operating in another EEC country that is not tightly regulated should fail because of activities that would be illegal in Germany, German taxpayers may end up responsible for something over which their government had no control.

On the other hand, if regulation is centralized, there is potential that regulators will abuse their power, increasing the cost of liquidity and shutting some borrowers out of financial markets.

Thus a major problem for the liberalization expected in 1992 and beyond is to standardize bank regulation and risk control across the individual countries that make up the EEC, without an overregulated market. For example, should reserve requirements be those of the United Kingdom, which are zero, or Germany, which are substantial? Should banks be supervised by the bank authorities in the country in which the banks operate, or should they be supervised by the authorities of the home country? Should all potential borrowers be free to issue securities in the open market, as is the case in the United Kingdom, or should the banks decide which borrowers have access to open markets, as is the case in Germany?

Thus Eurocurrency banking markets will probably remain large relative to Eurocurrency securities markets. This does not mean that the banking system's role will remain broad, however. It only means that the banking system's size must now be measured relative to world securities markets, regardless of whether securities are issued in the home country of the issuer or not.

Perhaps the strategies pursued by American banks in a liquid international financial market provide a better indication of banks' future role than do numbers on the relative sizes of bank and bond markets. In the mid-1980s, the major U.S. banks decided that their future overseas lay not in lending to large corporations, but in buying securities companies. The United Kingdom liberalized its regulations to permit bank ownership of securities firms in a move that was known as the "Big Bang."

The immediate reason for this decision by U.S. banks was that the profits from lending to large customers who have the alternative of issuing securities was too small to make the transaction worthwhile. In terms of the model we developed in Chapter 14, this implies that large borrowers were not willing to cover banks' monitoring costs.

In late 1990 and early 1991, many of the major U.S. banks that saw such a bright future in entering the securities business have decided to dramatically scale back their investment banking activities overseas. (See Box 15.5.) This does not imply that they intend to get back into the business of lending to customers who have securities market alternatives.

Past experience makes it unlikely that U.S. banks will supply dollar credits to international customers who do not have access to securities markets. In the late 1970s and early 1980s, U.S. banks became heavily involved in supplying dollar credits to developing countries. These customers looked like the customers that banks are familiar with domestically. They did not have access to security credit because their situation was precarious enough to need strict lender supervision. The large U.S. banks loaned large sums of money relative to their capital to these customers, especially to Latin American countries. At some of the major New York banks, these loans represented 200 percent of the lender's capital.

In the mid-1980s, world commodity prices fell, and since many developing countries depended on income from commodity exports to pay interest and principal on their loans, they failed to meet their debt obligations. This caused a dramatic decline in the value of the developing country debt held by the banks. For example, today the secondary market value of Argentine debt is about $0.20 on the dollar, the value of some Brazilian debt is $0.25 on the dollar, and the value of Mexican debt is $0.45 on the dollar.

Because many debtors are either not paying interest or are only paying interest periodically, the major banks began accruing interest on much of their loans to developing countries by increasing principal. At the same time, they have tried to negotiate agreements for lengthening debt maturity and lowering interest payments.

The role of banks in the market for developing country debt appears to be analogous to the role they have played in the leveraged buyout market in the United States; that is, they have taken the role of managing a debtor through a crisis. However, the impact on bank balance sheets and income statements has been devastating. In 1987 and 1989, the large New York banks reported substantial losses as they increased their loan reserves to account for expected losses on debt to developing countries (see Chapter 19).

Why, if this is what banks are supposed to do, has lending to developing

The Shrinking European Activities of U.S. Banks

In August 1990, the BIS reported that for the first 6 months of 1990, U.S. overseas banking assets fell by $47 billion, or 8 percent. The BIS said that the reduction was the sharpest on record—exceeding the 4 percent decline in assets that occurred in the first half of 1989.

There are two major reasons cited for the decline. One is that domestic banking business is more profitable than overseas banking. This is reflected in the reported 1989 profits for the U.S. banks with major overseas operations. Chase lost $943 million, Manufacturers lost $919 million, Chemical lost $615 million, BankAmerica lost $477 million, and Citicorp lost $467 million.

Much of this loss is due to loans made to developing countries in the late 1970s and early 1980s that are not paying interest. However, the shrinkage of assets overseas also indicates that the spread between the cost of funds and loans to borrowers from developed countries has become too narrow to be attractive. This is a natural outcome of the increasing liquidity of overseas dollar markets.

The decline in profitability of overseas business is not a new phenomenon. It had been of concern to American bankers since the mid-1980s. At first, the American bank response was to build an overseas securities business, especially in London. However, this strategy appears not to have provided a solution. Chase, Citicorp, and Security Pacific have all announced that they are closing or selling many of their overseas securities businesses.

countries had such a negative impact? A major reason is the sheer size of exposure to a particular borrower. However, another reason is that banks do not have the same leverage to negotiate with countries as they do with companies. When they lend to companies, they can threaten to seize assets under a court of law. When they lend to countries, their right of seizure is limited by the willingness of the country to accept the seizure. In the Latin American case, the banks have threatened to exercise the right of setoff against deposits held, which has been of some value in speeding negotiations, but they cannot take the party to court to force bankruptcy.

In summary, it is difficult for U.S. banks in the international marketplace to play the specialized role they have played domestically because their legal options are more limited as long as the candidates for bank loans are countries rather than companies operating in economies where lenders have clear rights. Thus it is unlikely that traditional lending activities will supplant the business of providing liquidity to dollar markets overseas. Unless the legal environment changes, the international activities of U.S. banks will shrink as liquidity of the international marketplace expands.

CONCLUSION

In this chapter we studied Eurodollar banking and securities markets. We saw that until the mid-1980s, the overseas dollar market was less liquid than the domestic dollar market. As a result, interest rates on Eurodollar CDs were higher than those on domestic CDs of the same maturity. The domestic market could not export liquidity to Europe through arbitrage because there is no cash, or same day, settlement and delivery for money market instruments in Europe as there is in the United States.

However, liquidity in the European market increased as the number of market participants increased. We measured the number of market participants by the volume of transactions that occur over CHIPS, the primary clearing system for Eurodollar transactions. We saw that as this volume increased, the dependence of the overseas market on the domestic market for liquidity declined, and the spread between Eurodollar and domestic CDs diminished.

We noted that the Eurodollar market is free of most regulations that are applied to banks and securities markets domestically. We found that lack of reserve requirements on Eurodollar deposits was not an important reason for the development of this market. However, it is likely that once the market became liquid, the lack of reserve requirements permitted banks to play a larger role in financial markets than they would have if reserve requirements had been applied. Nevertheless, we believe that over time banks will play the same specialized role in liquid international financial markets as they do in the U.S. domestic market.

KEY TERMS

Eurodollar market

Bank for International Settlements (BIS)

cross-border position

current account

Eurocurrency securities

Eurobond market

interest rate parity theorem

EXERCISES

1. What do we mean by the liquidity of a payments system? Define a measure of the liquidity provided by a payments system.

2. What do we mean by the credit risk of a payments system? Define a measure of the credit risk of a payments system.

3. Between 1972 and 1974, the Eurodollar market, measured by the balance sheets of the overseas branches of U.S. banks, doubled in size. The large increase in dollars held overseas resulted from the accumulation of dollars in the hands of oil-producing countries after the first oil shock. Some commentators at the time worried about how all these overseas dollars would be recycled. That is, they saw dollars leaving the U.S. economy, which would cause domestic spending to decline unless the dollars were "recycled" back to the United States. However, at the same time that increasing amounts of dollars were held overseas, the domestic offices of U.S. banks increased their loans to their foreign branches. This appears to be the opposite of recycling—that is, American banks appeared to be contributing to the dollar outflow. Give an alternative, payments-related explanation for the actions of American banks. (Before you answer this question, you might want to work through exercises 4 through 6.)

4. Assume that an Indonesian sells 5 barrels of oil to an American for $100. The American, who banks in New York, tells his bank to pay $100 to a bank in London where the Indonesian keeps her dollar account. The Indonesian buys a CD issued by her London bank. Describe the balance sheets of the London and New York banks after this transaction.

5. Now assume that the Indonesian's London bank (call it bank L1) makes an interbank loan to another London bank (L2). L2 buys a Treasury bill from the original American bank. Show the balance sheets of the American bank and banks L1 and L2. Does either London or New York have a net "due to" position relative to the other?

6. Now assume that the Indonesian decides to sell her CD to a London dealer. Assume that the London dealer must finance the CD with a bank loan from a third London bank (L3) because there is no investor willing to hold the CD. Describe the balance sheets of all the banks concerned. Is a net "due to" position created for New York?

7. Did the Eurodollar market develop as a means to escape U.S. domestic reserve requirements?

8. In the late 1970s, U.S. bank regulatory authorities, especially the Federal Reserve Bank of New York, became concerned about the rapid growth of the Eurodollar market because it operated beyond its control, so it permitted large banks to establish international banking facilities in the United States. Through these facilities banks are permitted to take deposits and make loans to non-U.S. residents. The profits from the facilities are not subject to state income taxes (state permission is necessary for this), and deposits are exempt from reserve requirements. However, deposits issued by these facilities must have a minimum maturity of 2 days. Why do you suppose the Fed thought it necessary to place this restriction on the business?

9. Assume that investors prefer to hold Eurodollar deposits rather than open-market securities. Assume also that Eurodollar borrowers prefer to borrow from the London office of the same bank they use for their domestic business. Show how such a situation can lead to a large interbank market.

10. Assume that the dollar equals 2 deutschemarks. The future exchange rate on a 1-year contract is 2.1 deutschemarks. The U.S. interest rate is 10 percent. The deutschemark interest rate is 5 percent. Explain how an arbitrager can make money.

11. Explain how active foreign exchange markets improved the liquidity of the Eurodollar market.

12. Explain the obstacles that American banks face in building a profitable international business.

13. For the payments systems associated with the major currencies (British pound, dollar, deutschemark, and yen), construct a liquidity–credit risk frontier.

14. Discuss a central bank's objectives or constraints that lead to its choosing a point on this frontier.

15. Will a central bank's choice of a point on the frontier be affected by the other central banks' choices so that the equilibrium will be the outcome of a game?

16. Will the currency with the most liquid payment system automatically become the vehicle currency?

FURTHER READING

Key, Sydney J. "Mutual Recognition: Integration of the Financial Sector in the European Community," *Federal Reserve Bulletin*, September 1989, pp. 591–609.

C H A P T E R

16

Monetary Policy in
International Financial Markets

Every year the leaders of the major industrial countries meet in a summit to attempt to coordinate economic policy. Frequently, the most important problem on the agenda concerns the appropriate levels of **exchange rates,** the prices of each country's currency in terms of the others. Sometimes there is an agreement that a currency is too expensive in terms of other currencies and should depreciate, as occurred in 1985, when it was thought that the dollar was overvalued. Sometimes there is an agreement not to allow exchange rates to move outside some prescribed range, as occurred in 1987. The implementation of such policy goals is generally a task for central banks.

A central bank's actions, however, also affect foreign securities markets. We can interpret "foreign markets" in several ways: markets in securities denominated in foreign currencies located abroad, markets in securities denominated in foreign currencies located domestically, and markets in securities denominated in a given central bank's currency but located in another country.

The coexistence of many currencies brings with it the problem of how to price one currency in terms of another, that is, how to determine the exchange rate. We will find that the exchange rate is determined through the supply and demand for currencies and through arbitrage in securities and goods markets. Initially, we will analyze the effect of monetary policies on **floating exchange rates** based on an assumption that each central bank acts only on domestic securities markets denominated in its own currency. Under this simplistic assumption, each central bank seeks to stabilize or provide liquidity to its own domestic securities or goods markets without regard to the exchange rate, letting the exchange rate attain any market-clearing level.

If, on the other hand, a central bank seems to affect the exchange rate as one of its policy goals, it can do so by altering its interventions in domestic securities markets in several ways. If it aims to have a sporadic, though active effect on the exchange rate, it can establish an exchange rate policy known as a **managed float.** During most of the period between 1973 and 1991, the exchange rates between the U.S. dollar, the pound sterling, the yen, and the deutschemark were determined with managed floating policies. If a central bank aims to allow the exchange rate to move only within well-defined limits, it is operating in a **target zone.** The currencies in the European Monetary System (EMS), for example, have followed a target zone policy since 1979. If a central bank intervenes to peg the exchange rate at a given level, it is operating a **fixed exchange rate** system. A gold standard and the monetary system operated under the Bretton Woods agreement from 1946 through 1973 are examples of fixed exchange rate systems.

Given their interest in exchange market intervention, central banks are major market makers in multiple currencies. To play the role of a market maker, central banks must take positions in foreign currencies; they must either hold foreign-denominated liquid assets or have lines of credit in foreign currencies, typically with other central banks.

The bulk of foreign-denominated liquidity available to central banks is their asset holdings of foreign exchange. For example, at the end of 1987, central banks held an aggregate of $453 billion in foreign exchange. Typically, these are liquid securities denominated in U.S. dollars, British pounds, Japanese yen, and German deutschemarks. Gold is still denominated as a form of international reserves, primarily as a hangover from the prefloating era when gold was the principal foreign reserve along with the dollar. The value of gold in official reserves in 1987 was $322 billion at current market prices. In addition, central banks maintain substantial credit lines with each other and with international organizations such as the International Monetary Fund (IMF).

EXCHANGE RATE DETERMINATION

By concentrating on arbitrage between financial and goods markets in different countries, we can form a simple framework for studying the determination of exchange rates.

Interest Rate Parity

The arbitrage that we briefly studied in Chapter 15 produced the **interest parity** relation: The interest rate on domestically denominated securities equals the interest rate on foreign-denominated loans of comparable default risk and maturity *plus* the percentage by which the forward exchange rate exceeds the spot exchange rate.

To see that the interest parity relation should generally hold, consider the two possible methods of investing $1 for 3 months depicted in Figure 16.1. An investor can buy a U.S. T-bill that will pay back $1 + r_\$$ dollars in 3 months. Alternatively, he can buy e yen for the dollar on the spot market for yen. A ¥1 investment in yen-dominated 90-day loans (called *gensaki*) will yield $1 + r_¥$ yen in 3 months, so the e yen purchased will pay $e(1 + r_¥)$. Currently, the forward exchange rate is f yen per dollar, so the yen payoff in 3 months can be sold for a guaranteed $(1 + r_¥)e/f$ dollars.

The original dollar can be invested either directly in U.S. T-bills or in a round trip through the yen exchange and securities markets. Both methods will deliver

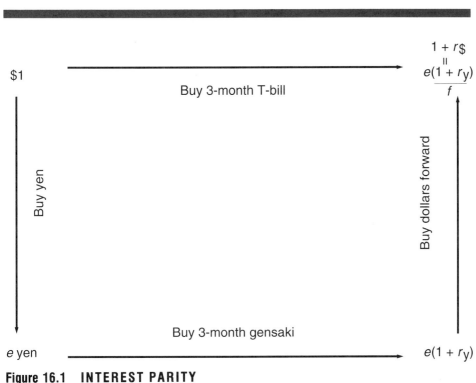

Figure 16.1   INTEREST PARITY

guaranteed dollars in 3 months. For an investor to be indifferent between the two methods, the payoffs must be equal:

$$1 + r_\$ = \frac{(1 + r_¥)e}{f} \quad \text{or} \quad 1 + r_¥ = \frac{(1 + r_\$)f}{e}$$

Notice that $f/e = 1 + (f - e)/e$, so

$$(1 + r_¥) = \left(\frac{1 + (f - e)}{e}\right)(1 + r_\$) = 1 + r_\$ + \frac{f - e}{e} + \frac{(f - e)r_\$}{e}$$

Eliminating the 1 from both sides and dropping the final term, that is, $r_\$ (f - e)/e$, because it is typically very small, we have the usual way of writing the interest parity condition:

$$r_¥ = r_\$ + \frac{f - e}{e}$$

Table 16.1 lists 3-month Eurodollar and Euroyen interest rates along with current and forward exchange rates between yen and dollars. Since the yields on the deposits are listed on an annual basis, as if the deposits were to be rolled over three times at the same interest rate, we must multiply $(f - e)/e$ by 4 to maintain comparability. In the table, the yields on Eurodollars are 3.34 percent higher than the yields on Euroyen. On July 13, 1989, the dollar exchanged for ¥139.45, but dollars for delivery in 90 days exchanged for ¥138.29 in the forward market. Since the forward rate is less than the current exchange rate, $(f - e)/e$ is a negative number. Note how closely the simple expression for interest parity holds.

Formally, interest parity is a relationship that holds between interest rates,

---

Table 16.1 INTEREST AND EXCHANGE RATES IN LONDON, JULY 13, 1989

90-day Eurodollar = $r_\$$	8.75% (annual rate)
90-day Euroyen = $r_¥$	5.41% (annual rate)
Spot yen = e	139.45 ¥/$
90-day forward yen = f	138.29 ¥/$
$\dfrac{4(f - e)}{e}$	−3.33% (annual rate)

$$r_¥ = 5.41\%$$
$$r_\$ + \frac{4(f - e)}{e} = 8.75 - 3.33 = 5.42\%$$

---

current exchange rates, and forward exchange rates. In this form, it is known as **covered interest parity** because all payoffs are certain when the original transactions are made. In a different theoretical version known as **open interest parity,** the expected future spot exchange rate $e^\star$ is substituted for the forward rate f. Open interest parity would be associated with a situation in which the buyer of yen securities does not lock in the future exchange of his yen payoff for dollars in the forward market. Instead, the investor simply will sell his yen for dollars in 3 months at the then–existing spot exchange rate. Under open interest parity, the two investment methods are *expected* to have the same payoff in dollars, but there is some risk that the exchange rate will not materialize as anticipated in 3 months.

We will find it convenient to use the open interest parity concept to study exchange rate determination. Let e be the current, or *spot,* exchange rate between yen and dollars, say, 138 ¥/$, and let $e^\star$ denote the exchange rate expected to prevail one period from now. The interest rates on one-period yen and dollar loans are $r_¥$ and $r_\$$, respectively. The open interest parity relation is then

$$r_¥ = r_\$ + \frac{e^\star - e}{e}$$

If $e^\star$ is greater than e, the exchange rate between the yen and the dollar is expected to *depreciate;* it will cost more yen to buy a dollar in the future. Therefore, a lender of yen will demand a higher interest rate than a lender of dollars to compensate for the expected percentage loss in the value of the yen relative to the dollar. If $e^\star$ is less than e, the yen is expected to appreciate, and yen interest rates will be less than dollar interest rates.

The Real Exchange Rate

As in other markets, we expect that international trade in goods will tend to equalize goods prices across trading countries. One way of measuring the relative costs of goods in two different countries is known as the **real exchange rate.** The real exchange rate between Japan and the United States, for example, serves as a measure of how many Japanese goods would exchange for a unit of U.S. goods. Since there are many different kinds of Japanese and U.S. goods, the comparison is typically made between the baskets of goods contained in a price index such as the consumer price index (CPI). For the Japanese, the real exchange rate would be

$$\frac{P_\$ e}{P_¥} = \frac{\text{dollar/U.S. goods} \times \text{yen/dollar}}{\text{yen/Japanese goods}} = \frac{\text{yen/U.S. goods}}{\text{yen/Japanese goods}} = \frac{\text{Japanese goods}}{\text{U.S. goods}}$$

If $P_\$$ and $P_¥$ are the U.S. and Japanese consumer price indexes, respectively, the real exchange rate measures how many units of the Japanese consumption basket would exchange for a unit of a U.S. consumption basket.

Purchasing Power Parity

If all goods in the baskets are identical and freely tradable, and if transport costs are minimal, we would expect that trade would drive their relative price to 1 so that $P_¥ = P_$e$. This relationship is known as **purchasing power parity.** One yen spent on goods in Japan will buy a certain amount of goods. With purchasing power parity, that same yen converted to dollars at prevailing exchange rates will buy an identical amount of goods in the United States.

If purchasing power parity holds, movements in the exchange rates would be associated with similar price-level movements. For example, suppose e rises by 10 percent with no movement in the U.S. price level. To maintain purchasing power parity, the Japanese price level also must rise by 10 percent.

While it is an attractive abstraction, purchasing power parity has been shown not to be satisfied in reality. There are several reasons for this. First, there are *restrictions to trade* in the form of tariffs, quotas, and transport costs. These prevent the prices of tradable goods from equalizing across countries. Second, there are *different goods in the consumption baskets* of each country that are not readily tradable. Examples are housing and personal labor services. If the prices of these goods move relative to the prices of tradable goods, then associated price-level movements would cause purchasing power parity to fail.

Movements in the Real Exchange Rate

Since purchasing power parity is typically violated, the real exchange rate will differ from unity. It will fluctuate with real changes in trade barriers and relative prices between tradable and nontradable goods. However, it also will fluctuate with changes in nominal exchange rates if some of the prices of goods in the consumption basket are slow to adjust.

For example, suppose that in period 1 the values of the price levels are $P_¥ = 130$ and $P_$ = 130$ and the nominal exchange rate e is 140 ¥/$. The real exchange rate, in contrast, is

$$\left(\frac{P_$e}{P_¥}\right)_1 = \frac{130 \times 140}{130} = 140$$

In period 2, the nominal exchange rate falls to 120 ¥/$, so the yen appreciates. If the price levels do not adjust immediately, the real exchange rate will change to

$$\left(\frac{P_$e}{P_¥}\right)_2 = \frac{130 \times 120}{130} = 120$$

Since it takes fewer Japanese goods to buy a U.S. good, the nominal yen appreciation coincides with a real exchange rate appreciation.

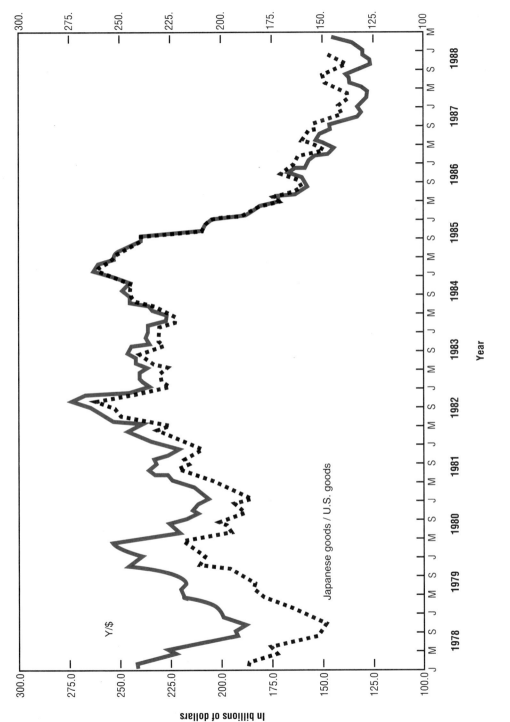

Figure 16.2 YEN/$ NOMINAL AND REAL EXCHANGE RATES

Figure 16.2 plots the real exchange rate against the yen per dollar nominal exchange rate. Movements in the nominal exchange rate are associated with movements in the real exchange rate. This is explainable if price levels move sluggishly. A change in the nominal exchange rate will then change the real exchange rate.

THE MONEY MARKETS AND EXPECTED EXCHANGE RATE DEPRECIATION

In Chapter 7 we examined the conditions for equilibrium in a domestic money market. Real money demand depends on real income and the nominal interest rate. Given real income, the interest rate and price level adjust to equate the real demand and real supply of money.

Figure 16.3 depicts this money market equilibrium in both the yen and dollar money markets. The demands for real yen and dollars are the usual downward-sloping curves. In this international economy, the yen money market consists of yen currency plus all yen-denominated Japanese bank deposits and Euroyen, and

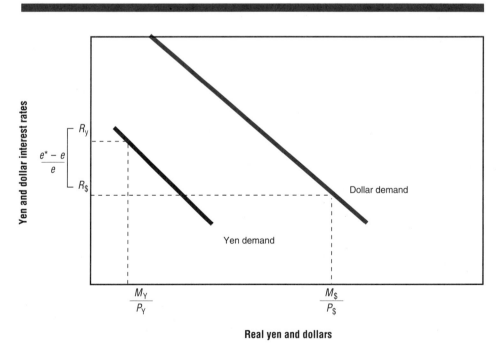

Figure 16.3 YEN AND DOLLAR MONEY MARKET EQUILIBRIUM

the dollar money market consists of dollar currency plus U.S. bank deposits and Eurodollars. Both domestic and Eurocurrency deposits affect the demand for good funds in Japan and the United States, as we saw in Chapter 15. Assuming that real yen balances are at a level $M_{¥}P_{¥}$, the yen market clears at an interest rate $R_{¥}$. The dollar market clears at an interest rate $R_{\$}$ with real balances of $M_{\$}/P_{\$}$. By interest parity, the difference between the interest rates measured on the vertical axis is $(e^{\star} - e)/e$, the anticipated percentage depreciation of the yen.

Figure 16.4 plots the anticipated depreciation rate against the current value of the exchange rate for a fixed value of $e^{\star}$, the expected future exchange rate. As the current value of the exchange rate rises, the ratio $e^{\star}/e$ falls, so the curve has a negative slope. When e is low enough that $e^{\star}$ exceeds e, anticipated depreciation is positive. For a high enough value of e, however, anticipated deprecation is negative; that is, the exchange rate is expected to appreciate. The position of the curve depends on the value of the expected future exchange rate; a higher $e^{\star}$ would shift the relation between e and $(e^{\star} - e)/e$ upward to a curve like 2. A given anticipated rate of depreciation would then be associated with a higher spot exchange rate.

Now we can relate Figure 16.3 to Figure 16.4 to describe the behavior of the current exchange rate. The supplies of real balances in yen and dollars are associated with an anticipated depreciation $(e^{\star} - e)/e$ in Figure 16.3. Suppose the expected

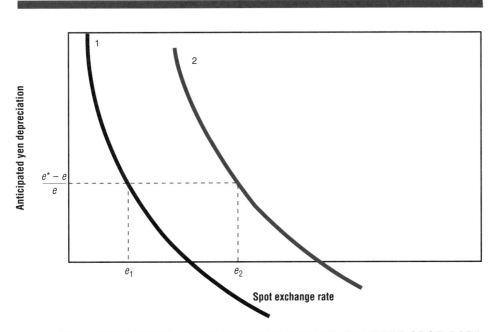

Figure 16.4 ANTICIPATED DEPRECIATION VERSUS CURRENT SPOT RATE

future exchange rate is that associated with curve 1 in Figure 16.4. For the depreciation rate given by Figure 16.3, we determine in Figure 16.4 the associated current exchange rate e.

The Impact of Money Market Shifts on the Exchange Rate

Now let's see how monetary shifts may affect the exchange rate. First, we will assume that price levels move slowly. By this we mean that monetary shifts have no impact on price levels in the period that they occur; in the period after the monetary shift, however, the price level will fully adjust to its long-term value. Next, we will examine exchange rate movements when price levels adjust immediately to monetary changes.

Sluggish Price Level Movements

Suppose we start in Figure 16.5 with an era of monetary stability. Money supplies in both countries have been such as to maintain stable price levels, so people expect no inflation. Nominal interest rates will then equal real interest rates in the two countries, and the price level and real money stocks will be determined as in Chapter 7. If real interest rates are also the same in the two countries, there will be no nominal interest rate differential. Thus the anticipated depreciation of the exchange rate will be zero. Since $(e^\star - e)/e = 0$, the expected future exchange rate equals the current rate e_1 in Figure 16.6.

The nominal exchange rate will be set at a level such that the real exchange rate $P_\$ e/P_¥$ is at its "long-run" level, at which there is no tendency for trade in goods to cause price-level movements.

An Increase in $M_¥$

Now suppose that the Bank of Japan permanently and unexpectedly increases the Japanese money stock by expanding its holdings of yen securities. This causes a shift in $M_¥$, raising $M_¥/P_¥$ if $P_¥$ is temporarily sluggish. In Figure 16.5, real balances shift rightward to $M_{¥2}/P_{¥1}$, lowering the yen interest rate to $R_{¥2}$. The anticipated depreciation rate becomes negative because $(e^\star - e)/e = R_{¥2} - R_\$$. That is, the expected future value of the yen $e^\star$ is less than the current value e.

What is the value of $e^\star$, the expected exchange rate next period? Remember, we assume that the price levels will adjust to their long-term market-clearing values in the next period. Since the Japanese money stock has increased permanently, the Japanese price level will rise proportionally to clear the money market, as we showed

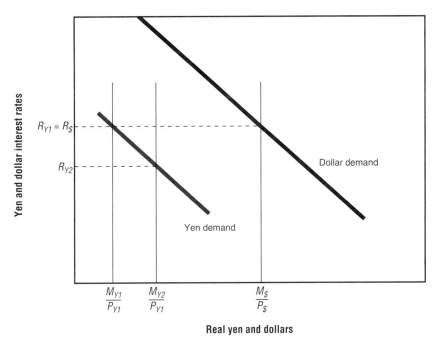

Figure 16.5 plot area contains:

Yen and dollar interest rates (vertical axis label)

$R_{Y1} = R_\$$

R_{Y2}

Dollar demand

Yen demand

$\dfrac{M_{Y1}}{P_{Y1}}$ $\dfrac{M_{Y2}}{P_{Y1}}$ $\dfrac{M_\$}{P_\$}$

Real yen and dollars

Figure 16.5   MONETARY EQUILIBRIUM WITH STABLE PRICE LEVELS AND EXCHANGE RATES

in Chapter 7. For instance, if the money stock increases by 10 percent, the price level will increase by 10 percent. The real exchange rate also will return to its long-term value in the next period. Initially, the real exchange rate was $P_\$ e/P_{¥1}$. If $P_¥$ rises next period, the exchange rate next period must rise proportionally to restore the long-term value of the real exchange rate. If $P_¥$ rises by 10 percent, next period's exchange rate will be 10 percent higher than the value of the exchange rate prior to the monetary expansion. Since market participants can foresee this increase, $e^\star$ will rise by 10 percent over its value before the increase in $M_¥$.

What is the value of the current exchange rate e? In Figure 16.6, the relation between the anticipated rate of depreciation shifts outward from curve 1 to curve 2, reflecting the increased value of $e^\star$. Given the negative value $(e^\star - e)/e$ from interest parity, we can determine the new value for the current exchange rate. The current exchange rate jumps up (depreciates) with the unanticipated increase in the Japanese money stock. Since in the next period the exchange rate is expected to fall (appreciate) to level $e^\star$, the current rate must have increased to level e_3, which is higher than its long-term value. If the yen money supply rises by 10 percent, the spot exchange rate will jump by more than 10 percent. The long-term value will

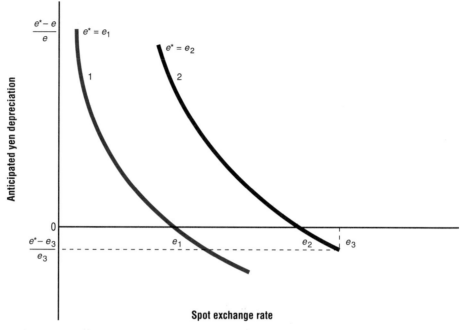

Figure 16.6   ANTICIPATED DEPRECIATION

be e_2, since the expected depreciation will be zero after it is attained. Next period the exchange rate will then appreciate to e_2 so that the long-term exchange rate increase is exactly 10 percent.

This more than proportional initial increase in the spot exchange rate is known as **exchange rate overshooting.** It happens if price levels adjust sluggishly. Interest rates must then adjust more in the short term to maintain money market equilibrium. These large interest rate movements are then passed on to the exchange markets through securities market arbitrage.[1]

The rise in the spot exchange rate with the price levels fixed raises (depreciates) the real exchange rate for the Japanese. The acquisition of U.S. goods now costs more Japanese goods than before.

Finally, the eventual rise in the price level will reduce Japanese real balances to their original level. The Japanese money market in Figure 16.5 will return to its original status: There will be no further expected inflation, and Japanese and U.S. interest rates will once again be equal.

1.   The overshooting concept was originally presented in Rudiger Dornbusch, "Expectations and Exchange Rate Dynamics," *Journal of Political Economy,* December 1976, pp. 1161–1176.

Flexible Price Levels

If the Japanese price level is flexible (a change in our assumptions), it will respond immediately to the increase in the money stock with a proportional jump upward. Then there will be no change from the original situation in the money markets in Japan: Both the Japanese real money stock and the interest rate will be unchanged. The anticipated rate of depreciation of the exchange rate will remain constant at zero. To maintain the real exchange rate, the spot exchange rate must immediately jump upward by the same percentage as the Japanese price level to the value e_2. To maintain the zero anticipated rate of depreciation, the expected future exchange rate $e\star$ also must jump by the same percentage.

Other Money Market Shifts

Similar exercises can be performed if other aspects of the money market shift in either country.

1. A one-time increase in the U.S. money stock will have analogous, though opposite, effects on the exchange rate: It will appreciate the spot exchange rate, that is, reduce the number of yen exchanging for a dollar. In addition, it will cause overshooting and anticipated future depreciation *if price level movements are sluggish*.

2. An unexpected income increase in Japan will shift out the money demand function and raise the interest rate if price-level movements are sluggish and there is no increase in the nominal money stock. This combination of events generates an anticipated future depreciation of the yen. In the next period, the Japanese price level will *decline* to its long-term level, as in Chapter 7. To restore the real exchange rate, the future nominal exchange rate $e\star$ also must decline in proportion to the price level. The spot exchange rate must then have fallen (appreciated) by more than $e\star$, since the exchange rate is expected subsequently to depreciate.

A Rise in the Rate of Money Creation

Suppose that the Bank of Japan decides to increase permanently the rate of money growth from zero to 10 percent per period. In Chapter 7 we learned that the Japanese price level will then rise steadily by a rate of 10 percent per period, so the nominal interest rate will also rise, from the real interest rate to the real interest rate plus 10 percent. *If the price level is immediately flexible,* it will also jump up at the time of the policy change because of the fall in real money demand.

There will then be a 10-percent difference between the yen interest rate and the dollar interest rate. This will imply a 10 percent per period anticipated depreciation of the yen. This rate of depreciation will continue indefinitely so that in every period $e\star$ will be 10 percent higher than in the previous period. To maintain the real exchange rate at its normal level, the spot exchange rate at the time of the announcement will jump up by the same percentage as the Japanese price level. It will then continue to depreciate at a rate of 10 percent per period.

FIXED EXCHANGE RATES

In addition to their other goals, central banks concern themselves with controlling the movements of exchange rates by controlling their liabilities and assets. A polar case of such control is a policy to maintain a fixed exchange rate between two currencies. While it lasts, a fixed exchange rate eliminates uncertainties about the exchange rate and limits the discretion of the central bank. We will consider various methods by which central banks can fix exchange rates.

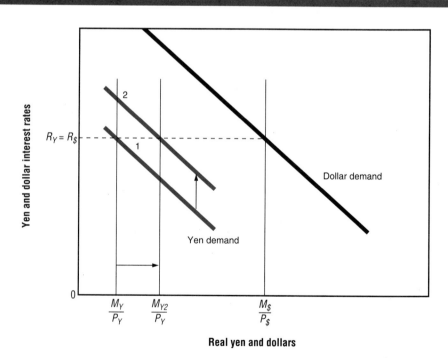

Figure 16.7   MONEY SUPPLY SHIFT KEEPS EXCHANGE RATE FIXED

As one method of fixing exchange rates, a central bank could offset with money supply changes any forces causing the exchange rate to move. For example, if Japan wishes to fix the yen per dollar exchange rate at 140 ¥/$, it could expand the yen monetary base and the yen nominal money supply whenever there was a tendency for the exchange rate to fall from 140, and it could reduce the yen monetary base whenever the exchange rate began to rise. We have seen that the exchange rate would appreciate if Japanese real income grew or if there were a monetary expansion in the United States. An increase in the Japanese money supply by an appropriate amount would preclude any movement in the exchange rate.

In Figure 16.7, suppose that a real income rise shifts the Japanese demand for money up to curve 2. This creates deflationary pressure in Japan; with no monetary action, the price level will tend to fall, and the exchange rate will appreciate. If the Bank of Japan simultaneously expands the money stock appropriately, it will shift the supply of real balances to $M_{¥2}/P_¥$, thus maintaining the old price level and exchange rate.

Which Assets Does the Central Bank Use to Fix the Exchange Rate?

In principle, a central bank can control the money stock as required for fixed exchange rates by acquiring or selling any asset, denominated either in domestic or foreign currencies. In practice, central banks operating fixed exchange rate policies follow the direct route of promising at any moment to buy or sell foreign good funds on demand for domestic good funds at the fixed rate. This converts the central bank into a continuously operating market maker in foreign exchange that will trade any amount of foreign currency at an unchanging bid and offer price. Other market makers may trade foreign exchange inside the central bank's spread, but a person seeking to acquire foreign currency to make a payment may find that the other dealers will not beat the central bank's official offer price. At such a time, the central bank will sell foreign exchange.

As a source of liquidity to the exchange market, the central bank must occasionally receive or deliver foreign good funds, so it must either hold foreign-denominated liquid assets or have a line of credit in foreign funds with other central banks. For this reason, foreign-denominated assets and liabilities will appear on the balance sheet of any central bank that intervenes in exchange markets.

In Table 9.4 we examined the detailed balance sheet of the Federal Reserve. There we noted that the Fed held $35.6 billion in assets denominated in foreign currencies. The Fed uses these assets to intervene in foreign exchange markets. In addition, the Fed maintains lines of credit with other central banks that give it access to additional foreign exchange. Actually, the Fed plays a relatively passive role in intervening to stabilize exchange rates between the dollar and other currencies. The main job is left to the intervention of foreign central banks.

Classifying Foreign Reserves on the Central Bank Balance Sheet

Table 16.2 represents the balance sheet of a central bank that uses foreign exchange to peg its exchange rate with foreign currencies. As one asset, it holds liquid foreign-denominated securities called **foreign reserves.** In addition, it holds domestically denominated securities called **domestic credit.** The central bank's liabilities consist of its currency in circulation and private bank deposits denominated in domestic currency. Other assets, liabilities, and capital of central banks generally are relatively small, so we ignore them here. The sum of currency and deposits is defined as the monetary base. In addition, the central bank may owe foreign currency to other central banks or private firms from previous borrowings. These are called **borrowed reserves.** Reserves minus borrowed reserves are referred to as **net reserves.**

Since assets must equal liabilities plus capital, and since other central bank assets and capital are usually relatively small, we can express the monetary base of the country approximately as

$$\text{Monetary base} = \text{domestic credit} + (\text{reserves} - \text{borrowed reserves})$$

To analyze a fixed exchange rate system, it is convenient to interpret the monetary base simply as the sum of domestic credit and net reserves.

The Loss of Money Stock Control Under Fixed Exchange Rates

Suppose that a central bank operating a fixed exchange rate wishes to expand domestic credit to support domestic financial market prices. As we saw earlier, the expansion of domestic credit tends to expand the monetary base and the money supply. Under a floating exchange rate with an inflexible price level, this would expand real balances and depress the domestic interest rate as in Figure 16.5. Yet, since the exchange rate is now fixed, there can be no anticipation of depreciation, so domestic interest rates cannot diverge from foreign rates. The real money supply therefore cannot change. Of course, the real money supply would stay constant if the price level jumps up proportionally to the money supply. For this to happen, however, the nominal exchange rate must eventually depreciate to restore the real exchange rate to its long-term value. Again, if exchange rates are fixed, this will not be possible.

Only if the central bank reabsorbs the increased monetary base can the real money supply stay unchanged with the rise in domestic credit. However, a fixed exchange rate system that guarantees central bank exchanges of foreign for domestic currency provides an automatic mechanism for offsetting the rise in domestic credit.

Table 16.2 CENTRAL BANK BALANCE SHEET

ASSETS	LIABILITIES
Foreign reserves	Borrowed reserves
Domestic credit	Monetary base

After they sell domestic securities to the central banks, participants in financial markets will find that they have more real money than they want, given the price level and interest rate. They can get rid of this excessive cash by buying foreign exchange from the central bank at the fixed exchange rate. Therefore, the increase in domestic credit is matched by an offsetting sale of reserves, leaving the nominal stock of money unchanged. We can express this result as

Change in domestic credit = minus the change in reserves

This leaves the monetary base unchanged in the presence of domestic credit movements. In the fixed exchange rate system, the central bank then sacrifices control of the money stock to the pegging of the value of foreign currency. More generally, we have already seen that the central bank can fix the exchange rate without using the instrument of direct exchange market intervention: It can simply set the monetary base through open-market operations in domestically denominated securities to preclude exchange rate movements.

Speculative Attacks on Fixed Exchange Rates

If a central bank subordinates the fixed exchange rate to some other domestic goal, it cannot peg the exchange rate indefinitely. If it increases domestic credit to satisfy other goals, it will generate an equal reduction in its holdings of foreign reserves. Large enough expansions of domestic credit will eventually exhaust central bank foreign exchange reserves and credit lines. If domestic credit expands still further, the central bank will be unable to keep its promise to exchange foreign funds for domestic funds at the fixed exchange rate. At this point, the exchange rate system must change. For example, the central bank may allow the currency to start floating indefinitely. After allowing the exchange rate to float for some period, it may then establish a new devalued fixed exchange rate.

If domestic credit expands without an accompanying increase in the domestic demand for money, we have seen that foreign reserves decline. Because there are limits to the extent of central bank intervention to preserve the fixed rate, the public eventually will launch a speculative attack against the central bank's remaining reserves, replacing them with domestic currency and wiping them out at one stroke.

Such an attack is a natural outcome for a fixed exchange rate system headed for certain collapse. To see this, suppose that as the central bank expands domestic credit, reserves gradually fall to their minimum limit without a run on reserves by market participants. Figure 16.8 plots domestic credit rising through time as the central bank pursues its principal domestic goals. We presume that the minimum level of reserves is zero, although it might attain any value, positive or negative, beyond which the central bank will not intervene. With a fixed exchange rate system, reserves fall steadily through time to preserve the money stock at a constant level. Suppose that the central bank smoothly runs out of reserves at time B with no speculative attack. Before time B, the fixed exchange rate system is in operation, so the money stock is constant. Since there is no anticipated depreciation of exchange rates, domestic and foreign interest rates are the same.

After time B, the fixed exchange rate is terminated because there are no further central bank reserve sales. The money stock now grows steadily with domestic

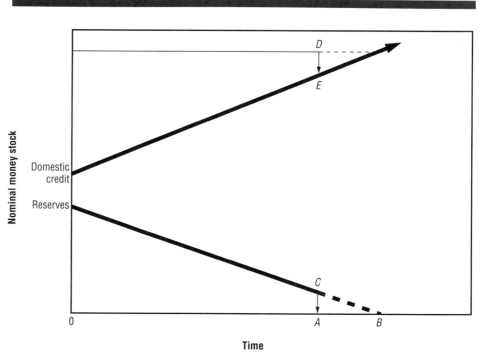

Figure 16.8   ATTACK ON FIXED EXCHANGE RATE REGIME

credit. As we saw earlier, there will be a steady depreciation of the exchange rate, so domestic interest rates will jump up at time B. There will then be a smaller demand for domestically denominated real money. To reduce the real money stock to the lower level demanded, the exchange rate and the price level must suddenly jump upward at time B, as we learned previously.

Now imagine the opportunities for a speculator prior to time B. The speculator can foresee a large depreciation in the exchange rate at time B. How can she profit from this knowledge? A moment before time B when the central bank is still selling reserves, the speculator can buy the remaining foreign reserves from the central bank at the fixed exchange rate in exchange for domestic currency. When time B arrives and the exchange rate depreciates, she can sell the foreign exchange for much more domestic currency than she originally paid for it and thereby avoid the real losses from the depreciation.

As always, there are many speculators awaiting opportunities like this, and each will try to buy the remaining reserves before the others as long as there is an opportunity to profit. The competition among them to make off with the central bank's reserves will cause them to attack the central bank at a time such as A when there is still a substantial amount of reserves. A shift to a floating exchange rate at time A will still cause domestic interest rates to jump up and real money demand to jump down. The real money supply will not be reduced by a jump up in the price level and exchange rates at time A, however. Rather, the nominal money stock will jump down by $DE = CA$, since speculators dumping domestic currency on the central bank in exchange for foreign reserves will force a sudden reduction in the monetary base. Thus competition among speculators precludes the exchange rate jump by forcing the collapse of foreign reserves and the end of the fixed exchange rate at time A. See Boxes 16.1 and 16.2.

An Abortive Speculative Attack

In reality, speculators do not know exactly what the policy response of a central bank will be if the fixed exchange rate is threatened. The central bank may expand its credit lines with other central banks and expend more foreign reserves than the speculators had thought. Speculators may then attack a fixed exchange rate only to find that the central bank sells more than enough reserves to meet their demands. The speculators would then resell their acquired reserves to the central bank and pay off their loans in domestic currency to await another opportunity.

Alternatively, a central bank may surprise speculators by floating or devaluing an exchange rate earlier than expected if it does not want to have its hands tied in the provision of liquidity to domestic markets. For example, suppose that the Bank of Japan, having fixed the exchange rate with the dollar at 120 ¥/$, suddenly devalues to a new fixed rate of 240 ¥/$. The anticipated depreciation rate will still be zero

Box 16.1

The Banking Holiday of 1933

Prior to March 1933, the United States maintained a gold standard that pegged the dollar to gold at $20.67 per ounce. Federal Reserve notes were redeemable in gold coin, so the Fed maintained a gold reserve of $3.25 billion to back its note circulation of $3.4 billion in February 1933. In addition, the U.S. Treasury circulated $650 million in gold certificates, which it also guaranteed to exchange for coin, and it maintained a 100-percent gold reserve against these notes. It appeared that U.S. currency had a very large gold backing.

Nevertheless, this was the worst period of the Great Depression, and there was strong pressure to inflate the economy by expansion of domestic credit. First, private bank note circulation was expanded to $861 million by February 1933, one-fourth the amount of Federal Reserve notes in circulation. These were currency notes authorized under the National Banking Act of 1863 and guaranteed by the Treasury. Second, in early 1933, farming interests, as they did traditionally when farm prices were depressed, pushed for an increased circulation of silver certificates and even a return to bimetallism's free coinage at the old mint rates of $1.29 per ounce. The price of silver was then $0.25 per ounce. Recall from Chapter 8 that this would have driven gold from circulation and perhaps raised the price level several fold. Also, there was a movement simply to devalue gold. The incoming Roosevelt administration issued no statement of support for the continuation of the gold standard, so speculation against the dollar began.

In the context of the accompanying figure, imagine that prior to 1933 domestic credit growth was relatively slow so that the slope of the anticipated domestic credit path was quite flat. Any speculative attack would be far in the future, if, indeed, one would ever occur. Suddenly, however, because of the new effort to expand the money supply, everyone realizes that domestic credit will grow much faster than they had anticipated. A speculative attack will then happen much sooner at a time such as A, perhaps immediately. This happened in February and March of 1933.

The accompanying table reports the gold holdings of the Fed and the Federal Reserve Bank of New York, which felt the brunt of the attack. By March 4, in less than a month, the New York Fed's physical supply of domestic gold had fallen by almost 60 percent, and the Fed expected further foreign gold withdrawals on that day of $700 million more. This forced the Fed to seek a suspension of the convertibility of the dollar to gold. The means of doing this was the declaration of the famous **Banking Holiday of 1933,** in which the entire financial system was closed for the next week. A defaulting Fed, not panicked depositors, forced the closing of the banking system. The new administration then made it illegal for U.S. residents to hold gold and nationalized the entire gold stock. By February 1934, gold was officially devalued by 59 percent to $35 per ounce, thereby confirming the fears of the speculators.*

*For a detailed account of this event, see Barrie Wigmore, "The Role of Gold in the Bank Holiday of March, 1983," *Journal of Economic History,* September 1987, pp. 739–756.

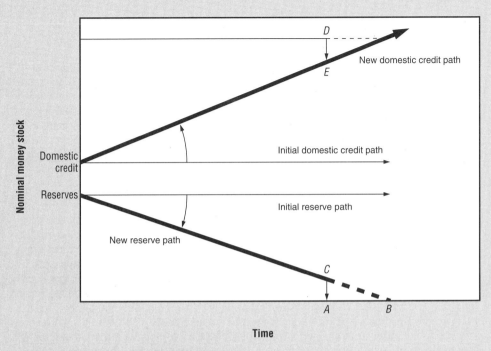

ATTACK ON A GOLD STANDARD

FEDERAL RESERVE GOLD HOLDINGS, 1933

Date	Fed System Gold Reserves ($Billions)	N.Y. Fed Gold ($Millions)	Gold in N.Y. Fed Treasury Account ($Millions)	Foreign Gold at N.Y. Fed
Feb. 8	3.25	917	531	112
Feb. 15	3.20	791	531	144
Feb. 21	3.12	744	531	201
Mar. 1	2.89	711	496	298
Mar. 4	—	381	380	391
Mar. 8	2.68	725	—	391

Source: From Barrie Wigmore, "The Role of Gold in the Bank Holiday of March, 1933," *Journal of Economic History,* September 1987, pp. 745–746.

Box 16.2

The 1971 Attack on the Dollar

From the end of World War II to 1973, the industrial countries operated a system of cooperatively fixed exchange rates known as the **Bretton Woods system,** the basic agreement for which was signed in Bretton Woods, New Hampshire, in 1944. Under this agreement, each country would fix its exchange rate to the U.S. dollar. In turn, the United States agreed to buy and sell gold to foreign central banks at the pegged rate of $35 per ounce. Foreign central banks would actively intervene in exchange markets to maintain their currencies at the pegged rate, and they maintained reserves of dollar securities and gold to do so. Each country was expected to operate a monetary policy that would be consistent with the maintenance of a fixed exchange rate.

To avoid too rapid adjustments in monetary policy when they were experiencing a drain on their reserves, central banks had access to lines of credit from the **International Monetary Fund (IMF).** The IMF was established by the Bretton Woods agreement to provide, first, a means of cooperative financing of temporary reserve outflows and, second, cooperative exchange rate realignments when countries experienced chronic reserve outflows or inflows. Each member of the IMF was required to deposit a quota of funds, one-fourth of which was in gold and the remainder in its own currency. Each member could then draw up to its gold quota in other currencies from the IMF for exchange market intervention. Furthermore, members could borrow up to their full quotas from the IMF in reserve currencies. As a member's borrowing increased, the IMF could negotiate programs to adjust the country's monetary and fiscal policies, with the aim of ending the reserve outflow. Effectively, the IMF provided formal credit lines in reserve currencies for use in exchange rate stabilization.

Such a system could operate initially because the United States had a large gold reserve relative to dollar claims against it by foreign central banks. This situation did not last for long.

The U.S. gold stock was effectively static, yet there was a tendency for foreign central bank dollar claims against the United States to expand over time. First, the real economies of the European countries grew relatively much faster than the U.S. economy during the 1950s and 1960s. This raised the demand for money in these countries and, in the absence of matching domestic credit increases, led to a dollar reserve inflow on their central bank balance sheets through the policy of maintaining the fixed exchange rate. Second, the United States began a rapid increase in its money supply in the 1960s to finance the Vietnam war and the Great Society social programs. In the context of Figure 16.8, this would normally have led to an outflow of gold reserves, but in the Bretton Woods context, the United States did not have to maintain the fixed exchange rates with other currencies directly through gold sales. Rather, the other countries had to maintain fixed rates through dollar purchases. This expansion of foreign money supplies through the fixed exchange rate policy led to a general round of inflation driven by the loose U.S. monetary policy.

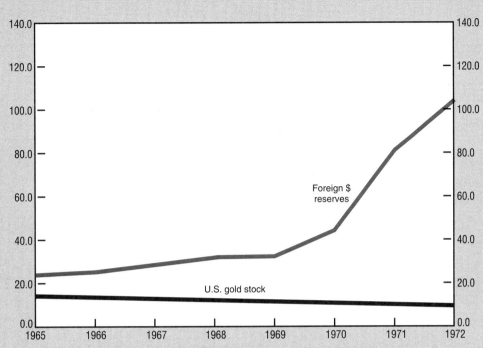

FOREIGN DOLLAR RESERVE HOLDINGS VERSUS U.S. GOLD STOCKS

The rise in foreign central bank dollar claims relative to their gold backing generated what became known as the **"confidence problem"**—the potential inability of the United States to make good on its promise to convert the dollar claims to gold (see accompanying figure). Once other countries became skeptical of the ability or willingness of the United States to convert dollar claims, it became reasonable for central banks to begin converting their dollar claims into gold, thereby leading to a drain in U.S. gold reserves. There was also a drain of gold to the private gold market of the kind described in Chapter 8, owing to the requirement that the dollar be pegged to gold at $35 per ounce despite a rising world level of nominal money and prices.

This situation is similar to the case portrayed in Figure 16.8, where the money supply represents the foreign central banks' holdings of dollar reserves. With their demand satisfied, central banks did not permit further expansion of dollar reserves. As the U.S. supply of dollar reserves expanded, the dollars were converted to gold, so U.S. gold stocks declined. The question was whether the gold stocks would run out smoothly. Not if the foreign central after the devaluation, because a new fixed exchange rate has been established. The supply of real money will be unchanged, although the price level and money stock will double once prices adjust.

Even if the Bank of Japan creates no additional domestic credit at the moment of devaluation, the nominal money stock will jump because of an inflow or sale of reserves to the central bank. The devaluation reduces real balances below their desired level. People will restore their yen balances by exchanging dollars for yen with the Bank of Japan. The inflow of dollars at the devalued exchange rate will then permit a further creation of domestic credit, and a sequence of recurrent devaluations may occur.

TARGET ZONES: THE EUROPEAN MONETARY SYSTEM

A system intermediate between a fixed exchange rate and a floating exchange rate system is known as a **target zone.** Within certain upper and lower limits, the exchange rate is permitted to float freely. Occasionally, the central bank will intervene in the exchange market to make sure that the exchange rate does not move out of the zone.

Figure 16.9 illustrates the concept of a target zone. If the exchange rate lies between 140 and 120 ¥/$, it is allowed to fluctuate freely with shifts in the demand for or supply of money in Japan and the United States. If it hits the upper value of 140 ¥/$, either the Bank of Japan will sell dollars or the Federal Reserve will buy

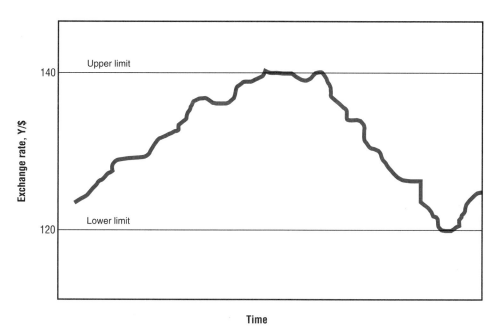

Figure 16.9   TARGET ZONE BAND

yen. If it hits the lower value of 120 ¥/$, the Bank of Japan will buy dollars or the Federal Reserve will sell yen.

What forces would cause the exchange rate to float up to 140 ¥/$? Suppose that the demand for money in the United States shifts upward or that the Fed reduces the U.S. money stock. Either event would cause the yen to depreciate relative to the dollar. If the fluctuation in dollar demand were sufficient, the yen might reach the exchange rate of 140 ¥/$ and trigger a sale of dollars, either directly from the Bank of Japan's holdings or by means of a loan from the Fed. The sale of dollars for yen would reduce the yen monetary base and possibly increase the dollar monetary base, thereby causing appreciation of the yen exchange rate.

The **European Monetary System (EMS)** is an explicit target zone system among the currencies of the countries of western Europe. It has been formally in operation since 1979.[2] Each currency in the system, the deutschemark, the French and Belgian francs, the British pound, the Italian lira, the Dutch guilder, and so on, is assigned a bilateral exchange rate with each of the other currencies. The actual exchange rates are permitted to float up to 2.25 percent above and 2.25 percent

---

2. For a description of the EMS, see Horst Ungerer et al., "The European Monetary System: Recent Developments," IMF Occasional Paper 48, Washington, December 1986.

below this central rate. The European currencies then float against the dollar in group formation.

Each central bank is responsible for intervening in the exchange markets to maintain the exchange rate between its currency and the other currencies in the system. When the exchange rate between two currencies actually reaches an upper or lower limit, both central banks are responsible for interventions to prevent the exchange rate from moving outside the band. For example, if the deutschemark has appreciated against the French franc, the Bundesbank must supply a deutschemark credit line to the Bank of France. The Bank of France can then sell deutschemarks for francs to keep the franc from further depreciating.

It may appear that the Bundesbank's supply of deutschemarks is effectively controlled by the Bank of France, since this process has created deutschemark deposits at the Bundesbank. The Bundesbank, however, can sterilize any deutschemark monetary effects of its loan by selling off some other asset that it holds. Thus it can preserve its own price-level stability. Eventually, the Bank of France must settle its debt with the Bundesbank. If the Bank of France finds that it must keep borrowing to preserve its target zone so that its deutschemark debt is mounting, it may have to seek a realignment of its central exchange rate with the deutschemark and other EMS currencies. This can occur only after a political bargaining process among the members of the EMS. In the first years of the EMS, such realignments occurred frequently. In recent years, however, the monetary policies of the EMS countries have approached that of the Bundesbank, so there have been no realignments.

BALANCE ON CURRENT ACCOUNT: WHY INTERVENE IN EXCHANGE MARKETS?

Central banks aim to control exchange rates in the belief that exchange rates affect exports and imports of goods and services and of capital. By altering exchange rates, they can change behavior in the *external sector* of the economy. Net trade in goods and services is one form of expenditure for domestic goods and services, so an alteration in net trade will affect the total demand for domestically produced goods. Also, exchange rate movements affect the demands for goods in export industries and in domestic industries that compete with imports.

Since a central bank may wish to change demands in its country's external sector, it is now useful to consider a standard central bank view of the effect of exchange rates on external flows of goods and services.

Balance of Payments Accounting Definitions

At this point, a few definitions from balance of payments accounting will be useful. A country's **balance of payments** accounts are designed to measure its payments and receipts to and from other countries for sales of goods, services, and capital and for public and private transfers of funds. The balance of payments accounts are subdivided into two key accounts known as the **current account** and the **capital account** (see Table 16.3).

The current account measures payments for trade in goods and services. Under that general heading, the *merchandise trade account* encompasses agricultural and manufactured products. Trade in services is separated into the *service account* and includes direct foreign purchases of domestic labor, earnings on capital previously exported abroad but owned by domestic residents, insurance payments, and payments for shipping. The capital account measures trade in assets: cash, financial assets, and directly owned real assets such as land, buildings, and machinery.

As a convention, balance of payments accounting categorizes any transaction generating an *inflow of cash* to domestic residents as a *credit* item. Any transaction generating an *outflow of cash* is a *debit* item. For example, a sale (export) of domestic wheat to foreigners is a credit item on the merchandise trade account, whereas an import of foreign steel is a debit item. A domestic lawyer's fee paid by a foreign company is a credit item on the service account, whereas the payment of a dividend by a domestic company to a foreign shareholder is a debit item. The sale of the domestic government's bonds to foreigners is a credit item on the capital account because it generates an inflow of cash. The purchase of land from a foreigner by a domestic resident is a debit item on the capital account.

The balance on the merchandise trade account is determined by summing all

Table 16.3   1989 U.S. BALANCE OF PAYMENTS ACCOUNTS ($BILLIONS)

A. Current account		−110.8
Merchandise		
Exports	378.4	
Imports	−500.6	
Other goods and services		
Credit	249.6	
Debit	−227.0	
Official transfers	−13.3	
B. Capital account		
Direct and long term		79.6
Direct investment in U.S.	63.9	
Direct investment abroad	−33.9	
Portfolio investment	47.4	
Short term		13.0
Errors and omissions		37.0
C. Liabilities constituting foreign authorities' reserves		7.8
D. Total change in reserves		−28.4

Source: From International Monetary Fund, *Balance of Payments Statistics,* May 1990, p. 22.

the credit items, summing all the debit items, and taking the difference between the two. If the credit items exceed the debit items, there is a *surplus* on the merchandise trade account; that is, the value of goods exported exceeds the value of goods imported. The balances on the service account, the current account, and the capital account are determined in a similar manner.

Table 16.3 presents the important categories of the U.S. balance of payments accounts for 1989. The current account for 1989 was in deficit by $111 billion owing primarily to a deficit on merchandise trade. Official U.S. authorities such as the Fed added to this deficit by buying about $28 billion in foreign reserves. This appears as the item labeled "Total Change in Foreign Reserves." This total deficit was offset by a surplus on the long- and short-term capital accounts of $93 billion and acquisition of $8 billion in U.S. securities as foreign exchange reserves by foreign authorities. An item called "Errors and Omissions" of approximately $37 billion provides the balance between the measured current and capital accounts. The accounts that we have reported in Table 16.3 do not quite add to zero because we have left out a few minor items.

Current Account Surplus Equals Capital Account Deficit

As a definitional matter, whenever there is a surplus on the current account, it must be balanced by an equivalent deficit on the capital account, adding official reserve changes into the capital account. Conversely, a deficit on the current account is matched by a surplus on the capital account. To see this, suppose that a country's only current account item is the sale of a bushel of wheat worth $2, so the current account is in surplus by $2. Since foreigners have bought more goods and services than they have sold to domestic residents, they must somehow have financed the shortfall. They can finance the $2 by selling $2 worth of their assets to domestic residents or by writing $2 worth of IOUs to domestic residents. In either case, domestic residents have bought $2 worth of assets from foreigners, and this will be entered on the capital account as a $2 debit item because it entails an outflow of cash.

The Balance on Current Account

Why would a country have deficit or surplus on its current account? We have seen that individuals tend to smooth out their consumption in the presence of changes in income. If future income is expected to be much greater than present income, they will seek to borrow resources now for consumption and repay the loans later. A similar argument applies to an entire country filled with individuals who expect to have a much higher income in the future than in the present.

In Figure 16.10, suppose that the quantities of goods available for consumption

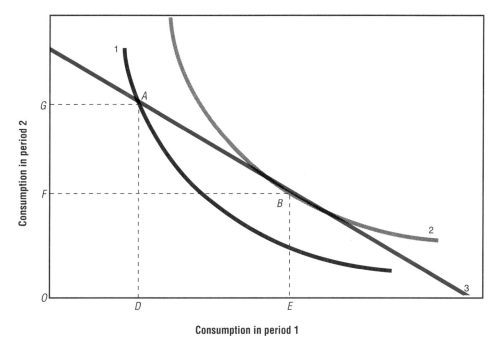

Figure 16.10 EXPORTS AND IMPORTS OF GOODS AND CAPITAL

for the representative person in a given country are indicated by point *A*. There will be more goods available in period 2 than in period 1. If the country did not engage in trade, it would have to consume the amounts of goods in each period represented by point *A* and attain the level of utility indicated by indifference curve 1. If it could borrow from the rest of the world at an interest rate indicated by the slope of line 3 through point *A*, it could consume at a preferred point *B*. In period 1, it would have an income of *OD* and consume *OE*, so it would incur a deficit on its current account of *DE*. This would be balanced by a surplus on its capital account of *DE* generated by the bond it sold to foreigners to finance the goods imports. In period 2, it would have an income *OG* and consume *OF*, so it would have a surplus on its current account *FG*. On its capital account it would have a deficit of *FG*, since it would buy back the bond it had sold.

Of course, not all the imports need be used for consumption. If investment opportunities in a given country are favorable, investment projects will earn high returns and greatly expand future income. To smooth income, residents of a country may borrow the capital from abroad rather than save out of current consumption to undertake the investment. Again, the country would run a deficit on current account, financed through bond sales, in which the goods imported may directly or indirectly be invested rather than immediately consumed.

Smoothing of consumption in the presence of expanding income is a major reason for current account deficits, and these may continue indefinitely. They are not a new phenomenon. Indeed, for most years through 1914, the United States persistently had current account deficits, reflecting foreign investment in the ever-expanding economy.

The Real Exchange Rate and the Balance on Current Account

Current account imbalances also may be driven by monetary forces that temporarily alter the real exchange rate. For example, consider again the example in Figures 16.2 and 16.3. A Bank of Japan money expansion temporarily depreciated the real exchange rate, making Japanese goods relatively cheaper than U.S. goods. We would expect that arbitrage in the goods market would lead to an increase in the U.S. demand for Japanese goods and services and a reduction in the Japanese demand for U.S. goods. Therefore, the balance on current account would be affected. We might reasonably suppose that a real exchange rate decline as a result of monetary forces would be associated with an increase in the surplus on the Japanese current account. When the price level in Japan eventually adjusted, this source of surplus on current account would disappear.

Once again, the presumption of slowly adjusting prices leads us to conclude that monetary policy has a real impact. If a central bank is concerned about fluctuations in the current account balance and their effect on aggregate demand, it then has a rationale for interventions in the exchange markets.

CONCLUSION

Central banks have traditionally intervened in markets for foreign exchange to make some assets denominated in domestic currency liquid in terms of foreign currencies. In the course of time, their efforts to extend such liquidity have varied. Before 1973, central banks maintained fixed exchange rates as a primary goal. They acted directly and continually as market makers in exchange markets and used their own resources and lines of credit with foreign central banks to peg exchange rates. The constant provision of liquidity to foreign exchange markets at fixed exchange rates occasionally became either too costly or too restrictive for central banks that wanted to extend liquidity to more domestic markets. At such times, central banks devalued the exchange rates or ceased their constant intervention entirely. Usually, such changes were associated with speculative attacks on central bank holdings of liquid assets denominated in foreign currencies. Prime examples of such attacks are the collapse of the gold dollar in 1933 and the end of the Bretton Woods system from 1971 to 1973. Since 1973, central banks of the large industrial countries have acted more sporadically as market makers in foreign exchange. They now occasionally maintain informal zones in which exchange rates are allow to float, but they intervene as major market makers to ensure that exchange rates do not move outside the zone. The European Monetary System is a formal target zone system that ties most western European currencies to each other in narrow bands.

KEY TERMS

exchange rate

floating exchange rate

managed float

fixed exchange rate

interest parity

covered interest parity

open interest parity

real exchange rate

purchasing power parity

exchange rate overshooting

foreign reserves

domestic credit

borrowed reserves

net reserves

Banking Holiday of 1933

Bretton Woods system

International Monetary Fund (IMF)

"confidence problem"

target zone

European Monetary System (EMS)

balance of payments

current account

capital account

EXERCISES

1. Suppose that the annualized 3-month yield in the Eurodollar market is 5 percent and in the Eurodeutschemark market is 8 percent and that the current spot rate is 1.7 DM/\$ and the 3-month forward rate is 1.9 DM/\$. In which currency should you borrow and in which currency should you lend?

2. With a sluggishly moving domestic price level and a flexible foreign price level, analyze exchange rate and price-level movements if the money demand curves in two countries shift outward equally because of real income increases in both countries.

3. As in exercise 2, analyze exchange rate and price level movements if the nominal money stocks of two countries increase by the same percentage.

4. With flexible domestic price levels, answer exercises 2 and 3 once again.

5. Suppose the yen price level is 180, the dollar price level is 120, and the yen per dollar exchange rate is 120. What is the real exchange rate between Japanese and U.S. goods?

6. Must a central bank intervene directly in the market for foreign exchange to influence the exchange rate?

7. Distinguish between a central bank's holdings of gross and net reserves.

8. A country temporarily maintains a fixed exchange rate system but generates domestic credit at a rate that guarantees an eventual end of the fixed rate. In defending the system, the country will expend foreign reserves, but it will not maintain the fixed rate if net reserves fall below R. Show that the fixed exchange rate system will end with a speculative attack on the remaining reserves rather than with a continuous decline of reserves until R is reached.

9. Why does a central bank lose control over the amount of base money when it operates a fixed exchange rate?

10. In a system such as the EMS, why can the country with the tightest monetary policy eventually force the adherence of the other countries to its policy?

FURTHER READING

Dornbusch, Rudiger. "Expectations and Exchange Rate Dynamics," *Journal of Political Economy*, December 1976, pp. 1161–1176.

Krugman, Paul, and Maurice Obstfeld. *International Economics*. New York: Harper-Collins, 1991.

Wigmore, Barrie. "The Role of Gold in the Bank Holiday of March, 1933," *Journal of Economic History*, September 1987, pp. 739–756.

The Liquidity Requirements of Financial Innovation

17

Financial Innovation and the Creation of Bank-Like Deposits

Banks have traditionally made liquidity available through their liquid loan and deposit liabilities. Through innovations in financial products, other financial institutions such as investment banks, mutual funds, and pension funds also can often provide deposit-like liquidity to their liabilities, even when their asset composition is not itself substantially liquid. They can do this by following sometimes complicated strategies of holding and trading appropriate combinations of assets. To the extent that such strategies can be carried out with transactions costs that are as low as bank operating costs, other institutions apparently can provide perfect substitutes for deposits.

In such a situation, there should be nothing special about the types of liabilities banks supply and the assets they hold. Indeed, we will see that bank deposits can be interpreted as a packaging of other kinds of securities such as stocks and options. This interpretation, however, hinges crucially on the existence of liquidity in the markets for these securities. If market participants believe that these markets are sufficiently liquid, they will substitute out of bank deposits to gain potentially higher returns. These methods apparently avoid the cost of reserves, but we will see that establishing positions in financial markets generally forces trading through clearinghouses that require access to bank credit lines.

Since options typically comprise a principal security in the portfolio that mimics

451

bank liabilities, we will expend some effort discussing what options are and how to price them when markets are liquid. We will then see that the payoffs of bank deposits can be mimicked with appropriate combination of options and other securities by developing the concept of **put-call parity,** a relationship that should hold among the prices of stocks, options, and loans. Next, we examine how pension funds and mutual funds in stocks or other securities can provide bank-like securities if they follow an appropriate trading strategy. We will see, however, that such strategies always lean on bank lines of credit.

OPTIONS

A central problem in finance concerns how to price particular types of financial instruments. For example, we may wish to price a pure discount bond that promises to pay $1 million in 1 year. In Chapter 2 we evaluated this contract by discounting the future payment to the present with an appropriate market rate of interest.

Similarly, we wish to price assets known as **options,** which have more complicated payoffs. What is an option and what commitments does a person buying or selling an option make? A buyer receives a right to trade a particular asset at a given price and amount at some specified time. The rights vary depending on the type of option contract. A right labeled a **call option** guarantees the *purchase* of an underlying security at a prearranged price. The most common underlying security consists of stock in a particular company. Other options traded on organized markets have as underlying securities whole baskets of stocks such as those contained in the S&P 500 index, foreign currencies, or bonds. Another type of right, the **put option,** guarantees the *sale* of an underlying security to another party for a given price. Since these rights are valuable, the problem of determining their proper price arises.

Options Vocabulary

A technical jargon is associated with the option markets. The contractual price at which a holder has the right to trade the underlying asset is called the **strike,** or **exercise, price.** For example, a standard call option contract typically contains the right to purchase 100 shares of a stock at the strike price. Alternatively, a put option is the right to deliver the shares for the strike price.

The act of choosing to take delivery or, in the case of a put option, of delivering the shares, is called **exercising** the option. Any option will have an expiration date, by which time the owner must choose to exercise or not. The call option will be exercised if the value of the underlying security exceeds the strike price at the expiration date; in this case, the option is *in the money.* Otherwise, it is **out of the money.** In practice, rather than exercise them, holders of options almost always sell out their positions to gain the payoff from the option. We will discuss this payoff later.

Options are also differentiated by the meaning of the expiration date. A **European option** conveys the right to buy or sell for the strike price only on the expiration date and not before. Alternatively, an **American option** gives the right to exercise any time on or before the expiration date. In our discussion, we will consider only European options to simplify matters.

Pricing a Call Option

To price an option appears difficult because of the uncertainty of the future payoff. The holder may or may not exercise the option. The seller may or may not receive a payment in exchange for the underlying security, depending on the market price of the security at the exercise date. An option contains a contingency, namely, a possible event that may not occur.[1]

We will now develop a simple model to find the price of a call option on one share of a stock.[2] For simplicity, the stock will pay no dividend during the period being examined. We will denote the current price of the stock by A; the price next period may either be aA—that is, $a \times A$—the lower of two possible prices, or bA, where $b > a$. Only these prices are possible in the next period. A short-term, liquid loan market also exists in which people can either borrow or lend risklessly at the market interest rate; R will represent 1 plus the rate of interest for one-period loans. Notice that by this assumption there is no cost of acquiring or placing funds, so there is no need for banks. *All markets are fully liquid, so arbitrage across markets can readily occur.*

We assume that $b > R > a$ so that the possible capital gains on the stock may exceed or fall short of the payoff on risk-free loans. Otherwise, the market either for the stock or for loans would not exist. For instance, if both b and a exceed R, people would always prefer to buy the stock. No one would want to lend. Arbitrage would then bid up the rate of interest. Everyone would try to borrow to buy the stock, and the price of the stock also would rise. In turn, this would affect A, a, and b. Conversely, if R exceeds b and a, nobody would buy the stock. Under no circumstances would the stock do better than the loan. The price of the stock would tend to collapse. Everybody would try to make loans, and that would tend to drive interest rates down.

We also assume that a call option on the stock exists in the financial markets. The option gives the holder the right to purchase a share of the stock next period at the strike price S. Our task is to price the call option. C denotes the value of the

---

1. Since any bond may default, we will see that a certain option aspect exists even for bonds. Usually, we treat U.S. government bonds as default free, however.

2. This model can be found in more detail in J. Cox, S. Ross, and M. Rubinstein, "Options Pricing: A Simplified Approach," *Journal of Financial Economics,* September 1979, pp. 229–263.

call option that we are trying to find. We will assume that $bA > S > aA$ so that the option may or may not be exercised.

If next period's realized stock price exceeds the strike price, then the holder can exercise the option and gain the difference between the future market price and the strike price. The seller of the option (the short position) must pay the difference between the future stock price and the strike price. If the future price is less than the strike price, the option will not be exercised and no funds will move.

Mimicking an Option's Payoffs

One way to price the call option is to examine all possible future payoffs and mimic them with a position in stocks and loans. We can determine the current price of this position in stocks and loans, and through an arbitrage argument we can then price the call option. This method requires us to determine the future flows of cash expenditures and receipts associated with each possible security.

We must first determine the position in the stock itself that mimics the option payoff. We will denote this stock position by x. A positive value of x shares indicates a *long* position; that is, we own the stock and would benefit from rises in its price. Alternatively, x may be negative, which indicates a *short* position in stocks. A person can be short simply by borrowing the shares and then selling them, but the shares, as a liability of the borrower, must be returned in the future. The future delivery of the shares to the person from whom they were borrowed entails a future cash outflow to reacquire them at then-current market prices. Therefore, a person short in shares would benefit from a fall in their price.

Finally, the portfolio holder can take a position in loans by lending out or borrowing y dollars this period. A positive value of y will indicate that the portfolio holder is making a loan. If he borrows instead, then y will take on a negative value. Again, the loan market must be so liquid that borrowing and lending can proceed at the same rate R with no bank intermediation and consequently no payment of the cost of reserves.

The entries in Table 17.1 represent the next period payoffs associated with each security depending on whether S exceeds or is less than the stock price next period. Remember that we do not yet know the exact values of positions x and y that mimic the payoff of the call option. Next period the stock may be worth either aA or bA;

Table 17.1 NEXT PERIOD PAYOFFS FROM SECURITIES

	$aA < S$	$bA > S$
1. Call option	0	$bA - S$
2. Stock	aAx	bAx
3. Loans	Ry	Ry

these possibilities are represented in Table 17.1 by $aA < S$ and $bA > S$, respectively (see Table 17.2).

If the low price occurs, the call option will not be exercised because exercise would require payment of S for a share worth only aA. The option will expire, and no inflows or outflows will be associated with it. If, however, the high price materializes, the market price of the stock will exceed the strike price, and the holder of the option will exercise it. The option payoff will be the difference between the market price of the stock and the strike price, $bA - S$.

We turn now to the stocks. When the low stock price occurs, the stock holdings would be worth aAx, the price per share multiplied by the number of shares. For example, if the mimicking position contains 100 shares with a per share price of $50, this yields $5,000 positive inflow. If the portfolio is short so that x is negative, this is an outflow. In the high price outcome, the shares of stock are worth bAx.

Finally, we turn to the loans. In both contingencies, these yield an inflow of Ry dollars, the original loan plus the interest payment.

The problem is to arrange the portfolio of stocks and loans to mimic exactly the outcome of the call option under either future possibility. We can derive this portfolio by choosing x and y so that the sum of the payoffs on stocks and loans exactly equals the payoff on the option in each contingency. This yields two equations in two unknowns:

$$aAx + Ry = 0$$

$$bAx + Ry = bA - S$$

We can solve these to yield x and y as functions of the stock price, the possible returns on the stock, the strike price, and the interest rate.

The solution is

$$y = \frac{-a(bA - S)}{R(b - a)} \quad \text{and} \quad x = \frac{bA - S}{bA - aA}$$

Table 17.2 DEFINITIONS OF VARIABLES IN OPTION PRICING EXAMPLES

A	Current price of the stock
aA	Lower possible stock price in next period
bB	Higher possible stock price in next period
C	Price of the call option
P	Price of the put option
R	One plus rate of interest for one-period loans
S	Strike price
x	Position in stocks that mimics the option payoff
y	Position in loans that mimics the option payoff

Notice that $1 > x > 0$, since $bA > S > aA$. Also, y is a negative number, since $bA > S$ and $b > a$. A negative position in loans means that cash must be borrowed to establish the mimicking portfolio. We conclude that a long position in a fraction of a share of stock, partly financed by borrowing, will mimic the payoff on a call option.

The intuition for this result is straightforward. In the case of a high stock price, the holder of the call option will receive a share of stock, and this is equivalent to a long position in stock. Simultaneously, the holder will pay out cash to cover the strike price, and this obligation is equivalent to a short position in loans—that is, to having borrowed cash that must be repaid.

Finally, we price the call option. We know that selling a call and buying the mimicking portfolio has no future net cash flow implications whatever. Under either contingency, there is a zero net payment outcome. If calls have a higher price than the portfolio that hedges them, an arbitrager can profit now by selling calls, hedging this short call position by buying the hedging portfolio. If the hedging portfolio costs less than the call, the arbitrager realizes an immediate profit with no current or future commitment of her own capital. For example, suppose that calls are selling for $25 each and the hedging portfolio against one call is valued at $20. Selling one call will realize $25, sufficient to buy the $20 hedging portfolio and to yield a pure profit of $5 with no effect on the future cash position.

Typically, we assume that such easy profit opportunities do not exist. Since everyone will try to sell call options and buy the hedging portfolio, the price of the option will rise and the portfolio price will fall. Competitive pressure will drive the price of the hedging portfolio and the value of the call option to equality. We can use a similar argument to show that the price of the call option will not be less than the value of the hedging portfolio, again because arbitrage opportunities would arise.

We conclude that the value C of the call option must equal the net value of the shares and loans in the mimicking position.

$$C = Ax + y = \underset{(1)}{A} \underset{(2)}{\left(\frac{bA - S}{bA - aA} \right)} - \underset{(3)}{\frac{a}{S}} \underset{(4)}{\frac{bA - S}{b - a}} \underset{(5)}{\frac{S}{R}} \qquad (17.1)$$

where   (1) is the value of a long position in one share,
        (2) is the fraction of a share implied by holding one call
        (3) is the short position in loans,
        (4) is the fraction of the loan with face value S represented by one call, and
        (5) is the present value of a promised payment of S dollars.

From the price solution, we can determine the following propositions.[3]

3. Although this is a very simple model, these results hold generally for option pricing models. Specifically, they hold for continuous-time pricing models of the Black-Scholes variety.

1. A rise in the current price of the stock or of the market interest rate will raise the price of the option.

2. A rise in the current price of the stock will increase the long share position and the short loan position required to mimic the option.

3. A call option has a value equivalent to the value of a fraction of a share of stock *minus* the value of a fraction of a loan paying S next period.

PRICING STOCKS AND BONDS WITH OPTION METHODS

The use of option pricing methods has become widespread not only for explicitly pricing call and put options on stocks but also for interpreting more complex financial instruments such as a company's stocks and bonds. To see how option pricing methods might be applied, let's begin with a brief review of facts about the corporate form of organization.

A corporation has many assets, such as manufacturing plants, financial claims, real estate, and so on. Its liabilities consists of bonds and other debt and of shareholders' equity. The bondholders (and other creditors) have first claim on the assets. That is, they must be paid before anyone else. The shareholders also have specific rights, however. Among these are a residual right to the assets after the bondholders are paid and the right to determine who manages the company.

An important feature of the corporate form of organization is that shareholders are not responsible for losses beyond their equity position. If the corporation goes bankrupt, the equity holders lose only the value of their shares; the bondholders cannot reach further into the personal wealth of the equity holders. If the value of the corporation's assets is insufficient to pay the corporation's debts, then the equity holders can simply turn over the remaining assets to the bondholders through a bankruptcy proceeding. There may not be enough assets to pay off all bonds fully, but this is not the shareholders' responsibility. Payment to creditors depends solely on the value of the corporation's assets; investors know that all private bonds involve some risk of default.

We can characterize this situation as an equity holder's call option on the assets of the firm. Suppose that the company's liabilities consist purely of discount bonds payable next period. If the equity holders make this payment, they receive full control of the remaining assets. If they do not, they are in default, and the bondholders receive the assets. This arrangement is a call option held by the equity holders, where the strike price is the face value of the bonds. In effect, equity is a call option.

An Example

As an example, consider the Barnes-Wentworth Oil Company, which incurs a debt to J. R. Ewing of $1 million payable in 1 year. It has borrowed the money to drill for oil in the Gulf of Mexico. There is a chance that the hole will yield $10 million in oil within the next year. Alternatively, it may yield nothing, in which case Barnes-Wentworth's assets are worthless.

As current assets, Barnes-Wentworth holds only a "lottery ticket" (the right to drill oil) that may pay something next period. The lottery ticket has a value because its outcome has not yet been realized. On the liability side, the company has a $1 million note payable next period. If the oil field comes in, Barnes-Wentworth will want to keep control of this new asset. It will pay $1 million to J. R. Ewing and retain assets worth $10 million. Meanwhile, J. R. Ewing, in effect, holds title to the firm's assets, and the firm has a call option with an exercise price of $1 million. If the oil does not materialize, the firm's assets are worthless; it will choose to default on its debt and go into bankruptcy. J. R. Ewing then holds a worthless asset, because Barnes-Wentworth has not exercised its out of the money call option.

An Alternative Explanation

Our discussion thus far has interpreted equity as a call option on the assets of the firm. However, there is an alternative and equivalent way to interpret the liability structure of the firm. First, we assume that J. R. Ewing holds Barnes-Wentworth's default-free note of $1 million face value. (Default free? Yes, if we interpret the note as the personal note of the fabulously wealthy equity holders that will be paid in any circumstance.) Simultaneously, we assume that J. R. Ewing has sold the company a put option, giving the equity holders the right to sell the company's assets to J. R. Ewing for the strike price of $1 million. Suppose that the oil field comes in. The company will pay off the default-free loan, but it will not exercise the put. Alternatively, suppose that the oil field does not come in. Barnes-Wentworth will still pay off the $1 million default-free loan. It also will exercise the put. J. R. Ewing must buy the assets for $1 million. The equity holders have paid $1 million dollars to their creditor, J. R. Ewing, but the creditor has to pay it back to purchase the company's assets.

In this situation, we can interpret the credit position as a combination of two different assets: the holding of a default-free loan and a short position in a put (in options market jargon, J. R. Ewing *wrote* a put). In originally acquiring the bond, J. R. Ewing presumably contracted for the current interest rate on default-free loans and then delivered funds equal to the discounted present value of $1 million to the company. In addition, the company must have paid J. R. Ewing the current market price of the put. On net, J. R. Ewing must have delivered to the company some amount less than the discounted present value of $1 million, the difference representing the value of the put option. Alternatively, as the expected loss due to default, we can view the difference as a payment that the equity holders must make to J. R. Ewing in return for their right to declare bankruptcy.

PUT-CALL PARITY

In the preceding section, the equity in Barnes–Wentworth was interpreted as a call option on Barnes–Wentworth's assets. Equivalently, equity can be interpreted as the holding of positions in three different assets and liabilities: the productive assets of Barnes–Wentworth, a put with which those assets may be delivered, and borrowed cash. Since the equity has the same value regardless of how we interpret it, the current value of the call option must equal the current value of the underlying assets *plus* the current value of the put (these are the assets of the equity holders) *less* the current value of the note (their liability, since they sold a note, means they have a short position in loans).

This equality illustrates put–call parity. The relationship holds for puts and calls on the same underlying security where both options have the same strike price and the same expiration date. The face value of the loan also equals the strike price. Let C, P, and A represent the current values of the call, the put, and the underlying asset, respectively. Suppose that the options expire in 1 year. Let R be 1 plus the interest rate on 1-year, riskless loans, and let S represent the strike price and the face value of a loan. The current value of the loan is S/R. Then the put–call parity derived in the preceding example can be described as

$$C = A + P - \frac{S}{R}$$

More generally, if these are marketable puts and calls for shares of stock of the sort typically traded on options exchanges, the put–call parity relationship also holds. This can be determined by considering next year's payoffs on a portfolio that consists of holding long positions of one share of stock and one put and a short position of one call option (that is, the portfolio owner has bought one put and sold one call). The payoffs depend on A', the value of the stock next year (see Table 17.3).

The payoffs depend on the relationship of next year's stock price to the strike price. Under any circumstances, the stock price will be worth A', an amount that is not known currently. Suppose, however, that the stock price exceeds the strike price. Then the put will not be exercised, since it is out of the money, and it will have a payoff of zero. The call option, however, will be exercised by whoever holds it. Since this portfolio is committed to deliver shares worth A' in return for S in cash, it must actually pay out $A' - S$ on net, which explains the negative sign attached to this item in the call line of the table. Summing the payoffs from all the positions for the case where $A' > S$, we find that the net payoff is S.

Suppose now that $A' < S$. In this case, the put will be exercised, and a share

Table 17.3 SECURITY PAYOFFS

	$A' < S$	$A' > S$
1. Stock	A'	A'
2. Put	$S - A'$	0
3. Call	0	$-(A' - S)$
4. Total	S	S

of stock worth A' will be delivered in return for S. The net payoff from the put is then $S - A'$. Since the call is out of the money, its holder will not exercise it, so it yields a zero payoff for the portfolio. Summing again across positions, the net payoff is S.

We have shown that under any circumstance this portfolio will have a payoff of S next year. However, this is exactly the payoff of a 1-year discount loan with face value of S. We know that the present value of the loan is S/R. Since the preceding portfolio is equivalent to the loan in payoff implications, market forces should arise to make its current value also equal to S/R.

To convince yourself of this, note that the current value of the portfolio is $A + P - C$, where A is the current market value of the stock, P is the current value of the put, and C is the current value of the call. The current value of the call affects the portfolio value negatively, because a short position is a liability. We claim that

$$\frac{S}{R} = A + P - C \qquad (17.2)$$

If the equality does not hold, arbitrage profits are readily available.

Suppose, for example, that at current market prices $S/R > A + P - C$. How can an arbitrager profit from this situation? By selling a bond with face value S, she can obtain more than enough current funds to acquire the portfolio. The bond requires a future delivery of S dollars by the arbitrager, but the portfolio will deliver S dollars to her. Therefore, the future payoff implications wash out, and the arbitrager would pocket the difference between the proceeds of the bond sale and the cost of the portfolio as a pure profit.

There are, however, many arbitragers looking for such opportunities, and their attempts to gain profits quickly shift the asset prices. For example, increased buying demand for puts would raise put prices, whereas increased supplies of calls would reduce call prices. Both movements would raise the value of our hypothetical portfolio until it attains equality with the value of the bond. Similarly, arbitrage would keep the value of the portfolio from exceeding the value of the bond.

CREATING DEPOSIT-LIKE SECURITIES
WITH HEDGED ASSETS

We now consider how a nonbank institution such as a pension fund or a mutual fund, which holds risky assets and has no equity cushion, can yet apparently offer deposit-like liabilities to their shareholders. By "deposit-like," we mean that a fund can guarantee a minimum capital value on its liabilities deliverable in cash on short notice, regardless of the value of its underlying risky assets. Given the previous discussion in this chapter, you may guess that a fund can do this by hedging its risky assets with options.[4] From our previous discussion of the sources of liquidity, however, you may wonder how the cash materializes without the access to bank lines. We will find that, in fact, access to liquidity through the banking system is vital to the delivery of the promised cash. Provision of such liquidity is the crux of why securities markets organize themselves to be so dependent on the banking system.

Static Hedging with Actual Options

To make matters concrete, let us suppose that a mutual fund acquires 100 shares of a stock for $100 per share and also holds a small amount of cash.[5] Suppose further that as liabilities it issues 100 shares of its own; each mutual fund share would then be worth 1/100 of the value of the assets. The fund agrees to redeem shares in cash on a day's notice at the prorated value of the fund's assets. If the stock price falls to zero, the mutual fund shares in aggregate would be worth only the small amount of cash held by the fund plus interest earnings. Since shares in this fund are not readily convertible into a fixed amount of good funds, they lack the liquidity and safety of bank deposits. Of course, if the stock price doubles to $200, the mutual fund shares will nearly double, so shareholders will receive the upside gain.

Now suppose that shareholders do not wish to bear the major downside losses associated with stock price declines, but they do want to realize any upside returns resulting from upward movement of the stock price. Also, they want their claims

---

4. There are other methods for placing a floor under the portfolio value, and we may refer to them generally as **stop-loss techniques.** Here we will describe static and dynamic hedges. A classic alternative method is to give a stop-loss sale order to a broker, telling the broker to sell the portfolio whenever the share price reaches the desired floor value. Provided that markets are liquid so that an investor can sell all the shares he wants at a price near to the most recent transaction price, stop-loss strategies can make a portfolio of stocks alone de-

posit-like. See Chapter 18 for a consideration of what happens when markets are not liquid.

5. Normally, a mutual fund would be diversified among many different stocks. For instance, it may purchase a "marketbasket" of stocks such as the S&P 500 on a market-value-weighted basis. Then the option to hedge this position would be a stock index option. The logic of the argument, however, would be identical.

to be readily convertible to good funds on short notice. They want to be able to cash out their capital at any time at a guaranteed minimum price for sudden spending needs, but they also seek the high average returns of stock market investment.

The mutual fund management can cater to these demands by holding onto its stock portfolio while simultaneously using its cash to acquire a put option on the stock that it holds. Suppose that for a price P a put option on 100 shares of stock with a strike price of $100 is available on the market. To make matters simple, suppose that the cash held by the fund exactly equals P so that the initial value of the fund's assets is $10,000 + P$.

If the fund buys a put on its stock, it can create a pattern of payoffs to its portfolio that is described in Figure 17.1. If at the expiration date of the option the stock price exceeds $100, the put options are worthless, and the cash payoff per mutual fund share just equals the stock price. The payoff per mutual fund share rises dollar for dollar with further rises in the stock price on the expiration date. If the stock price is less than $100, the put is exercised, and the payoff per mutual fund share is $100 regardless of how low the stock price falls. The mutual fund has thus placed a floor under the capital value of its shares, guaranteeing that they will be worth a minimum of $100 while paying off any upside gain in stock prices.

Line 1 in Figure 17.1 represents the payoff to an unhedged fund. If the stock price is zero, the payoff per share is $RP/100$, where R is the payoff on loans, because

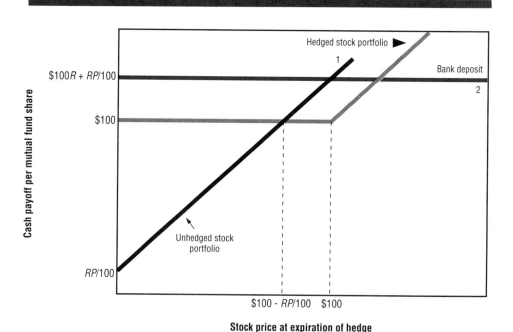

Figure 17.1 PAYOFFS ON A HEDGED MUTUAL FUND

the fund initially held an amount P of fixed-interest securities. The payoff then rises dollar for dollar with the stock price. There is no floor, so in the range of stock prices between zero and $100 − RP/100$, the unhedged fund performs worse than the hedged fund. For prices above $100 − RP/100$, however, the unhedged fund performs better. Thus, to create a liquid deposit-like asset, the shareholder must give up some upside return.

You should also notice that the hedged fund does not guarantee quite as high a floor as a bank deposit. The bank deposit promising a fixed payoff R would pay $R(\$100 + P/100)$ on the original capital that was instead invested in the mutual fund share. This is indicated by line 2 in the figure.

Hedging a stock or a basket of stocks with a put that exists on the market is called **static hedging** because once the hedge is in place, no adjustments need be made to the portfolio until its expires. Of course, part of the portfolio would have to be sold whenever a shareholder wanted delivery of good funds. The relation between puts and shares, however, would not change.

Dynamic Hedging with Portfolio Insurance

Unfortunately, because few put contracts exist on the market, a mutual fund will not easily find a put with exactly the characteristics it may want. For example, puts with the appropriate strike price may not exist, so the fund cannot create a static hedge to produce the capital guarantee and degree of liquidity that its shareholders expect. Alternatively, puts covering the entire basket of securities held by the fund may not exist.

To circumvent the lack of appropriate put contracts, the mutual fund can manufacture **synthetic puts** to provide the deposit-like properties demanded by its customers. The method of creating a synthetic put by dynamic hedging is known as **portfolio insurance.** We will now see how the put option can be mimicked by a short position in the stock (selling stock) and a long position in loans.

To provide a hedge for the mutual fund's stock holdings, we want to tailor-make a put that would place a floor under our portfolio value. Consider the problem for a mutual fund with a large variety of stocks that fluctuate with market price. It wants to make sure that if the general stock market price falls below a certain level, the fund will be protected in the sense that it can still convert its portfolio into a predictable amount of good funds.

Let us rewrite equation 17.2 to express the value of a put. The value of the put is equal to the value of a long position in the call *plus* a short position in one share *plus* a long position in loans worth S/R. We do not have the appropriate call directly available, but again we have the ability to create a synthetic call option through share and loan positions.

Remember that the value of the call equals the value of a fractional position in shares minus a fractional position in loans. Option pricing equation 17.1 indicates that the share fraction x itself depends positively on the share price; if the share price rises, x rises, so an increased shareholding is required to mimic the call, and vice versa. The face value of the loan is the strike price S, and the call implies a liability of a part of the present value of this loan, S/R. The number of loans of face value S required to mimic the call also shifts positively with changes in the stock price.[6]

Let us substitute into put-call parity equation 17.2 the appropriate share and loan positions for the call option derived in equation 17.1 to determine how to create this synthetic put. Gathering terms in shares and loans, we derive

$$P = -(1 - x)A + \left(1 + \frac{\gamma R}{S}\right)\frac{S}{R} \tag{17.3}$$

Effectively, this implies that a put consists partly of a short position in stock, since x lies between 0 and 1. The short stock position of $(1 - x)$ shares has a market value of $(1 - x)A$. This value enters negatively into the value of a put because a short stock position is a liability. The loan position is $(1 + \gamma R/S)S/R$. This is a long position in loans because $\gamma R/S$ is between 0 and -1, but it is a long position in a fraction of a loan with a face value of S. Therefore, the formula tells us that the value of a put can be mimicked by selling $(1 - x)$ shares of stock short and acquiring $(1 + \gamma R/S)$ loans with a face value of S.

Now it is possible to imagine actually creating this put synthetically by taking positions in stock and loans. We have to adjust the amount of the short sale and the loan holdings upward or downward depending on what happens to the stock price. For instance, suppose that the stock price starts to fall. Should we increase or decrease our short position? Since x falls toward zero with a fall in the stock price, the short position $-(1 - x)$ increases in absolute magnitude (becomes more negative). We should increase our short position by selling shares. If the stock price continues to fall, we should sell more shares to keep mimicking the put. Also, we should acquire more cash claims, lending out more funds.

If we want to design a particular put, equation 17.3 tells us how to do it. We can choose the strike price we prefer to guarantee a conversion of our portfolio to a certain amount of cash, so we can construct the put by taking a position in shares and loans implied by the equation. Then we have an effective hedge for the mutual fund.

The Use of Stock Index Futures

Although it is theoretically coherent, the preceding technique is not how portfolio insurance is carried out in practice. Implementing portfolio insurance by direct sales of shares can be very costly. For instance, many pension funds and mutual funds are comprised of stocks of the S&P 500. A portfolio holding the S&P 500 would

---

6. Recall that the fraction of a loan promising to pay S in a call option is $\gamma R/S = -[(aA/s)(b - S/A)]/(b - a)$. When A falls, both terms in the numerator fall, so this fraction falls. A smaller loan is needed in a portfolio that mimics a call option.

have to buy and sell all the shares in the index every day to make the dynamic hedge work. This would be very expensive.

To implement a portfolio insurance scheme, practitioners actually take positions in the "stock index futures market." This is a market that started in 1982 in the Chicago Mercantile Exchange.

Normally, a futures contract involves a promise to deliver a given quantity of a commodity at a specific future date for a predetermined price. Few holders of futures contracts actually require delivery; rather, they sell the contracts at their current market value. From the current market value is subtracted the prearranged futures price, and the difference is settled in cash. Ideally, the current value of the commodity at the time of expiration determines the settlement to be made.

Stock index futures contracts use certain stock indices as their standard for settlement, notably the S&P 500 index. In the stock index futures contract, no delivery of shares is promised. Settlement is in cash. An index has no units, so the S&P 500 index is multiplied by a conversion factor of $500 to express the index in dollar amounts. By convention, the dollar amount delivered is determined by taking the S&P 500 index value A' on the delivery date, multiplying by $500, and subtracting the contracted future price index, which we label F, also multiplied by $500. If you write a contract—that is, take a short position in the contract—you are promising to deliver to the buyer of the contract an amount A' multiplied by $500 at the delivery date less the futures price F times $500. See Box 17.1.

For example, if the futures price F is 200, the buyer of the contract agrees to pay that amount on the expiration date. You might think that A' will have a value of 150 at the expiration date. The profit you expect to make is the difference between the futures price of 200 and $A' = 150$ multiplied by $500, or $25,000. If A' indeed turns out as you expected, the buyer of the contract must deliver $25,000, the net of the cash delivery commitments of the buyer and seller. Of course, the buyer is betting that the index will have a value of 200 or more.

Suppose that you consider writing (selling) a contract whereby you gain on a downward movement in stock prices. What is the position that you are assuming in equities if you have agreed to deliver shares in the future? This is the equivalent of a short position in shares. Simultaneously, however, you are taking a long position in cash because you will receive the cash in the future. This is the equivalent of making a loan. The cash to be received in the future is usually referred to as a **synthetic T-bill,** since it represents a certain amount that will be delivered in the future just like a T-bill. Of course, it is not default free and it lacks the liquidity of a T-bill, so this term is a misnomer. The loan aspect of the futures contract leans on access to bank lines of credit, so we may more accurately call it a synthetic certificate of deposit or synthetic commercial paper.

This combination of positions, however, is exactly what you would want to take if you wanted to create a synthetic put. By writing an index futures contract, you can mimic the short position necessary to create a put. How many futures contracts you have to write depends on the short stock position derived in put equation 17.3. The larger the short position, the more futures contracts you have to write. Also, from the put equation, the larger the short position you want to assume because of the fall in stock prices, the larger is the cash position. Writing a futures contract automatically increases your cash position.

Therefore, instead of using stock and certificate of deposit transactions for portfolio insurance, the puts can be mimicked simply by taking positions in futures markets, by writing index futures contracts.

Program Trading

Independent of the group of people who trade in futures in order to provide portfolio insurance are those called **program traders,** who continuously track the price of the stock index relative to the price in the futures market. If these two prices do not line up in an appropriate manner, they take advantage of arbitrage opportunities.

There are two ways of acquiring the basket of stocks in the index on the expiration date of the futures contract. One is to buy the futures contract. The second is to buy the stocks in the index now and carry them until the expiration day of the futures contract. If the stocks in the index are bought now, however, cash must be delivered now. This cash can otherwise be lent in the form of acquiring a CD until the expiration day of the contract. As a compensation, the stocks do pay some dividends while they are held.

For instance, suppose that the value of the future stock index is F and that the value of the current index of stocks is A. One plus the market yield on CDs is R, and the percentage dividend yield on the stocks in the index is expected to be D. The cost as of the day of expiration of acquiring the stocks in the index now and holding them is $A(R - D)$. This cost is referred to as the **cost of carry.**

Suppose that $F < A(R - D)$. The futures contract price implies that for a future delivery of the S&P 500 index, the arbitrager will pay a relatively low price. The cost of acquiring actual S&P 500 shares is higher than that price at current market prices.

What would be the response of an arbitrager to this differential? Using the economic principle of buy where prices are low and sell where prices are high, she would sell stock now and buy stock index futures. Suppose that she borrows the stock and sells it now at the high price. This commits her to future delivery of the shares. Simultaneously, she buys future shares at a low price, leaving the net as a profit. Effectively, she has covered her position by taking a long position in the futures market and a short position in the stock market.

Margin Requirements for Short Selling Stock

The amount of margin deposited by a short seller of stock with the stock lender depends on whether the short seller is a broker-dealer or simply a customer. If the short seller is a broker-dealer who borrows stock from another dealer, the margin deposit with the lender equals the value of the stock at the close of the last day's business. If the stock price rises after the stock is borrowed, the short seller must add to the margin deposits with the lender. Acceptable collateral for margin includes Treasury securities, CDs, bankers acceptances, and irrevocable letters of credit.

If the short seller is a customer, the Federal Reserve's Regulation T requires an additional initial deposit of 50 percent of the market value of the stock with the lender.

Futures and Option Exchange Clearinghouses
and Margin Requirements

In practice, the operation of futures and option markets is more complicated. At the heart of both types of markets lies a clearinghouse that guarantees that buyers and sellers will deliver cash or securities on the expiration dates. Buyers and sellers of options and futures contracts do not enter into contracts with each other. Rather, a clearinghouse writes the contract with the buyer and buys from the writer. Since performance on each contract depends only on the creditworthiness of the clearinghouse, contracts are uniform and market liquidity is increased.

For all options, regardless of the exchange on which they trade, the Options Clearing Corporation (OCC) serves as the clearinghouse. Stock index futures are guaranteed by the clearinghouse associated with the exchange on which they trade. For example, the S&P 500 index futures contracts are traded on the Chicago Mercantile Exchange, and they are guaranteed by the Chicago Mercantile Exchange Clearinghouse (CMECH).

Margin on Futures Contracts. In taking a position on both sides of a futures contract, a clearinghouse bears a risk that one of the parties will default. To protect itself against default, the clearinghouse requires a **margin** deposit at the start of the futures contract. Members of the clearinghouse, known as clearing members, include the well-known investment banks. Clearing members must make margin deposits of $10,000 with the CMECH for contracts traded for their own accounts. For customers of clearing members, the CMECH may require a $20,000 deposit by each party of an S&P 500 contract as initial margin if they are classified as speculators. A speculator does not have a position in actual shares that balances his or her futures position. If customers are classified as **hedgers,** the CMECH requires a smaller margin of $10,000. A hedger has a stock position that is the opposite of its futures position.

These deposits by customers are placed in the hands of the clearing members, who are the customers' agents. From the margin delivered by customers on each contract, the clearing member must deliver $10,000 to the CMECH into special margin accounts in their names at banks selected by the CMECH. The deposits of customers of clearing members may take the form of a T-bill, cash, a letter of credit from a bank, or securities listed on the New York Stock Exchange (credited at 70 percent of their market value). For clearing members' deposits at the CMECH, however, the first $25,000 must be in cash—that is, bank deposits—after which Treasury securities and bank letters of credit are acceptable. The bank letters of credit must be irrevocable and callable within 60 minutes.

As an example of the margin deposit required at the CMECH, suppose that the S&P 500 futures index is currently 310. An S&P 500 contract has a value of $500 × 310 = $155,000, so the margin deposit represents about 6.5 percent of the contract value. Margin requirements are adjusted upward if average daily stock price movements increase, however.

In a process known as **marking to market,** each contract is repriced by the CMECH at the end of each day according to the S&P 500 futures index established in the day's trading. For example, suppose that MM Enterprises buys a futures contract on May 1 when the S&P 500 futures index is 310. The contract is sold by the Methuselah Pension Fund. Each party deposits the required $20,000 with the clearing members who served as their brokers. Of this amount, the clearing members deliver $10,000 for each contract into margin accounts at the CMECH. On May 2, the S&P 500 futures index closes at 290. The contracts that are outstanding from before May 2 are then rewritten by the CMECH at the futures index of 290. This marking to market is done to make all outstanding contracts uniform so that the market will not be segmented. It also forces an immediate settlement of any losses. In this case, MM Enterprises has lost $10,000—that is, $500 × (310 − 290). It agreed on May 1 to buy for 310 × $500 something that is worth only 290 × $500 on May 2. On the other hand, Methuselah Pension Fund has gained $10,000—it sold for $500 × 310 on May 1 something that is worth only $500 × 290 on May 2.

MM Enterprises is required to settle this loss, and Methuselah Pension Fund will be credited with its gain immediately. The CMECH deducts $10,000 from the margin account maintained by the clearing member for MM Enterprises and credits the margin account maintained for Methuselah Pension Fund with $10,000. If Methuselah Pension Fund's margin account exceeds the amount required for initial margin, Methuselah Pension Fund can have access to the excess cash. On the other hand, if MM Enterprises' margin account falls to a minimum **maintenance margin** set by the CMECH, a **margin call** is made by the clearing member. MM Enterprises must then deliver sufficient additional cash, known as **variation margin,** to top its margin account with the clearing member back up to the initial margin requirement of $20,000. In this example, if the maintenance margin is $10,000, the futures index fall on May 2 will trigger a variation margin call of $10,000 to MM Enterprises. If MM Enterprises does not deliver cash quickly to its margin account, its contract will be sold by the clearing member. In addition, the clearing member's margin account at the CMECH has lost $10,000, so the CMECH requires that the clearing member deposit an additional $10,000 of margin. After each day's business, similar margin computations are made.

Buyers or sellers of contracts will usually have prearranged lines of credit with banks to deliver funds to the CMECH in case of margin calls. Such lines make the index futures market liquid. In their absence, margining of contracts could not proceed smoothly, and the clearinghouse's guarantee might not be credible.

Margin on Options Contracts. Buyers of options simply pay the premium and either exercise the option or not. Writers of options may suffer losses that are quite large if stock prices move sufficiently, so the Options Clearing Corporation imposes margin requirements to guarantee that writers of options will not default. For example, for broadly based index options, the seller must maintain margin equal to the option premium received on the sale plus 15 percent of the market value of the index minus the value by which the option is out of the money.

For example, suppose that the S&P 500 index is 300 so that the value of the index is $500 × 300 = $150,000. Suppose that S&P 500 call options with a strike price of 310 currently sell for $1,000. The amount of margin required from a writer of a call is

$1,000	The call premium
+ $22,500	0.15 times the current value of the index of $150,000
− $5,000	Amount by which the call is out of the money (10 × $500)
$18,500	Total margin

For the margin required for a short put, suppose that an S&P 500 put option with a strike price of 310 currently sells for $12,000. The margin required from a writer of the put is

$12,000	The put premium
+ $22,500	The current value of the index
− 0	Amount by which the put is out of the money
$34,500	Total

Cash Requirements for Arbitrage

Put-Call Parity Arbitrage.   We now consider how heavily dependent financial innovations are on the delivery of cash through bank lines. Specifically, through an example, we will analyze once again the arbitrage that gives us put-call parity in the light of how much cash the arbitrager must deliver to carry out the required transactions in securities markets. Suppose that instead of the equality in equation 17.2, market prices are such that

$$\frac{S}{R} < A + P - C$$

Then there is an opportunity for an arbitrager to profit by buying a CD or commercial paper with a par value of S (the strike price in the options) and selling the portfolio consisting of the shares in the stock index, the put, and the short call. In other words, the arbitrager will short sell the shares in the stock index, write a put, and buy a call option.

Specifically, suppose that $S = \$155,000$ (that is, $500 × 310$), the exercise date is 1 year from now, the interest rate on certificates of deposit is 5 percent per year, the call option premium is $1,000, and the put option premium is $12,000. The current value of the stock index is $150,000 (that is, $500 × 300$). Then the current price of the CD is $155,000/1.05 = \$147,620$, and the value of the portfolio is $161,000 = \$150,000 + \$12,000 − \$1,000$. The arbitrager should buy the cheap CD and sell the expensive portfolio. This will produce a profit of about $13,380 with no risk. This calculation, however, does not account for the commitment of cash that the arbitrager must make.

Table 17.4 indicates how much cash the arbitrager must deliver out of pocket to carry out the arbitrage. First, the arbitrager must deliver $147,620 to the bond

Table 17.4 NET CASH DELIVERIES REQUIRED FROM ARBITRAGER

1.	$147,620	Payment to CP dealer
2.	75,000	Net cash needed for short sale margin
3.	1,000	Premium for call purchase
4.	22,500	Margin for writing the put
	$246,120	Total

seller. Next, the arbitrager has sold the shares short, so she must deliver the proceeds of $150,000 plus an additional $75,000 in cash to serve as margin for a net cash drain of $75,000. Next, the arbitrager must deliver $1,000 to purchase the call option. Finally, the arbitrager must deposit the put premium of $12,000 plus $22,500. The total cash that must be delivered is $246,120.

Program Trading Arbitrage.   Suppose that Trader Vic, a program trader and CMECH clearing member, observes that the S&P 500 futures index is 310. The current yield on CDs is 5 percent per year. The stocks in the S&P 500 basket have a current market index of 300, and the stocks are expected to yield dividends at a rate of 3 percent per year. In this case, the value of the futures contract is $155,000 (that is, $500 × 310). The cost of carrying the stock position is $153,000. The cost of carry is determined by multiplying the current index value of $150,000 (that is, $500 × 300) by (1 + 0.05 − 0.03). Immediately, Vic's program launches an order to buy the shares in the index and sell an index futures contract, thereby earning $2,000 per contract. As a consequence, liquidity is increased in both markets. How much cash does Trader Vic need for this transaction?

He must deliver $150,000 to buy the shares. In addition, he must deposit $10,000 of margin with the CMECH, for a total of $160,000.

FINANCIAL INNOVATION LEANS ON THE LIQUIDITY OF THE BANKS

As we indicated in Chapter 13, prior to January 1, 1991, nonpersonal domestic CDs were subject to a 3-percent reserve requirement. Commercial paper, which has the same liquidity characteristics, was not. Therefore, an expansion of the commercial paper market increased the amount of comparatively liquid securities that could be created for a given reserve base. We presented evidence in that chapter that the availability of close substitutes for bank liabilities subject to reserve requirements made reserve requirements nonbinding, which reduced the cost of liquidity for everyone.

In this section we look at the market for synthetic CDs like the one created in equation 17.2 in the same light. That is, was this market also a method of creating a security with the liquidity of a CD that was not subject to reserve requirement? To analyze this problem, suppose that reserve requirements are binding, there is no commercial paper market, and the cost of liquidity is high because the amount of good funds to settle payments in the system is greater than the banks want. This means that the opportunity cost of holding a CD instead of a less liquid security is high—that is, the interest rate on the CD is relatively low.

Let's assume that, based on equation 17.2, an entrepreneurially minded broker sees an opportunity to create a synthetic CD by converting a relatively illiquid security, a share of stock, into a synthetic CD. The expected return on the stock is high relative to the interest rate on the liquid CD because reserve requirements are binding. Note that the expected return on the stock is relatively high because an investor must pay for the high cost of liquidity in the event that he must sell it to deliver cash. If the broker can create a liquid security from the stock without paying for reserves, she can make a riskless profit by selling the new security for a higher price (lower return) than she must pay to create the new security.

She knows that according to equation 17.2, she can create a synthetic CD with a portfolio that is long in stock, long a put, and short a call. Since she sees no instrument that is subject to reserve requirements in any of the instruments in this portfolio, she thinks that the portfolio has a lower price (higher return) than the CD. She spots an arbitrage opportunity.

As we indicated earlier, whatever happens to the price of the stock, the broker can guarantee the same payoff as a bank CD to the investor. Thus she incurs no risk. Before we can conclude that she has found a riskless way to make a profit, however, we must determine whether she must indirectly hold reserves to create the synthetic CD.

She may have to put up some margin on the call option she writes, but we will make the assumption that there are no margin requirements. Despite this assumption, we shall see that the broker must implicitly hold some of her portfolio in the form of reserves because the individual from whom she buys the put must hold a CD, assuming he writes the put from a hedged position.

Consider equation 17.3. The hedged portfolio against the put consists of shorting stock and holding a fraction of the value of the broker's portfolio, S/R, in the form of a bank CD. Since the reserve requirement is binding, the interest rate on the CD is lower relative to interest rates on less liquid securities than it would be if the requirement were not binding. According to equation 17.3, the lower the return R on CDs, relative to the interest rate on less liquid securities, the higher is the price of the put relative to the price of less liquid securities such as stock. The existence of a binding reserve requirement forces the broker to pay more for the put relative to the price of the stock, which reduces her gain.[7]

---

7. The relative price the broker receives for the call she sells is also lower in the case of binding reserve requirements. This follows from equation 17.1.

Nevertheless, the broker does conserve on the use of reserves to some extent. Since $(1 + \gamma R/S)$ in equation 17.3 is a positive fraction, she pays for fewer reserves than she would have to pay on a real CD. As a result, this financial innovation has increased the supply of liquid securities that can be supported by a given reserve base. Banks can then shrink their balance sheets and reduce their reserve holdings without reducing the total supply of CDs and synthetic CDs. The supply of synthetic CDs will expand until the quantity of reserves held relative to liquid instruments in the financial markets is exactly what the market wants to hold, just as in the case of the commercial paper arbitrage described in Chapter 13. This will cause the return on the bank CD to rise relative to the expected return on the stock, eliminating the arbitrage opportunity.

The removal of reserve requirements on CDs in January 1991 has eliminated the necessity of expanding synthetic CDs and commercial paper to increase the number of liquid securities to reduce bank reserves to a level desired by banks. Because all these instruments are perfect substitutes from the investor's point of view, however, elimination of reserve requirements will not necessarily cause the expansion of bank CDs relative to commercial paper or synthetic CDs.

THE SWAP MARKET

Starting in the early 1980s, a vast market involving swaps of different streams of payments has emerged as a major banking business. The market has two principal instruments. The first is the **interest rate swap** in which interest payments from different types of nominal securities denominated in the same currency are exchanged. The second is the **currency swap** in which streams of interest payments from two securities denominated in different currencies are exchanged. Banks are the major market makers in these markets, and they generally take one side of each swap contract.

An Interest Rate Swap

As an example of how an interest rate swap works, we suppose that the Mississippi Company takes out a 5-year bank loan from Banque Royale. The company can access the public market for long-term funds only at a very high interest cost because it is a risky company. However, it can borrow long-term from a bank at a lower cost if it is willing to submit itself to stringent monitoring that is typical of a bank loan contract. The bank loan contract specifies that the company's interest payments are based on the 6-month LIBOR rate plus 90 basis points. Hence, this is a floating rate loan contract.

Banque Royale does not want to make a long-term loan at a fixed–interest rate because most of its liabilities are short term. Banks are in the business of converting loans to illiquid borrowers, like the Mississippi Company, into liquid assets for investors in the form of deposits. Because deposits are liquid, they must, of necessity, be short term. Since the bank specializes in monitoring credits, it can convert long-term loans into short-term deposits. However, it may not want to absorb the interest rate risk associated with making the long-term loan liquid. After all, its comparative advantage is in monitoring behavior, not absorbing interest rate risk.

The Mississippi Company, as a struggling company that must borrow from a bank, faces many business risks. One risk that it would rather avoid is interest rate risk. Let us assume that it signs relatively long-term contracts with its customers, so its cash flow does not increase when interest rates rise. It would therefore prefer to borrow at a fixed interest rate.

Borrower and lender can be accommodated in the swap market. Suppose that the South Sea Company is a highly rated corporation with access to the fixed rate public debt market. South Sea Company can easily absorb some interest rate risk, so it is willing to trade fixed interest payments for floating payments in the form of a swap. The Mississippi Company borrows $100 million at floating rates from Banque Royale, and the South Sea Company issues a fixed rate bond for $100 million. They agree to swap interest rate payments. The South Sea Company makes a floating rate payment to the Mississippi Company, and the Mississippi Company pays a fixed interest rate to the South Sea Company. From the payments received from the South Sea Company, the Mississippi Company can pay Banque Royale a floating rate while reducing its interest rate exposure because it pays a fixed rate to the South Sea Company.

At what price will the interest payments be exchanged? Suppose that the South Sea Company can borrow in the fixed rate bond market at 8 percent per year. It can also borrow in the short-term market at LIBOR plus 10 basis points. This liability might be in the form of 6-month Euro-commercial paper, so, unlike the Mississippi Company's bank loan, this liability is short term as well as floating rate. The Mississippi Company has access to the junk bond market at an interest rate of 10 percent. Thus, it pays 200 basis points more than the South Sea Company in the public fixed rate market but only 80 basis points more in the floating rate bank loan market. The bank loan has a relatively low interest rate because the Mississippi Company must submit itself to stringent monitoring controls when it borrows from the bank.

The South Sea Company should be able to achieve a more favorable funding cost in a swap with the Mississippi Company than it could receive in the public market because it absorbs some risk with the swap. If the Mississippi Company should fail to make fixed rate payments to the South Sea Company, the South Sea Company would stop making floating rate payments to the Mississippi Company, but the South Sea Company would still have to make payments on fixed rate debt.

Suppose that the South Sea Company agrees to pay the Mississippi Company LIBOR in exchange for a fixed rate payment of 8.5 percent. The Mississippi Company must pay Bank Royale LIBOR plus 90 basis points. Thus, its payment to the bank net of its receipts from the South Sea Company is 90 basis points. In addition, it must pay a fixed 8.5 percent to the South Sea Company, so its total cost of fixed rate funds is .90 + 8.5 = 9.4 percent. Its cost of fixed rate funds, after submitting itself to stringent bank monitoring, is 60 basis points lower than issuing a junk bond.

The South Sea Company must pay LIBOR, which is 10 basis points less than it would have to pay if it issued Euro-commercial paper. In addition, it receives 8.5 percent fixed but must pay only 8 percent. Hence, its total compensation for bearing the risk of being saddled with a fixed rate liability is .10 + .50 = 60 basis points. In practice, the compensation paid to each party is subject to negotiation.

A Currency Swap

A currency swap is like an interest rate swap except that the two parties to the swap exchange interest payments denominated in different currencies and also swap principal. Investors may wish to use such swaps if they can reduce their exposure to currency risk by doing so. For example, suppose the exchange rate between DM and U.S. dollars is 2 and that the rate is not expected to change. In addition, suppose that Metropolitan Life Insurance Company wants to buy Daimler-Benz bonds for portfolio diversification; but because its insurance liabilities are denominated in dollars, it does not want the currency risk associated with a DM bond. A German insurance company, on the other hand, wants to buy IBM bonds for portfolio diversification, but it also does not want the currency risk.

Daimler-Benz and IBM also prefer to issue bonds in their own currencies because most of their cash flow is denominated in the home currency and they do not want the currency risk either. The problem can be solved in the swap market. Metropolitan can buy DM Daimler-Benz bonds, and the German insurance company can buy IBM dollar bonds. The two insurance companies can agree to swap the original payment to buy the bonds and interest rate receipts. The companies will also swap repayment of principal at maturity. Alternatively, IBM can issue a DM bond to the German insurance company, and Daimler-Benz can issue a dollar bond to Metropolitan; then Daimler-Benz and IBM can swap principal and interest payments.

Because we have assumed that the DM–dollar exchange rate is not expected to change, long-term interest rates in the two currencies must be equal. Suppose that Daimler-Benz and IBM both have the same high credit rating, so their cost of borrowing fixed rate in their respective currencies is the same, say 8 percent. However, Metropolitan is willing to hold a dollar-denominated Daimler-Benz bond for 7.9 percent per year because this presents a previously unexploited opportunity to diversify its portfolio. Likewise, the German insurance company is willing to hold a DM-denominated IBM bond at 7.9 percent per year. IBM can issue a DM denominated bond, and Daimler-Benz can issue a dollar denominated bond. IBM can then swap DM for dollar payments on a two for one basis with Daimler-Benz, and both will gain 10 basis points.

Banks in the Market for Swap Contracts

The principal of the interest rate loans is not swapped—only a stream of interest payments is swapped. The principal upon which the amount of cash to be swapped is based is called the **notional principal amount.** For currency swaps, both principal and interest are swapped. In mid-1990, the world total notional principal on interest rate and currency swaps was $2.4 trillion.

Commercial banks both make the market in swaps and offer themselves as a counterparty in nearly every swap contract. For example, in 1989, 10 U.S. banks accounted for one side in 70 percent of global swap contracts.

In the context of our earlier interest rate swap example, the Mississippi Company and the South Sea Company will not actually contract directly with each other. First, the Mississippi Company will negotiate to have a bank, the Sword Blade Bank, assume the role of the long-term lender—that is, the Sword Blade Bank takes the place of the South Sea Company. For the Sword Blade Bank, this is the first leg of two swap contracts. The bank, however, assumes some interest rate risk in this contract. It pays LIBOR minus 8.5 percent per year on net. If LIBOR rises above 8.5 percent, the Sword Blade Bank will have to make positive payments on the swap.

To cover against interest rate movements, the Sword Blade Bank can enter another swap as a fixed rate payer to the South Sea Company—that is, the bank can assume the role played by the Mississippi Company in the earlier example. The two swaps taken together eliminate the bank's interest rate risk—that is, any loss the bank makes on one contract through interest rate movements is offset by the gain on the other contract.

In making the market, Sword Blade Bank posts fixed rate yield quotations for entering a contract either as a fixed rate payer or as a floating rate payer. For example, Table 17.5 lists interest rate swap quotations for 6-month LIBOR floating rate payments for various maturities. The convention is to list the yield on the fixed rate security that is to be swapped for the LIBOR payments. In the table, an offer price indicates that the bank will assume the role of the floating rate payer and will receive the fixed payment, and a bid price means that the bank will be the fixed rate payer. For a 5-year swap, an offer of 8.38 indicates that the Sword Blade Bank will deliver LIBOR every 6 months on the notional amount of the swap in return for a fixed payment of 8.38 percent per year of the notional amount. For the same swap, a bid of 8.33 indicates that the Sword Blade Bank will deliver a fixed payment of 8.33 percent of the notional amount in return for 6-month LIBOR payments. If the Sword Blade Bank both buys and sells a swap, it is perfectly hedged against interest rate movements, and it receives a 5 basis point (8.38 − 8.33) annual income for having made the market.

The bank makes a spread because it absorbs some risk in the swap. First, it may not be able to hedge a swap contract instantly, so it bears interest rate risk. Second, it guarantees fixed payments to the South Sea Company, even if the Mis-

Table 17.5   SWORD BLADE BANK INTEREST RATE SWAP QUOTATIONS (6-MONTH DOLLAR LIBOR)

Maturity	Bid	Offer
2 years	7.30	7.36
3 years	7.76	7.81
5 years	8.33	8.38
7 years	8.59	8.64
10 years	8.73	8.78

sissippi Company should default on its obligation to pay the bank the fixed rate in exchange for LIBOR. Thus, if short rates should unexpectedly fall and the Mississippi Company defaults, the bank would suffer a loss. However, even when the bank guarantees a swap, each counterparty receives compensation for some remaining risks of entering the swap contract. The South Sea Company still faces interest rate risk that it might otherwise have not accepted. It also faces the risk that the bank might default on its end of the bargain. The Mississippi Company will still pay a lower fixed rate than it would pay in the open market because it still subjects itself to the monitoring straightjacket of a bank loan.

Why Do Banks Dominate the Swap Market?

Since anyone can make the market in interest rate swaps, we must inquire why banks so dominate the market. We have emphasized that banks specialize in netting payments across customers. Banks must deliver reserves only against net due to position. They have many customers that receive and make payments throughout the business day. Their large customer base makes it likely that a bank's net position at any one time will be small relative to the amount of payments received and sent; thus, they are able to promise liquidity to their customers while holding a relatively illiquid asset portfolio.

The problem of creating a liquid swap market is similar. A market maker in swaps that has access to many potential counterparties can effectively guarantee market access to a customer while reducing its own exposure to a minimum. Banks have access to customers with a wide range of access to credit markets. They know large corporate clients in their role as provider of wholesale payments. They know risky corporations in their role of providing loans to customers that require monitoring. The large customer base of money center banks permits the most efficient netting of swap contracts. Banks must play a role in guaranteeing these contracts because the counterparties do not know each other.

CONCLUSION

Institutions other than banks can supply securities with bank deposit-like characteristics to households. They can do this while holding assets whose value fluctuates greatly without providing a cushion of equity protection to their "depositors." Their method consists simply of selling the risk associated with falls in their assets' value through options or futures markets to speculators who are more willing to bear the risk than households. Thus the risks associated with providing liquidity are distributed throughout the economy to a wide range of nonbank risk bearers.

In this chapter we have analyzed various techniques that bestow deposit-like characteristics to illiquid securities. If these devices, which include options and futures contracts, could create liquidity in securities without generating additional demands for bank lines, banks would go out of business. No one would want to pay for the reserves they hold at the central bank.

Users of options and futures contracts must put up margin to ensure that they perform as promised, however. For example, an arbitrager cannot take advantage of a discrepancy between the price of a CD and a theoretically equivalent portfolio of stocks, puts, and calls without having access to a substantial amount of cash on short notice.

Even the theoretical possibility of creating a synthetic CD founders on the necessity of the writer of a put to hold a liquid asset to hedge positions. Because the writer of the put must hold a CD that is smaller in value than the synthetic CD, however, expansion of the synthetic CD market has functioned as a way to conserve on reserves.

KEY TERMS

put-call parity	portfolio insurance
option	synthetic T-bill
call option	program trading
put option	cost of carry
strike (exercise) price	margin
exercise	hedger
in the money	marking to market
out of the money	maintenance margin
European option	margin call
American option	variation margin
stop-loss techniques	interest rate swap
static hedging	currency swap
synthetic put	notional principal amount

EXERCISES

1. Prove that a rise in the current price of a stock or of the market interest rate will raise the price of an option.

2. Prove that a rise in the current price of a stock will increase the long share position and the short loan position required to mimic an option.

3. Prove that a call option has a value equivalent to the value of a fraction of a share of stock minus the value of a fraction of a loan.

4. During the crash of October 19–20, 1987, enormous spreads developed between the prices of S&P 500 stocks and the S&P 500 index futures contract, especially at the start of trading. On these days, specialists could open trading in many of the stocks on the New York Stock Exchange only after long delays. Explain how problems in opening stocks might account for this spread.

5. "Normally, options trading–oriented investors are far less active in the futures market. This spillover of trading activity was especially large because the week's fall in stock prices had essentially eliminated all at-the-money options, which meant that investors could not roll their positions into a new contract month. Most listed option strike prices were above the prevailing market levels. Since it became difficult to establish, or to maintain, efficiently hedged positions using options, many options trading–oriented investors shifted their hedging activity to the futures market."

   a. Explain the problems of a portfolio manager who wants to hedge a stock position when she is unable to buy at-the-money options.

   b. Explain how she can overcome this problem by shifting her business to the futures markets. Describe in detail exactly how a hedge can be constructed through the futures market.

6. Suppose that a put and a call option on a stock index have the same exercise price S and the same exercise date 1 year from now. The put price is P, and the call price is C. The stock index has a price A, and the conversion factor is $1 for each index point. Show that a portfolio long one put option and one unit of the stocks in the stock index and short one call option has the same value as a 1-year CD with a face value of S.

7. Show that if there is divergence from put-call parity, an arbitrager can profit by establishing the appropriate self-financing portfolio of assets and liabilities.

8. On February 28, the Chicago Mercantile Exchange began trading a new index future, the S&P 5, which consists of five growth stocks (they pay no dividends) chosen to reflect the fortunes of small companies traded on the New York Stock Exchange. The five firms on February 28 are as follows:

Firm	Price	Shares Outstanding
A	50	10,000
B	43	15,000
C	61	40,000
D	19	20,000
E	28	25,000

    a. Calculate the S&P 5 for February 28. The base-year value for the S&P 5 is $777,500. The method of calculation is identical to that for the S&P 500.

    b. The S&P 5 futures contract is an agreement to buy $500 times the futures value of the S&P 5 on a specified date in the future. Suppose that the yield to maturity on a 6-month CD is 5 percent on February 28. What do you predict will be the price on a futures contract expiring in August?

9. XYZ Investors, a clearing member of CMECH, has three customers interested in S&P 5 futures. X, the first customer, suffers from a rash immediately before a bear market begins. He broke out the morning of February 27 and plans to profit from the impending downturn. Y has a sophisticated econometric model that shows unambiguously that the biggest bull market in history is about to begin. He too plans to profit. Z manages a portfolio that mimics the S&P 5, and she wishes to hedge against a market downturn. Initial margin for speculators is $6,000, and maintenance margin is $4,000. For hedgers, initial margin is $4,000 and maintenance margin is $3,000.

    a. In trading on February 28, X and Y open contracts, whereas Z does not. How much initial margin is deposited by XYZ Investors with CMECH on March 1 if the futures price coincides with the current index value?

    b. The S&P 5 futures contract falls 2 points on March 1. At this point, Z begins to initiate a hedge and sells a contract. How much initial margin is deposited with CMECH on March 2? How much variation margin is paid to CMECH on existing contracts on March 2? How much does CMECH pay out to gainers on March 2?

    c. On March 2, the S&P 5 futures contract falls another 5 points. Describe the activity in customer margin accounts before trading opens on March 3. Describe the margin paid to CMECH and received from CMECH by XYZ Investors.

In exercises 10 to 15, let S = $100, the interest rate on CDs be 5 percent per year, the index price be $100, the call option price (premium) be $7, and the put option price (premium) be $3. The arbitrager is a partner in a large investment firm, a clearing member of all exchange clearinghouses.

10. Suppose that the arbitrage in exercise 7 involves buying a CD. How much cash must the arbitrager deliver for the CD purchased? When are the funds delivered?

11. Describe how the Options Clearing Corporation calculates margin requirements for options. How much cash must the arbitrager deliver to the OCC for this transaction to cover required margin?

12. Suppose that instead of buying a call option, the arbitrager manufactures a synthetic call by using stock index futures contracts. This involves buying y futures contracts and trading z additional dollars' worth of CDs. Does this require an acquisition of z dollars' worth of CDs or a sale? What is the net amount of cash that she must deliver today on all her CD transactions?

13. Describe the margining rules and margin account operations of the CMECH. If there is a 10 percent initial margin, how much cash must the arbitrager deliver to the CMECH to manufacture a synthetic call?

14. After the arbitrager establishes all the positions indicated, the stock index falls precipitously by half. Will the arbitrager need more or less cash to maintain the hedge? Describe these changed cash requirements market by market.

15. Discuss how the ability to construct arbitrages or derivative securities is dependent on access to the liquidity of the banking system.

FURTHER READING

Black, Fischer, and Myron Scholes. "The Pricing of Options and Corporate Liabilities," *Journal of Political Economy,* May 1973, pp. 637–654.

Cox, J., S. Ross, and M. Rubinstein. "Options Pricing: A Simplified Approach," *Journal of Financial Economics,* September 1979, pp. 229–263.

Kolb, Robert. *Understanding Futures Markets.* Glenview, Ill.: Scott-Foresman, 1988.

Sofianos, George. "Margin Requirements on Equity Instruments," *Federal Reserve Bank of New York Quarterly Review,* Summer 1988, pp. 47–60.

18

Liquidity Crises in Financial and Banking Markets

Throughout our study of banking we have emphasized that a primary role of banks is the provision of liquidity and payment services to financial and goods markets. The Federal Reserve was itself created in 1913 principally because of the perception that the private banking system occasionally failed to provide sufficient liquidity. Shortages of liquidity occurred seasonally on a small scale, and large-scale panics took place regularly prior to the founding of the Federal Reserve.

Many of the powers of the Federal Reserve are aimed at helping banks to create liquidity, and one of the Fed's primary goals is to maintain the stability of the banking system and "orderliness" (liquidity) in financial markets when demands for liquidity suddenly increase. The timely provision of liquidity can prevent needless costly bankruptcies among financial and other business institutions, thereby increasing the stability of important sectors of the economy.

Why is it desirable that one of the Fed's policy goals be the maintenance of **orderly markets**? What are the gains and costs of such a policy compared with a system without a central bank? To address these issues, we will first consider how potential shortages of liquidity affect behavior in banking and financial markets. We will examine especially how liquidity crises can break out in securities markets and how banking panics can occur.

LIQUIDITY IN SECURITIES MARKETS

We begin by analyzing the effects of insufficient liquidity on stock prices. Suppose that an important segment of stockholders use a **stop-loss trading strategy** in which sales are triggered only when stock prices fall to a certain value. These stockholders make use only of the latest market price in determining whether to sell and do not concern themselves with gathering information on prospective stock earnings. This sort of behavior is often referred to as **information trading** or **noise trading.**

Stop-Loss Strategies

We can interpret stop-loss strategies as a willingness to fully bear the risk of stock price movements if a stockholder's wealth is above a certain minimum value. When her wealth falls below that value, however, the stockholder is completely unwilling to bear further risk of stock price movements and shifts to the immediacy of cash or liquidity. For example, a person might be willing to bear the risk of holding stocks as long as she was assured that she would have at least enough to send her kids to college. If her stocks were worth more than this amount, she would stay entirely in the market. If their value fell to the cost of college tuition, she would jump out of the market into cash. Providing that the stock price did not take big jumps, she could guarantee a minimum value for her portfolio by keeping careful track of stock prices.

Stop-loss strategies exist in many forms. The selling strategy set forth above is a highly informal version in that it is known only to the shareholder. We will see that such strategies increase the responsiveness of the stock price to negative information about stock earnings. **Portfolio insurance** is a more formal version of the same sort of objectives. With portfolio insurance, however, there is no sudden movement out of the market. Rather, the portfolio insurer continually sells small amounts of shares as the stock price falls. Portfolio insurance also prescribes buying shares as the market price rises, unlike stop-loss selling.

Finally, a person financing a portfolio of securities with call loans is implicitly contracting with banks to sell the portfolio when its value reaches a minimum level. The borrower must have some equity—that is, some of her own funds—called **margin,** in her portfolio to acquire and maintain a loan. For example, currently in the United States, margin must be maintained at least at 25 percent of the value of the portfolio. The bank demands margin to guarantee that the loan will be repaid. With ample margin, the bank is assured that the loan is relatively riskless and therefore is willing to lend at relatively low interest rates. As market prices of securities fall, the bank's protection begins to evaporate, and at some point the bank will make a margin call, insisting on the delivery of additional securities or cash to serve as collateral. If the margin call is not met by the borrower, the lender can immediately sell the collateral to recover the value of the loan.

All these techniques are *strategies,* or trading rules, of market participants. Other market participants may have no knowledge of the existence of such traders because the potential sell orders lie buried in the future. They will explode on the market only if tripped by the proper contingency. When the time comes for these sales to occur, the sellers may find no buyers prepared to take the other side of the market at the last reported price, and the price may suddenly collapse. For any one small player, the assumption of price continuity is probably reasonable, so it is also reasonable to follow a stop-loss strategy. If all selling strategies are triggered simultaneously, however, they will prove to be infeasible.[1]

How can the strategies be made feasible? That is, how can they all coexist without surprising the market? These strategies are methods to mimic the possession of a put option on stock. If the stop-loss seller simply acquired a put, she would guarantee her floor price. Simultaneously, she would have alerted the markets to her presence; the put price would increase to reflect the market's anticipation of selling pressure when stock prices hit a particular level.

Stock Prices with Unknown Stop-Loss Strategies.

Suppose at first that holders of shares generally do not know the hedging strategies in the minds of participants in the markets; they find out about these strategies only as the stock price declines as a result of negative information about earnings. This lack of knowledge permits a potentially chaotic situation to arise in which large, discontinuous declines in stock prices are caused by only small increments in negative earnings information.

We can analyze stock price behavior in the context of Figures 18.1 and 18.2. In Figure 18.1, the supply of stock is fixed at x. Line 1 represents a downward-sloping demand curve for shares. The number of shares demanded depends negatively on the stock price, given the anticipated dividends. The position of the demand curve depends on the amount of dividends that market participants believe the stock will pay on a regular basis. Lower anticipated dividends are bad news that shift the demand curve to the left to a position represented in line 2, for example.

Some shares are demanded by people who base their trades on information about the anticipated dividend stream of the stock. If the anticipated dividend stream remains unchanged, then they will reduce their demands for the stock as its price rises, because a price rise causes the anticipated return on the stock to fall. The presence of these information-based traders gives the demand curve in Figure 18.1 its negative slope. If the anticipated dividend should fall, the stock would be earning a lower yield at any given price. Again, this would cause a decline in the shares demanded by the informed traders, and this is the source of the leftward shift in the demand curve, depicted by line 2 in Figure 18.1.

The equilibrium stock price, given a certain value of dividends, is found at the intersection of the demand curve with the vertical supply line. For instance, if

---

1. Sanford Grossman presents a detailed discussion of the infeasibility of unsignaled strategies in his "An Analysis of the Implications for Stock and Futures Price Volatility of Program Trading and Dynamic Hedging Strategies," *Journal of Business,* Vol. 61, No. 3 (1988), pp. 275–298.

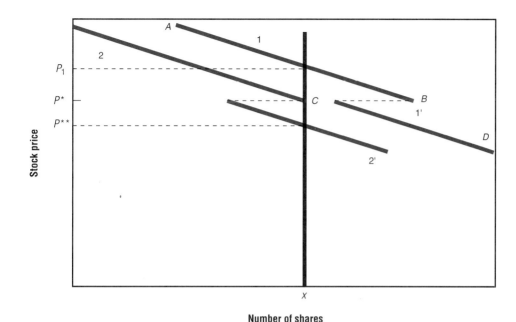

Figure 18.1 SHARE DEMAND WITH STOP-LOSS PLAYERS

dividends are such that line 1 is the relevant demand curve, the equilibrium stock price is P_1. A lower dividend will cause the demand curve in Figure 18.1 to shift leftward, producing a new equilibrium at a lower price.

Shareholders who are playing a stop-loss strategy will hold the shares only as long as the price is above $P\star$. When the price falls to $P\star$, they will sell all their shares and leave the market for good. In Figure 18.1, the combination of traders following a stop-loss strategy with the information-based traders can be depicted as a discontinuity in the demand curve. Segment CD on line 1 represents the demand of informed traders when the market price is below $P\star$. Segment AB is a uniform rightward shift of the informed traders' demand curve if we add in the holdings of the stop-loss players when the market price exceeds $P\star$. At prices higher than $P\star$, these players want to hold a relatively large amount of shares, and their demands must be added to those of the other traders. As dividends fall, the demand curve will shift to the left, and the equilibrium price will decline.

Once the demand curve reaches the position represented by the lines 2 and 2′ in Figure 18.1, a small further decline in dividends will cause a discontinuous fall in price to $P\star\star$ in both figures. This is a market crash brought about by a very small increment in negative news about dividends. The relation between anticipated dividends and equilibrium stock price when stop-loss traders are still in the market

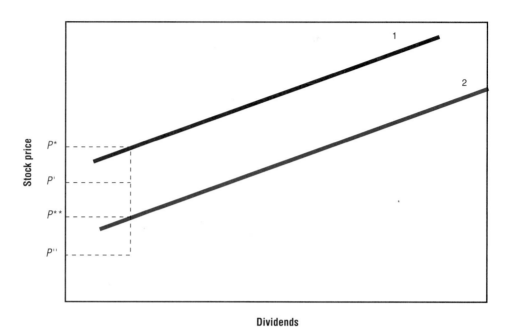

Figure 18.2   DIVIDEND-PRICE RELATION WITH SURPRISE STOP-LOSS TRADERS

is depicted in Figure 18.2 as line 1. If stop-loss traders are out of the market, a given dividend will be associated with a lower equilibrium price; this relationship is depicted as line 2 in Figure 18.2. The market price falls continuously along line 1 in Figure 18.2 as long as the equilibrium price exceeds $P^\star$. When the price reaches $P^\star$, the stop-loss sales occur, and the price falls discontinuously. This discontinuity is depicted in Figure 18.2 as a shift from the relationship along line 1 to that along line 2.

Let's look at this from another point of view. The stop-loss traders implement their strategies to guarantee that they can get out of the market at some desirable minimum price $P^\star$. For this strategy to work, however, the stock price must be continuous at $P^\star$. For any one stop-loss trader, the price would indeed be continuous when he attempts to sell at $P^\star$. The amount of shares he wants to sell would be small enough that the other traders could absorb them without disturbing prices. When all stop-loss traders attempt to sell simultaneously, however, the remaining traders will not absorb the shares sold at $P^\star$. The price then falls precipitously, and stop-loss sellers as a group fail to sustain a floor value of $P^\star$ on their shares. Although the strategy works perfectly well for any individual, a large-scale attempt to implement it will tend to fail.

In setting up this picture of the stock market, we have implicitly assumed that the information-based traders do not suspect the existence of the stop-loss traders. The trigger price $P^\star$ creates an invisible pitfall in the previously unexplored downside of the stock price.

Stock Prices with Known Stop-Loss Strategies.   Suppose now that all traders are aware of the presence of the stop-loss players in the market. Information-based traders, realizing that there will be a large selloff when the price reaches $P^\star$, will insist on a high yield on their stocks even when prices exceed $P^\star$. The relationship between stock prices and dividends then changes to that depicted by the curve ABC in Figure 18.3.[2] The segment AB reflects the demands only of the information-based investors at prices below $P^\star$, when they hold all existing shares. The segment BC results from the demands of both groups. Line 1 in this figure is identical to line 1 in Figure 18.2: It represents the price response to dividend movements when the information-based traders do not know that the stop-loss players are present in the market.

For a given dividend, the deviation of the points on BC from points on line 1 reflects the price discount required by information-based traders when they understand that other traders may dump their shares. A large discount implies a relatively low price and a relatively high current yield on the stocks. Notice that for dividends above but near $D^\star$, the price decline for a given decline in dividends is large, so prices are volatile in this region. The high current yield will offset the relatively high capital losses that traders anticipate because of the impending selloff. Traders expect capital losses because a given fall in dividends will cause prices to fall by more than the same dividend increase will cause prices to rise. If dividend increases and falls of given sizes are equally probable, traders expect that, on average, prices will fall. When the dividend is near $D^\star$, traders know that stop-loss sales are imminent, so they require a maximum discount. For higher dividends, the discount is small, since it is unlikely that the stop-loss strategy will be implemented.

If dividends actually reach $D^\star$, prices fall to $P^\star$, and the stop-loss players dump their stocks and leave the market. Any further declines in dividends will then move the stock price along the segment AB as before, because the only shareholders are information based.

Why will remaining investors hold the dumped shares with no radical price adjustment? Notice that just prior to the selloff, the high current yield, approximately equal to $D^\star/P^\star$, is offset by large anticipated capital losses as the price-dividend relation is at its greatest curvature. Just before and just after the selloff, the current yield on the stock is approximately unchanged at $D^\star/P^\star$. After the selloff, however, anticipated rates of price decline are suddenly much smaller, since the stop-loss traders have now bailed out. The price-dividend relation is now given by line 2,

2.   Paul Krugman, in "Trigger Strategies and Price Dynamics in Equity and Foreign Exchange Markets," NBER Working Paper No. 2459, December 1987, presents a clear intuition of this relationship. Figure 18.3 was developed by Krugman.

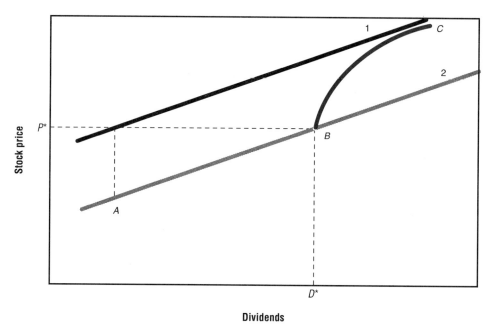

Figure 18.3   DIVIDEND-PRICE RELATION WITH KNOWN STOP-LOSS TRADERS

where price increases or falls of given amounts are equally probable. Expected capital gains and losses are then zero. The total return on the stock, current yield plus capital gains, therefore jumps upward at the time of the selloff. The higher return increases the demand of the remaining players sufficiently to absorb the dumped shares.

Finally, you should notice that knowledge of the presence of the stop-loss players will precipitate the price fall to $P\star$ when dividends are at a much higher level than in the case of ignorance.

Liquidity Events

In the two examples of selloffs that we have just studied, stock prices move for a good reason: the sudden unwillingness of a group of shareholders to bear risk after stock values fall below a certain value. Prices always reflect the underlying worth of the asset, whether or not price movements come as a surprise.

We now add to these scenarios the possibility that prices may deviate significantly from the equilibrium levels that we have derived because of liquidity problems. In each example there was a sudden upsurge of trading, and such trading would normally require a surge in the use of the payments system and of short-term credit markets. The buyers must write checks or electronic payment orders and arrange short-term financing to carry their new positions in stock. These massive, though temporary increases in the demand for liquidity can be referred to as **liquidity events.** In our analysis we have implicitly assumed that the payments system and credit markets could smoothly handle these increased demands for services.

Typically, when large sales of stock suddenly occur, the ultimate demanders of stock are not the initial buyers. The initial buyers are the market makers, whose function is to accommodate temporary imbalances in buy and sell orders. These market makers may range from stock market specialists and professional dealers to industrial firms with cash; they all recognize a profit opportunity. The market makers would buy temporarily for inventory and sell as the demands of the final investors gradually appear on the market. To undertake this service, of course, the market makers need sufficient credit lines so that their payments orders are accepted and they can get short-term financing to carry their positions. In short, the market makers who provide liquidity to the market must themselves have access to liquidity.

To pay for their costs in providing this service, market makers require some revenue. Revenue arises from the difference between the price at which they ultimately sell the stock acquired in a liquidity event and the price at which they buy the stock. In the preceeding examples we have depicted the price at which they sell the stock to final buyers. To generate revenues sufficient for the market makers to supply liquidity services, the prices paid to the stop-loss sellers must actually be less than the prices indicated in the figures. For example, the stock price in Figure 18.2 may fall temporarily to P'' if market makers absorb part of the selloff before ultimate holders of the stock begin to buy. If ample liquidity is available to the market at the time of the liquidity event, however, the price differential will be small.

Liquidity Stringencies.   What would happen if potential buyers were constrained in intraday credit on the payments system and in short-term loans to carry their securities inventory overnight? In other words, what would happen if liquidity were unavailable in the stock market?

To address this question, we first consider a simple example of how a sale of stock would affect the balance sheets of market participants. The market will consist of a seller of stocks, a potential market maker, the banks associated with these two players, and the banks' clearinghouse.[3] The market provides adequate liquidity to undertake the payments for and financing of the transaction; all checks will be honored, and financing will be available for the market maker to carry a stock position.

3.   We will ignore the complications that arise from the 5-day settlement lag ᴄ n shares and on the con-   trol of credit and the provision of liquidity through the stock market's own clearinghouse.

Table 18.1 PAYMENTS IMPLICATIONS OF A STOCK TRANSACTION

Seller

ASSETS		LIABILITIES
Stock	− $100	
Due from seller's bank	+ $100	

Market Maker

ASSETS		LIABILITIES	
Stock	+ $100	Due to market maker's bank	+ $100

Seller's Bank

ASSETS		LIABILITIES	
Due from market maker's bank	+ $10\	Due to seller	+ $100

Market Maker's Bank

ASSETS		LIABILITIES	
Due from market maker	+ $100	Due to seller's bank	+ $100

The seller suddenly decides to sell $100 worth of shares at the current market price, and the market maker decides to add the shares to her inventory. Table 18.1 indicates the payments implications of this transaction on the balance sheets of the players during the day that the market maker writes his check. The seller delivers the $100 of shares and receives a "due from" of $100 from her bank after depositing the check. The market maker adds the shares as assets, balancing them with a "due to" to his bank of $100. The seller's bank has a "due to" of $100 to the seller and a "due from" of $100 from the market maker's bank. The market maker's bank has a "due to" to the seller's bank of $100 as a liability and a "due from" of the market maker as an asset.

At the end of the day, the clearinghouse settles the payments, clearing the "due to's" and "due from's" off the balance sheets. If the market maker has a $100 deposit in his bank, the bank extinguishes it to cancel the "due from" it holds on its customer. The bank also delivers $100 in cash or borrows $100 from the seller's bank to settle its "due to" of $100. The seller's bank credits its customer with $100 of additional deposits and reduces its "due to" to its customer by $100.

In this case, the amount of deposits in the banking system does not expand. Already existing deposits are simply transferred from buyer to seller. The market maker himself holds all the liquidity that is needed to finance the acquisition.

Call Loans.   Typically, market makers do not devote large amounts of their capital to holding bank deposits. Instead, they may approach the banks for loans to finance their purchases, having previously established a line of credit. The banks can supply credit in the form of call loans to the market maker. The banks, however, must themselves finance the call loan.

Table 18.2 presents the end-of-day balance sheet changes if positions are fi-

Table 18.2   END-OF-DAY POSITIONS

Seller		Market Maker	
ASSETS	**LIABILITIES**	**ASSETS**	**LIABILITIES**
Stocks −$100		Stock +$100	Call loan from market maker's bank +$100
Bank deposits +$100			

Seller's Bank		Market Maker's Bank	
ASSETS	**LIABILITIES**	**ASSETS**	**LIABILITIES**
Interbank loan to market maker's bank +$100	Deposit by seller +$100	Call loan to market maker +$100	Interbank loan from seller's bank +$100

nanced through an expansion of call loans and deposits. The seller's stock assets fall by $100, but her bank deposits rise by $100. The market maker adds stock worth $100 to his assets, but he has new liabilities $100 in call loans from his bank.[4] The seller's bank has $100 of additional deposits, and the market maker's bank has additional assets of $100 in call loans. An easy way to handle this imbalance is for the seller's bank to make $100 interbank loan to the market maker's bank. Indeed, when the market maker's bank finds that it must deliver $100 at clearing time, it will seek an interbank loan.

Effectively, the seller of the stock has converted a direct claim on a long-term, risky security to an indirect claim. She now holds a bank deposit backed by her bank's assets, one of which is a claim on another bank with assets collateralized partly by the original shares. A string of credit and payment transactions intermediated by the banking system has permitted the stock transfer to proceed smoothly.

What happens if the banking system has no excess reserves and is therefore constrained from expanding deposits? The banks can still put these transactions through by selling $100 worth of some other security to another depositor or by not rolling over $100 of loans coming due. Doing this would remove $100 of other securities from the banking system's asset column and $100 of other deposits from its liabilities, thereby allowing the banks to supply $100 of deposits to the seller. Indeed, the seller herself may purchase one of the bank's assets rather than hold deposits. She could, for example, enter into a repurchase agreement for government securities held by the bank. In effect, the seller would then have swapped her stock

---

4. This assumes that the bank will finance the market maker's stock without requiring margin or equity from the market maker. If the bank requires some equity, and if the market maker has no further nonmargined assets, he will not get the necessary financing from the bank.

for a Treasury security, and the bank would have swapped a Treasury security for a call loan. To encourage one of its depositors to purchase a security, it would have to offer some price reduction or, equivalently, a higher yield. The sudden demand for liquidity in the stock market could thus push up interest rates in other markets.

Under the current rules governing reserve accounting in the United States, bank deposits can expand massively on any one day. Recall that required reserves are computed on the basis of average deposits over a 2-week accounting period. Therefore, banks can briefly finance market makers faced with carrying large positions. In the absence of increases in reserves by the Fed, however, the banks would later have to contract their deposits severely during the succeeding days of the reserve accounting period. Again, this would push up interest rates in their loan markets.

The Effect of Large Liquidity Demands on Stock Prices

In the preceeding examples, the banks are willing to provide enough liquidity for market makers to absorb the sudden stock sales. They would, however, charge market makers a rate of interest commensurate with the yields they forgo in the loan market. Market makers must earn at least the interest charge on carrying their stock positions. If they immediately find final buyers for the shares, their costs are small. The longer they must hold the stock until final buyers appear, the higher are their costs.

Market makers would therefore set their bid price sufficiently below their expectation of the ultimate equilibrium price, at which they would sell their inventory, to pay for expected interest charges. These charges depend on how long market makers expect it will take for final buyers to appear.

In brief, with a large magnitude of stock sales, there arises a larger demand for liquidity through the banking system. In turn, this increases the price of liquidity and depresses the market bid price.

What Happens When Banks Refuse to Lend on Stock Market Collateral?

In our examples of security transactions we have assumed that banks are willing to provide all the credit necessary to complete the transactions. Suppose now that the banks are unwilling to accept payment promises from the potential buyers, such as market makers, or even to make overnight loans to them.

To supply such credit, the banks must have confidence in the solvency of market makers and in their ability to clear their checks at the end of the day. Yet a sudden price fall of the sort that we have just studied would probably come as a surprise; no one would know the extent of the selling pressure. Banks might think that the market makers were jumping into the market at too high a price and might quickly become insolvent, wiping out a portion of the loans. The increased risk might cause the banks to hesitate on committing loans until the new equilibrium price became clear.

The cutoff of liquidity to the market would cause prices to fall well below the equilibrium $P^{\star\star}$ depicted in Figure 18.2. Of course, prices would eventually reach a level low enough that some market makers would be able to acquire the shares with their available liquidity. Also, banks would eventually realize that they could profit handsomely enough from high yields on call loans to justify the risk of lending. With a price P'' far enough below $P^{\star\star}$, market makers would recognize that they could profit from temporarily financing an increased securities inventory even with high-interest-rate call loans. Ultimate buyers also would eventually realize that market fundamentals justified the somewhat higher equilibrium price $P^{\star\star}$, and they eventually would relieve the market makers of their inventory. The losers would be the sellers playing a trading strategy based only on market price, which causes them to sell in the teeth of an illiquid market. The winners would be those long in cash or access to cash.

Snowballing Liquidity Problems

In our example we have assumed that only one group of sellers dumps stock at a given market price. Suppose now that several groups play stop-loss strategies; some sell at price $P^{\star}$, but progressively more groups sell as prices fall further. These groups may consist of more final holders of securities, but they also would consist of potential market makers who already hold inventories of securities financed by call loans.

A lack of liquidity in the market may cause a snowballing of sell orders. If the price falls below its equilibrium as a result of liquidity problems, further sales may be triggered. Banks may make margin calls on their loans to security holders. This may either bankrupt the security holders or force them to sell their stocks. In either case, it precludes their entry as market makers in the stock. This expanding volume of trades in the security generates an expanding demand for liquidity along with a possibly diminishing supply. See Box 18.1.

Banks as Market Makers in Liquidity

A snowballing liquidity event such as that associated with the 1929 stock market crash is fortunately extremely rare, although it is often invoked as a standard explanation of stock price collapses. The banking industry exists to seek out and supply liquidity as it is demanded. It is the ultimate market maker in cash. Other institutions may specialize in making markets in particular securities, but they simply serve to

Box 18.1

The Crash of 1929

The stock market **Crash of 1929** provides a prime example of the effect of margin-related sales on liquidity in the stock markets. At its peak at the beginning of September 1929, the Dow Jones industrial average (DJIA) was 381. It reached a low of 230 on October 29, 1929.* This was a fall of about 40 percent in 2 months. It may have been an appropriate price fall given changes in the underlying economy, but during the decline there were large price fluctuations as a result of sporadic liquidity problems.

Prices fell gradually until Wednesday, October 23, when a sudden price drop drove the DJIA to 305, a 1-day decline of 6 percent. An outburst of sell orders on October 24 ("Black Thursday") drove prices down temporarily by 33 points to 272. Trading volumes on this and succeeding days of the crash reached unusually high levels. This led to the intervention of a "Bankers' Pool" into the market, which provided sufficient liquidity so that prices closed down by only 6 points at 299. The Bankers' Pool was a group of New York City commercial and investment bankers that pooled funds together both to provide liquidity to the market and to speculate on stock. The Bankers' Pool was therefore equivalent to the market makers in our earlier examples.

The huge volume of trading during the week of Black Thursday caused delays in the assessment of customer positions. By the weekend, the New York Stock Exchange and its firms finally sorted out the losses, and margin calls to customers forced additional selling on Monday, October 28, and Tuesday, October 29. The DJIA fell to 230 on October 29, a 2-day loss of 20 percent. On October 30 and 31, prices rebounded to 273; they fell again to 231 by November 6.

At the end of September 1929, margin accounts in brokerage firms on the New York Stock Exchange (NYSE) amounted to $8.5 billion, or 9.8 percent of the market value of all shares trading on the exchange.† By the end of the year, margined accounts fell by $4.6 billion. The accompanying figure dramatically indicates the withdrawal of credit from the stock market. The following table shows the impact of margin-related sales on the total sales volume of the stock market.

Month	Percent Value of Margin Sales to All Sales	Value of Margin Debt	
		Total ($Millions)	Percent of Total NYSE Value
October 1929	23.3	$6109	8.51
November 1929	46.1	4017	6.32
December 1929	0.6	3990	6.17

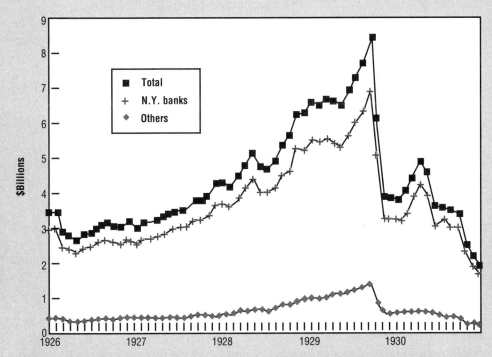

SOURCES OF NYSE BROKERS' LOANS *Source:* From Eugene N. White, "When the Ticker Ran Late: The Stock Market Boom and Crash of 1929," in Eugene N. White (Ed.), *Crashes and Panics: The Lessons From History*. Homewood, Ill.: Dow Jones-Irwin, 1990, p. 162.

The sudden price falls may be attributed to the liquidity impact of major sales associated either with margin calls or with individual stop-loss strategies. To marshall sufficient liquidity to handle the large sales volumes required a price fall large enough to compensate the market makers for their costs and the risks of buying for inventory. The rebound of prices signaled the market makers' chance to sell off their inventories to final holders. The liquidity problems then repeated themselves as additional stop-loss strategies, either explicit or implicit, were triggered by further assessments of stockholders' positions.

*For detailed information on price movements during the Crash of 1929, see Barrie Wigmore, *The Crash and its Aftermath* (Westport, Conn.: Greenwood Press, 1985), Chapter 1.

†See *Report of the Presidential Task Force on Market Mechanisms,* January 1988, pp. viii–13, for more details. This is the source of the data in the table.

pass on shifts in liquidity demand in their markets to the banking system. It is the banking system's business to match supplies and demands for liquidity. Usually the banking system is fully loaned up and cannot expand its balance sheet. It then makes the market in liquidity by shifting the components of its balance sheet among demanders of liquidity.

The Central Bank and the Provision of Liquidity

A large liquidity event may cause a large general increase in interest rates if the banks can respond only by shifting assets on their balance sheets and not by expanding the supply of liquidity. To encourage current depositors to swap deposits for assets currently on its balance sheet, a bank may have to offer a substantial price reduction. In turn, the bank must pass these costs on to the market makers in the form of high rates on call loans, thereby forcing a low stock price on the market and perhaps bankrupting market makers who are financing large stock inventories. Such bankruptcies may be very costly to sort out and may lead to a lack of confidence in trading institutions.

An alternative is possible, however. If a large security price movement is clearly the result of liquidity problems, costly bankruptcies of market makers can be avoided by a costless expansion of bank balance sheets to finance the market makers' holdings. Effectively, the sellers of the securities would lend to the banks through a deposit expansion, and the banks would lend to the market makers, as above. When the final buyers buy from the market makers, they would extinguish their bank deposits in exchange for the securities. The market makers would simultaneously extinguish their loans, and the banking system would contract back to a normal level, as we learned in the example of Table 18.2.

A banking system with no reserve requirements could undertake this liquidity expansion provided that depositors trusted the banks. In the U.S. system with required reserves, the expansion could be undertaken only through a simultaneous expansion of reserves at the Fed. Indeed, the Fed's policy of maintaining orderly financial markets—that is, of maintaining the "depth, breadth, and resiliency" of markets—aims rather vaguely at ensuring price continuity and narrow bid-ask spreads to prevent unnecessary losses arising purely from liquidity problems.

The Fed's role as lender of last resort means that it will buy eligible assets from banks in the presence of a liquidity disturbance. Provided that the additional reserves are left in the banks, the banks can then both replace these assets with loans to the financial sectors demanding liquidity and expand their balance sheets with further loans and deposits. If prices are depressed purely as a result of a liquidity event, then all these transactions can be quickly undone as the market makers sell their securities to the final buyers. The banks then can extinguish their loans to the dealers, and the Fed sells its newly acquired securities back to the banks. Bank and Federal Reserve balance sheets return to their preselloff sizes, and there is no monetary expansion. A perfect example of such a pure liquidity event is the Bank of New York computer collapse discussed in Chapter 12.

Example: The Crash of 1987. Now let us examine a popular explanation for what happened when the stock market crashed on Monday, October 19, 1987. Several studies have argued that an initial downward movement in stock prices was exacerbated by the existence of many large players using trigger-price strategies. Many used formal methods such as portfolio insurance; others used more informal stop-loss strategies. In addition, margin calls forced yet more sales. Together these created a liquidity event that caused extreme price fluctuations at the time of the crash.

Large stock price falls in the week prior to October 19 had weakened the liquidity positions of many potential market makers. These earlier falls may have been driven by changes in fundamental values—that is, changes in the underlying dividend earnings of the stocks or long-market discount rates. The initial price fall on October 19 alerted the computers of portfolio insurance managers. This led to orders to write futures contracts, driving down the price of the futures contracts and unstably widening the difference between stock and futures prices. Immediately the computers of the arbitragers were alerted that stock prices were high relative to futures market prices. They sold stock, further lowering the stock price, and bought stock index futures. Registering yet another decline in the stock price, portfolio insurers sold still more futures, widening the gap between spot and futures prices. The process continued and created a cumulative situation of ever-deepening decline, according to this line of argument.

Of course, for this argument to work—that is, to argue that the combination of program trading and portfolio insurance somehow caused a move of market values from fundamental values—requires that there be no other speculators in the market who recognize the opportunity and jump in to buy up stocks and move prices back. Somehow that group disappeared in 1987, and their disappearance removed the normal liquidity in the market. In fact, trading could not occur in many shares and in stock index futures, thereby destroying the illusion that everyone could liquidate to preserve capital value. Any individual could always cash out at the chosen floor value of his or her shares, but investors as a whole could not.

In a situation with no liquidity problems, this cumulative price collapse would normally occur only if the fundamental values of the shares suddenly declined. Of course, the pace of decline might be accelerated by the computerization of trades; the portfolio insurance/program trading combination would be one way in which the price drop would be implemented almost instantly. There is nothing inherently wrong with this combination of strategies if it is just a method of quickly moving prices to their fundamental values.

Figures 18.4 and 18.5 indicate that there were liquidity problems on October 19 and 20. Trading in S&P 500 index futures was dominated by portfolio insurance on both days, as indicated by the percentage of futures trading volume represented

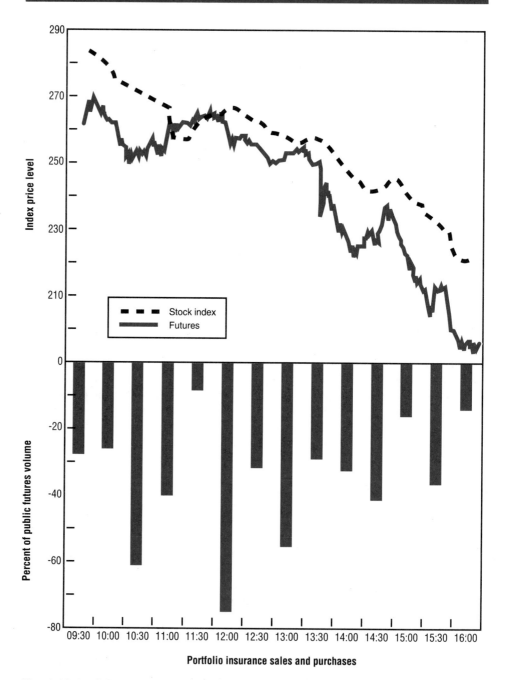

Figure 18.4   S&P 500 INDEX AND FUTURES CONTRACTS, MONDAY, OCTOBER 19, 1987 *Source:* From *Report of the Presidential Task Force on Market Mechanisms,* Washington, 1988, p. 31.

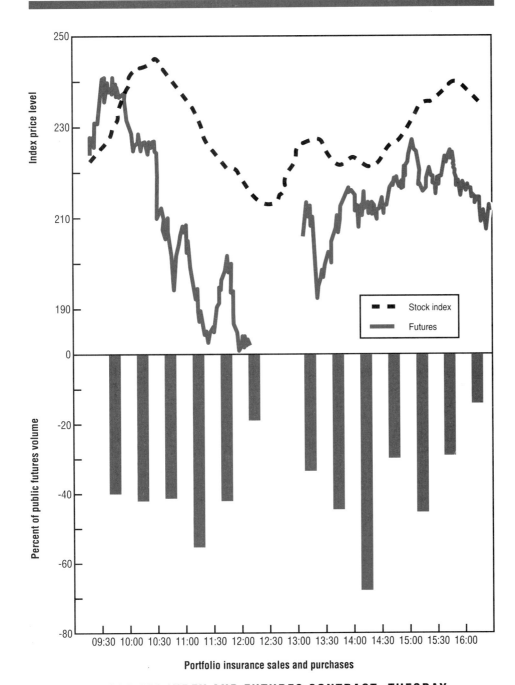

Figure 18.5   S&P 500 INDEX AND FUTURES CONTRACT, TUESDAY, OCTOBER 20, 1987 *Source:* From *Report of the Presidential Task Force on Market Mechanisms,* Washington, 1988, p. 31.

by portfolio insurance transactions. A wide spread developed between the stock and futures price indexes. The S&P 500 stock index dropped from 283 to 220 on October 19. On October 20, it jumped up to 240, fell back to about 210, began fluctuating as liquidity flowed back into the market, and ended day at 237, a bit more than 10 percent above its low for the day.

Banks became concerned with the position of brokerage firms on October 19 as exchange clearinghouses issued margin calls. This concern led banks to withdraw lines of credit from some firms and created a general reluctance to lend further to the markets. At 8:15 A.M. on Tuesday, October 20, the Fed announced, "The Federal Reserve affirms its readiness to serve as a source of liquidity to support the economic and financial system." In other words, it was prepared to lend to banks and make open-market purchases to increase reserves and provide liquidity to meet demands.

Nevertheless, on Tuesday, "some market makers did curtail their market making activities, especially in the case of block trading where temporary commitments of capital were required, because they feared that loans or credit lines from commercial banks might be exhausted or withdrawn."[5]

What Happens When a Central Bank Mistakes a Fundamental Price Decline for a Liquidity Problem?

In the context of Figure 18.3, everyone can foresee an increase in demand for liquidity, and a riskless increase in liquidity supply can be provided, as discussed earlier, to prevent fluctuations in other securities markets while the transfer of shares from sellers to final buyers is implemented.

What can we say about a situation such as that depicted in Figure 18.2, however, where the liquidity event comes as a surprise and the equilibrium price is uncertain? Suppose that market makers erroneously believe that P' will be the equilibrium price. They start buying securities at P' and demand liquidity to finance the position. Suppose that the central bank also believes that demands for liquidity at P' are reasonable and that a failure to supply them will trigger a needless liquidity crisis. It expands reserves and pressures the banks it regulates to make call loans collateralized by the securities evaluated at a price P'. It also pressures the banks not to issue margin calls to security holders with insufficient margin at price P'.

In this event, however, the central bank is incorrect. The security price eventually falls to $P**$, bankrupting the market makers and leaving bad loans on the books of the banks. If the central bank then reduces reserves to their original levels through security sales, the capital position of the banks will be weakened. Depositors will have less confidence in them, and they will be less able to provide liquidity services in the future.

Alternatively, to reduce the damage to the banks from this mistake, the central bank may not reduce reserves to their preselloff level. As we learned in earlier

---

5. This claim is from the *Report of the Presidential Task Force on Market Mechanisms,* 1988, p. 52. For additional descriptions of the disappearance of liquidity from the markets, see Sanford Grossman and Merton Miller, "Liquidity and Market Structure," *Journal of Finance,* July 1988, pp. 617–634.

chapters, doing this would lead to a permanent expansion of the money stock and a rise in the price level.

How would this inflation help the banks? Consider a bank's preselloff balance sheet in Table 18.3. Initially, as in panel (a), the bank has nominal assets of $900 million in loans and $100 million in reserves. It has $900 million in deposits and $100 million in capital. The required reserve ratio is 1/9, or 11 percent.

During the crash in stock prices, the central bank adds $100 million in reserves by buying Treasury securities on the open market. The bank adds the $100 million paid to the seller of the Treasury securities to its reserves and is pressured by the central bank into making $800 million in call loans to market makers buying at P'. These are balanced by an inflow of $900 million in new deposits with the expansion of its balance sheet. These changes are depicted in panel (b).

Suppose that the central bank, believing this to be a short-lived liquidity problem, intends soon to return reserves to their old $100 million level to avoid inflation. The stock will then be worth only $P^{\star\star}$ in this case. Suppose that the call loans will then be defaulted and be worth only $400 million on liquidation. The bank's capital will then be wiped out, and it will be unable to pay $300 million to its depositors.

To derive this result, remember that reserves will fall back to $100 million if the central bank sells securities for $100 million to a depositor at one of the banks. This immediately reduces deposits to $1.7 billion. The bank must now contract its deposits by another $800 million to meet reserve requirements. It can do this by selling some of the loans and securities taken as collateral for the defaulted call loans. The total value of its reserves, loans, and securities held as collateral is $1.4 billion (that is, $100 million + $900 million + $400 million). Against this, it has $1.7 billion remaining in deposit claims. It can sell the collateral, now worth $400 million, and $400 million in loans to reduce its deposits. This leaves it with a balance sheet as in panel (c). The bank is now insolvent.

If the central bank does not extinguish the new reserves, the money supply and price level eventually will approximately double. This should double the nominal price of the stock to $2 \times P^{\star\star}$. Suppose that the value of the stock collateral now exceeds the nominal amount of the call loans. The call loans will then all be repaid to the bank. The bank's reserves, loans, and deposits will still have the nominal values of panel (b). The nominal value of bank capital is still $100 million. The bank has moved from insolvency to solvency. Its real size has fallen in half (its nominal value divided by the doubled price level), but the price level increase has preserved its role as a market maker in cash.

Here we have a case where a central bank acts to maintain orderly securities markets by channeling liquidity through the banking system to support purchases by market makers. If the price fall has arisen only from a momentary liquidity problem, the intervention will stabilize security prices at little cost. The central bank has extended liquidity to a set of securities and thereby increased their values. If the price should fall for fundamental reasons, however, the central bank's intervention through the banking system will cause a large amount of potentially bad loans to be made, thereby threatening banks and market makers. The central bank is then

Table 18.3 BALANCE SHEET EFFECTS OF CALL LOAN DEFAULT ($MILLIONS)

a. Preselloff Bank Balance Sheet

ASSETS		LIABILITIES	
Reserves	100	Deposits	900
Loans	900	Capital	100

b. After Provision of Liquidity to the Stock Market

ASSETS		LIABILITIES	
Reserves	200	Deposits	1,800
Loans	900	Capital	100
Call loans	800		

c. After Default

ASSETS		LIABILITIES	
Reserves	100	Deposits	900
Loans	500	Capital	−300

Box 18.2

The Mississippi Bubble: Using Liquidity to Support Stock Prices

The **Mississippi Bubble** of 1719–1720 is considered one of the most famous examples of a speculative mania. Actually, it is a better example of what happens when a central bank attempts to peg the value of a stock at a level well above its fundamental value. It is the first case of the operation of a system of "managed currency," a system based purely on the use of paper legal tender currency of the sort that has dominated modern economies since 1971.

John Law was the financial genius behind the Mississippi Bubble. A Scotsman, Law became an important financier in France, forming a bank in 1716. Years earlier, Law had published a book on economic activity in which he argued that a depressed economy could grow if firms could issue securities that circulated as money—that is, the securities should be highly liquid to maximize demand for them.* The funds from such securities sales would then be used to undertake profitable investments that would in turn justify the high value attached to the original securities. Law argued that the increase in the supply of money would not cause inflation—instead, it would increase real money demand because it would cause an expansion of real income.

In 1716, France was impoverished, having just emerged from the long series of wars of Louis XIV with a huge national debt. Winning the political favor of the Regent of France because of the attractiveness of his monetary theories and his skill in finance, Law formed the Compagnie des Indes in 1719. In a short period, Law's company had taken over all the colonial trading companies of France through mergers and acquisitions. This included a monopoly right to develop the colony in Louisiana, from which the name Mississippi Bubble comes. In addition, as his power grew, Law bought the rights to the French mint and to the collection of all French taxes. He also refinanced the entire national debt starting in the fall of 1719 with a series of exchanges of Compagnie des Indes stock for government bonds that would continue through 1720. Effectively, he privatized most of the French Treasury under his company, and he became officially the Controller General of the French Treasury in January 1720.

Simultaneously, his bank was nationalized as the Banque Royale, placed under Law's control, and given the right to issue legal tender paper money known as *livre tournois*.

Throughout this growth process, Law issued ever-increasing numbers of shares in the Compagnie des Indes to finance his acquisitions. Share prices rose from 500 livres per share to 10,000 livres per share in 6 months. By January 1720, the market value of all shares issued reached about 5 billion livres, about one-sixth of all the wealth of France. The movement of share prices is indicated in the accompanying Figure A.

Unfortunately, not everything was as it seemed. The Banque Royale had issued increasing amounts of paper currency in 1719 to provide liquidity to market the new stock issues—

*The book was John Law's *Money and Trade Considered: With a Proposal for Supplying the Nation with Money.* Glasgow: Foulis, 1760.

Box 18.2 (continued)

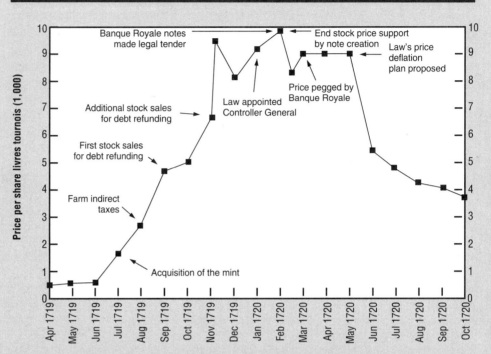

Figure A   COMPAGNIE DES INDES STOCK PRICE   *Source:* From Peter M. Garber, "Famous First Bubbles," *Journal of Economic Perspectives,* Spring 1990, pp. 35–54.

that is, it made loans to speculators and market makers. As the newly issued stock and the debt refinancing hit the markets in 1719 and early 1720, the Banque Royale began to increase the supply of liquidity very rapidly. The paper currency in circulation more than doubled from 600 million livres to 1.3 billion livres in early 1720 (see accompanying Figure B). Nevertheless, the increasing supply of company shares began to depress the market price below 10,000 livres. Law resolved to peg the share price at 9,000 livres in March 1720 and intervened actively for the next 3 months.

How could Law peg the value of one-sixth of French wealth? This is simple when you control the supply of legal tender. He required the Banque Royale to exchange paper currency for shares at the pegged price. The effect of this intervention was a further doubling of the Banque Royale's notes from 1.3 billion lives to 2.7 billion livres in 3 months. Also as

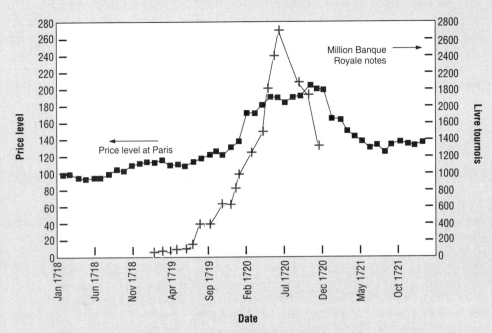

Figure B MISSISSIPPI BUBBLE MONEY AND PRICE DATA   *Source:* From Peter M. Garber, "Famous First Bubbles," *Journal of Economic Perspectives,* Spring 1990, pp. 35–54.

a result of this policy, the shares outstanding were effectively converted into 9,000-livre notes.

As you might expect, the effect of providing liquidity to prop the stock market at the "wrong" level was an inflation. As depicted in Figure B, the price level nearly doubled in 1 year. Recognizing that his pegging operation was inflationary, Law ceased the Banque Royale's intervention and began to withdraw its currency from circulation. The result was a collapse of share price to 2,000 livres in a few months and a significant reduction of the price level.

Many investors in his company suffered great losses, and together with his political enemies, they forced Law to flee France. Although he initially became very wealthy from this experiment, Law believed in his program, so he never protected his wealth by putting it into assets outside France. As a result, he was impoverished by the collapse of his scheme. The French had moved so rapidly from extreme optimism for the prospects of Law's enterprise to despair that for many decades after 1720 the word *"banque"* carried a negative meaning, an attitude that retarded the development of French finance.

left with a choice. It can allow the banking system to collapse so that many other markets will be left without a liquidity source until the system can be reorganized. Alternatively, it can restore the banks directly through an inflation. We can conclude that in deciding the nature of markets that it wishes to make liquid, a central bank always faces the tension between the potential losses that may arise either through general inflation or bankruptcy of the banking system and the gains in security values that arise from added liquidity. See Box 18.2.

BANKING CRISES

Outbreaks of illiquidity in financial markets have often occurred and still occur, even without problems in the banking sector. The major panic of 1914 and the stock market crashes of 1929 and 1987 occurred without banking panics, and illiquidities have recently broken out in commercial paper markets and in markets for foreign currencies without banking difficulties.

In many historical cases, however, financial crises and banking panics have broken out simultaneously. A **banking panic** occurs when a large segment of the banking system's creditors demand delivery of more liquidity than the affected banks can supply. From 1793 to 1857, the United States experienced 11 large banking panics, and major banking panics also occurred in 1873, 1893, 1907, 1930, 1931, and 1933. Since 1933, after the advent of deposit insurance and active Federal Reserve intervention, there have been no large banking panics, even though large segments of the banking system have occasionally become insolvent. Those runs which have occurred, such as that on Continental Illinois Bank in 1984, have typically been caused by uninsured large depositors of insolvent banks attempting to extract their funds. Usually, even in these cases, the Federal Reserve provides sufficient loans to the banks to permit the large depositors to withdraw their funds without loss, thereby effectively insuring them.

What Happened in Widespread Bank Runs?

As financial institutions with very short-term liabilities, banks are required to deliver cash, or good funds, to their creditors on short notice. The cash or reserves held by banks is a small fraction of bank liabilities, and banks cannot themselves create cash. This makes the banking system as a whole vulnerable to illiquidities if depositors suddenly demand payment.

For any one bank, sudden large withdrawals need not be a great problem provided that it has lines of credit with other banks. We saw in an earlier chapter that membership in a clearinghouse provides a bank a natural source of funds. If the withdrawals take the form of depositors writing large amounts of checks for deposit in other banks, the bank will have a net clearinghouse debit at the end of the day. As a clearinghouse member, it can call on other member banks to lend it funds collateralized by its liquid assets. Deposits will simply be replaced by interbank loans on the liability side of its balance sheet. Other banks will balance their new deposit liabilities with loans to the affected bank.[6]

If depositors distrust the banking system enough to withdraw and hoard cash rather than to redeposit it, the reserves held by the clearinghouse and its members may not be sufficient to pay off depositors. Then banks have to call in loans to get cash or dump loans on the market for what they will bring. These actions raise interest rates, reduce the value of the banks' asset portfolio, and thus encourage hoarders of cash to return it to the banks. The calling of loans also reduces the liquidity available to the securities markets and causes sudden price declines, thereby converting the banking crisis into a financial crisis. If continued attempts to pay cash to depositors threaten the solvency of the banks, banks finally suspend cash payments to their remaining liability holders.

A suspension of convertibility of deposits to cash causes the deposit price of cash to rise—that is, a market arises in which $1 of cash exchanges for more than $1 of bank deposits. The interbank payments system, however, can continue to operate with net "due to's" covered by interbank lending. This situation continues until cash hoarders redeposit enough funds in the banking system for convertibility to be reestablished.

The Fragility of a Banking System and the Contagion of Fear

Economists have several explanations for why large numbers of depositors suddenly demand payment in cash from large segments of the banking industry. Elements of each explanation are probably present in varying degrees in each panic episode. The first and probably most widely invoked explanation for widespread bank runs turns on the fragility of a fractional reserve banking system when the supply of cash cannot be expanded rapidly. If depositors suddenly demand cash for their deposits

---

6. Private clearinghouses prearranged lines of credit to members to handle periodic problems with individual banks. The clearinghouse regulated and examined the activities of its members, and if the clearinghouse believed that a bank facing large withdrawals was sound, other members would lend to it freely. See Gary Gorton, "Clearinghouses and the Origins of Central Banking in the U.S.," *Journal of Economic History*, No. 42 (June 1985), pp. 277–284, for a detailed discussion of the behavior of pre-Fed clearinghouses. Also see Gary Gorton and Donald Mullineaux, "The Joint Production of Confidence: Endogenous Regulation and 19th Century Commercial Bank Clearinghouses," *Journal of Money Credit and Banking*, Vol. 19. No. 4 (1987), pp. 455–468 and R. Timberlake, "The Central Banking Role of Clearing Associations," *Journal of Money Credit and Banking*, Vol. XVI, No. 1, (February 1984), pp. 1–15.

and hoard all the cash they receive, it is impossible for the entire banking system to acquire sufficient cash to pay off all its depositors. Dumping its securities on the asset markets in the presence of no source of liquidity would only depress securities prices, thereby making the banking system insolvent.

With a fragile banking system, it is easy to invoke psychological forces or crowd behavior to explain banking panics. Depositors simultaneously awaken with a belief that all other depositors are about to withdraw their funds from banks. Among individual depositors, this leads to a **contagion of fear** that their deposits will be lost or at least frozen if they do not immediately run to the bank and convert their deposits to cash. Given that they believe that all other depositors are about to run the bank, it is rational for each individual depositor to run to the bank, and this ratifies the original belief. If the banks attempt to keep paying out cash, the banking system may indeed become insolvent. If it suspends cash payments, it may disrupt the payments plans of depositors. In either case, it is reasonable for the depositor to attempt to withdraw cash.[7]

Of course, the banking system was always fragile in this way, yet system-wide banking panics occurred only infrequently. What would cause the psychologies of depositors to congeal at one moment to foment a panic? One possibility is that the publicly reported insolvency of an important bank or other financial institution might lead everyone to believe that all depositors were about to react by withdrawing funds. This would be sufficient to trigger the liquidity crisis.

Widespread Bank Runs as a Way to Audit Bank Solvency

In an alternative explanation, a sudden publicly reported insolvency of an important financial institution is also key in triggering a system-wide bank run.[8] The emphasis in this explanation, however, is on depositor concerns about the solvency of their own banks and not on possible temporary illiquidities in the banking system.

A sudden important bankruptcy alerts depositors that financial institutions may not have been as carefully audited and regulated as they had thought. Depositors then worry not so much about the behavior of other depositors as about the solvency of their own bank. They wonder if their bank has been run poorly and if it is holding bad assets on its books. Each individual depositor does not worry about what other depositors will do or if his or her bank will be temporarily illiquid. Rather, each

7. The contagion of fear approach is the dominating explanation in Milton Friedman and Anna Schwartz's classic, *A Monetary History of the U.S.* (Princeton, N.J.: Princeton University Press, 1963). A more recent formal theory expounding this view can be found in Douglas Diamond and Phillip Dybvig, "Bank Runs, Deposit Insurance, and Liquidity," *Journal of Political Economy,* June 1983, pp. 401–419.

8. This explanation is proposed formally in Gary Gorton, "Bank Suspension and Convertibility," *Journal of Monetary Economics,* March 1985, pp. 177–194.

worries about getting his or her funds out of the bank before it is declared insolvent and he or she is forced to wait through claims in long bankruptcy hearings. Thus this is not a panic contagion of fear having to do with the chronic lack of liquidity in the system; it is a well-founded response to possible insolvency. Withdrawals under these circumstances may cause a system-wide liquidity problem, but illiquidity is not the driving force.

Many banks in the system will not suffer a run because their depositors remain confident in their solvency. To get loans from such strong banks or, equivalently, to continue to use the clearing system, banks that do suffer a run will submit themselves to audits by their clearinghouses or by lender banks. These institutions will examine the assets of the run banks and base loans on the quality of the assets. That the run banks can receive large loans from other banks in their clearinghouse signals depositors that their banks have successfully passed an audit and that they are probably solvent after all. Depositors will then readily redeposit their withdrawn funds, and the bank can resume normal operation.

If a bank really is insolvent, an audit by other banks will preclude its receiving loans, and the run will close it down. Thus a bank run serves as the market's method of forcing poorly run banks out of operation. This actually may benefit a bank's depositors, because the management of an insolvent bank that is still operating is tempted to make highly risky gambles to put itself back "above water," as we will see in Chapter 20 when we study the S&L crisis of the late 1980s.

To the extent that the remaining assets can be sold at reasonable prices, a bank closing protects the depositors from the burden of further losses to the capital value of their deposits at the cost of making deposits illiquid. More generally, the cost of throwing out the bad apples all at once is a liquidity crisis in the banking and financial system.

Banking Panics as Corners of the Money Market

Prior to the existence of the Fed, mobilizable cash reserves always lay in the hands of only a few money-center banks, members of the New York Clearinghouse Association. There has always been a suspicion that these banks took advantage of liquidity problems in other financial institutions to squeeze, or corner, the money markets through what was known as the "**Money Trust.**"[9] Indeed, the power to expand cash reserves granted to the Fed served to make such corners impossible.

A Stock Market Corner. To understand the rather grandiose concept of a money market corner, it is useful first to paint a simple picture of a corner in the stock market. Such corners, of course, are currently illegal price manipulations under

---

9. R. Glen Donaldson, "Interbank Trade and the Financing of Bank Panics," Financial Research Center Memorandum 124, Princeton University, 1991, provides the only formal model of how such a corner or squeeze might occur.

Table 18.4 FINANCING SHARES WITH CALL LOANS

Stockholder				Broker			
ASSETS		LIABILITIES		ASSETS		LIABILITIES	
Shares owed by broker on call	100	Broker's call loan	$100	Shares	100	Shares owed to stockholder on call	100
Bank deposits	$100	Net worth	$100	Call loan to stockholder	$100	Call loan from bank	$100

Short Seller				Bank			
ASSETS		LIABILITIES		ASSETS		LIABILITIES	
				Reserves	$ 10	Deposits of stockholder	$100
				Call loan to broker	$100	Capital	$ 10

the Securities Act of 1933. Even prior to their illegality, corners were hard to pull off, even by the greatest stock market operators.

Table 18.4 depicts the balance sheets of several stock market players: a holder of stock, the holder's broker, a short seller of stock and her broker, and a bank providing call loans to the market. Each balance sheet portrays the initial position of each player. Each of these players is representative of a large group of competitive players assuming a similar role.

The stock owner has bought 100 shares of stock on margin for a total of $100 and has deposited them with his broker as collateral. We will assume a zero margin requirement for simplicity. In his asset column, he has a claim on 100 shares of stock from the broker; he also has $100 of bank deposits. As liabilities, he has $100 of call loans from the broker. He also has $100 of net worth. He can call for delivery of the shares from the broker at any time by paying off the call loan.

We will register the 100 actual shares as assets of the broker, although he is only holding them as collateral. The broker also holds a $100 promissory note from her client in the form of the call loan. As liabilities, the broker has borrowed $100 in a call loan from the bank and owes 100 shares of stock to her client. Notice that the cash and stock assets and liabilities of the broker are perfectly balanced; she is unaffected by changes in stock prices and interest rates.

The bank has $100 of call loans to the broker and $10 of cash reserves financed by $100 in deposits and $10 of capital.

Now suppose that another customer of the broker wishes to speculate on a price decline by short selling the stock. He borrows the 100 shares from the broker, sells them on the market for $100 and deposits the $100 with the broker as collateral against the delivery of the stock. The broker deposits the $100 in the bank. The broker's and short seller's new balance sheets are given in Table 18.5. The broker has lent out the original 100 shares, so they are removed from the balance sheet but

Table 18.5 CORNERING A SHORT SELLER

Stockholder

ASSETS		LIABILITIES	
Shares owed by broker on call	100	Broker's call loan	$100
Shares	100	Net worth	$100

Broker

ASSETS		LIABILITIES	
Shares owed by short seller on call	100	Shares owed to stockholder on call	100
Bank deposits	$100	Call loan from bank	$100
Call loan to stockholder	$100	Deposits of short seller	$100

Short Seller

ASSETS		LIABILITIES	
Deposit with broker	$100	Shares owed to broker on call	100

Bank

ASSETS		LIABILITIES	
Reserves	$ 10	Deposits of broker	$100
Call loan to broker	$100	Capital	$ 10

are replaced by the short seller's promise to deliver 100 shares on demand from the broker. In addition, the broker adds a liability of $100 on demand to the short seller and an asset of $100 in bank deposits. For the bank, the only change is a reduction of $100 in the deposits of whoever buys the shorted stock. The broker's deposits rise by $100.

Why might the stockholder and short seller decide to take these positions? If the stockholder expects the price of stock to rise, he can profit by buying stock and financing with call loans. If the price actually does rise, he keeps the difference between the shares' value and the loan. If prices fall, however, the broker will make a margin call, insisting on the delivery of cash or other liquid securities to increase the collateral. To avoid having his stock position sold out, the stockholder must have access to liquidity; he must be able to sell some other asset for cash or to have it accepted as collateral. For the short seller, the situation is reversed. He wins on a price fall and loses on a rise. If prices rise, the short seller must top up his cash collateral to prevent the broker from calling in the shares that he owes.

For simplicity, let us assume that the new buyer of the shares is the original holder of the shares. His balance sheet in Table 18.5 indicates a rise in actual shares held of 100 shares and a reduction in bank deposits of $100.

Finally, suppose that the 100 shares constitute all the shares available on the market. If the holder of the shares calls for the delivery of the shares owed to him and withholds the actual shares from the market, neither the broker nor the short seller can purchase shares at any price to make good their commitment. The holder of the shares has **cornered the market.** He has contracts obliging others to deliver a certain commodity or security to him on call, yet he controls the entire available supply of the security. He can name the cash price of shares at which he will allow

Box 18.3

The Panic of 1907

The **Panic of 1907** provides an example of how a money market corner might occur. It was set off October 1907 when a syndicate of stock operators tried to corner the stock in a copper company, the equivalent action of the stockholder in Table 18.5. The syndicate, whose position was financed by several banks and trust companies, failed in its attempt to corner the stock, and the market price of the copper stock plummeted. The syndicate failed because it could not get sufficient liquidity in the form of call loans from banks to keep the price of shares high. This caused depositors to question the solvency of the syndicate's banks, which had made large loans against the collateral of the collapsed stock, and led to bank runs.

The bank runs spread to the larger trust companies, notably the Knickerbocker Trust and the Trust Company of America. These trust companies were state-chartered New York banks that held relatively few cash reserves. They attempted to raise cash by calling in their call loans to brokers, which triggered a rapid price decline in the stock and bond markets. Thus breaking the corner attempt generated a generally increased demand for liquidity.

the broker and short seller to settle their obligation to him in cash, and he will generally seek a good portion of their wealth.

Of course, this is a transparent case of a corner that both the broker and short seller can recognize. If the short sellers do not know that the available supply of shares is under the control of a single individual, they may fall into a corner. They may believe that the stock price has been bid higher than some appropriate value and attempt to profit from an anticipated fall.

The short sellers may even be correct in their beliefs. If the stockholder is consciously attempting a corner, he may try to drive the stock price above an appropriate value. Two circumstances make this possible. First, the stockholder must have access to sufficient liquidity to finance his growing purchases at increasing prices. Second, the potential short sellers must lack the liquidity to take an increasing short position.

The stock price in this situation departs from some reasonable underlying value for reasons having nothing to do with the stock itself. Rather, the market is simply betting on which side has greater access to liquidity. Corners are about access to liquidity, not about the specific security involved in the corner.

The solvency of members of the New York Clearinghouse Association, primarily large national banks rich in cash reserves, was not in question. Typically, in times of liquidity crisis, these banks would pool all their reserves under one manager to be marketed to those demanding liquidity. The natural manager of the pool was the premier investment banker of the day, J. P. Morgan, who was in a position to evaluate all the securities in the market. Remember that in times of liquidity crisis, those who have shorted cash in financial contracts have their short position called. They must either deliver cash or have their collateral sold out on the market. Yet, in this case, there was no liquidity on the market because only one player controlled all the available liquidity. The cash market was cornered, and the short players had to make their best deal with Morgan, exchanging securities for cash at low prices.

Bank suspensions rose as a result of runs, and stock prices collapsed, creating demands for liquidity and raising call loan rates. Total deposits fell as they were converted to currency hoarded by the public. Clearinghouse banks sold their cash in exchange for large amounts of securities.

The clearinghouse banks did serve as a large supplier of liquidity, and Morgan was credited with having reduced the potential severity of the panic. Nevertheless, it was generally recognized that with no possibility of expanding legal tender cash in crises, there was a continuing risk of money market corners. This realization generated an effort to nationalize the function of providing liquidity in times of crisis, from which emerged the Federal Reserve Act of 1913.

A Money Market Corner. Now let's turn to the meaning of a money market corner. Again, consider each player's position in Table 18.5. This time, however, push their stock positions to the back of your mind and focus on their cash positions. The stockholder has sold cash short: He has promised to deliver cash on call. The other players are long in cash; each player's cash position is just the opposite of his or her stock positions.

Suppose that the bank controls all the available cash and that the broker calls in the stockholder's loan. The only source of funds for the stockholder is either the bank itself or one of the bank's depositors. If neither the bank nor its depositor will provide a loan to replace the broker's loan, the stockholder will have to market his shares for what they will bring to get cash to pay off the loan.

Effectively, the combination of the broker and the bank have cornered the money market. They hold contracts obliging others to deliver cash while controlling all the available cash. They can name the share price of cash at which they will allow the stockholder to settle his obligation to them in shares.

Note that breaking up an attempt at a stock corner involves cutting the liquidity

Box 18.4

The Hunt Brothers' Silver Corner and the Fed's Corner on Money

Although it was formed specifically to prevent liquidity crises, the Fed itself occasionally restricts the availability of liquidity when it believes that excessive bank credit is channeled into speculative activities rather than into production and distribution activities. The collapse of the silver speculation of 1979–1980 provides a classic example of this, showing that a corner on liquidity can counter a corner on a commodity or a security.

In this speculation, Nelson Bunker Hunt and William Herbert Hunt acquired a large portion of the available supply of silver bullion and coin while simultaneously buying a huge quantity of silver futures contracts. Since the Hunts were buying futures, other speculators were selling silver futures or going short silver. Since the Hunts also controlled most of the deliverable supply, they were in a position to work a classic corner on silver. The extent of the Hunt brothers' holdings is shown in the accompanying table.

The speculation occurred in the last 3 months of 1979 and the first 3 months of 1980, finally collapsing on March 27, 1980. During this period, the silver holdings of the Hunts or of corporations controlled by them reached a peak of 123 million ounces. The total industrial silver use in the United States was 175 million ounces in 1979, and the total world supply of silver in 1979 was 425 million ounces. In addition, other speculators allied with the Hunt brothers acquired large silver holdings. Together, this group controlled most of the deliverable supply.

Simultaneously, the Hunt brothers acquired a large number of commitments under which they could demand delivery of silver on the futures markets, the Comex in New York and the Chicago Mercantile Exchange. A silver futures contract is a commitment to deliver silver at a given date in the future for a price agreed on now. If you buy a contract, you are commiting to deliver a market-determined amount of cash for a standard unit of 5,000 ounces of silver.

As security that you will carry out your promise, you must deposit a cash margin with your broker. At the time, the required margin was about 5 percent of the value of the contract, which was 5,000 ounces multiplied by the futures price. Similarly, the seller of the contract must deposit a cash margin to guarantee that she will deliver the silver. The margin deposit is adjusted at the end of each day depending on the day's change in the price of new futures contracts. If the futures price rises, the value of the silver to be delivered rises relative to the originally contracted cash payment plus the margin deposit, so the short seller must increase her cash deposit with her broker. Since the value of the silver receivable by the buyer plus his margin deposit has risen relative to the cash that he must deliver, the buyer can withdraw cash from his broker.* If the price falls, the opposite adjustments are made.

Note that price changes entail demands for liquidity. If margin calls are not met, positions must be sold immediately.

*The cash paid by the short seller is simply transferred to the account of the buyer of the contract through the futures exchange's clearing system at the end of each day.

HUNT BROTHERS' SILVER AND SILVER FUTURES HOLDINGS (MILLIONS OF OUNCES)

	August 1, 1979	January 1, 1980	March 28, 1980	May 2, 1980
Silver bullion and coins	42	87	123	71
Futures contracts on futures markets	74	93	9	3
Other forward contracts	—	3	12	11
Loans from banks and brokers with silver collateral ($millions)	308	271	953	391

Source: From U.S. House of Representatives, Subcommittee of the Committee on Government Operations, *Hearings: Silver Prices and the Adequacy of Federal Actions in the Marketplace,* 1979–80, H.R. 97-395, 96th Congress, 2d Session, 1980.

The accompanying figure depicts the effects of these transactions on the futures prices for silver in 1979 and 1980, and the effect on the spot, or cash, price was similar. The price had been around $5 per ounce for years, but it suddenly jumped to $10 at the end of 1979, reaching a peak between $40 and $50 per ounce at the end of January 1980. It remained at about $35 per ounce until March 1980, when it collapsed to $12 per ounce.

While prices rose, the Hunts faced no problems with liquidity. Margin calls went to sellers of futures contracts, and the Hunts could draw on their margin accounts to finance further spot silver and futures contract acquisitions.

Pressure against the silver speculation quickly took the form of an attack against the Hunts' liquidity. In October 1979, the Fed asked its member banks to avoid making loans for speculation in commodities, but the banks paid little attention to this request. The authorities on the futures markets steadily increased margin requirements against contracts. In January 1980, to force the Hunts to sell off contracts, the exchanges placed ceilings of 2,000 contracts on speculators' positions.

These actions drove the futures prices to below $29.75 per ounce by March 10, 1980. To meet margin calls and finance their positions, the Hunts had to borrow heavilily from brokers and banks, as indicated in the accompanying table, absorbing 13 percent of all new bank credit in the United States during February and March.† On March 14, the Fed requested once again that banks limit the extension of credit for commodity speculation. By March 27, the Hunts could not acquire sufficient cash to meet margin calls, and their positions began to be sold, driving the price of silver immediately to $12 per ounce. The Hunt brothers absorbed a loss of $1 billion on their broken attempt to corner the silver market.

You should note that the inability of the Hunt brothers to meet margin calls at the time did not indicate that they were insolvent. The Hunts were immensely wealthy, with stocks in

†See U.S. House of Representatives, Subcommittee of the Committee on Government Operations, Hearings: *Silver Prices and the Adequacy of Federal Actions in the Marketplace, 1979–80* (H.R. 97-395, 96th Congress, 2d Session, 1980), pp. 58 and 148.

Box 18.4 (continued)

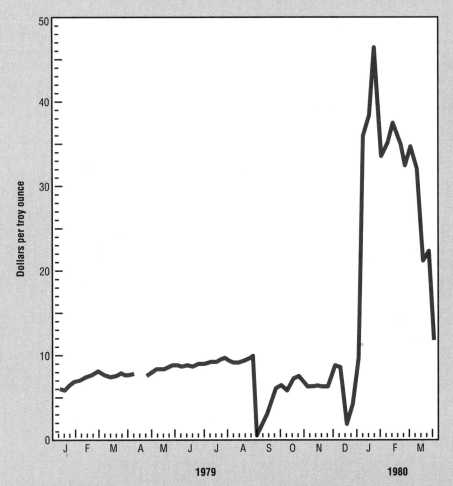

SILVER: NEAREST FUTURES CONTRACT, CHICAGO BOARD OF TRADE, JANUARY 1979 to MARCH 1980 *Source:* U.S. House of Representatives, *Hearings: Silver Prices and the Adequacy of Federal Actions in the Marketplace, 1979–80,* H.R. 97-395, 96th Congress, 2d Session, 1981, p. 38.

oil and other industries far exceeding the value of their margin requirements. Lenders normally would have unhesitatingly extended loans against such collateral. The central bank, however, cut this source of liquidity and effectively cornered the Hunts in the money market.

of the stockholder attempting the corner. A corner on cash is the countermove to an attempted corner on a security or commodity.

Of course, the pre-Fed money market was so large and competitive that it would have been a rare event for a money market corner to have occurred. However, the very scale of such a corner would imply that it would be associated with a large financial crisis, since most securities were financed on call loans. Such a withdrawal of liquidity would have generated a precipitous decline in the cash prices of securities. Banks with large cash reserves to inspire the confidence of their depositors, such as clearinghouse members, would have been in a position to buy securities cheaply. Other banks with small cash reserves might suffer runs when their depositors observed the fall in the market value of their assets; these banks would not be in a position to extend call loans or purchase dumped securities. See Boxes 18.3 and 18.4.

THE CME LIQUIDITY CRISIS: PAYMENTS SYSTEM LIQUIDITY AVERTS FINANCIAL CHAOS

So far we have developed a scenario in which a central bank can provide liquidity to a market under stress, thereby alleviating any liquidity problems. We have not examined technical details on the timing of the provision of liquidity. Now we will consider a concrete case of liquidity crisis on the S&P 500 index futures market of the Chicago Mercantile Exchange that occurred on October 20, 1987. This case provides a striking example of how gridlock in the payments system can trigger a liquidity crisis. It also shows how suddenly a liquidity problem may materialize and how timely and well directed a central bank provision of liquidity must be to contain the problem.

The Chicago Mercantile Exchange Clearing House (CMECH) normally calculates initial and variation margins on its contracts after the day's trading has been verified. At 5:00 A.M. the next day, the CMECH distributes payment or collect messages to four Chicago banks designated as settlement banks. Each member of the exchange maintains accounts for itself and its customers at one or more settlement banks. Settlement banks receive a pay message for customers and members who must add to their margins and a collect message for those who are to receive payment in their margin accounts. By 7:00 A.M., each settlement bank must confirm that it will make all required payments to the CMECH on behalf of its customers.

On October 20, 1987—the day after the stock market crash—settlement banks delayed their confirmations that they would make the payments of margin calls for some large member firms with sizable obligations from the previous day's trading. The Chicago settlement banks were unwilling to guarantee that payments would be made until they verified that sufficient funds had been transferred to them from the member firms' New York banks.

Normally, the firms' lines of credit with the settlement banks were large enough to provide funds for margin payments if their deposit accounts were short of funds. On October 20, however, the payments required were so large that they exceeded the firms' lines of credit. The settlement banks did not wish to expand the lines because of credit risk and a potential liquidity problem. If they had given the firms deposit credit, the settlement would have proceeded. Customers receiving margin would have immediately received credits in their deposit accounts in Chicago. However, the customers might have immediately swept these funds into their accounts in New York.

The settlement banks would then have gone immediately into a net debit position on funds transfer over Fedwire at the start of the business day. Recall that the Federal Reserve places a cap on daylight overdrafts of Fed accounts for individual banks. It also caps total overdraft lending by one bank to clearing members of futures exchanges. Having their funds swept out at the start of business would immediately have placed the settlement banks over their cap, thereby forcing them to the fed funds market to gain liquidity. In brief, the settlement banks did not want to start business short of liquidity on the day of the largest liquidity crisis in half a century.

In addition, if the firms receiving credit did not move funds back into their accounts before the end of the day, the settlement banks would have been forced to make them overnight loans, exceeding the prudential limits imposed by the Fed on such credit.

Frantic early morning calls were made to the New York banks to get payments sent to Chicago over Fedwire, but in the prebusiness hours the relevant bank officials could not be found. Finally, officials at the Federal Reserve assured the Chicago banks that sufficient liquidity would be available to them directly, and they committed to extend funds to the clearing members. Settlement of the previous day's margin was made just prior to the opening of trade on October 20. We should notice, however, that a general liquidity increase by the Fed through open-market purchases would not have alleviated this problem, since such funds would have gone to banks in New York initially.

CONCLUSION

Liquid securities markets require the availability of a market maker ready to supply cash immediately in exchange for sales and to supply securities in exchange for cash. Occasionally, selling or buying pressures may overwhelm the available liquidity in the market, leading to price discontinuities and cascading sales or purchases known as crashes or panics.

As the market maker in cash, the banking system plays a key role in supplying liquidity to the securities market through loans to market makers. Private banks, however, may lack a sufficient supply of liquidity to stem a liquidity crisis. A central bank's most basic role is to provide sufficient liquidity to ensure that liquidity crises do not occur in financial markets. The central bank must determine whether a large price fall in securities markets arises from a liquidity problem or from a dramatic change in underlying securities values. If it is a liquidity problem, an intervention will stabilize the markets and prevent needless bankruptcies. If not, an intervention can lead to inflation if the central bank attempts to prop securities prices at too high a nominal level.

KEY WORDS

orderly markets	Crash of 1987
stop-loss strategy	Mississippi Bubble
portfolio insurance	banking panics
margin	contagion of fear
liquidity events	"Money Trust"
liquidity stringency	cornering a market
Crash of 1929	Panic of 1907

EXERCISES

1. A nationalized central bank providing an "elastic" currency is vital to the mitigation of financial panics, since the private banking system is incapable of providing such elasticity. Discuss.

   In exercises 2 to 4, suppose that two types of participants trade on securities markets: (1) risk-neutral traders who base their demands for securities purely on anticipated returns formed on the basis of the most up-to-date information and (2) risk-averse traders who follow a stop-loss strategy. With this strategy, a trader will hold his or her securities if their price exceeds some minimum value. If the price falls to the minimum value, the trader will sell all his or her securities for cash.

2. Characterize the attitude toward risk of the stop-loss trader as a function of wealth.

3. Suppose that the information-based traders do not know of the existence of the stop-loss traders. Describe the dynamics of securities prices as negative information about returns gradually trickles in. Provide an intuitive explanation.

4. Suppose that the information-based traders know the floor price at which the stop-loss traders sell. Describe the dynamics of securities prices as negative information about returns gradually trickles in. Provide an intuitive explanation.

5. What is a rationale for a central bank to stabilize interest rates rather than to control the stock of money?

6. Explain how call loans provided by banks generate liquidity in a securities market when a seller insists on holding the bank deposit received in payment.

7. What happens to a securities market when banks refuse to lend on securities in the presence of large sales volumes?

8. What happens to the banking system when a central bank mistakes a fundamental price decline for a liquidity problem and encourages banks to lend freely on the basis of security collateral?

9. Why are banks subject to runs by customers? Are other institutions subject to similar runs? What characteristics of the assets and liabilities of these institutions make them subject to runs?

10. Discuss the nature of a corner on securities or commodities. Show that a counter to a corner on securities is a corner on cash.

11. What is a corner on the money market?

12. Construct a situation in which a cap on bank overdrafts at the Fed can exacerbate a liquidity crisis.

FURTHER READING

Donaldson, R. Glen. "Interbank Trade and the Financing of Bank Panics," Princeton University: Financial Research Center Memorandum No. 124, 1991.

Gorton, Gary. "Bank Suspension and Convertibility," *Journal of Monetary Economics,* March 1985, pp. 177–194.

Gorton, Gary, and Donald Mullineaux. "The Joint Production of Confidence: Endogenous Regulation and 19th Century Commercial Bank Clearinghouses," *Journal of Money Credit and Banking,* Vol. 19. No. 4 (1987), pp. 455–468.

Grossman, Sanford. "An Analysis of the Implications for Stock and Futures Price Volatility of Program Trading and Dynamic Hedging Strategies," *Journal of Business,* Vol. 61, No. 3 (1988), pp. 275–298.

Grossman, Sanford, and Merton Miller. "Liquidity and Market Structure," *Journal of Finance,* July 1988, pp. 617–634.

Krugman, Paul. "Trigger Strategies and Price Dynamics in Equity and Foreign Exchange Markets," NBER Working Paper No. 2459, December 1987.

Report of the Presidential Task Force on Market Mechanisms. Washington, January 1988.

Wigmore, Barrie. *The Crash and its Aftermath.* Westport, Conn.: Greenwood Press, 1985, Chapter 1.

Bank Risk and Government Policy

C H A P T E R

19

The U.S. Bank Regulatory System

The system for regulating commercial banks in the United States is in shambles. The Federal Deposit Insurance Corporation (FDIC), the federal agency that insures bank deposits, is widely predicted to go bankrupt soon after the end of 1991. As of this writing, the whole bank regulatory system is in for a major overhaul. The Treasury has made a formal proposal about what the new regulatory structure should look like, and Congress will undoubtedly have many ideas of its own.

In this chapter we consider the need for bank regulation and how the system in place in 1990 evolved to meet the need. We then analyze how the system works and why it has gone awry. We discuss what regulators are doing to improve the existing system and the various proposals for reform. We evaluate these proposals to determine whether they can really improve on the current regulatory system.

THE PURPOSES OF BANK REGULATION

As we have seen throughout this book, banks play a crucial role in the payments system. In the wholesale market for large dollar payments, on a typical day banks pass billions of dollars among themselves via electronic signals over Fedwire and CHIPS, but actual transfers of funds do not take place until settlement.

Individual banks do not have time to check the credit quality of other banks sending them payments messages to be settled later with funds transfers. Thus both CHIPS and Fedwire have created insurance systems to protect individual banks from the failure of a sending bank to actually make good on its payment message. In the case of Fedwire, the Federal Reserve is the insuring agent.

Consumers and small businesses also use banks for payments. Their normal procedure for making a payment is to go to the bank to obtain cash from their bank deposit, write a check drawn on that deposit, or use a credit card. The safety of the bank deposit has, for these customers, become as important as the safety of payments made over Fedwire for wholesale customers. The **Federal Deposit Insurance Corporation** (**FDIC**) is the insuring agent for retail deposits.

Moral Hazard and Bank Supervision

Insuring deposits or payments messages subjects the insurance agency to the same moral hazard problems we discussed in Chapter 3. Given a price for insurance, the insured entity has an incentive to cheat—that is, to take on more risk than the insurance agency is getting compensated for.

For example, banks that collect deposits insured by the government have an incentive to hold risky assets. Depositors do not care about the risk profile of the bank; their money is perfectly safe. As a result, they do not have to be compensated with a higher expected return for holding their deposit in a risky bank. This places the stockholders or the managers (or both) in a position to reap exceptionally high expected returns from taking on risk. They can pocket what would, without deposit insurance, have to be paid to depositors as compensation for bearing risk.

A solution to the moral hazard problem is bank supervision. Bank regulators from the Federal Reserve, the FDIC, and other agencies employ a battery of bank examiners to check up on the quality of bank assets and management. These agencies also have established rules for what banks can and cannot do, and they have established accounting standards that banks must meet.

Insuring and Supervising Wholesale versus Retail Banking Markets

Conceptually, the problems of insuring and supervising wholesale and retail banking markets are quite distinct. The major concern in wholesale banking is to maintain confidence in the payments system. Thus the Fed ensures that payments messages sent over Fedwire can be converted into good funds at the end of the day. If a bank cannot settle, the Federal Reserve can make short-term loans through the discount window. As long as a borrowing bank has liquid assets that the Fed can hold as collateral and seize in the event of default, there is little danger that the Fed will experience large losses in insuring wholesale payments.

The experience of the stock market Crash of 1929 extended the Fed's role to include providing liquidity support in the event of a crisis in financial markets. This type of support can be carried out through discount window loans as well, with little chance of loss to the Fed, as long as the crisis is truly temporary and banks have enough liquid assets that the Fed can discount.

On the retail side, deposits, rather than transactions among banks, are insured, which requires detailed knowledge of all the assets and activities of individual banks, for in the event of a bank failure, liquid assets are not sufficient to pay off the insured depositors, whose claim on the bank often equals more than 70 percent of total assets. If a bank's assets are sufficiently impaired, the insurance fund could be forced to disburse a large sum of money to meet its obligations. Thus strict supervision is necessary to prevent such losses to the insuring agency.

Events in the 1980s proved that the conceptual distinction between wholesale and retail insurance is untenable. To safeguard the wholesale payments market, regulators found it necessary to insure wholesale liabilities, just as they insure retail deposits. The expanded obligations of the FDIC have driven it close to bankruptcy. In the sections that follow, we will briefly trace the history of the U.S. bank regulatory system to see how this came about.

EVOLUTION OF THE U.S. REGULATORY SYSTEM

At the beginning of the twentieth century, the U.S. banking system consisted of two classes of commercial banks, state-chartered banks and national banks. The powers of **state banks** were determined by the laws of the various states, and the states also assumed responsibility for examining the financial condition of these institutions. **National banks** were chartered by the federal government, and their powers were determined by federal law. The **comptroller of the currency**, an official appointed by the President, was responsible for regulating and examining the financial condition of these institutions.[1]

The two groups of regulators set capital and reserve requirement standards as well as standards for the riskiness of assets for the banks they supervised. Bank capital, which corresponds to the net worth or capital in a nonfinancial corporation, absorbs fluctuations in income arising from interest rate risk and unexpected loan

---

1. For a thorough discussion of the U.S. regulatory structure at that time, see Eugene Nelson White, *The Regulation and Reform of the American* *Banking System, 1900–1929* (Princeton, N.J.: Princeton University Press, 1983).

losses. Thus the imposition of capital standards was an attempt to improve the ability of banks to survive these risks and to meet their obligations to their depositors.

Reserve requirements were set to ensure that banks had sufficient liquidity to meet demands for cash from their depositors. Reserves were assets on a bank's balance sheet that were either cash or assets easily convertible into cash. Cash was defined as gold and silver coin and Treasury paper currency. Assets easily convertible into cash were defined as deposits held at other banks, particularly deposits held in banks in large cities, designated as reserve city banks.

The Correspondent Banking System
Before the Federal Reserve

These interbank or correspondent bank deposits and the relationship between a bank and its reserve city bank correspondent represented the major source of liquidity in the banking system prior to 1914. If a merchant in a small city or town or a farmer wished to pay a supplier in a large city, good funds would be delivered to that supplier from the correspondent balances held by the local bank at a bank in the large city. Correspondent bank balances naturally tended to pile up in the major cities because they were focal points of trade and industry. In the early twentieth century, over 50 percent of these balances were held in the banks of only three cities, New York, Chicago, and St. Louis, and 70 percent of these were held in New York. These cities were called **central reserve cities.**

Central reserve city banks invested their bankers' balances in the **call money market,** which represented loans to securities brokers and dealers for the purchase of stocks and bonds. The interest that the central reserve city banks earned on these balances was credited to the accounts of their smaller bank customers, less deduction of charges for processing checks paid from their accounts.

Because the economies of the smaller towns and cities were primarily agricultural at that time, the small banks' demand for funds was seasonal, rising from planting time through the harvest when payments were made to labor and for materials and then declining into a surplus after the crop was sold. To accommodate the increase in seasonal demand for funds, the central reserve city banks would discount loans made by their correspondents, thus providing them with additional reserves, in the form of either legal currency or correspondent balances. Central reserve city banks discounted loans by purchasing them from the country bank that originated them at a price less than the full face value of the loan.

In this way, the seasonal cash demands of the West and the South could be met. During periods of surplus cash in these two regions, the country bank would repurchase the loans it had sold to its correspondent, although at the full face value of the loan, and it would request that the reserve city bank invest the remaining surplus funds in the call money market. The seasonal increase in demand for reserves naturally led to seasonality in interest rates. They would rise during planting time and fall after the harvest.[2]

Clearinghouses

Within the reserve cities, groups of banks formed clearinghouses to reduce the cost of settling payments-related debts among member banks. Clearinghouse members would collect all checks drawn on other members at a single location, and rather than transfer good funds on each item separately, the members would settle with each other on a net-due basis. The clearinghouse not only simplified the act of settlement, but also reduced the demand for cash.

The Discount Function of the Clearinghouse. When the country banks needed cash during the growing season, they would drain cash from the reserve city banks to meet that need. Sometimes, when cash became particularly tight in the reserve cities, clearinghouse member banks would not settle with each other in cash. Instead, they would deliver loans and securities to the clearinghouse for discount. The clearinghouse would issue script based on a percentage of the face value of the loans and securities accepted. The members could then use this script to settle their net positions with the clearinghouse.

Occasionally, cash would become so scarce that banks could not guarantee conversion of their deposits to cash on demand by the nonbank public. Such events were called *panics,* and a classic panic, described in some detail in Chapter 18, occurred in 1907. Since cash consisted only of Treasury currency and coin, the correspondent banking and clearinghouse networks could not increase the supply by discounting more loans and securities. Banks that were threatened by runs would then suspend the conversion of deposits into cash, but they would otherwise remain open for business. When cash in the banking system returned to "normal" levels, convertibility resumed.

The clearinghouse and correspondent bank systems functioned as market makers for its members and bank customers, respectively. They would always be willing to quote a price for eligible assets for discount, thereby providing liquidity to the market. Their price at times of suspension (that is, when deposit to currency convertibility was suspended) had to be quoted in deposits rather than cash, but they always made a market in certain designated assets.

Bank Insolvency and the Clearinghouse. Clearinghouse members held non-interest-bearing reserves at the clearinghouse to provide collateral for net "due

---

2. See Jeffrey A. Miron, "Financial Panics, the Seasonality of the Nominal Interest Rate, and the Founding of the Fed," *American Economic Review,* March 1986, pp. 125–140.

to" positions at settlement time. If a member bank had a net "due to" position arising from payments due to other clearinghouse members, the clearinghouse would guarantee delivery of reserves, even if the paying bank's reserve account was short of funds. In that event, it would lend reserves to that bank by discounting its high-quality paper.

The purpose of the clearinghouse was not to ensure the solvency of its member banks or protect the banks' customers from bankruptcy of a member bank. The sole purpose was to protect the claims of the other members against default on net "due to's." By discounting a bank's high-quality paper, the clearinghouse actually increased the risk to a bank's depositors. It took first claim to the best assets, leaving the remaining creditors (including the depositors) holding claims to the leftovers. The objective of the clearinghouse was thus to place its members in the most favorable position in the event of a bankruptcy of one of the member banks.

The suspension of conversion of deposits to currency was never declared for individual banks because inconvertibility could only be a system-wide problem that occurred when there was insufficient cash to cover the amount of high-quality paper presented for discount.

During the Panic of 1907, the glaring inadequacies of the private clearinghouse system as a method of providing adequate liquidity when the demand for cash rose created a demand for reform. The dependence of the stability of financial markets and the banking system on the actions of a few individuals, namely, J. P. Morgan and his friends, was unacceptable.

ORIGINS OF THE FEDERAL RESERVE

Commentators approaching the question of reform believed the problem had two aspects. The first was a need to expand the currency when the demand for currency rose relative to deposits. The second was the need to give all banks access to a market for loan discounts. The movement for reform eventually resulted in the passage of the Federal Reserve Act in 1913 and the opening of the Fed in 1914.

The Federal Reserve Act established the Federal Reserve System, whose aim was essentially to function as a government-sponsored clearinghouse. It had the power to clear payments and to discount loans and securities. The major difference between the Federal Reserve System and the private clearinghouses was that the Fed was given the right to create currency for the loans and securities it discounted.

Organization and Membership in the Fed

The Federal Reserve Act established 12 Federal Reserve districts in the United States. The legislation mandated a decentralized system because country bankers feared that the system would be dominated by the large central reserve city banks, primarily those in New York.

A Federal Reserve bank was established in each district, and a Board of Governors of the system was established in Washington to coordinate the actions of the district banks.[3] All national banks had to become members of the system, and state-chartered banks were invited to become members on a voluntary basis. Members were required to hold reserves with the Federal Reserve bank in their district.

Reserves held at the Fed did not pay interest. Many smaller banks viewed this as a burden. They used the Fed like a correspondent bank—that is, the Fed discounted loans to provide liquidity and provided check-processing services. There was one fundamental difference, however. Their correspondent bank paid interest on bankers' balances, whereas the Fed did not.

The large banks, on the other hand, viewed the Fed as a substitute for the clearinghouse. That is, the Fed netted payments among the member banks, and reserves were transferred only to cover net "due to" positions at settlement. Of course, the Fed also provided netting services for small banks, but small banks were rarely in a position where netting significantly decreased their need to transfer reserves. Since clearinghouse reserves did not bear interest, the large banks were quite satisfied to hold non-interest-bearing reserves with the Fed and substitute Fed services for the services of private clearinghouses.

Other benefits of membership included access to the discount window, the privilege of discounting high-quality loans and securities to obtain additional reserves. They also included access to the check-clearing services of the Federal Reserve System. Naturally, banks that were most actively engaged in the interbank payments system found membership most attractive. These were primarily the large banks in the major cities.

Thus the cost of membership was higher for small banks than for large banks, and many state banks refused to join. In 1929, state banks made up 69 percent of the 24,500 banks then in existence. Only 7 percent of the state banks were members of the system. Large state banks, however, tended to be members. The total deposits of the 7 percent of the state banks that were members exceeded the total deposits of the 93 percent that were not members.[4]

Should Fed Membership Be Universal?

Prior to the Great Depression of the early 1930s, the inability of the Fed to attract universal membership was of great concern to commentators who believed that universal access to the discount window in times of crisis was vital.[5] The validity of this view depends on how the political and business leaders of the time interpreted the role of the Federal Reserve System.

3. Originally, the board was known as the Federal Reserve Board.

4. Miron, *op. cit.*, p. 132.

5. Miron, *op. cit.*, p. 127.

Debate over the Purpose of the Discount Window. The pre-Depression role of the Fed turned on whether it discounted different securities from those discounted by correspondent banks or clearinghouses under the previous system. If it maintained the pre-Fed standard for discounting, members could discount their own eligible paper, say Treasury bills, at the Fed and receive cash or reserves for their accounts. Nonmembers could gain access to Fed liquidity by forming correspondent relations with members. Members could provide credit to nonmembers by discounting Treasury bills presented by nonmembers. Members could finance such loans by presenting Treasury bills at the discount window.

On the other hand, if the purpose of the Fed was to extend the eligibility of paper for discount beyond what the private market had considered eligible, the extent of membership was an important issue. While a member bank could present low-quality paper, say, a commercial real estate loan, to the Fed, it would be unwilling to accept the same quality paper as collateral from its correspondent, because the member, not the Fed, would suffer the loss if the nonmember defaulted on the loan. As a result, nonmember "due to's" would be riskier than members' "due to's." Hence the universal acceptability of bank "due to's" and, consequently, the liquidity of the payments market would depend on the universality of membership.

Universal Access to Federal Reserve Services. The problem of attracting small state-chartered banks into the Federal Reserve System continued up to the passage of the Monetary Control Act of 1980. In the 1970s, when high inflation drove nominal interest rates on short-term CDs close to 15 percent, many small state banks that were members quit the system because the cost of holding reserve requirements was too high.

In response, Congress passed the **Monetary Control Act of 1980,** which made reserve requirements universal on all transaction accounts issued by commercial banks and thrifts. Thus Fed membership, at least as far as being subject to reserve requirements, has become universal. In addition, all institutions holding reserve requirements were given access to the discount window, Fedwire, and check-processing services of the Fed. These services are now provided to members and nonmembers alike for a fee that is supposed to be based on the cost of providing them.

Bank Insolvency and the Federal Reserve

Whether the Fed's role was to make the payments system safer for individual banks or simply to increase reserves to prevent financial panics, it was not meant as a vehicle to protect depositors from the consequences of bank failure. Thus, in terms of the goals we established at the beginning of this chapter, the Fed's role was, at best, to improve the safety of the wholesale payments market; it did not exist to protect the deposits of retail customers.

Figure 19.1 presents the number of bank failures from 1920 through 1990. In

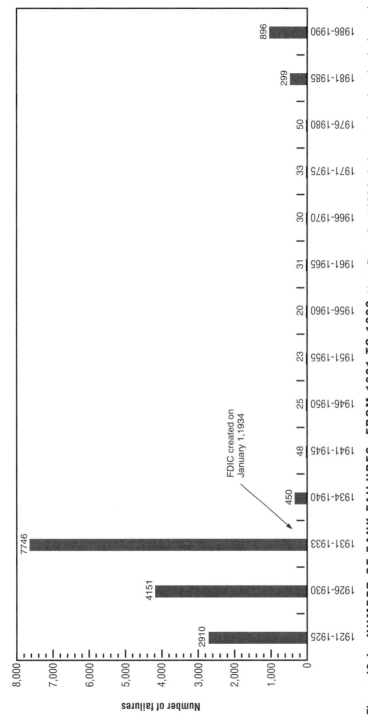

Figure 19.1 NUMBER OF BANK FAILURES, FROM 1921 TO 1990 *Note:* Data after 1933 include mutual savings banks insured by the FDIC. *Source:* Adapted from Milton Friedman and Anna Jacobson Schwartz, *A Monetary History of the United States, 1867–1960,* Princeton, N.J., Princeton University Press, 1990, p. 468, Table 16, and the Federal Deposit Insurance Corporation, *1990 Annual Report,* Table 122.

the 1920s and early 1930s, bank failures were high, despite the existence of the Fed. During the early years of the Great Depression, bank failures become endemic, and in 1934, Congress saw the need to establish a whole new agency to cope with the problem. As Figure 19.1 indicates, with the institution of government deposit insurance, the bank failure problem dramatically declined in importance until the late 1980s.

The new agency that performed this seeming miracle was the Federal Deposit Insurance Corporation (FDIC). This agency continues to provide deposit insurance: If a bank goes bankrupt, the FDIC guarantees that depositors will not lose their funds. This philosophy of depositor protection has become the main focus of the U.S. bank regulatory system in recent years. We now turn to a description of how the system functioned as of year-end 1990.

THE STRUCTURE OF THE BANK REGULATORY SYSTEM BEFORE 1991

The Regulatory Agencies

The federal regulatory structure for commercial banks in the United States is complicated because banks can be chartered either by a state or by the federal government. As we saw earlier, state-chartered banks have the option of joining or not joining the Federal Reserve System, whereas national banks must be members. National and state-chartered member banks also must belong to the Federal Deposit Insurance Corporation. State nonmember banks may join the FDIC, and some states require membership. Virtually all commercial banks in the United States are insured by this agency. In addition, as we have seen, the Comptroller of the Currency regulates

Table 19.1   U.S. COMMERCIAL BANK DOMESTIC ASSETS BY MEMBERSHIP STATUS, MARCH 31, 1990 ($BILLIONS)

	Assets	Percent of Total Assets	Number of Banks	Percent of Total Banks
Total commercial banks	2,915,424		12,572	
Federal Reserve members	2,165,268	74.27	5,138	40.87
National	1,743,762	59.81	4,114	32.72
State	421,505	14.46	1,024	8.15
Nonmembers	750,157	25.73	7,434	59.13

Source: From *Federal Reserve Bulletin,* January 1991, Table 4.22.

national banks, and state regulatory authorities do the same for state member and nonmember banks.

To further complicate matters, the Federal Reserve has oversight authority for bank holding companies. A **bank holding company (BHC)** is a legal entity that owns one or more banks. That is, it holds the stock of a bank or banks, and the stock of the holding company is, in turn, held by investors. This might seem somewhat bizarre, since investors can own a bank directly. However, there are some regulatory advantages to the bank holding company form of organization, as we will see later in this chapter. Over half the banks, with over 90 percent of the banking assets, are owned by bank holding companies.

This structure generates a great deal of overlap in the regulation of commercial banks. The FDIC has the right to regulate virtually all the commercial banks in the country, and the Federal Reserve, because of its authority over holding companies, has the right to regulate the organizations that control almost all the bank assets. The Comptroller of the Currency has supervisory authority over more than half the assets in the commercial banking industry as well. In practice, primary supervisory authority for banks has been divided among the three agencies as follows: The Federal Reserve supervises state-chartered member banks, the FDIC supervises state-chartered nonmember banks, and the Comptroller of the Currency supervises national banks. Table 19.1 summarizes which agency has primary responsibility for which banks and how large a segment of the industry each regulates. (The Fed currently has sole authority to regulate BHCs, which is not described in the table.)

The Federal Reserve System is overseen by a Board of Governors, made up of eight individuals appointed by the President and approved by the Senate. The term is 14 years, except for the chairman, whose term is 4 years. As we indicated earlier, the system consists of 12 districts, each of which has a Federal Reserve bank. In addition, each reserve district has several branches in the major cities in its district (see Figure 19.2). The Board of Governors sits in Washington, D.C., and it determines system-wide policy on all major supervisory issues. The chairman of the FDIC and the Comptroller of the Currency are also appointed by the President with the consent of the Senate.

Regulation of the thrift industry is somewhat different. We will consider its regulatory structure in Chapter 20.

The Role of the Discount Window

With the passage of the Monetary Control Act of 1980, domestic offices of all depository institutions must maintain reserves on transaction deposits, nonpersonal time deposits, and Eurocurrency liabilities with the Federal Reserve. Table 19.2 summarizes the required reserves on the three types of accounts. Note that reserve requirements on time and Eurocurrency liabilities are currently zero, but the Fed has legislative authority to reimpose them at any time. Note also that smaller institutions have lower reserve requirements than larger ones.

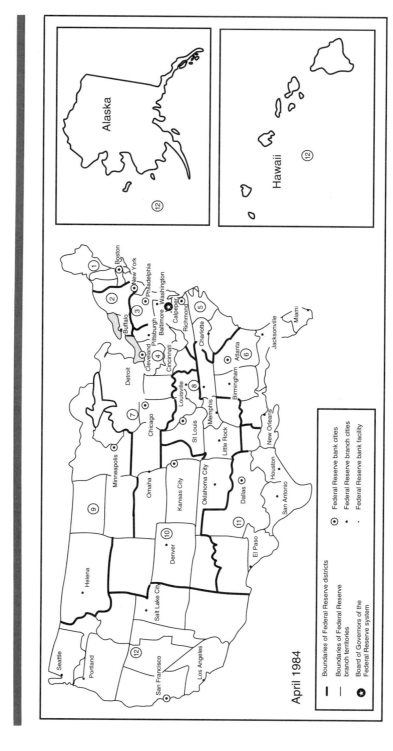

April 1984

Boundaries of Federal Reserve districts

Boundaries of Federal Reserve branch territories

Board of Governors of the Federal Reserve system

⊙ Federal Reserve bank cities

• Federal Reserve branch cities

· Federal Reserve bank facility

Figure 19.2 BOUNDARIES OF FEDERAL RESERVE DISTRICTS AND THEIR BRANCH TERRITORIES

Table 19.2 RESERVE REQUIREMENTS AT BANKS AND THRIFTS

	Percent of Deposits	Effective
Institutions with less than $41.1 million in *transaction deposits* and the first $41.1 million at all other institutions	3	12/18/90
Transaction deposit volume above $41.1 million	12	12/18/90
Nonpersonal time deposits	0	12/27/90
Eurocurrency liabilities	0	12/27/90

Source: From *Federal Reserve Bulletin,* January 1990, p. A8.

The Monetary Control Act also provides that all institutions subject to reserve requirements shall have access to the discount window and to Fedwire. The question we need to consider is whether universality of access has enhanced the role of the discount window as a tool for maintaining bank solvency.

The Federal Reserve recognizes three major types of credit extended through

Table 19.3 AVERAGE WEEKLY BORROWINGS FROM FEDERAL RESERVE DISCOUNT WINDOW* ($MILLIONS)

	Adjustment Credit	Seasonal Credit	Other Extended Credit	Total Credit
December 1982	477	33	187	697
December 1983	676	96	2	744
August 1984	628	346	7,036	8,010
December 1984	469	113	2,604	3,186
June 1985	389	151	655	1,205
December 1985	763	56	499	1,318
June 1986	164	108	531	803
December 1986	486	38	303	827
October 21, 1987†	342	183	482	1,007
December 1987	201	93	483	777
June 1988	218	311	2,544	3,083
December 1988	342	130	1,244	1,716
June 1989	142	431	917	1,490
December 1989	161	84	20	265
June 1990	224	311	346	881

Source: From *Federal Reserve Bulletin,* Table 1.12, various issues.

*Monthly averages of biweekly averages of daily figures.
†Biweekly averages of daily figures.

the discount window.[6] These purposes are distinguished by three classifications: adjustment credit, seasonal credit, and other extended credit. In all three cases, institutions borrow from the Fed by means of a discount on eligible paper or by means of advances. Both types of credit represent collateralized borrowing, but a **discount** is technically a sale of an asset to the Fed at a price less than face value. An **advance** is a loan collateralized by an asset. The interest rate charged is the discount rate we have encountered before. Today most lending is through advances rather than discounts. The Fed determines what is acceptable collateral. Generally, it includes U.S. government and agency securities, state and municipal notes and bonds, mortgages on one- to four-family residences, and consumer and business notes of indebtedness.

Table 19.3 summarizes selected monthly averages of the type of credit extended by the Federal Reserve between 1982 and 1990. Note that short-term adjustment credit has, with the exception of 1984 and 1988, been the major type of credit extended. We will consider all types of Fed credit in more detail in the following sections.

Adjustment Credit

Short-term **adjustment credit** is, by the Fed's definition, meant to be used for "the coverage of sudden, unforeseen deposit outflows, the need to counter temporary and unexpected difficulties in obtaining funds from other sources, and, in some circumstances, the accommodation of unexpected increases in loan demand."

In a broad sense, banks can obtain adjustment credit to settle daily "due to's" either in the overnight fed funds market or through selling U.S. government securities under agreement to repurchase. The interest rate in these markets is set privately by the marketplace, although, as we have seen, Federal Reserve open-market operations affect the fed funds rate. Usually, however, the Fed's discount rate is lower than the fed funds rate, so institutions have a strong incentive to seek funds through the "window." The Fed is aware that its short-term adjustment credit represents a subsidy, so it is careful to monitor the extent to which an individual institution uses the discount window.

> In judging whether a user is relying unduly on adjustment borrowing, the Reserve Bank discount officer takes into account the institution's indebtedness in relation to its total deposits, the frequency and duration of its past borrowings, any special circumstances affecting its current position, and efforts it has made to obtain funds from other reasonably available sources.

The Fed is obviously effective at preventing habitual dependence on the discount window, because adjustment credit is dwarfed by borrowing in the fed funds market.

6. Board of Governors, *The Federal Reserve System: Purposes and Functions* (Washington, D.C., 1984), pp. 58–62.

Box 19.1

Adjustment Credit and the Stock Market Crash of 1987

In Table 19.3 we listed "short-term adjustment credit" for the 2-week period ending on October 21. The stock market crash occurred on October 19, 1987. Banks make loans for carrying securities to brokers, dealers, and ordinary investors on "margin," which means that they lend funds for purchase of the security collateralized by the value of the security. The Fed does not permit banks, or other lenders, to lend funds equal to the market value of the security; they restrict new security loans to only 50 percent of the current market value. After the security loan is made, margin must be maintained at least at 25 percent of the security's current market value. Therefore, if the security price falls by more than one-third, cash must be delivered to top up margin.

When securities prices fell on October 19, many investors who had borrowed to buy securities were forced to pay off part of their loan because the value of their securities had fallen and their loan exceeded 75 percent of the new value. To stem the fall in stock prices, the Fed encouraged banks to provide securities credit so that potential buyers could have access to funds to buy securities from those forced to sell. The Fed's encouragement was backed by a promise to extend credit to banks through the discount window so that they would not have to sell other assets to meet credit needs.

The actual amount of borrowing from the Fed on October 19 is hard to discern from the reserve accounts because the figure is subsumed in the 2-week averages. However, if we consider only the balance sheets of the large New York City banks, which report every Wednesday, we can get a closer approximation than the 2-week average. On Wednesday, October 21, the large New York City banks had borrowed $2.4 billion from the Fed. The previous week they had borrowed nothing.

For example, in October 1990, borrowings through the discount window totaled, on average, $57 million per day. In that same period, the average volume of fed funds purchased by commercial banks (that is, borrowing in the fed funds market) equaled $191 billion. See Box 19.1.

Seasonal Credit.   **Seasonal credit** is primarily a subsidy to small country banks that "lack effective access to national money markets" to finance agricultural borrowing during the growing season, and the Fed recognizes it as such:

> Without an assured source of seasonal credit, these smaller institutions typically would accumulate short-term securities as a pool of liquidity on which they would draw to meet peak seasonal needs for funds. To the extent that resources were tied

up in this way during the off-peak season, some needs for credit for desirable projects might not be accommodated.

As Table 19.3 indicates, much less credit is extended for seasonal purposes than for other reasons.

Extended Credit and Insolvency Protection: The Case of Continental Illinois.

The purpose of other **extended credit** is to prevent a run on an insolvent bank. The explosion in other extended credit in the summer of 1984 was due to the imminent collapse of the Continental Illinois Bank, which at the time was the seventh largest bank in the United States, with some $43 billion in assets.

The Fed recognizes that extended credit is meant to buy time so that an institution that is about to fail can be dissolved in an orderly fashion or so that a buyer can be found. It is not meant to bail out all the liability holders in a failing bank. By law, only deposits of less than $100,000 are protected, and technically, the FDIC is responsible for the protection of insured depositors at banks. However, as we shall see, the Fed's actions in the case of Continental changed market perceptions of the role of insurance in large bank failures. This, in turn, enlarged the role that the FDIC plays in bank failures, much to the detriment of the solvency of the FDIC.

Continental Bank, with over 90 percent of its liabilities technically uninsured, looked like a bank that, if treated by the book, should have been allowed to fail without much loss to the government. In March of 1984, Continental reported negative operating income resulting from heavy losses on loans in energy-producing states, and the uninsured liability holders began a bank run. Regulators and politicians decided that its failure could disrupt the money markets, possibly creating a crisis of confidence in the U.S. banking system. The only way they could prevent the crisis was to replace fleeing funds with extended credit from the Federal Reserve. The Fed poured money into the bank equal to over $7 billion by August 1984.

Realizing that further "liquidity assistance" by the Fed would only be used to finance the bank run, on May 17, according to congressional testimony, the Fed and the FDIC proposed a plan that would guarantee the funds of all uninsured depositors and general creditors of the bank. When this plan was put into effect, the run ceased. After August, there was no further increase in extended credit by the Fed. By the end of the year, extended credit had fallen to $2 billion.

The market viewed the actions in the Continental case as confirmation of the **"too big to fail" doctrine.** That is, the market has come to believe that the government will not let a large bank fail. Consequently, all liability holders, whether technically insured or not, are safe in a large bank. The doctrine was put to the test in Texas in 1988 when two large banks with almost 60 percent of their liabilities uninsured were about to collapse. This time the FDIC announced that all liability holders (excluding bondholders) would be protected. However, the Fed reportedly had to supply extended credit until the FDIC made its announcement, indicating the market has some residual doubts about the applicability of the "too big to fail" doctrine in specific cases. The FDIC assumed control of the banks and auctioned them off in what is known as "assisted transactions." As we will see in Chapter 20, these assisted transactions have cost the FDIC quite a bit of money and have driven the FDIC itself to the verge of bankruptcy.

The confirmation of the "too big to fail" doctrine implies that wholesale liabilities are almost certainly insured. Thus the distinction between liquidity assistance and insurance has become almost meaningless. Preserving liquidity in wholesale markets now means preserving the value of wholesale bank liabilities. Thus the problem of insuring both retail and wholesale activities is now practically the same. The regulators must closely supervise the risk of bank balance sheets and activities. It is not sufficient for wholesale banks to merely maintain enough liquid assets to guarantee Fed loans made through the discount window. We now turn to how banks are supervised.

THE SUPERVISORY PROCESS

In Chapter 3 we discussed ways in which households meet their need for all kinds of insurance. We noted that the price of insurance is determined by the frequency with which the insured event is expected to occur among the members of the insurance pool. We also discussed the problem of moral hazard: the extent to which the mere existence of insurance changes the behavior of the insured party so that the insured event is more likely to occur.

For the federal regulatory system to operate as an insurance agency to protect against losses to depositors, it must solve the same two problems. It must be able to predict the rate of bank failures and protect itself against the possibility that the existence of insurance will cause the risk of failure to rise. The supervisory process is used to assess the riskiness of banks and to control behavior to prevent excessive risk taking. In this section we discuss how this system operates and evaluate its success.

In 1978, Congress mandated the establishment of the Federal Financial Institutions Examination Council to standardize supervision of financial institutions across the federal agencies that regulate banks and thrifts. We will therefore discuss the supervisory process for banks regardless of whether the primary federal regulator is the Fed, the Comptroller of the Currency, or the FDIC.

Bank Examinations

Each regulatory agency has responsibility for conducting examinations of the institutions under its control. These examinations are carried out periodically on an unannounced schedule, but they are generally done at least every 2 years. The Board of Governors of the Federal Reserve states that the objectives of the **bank examination** are as follows:

1. An appraisal of the soundness of the institution's assets

2. An evaluation of internal operations, policies, and management

3. An analysis of key financial factors, such as capital, earnings, liquidity, and interest rate sensitivity

4. A review of compliance with all banking laws and regulations

5. An overall determination of the institution's solvency[7]

If the regulatory agencies were private insurance companies, they would use the preceding information to determine the riskiness of the client and the price of his or her insurance. In addition, they would institute procedures to prevent moral hazard. The federal insurance agencies do not price insurance based on differences in risk. Instead, they charge a flat fee based on total domestic deposits, including those which are not legally insured. The cost of insurance has been rising for several years because of the dire financial condition of the FDIC. We consider proposals to revamp the FDIC in the next chapter.

Regulatory Powers to Prevent Unsafe Banking Practices

If a bank is found to be engaged in unsafe practices, the regulatory agency may write a memorandum to senior management and the board of directors of the institution. The memorandum states the problem and requests that management and the directors remedy the situation. This sounds mild, but the regulators wield awesome powers.

Cease and Desist.   If the solvency of the bank is at risk, the regulators have cease and desist powers and the power to remove senior management. Through **cease and desist orders,** the regulatory agencies can stop an institution from engaging in a practice they consider harmful to safety and soundness.

However, it is often difficult to regulate the safety of an institution through cease and desist powers because it is often impossible for a financial institution to extricate itself from an unsound practice by the time the regulators recognize the problem. For example, in the 1980s, many developing countries stopped payment on loans that major U.S. banks had provided in the 1970s. In 1990, the Bank of New England went bankrupt because of real estate loans made earlier in the decade. We will describe these situations in some detail below. In the Continental Illinois case, the market forced the regulators to recognize a problem. By then, it was too

---

7. *Ibid.,* p. 90.

late to change internal policy, and the rescue package included the purchase by the FDIC of $5 billion in face value of nonperforming loans at a purchase price of $4.5 billion.

Loans that are not paying interest do not provide revenue to cover interest and noninterest expenses. A bank can still meet these obligations, that is, stay out of bankruptcy, if it can reduce payments to shareholders sufficiently to offset the decline in revenues. If a bank has a high capital-to-asset ratio, expected dividends will be high relative to mandatory interest payments. Consequently, the bank can free up more funds to pay interest in the event of loan defaults. Thus capital can provide a cushion to ensure that depositors will be paid even if interest revenue should decline as a result of loan defaults.

Latin American loans—or other risky loans—cannot be removed from banks' balance sheets by cease and desist powers. They can only be sold at a loss based on the market's expectation of the debtor's ability and desire to resume interest payments. A mistake in providing credit cannot be remedied after the fact, so the regulatory authorities must find ways to prevent mistakes from happening.

However, cease and desist orders can prevent an incompetent management from further destroying the value of a bank and thereby increasing the potential liability of the regulatory agencies. Their effectiveness depends on their issuance *before* a bank slides into bankruptcy. In 1990, the Bank of New England was under a cease and desist order, but the quality of its assets had deteriorated to such an extent that it was declared insolvent in January 1991.

Increased Loan Loss Provisions.   The regulatory authorities can "suggest" that a bank increase its provisions for loan loss against loans they consider risky. For management that wishes to avoid trouble, this suggestion should be taken as a requirement. As shown in Chapter 10, a bank voluntarily makes provisions for loan loss out of current income, reducing its capital-to-assets ratio if income is inadequate to cover the provisions. By forcing a bank to increase its reserves, regulatory authorities can therefore force a bank to reduce its capital-to-asset ratio. This, in turn, can force a bank to take action to strengthen this ratio, as we shall see. When regulators force a bank to increase its provisions, it is done in secret so as not to further erode public confidence.

Declaration of Impairment.   When a bank's soundness is impaired, the regulatory agencies have statutory authority not only to remove management but also to take over operation of the institution or find a buyer for it. The definition of "impairment" is based on an accounting standard of capital relative to total assets. Bank assets and liabilities are assigned a **book value** based on the cost of acquiring them.

For example, if a bank buys a bond paying $100 per year for $1,000, the accounting or book value of that bond is $1,000. Assets are evaluated at this price even if interest rates should rise. If we assume that the value of liabilities is also unaffected by the risk in interest rates, then the book value of capital, or equity (defined as assets minus liabilities), will remain the same. However, if we acknowledge that changing interest rates affect the market value of assets and liabilities, then the market value of the bank's capital also changes. Table 19.4 shows how this might happen.

The book value of equity will not be affected by the increase in interest rates, and by the Fed's definition, the bank in case 2 of Table 19.4 is not impaired by the rise in rates. However, the consequent decline in market value of a bank's stock can

Table 19.4   CHANGES IN BANK CAPITAL

Assume that a bank has the following balance sheet:

ASSETS	LIABILITIES	
Bonds $1,000	Deposits	$900
	Equity	$100

The bond yields $100 per year; deposit costs are variable. The bank's income statement would vary, depending on our interest rate assumptions.

Case 1. Bond Interest Rate is 10 Percent and Deposit Costs Are also 10 Percent

Bonds pay	$100
Deposit costs at 10%	90
Net income	10
Return on equity	10%

Case 2. Bond Interest Rate is 10 Percent and Deposit Costs Rise to 10.5 Percent

Bonds pay	$100
Deposit costs at 10.5%	95
Net income	5
Return on equity	5%

Effect of case 2 on market values:

$$\text{Market value of bond at } 10.5\% = \frac{1,000}{10.5/10} = \frac{1,000}{1.05} = 952.38$$

$$\begin{aligned} \text{Market value of capital} &= \text{assets} - \text{liabilities} \\ &= \$952.38 - \$900 \\ &= \$52.38 \end{aligned}$$

Book value is unchanged.

still create opportunities for the Fed to use its definition of impairment to control bank behavior.

In the example in Table 19.4, net income declined from $10 to $5 as a result of the rise in rates. Let us assume that the bank in Table 19.4 had planned to retain $8 in earnings to increase its capital and expand its assets by $80. This would have permitted it to retain a constant capital-to-assets ratio of 10 percent. Although in case 2 it no longer has enough earnings to maintain a constant capital-to-assets ratio while expanding, it might decide to expand anyway by reducing the ratio. This might lead the regulators to declare that the soundness of the bank has been impaired.

The ability to control the growth of an unsound bank by setting standards for the capital-to-assets ratio is an increasingly important regulatory tool. In fact, the regulators are moving toward making control of this ratio the most important element in bank supervision.

BANK CAPITAL

In 1987, the Federal Reserve proposed capital guidelines for approval by all federal regulatory agencies. In 1990, they were approved by all the agencies and scheduled to go into full effect in 1992. The guidelines establish requirements for a capital to weighted risk assets ratio and a capital to total assets ratio.

The guidelines require that, by 1992, bank holding companies maintain a tier 1 ratio of capital to weighted risk assets of 4 percent. Tier 1 capital is defined as equity capital. In addition, the soundest banking companies must maintain a 3-percent ratio of tier 1 capital to total assets. Those deemed more risky by the regulators must hold a higher ratio. Bank holding companies also must maintain an 8-percent tier 1 plus tier 2 ratio of capital to risk assets. Tier 2 capital includes loan loss reserves, perpetual preferred stock, and subordinated debt. Preferred stock is stock that has a priority claim on dividends before other shareholders, who are known as common shareholders, are paid. Subordinated debt is a bond whose claim in bankruptcy court is inferior to depositors.

Weighted risk assets are calculated based on procedures established by the regulators. U.S. government and U.S. government–guaranteed securities are given a zero risk weighting, meaning that they are not included in risk assets at all. Securities guaranteed by U.S. government agencies and general obligation municipal bonds are given a 20-percent weighting, meaning that 20 percent of their book value is included in risk assets. Home mortgages are included in a 50-percent weighting category, and other loans are in the 100-percent category.

Off-balance-sheet items are also assigned to a risk class. Those, such as standby letters of credit, which obligate a bank to lend are given a 100-percent risk weighting. Less firm commitments are placed in lower categories. Lines of credit that the bank can unconditionally cancel at any time fall into the zero risk weighting category.

Goodwill.   Another aspect of the new capital requirements is that goodwill cannot be considered equity capital. **Goodwill** is an asset that develops when one company acquires another and pays more for it than the book value of its shares. The shares of an acquired bank must appear on the acquiring bank's balance sheet at the price paid, but the assets of the acquired bank must appear on the acquiring bank's balance sheet at their original book value. Assuming a purchaser pays more than book value for the equity, assets would be less than liabilities plus equity capital. The difference must be carried as goodwill on the asset side of the balance sheet. Table 19.5 works through an example of how goodwill arises in an acquisition.

In determining the regulatory capital-to-assets ratio, an amount equal to goodwill must be subtracted from the equity account, so an acquisition that creates a lot of goodwill will reduce the regulatory capital-to-assets ratio. A bank will not be able to consummate the deal if the ratio of equity to risk assets would fall below 4 percent of risk assets. If a potential acquirer were unwilling to sell additional equity, it would not be able to grow through acquisition.

Why do the regulators subtract goodwill from assets in determining a bank's capital-to-assets ratio? Partially, it is because the whole regulatory system works on the principle of book value rather than market value. A bank holding company cannot write up the value of its assets when interest rates fall, so it should not be able to write up the value of an asset it acquires either.

Perhaps a more fundamental reason is that the regulators believe that by not

Table 19.5   THE CREATION OF GOODWILL: BANK A PURCHASES BANK B FOR $10 MILLION IN CASH

Assets	Bank A	Bank B	Payment to Stockholders	Bank A after Acquisition
Cash and "due froms"	20	8	(10)	18
Securities	40	16		56
Loans	120	50		170
Other assets	20	6		26
Goodwill	0	0		4
Total Assets	200	80		274
Liabilities and Capital				
Deposits	170	68		238
Other liabilities	18	6		24
Equity	12	6		12
Total Liabilities	200	80	(6)	274

Note: The stockholders of bank B originally invested $6 million in their bank. Bank A's stockholders paid bank B's stockholders $10 million for their bank. Thus bank B's shareholders received their original investment, which is indicated by the withdrawal of $6 million in equity. The difference between what bank B's shareholders paid in and what they received, $10 million, must be accounted for as goodwill.

counting goodwill, a bank holding company is forced to be very conservative about how it finances an acquisition. As we indicated earlier, subtracting goodwill means that liabilities increase faster than assets in an acquisition, and equity declines. This must be offset by the issuance of more equity. If an institution cannot raise the additional equity, it cannot finance the acquisition. Thus this represents another important attempt by the regulatory agencies to control the growth of what they perceive to be weak institutions.

Table 19.6 RISK-BASED CAPITAL FOR THE 25 LARGEST U.S. BANK HOLDING COMPANIES

Rank	Company	Head-quarters	Assets ($Billions) 12/31/89	Tier 1 Capital to Risk Assets (%) 12/31/89	Tier 1 and 2 Capital to Risk Assets (%) 12/31/89
1	Citicorp	NY	230.6	4.04	8.08
2	Chase Manhattan Corp.	NY	107.4	4.46	8.87
3	BankAmerica Corp.	CA	98.8	5.61	9.11
4	J. P. Morgan & Co., Inc.	NY	89.0	5.90	10.10
5	Security Pacific Corp.	CA	83.9	4.10	8.20
6	Chemical Banking Corp.	NY	71.5	4.65	8.74
7	NCNB Corp.	NC	66.2	5.00	8.62
8	Manufacturers Hanover Corp.	NY	60.5	5.69	10.24
9	First Interstate Bancorp.	CA	59.1	3.66	7.32
10	Bankers Trust New York Corp.	NY	55.7	4.34	8.08
11	Bank of New York Co.	NY	48.9	4.61	7.58
12	Wells Fargo & Co.	CA	48.7	4.95	9.91
13	First Chicago Corp.	IL	47.9	4.70	8.00
14	PNC Financial Corp.	PA	45.7	7.48	9.73
15	Bank of Boston Corp.	MA	39.2	N.A.	N.A.
16	Fleet/Norstar Financial Group	RI	33.4	7.26	10.70
17	First Union Corp.	NC	32.1	6.49	11.05
18	Mellon Bancorp.	PA	31.5	4.60	8.79
19	SunTrust Banks, Inc.	GA	31.0	7.03	11.01
20	First Fidelity Bancorp.	NJ	30.7	5.62	9.61
21	Bank of New England Corp.	MA	29.8	N.A.	N.A.
22	Continental Bank Corp.	IL	29.5	5.40	6.80
23	Barnett Banks, Inc.	FL	29.0	6.09	8.61
24	Shawmut National Corp.	CT	27.9	5.01	8.74
25	Marine Midland Banks, Inc.	NY	27.1	3.77	7.54

Source: Adapted from American Banker, *Top Numbers, Part 2, 1990 Update,* pp. 59, 65, and 66.

Note: Tier 1 capital consists of common stock, non-cumulative perpetual preferred stock, and minority interest in equity accounts of consolidated subsidiaries less goodwill, less 50 percent of investments in certain subsidiaries and 50 percent of reciprocal holdings of the capital instruments of other banking companies.

Tier 2 capital consists of qualifying loan loss reserves, perpetual preferred stock, mandatory convertible notes, perpetual debt, and subordinated term debt less 50 percent of investments in certain subsidiaries and 50 percent of reciprocal holdings of the capital instruments of other banking companies.

Box 19.2

Citicorp Tries to Reduce its Capital Requirement

Citicorp, like many other large bank holding companies, created programs to give their more risky clients access to the commercial paper market. Their clients pledged inventory as collateral for the commercial paper issue, and Citicorp offered a credit line to back up the issue. With the line, the customers' commercial paper received the highest-quality rating, equal to Citicorp's commercial paper rating.

Under the risk-based capital requirements, standby letters of credit, which represent a firm commitment to lend in the event that a company cannot roll its commercial paper over, are given a 50-percent weighting. This means that banks must hold 50 percent of the capital requirement against them. For example, if a bank has standbys of $5 billion, it would need to hold 2 percent tier 1 capital, or $20 million, and 2 percent tier 2 capital.

However, Citicorp structured its credit facilities as "standby reimbursement agreements" rather than standby letters of credit. The difference in the wording of the two credit lines exempts the reimbursement agreement from capital requirements, but the market has accepted it as an absolute commitment to lend, just like the standby letter of credit. Thus Citicorp issued $20 billion in reimbursement agreements without having to set aside capital to cover them.

All would be well, except that, as of this writing, Citicorp's P1 commercial paper rating (the highest-quality rating) is in danger of being lowered, which, of course, also would lower the rating on the commercial paper issued by their clients and backed up by the credit facility. If Citicorp's rating is reduced, there is a significant chance that its clients' commercial paper cannot be rolled over. The market for low-grade commercial paper is drying up because the SEC has recently limited the amount of such paper that money market mutual funds may purchase. Citicorp would have to make loans to its clients under the reimbursement agreements.

This would require Citicorp to come up with $800 million in tier 1 and $800 million in tier 2 capital. As Table 19.6 indicates, as of year-end 1989, Citicorp is just barely in compliance with the guidelines for tier 1 capital. The decline in their commercial paper rating would force them into the market for equity at a time when their stock price is depressed.

Source: From *American Banker,* Tuesday, February 19, 1991, pp. 1 and 14.

The Impact of Capital Regulation on Large Banks. Table 19.6 indicates the ratio of capital to risk assets (both tier 1 and tier 2) for the largest 25 banks in the United States as of the end of 1989. As you can see, all the major bank holding companies meet the capital guidelines, but some, notably Citicorp, just barely do so. See Box 19.2.

Table 19.7 lists the capital-to-assets ratio for the 25 largest banking companies in the world. As indicated in the footnote to the table, the definition is not the same as the definition of tier 1 capital used by the Fed. Nonetheless, as you can see, most of the large banks, which are Japanese, do not meet the minimum 3-percent ratio of capital to total assets required by the Fed for the safest U.S. bank holding companies.

Table 19.7 TOP 25 BANK HOLDING COMPANIES IN THE WORLD, RANKED BY ASSETS ON DECEMBER 31, 1989 OR NEAREST FISCAL YEAR END

Rank	Bank	Country of Origination	Deposits in Billions of U.S. Dollars	Equity-to-Assets Ratio (%)
1	Dai-ichi Kangyo Bank, Ltd., Tokyo	Japan	403.4	2.91
2	Sumitomo Bank, Ltd., Osaka	Japan	368.2	3.49
3	Fuji Bank, Ltd., Tokyo	Japan	362.6	3.12
4	Mitsubishi Bank, Ltd., Tokyo	Japan	360.0	2.89
5	Sanwa Bank, Ltd., Osaka	Japan	353.7	3.11
6	Industrial Bank of Japan, Ltd., Tokyo	Japan	256.9	3.17
7	Credit Agricole Mutuel, Paris	France	242.3	4.88
8	Banque Nationale de Paris	France	231.8	2.67
9	Tokai Bank, Ltd., Nagoya	Japan	227.7	2.85
10	Citicorp, New York	U.S.	227.0	4.44
11	Norinchukin Bank, Tokyo	Japan	220.0	0.57
12	Mitsubishi Trust & Banking Corp., Tokyo	Japan	213.5	2.97
13	Credit Lyonnais, Paris	France	211.0	3.18
14	Barclays Bank Plc., London	U.K.	205.5	5.12
15	Mitsui Bank, Tokyo	Japan	203.3	2.69
16	Deutsche Bank, Frankfurt	Germany	202.6	4.18
17	Bank of Tokyo, Ltd.	Japan	200.5	2.90
18	Sumitomo Trust & Banking Co., Ltd., Osaka	Japan	190.9	2.36
19	National Westminster Bank Plc., London	U.K.	187.1	5.12
20	Mitsui Trust & Banking Co., Ltd., Tokyo	Japan	182.6	2.08
21	Societe Generale, Paris	France	176.0	2.29
22	Long Term Credit Bank of Japan, Ltd., Tokyo	Japan	174.2	3.50
23	Taiyo Kobe Bank, Ltd., Tokyo	Japan	173.0	2.42
24	Yasuda Trust & Banking Co., Ltd., Tokyo	Japan	157.8	2.95
25	Daiwa Bank, Ltd., Osaka	Japan	155.5	2.11

Source: American Banker, *Top Numbers: Part Two, 1990 Update,* p. 130.

Note: **Equity** includes shareholder's capital, which includes the value of common and perpetual preferred stock, surplus, undivided profits, and capital reserves. Minority interest is excluded whenever possible. **Total assets** excludes contra accounts and contingent liabilities.

How an Increase in Provisions for Reserves Decreases
Capital for Regulatory Purposes

On February 20, 1991, Chairman Greenspan of the Fed appeared before the Senate Banking Committee to testify about the credit crunch that he feared would prolong the recession. He stated that because regulators had tightened credit standards, banks would be unable to supply the credit necessary to get the economy moving again. He said that the tightening was an exaggerated response to loose credit standards that regulators had applied in the mid-1980s.

However, in 1991, banks faced a serious problem resulting from lax credit standards that made it difficult for them to expand lending, no matter what the policy of regulators might be. This problem is illustrated for money-center banks in Table 19.8. They faced a substantial, and increasing, ratio of past due and non-accrual loans (problem loans) to total loans (see Table 19.8, line 1). Even more troublesome was the increase in the problem loan ratio relative to reserves for loan loss (see Table 19.8, line 1 divided by line 5). This meant that the New York banks would have to increase reserves, which, as we explained in Chapter 10, must be replenished through provisions for loan loss. Recall that if provisions exceed net income, equity capital must decline.

The impact of increasing loan loss reserves on the equity-to-assets ratio for the major money-center banks is illustrated in Table 19.8. Problem loans at these banks have been a drag on performance since the mid-1980s, primarily because the banks had committed a high percentage of their assets to foreign, particularly Latin American, loans. Many Latin American economies were dependent on commodity exports

Table 19.8 PROBLEM LOANS AT NEW YORK MONEY-CENTER BANKS

	1987	1988	1989	1990*
1. Problem loans to total loans	5.70%	5.93%	5.96%	6.40%
a. Real estate loans	2.65%	3.27%	4.41%	7.46%
b. Commercial and industrial loans	6.47%	6.26%	5.70%	5.68%
c. Consumer loans	2.30%	2.36%	2.55%	2.82%
d. Foreign loans†	9.90%	11.66%	10.84%	8.77%
2. Foreign loans to total assets	23.70%	21.06%	19.66%	19.13%
3. Provisions for loan loss to assets (flow)	2.04%	0.54%	1.73%	0.76%
4. Return on assets	−0.63%	1.03%	−0.51%	0.43%
5. Retained earnings to assets	−0.89%	0.75%	−0.83%	0.05%
6. Loan loss reserves to assets (stock)	2.53%	2.40%	2.98%	2.43%
7. Equity capital to assets	4.51%	5.42%	4.79%	4.93%

Source: From Board of Governors of the Federal Reserve System, *Consolidated Financial Statements for Bank Holding Companies* (FR Y-9 C), Washington, 1991.

*Annualized data from September 1990.
†Also distributed among other categories.

to provide cash for debt servicing. In the mid-1980s, energy prices fell by some 50 percent, and other commodities, such as copper, experienced steep price drops as well. As a result, there was no cash to pay principal and interest on the loans.

In 1987, Citicorp decided to recognize the risk of default of its Latin American debt by increasing its loan loss reserves. Other money-center banks reluctantly followed suit. This created large losses at the major New York banks because provisions for loan loss were greater than net income (see Table 19.8, lines 3 and 4).

In 1988, however, money-center banks appeared to have a good year. Provisions were low, so net income and retained earnings were high; consequently, capital-to-assets ratios improved. However, in 1989, another large provision was made to cover Latin American debt. This time Morgan, the most strongly capitalized money-center bank, made the decision to increase reserves, and again reluctantly, the other banks followed suit. Capital-to-assets ratios fell sharply as provisions exceeded income.

In 1990, the domestic real estate loans turned into the new problem facing banks (see Table 19.8, line 1a). This time the money centers did not increase their reserves to cover the increase in problem loans (see Table 19.8, lines 1 and 6). Hence net income remained positive, and capital-to-assets ratios rose. The market, however, did not believe that the reported earnings were real. That is, it believed that these banks would eventually have to increase reserves. Consequently, bank stocks fell sharply, until the Fed lowered the discount rate in early 1991.

Capital Regulation as a Substitute for Principal-Agent Theory

When we studied the incentive effects of firm liability structure in Chapter 2, we found that the capital-to-assets ratio of a firm is determined by the stockholders' need to police management. Highly leveraged firms must meet large interest payments relative to total revenue. Since management usually wants to avoid bankruptcy, a high degree of leverage forces them to operate in a conservative manner. If principal-agent theory explained the differences in leverage ratios across banks, we would not need capital requirements. The most highly leveraged banks would not necessarily have higher probabilities of bankruptcy than the least leveraged, since high leverage is one way that owners encourage more conservative behavior on the part of management. Public regulation of the leverage ratio would be pointless because the market would establish the best leverage ratio to reduce management risk taking.

The reason that regulators are not guided by the conclusions of principal-agent theory is the fact that bank liabilities are insured. Since depositors and other bank liability holders are insured, they do not care about the riskiness of their bank. They enjoy a risk-free rate of return on their liabilities regardless of the riskiness of their bank's portfolio. A high degree of leverage can then yield a gain to both stockholders and management, and also managers may be persuaded by the potential gain to bear the increased risk of bankruptcy by holding a risky, high-payoff asset portfolio. Thus leverage becomes a way of gambling at the government insurance agency's expense rather than a way of containing the negative consequences of management independence.

Table 19.9 provides an example of such behavior. We consider the problem of insurance and bank risk in some detail in Chapter 20.

Table 19.9 INSURANCE INCENTIVE TO INCREASE LEVERAGE

Assumptions: Risk-free interest rate is 5 percent
Bank loans earn 6 percent, and deposits pay 5 percent for interest

Balance Sheet

ASSETS		LIABILITIES	
Loans	$1,000	Deposits	$900
		Equity	$100

Income Statement

Income	$60
Deposit expense	45
Net income	15
Return on equity	15%

Now the bank increases its leverage. Deposits are insured.

Balance Sheet

ASSETS		LIABILITIES	
Loans	$1,000	Deposits	$950
		Equity	$50

Income Statement

Income	$60
Deposit expense	47.5
Net income	12.5
Return on equity	25%

Without insurance, assume that deposit expense would rise to 5.5 percent with the increase in leverage.

Income Statement

Income	$60
Deposit expense	52.5
Net income	7.75
Return on equity	15.5%

Conclusion: Insurance makes leverage more attractive.

Supervising Banks Through Capital Regulation. The insurance system sets up incentives to take risk that are difficult for regulators to thwart. Capital regulation, upon which regulators are increasingly dependent, may not save the FDIC from future losses. This is illustrated in the case of the Bank of New England, which was declared insolvent in January 1991. In 1988, the Bank of New England, with $33 billion in assets, reported a healthy capital-to-assets ratio of 5.1 percent. Its loan charge-off ratio was only slightly above the industry average, and nonperforming loans were well within the industry norm as well. Yet the very next year, its capital-to-assets ratio became negative as it took large provisions to cover expected loan losses. Thus, in 1 year, the Bank of New England went from an institution that apparently satisfied the regulatory guidelines to a bank that had no equity at all.

The Impact of Capital Regulation on Risk and Liquidity Premiums

What effect will stringent capital requirements have on the banking system and on the financial markets that depend on them for liquidity? To analyze this problem, we consider the impact of this policy under the assumption that it succeeds at its purpose, which is to reduce the risk exposure of the FDIC. We assume that it succeeds because shareholders are forced to put up more of their own money, which they would lose in the event of bankruptcy. This decreases the expected gain from investing in a risky portfolio.

The impact of a reduction in the FDIC subsidy on liquidity premiums depends on who benefited from the subsidy in the first place. Since the subsidy represented a gain to banks, it should have caused the banking system to expand. It also created an incentive to increase risk; hence it should have led to higher leverage ratios and riskier loan portfolios. The expansion effect and the leverage effect should have led to lower liquidity premiums (higher returns on liquid securities) as a result of the expansion of liquid bank liabilities. The loan effect should have reduced risk premiums as a result of the increased demand for risky loans by banks.

Thus the most likely outcome of a decrease in the FDIC subsidy is higher liquidity premiums. This will lead to an increase in the return on CDs and commercial paper relative to demand deposits and overnight repurchase agreements. In turn, the capital requirement will raise the required return on less liquid assets relative to commercial paper. There will be fewer liquid assets and, consequently, less settlement in good funds. Thus the banking system will shrink relative to financial markets in general.

Not all banks are faced with the problem of shrinkage. As we will see below, smaller banks meet the capital requirements with ease. Many of these have room to expand to replace the capacity of those which are forced to shrink. However, the presumption is that the reduction in the subsidy will cause the industry as a whole to shrink, causing the cost of liquidity to rise.

Threats to the Solvency of the FDIC

Ironically, the bank holding companies that are the greatest threat to the solvency of the bank insurance fund are those which have the fewest insured deposits to total liabilities. This is illustrated in Figure 19.3, in which we plot the ratio of insured deposits to total liabilities against average loan loss reserves to assets over the years 1985 through 1989. It is also apparent, from Figure 19.4, that the banks with the lowest ratio of insured deposits are also the largest banks in the country.

At the beginning of 1991, the FDIC fund to insure deposits totaled $9 billion. In 1990, it lost almost $4 billion. The FDIC expected that with the losses associated with the Bank of New England and other expected failures, the fund would decline to $4 billion by the end of 1991. A few more large bank failures, which are not unexpected, would wipe out the fund.

It is clear that supervision has not adequately protected the banking system from risk, and the largest bank holding companies represent the greatest potential liability of the FDIC. As a result, Congress and the Bush administration are, as of

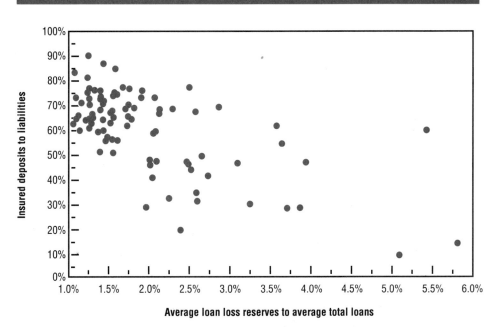

Average loan loss reserves to average total loans

Figure 19.3   RISKY LOANS VERSUS INSURED DEPOSITS   Average for the Top 96 Bank Holding Companies *Note:* Insured deposits include the following: demand deposits, NOWs, money market deposits, other savings, and time deposits less than $100,000. *Source:* From Board of Governors of the Federal Reserve, *Reports of Condition and Income for Bank Holding Companies,* 1985, 1986, 1987, 1988, 1989, and September 1990.

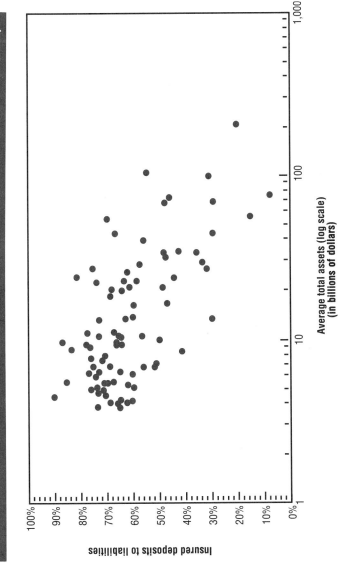

Figure 19.4 INSURANCE VERSUS BANK SIZE *Average for the 96 Largest Bank Holding Companies Note:* Insured deposits include the following: demand deposits, NOWs, money market deposits, other savings, and time deposits less than $100,000. *Source:* From Board of Governors of the Federal Reserve, *Reports of Condition and Income for Bank Holding Companies,* 1985, 1986, 1987, 1988, 1989, and September 1990.

this writing, considering ways to strengthen the banking system, particularly the large banks. The proposals focus on deregulating the banking system with the hope of attracting additional capital to the industry. (See a description of the Treasury proposal for bank reform in Box 19.3.) We now turn to an analysis of whether deregulation will achieve the aim of strengthening the banking system.

REFORMING THE BANKING SYSTEM

The Treasury proposal for reform of the U.S. banking system, by encouraging banks to engage in a broader range of activities and permitting ownership of banks by industrial companies, breaks with a strong tradition in American banking. The

The Treasury would permit well-capitalized bank holding companies to engage in a variety of new activities. For example, they could own financial affiliates that underwrite corporate securities and provide all kinds of insurance. Currently, bank holding companies are severely restricted in their ability to enter these businesses. The Treasury also would permit banks to manage mutual funds.

The hope is that the expansion of powers will improve bank income, making their equity more attractive to investors. To further improve the market for bank equity, the Treasury also would permit industrial companies to own banks, which is currently strictly prohibited.

The proposal includes safeguards to prevent banks from lending money to nonbank affiliates in the holding company. Most of these safeguards are already in place. They will be described in the text.

The Treasury also would eliminate restrictions on interstate branching. Currently, banks are not allowed to branch across state lines. By permitting banks greater geographic diversity in their business, the Treasury hopes to stabilize their earnings, again making their equity more marketable.

The proposal also would reassign regulatory authority among the various agencies. It would eliminate duplication; only one regulator would be responsible for each bank. Insured state-chartered banks would be regulated solely by the Fed. Insured national banks would be regulated solely by the Comptroller of the Currency. Bank holding companies would be regulated by the agency that regulates the main bank in the holding company. The FDIC would lose its regulatory authority.

The proposed reassignment of regulatory authority has created opposition among the agencies affected. The Fed is opposed because it would end up regulating mostly small banks; it believes its major role in the payments system requires it to have authority over large banks. The FDIC says it needs to regulate the banks it insures. The Treasury has indicated that its proposal to exclude the FDIC from supervision was a mistake.

tradition is that banking should be kept distinct from other lines of commerce. For example, in 1905, a New York State commission to investigate alleged fraud in the insurance industry recommended that banks be prohibited from entering the insurance business. The commission's recommendation was accepted by the state legislature, and the principle was adopted generally by other states.

The tradition is based on the notion that bankers' judgments on matters of credit should be free from the possibilities of conflicts of interest. We saw in Chapter 14, for example, that banks play a distinct role in managing credit crises in individual firms. In the United States, they exercise this power through control of the bank deposit. For other creditors to trust their judgments as honest brokers, banks eschew holding securities that are commonly held by other investors.

The Treasury argues that this limitation on banks has lessened their ability to raise equity capital and has consequently contributed to the deteriorating financial condition of the banking system and the near bankruptcy of the FDIC. In this section we consider the history of the American tradition of separating banking from other lines of commerce and comment on the effects of removing these restrictions.

The Evolution of Bank Holding Companies

Commercial banking historically remained separate from other lines of commerce until World War I. National banks were restricted to activities narrowly defined as banking, mainly taking deposits and making commercial loans. Most states had similarly restrictive laws. During World War I, the U.S. Treasury used deficit finance to fund the war effort, which required the flotation of a large quantity of Treasury bonds. The Treasury needed to find a low-cost way to reach the buying public. Securities firms did not provide brokerage services to the general public at the time; commercial banks were the only financial institution in contact with the broad public.

The Treasury asked the banks to sell bonds, and many banks established **subsidiary companies,** known as **security affiliates,** to underwrite war bonds. When one company wholly owns or holds enough shares to control another company, the latter company is known as a subsidiary of the former. National banks had to establish security affiliates because they were prohibited from directly engaging in the securities business. In this context, we define the securities business as the underwriting of securities and their sale and purchase for the bank's own account.

A usual form of corporate organization used by banks was to establish a holding company to own the stock of both the bank and the affiliates engaged in underwriting securities. Thus the bank holding company was born.

After World War I, the government budget quickly returned to surplus, and the amount of its outstanding debt began to shrink. The securities affiliates of banks now began underwriting the bonds and, in some cases, the equity of private corporations. After the stock market crash in October 1929, many people believed that banks had used their securities affiliates to speculate in the stock market and that the collapse of securities affiliates contributed to the collapse of the banking system. The classic example of this was the failure of the Bank of United States (see Chapter 20).

That the collapse of a securities affiliate can, at least conceptually, drag down a bank is illustrated in the balance sheet presented in Table 19.10. The table illustrates that equity in the affiliate effectively can be financed by deposits through loans from the bank rather than by equity in the bank holding company. If the affiliate goes under, the value of the bank's assets falls below the value of its deposit liabilities.

Adding to the general concern that banks were playing the stock market with depositors' money was the perception that conflicts of interest encouraged banks to take extreme risks. It was argued that a bank has an incentive to lend money to a financially distressed affiliate that it would not have if the affiliate were, in fact, independent of the bank.

Table 19.10 BANK HOLDING COMPANY AFFILIATE BANKRUPTS A BANK ($BILLIONS)

Bank Holding Company				Bank			
ASSETS		**LIABILITIES AND NET WORTH**		**ASSETS**		**LIABILITIES AND NET WORTH**	
Equity in bank	5	Loans from bank	15	Loan to bank holding company	15	Deposits	95
Equity in affiliate	15	Equity	5	Other loans	85	Equity	5

Affiliate Goes Bankrupt

Bank Holding Company				Bank			
ASSETS		**LIABILITIES AND NET WORTH**		**ASSETS**		**LIABILITIES AND NET WORTH**	
Equity in bank	5	Loans from bank	15	Loan to bank holding company	5	Deposits	95
Equity in affiliate	0	Equity	−10	Other loans	85	Equity	−5

To see this argument, consider again Table 19.10. The affiliate and, consequently, the bank are already bankrupt. If the bank's stockholders can hide the true financial condition of the affiliate from the public and raise additional deposits to make further loans to the affiliate, they have nothing to lose. After all, inaction means they have already lost their entire investment, so why not try to salvage something by throwing good money after bad? If they do not succeed, only the depositors lose.

These concerns, coupled with the sensational example of the Bank of United States, led to the passage of the Glass-Steagall Banking Act in 1933. This law prohibited banks from owning affiliates that are principally engaged in underwriting corporate securities and certain securities of state and local governments as well.

The Regulation of Bank Holding Companies

The Glass-Steagall Act prohibited banks from forming affiliates to engage in underwriting corporate securities, but it did not regulate the establishment of affiliates to carry on other activities that banks were not allowed to engage in directly. For example, banks were prohibited from engaging in most insurance underwriting, but they could legally do so by establishing an affiliate.

The same conflict of interest arguments that we discussed earlier were made to argue that the ability of banks to establish affiliates in general should be strictly regulated. The result was the Bank Holding Company Act of 1956. This act regulates the nonbank activities of holding companies that own more than one bank. It established a doctrine that bank holding companies could only engage in activities that are "closely related" to banking. The Federal Reserve was given authority to define these activities and regulate bank holding companies, even if none of the banks in the holding company were members of the Federal Reserve System.

It did not take long for large banks to realize that they could expand their activities beyond those considered "closely related" to banking by forming single-bank holding companies, which were exempt from the 1956 law. The 1956 law had only covered holding companies that held *more* than one bank. In 1970, Congress decided to close this loophole by amending the law to include regulation of single-bank holding companies as well. The Bank Holding Company Act as amended in 1970 is the primary law regulating the activities permissible to commercial banks through holding companies.

Holding companies may "undertake certain activities that the Federal Reserve Board determines to be so closely related to banking, or to managing or controlling banks, as to be a proper incident to banking and that would result in benefits to the public."[8] Until recently, the Board of Governors defined this narrowly to restrict bank holding companies to owning businesses that are similar to banks, such as finance companies and thrift institutions. They also could establish securities affiliates to engage in underwriting securities not prohibited by the Glass–Steagall Act. However, in the late 1980s, the Fed began to liberalize its stance.

Cracks in the Wall Around Banking

In the 1980s, the Fed became concerned about the soundness of the money-center and other large bank holding companies. Recall from Figures 19.3 and 19.4 that the large bank holding companies have taken on more risk than the smaller companies. The Fed came to believe that this happened because large corporations no longer depended on banks to finance their activities. The most commonly cited evidence for this proposition is the rise in the commercial paper market, which we observed in Chapter 14. The Fed reasoned that because large corporations, which were generally low-risk customers, no longer needed big banks, big banks were forced to find new, riskier customers. The result was a deterioration in the quality of their balance sheets.

The Fed's remedy for this problem was to let bank holding companies back into the securities business, because, they reasoned, this would bring the large corporate customers back to the banks. To get bank holding companies into the securities business, the Fed had to find a way around the Glass–Steagall Act. They did this by interpreting the words "principally engaged."

---

8. Board of Governors, *op. cit.*, p. 98.

Box 19.4

Bank Holding Company Inroads
into Securities Underwriting

In mid-1989, the Fed granted approval for bank holding companies to own a securities affiliate that underwrites corporate debt and asset-based securities, as long as that affiliate is not "principally engaged" in the business. As of this writing, five domestic bank holding companies, all headquartered in New York and California, have been given permission to underwrite corporate debt.

In September 1990, J. P. Morgan, a large New York holding company that does not engage in retail banking, received permission to underwrite equity securities under the same exception the Fed made to the Glass-Steagall Act to permit bank holding companies to underwrite corporate debt. In January 1991, three more bank holding companies, one American and two Canadian, also were given permission to engage in this activity.

So far only two domestic bank holding companies play a significant role in underwriting corporate securities. They are Morgan and Citicorp. According to Securities Data Corporation, in 1990, Morgan and Citicorp each had 1.3 percent of the market for underwriting corporate debt. In contrast, Merrill Lynch, the largest domestic underwriter, had 17.3 percent of the market. Analysts expect the banking companies to have a long, hard climb to catch up to the leading investment banks in the domestic market.

Source: Data are quoted from *American Banker,* January 3, 1991, pp. 1 and 10.

Banks are not allowed to own affiliates that are "principally engaged" in underwriting corporate securities. However, because the Glass-Steagall Act did not define this term, the Fed chose to define it as prohibiting affiliates that received more than 10 percent of their revenue from underwriting corporate securities. The courts upheld this interpretation. Several large bank holding companies have been given permission to engage in underwriting corporate securities. See Box 19.4.

Funding Holding Company Subsidiaries

The Fed believes that bank holding companies can engage in underwriting through subsidiaries with little danger that bank depositors will be hurt by conflicts of interest because the Bank Holding Company Act strictly regulates transactions between banks and other affiliates owned by a single holding company. The separation of the bank from the other subsidiaries of a holding company is known as a **firewall.** Thus, they argue, the transaction described in Table 19.10 cannot possibly occur today. The bank would be prohibited from making a loan to the holding company for the purpose of funding the securities affillitate.

Why Firewalls Are Ineffective

Unfortunately, firewalls are probably not a foolproof method of protecting a bank's decisions from events affecting the remainder of a holding company. For example, consider the balance sheet in Table 19.11 of the Infinite Horizons Corporation, a holding company that owns the controlling equity of the Disolvem Chemical Company and the Number One Bank. The bank has a book value of $1 billion, and the chemical company has a book value of $2 billion. These assets are financed with $1.5 billion in bonds and commercial paper and $1.5 billion in equity. We assume that the holding company's cost of debt is 12 percent, so its interest expenses equal $180 million per year.

Number One Bank is managed independently of Disolvem and scrupulously avoids lending to either Infinite Horizons or Disolvem. Soundly operated, the bank holds high-quality assets and pays a steady stream of earnings to Infinite Horizons in the form of dividends, equal to 12 percent of the book value of its equity, or $120 million per year. The chemical company is somewhat riskier than the bank. It usually pays a dividend of 15 percent of its book value, or $300 million, to the parent company. These dividends are more than sufficient to pay the interest on the holding company's bonds and commercial paper. The firewalls have prevented Infinite Horizons from misusing the resources of Number One Bank by precluding direct loans.

Now suppose that one of Disolvem's plants accidently releases a compound that turns Lake Michigan into airplane glue. The Environmental Protection Agency (EPA) sues Disolvem, and it is clear that within 2 years the courts will close Disolvem and liquidate its assets. The earnings from Number One Bank alone will be insufficient to service the bond and commercial paper claims against Infinite Horizons. The holding company will be bankrupt, and its controlling stock in the bank will be sold to pay off the bondholders. Infinite Horizons' management will be out of a job.

Table 19.11 INFINITE HORIZONS' BALANCE SHEET ($MILLIONS)

ASSETS		LIABILITIES	
Stock in Disolvem Chemical Company	2,000	Bonds and commercial paper	1,500
Stock in Number One Bank	1,000	Capital	1,500

How can Infinite Horizons' management avoid this fate? Its only choice is to replace the conservative banker who manages Number One Bank with a risk taker given the task of generating high current returns and dividends. High enough current earnings on Number One Bank stock may be sufficient to service bondholders of Infinite Horizons, allowing the management to retain control. Thus the failure of Disolvem turns the formerly soundly managed bank into a gambler. If the strategy fails, the bank and the holding company will go bankrupt, and the FDIC will have a liability. The firewall has not prevented the holding company from pushing Number One Bank's management into unsound practices.

Evaluating the Treasury's Proposal

The Treasury argues, along with Fed, that the capital position of large bank holding companies will only improve if banks are allowed to engage in a broader range of activities. Thus their proposal would repeal the Glass–Steagall Act. It also would go further than this: It would permit industrial companies to own banks. The Treasury argues that broader ownership potential is necessary to improve the market for bank stocks.

Can deregulation save the large bank holding companies? The argument hinges on whether broader powers for bank holding companies can improve the profitability of their bank subsidiaries. The perceived weakness of the money-center banks is that the *banking business* is unprofitable. If the new powers do nothing for the banking business, it will not be attractive for investors to use the profits from viable businesses to subsidize the weaker banking business.

In Chapters 13 and 14 we saw that banks play a crucial role in supplying liquidity to the markets that large corporations depend on to raise capital. Thus the role of banks in wholesale credit markets remains crucial, but the scope of their participation has narrowed. The argument for broader securities powers is that the same information banks accumulate to price lines of credit can be used to price securities issued by the firms that have the lines. Thus there are economies of scope in permitting banks to supply both lines of credit and underwrite securities.

Economies of scope are gains achieved by performing two or more businesses within the same organization. They most often arise when two businesses can be run using the equipment that would have been needed to run one alone. For example, a beef slaughterhouse can achieve economies of scope by selling beef and hides.

We pointed out the problem with this argument in Chapter 14. Specifically, in Box 14.6 we saw that Citicorp attempted to gain from economies of scope but had to back off because of potential conflicts of interest. We suspect that when bank holding companies attempt to achieve economies of scope between providing liquidity to securities markets and dealing in the securities themselves, they will run into similar problems. Hence we are skeptical that broader securities powers can cure the ills of large money-center banks.

Reform of Laws Governing U.S. Banking Structure

The Treasury's proposal also includes the removal of interstate branching restrictions, and this is designed to encourage the formation of large banks that operate on a nationwide scale. Many political leaders are disturbed that only one American bank is listed among the top 25 banks in the world. They believe that geographic deregulation will cause the banking industry to consolidate, creating large banks that can more efficiently compete with foreign banks. This, in turn, should improve the financial health of large banks, permitting them to raise capital more easily. In this section we evaluate the impact of geographic deregulation on U.S. banking structure.

As of the beginning of 1991, banks were still prohibited from branching across state lines. This was so because state law governed branching; for example, some states, such as Illinois, prohibit branching altogether. Others, such as Texas, permit branching, but on a limited basis, such as within the county in which a bank has its head office or within counties contiguous to that county. Other states, such as New York and California, permit banks to branch statewide. It is because of the restrictive branching laws of many of the states that there are over 12,500 banks in the United States.

The reason states have control over branching goes back to the dual nature of the American banking system. Recall that banks can be chartered by either state authorities or federal authorities. No state has permitted a bank controlled by regulators of another state to do business within its borders.

Bank holding companies, however, have been permitted to own banks in more than one state, although this too has been subject to state regulation. The Douglas Amendment to the Bank Holding Company Act of 1956 gave a state the authority to deny bank holding companies owning banks in other states from doing business within its borders.

Over the past decade, all but five states have liberalized their laws to permit out-of-state holding companies to own banks within their borders. To determine the impact of the Treasury's proposal on American bank structure, we will investigate the effect of the liberalization that has occurred to date on the national market share of the largest bank holding companies. Our analysis is confined to the period 1976 through 1987 because 1987 data are the most recent available from the Fed.

The data presented in Table 19.12 indicate that the share of domestic banking assets held by the 10 largest bank holding companies declined slightly over the period, despite the liberalization of state restrictions. Bank holding companies in the size category 25 to 100 experienced the largest gains.

Part of the reason for this is that most states placed restrictions on which out-of-state bank holding companies could enter their markets. For example, many formed regional compacts that only opened their markets to holding companies from neighboring states. Table 19.13 indicates the share of banking assets held by the largest 10 holding companies in each region of the country.

For some regions, especially New England, the share of assets held by the top

Table 19.12 SHARES OF DOMESTIC BANKING ASSETS, ACCOUNTED FOR BY THE LARGEST BANKING ORGANIZATIONS

		Rank by Asset Size		
Year	1 to 10	11 to 25	26 to 50	51 to 100	Top 100
1987	20.2	14.6	13.5	13.2	61.5
1986	20.0	13.5	12.7	12.9	59.1
1985	20.3	12.8	12.6	12.0	57.7
1984	20.3	12.8	10.4	11.5	55.0
1983	21.0	12.8	9.4	11.1	54.3
1982	21.8	12.4	8.8	10.6	53.6
1981	21.1	12.0	8.5	10.1	51.7
1980	21.6	11.5	8.5	9.8	51.4
1979	21.3	11.3	8.9	9.7	51.2
1978	21.1	11.3	8.7	9.7	50.8
1977	21.0	11.0	8.5	9.7	50.2

Source: From *Federal Reserve Bulletin*, Vol. 75, (March 1989), p. 126.

Table 19.13 GEOGRAPHIC DISTRIBUTION OF DOMESTIC BANKING ASSETS, 1987

Region	Number of Banking Organizations	Banking Assets (Billions $)	Percent Change in Assets 1976–1987	Percent Change in No. of Organizations 1976–1987	Share of Assets Held by the 10 Largest Organizations (%)	
					1976	1987
Northeast	198	155.3	306.5	− 33.1	51.9	77.8
Midatlantic	484	695.3	234.3	− 34.3	58.5	58.1
Southeast	1548	459.8	117.3	− 28.5	18.3	43.5
Midwest	3875	604.6	143.8	− 26.4	24.5	29.4
Southwest	3450	335.4	132.2	− 1.8	24.0	35.9
West	652	349.2	171.4	52.3	75.1	70.4

Source: From *Federal Reserve Bulletin*, Vol. 75 (March 1989), p. 129.

Note: The regions are defined as follows: Northeast = Connecticut, Maine, Massachusetts, New Hampshire, Rhode Island, and Vermont; Midatlantic = Delaware, New Jersey, New York, and Pennsylvania; Southeast = Alabama, District of Columbia, Florida, Georgia, Maryland, Mississippi, North Carolina, South Carolina, Tennessee, Virginia, and West Virginia; Midwest = Illinois, Indiana, Iowa, Kentucky, Michigan, Minnesota, Missouri, Montana, North Dakota, Ohio, South Dakota, and Wisconsin; Southwest = Arkansas, Arizona, Colorado, Kansas, Louisiana, Nebraska, New Mexico, Oklahoma, Texas, and Wyoming; West = Alaska, California, Hawaii, Idaho, Nevada, Oregon, Utah, and Washington.

10 holding companies increased dramatically. Are the New England results indicative of what will happen to the share of the nation's largest banking companies after the legalization of nationwide interstate branching? A closer look at the regional results leaves room for doubt.

The West, which has three of the largest retail banking companies in the country, actually experienced a decline in market concentration. This occurred despite the fact that the large California bank holding companies aggressively expanded outside their home state, purchasing banks in Oregon and Washington. While they were busy doing this, they saw their share of the California market fall from 78 to 67 percent.

The Midatlantic region, which is home to the large New York banks, experienced no change in concentration. This was partly due to the fact that states in the region refused to form pacts with New York, for fear that the New York banks would dominate their markets. However, New York State has been a statewide branching state since the mid-1970s, and the New York City banks have failed to penetrate the upstate market. This indicates that it is not so easy for large banks to penetrate a market, even if the law permits such expansion. In 1989, New Jersey permitted New York bank holding companies to own banks in New Jersey. So far, only one of the major New York banking companies has taken advantage of the offer, and the bank it owns is not among the top three banks in the state.

There is no obvious trend toward large bank dominance because there are few economies of scale in banking for which it is necessary to form large banks. For example, much of the business of financial firms requires processing large quantities of data and paper. Loan payments must be received and credited to the proper account. Interest payments must be credited to depositors, and monthly statements must be prepared. Because these "back office" activities are computer intensive, they are subject to some economies of scale. However, small banks can, and do, hire independent firms to do their processing for them. See Box 19.5.

The major problem that financial companies have in getting big is obtaining access to large numbers of customers. For example, the concentration ratio among consumer finance companies is fairly high—the top three companies have over 60 percent of the market. However, the top three firms are the finance company subsidiaries of the big three automobile companies. Their market share is derived from their access to consumers through car dealerships.

On the other hand, the concentration ratio of business loans provided by finance companies is much lower. The top three firms have only about 32 percent of the market. Again, these are the subsidiaries of the automobile companies. Recall from Chapter 14 that automobile credit makes up a large portion of the business loans at finance companies, although not as large a portion as in the consumer market. Consequently, the automobile finance subsidiaries have a lower share of the business market. With the diversity of the equipment to be financed, no company has dominant access to the customers. Thus the shares of the largest firms are much smaller.

In retail banking, the primary vehicle for customer acquisition is the local branch network. The local bank maintains its advantage, even with nationwide ATM networks, for various reasons. One is that small businesses are the major beneficiaries of a conveniently located branch. Convenient cash pickup and delivery is crucial to a small retailer. Second, network ATMs do not perform all the functions of own-bank ATMs. For example, the customer of an out-of-state bank usually cannot make deposits in a network ATM. Also, banks are charged a fee when its customer uses another bank's ATM, which is often passed on to the customer. However, perhaps the biggest reason for the dominance of the local bank in its own market is the convenience that the local branch provides for opening up an account.

Thus a bank holding company establishing a nationwide business must go through the expensive task of buying banks in the major markets across the country or opening up new local branch networks. None of the large bank holding companies currently has the financial resources to make itself a dominant player nationwide. Ironically, as Figures 19.3 and 19.4 indicate, it is the smaller bank holding companies that are healthier than the large ones. Thus the Treasury's recommendation for interstate branching, while a desirable move, will not create a few large, highly capitalized banking companies that dominate the national market.

A large bank holding company operating nationwide would have the advantage of diversification. Recall from Box 3.3 that over the last 5 years, the return on bank assets has varied significantly across Federal Reserve districts. However, the operating aspects of banking make it difficult to achieve the scale required for diversification. The acquisition of retail customers is very costly. See Box 19.6.

CONCLUSION

In this chapter we have traced the evolution of the U.S. bank regulatory system. We have found that it first evolved to increase the liquidity of payments markets. The experiences of the Great Depression extended the role of regulation to insuring retail deposits. The experiences of the 1980s led to the "too big to fail" doctrine, which essentially provided for insurance of all liability holders of large banks. This policy has led to the near bankruptcy of the FDIC. The remedy for the problem—broader powers for bank holding companies—appears unlikely to solve the problem.

Box 19.6

Banking Structure in Japan

As we have noted, Japan is the home of the largest banking organizations in the world. Does this mean that the Japanese banking market is dominated by a few large banks? The accompanying table indicates that the largest 13 banks in Japan, known as "city banks," have over 45 percent of total domestic bank deposits, compared with 23.5 percent for the 13 largest in the United States.

To arrive at this number, we have defined bank deposits relatively narrowly. We have excluded the large postal savings system in Japan, which is run by the government and offers the public a bank-like deposit. On March 31, 1990, the postal savings system had deposit liabilities of $1,007 billion. If these were added to the bank deposit total, the share of city banks would fall to 34.9 percent. In addition, Japan has a large number of cooperative banks with deposits of about $750 billion, about $250 billion smaller than the U.S. thrift and credit union industries combined.

Despite the relatively high concentration ratio, Japan does not really have nationwide banking. As of September 1990, 92 percent of the domestic branches and subbranches of the seven largest Japanese banks were located in the three largest metropolitan areas—Kanto (Tokyo), Kinki (Osaka), and Aichi (Nagoya). In addition, in March 1990, the city banks had only 21.4 percent of the total domestic bank branches, less than half their deposit share.

The markets outside the major metropolitan areas are serviced by 132 "regional banks." The city banks were effectively prohibited from branching extensively into these markets

KEY TERMS

Federal Deposit Insurance
  Corporation (FDIC)

state bank

national bank

Comptroller of the Currency

central reserve cities

call money market

discount

Monetary Control Act of 1980

bank holding company

advance

adjustment credit

seasonal credit

extended credit

"too big to fail" doctrine

bank examination

cease and desist orders

book value

CONCENTRATION RATIOS IN JAPAN AND THE UNITED STATES (US $MILLIONS), MARCH 31, 1990

	Japan	United States
A. Domestic deposits of the 13 largest commercial banks	1,477,282	516,659
B. Total domestic deposits at all commercial banks	3,227,542	2,201,899
Concentration ratio (A/B)	45.77%	23.46%

Source: From *Federal Reserve Bulletin,* January 1991, p. A73; Consolidated Financial Statements for Bank Holding Companies as reported to the Board of Governors of the Federal Reserve System; Bank of Japan, *Economic Statistics Monthly,* July 1990, pp. 33–36.

Note: Conversion rate: ¥130 = $1.00.

because they are limited in the number of branches they are allowed to open in a given year. However, there is no rule against the acquisition of regional banks by city banks. In fact, recently, Sumitomo Bank bought a regional bank that operates in the Tokyo metropolitan area. However, there has as yet been no interest in the acquisition of a regional bank operating outside the major markets. This pattern is similar to the lack of interest displayed by the New York City banks in upstate New York markets.

weighted risk assets   security affiliate
goodwill   firewall
subsidiary company   economies of scope

EXERCISES

1. To ensure the delivery of payments, the traditional clearinghouse held reserves to cover net "due to" positions. Yet banking crises, such as the one in 1907, occurred with some regularity. Why was a banking system that guaranteed net "due to's" among banks inadequate to ensure financial stability?

2. The Fed was formed to provide a more elastic currency, which meant that it would expand reserves in a period of financial crisis. In comparison, the private clearinghouse could not expand reserves without buying them on the open market through sales of short-term bank bills. If the Fed expanded reserves through buying the same bills, what would the creation of the Fed imply for the price of bills in a liquidity crisis? Would this change the interest rate at which lenders would be willing to hold bills in normal times?

3. Consider a financial system that consists of banks and stock brokerage houses. The banks are constrained by regulation to hold short-term loans as assets and deposit-like accounts as liabilities. The central bank guarantees that intraday payments messages will be converted to good funds at settlement. All payments are made through accounting-entry bookkeeping in the banks. The stock brokerage houses are completely unregulated.

    a. Describe the effect on the allocation of resources if bank regulation were terminated.

    b. Suppose that a large percentage of banks suddenly became insolvent. Under what circumstances would this event have a strong impact on the allocation of resources? Are banks then "special" financial intermediaries that require regulation and protection?

4. Explain how federal regulatory policy led finally to the "too big to fail" doctrine.

5. In recent large bank failures, the federal regulatory authorities have had to announce their intention to bail out all liability holders (except bondholders) before the market for wholesale liabilities stabilized. What does this imply about the firmness of the market's belief in the "too big to fail" doctrine?

6. Why are reserve requirements lower for small banks than for large banks?

7. Why are cease and desist orders often ineffective at preventing bank failure?

8. Explain how goodwill can arise in an acquisition. Why don't bank regulators count goodwill as capital?

9. What is the justification for regulation of bank capital? Explain how government insurance encourages leverage.

10. How do you suppose banks will attempt to get around capital regulation?

11. Provide arguments both for and against allowing depository institutions to undertake investment banking activities either directly or through securities affiliates.

12. Who gains from the continued existence of the Glass–Steagall Banking Act of 1933?

13. What is the purpose of separating banking from commerce?

14. Explain why firewalls are not foolproof.

15. Discuss the impact of product deregulation on the viability of the large money-center banks.

16. What forces will retard rapid consolidation of the U.S. banking system, even if Congress passes interstate banking?

FURTHER READING

Amel, Dean F., and Michael J. Jacowski. "Trends in Banking Structure Since the Mid-1970s," *Federal Reserve Bulletin,* March 1989, pp. 120–133.

Board of Governors of the Federal Reserve System. *The Federal Reserve System, Purposes and Functions.* Washington, 1984.

Dykes, Sayre Ellen. "The Establishment and Evolution of the Federal Reserve Board: 1913–1923," *Federal Reserve Bulletin,* April 1989, pp. 227–243.

"Final Rule: Amendments to Regulations H & Y (Risk-Based Capital Regulations)," *Federal Reserve Bulletin,* March 1989, pp. 152–187.

Miron, Jeffrey A. "Financial Panics, the Seasonality of the Nominal Interest Rate, and the Founding of the Fed," *American Economic Review,* March 1986, pp. 125–140.

White, Eugene Nelson. *The Regulation and Reform of the American Banking System, 1900–1929.* Princeton, N.J.: Princeton University Press, 1983.

20

Rogue Banks: Moral Hazard
in the Banking System

How do banks turn bad? We have considered the operation of the U.S. bank regulatory system, concentrating mainly on the tools of the regulator. We now examine problems that arise when banks circumvent the regulator or when the regulator colludes with banks to engage in imprudent behavior. This is the problem of moral hazard: Bank management can find ways to increase the risk of the bank's activities and turn the bank's resources to its own advantage without the knowledge of the bank's creditors. Such acts need not even be fraudulent or illegal. Any losses that accrue can be attributed merely to bad business decisions rather than to prosecutable violations. The role of prudential regulation, of course, is to prevent this from happening.

SOUND BANKING PRINCIPLES

Prudent behavior for banks can be summarized in a few guiding principles that are useful for banks anywhere in the world.[1]

1. A more detailed description of these principles and the moral hazard problems that can arise in bank management can be found in Aristobulo de Juan, *Does Bank Insolvency Matter?* (Washington, D.C.: The World Bank, November 1988).

1. *Avoid overextension and quick growth.* The rapid expansion of its balance sheet can lead a bank to lend too much relative to its capital. It also can generate loans in areas of activity with which the bank's management is unfamiliar. The rapid expansion may arise because depositors are being offered deposit rates that are much higher than low-risk lending can sustain.

2. *Diversify loans to avoid lending a significant portion of bank capital to a single borrower or group of borrowers subject to the same credit risks.* A failure of a single company or problems in a single industry or locality can wipe out bank capital if there is insufficient diversification. Individual loans therefore should be limited to fractions of bank capital.

3. *Avoid loans to borrowers connected with the bank.* Such loans may be to companies connected with the bank through a complicated corporate structure. They may be to the bankers themselves, to their friends and relatives, or to their political protectors. Loans of this sort can readily be used to strip the bank of its assets through some kind of fraud.

4. *Avoid mismatching of liabilities and assets.* A typical mismatch occurs when a bank holds long-maturity assets and short-maturity liabilities. Then a rise in interest rates can wipe out bank capital and lead to collapse of the institution. Similarly, a mismatch in the currency composition of assets and liabilities can create an insolvency in the presence of exchange rate movements. For example, if assets are denominated in dollars and liabilities are denominated in deutschemarks, a fall in the deutschemark value of the dollar can drive the value of assets below the value of liabilities.

The Frequency of Problem Banks

Failure to observe one or more of these simple principles lies behind almost every individual or system-wide banking insolvency. Such problems arise regularly in many countries. A partial list of recent troubled banking systems in various countries includes the following:[2]

—— Argentina: A banking crisis from 1980 to 1982 caused the liquidation of 71 of 470 financial institutions.

—— Chile: From 1981 to 1983, the government liquidated, restructured, or recapitalized insolvent institutions holding up to 45 percent of the financial system's assets. In September 1988, the central bank held bad bank loans equaling 19 percent of GNP.

—— Spain: From 1978 to 1983, financial institutions holding 20 percent of Spain's deposits had to be rescued by the government.

2. For a more complete list of countries with banking problems, see The World Bank, *World De-* *velopment Report, 1989* (New York: Oxford University Press, 1989), pp. 71–72.

—United States: From 1981 to 1988, 1100 S&Ls were closed or merged. In 1989, 600 more were insolvent, although not yet closed. These had assets totaling more than $250 billion. Their insurer, the Federal Savings and Loan Insurance Corporation, had a capital deficit of $14 billion at the end of 1987. In March 1990, 290 thrift institutions with assets of $130 billion were in conservatorship.

—United States: From 1985 to 1989, 803 banks insured by the FDIC with assets totaling $100 billion failed or had to be merged.

THE BANK OF UNITED STATES COLLAPSE

To see how violations of the prudential principles, notably principle 3, can lead to banking problems, it is helpful to consider a famous example, the collapse of the **Bank of United States** in 1930.

The bank, with over $200 million in deposits, failed in December of that year. It was the largest bank failure during the Great Depression. Because of its name, much of the public erroneously assumed that it was an official institution, so its failure engendered a lack of confidence in the whole U.S. financial system.

The bank failed because it had engaged in fraudulent practices by lending to a complex array of corporate affiliates. Thus the bank could have been saved only if other banks had been willing to bail it out by buying assets at prices far above those justified by the earnings of the assets.[3]

The story began in 1927, when the founder of the Bank of United States, Joseph Marcus, died. At his death, the bank, which was chartered by the State of New York, had about $70 million in deposits. It was a member of the Federal Reserve System and was primarily engaged in lending money to the garment district of New York City.

Upon the death of Marcus, his son Bernard and his partner Saul Singer took control of the bank. They established an affiliate corporation called City Financial Corporation that issued two classes of stock, A stock and B stock. Class B shares, the voting shares, were issued only to the two partners. Class A shares were sold to the public for cash. Class A shareholders had no voting rights.

The cash raised from stock sales was partially used to buy stock in the bank. The remaining cash was used to take equity interest in real estate deals that were partially financed by loans from the bank. The establishment of the affiliate enabled Marcus and Singer to engage directly in dealing in equities and in the purchase of real estate; it was otherwise illegal to do so through a New York–chartered bank.

The partners next established a syndicate with the other directors of the Bank

---

3. We base our account on M. H. Werner, *Little Napoleon and Dummy Directors* (New York: Harper Brothers, 1933), and Paul Navazio, "Analyzing the Failure of the Bank of United States," Working Paper, University of California, Davis, 1984.

of United States to expand the capital resources of City Financial Corporation. They sold additional class A stock to syndicate members below its market price to raise $2.45 million. A sale of stock below its market price effectively dilutes the ownership of the other shareholders.

Meanwhile, the resources of the Bank of United States were expanded by the merger of the bank with the Central Mercantile Bank, a New York bank with total deposits of some $50 million. The merger was achieved by exchange of shares. The shareholders of Central Mercantile Bank received $1\frac{1}{2}$ shares of Bank of United States stock for every share of their stock in the old bank.

In the fall of 1928, Marcus and Singer formed a second affiliate, the Bankus Corporation, which bought most of the shares of City Financial Corporation. With $9 million borrowed from City Financial Corporation, Bankus Corporation bought 360,000 shares of Bank of United States stock. This represented half the 720,000 shares outstanding. The remaining 360,000 shares were surrendered by their owners, who were reissued a unit consisting of one share of Bankus Corporation and one share of Bank of United States stock. Then the 360,000 Bank of United States shares held by Bankus Corporation were combined with an additional 360,000 Bankus Corporation shares that were exchanged for 720,000 of City Financial Corporation shares. The result of all these transactions was an extremely close connection between the owners of the Bank of United States and the two affiliates. The three firms were all controlled by Marcus and Singer.

The partners then undertook another bank merger with the Municipal Bank and Trust Company together with its securities affiliate, Municipal Financial Corporation. The deal was consummated by swapping Municipal stock for Bankus–Bank of United States stock at below the market price of Bankus, which was about $200 per share in May 1929. The acquisition of the Municipal Bank completed the growth of the Bank of United States to a system with $230 million in deposits and $293 million in assets. Figure 20.1 depicts the rapid evolution of the Bank of United States corporate structure.

This was the beginning of trouble for the partners and ultimately for the depositors of the Bank of United States. The former Municipal Bank and Trust Company shareholders began to sell their shares in Bankus–Bank of United States, and the price began to fall. To support the price, Marcus and Singer began to buy shares through the syndicate. However, they could not buy enough to stop the slide, so in July 1929 they offered shares to Bank of United States depositors and agreed to repurchase the shares if the price fell below $198. This was at a time when they had briefly manipulated the price up to $208 per share. The share price immediately slid to $187 in August 1929, and the Bank of United States later failed to keep this repurchase promise. In this way, $6 million in deposits were converted to shares in the Bank of United States.

The price of the bank stock continued to fall despite these efforts, so Singer and Marcus decided that the affiliates should buy the stock with loans financed from the bank. Thus bank depositors' money was used directly to attempt to support the price of the bank stock. Singer assured the directors of the bank that the loans were sound because they were backed up by the real estate investments of the affiliates.

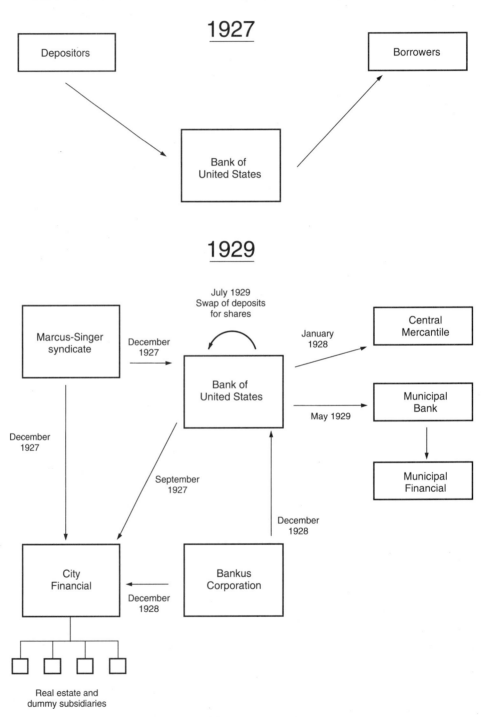

Figure 20.1 DEVELOPMENT OF BANK OF UNITED STATES

In December 1930, the New York State Banking Department examiners declared the bank insolvent. The loans made to support stock purchases by the affiliates were in default because the stock price had fallen and the affiliates' real estate investments had gone bad. Marcus and Singer were charged with fraud and spent time in prison. The bank's depositors eventually recovered 80 percent of their funds, but since many ended up as shareholders as well through the broken repurchase promise, this understates their loss. Under New York banking law, in case of a bank failure, stockholders could be charged up to the par value of their stocks by the bank regulators. The depositors entering the repurchase agreement lost both their deposits and the subsequent charges.

FRAUD IN TWO S&L COLLAPSES

As a more recent example of how violation of the principle of no lending to associated firms can lead to collapse, consider the cases of American Diversified Savings and North American Savings and Loan.

At the beginning of June 1987, the Federal Savings and Loan Insurance Corporation (FSLIC) announced that it would pay out $1.35 billion to liquidate two federally chartered S&Ls in California—American Diversified Savings and North American Savings and Loan. The move was considered unusual because the FSLIC had until then attempted to deal with failures by finding buyers for failed institutions so that their customers would experience minimum disruption. Also, the payout was large relative to the total insurance fund maintained by the FSLIC—it equaled 40 percent of the fund.

There is a strong suspicion that these two S&Ls failed because of fraud. State-chartered S&Ls in California had the right to make direct real estate investments—that is, they had the power to hold real estate directly instead of merely holding a mortgage on property. Federally chartered S&Ls were given this power by the Federal Home Loan Bank Board, a federal agency that no longer exists but at the time had power to regulate federally chartered savings and loans. We will consider in particular the case of North American Savings and Loan.[4]

North American was established by a California dentist in 1982. It had only one branch and made only a few mortgage loans. It obtained most of its deposits by soliciting nationwide through advertising, and it paid about 1.4 percentage points above the national average for its deposit funds. Under the Depository Institution Deregulation and Monetary Control Act of 1980 (DIDMCA), interest rate ceilings on S&L deposits had been gradually removed during the first half of the 1980s. North American's average deposit size was $90,000, so virtually all its liabilities were insured by the FSLIC.

4. From *The New York Times,* June 30, 1988, pp. D1 and D15.

In 1982, an investment trust bought a condominium development at Lake Tahoe for $3.6 million. The investment trust happened to be run by the same dentist who owned North American. According to the FSLIC in 1988, the dentist sought to disguise his interest in the trust and then to acquire an option to buy the property at an inflated value. The FSLIC claimed that the dentist paid nearly $3 million for the option, which he then donated to North American. In late 1983, North American exercised the option to buy the development, paying $14.7 million for the property. North American placed the asset on its books for $17.7 million (the purchase price plus the option price).

In the middle of 1984, the investment trust was dissolved, and investigators think that the profits filtered back to the dentist. Later that year North American sold the property for $20.5 million and provided a loan of $18.4 million to the purchaser to acquire the property. The dentist's top aide acted as real estate broker for the transaction and was paid $1 million.

In 1985, the buyer defaulted on the loan, and the property came into the possession of North American once again. In 1986 it was sold for $30 million to a company of which the dentist's aide was an officer. The aide again acted as real estate broker. The property was later sold again for $40 million to a company owned by the aide's father.

This series of transactions resulted in personal profits for the dentist and his top aide, but the FSLIC claimed they were also designed to inflate the value of North American's assets. In the end, the FSLIC estimated that the property was worth only $2.4 million rather than the final $40 million sale price.

Effect of Asset Inflation on S&L Balance Sheets

We can assume that the inflation of capital of North American resulted from financing of the property when it was resold. For example, let us assume that an S&L buys property for $15 million. It finances the purchase by attracting $15 million in deposits. If it sells that property for $30 million, it receives a gain of $15 million over the cash it originally paid, which shows up as an increase in capital of $15 million. This sets up the balance sheet depicted in Table 20.1a. Assets rise by $15 million to $30 million in cash, while deposit liabilities remain constant at $15 million.

If the S&L receives cash for the transaction from an independent buyer, this is a legitimate gain in capital. Suppose, however, that the property really is worth only $15 million but that the S&L sells it for $30 million to a relative of the S&L's owner. The buyer finances the transaction with a $30 million loan from the S&L, collateralized by the property. The S&L's balance sheet still looks like Table 20.1a, but now the assets consist of a $30 million loan rather than cash. The S&L's owners can convert their higher paper capital to cash by attracting $15 million in new deposits and paying the funds received to its stockholders as dividends or to its management as inflated salaries and bonuses. The new balance sheet of the S&L is presented in Table 20.1b. The assets consist of the $30 million loan to the buyer. The liabilities

Table 20.1 BANK POSITION AFTER REAL ESTATE SALE ($MILLIONS)

a. Cash Purchase				b. Bank Financed Purchase			
ASSETS		**LIABILITIES**		**ASSETS**		**LIABILITIES**	
Cash	30	Deposits	15	Loan	30	Old deposits	15
		Capital	15			New deposits	15

are $15 million in old deposits and $15 million in new deposits. By selling the property at a higher price than it is worth, the S&L can artificially raise the value of its assets relative to its liabilities.

Since the property was indeed worth only $15 million, the borrower will eventually go bankrupt, leaving the S&L with a bad loan of $30 million and a property collateralizing the loan worth $15 million. The S&L is insolvent to the tune of $15 million, the management and owners are richer by $15 million, and the insurer picks up the tab. (Of course, in the case of North American the property was not even worth $15 million to start with. The dentist had sold the property to North American at an inflated price, and subsequent sales also were inflated. The ultimate loss to the FSLIC approached $28 million.)

Recall that regulators use capital-to-assets rules to determine whether banks and thrifts are permitted to expand their businesses. Bank examiners basically check only a bank's bookkeeping to ensure that the paperwork for loans on the bank's balance sheet is in order and that payments are on schedule. One of the principles of bank examination, however, is not to question the business judgment of the bank: As long as loans are performing on paper, examiners will rate a bank as healthy.

The complicated series of transactions made it appear that North American was healthy. Ultimately, however, the FSLIC insurance fund was forced to bear the consequences.

LIQUIDATING A FAILED BANK: HOW THE FDIC RESCUES DEPOSITORS WHEN A BANK FAILS

The **Federal Deposit Insurance Corporation (FDIC)** keeps a "90-day list" of banks that are expected to fail within that time.[5] Banks are placed on this list after

5. For a detailed description of the actions of the FDIC in handling troubled banks, see Irvine H. Sprague, *Bailout, An Insider's View of Bank Failures and Rescues* (New York: Basic Books, 1986), or John F. Bovenzi and Maureen E. Muldoon, "Failure Resolution Methods and Policy Considerations," *FDIC Banking Review,* Fall 1990, pp. 1–11.

consultation with the various regulatory authorities—the Federal Reserve, the Comptroller of the Currency, and the state banking supervisors. The list is updated weekly.

As soon as a bank is placed on the 90-day list, bank examiners from the FDIC begin the process of determining the value of its assets, the extent of its liabilities, and the extent to which uninsured depositors might be able to withdraw their funds.

The appearance of a bank on the list also begins the process of determining how to rescue the insured depositors. The board of the FDIC has several options.

1. A **payoff** of the insured depositors and closure of the bank.

2. A **purchase and assumption (P&A)** transaction, in which another institution purchases some of the bank's assets and assumes the deposit liability.

3. A **deposit transfer,** in which the FDIC makes a cash payment to another institution to accept responsibility for deposit liabilities. The remainder of the bank is liquidated by the FDIC.

4. A **bailout** of the bank, that is, financial assistance to the bank to prevent its failure and permit its continued operation as an independent entity.

5. A **bridge bank** owned by the FDIC to operate the failed bank temporarily until its final disposition can be determined.

The choice of options has an economic impact on the participants. If a payoff of the insured depositors is chosen, noninsured creditors and stockholders are likely to lose their money. A deposit transfer is a variant of a payoff that is similar in its effects on stockholders and noninsured creditors. If the bank is purchased by a third party, the noninsured creditors will be paid off, but the stockholders are likely to lose their money. A bailout has distributive effects similar to a purchase.

Although the board of the FDIC makes the decision, it is not entirely free to choose between payoffs and purchases. The law requires that it attempt to minimize the cost of the choice to the FDIC. In its 1949 annual report, the FDIC stated that no depositor, insured or uninsured, had lost any money in a bank failure because all failed banks were sold to healthy ones. The sale process involves the FDIC in some possibly heavy costs, as we will see below. Therefore, this statement in 1949 raised some fury in Congress because it implied that all depositors were insured, and Congress feared this would create a moral obligation to all depositors that could only be met with taxpayers' money.

The FDIC was henceforth more careful to minimize the cost in deciding between payoff and purchase. How does it determine the cost of each option? The examiners value the bank's insured deposits and assets. The difference in these values is the cost of a payoff.

The value of the purchase option relative to the payoff option is determined as follows: The nonperforming loans are separated from the assets with some value— that is, those which are paying some income. The FDIC promises a prospective purchaser that it will make up the difference between the value of the performing assets and the value of all liabilities, including the uninsured liabilities, with a cash payment. The nonperforming assets are taken over by the FDIC to be liquidated separately. Prospective purchasers are then asked to bid on the value of this package.

Bids are accepted on the day that the bank is scheduled to fail. Bidders must be at least twice the size of the failed bank, and they must have adequate capital. Any of the regulators involved in the failure can force a prospective bidder off the list. The determination as to whether payoff is cheaper than purchase is determined by the size of the bid on the FDIC's package. The direct cash obligation of the FDIC is greater in the purchase case because all liability holders are then repaid, not just depositors. The price the bidder is willing to pay may more than offset this difference in FDIC outlays. If the FDIC accepts the bid, the winning bidder acquires the bank, and all liability holders of the former bank become liability holders of the winning bank.

If a payoff is chosen, the FDIC may become the receiver of the closed bank and immediately writes checks fully repaying the insured depositors. Alternatively, the FDIC may simply transfer the insured deposits to another institution along with the cash to cover them. The receiving institution may, in turn, pay a premium to the FDIC because it values the additional customers.

In both cases, purchase or payoff, the nonperforming assets are taken over by the FDIC. If recoveries are made—that is, if the nonperforming assets end up having some value—the uninsured creditors (in the case of a purchase) and the stockholders are paid after the FDIC recovers its funds from liquidation of the assets. This is the basis for our statement earlier that these two groups are likely to lose all their money, but the loss is not certain.

Table 20.2 TEN LARGEST FDIC FAILURE-RESOLUTION TRANSACTIONS THROUGH YEAR-END 1989

Date	Bank Name	Type of Transaction*	Assets ($Billions)
July 29, 1988	First Republic Bancorporation	BB	33.7
Sept. 26, 1984	Continental Illinois	OBA	33.6
Mar. 28, 1989	MCorp	BB	15.4
Apr. 20, 1988	First City Bancorporation	OBA	11.2
Apr. 28, 1980	First Pennsylvania	OBA	8.0
Sept. 1, 1985	Bowery Savings Bank	OBA	5.3
July 20, 1989	Texas American Bancshares	BB	4.3
Oct. 28, 1974	Franklin National Bank	P&A	3.7
Mar. 20, 1982	New York Bank for Savings	OBA	3.4
Nov. 28, 1981	Greenwich Savings Bank	OBA	2.5

Source: From John F. Bovenzi and Maureen E. Muldoon, "Failure-Resolution Methods and Policy Considerations," *FDIC Banking Review,* Fall 1990, p. 2.

*BB = bridge bank; OBA = open bank assistance; P&A = purchase and assumption.

Box 20.1

FDIC Resources

The FDIC acquires revenue by charging banks premiums against bank deposits. For example, in 1990, premiums for members of the **Bank Insurance Fund (BIF)** were set at $0.12 per $100 of deposits in banks, including uninsured deposits. In 1991, they were $0.195 per $100 of deposits. From such premiums, the FDIC builds an insurance fund consisting of cash and liquid earning assets such as Treasury securities that provide an additional revenue source. The FDIC has not directly used U.S. Treasury funds, although the Treasury will support the FDIC if its insurance fund becomes depleted.

The mounting failures of banks caused the Bank Insurance Fund balance to fall from $13.2 billion in December 1989 to $8.5 billion in January 1991. Without sufficient funds, the FDIC's illiquidity may cause it to avoid closing failing banks. Alternatively, although a payoff may be advantageous in the long run, the FDIC might instead choose a bailout to minimize the immediate reduction of its liquid assets.

To avoid constraining its range of action, the FDIC needs sufficient liquid assets. One way to get them is from an injection of funds from the Treasury, and the FDIC does have a $5 billion line of credit with the Treasury. Another way is to assess all the insured banks an amount that would immediately bring the fund to a comfortable level. Finally, the FDIC can borrow and increase its premium charge to generate the cash flow to pay off the loan.

For example, in January 1991, the FDIC's Bank Insurance Fund held a ratio of $0.43 per $100 of insured deposits, the lowest level since the Great Depression; and the fund was projected to fall to a ratio of $0.19 per $100 by the end of 1991 because of continuing bank failures. In December 1990, L. William Seidman, the chairman of the FDIC, proposed an assessment of $25 billion from the insured banks. In 1990, however, the banking industry registered profits of only $15.4 billion, so it opposed the proposal. As an alternative, in March 1991, Seidman proposed a plan to borrow $25 billion—partly from the Federal Reserve and the rest from the banks or the Treasury. He proposed that premiums be raised by $0.035 per $100 to finance the loan. These charges, of course, would show up in the form of an increased spread between deposit and lending rates.

In a bailout, formally called **open bank assistance,** the FDIC injects sufficient cash into the failing bank to cover the difference between the estimated market value of the bank's assets and its liabilities. In then finds private investors to inject new capital into the bank. The old management is usually replaced, and the FDIC forces some losses on the junior debt holders and old stockholders of the bank. Unlike the other methods, the bank never formally closes or ceases business activity.

Box 20.2

Who Pays for FDIC Insurance Premiums?

Banks pay insurance premiums to the FDIC at a predetermined rate per $100 of deposits, regardless of whether the deposits are legally covered by insurance. Only deposits of less than $100,000 are covered by FDIC insurance, so wholesale deposits pay the premium without receiving any explicit insurance. Who really pays this premium, and what effect do increases in the premium have on liquidity in financial markets?

Consider the position of an investor holding a large CD. The bank must pay an insurance premium of 23 basis points on the entire amount of the CD. If the bank tries to pass this cost on to the CD holder through a 23 basis point reduction in yield, CD holders will respond by shifting to commercial paper, which faces no charge for deposit insurance; so the large CD market will collapse. Since the large CD market still exists, however, we must conclude that the cost of the insurance premium is not passed on to wholesale depositors. Banks can cover the cost of premiums only by increasing the riskiness of their activities until the higher expected return on bank assets associated with higher risk covers the cost of insurance.

Now consider a demand deposit, which is subject to the insurance premium, whereas a repurchase agreement is not. Assuming the bank sells a repo backed by a government security, the return on the repurchase agreement is relatively low because of the favorable liquidity and risk characteristics of the underlying security. Insurance gives the demand deposit the same risk characteristics, so demand deposits should pay the same yield as repurchase agreements. If a bank tries to pass the cost of deposit insurance to wholesale demand deposits by paying a lower return on demand deposits than on the repo, depositors will switch to repurchase agreements. Nevertheless, the wholesale demand deposit market still exists, so again banks must cover the cost of insurance by taking risk appropriate to the level assumed in the premium.

Thus, banks can pay for the burden of the deposit insurance premium by taking on more risk. Therefore, if insurance is properly priced for the risk assumed, it should have no effect on liquidity premiums on the various securities in the market. Recall from Chapter 13 that liquidity premiums depend only on the reserve costs that a security is likely to impose on the banking system.

The FDIC can choose the bailout option when a failed bank is essential to provide adequate banking service in its community. Because it is believed that the failure of a major bank would disrupt the money markets, this condition has been used to justify the bailout of such banks as Continental Illinois in 1984. Table 20.2 indicates that large bank failures are most often managed with a bailout.

Finally, the FDIC may charter a bridge bank to take over the assets and some liabilities of the closed bank. The FDIC itself owns the bridge bank, which it may operate for up to 2 years while determining the final disposition of the bank. The bridge-bank option allows the FDIC to prevent the damage to a community that terminating the operation of a bank might cause while avoiding the moral hazard problem of operating a bank with negative capital. This option was permitted only starting in 1987, and the few cases of its use are primarily for large banks, as indicated in Table 20.2.

Of the 428 banks closed in 1988 and 1989, purchase and assumptions were used in 339 cases, insured deposit transfers in 52 cases, payoffs in 15 cases, and bailouts in 22 cases. See Box 20.1 and Box 20.2.

THE SHIFT FROM A GOOD BANK TO A BAD BANK

Aside from outright fraud, as in the case of North American, how does a bank turn bad? A bank can always run into a string of bad luck, wherein its borrowers default, wiping out its capital. Prior to deposit insurance, depositors were often alert to such possibilities, and they would frequently run the banks for self-protection. If the bank were indeed insolvent, a bank run served to minimize the damage of its insolvency by forcing a quick closing of the bank. With insured deposits, however, depositors are indifferent about the fate of their banks, and it falls to the insurer to act as watchdog and halt the activities of a failed bank.

Once a bank is insolvent, what further damage can its management do that requires the timely closure or restructuring of the bank? Banking institutions often have access to funds long past the time that they become insolvent. Stated differently, they are still liquid. This means that they can continue to borrow from depositors and relend to their bankrupt borrowers. The borrowers then use the new funds to pay interest and principal on old loans. The bank management can book the interest income as earnings and even pay out dividends to stockholders and bonuses to itself.

Once its bank is insolvent, management may as well carry on as long as possible, extracting what it can from the bank and hoping that a turn of events will make its bad loans good. To remain open, the bank management neglects to classify unpaid loans as "overdue," which would signal a problem. Rather, it reschedules the loans, stretching out payments, and it even makes new loans to its borrowers to cover the interest due on the old loans. We have seen how these practices became common in loans to less developed countries such as Argentina, Brazil, and Mexico after the debt crisis starting in 1982. The bank examiners classify as good all loans on which scheduled payments are being made, so most of the effectively defaulted loans on the books of an insolvent bank can be classified as "good."

Now let's examine in detail how a bank can cosmetically improve its books despite poor loan performance. First, Table 20.3 shows the balance sheet of a bank

Table 20.3 NORMAL DISPOSITION OF PAYOFF ON BANK LOAN

a. Initial Position				b. After Interest Payment			
ASSETS		LIABILITIES		ASSETS		LIABILITIES	
Loan to A	$100	Deposits	$90	Loan to A	$100	Deposits	$98
		Capital	$10	Loan to B	$ 8	Capital	$10

receiving a payoff on a normal, sound loan. Suppose the bank's initial position (see Table 20.3a) includes a loan outstanding of $100 to company A, funded by deposits of $90 and capital of $10. The loan must pay 10 percent in interest each period to avoid being classified as overdue. Depositors are paid 9 percent per period. Table 20.3b represents the situation one period later after company A has paid its interest of $10 to the bank. Depositors receive $8.10 in interest. We assume that $8 is reinvested in the bank, increasing deposits to $98. This leaves $1.90 in profit to be distributed as dividends to shareholders and as bonuses to management. The $8 increase in deposits fund a new loan to company B.

Let us begin again from the balance sheet in Table 20.3a. Now, however, it turns out that company A is bankrupt: Assets that collateralize the loan are worth only $40. For example, company A may have been an oil drilling company, and the price of oil may suddenly have fallen, collapsing new exploration and oil field development. The bank is itself insolvent because it has collateral of only $40 against $90 in deposits. Its management could honestly announce its insolvency to the world, forcing itself out of a job, *or* it could remain open by carrying company A with additional loans.

Company A has a payment of $10 in interest due on its loan. The bank can make sure the loan does not become overdue by lending an additional $10 to company A. Company A will then use the new loan to pay the interest due the bank. The balance sheet of the bank after this transaction is presented in Table 20.4a. The assets consist of the old and new loans to company A. From company A's

Table 20.4 KEEPING A BANKRUPT COMPANY AFLOAT

a. Relending Interest Payments				b. Income Statement			
ASSETS		LIABILITIES		RECEIPTS		PAYMENTS	
Old loan to A	$100	Old deposits with interest	$98	Interest income	$10	Interest expense	$8.10
New loan to A	$ 10	New deposits	$2			Dividends	$1.90
		Capital	$10				

interest payment, $8.10 is paid to depositors as interest, and again we assume that $8.00 is reinvested in the bank. To keep the shareholders happy, the remaining $1.90 is booked as profit and paid out as dividends. The bank will then have to attract $2 in new deposits to fund part of its new loan to company A.

The bank's income statement is summarized in Table 20.4b. The bank books interest income of $10, interest expense of $8.10, and profit and dividends of $1.90. The bank's books indicate that it is perfectly sound. Note, however, that the bank now has deposit claims of $100 against assets that still are worth only $40. If the bank had closed immediately, the insurer would have been required to pay $50, the difference between the original $90 in deposits and the $40 in assets. To stay open one more period so that its owners can extract an additional $1.90, the bank has increased the deposit claims to $100 against the same $40 in assets. The burden on the insurer has increased by 20 percent from $50 to $60.

This process could continue with ever-growing new loans to company A and expansion of the bank's balance sheet. Interest income would continue to rise, as would the book profits of the bank; the growth rate of the bank is at compound interest.

Banks of this type are referred to as the "**walking dead**" because they keep on operating and running up losses. Losses that will eventually have to be paid by the insurer will continue to grow until the bank is closed. Thus the management has every incentive to continue to attract funds to the insolvent bank. Note that these actions are not necessarily illegal: A case can always be made that actions that are ex-post unsound may be ex-ante sound business decisions. Bankers are typically not jailed for bad business judgment.

THE METAMORPHOSIS OF A ROGUE BANK

Unfortunately for the bank management, these cosmetic bookkeeping operations designed to fabricate a continual stream of book profits cannot last forever. The bank is likely to become ever more insolvent, and eventually, regulatory limits on loans to single borrowers can trigger the bank's closure. Because of the certain end of their control, the bank's management becomes desperate at some point and begins making new loans on high-risk projects. Although high risk, the new projects are not sure losers, unlike the bankrupt firms already on the bank's books. The bank management gambles that some of the projects will pay off extremely well, thereby restoring the bank's solvency and the longevity of management.

Suppose that the bank is currently in the position indicated by the balance sheet in Table 20.4a. It has $100 in old loans to the bankrupt company A, $10 in new loans to company A, $100 in deposits, and $10 in book capital. To remain open in the next period, the bank lends a further $11 (that is, 10 percent of $110) in interest

Table 20.5 BETTING THE BANK

a. Funding B's Loan with New Deposits

ASSETS		LIABILITIES	
Loans to A	$121	Old deposits	$100
Loan to B	$ 65	New deposits	$ 76
		Capital	$ 10

b. Income Statement

RECEIPTS		PAYMENTS	
Interest income	$11	Interest expense	$ 9.00
Fees	$15	Dividends	$17.00

to company A. The total of the loans to company A is now $121, which we book in the bank's balance sheet in Table 20.5a. The $11 in interest payments shows up as a credit item on the income statement in Table 20.5b; interest expense to depositors is $9.00.

Now, however, the management senses that it cannot continue in operation much longer without taking drastic action. It decides to make a large loan to company B to finance a high-risk project. The loan to company B is for $65, but the bank charges company B an upfront fee of $15 for the loan. Company B is willing to pay the fee because its project is of such high risk. If company B is successful, it will pay back $65 plus interest. On net, company B borrows $50 for its project, the $65 face value of the loan less the $15 fee. Effectively, company B will pay a very high rate of interest *if* its project is successful.

We book the loan to company B on the bank's balance sheet in Table 20.5a; the fee income appears as a credit item on its income statement in Table 20.5b. Note that because it is undertaking desperate measures, the bank can book high profits of $17 that it can pay out to management and shareholders.

The new loans to companies A and B total $76. To finance them, the bank must attract $76 in new deposits. To attract these new deposits from other banks, we assume that the bank raises its deposit interest rate to 10 percent. It also raises its loan rate to 13 percent. The higher interest rate attracts funds from other, sound banks that lack access to sound borrowers willing to pay loan rates sufficient for those banks to raise their own deposit rates. The sound banks therefore will shrink at the expense of the insolvent bank. Consequently, capital will be channeled away from sound investment projects to high-risk projects. Effectively, the presence of such **rogue banks** with insured deposits will lead to the subsidization of high-risk investments.

We have classified the loan to company B as high risk. Suppose that in the next period the highly probable bad outcome for company B does materialize so that B is bankrupt with worthless assets. Now the bank has claims only on assets worth $40, the value of company A's collateral. The bank's deposit liabilities are $176 plus

10 percent × \$176 = \$193.60. The insurance fund will now have to pay out \$153.60 to close the bank.

THE COLLUSION OF BANK REGULATORS

Why would a deposit insurer permit continual erosion of the insurance fund without making an attempt to close an insolvent bank? One reason is that paying off depositors requires the expenditure of the insurer's resources in one of the methods described earlier. If the loss to an individual bank or group of banks is large enough, the insurer's funds will be inadequate to close all the banks and pay off depositors. The insurer itself becomes bankrupt. Its management now is in the position of the management of an insolvent bank. It is willing to let the situation continue, hoping that the financial environment will restore solvency to the banks or that the government will provide sufficient funds to close the banks and pay off depositors. Depositors remain confident that eventually the insurer—that is, the government—will pay off; otherwise, they would withdraw their funds in a bank run. Until it receives sufficient funds from the Treasury, however, the insurer must let the situation continue. An example of such behavior is the operation of the Federal Savings and Loan Insurance Corporation from 1981 through 1989; the FSLIC could not close bankrupt S&Ls for lack of sufficient funds.

WHY DOESN'T THE TREASURY ACT?
THE CORRUPTION OF THE POLITICIANS

Appropriation of public funds to bail out an overextended deposit insurance fund is not an automatic action. It is a political act requiring the agreement of a congressional coalition strong enough to have its way. Suppose that the insolvent banks and their high-risk borrowers are politically influential. Important politicians connected to these institutions may then block action to appropriate funds to end the cumulating potential drain on the Treasury. If sufficient funds were appropriated by Congress, the insolvent bank managements would be thrown out, their shareholders would cease receiving dividends, their old defaulting borrowers would be thrown into bankruptcy, and new borrowers would be unable to obtain funds to finance high-risk projects in their political jurisdiction. Politicians associated with these interests, therefore, tend to drag their feet on ending the problem through an appropriation of funds because continuing the status quo gives their friends and their districts an unrestricted tap on the Treasury. Effectively, they can force an unvoted appropriation of tax dollars to subsidize their friends in this way.

THE INSOLVENCY OF THE S&LS

The collapse of U.S. thrift institutions in the 1980s serves as a classic example of the system-wide insolvencies that can arise in a banking system. In 1988, there were approximately 2,800 insured S&Ls with aggregate assets of $925 billion. From 1983 through third quarter 1988, however, 356 insured S&Ls with assets of $129 billion were closed or merged with Federal Savings and Loan Insurance Corporation (FSLIC) assistance. In 1989, the FSLIC itself was bankrupt and unable to close any additional insolvent S&Ls. The estimated liability of the insurance agency for deposits in S&Ls that had failed but could not be closed for lack of funds ranged upward from $50 billion. Hence a massive bailout funded by the U.S. Treasury was undertaken with the passage of the **Financial Institutions Reform, Recovery, and Enforcement Act of 1989 (FIRRE).** How could a problem of this magnitude occur?

The FHLBanks and the FSLIC

Prior to the reforms in 1989, the **Federal Home Loan Banks (FHLBanks)** and the **Federal Savings and Loan Insurance Corporation (FSLIC)** regulated the S&Ls. The FHLBanks were the central supplier of credit to the S&Ls. Established in 1932, it was a federal agency organized like the Fed into 12 district banks spread across the United States. Its purpose was to supply liquidity to S&Ls experiencing heavy savings withdrawals. Therefore, the assets of the FHLBanks consisted almost entirely of advances to S&Ls. The primary liabilities used to finance the advances were the consolidated obligations of the Federal Home Loan Bank Board (FHLBB), which were debt instruments sold to private buyers at market rates. Based in Washington, the FHLBB directed the regulatory operations of the FHLBanks. In emergencies, the U.S. Treasury was empowered to purchase $4 billion of FHLBB obligations. In addition, the Federal Reserve had authority to purchase and sell the FHLBB debt issues. Thus the FHLBB had a line of credit to the Fed.

The FSLIC completely insured S&L deposits against loss up to $100,000 per account. When an S&L became insolvent (in book-value terms), the FSLIC managed the liquidation, merger, or recovery of the S&L, sometimes infusing it with some of its own assets to ensure no loss to depositors. As of March 1981, its assets equaled $6.7 billion.

The Early 1980s

To determine how the S&L collapse developed, it is helpful to consider the nature of the system of S&Ls as of the early 1980s. The S&Ls were originally established as financial intermediaries to channel capital into housing construction. As a result, they were required to hold a large percentage of assets in long-term mortgages collateralized by residential and commercial real estate.

To fund these assets, they borrowed short-term deposits. Until the early 1980s, interest rate ceilings were imposed by the Federal Reserve on bank deposits and by the FHLBB on deposits in S&Ls. The S&Ls, however, were allowed to offer a deposit rate on passbook savings accounts that exceeded the rate permitted at banks by 25 basis points. Hence they had an advantage in attracting the funds of small depositors.

Because of the relative stability of market interest rates prior to the late 1970s, the dominant mortgage type was the fixed-interest-rate mortgage. By 1980, about 80 percent of S&L assets consisted of long-term fixed-interest mortgages. Thus regulation set up a classic mismatch of assets and liabilities on the balance sheets of S&Ls: The S&Ls were lending long term and borrowing short term.

This mismatch was not a problem while interest rates were stable, but in the late 1970s, interest rates on 3-month CDs began to climb rapidly, reaching 14 percent in 1979 and 18 percent in the summer of 1981. Only in September 1982 did they descend below 10 percent. The rise in interest rates meant that the S&Ls were primarily holding long-term mortgages paying interest rates that had been prevalent in a low-yield period. Specifically, 68 percent of the mortgages held on the books of S&Ls were paying rates of less than 10 percent at the end of 1980. Market interest rates on other long-term bonds were much higher than 10 percent. For example, 30-year U.S. Treasury bonds were yielding 12 percent, and by October 1981 they were paying 15 percent. Short-term market interest rates on instruments competitive with S&L deposit liabilities also were much higher than the earnings of S&L assets. For example, interest rates on 3-month bank CDs were 13 percent at the time.

Because the S&Ls paid low ceiling rates of only 5.25 percent on passbook deposits, depositors rapidly withdrew their funds and invested them instead in money market mutual funds or in other S&L accounts paying close to market rates. In addition, the S&Ls borrowed heavily from the FHLBanks at market rates. Hence the interest earnings of the S&Ls fell short of interest expense, and the book capital position of the industry began to erode. If we discount S&L assets (mostly mortgages) at the long-term interest rates prevailing at the end of 1980, then the market value of S&L mortgages was $150 billion less than book value.[6] Since total book value of S&L assets was $630 billion and capital on the books was $33 billion in December 1980, the entire S&L system could be considered insolvent in that readily available market evaluations of S&L assets were far exceeded by the value of S&L liabilities.

S&Ls did not close, however. Ongoing losses caused system-wide book capital to decline to $28 billion by the end of 1981 from $33 billion at the end of 1980. Despite this, S&Ls actually expanded their liabilities by 5.2 percent, or $33 billion, during 1981, funded by increases in deposits of 2.5 percent and an increase in borrowings from FHLBanks of $16 billion, or 34 percent.

6. See FHLBB, *Report of the Task Force on Savings and Loan Portfolio Profitability,* July 1981.

The 1981 "Walking Dead"

The FSLIC classified an S&L as a problem institution if it was insolvent or projected soon to be insolvent in book-value terms, not in market-value terms. Thus an S&L that was obviously insolvent in market terms was permitted to continue operations unhindered as long as its book capital did not fall too low. In addition, not accounting for current capital losses, it might earn large book profits and therefore pay dividends. Since the FSLIC had assets of only $6.7 billion in March 1981, it was not in a position to close many S&Ls that were insolvent even in book-value terms. Instead, the FSLIC gave capital notes, effectively IOUs of the FSLIC, to the S&Ls. The S&Ls could add these to their book capital to circumvent regulatory book capital requirements and remain in business. Thus the FSLIC relaxed accounting standards and the strictness of its regulation to avoid admitting its own insolvency.

In the fall of 1982, short-term interest rates on CDs finally fell to 10 percent, alleviating the drain on S&L capital and increasing the market value of assets. By that time, however, the true capital in many S&Ls had been reduced to negative values.

The Transformation to S&L Rogues

Two legal changes set the insolvent S&Ls in motion as rogue banks: the **Depository Institution Deregulation and Monetary Control Act of 1980 (DIDMCA)** and the **Garn–St Germain Act of 1982.** DIDMCA deregulated depository institutions by gradually terminating regulatory ceilings on deposit interest rates. By April 1986, both banks and S&Ls could offer any yield they wished to attract deposits. Normally, such a change would benefit the small saver. In the presence of massive insolvencies in the S&L system, however, it opened the door to an unlimited expansion of insolvent S&Ls. They regularly offered yields on deposits far above those which the solvent S&Ls and banks could offer, often as much as 2 percent more. As we noted earlier, North American paid 1.4 percentage points above market rates for its deposits and it advertised nationally for funds. Thus deregulation unleashed the vampire into the city.

Many S&Ls of dubious viability solicited deposits nationwide through brokers. It was partially through this channel that they bid for funds substantially above market interest rates. Figure 20.2 indicates the increase in brokered deposits from March 1987 through September 1988, at which time they represented 7.2 percent of total S&L deposits.

The Garn–St Germain Act of 1982 allowed S&Ls to expand the types of assets they held to include commercial loans up to 20 percent of assets and consumer loans up to 30 percent of assets. In 1985, the FHLBB issued a ruling permitting federally chartered S&Ls to take equity positions in real estate developments. Effectively, these deregulatory moves, aimed at letting the S&Ls grow out of their insolvency, greatly expanded the opportunities of the S&Ls to hold high-risk assets at just the

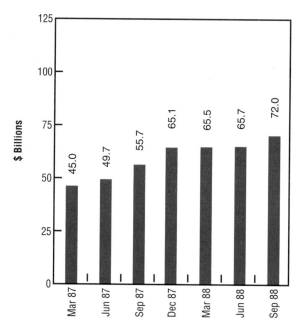

Figure 20.2 BROKERED DEPOSITS FOR ALL U.S. SAVINGS AND LOANS
Source: From American Banker, *Sheshunoff S&L Quarterly*, Sept. 1988, p. I.4.

moment that they had become fevered gamblers, although many state–chartered institutions had held these powers for some time. See Box 20.3 and Box 20.4.

Inevitably, a large share of the high-risk projects did not pay off, leaving the S&Ls in even worse condition by the end of 1985 than in the early 1980s. Losses were concentrated in regions where economic downturns had occurred, such as the oil-producing states. Regional downturns not only affected commercial ventures (and the loans that supported them), but also greatly depressed real estate prices. Since their collateral lost much of its value, S&L loans would have been defaulted in the absence of S&L rollovers. For example, as Figure 20.3 indicates, in the first 9 months of 1988, the S&Ls in the energy- and mineral-producing states of Texas, Oklahoma, and Alaska experienced much greater net income losses relative to assets than those of other regions of the country.

The FSLIC either liquidated or arranged for a purchase of the troubled S&Ls. Over the period from 1983 through the first 9 months of 1988, an increasing number of S&Ls had to be liquidated or sold because they had become insolvent in book-value terms, as we can see in Figure 20.4. These liquidations and arranged purchases drained the assets of the FSLIC to the extent that it lacked the resources to move quickly to close new problem S&Ls.

Box 20.3

Lincoln Savings: Bank of United States Revisited

When Charles Keating bought Lincoln Savings, a California S&L, in 1984 for $51 million, it was a conventional S&L with $1 billion in assets, primarily home mortgages. Lincoln went bankrupt in April 1989 at an ultimate cost of $2.5 billion to the Treasury, the largest loss of any thrift failure.

The Federal Home Loan Bank of San Francisco began investigating Lincoln in 1986 to determine if Lincoln was acquiring excessively risky assets. It determined that there were $135 million in unreported losses at Lincoln. The losses came from overappraisals of property values and losses on equity investments.

Danny Wall, chairman of the Federal Home Loan Bank Board, was responsible for regulating Lincoln through the local FHLBank. In May 1987, the FHLBank of San Francisco recommended that Lincoln be placed in receivership. Lobbied by five influential U.S. senators who had received large campaign contributions from Keating, Wall transferred regulatory authority over Lincoln from San Francisco to the FHLBB in Washington in October 1987 and allowed the S&L to remain open. From that time until it was closed, Lincoln's assets jumped from $3.9 to $5.5 billion.

Lincoln was owned by the American Continental Corporation, a holding company. When it took over Lincoln, the FSLIC found that Lincoln had sold $250 million in subordinate notes of American Continental to 23,000 small depositors by misrepresenting them as deposits in a repeat of the tactics of the owners of the Bank of United States. These were fraudulent sales that were worthless because they were junior claims on the thoroughly bankrupt holding company. The sales occurred in the lobbies of Lincoln's branches, and they effectively cut the former depositors out of any claims on the FSLIC because they were not insured deposits.

Because of his political influence, Wall was rewarded for his careful supervision by becoming the first director of the Office of Thrift Supervision, the regulatory successor of the FHLBB. In the first suit filed by the Resolution Trust Corporation (RTC) after its founding, Charles Keating, members of his family, and directors of American Continental were sued for $1.1 billion. The RTC charged that the defendants profited through insider dealing, illegal loans, sham real estate and tax transactions, and fraudulent sale of Lincoln stock to employees of American Continental.

Source: This account is drawn from *The Economist*, August 26, 1989.

The FSLIC required an injection of funds from the Treasury to liquidate problem S&Ls, but this, in turn, required an act of Congress. The congressional leadership dragged its feet on appropriating the funds, aiming to force FSLIC agreement not to close favored S&Ls. Finally, it passed the Banking Act of 1987, a temporizing measure that gave the FSLIC $10 billion to close the most troubled institutions. As

Box 20.4

Junk Bond Junkies

In the 1980s, a form of corporate finance known as high-yield, or junk, bonds became dominant in the financial restructuring of corporations. Companies took on a large amount of bond indebtedness, thereby increasing default risks. To reimburse them for such risk, bondholders paid low prices and therefore received high yields. Drexel Burnham Lambert (now bankrupt) was the premier investment bank that marketed junk bonds to a huge network of buyers developed by junk bond king Michael Milken. Among the many buyers in the network, S&Ls were major players.

S&L buyers of junk bonds added them to their holdings of already risky assets. It was natural for them to do so, of course, since there was little or no actual capital in the S&Ls. Once the liquidation of the S&Ls began after the passage of FIRRE, regulators ordered the S&Ls to eliminate the junk bonds from their balance sheets. Unfortunately, since the market for such bonds was highly illiquid, and since S&Ls had been major buyers, the selloff caused a collapse in prices. For many S&Ls this price decline threatened their remaining book capital. For example, the Columbia Savings and Loan Association of California had $4.1 billion in junk bonds and $284 million of book capital. Subsequent junk bond price declines finally put this and many other S&Ls into bankruptcy.

Source: Adapted from "Heard on the Street," *Wall Street Journal,* January 23, 1990.

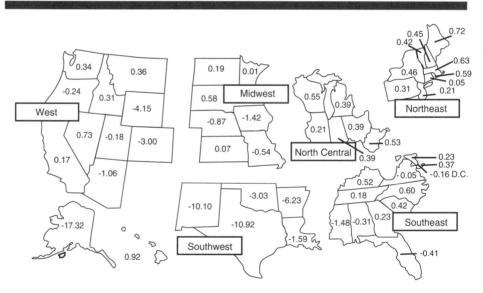

Figure 20.3 RETURN ON S&L ASSETS, FIRST THREE QUARTERS 1988
Source: From American Banker, *Sheshunoff S&L Quarterly,* Sept. 1988, p. I.10.

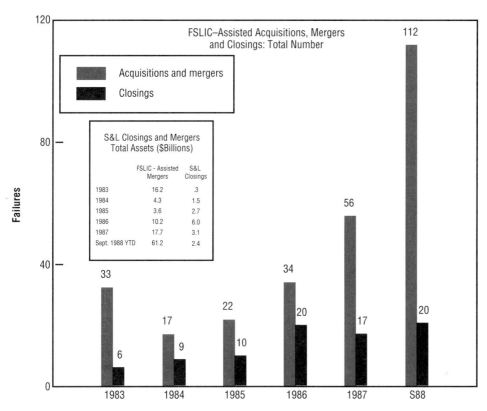

Figure 20.4 CLOSED S&LS AND FHLBB-ASSISTED TRANSACTIONS *Source:*
From American Banker, *Sheshunoff S&L Quarterly,* Sept. 1988, p. I.40.

you can see from the table in Figure 20.4, this was little more than a Bandaid compared to the assets involved. The remaining insolvent thrifts were permitted to continue running up losses.

THE S&L BAILOUT PACKAGE OF 1989 AND THE NEW S&L REGULATORY STRUCTURE

In August 1989, the first serious step to terminate hemorrhaging S&L losses was taken with the passage of the Financial Institutions Reform, Recovery, and Enforcement Act of 1989 (FIRRE). By this law, the FHLBB and the FSLIC were dissolved.

The former Federal Home Loan Bank system (the 12 district banks) was preserved but placed under the control of a new **Office of Thrift Supervision (OTS),** an office of the U.S. Treasury. The OTS is now the primary regulator of federal and state S&Ls and their holding companies, and supervision of S&Ls is now undertaken by the OTS and not at the FHLBanks.

The shape of the bailout package was curiously complicated. It reflected the continued political charade of pretending that the U.S. Treasury would not pay entirely for the S&L disaster. A high but unknown amount of funds had to be found to liquidate the failed thrifts; estimates of the cost ranged from $80 billion to $150 billion. Various political forces molded the bailout plan to avoid admitting that the liquidation of failed thrifts would eventually add up to $100 billion to the federal budget deficit. Thus the shoddy accounting procedures of the thrifts replicated themselves all the way to the federal government's budget reporting.

The complexity of the transitional regulatory environment is presented in Figure 20.5. A new liquidator of failed thrifts, the **Resolution Trust Corporation (RTC),** was established to replace the FSLIC as the conservator and receiver of depository institutions that failed either before or up to 3 years after the enactment of FIRRE. A conservator is appointed when the failed institution is kept temporarily in operation; a receiver is responsible for liquidating a closed institution. The FDIC, however, is the manager of the RTC. To obtain the funds necessary to liquidate failed thrifts and pay off depositors, the RTC had the right to sell up to $50 billion of bonds backed by the U.S. Treasury (but not listed as part of the government's deficit). In addition, in the first year of RTC operation, the Treasury transferred $18.8 billion to the RTC. Furthermore, a Resolution Funding Corporation (REFCORP) was established to provide further funds to the RTC by issuing up to $30 billion in bonds. Funds transferred by REFCORP to the RTC would reduce the RTC's ceiling on debt obligations. That is, if REFCORP provided $13 billion to the RTC, then the total amount of debt obligations that the RTC could issue would be reduced from $50 billion to $37 billion. REFCORP is owned by the FHLBanks. Funds for the payment of interest on its bonds come from the FHLBanks, revenues of the RTC, and as necessary from the U.S. Treasury. See Box 20.5.

Effectively, the RTC is a mega-financial institution managing and liquidating hundreds of billions of dollars of assets of the failed thrifts. It finances itself with deposits in the institutions that it does not close and with funds from the Treasury, REFCORP, and its own bonds. The funds that the RTC recovers by liquidating S&L assets will cover some of these latter sources of funds, but ultimately, the Treasury will have to pay remaining RTC and REFCORP obligations and materialize the losses incurred in the collapse of the S&Ls as an expenditure on its own books. That is, the taxpayers will have to pay the difference after the RTC does its best.

Deposit insurance and regulation for S&Ls were to be provided by the FDIC after passage of the law. The FDIC established a separate insurance fund for S&Ls; the fund was given the ironic acronym SAIF (Savings Association Insurance Fund). The separate FDIC insurance fund for deposits in commercial banks is called BIF (Bank Insurance Fund). SAIF is supported by premium assessments on SAIF

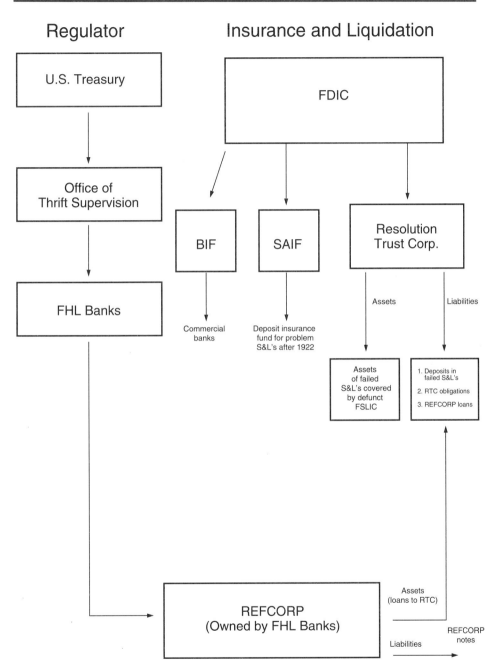

Figure 20.5   S&L REGULATORY STRUCTURE

Box 20.5

Two Years of RTC Operation

By March 1991, the RTC had spent most of the $50 billion authorized in the 1989 FIRRE Act. In less than two years, it had seized 565 S&Ls, of which it has sold or liquidated 370. It operated the remaining 195 seized S&Ls as a conservator, preparatory to selling or liquidating them. The original $50 billion covered losses that the RTC had realized through March 1991. To cover its projected losses from the sale or liquidation of the 195 S&Ls in its hands plus an additional 20 that it expected to seize in the next six months, the RTC received an additional appropriation from Congress of $30 billion in March 1991.

In addition, it was authorized to borrow an additional $47 billion for "working capital"—that is, cash payouts incurred in the sale of S&L deposits that were expected to be recovered in the future sale of the S&L assets acquired by the RTC in deposit transfers or liquidations. The RTC, having already sold $138 billion in seized assets since 1989, was still holding $155 billion in assets in March 1991, including $17 billion in real estate and $5.5 billion in junk bonds. Most potential buyers of S&Ls were interested in acquiring only the deposits and not the assets of the troubled institutions. Thus the RTC was forced to acquire funding to finance temporarily its holdings until it could liquidate them.

members, payments from the FSLIC resolution fund, discretionary payments from the Resolution Trust Corporation, and some payments from the Treasury. The FDIC can temporarily suspend deposit insurance for banks and S&Ls with no tangible capital. SAIF will be responsible for managing the closing of thrifts that fail after 1992.

FIRRE also established strict capital requirements for S&Ls. S&Ls are required to have core capital (mainly common and preferred stock and surplus and earlier FSLIC capital contributions) of at least 3 percent of assets and risk-based capital in amounts at least as stringent as those required for the commercial banks that we studied in Chapter 19. The Office of Thrift Supervision can restrict the asset growth of any S&L that fails to comply with the capital requirements.

New asset restrictions also were imposed on thrifts. For example, they can now hold only investment-grade debt, and their ability to make equity investments is severely limited. At its discretion, the FDIC may prohibit thrifts from engaging in activities posing a serious threat to SAIF. These changes reduced the ability of insolvent thrifts to gamble.

As part of FIRRE, thrifts were prohibited from making loans secured by non-residential real estate in excess of 400 percent of capital. Seventy percent of the portfolio assets of thrifts must be associated with housing construction or mortgage lending on housing. Thus thrifts are required to stay primarily within their original domain—loans to the housing sector—a continued violation of the principle of not concentrating lending in one sector.

CONCLUSION

Adherence to a few simple principles can generally prevent bank failures: diversifying loans and avoiding quick growth, avoiding loans to entities directly connected with the bank, and avoiding mismatches between assets and liabilities. The numerous bank and S&L failures that occurred in the 1980s are attributable to violations of one or more of these principles.

Depositors do not force the closure of an insolvent bank that has reliable deposit insurance. When a bank experiences such losses that it is insolvent, it can continue to book profits for an extended period by relending to failed borrowers and engaging in more risky lending financed with brokered deposits. It is the responsibility of the deposit insurer to prevent further losses in the operation of the insolvent bank. If the deposit insurer lacks funds to close failed banks, additional losses will accrue.

The massive S&L failures of the 1980s were caused by mismatches in maturity between assets and liabilities. The rise in market interest rates in the early 1980s generated large losses for the S&Ls. The lack of resources of the insurer, the FSLIC, prevented the early closure of insolvent institutions, which then engaged in high-risk lending to make themselves whole. Losses cumulated to such an extent that a massive liquidation of S&Ls was begun in 1989, made possible by a huge allocation of funds from the U.S. Treasury.

KEY TERMS

Bank of United States

Federal Deposit Insurance Corporation (FDIC)

payoff

purchase and assumption

deposit transfer

bailout

bridge bank

open bank assistance

Savings Association Insurance Fund (SAIF)

Bank Insurance Fund (BIF)

"walking dead"

rogue bank

Financial Institutions Reform, Recovery, and Enforcement Act of 1989 (FIRRE)

Federal Home Loan Banks (FHLBanks)

Federal Savings and Loan Insurance Corporation (FSLIC)

Depository Institution Deregulation and Monetary Control Act of 1980 (DIDMCA)

Garn–St Germain Act of 1982

Office of Thrift Supervision (OTS)

Resolution Trust Corporation (RTC)

EXERCISES

1. Interest ceilings on deposits were gradually terminated during the first half of the 1980s. How did this initially generate a cash flow problem for S&Ls and subsequently create an incentive for them to acquire risky assets?

2. Because premiums are not adjusted for risk, do banks whose deposits are insured by the FDIC have a competitive advantage over uninsured financial institutions?

3. List four signals of a troubled bank. Why do these signals indicate potential problems?

4. Suppose that Cole Lapse owns an S&L and also owns two real estate investment companies—Desert Development and United Wastelands. Cole's cousin, Dee Backle, owns a property containing toxic waste and faces potentially high cleanup costs. Backle sells the property to Desert Development for $1 million, and the deal is financed by a loan of $950,000 from Cole's S&L. The S&L charges 20-percent interest on the loan, and its cost of funds is 10 percent. After 1 year, Desert Development sells the property to United Wastelands for $10 million, and United Wastelands finances the purchase with a loan from Cole Lapse's S&L of $9.5 million. When the government sues to clean up the land 1 year later, United Wastelands goes bankrupt.

    a. Trace this sequence of transactions on the balance sheets of the S&L and of Desert Development.

    b. Suppose that the S&L pays out its increased book profits as dividends to its owner. How much does Cole Lapse pocket from this sequence of deals as the S&L owner and as the owner of the two real estate companies?

5. When a deposit insurer is illiquid (has little cash on hand), why does it prefer arranging a bailout or a purchase and acquisition to effecting a payoff or a deposit transfer?

6. When a legislature observes large-scale insolvencies among insured depository institutions, why does it hesitate to appropriate sufficient funds to the deposit insurer to end the cumulating losses? How can a region gain from such delay?

7. With hundreds of billions of dollars of assets, the RTC is now one of the largest financial intermediaries in the United States. Most of its assets are illiquid real estate, loans against real estate, and junk bonds. Given the illiquidity of its portfolio, why is the RTC in such a hurry to sell off its assets? Will such urgency tend to increase or reduce the ultimate losses of the Treasury?

8. Much of the loss currently associated with the S&L debacle was generated in the early 1980s when market interest rates rose dramatically. Rather than close many of them, the FHLBB and the FSLIC chose to allow the S&Ls to "grow out of the problem." Suppose that the S&Ls were insolvent in the amount of $50 billion at the end of 1981. Suppose also that these losses were not realized on the books

of the S&Ls and simply rolled over through expansion at a compound interest rate of 10 percent per year. By the end of 1988, how much of the loss of the S&Ls was attributable to the losses suffered from the interest rate mismatch in 1981?

FURTHER READING

Bovenzi, John F., and Maureen E. Muldoon. "Failure-Resolution Methods and Policy Considerations," *FDIC Banking Review,* Fall 1990, pp. 1–11.

Kane, Edward. *The S&L Mess: How Did It Happen?* Washington, D.C.: Urban Institute Press, 1990.

Werner, M. H. *Little Napoleon and Dummy Directors.* New York: Harper Brothers, 1933.

World Bank. "Financial Systems in Distress," in *World Development Report, 1989.* New York: Oxford University Press, 1989, Chapter 5.

21

Monetary Policy
and Economic Activity

W hat is the influence of monetary forces on real economic activity? This is the problem that has driven a central debate in economics for generations. Some economists believe that movements in the quantity of money have a major impact on the economy and that economic activity, which left unattended is subject to excessive fluctuations, can be managed with proper monetary policy and fiscal policy. Others dispute these beliefs, arguing that fluctuations either are not excessive or that they cannot beneficially be controlled with monetary policy. Typically, these disputes revolve around the effects on the business cycle—that is, movements of employment, unemployment, and output—of relatively minor monetary interventions by the central bank.

Despite the disagreement, there is widespread agreement about the impact of major shifts in the money supply on economic activity. Massive and ongoing creation of money will lead to hyperinflation. Massive and rapid reduction in the money supply will cause a depression. This agreement has been forged by our observations of the major economic disruptions of the first half of this century, notably the hyperinflations in Europe following World War I and the Great Depression of the 1930s.

For more normal periods, such as the pre-World War I period and especially the post-World War II period, the evidence does not speak as loudly about the relation between money and real economic activity, and this relative muteness has been the source of the endless theoretical disputes in macroeconomics about monetary policy. Most of the theories reach back and base themselves in the more extreme evidence from either the hyperinflations or the depression in their prescriptions for more normal times.

In this chapter we will examine the goals of monetary policy. We will study the evidence for the impact of money on economic activity in the extreme cases of the German hyperinflation and the U.S. depression. We will then consider evidence about the impact of monetary policy on unemployment and output in more normal times. Finally, we will examine the Keynesian, monetarist, and business cycle theories on which various policy prescriptions are based.

In previous chapters we assumed that monetary changes and policies were well known, that monetary policy shifts were incorporated immediately into expectations, and that prices were free to move flexibly. In such a situation, monetary changes affected only nominal quantities. This is a set of assumptions that economists would generally consider appropriate for a long-run situation.

For shorter horizons, some of the assumptions have to be relaxed, and most economists expect at least some temporary real impacts from monetary changes. For example, we expect that a sudden increase of reserves held by banks as deposits in the Fed will not affect the price level on the day it occurs or even on immediately succeeding days. Rather, it will exert a large effect on the Fed funds rate, as we saw in Chapter 13: The nominal and real Fed funds rate will fall.

Whether this fall in real rates can persist and spread across the term structure, thereby significantly affecting real output and employment, is a matter of debate. Economists used to know the answer to this question—an unequivocal yes. This confidence was reflected in the intensive textbook presentation of the Keynesian model, in which monetary policy could control real activity. With the collapse of confidence in the Keynesian model, the macroeconomics arena has been left in disarray. There are now many different answers to the issue of the impact of monetary policy on economic activity. Our presentation will track several of the main schools of thought on this issue.

THE RATIONALE FOR MONETARY INTERVENTION

We have seen in previous chapters how sudden shifts in demand for securities can cause bankruptcies in capital markets. Although bankrupt firms of market makers and speculators will eventually be replaced, such events can increase the riskiness of making markets. In turn, this will increase spreads and the cost of capital, thereby hindering flows of capital from savers to investors. To the extent that productive activities backing the securities truly are riskier, such bankruptcies are normal and reasonable outcomes: To prevent them through central bank intervention and the provision of liquidity would be a subsidy to risky investment and finance and would eventually lead to inflation. If, however, the disturbance is a purely temporary liquidity event, an intervention would simply lead the market to an appropriate equilibrium, avoiding costly bankruptcies with no inflation. Thus, as a matter of fundamental policy, central banks serve as lenders of last resort during financial crises. This is simply a banking way of saying that they serve as large-scale market makers in cash—that is, they operate as banks.

As a negative effect, the existence of a lender of last resort can induce financial intermediaries to undertake a portfolio of activities that is too risky. That is, intermediaries may take on risky projects because the claims against the projects that perform badly can be sold off in the midst of a crisis to the lender of last resort. Capital will thus flow away from less risky projects and consumption and into more risky and even bad projects.

The Many Goals of Monetary Policy

As lenders of last resort, central banks occasionally must take responsibility for supporting the nominal prices of securities by assuming a banking role as a market maker in liquidity. Indeed, central banks such as the Bank of England and the Federal Reserve originally were intended entirely to operate as banks in the provision of liquidity. Over the years, however, as ideas about the efficacy of monetary interventions have evolved, central banks have assumed several responsibilities, supporting many different nominal values. One obvious responsibility regarding a nominal quantity is the fixing of the prices between legal tender and precious metals or foreign currencies, that is, the establishment of a monetary standard. We examined the effect of fixing the value of the unit of account in terms of precious metals in Chapter 8.

Another responsibility is guaranteeing the exchange rate between money and bank liabilities—that is, the support of the value of bank deposits and interbank payment promises. This is typically done formally with the provision of deposit insurance, as we saw in Chapter 20, although a central bank may extend a large line of credit to a deposit insurer to make sure that deposits can be paid off quickly in system-wide banking insolvencies. Nevertheless, central banks will generally secure the value of large deposit liabilities by making loans to banks to ensure their liquidity. Remember, for example, the Fed's loans to the Continental Illinois Bank discussed in Chapter 19.

Another goal is the control of nominal interest rates. This goal may arise from a desire to provide a government with an easy source of finance. From 1942 to 1951, for example, the central Fed goal was to control a wide range of T-bill and Treasury bond rates. Alternatively, the goal may arise because the central bank aims primarily to serve a monetary role rather than a banking role. In a monetary role, the central bank assumes more grandiose designs and attempts even to control general economic activity. Nowadays, the controlled interest rate is the Fed funds rate—that is, the Fed adds or removes reserves from the system to affect the movements of this overnight interbank rate. The Fed, however, generally treats the Fed funds rate as an "intermediate target"—it is manipulated because it is somehow connected with the achievement of other, primary goals, such as the smoothing of economic fluctuations.

At other times, the Fed has concerned itself with controlling the rate of inflation, and perennially, there are suggestions that the Fed should control some price index or even nominal gross national product.

These goals of policy frequently conflict with each other. It is often possible for the Fed to use monetary policy to control several asset prices at once, but inevitably a time comes when it must place a priority on one goal and drop the others. Indeed, the history of the Federal Reserve can be related as a sequence of different assets whose price the Fed controlled.

The first was the gold standard era from 1914 to 1933, when the first priority was maintaining the fixed exchange rate between the dollar and gold. As long as this goal was met, the Fed also used its policy to manipulate the prices of securities such as commercial paper, bonds, and stocks. When the gold standard was threatened, however, the Fed ceased its attempts to prop up other prices, such as, for example, in 1931 and 1932, when in the midst of the Great Depression it raised its discount rates to stem outflows of gold reserves.

Finally, with the devaluation of the dollar in 1934, the Fed abandoned its commitment to a fixed exchange rate and began an era of giving priority to stabilizing the securities markets, especially markets for government securities. It followed this policy rigidly from 1942 to 1951 by either pegging or placing a floor under the prices of U.S. Treasury securities and less rigidly from 1951 to 1979 by imposing a policy of flexibly manipulating interest rates. Through 1973, there was ostensibly a peg of the dollar to gold. It was clear, however, that this was now a secondary goal; indeed, the peg to gold was effectively abandoned in 1971 when it became inconvenient.

The accelerating inflations of the 1960s and 1970s led to abandonment of the interest rate policy and adoption of a policy to control monetary aggregates from 1979 to 1982. This effort, in turn, was abandoned with the revival of an interest rate policy in 1982, with a monetary aggregate policy as a secondary objective. Finally, the rapid fluctuations of the dollar in the exchange markets led to the readoption of a goal of exchange rate targeting, formalized in the Louvre Accord of 1987. Throughout, the Federal Reserve sporadically maintained its policy of preventing liquidity crises. For example, it intervened strongly in the Crash of 1987 to provide liquidity.

Earlier epochs were marked by primary goals that survived for long periods of time. The 1980s saw rapid shifts from one policy to another. These constant shifts indicated an unsteadiness in Federal Reserve objectives. Under each objective, the Fed expands the delivery of liquidity to a specific market by directly becoming a market maker in that market. Assets in that market become more liquid than they were before. Their prices therefore rise with a liquidity premium, and their supply expands. The opposite happens in markets that fall out of favor as targets, and assets in those markets fall in value.

Why Stabilize Interest Rates?

We have seen in earlier chapters that the Fed, in its role as lender of last resort, wishes to prevent extreme fluctuations in interest rates that may be caused by major liquidity events. On a smaller scale, the Fed acts to stabilize interest rates even in the absence of financial crises. Since the stabilization of interest rates is the primary day-to-day operational policy of the Fed, we now consider its motivation.

This policy would be sensible if the major disturbances in the money market involved shifts in the demand for liquidity. Specifically, suppose that the demand for money in real terms can be depicted as in Figure 21.1. The demand curve is downward sloping because a rise in interest rates makes money holding more costly. The position of the demand curve is affected by the level of real income or economic activity. A higher level of activity shifts the demand curve outward: More real money is demanded for any given interest rate. The position of the demand curve may, of course, shift for reasons other than movements in income. Changes in payments technology or in the risks associated with holding other assets also may shift money demand.

Let the initial money supply be M_0 and the initial money demand be indicated by curve D_0D_0. The price level P_0 and interest rate R_0 would then produce equilibrium in the money market with a real money supply of M_0/P_0. Suppose now that some disturbance shifts money demand to curve D_1D_1. The demand for real money now exceeds the supply. In the absence of any change in the supply of money, three different changes can occur to restore equilibrium in the money market.

1. *Change in prices.* The price level may fall from P_0 to P_1, increasing the supply of real money to M_0/P_1. This, however, would cause real transfers from dollar debtors to dollar creditors as the real value of their debt rises and may generate bankruptcies.

2. *Change in income.* Real income y can fall to reduce real money demand sufficiently to offset the initial disturbance and shift money demand back to D_0D_0. The fall in real income implies a fall in employment of resources, which may be undesirable.

3. *Change in interest rates.* The nominal interest rate R may rise to choke back money demand. Unless expectations of inflation increased, the nominal interest rate rise also would be a real interest rate rise. The nominal interest rate rise, however, would reduce the value of securities.

While we have concentrated so far on the price level movement, all three responses may materialize, although most economists would think that the first response would be a rise in the interest rates because of a liquidity shortage. The

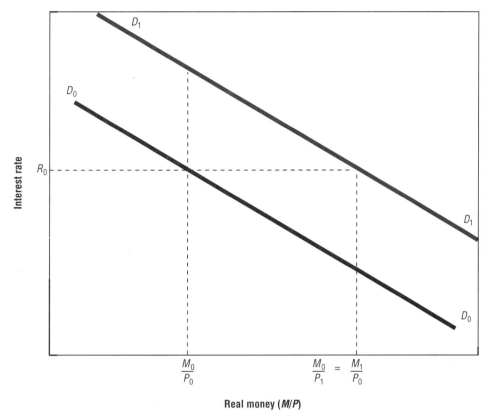

Figure 21.1 DEMAND FOR REAL MONEY

income effect might materialize if economic activity slowed in the medium term. Finally, however, the price level effect would dominate.

It is possible to avoid any response, however, by having the Fed expand the money stock. If the Fed can accurately observe the disturbance to money demand, it can simply increase the money stock to M_1, an increase in the real money stock to M_1/P_0 exactly equal to the amount by which money demand shifted (see Figure 21.1 again). There need then be no change in the price level, interest rates, or real income to maintain money market equilibrium. If the disturbance to money demand disappears later on, the Fed can reduce the money stock accordingly if it recognizes the change. The Fed is simply responding to increases in liquidity demand by costlessly increasing the supply of liquidity, thereby avoiding potentially costly fluctuations in the real economy.

Unfortunately, it is not usually possible to observe disturbances in money demand. Instead, the Fed might interpret movements in interest rates, which it can observe, as responses to money demand disturbances. An increase in money demand would tend to raise R. To offset demand disturbances, the Fed could then expand the money supply if R begins to rise. If R begins to fall, signaling a negative disturbance, the Fed would respond by reducing the money stock.

This policy's direct goal is to stabilize the nominal interest rate to prevent liquidity demand disturbances from having an impact on the price level and the real economy. It would be effective if the primary disturbance in the economy were one of liquidity demand.

Suppose, however, that the real interest rate also fluctuates as a result of technological changes. For instance, a breakthrough in semiconductor or software technology may make machine tools much more productive. The real rate of interest would then rise as producers scramble for the resources to undertake investments incorporating the technology. If the nominal interest rate rises because of an exogenous rise in real interest rates, the monetary authority might respond with a monetary expansion, thinking that a positive disturbance has increased the demand for real money. Without an increase in the money supply, the price level would tend to rise because of the reduced real money demand. The monetary expansion tends to increase the price level even more. Clearly, it is necessary to keep track of real interest rate movements generated from outside the monetary system to implement an appropriate response.

HYPERINFLATION AND DEPRESSION: HOW EXTREME EVENTS SET THE AGENDA FOR POLICY

Two major monetary disturbances in this century were the point of departure for most thinking about the impact of money on economic activity: the hyperinflations and the Great Depression. One or the other of these events generally serves as a template against which to assess current macroeconomic phenomena.

Hyperinflation

A **hyperinflation** is fuzzily defined as an extreme rate of increase in a country's price level over an extended period of time. Since money supplies also increase rapidly, hyperinflations are considered conclusive evidence that rapid inflation is driven by money creation. Hyperinflations typically are associated with wars and their aftermath. Hyperinflations broke out in Germany, Austria, Hungary, Poland, and the Soviet Union after World War I and in Greece and Hungary after World

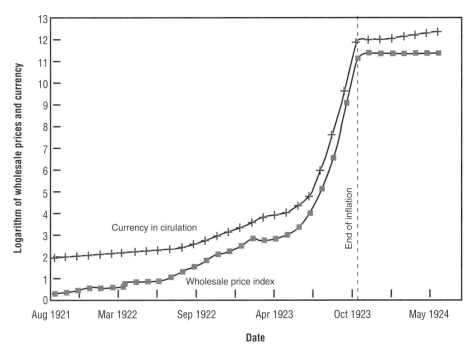

Figure 21.2 MONEY STOCK AND PRICE LEVEL IN THE GERMAN HYPERINFLATION

War II. More recently, hyperinflations have occurred in Bolivia, Peru, Brazil, and Argentina.

The German hyperinflation of 1921–1923 serves as the prime example of the connection between money and prices. Figure 21.2 depicts the money stock and price level in Germany during the hyperinflation. Figure 21.3 plots real money supplies M/P against time during the inflation. As inflation rates and expected inflation rates increased in 1922 and 1923, so did the opportunity cost of holding cash. As we would expect, the lower levels of real value of money are associated with higher levels of inflation.

What causes hyperinflations? Central banks do not permit hyperinflations merely to provide a pathologic monetary environment for the amusement of academic economists. The central banks are required to finance huge loans to governments that are so distrusted by the public that they can borrow nowhere else. All governments need to generate revenues to pay for their expenditures, and one source of revenues is taxation. The tax system, however, may not generate enough to

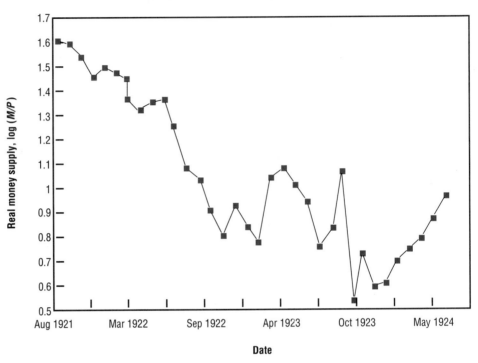

Figure 21.3   REAL MONEY STOCK IN THE GERMAN HYPERINFLATION

cover expenditures. In such cases, the government must borrow by selling its bonds. If the public does not wish to buy the bonds, the government can either reduce expenditures or force the central bank to buy the bonds. If the deficit funded by the central bank is large enough and chronic, a hyperinflation will ensue. Figure 21.4 depicts the real value of the deficits funded by the central bank in the German case. See also Box 21.1.

The parallel movements in money and prices are so dramatic that hyperinflations are often regarded by economists as pure monetary experiments. Nominal changes are so huge that they are thought to dwarf any real changes. Nevertheless, we should avoid the conclusion that the primary causal events in a hyperinflation are necessarily monetary. Hyperinflations typically arise in economies in which political control is so fragile that the government itself is on the verge of disintegrating. The only method left to the government to gather resources to prevent total collapse is to "print money"—that is, through money creation. For example, the German government in the early 1920s faced dual demands that were nearly impossible to fulfill. First was the need to make huge reparations payments to the victorious Allies of World War I. The other need was to fund its own internal activities, including

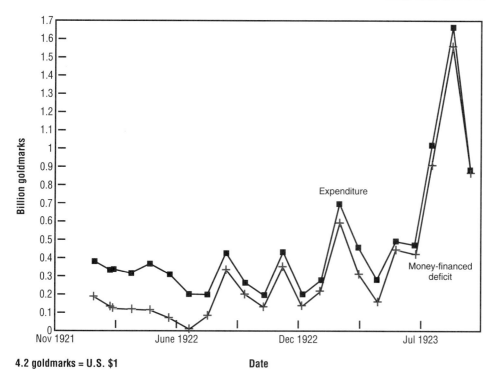

4.2 goldmarks = U.S. \$1   **Date**

Figure 21.4   GOVERNMENT EXPENDITURE AND DEFICIT FINANCED BY MONEY CREATION, GERMANY, 1921–1923

massive programs to subsidize heavy industrial investment. By the end of the inflation, it had stopped making reparations payments, but it made enormous payments to subsidize a general strike and other resistance against the French occupation of the Ruhr. Thus it engaged in a struggle with the French with the only weapon it was permitted: financial warfare.

Simultaneously, the German state was collapsing into its pre-1870 independent principalities under political and financial attack by the hostile French. The French and Belgians occupied the Ruhr, the industrial heart of Germany, and encouraged independence movements in the Rhineland. Bavaria was a semi-independent state by November 1923, the last month of the hyperinflation, when Hitler attempted his coup in Munich.

Associated with the collapse of the state in a hyperinflation are many dramatic real changes in the economy. On a macroeconomic level, economic activity can fluctuate enormously, depending on the policies of the government. In the German case, Figure 21.5 depicts the changes in unemployment.

Box 21.1

Hyperinflation as a Tax on the Public

The real value of the resources generated by money creation can be considered as a tax on money holders. Recall that the real value of the money held by the public at some time zero is M_0/P_0, the nominal money supply at time zero divided by the price level at time zero. The government creates an additional amount of nominal money between time zero and time 1 by selling $(M_1 - M_0)$ worth of bonds to the central bank. The central bank increases its assets by $(M_1 - M_0)$ bonds and its liabilities by an $(M_1 - M_0)$ increase in the deposits of the government. To pay its bills, the government then writes a check on its account, and $(M_1 - M_0)$ materializes as an increase in the monetary base, as in the accompanying table.

CENTRAL BANK MONEY CREATION

a. Immediately After Bond Sale		b. After Government Used Deposits to Purchase Goods and Services	
ASSETS	LIABILITIES	ASSETS	LIABILITIES
Government bonds $(M_1 - M_0)$	Government deposits $(M_1 - M_0)$	Bonds $(M_1 - M_0)$	Currency or deposits of public $(M_1 - M_0)$
			Government deposits 0

The value of the goods that the government acquires by this device is approximately

$$\frac{M_1 - M_0}{P_0} \qquad \text{Real revenue from money creation}$$

Dividing and multiplying the real revenue by M_0, we can convert this into

$$\frac{M_1 - M_0}{M_0} \times \frac{M_0}{P_0} = \text{inflation tax revenue}$$

Tax rate Tax base

The first term is the percentage growth or inflation of the money stock, and this can be interpreted as a tax rate. The second term is the initial real value of the money stock, and this can be interpreted as the real base against which the tax is levied. The product of the tax rate and tax base is the real revenue from inflation.

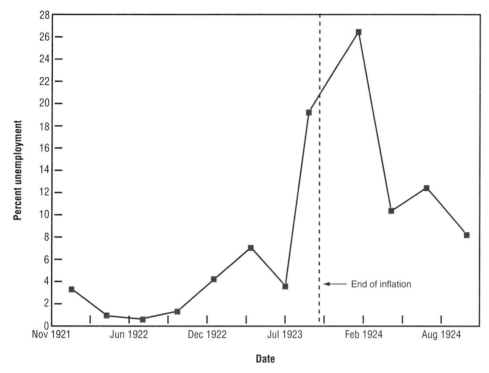

Figure 21.5 UNEMPLOYMENT PERCENTAGE DURING THE GERMAN HYPERINFLATION

On a corporate level, the organization of German industry also rapidly changed. Huge conglomerates formed, comprised of thousands of formerly independent companies, whose purpose was to use internal accounting to avoid settlement that required the use of rapidly depreciating money and to take advantage of the access of a few large firms to liquidity from the central bank. Such organizations were dominated by financiers skilled in being short in cash rather than by captains of industry skilled in production and marketing.

The faster the central bank creates apparent liquidity by printing money, the less liquidity there is as the real supply of good funds declines. Thus the whole focus of management changes, and investment decisions are driven by the desire to avoid liquid positions. Also, control over management disappears as the bond-holders' real position evaporates. Corporations become funded almost entirely by equity, with the associated loss of control over management and the increase in moral hazard.

In the German case, massive investments were undertaken during the inflation, but these proved to be so poorly conceived that a large fraction of the newly constructed capital was scrapped in the industrial rationalization in the years immediately following the inflation.

Most economists have observed the coincidence of hyperinflation and large-scale economic disturbances and have concluded that very high inflation rates inevitably create social losses. They also have concluded that large real economic and price level disturbances are driven by rapid increases in the money supply. Thus the lesson learned from the hyperinflations is to avoid too fast a rate of inflation. The Germans especially learned the lesson so well that they have ever since had inflation rates that are among the world's lowest.[1]

The Great Depression

Figures 21.6 and 21.7 depict the movements in U.S. money stock, monetary base, prices, and industrial production during the **Great Depression** of 1929–1933. The sharp decline in the stock of money in the form of bank deposits, punctuated by bank runs in 1930, 1931, and 1933, was associated with large falls in income, production, and prices. Unemployment rates hit unprecedented levels that persisted until the outbreak of World War II.

After many years of analysis and debate, most economists have concluded that a lack of energetic response by the Federal Reserve to the decline in the money stock associated with plunging bank deposits was a major cause of the depression.[2] The monetary base depicted in Figure 21.6 declined slightly in 1930 and then began to rise slowly. The Fed did not—in fact, could not—do much to expand the base to stabilize the money supply. Effectively, the Federal Reserve permitted the money stock to decline.

The reason the Federal Reserve could not expand the monetary base energetically was a legal requirement that its notes and deposits be backed by a minimum percentage of gold. Treasury securities did not count as backing for the Fed's liabilities. In 1932, this restriction was relaxed with the passage of the Glass-Steagall Act (not to be confused with the Glass-Steagall Banking Act of 1933 that separated investment and commercial banking). The Fed was then permitted to expand its holdings of Treasury securities. Fears of a collapse of the gold standard, however, prevented too rapid a monetary expansion. Thus the Fed was caught between two conflicting goals: the maintenance of the gold standard versus prevention of the

1. For detailed information about the German hyperinflation, see Constantino Bresciani-Turroni, *The Economics of Inflation* (Northampton: John Dickens & Co., 1937), and Carl-Ludwig Holtfrerich, *The German Inflation 1914–1923* (New York: Walter de Gruyter, 1986).

2. This is the Friedman-Schwartz indictment of the Federal Reserve that was published in their famous chapter on the Great Contraction in Milton Friedman and Anna J. Schwartz, *A Monetary History of the U.S.* (Princeton, N.J.: Princeton University Press, 1963). It has since gained widespread acceptance, even at the Federal Reserve itself.

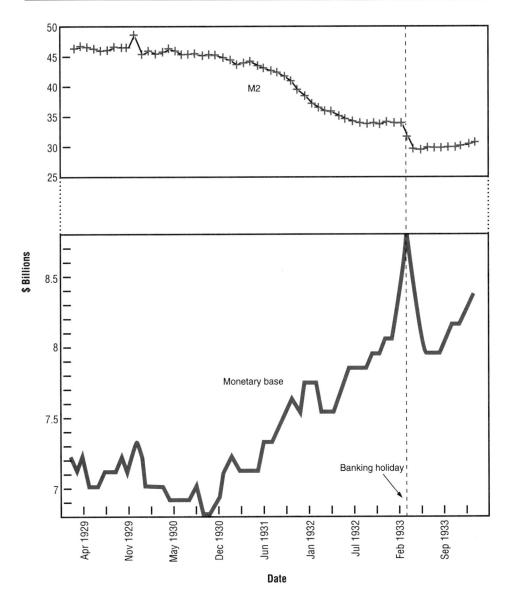

Figure 21.6   M2 AND MONETARY BASE IN THE GREAT DEPRESSION

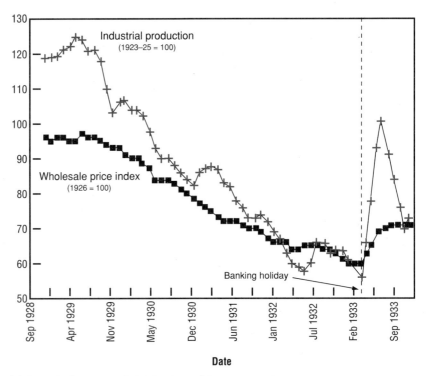

**Figure 21.7   PRICE LEVEL AND INDUSTRIAL PRODUCTION
IN THE GREAT DEPRESSION**

decline in the price level. This dilemma was finally resolved in March 1933 with the departure of the United States from the gold standard, but only after a run on the Fed's gold stock in February 1933 and the complete closing of U.S. banking and financial markets in March 1933.

The fall in prices and the industrial decline led to massive defaults on securities and bank loans. Banks lending heavily to particular industrial sectors or regions became insolvent and were run in several waves. The public held more cash and fewer deposits, and banks started to hold excess reserves to protect themselves against further bank runs. Thus the money supply declined further, again reducing the price level and triggering another round of defaults. All this could have been avoided with an appropriate expansion of the monetary base at the right time. The price level would have been stabilized, and the default risk would have been reduced.

The reduced price level during the Great Depression increased defaults on bank loans and effectively made many banks insolvent. Recently, economists have argued that when these intermediaries were run and forced to close, a valuable information capital, their specialized ability to distinguish credit risks among small, local firms dependent on them, was destroyed. This hole in the financial intermediation industry forced the pooling of less risky firms with riskier firms in the eyes of remaining lenders. These lenders perceived increased risk overall, a perception that raised these firms' cost of funds and forced them to reduce their level of activity. The restoration of the information capital with the entry of solvent intermediaries was necessarily a slow process. This destruction and degradation of the process of financial inter-mediation thus help to explain the protracted nature of the Great Depression. Al-though a sharp monetary decline might have set off the process, monetary forces by themselves should not have had such a long-term negative effect.[3]

The Great Depression triggered such an intense fear of deflation that monetary policy has been inflationary ever since. In only 1 of the 50 years since the Great Depression have consumer prices fallen, by 1 percent in 1949. The Great Depression also generated an aversion to the bankruptcy of important financial institutions, notably banks and S&Ls. Deposit insurance and stricter control over banks and thrifts were the results, as we have seen in other chapters.

THE EFFECTS OF POLICY ON ECONOMIC ACTIVITY

Why should the Fed direct its policy toward controlling fluctuations in nominal values? The reason is that most policymakers and economists believe that fluctuations in nominal quantities such as the price level, the nominal interest rate, and exchange rates can be used to control fluctuations in important economic activities such as total real output, investment and savings, exports and imports, and employment and unemployment levels. They also believe that the welfare of society would generally improve if these fluctuations were reduced in frequency and magnitude.

What are the fluctuations that policymakers wish to affect with monetary policy? In panels (a), (b), and (c) of Figure 21.8 we plot fluctuations of growth rates of real GNP, real consumption, and real investment, respectively, in the post World War II period. In panel (d) we plot the measured unemployment rates for the same period. These fluctuations are shown as deviations from the trend for these variables.

---

3. See Ben S. Bernanke, "Nonmonetary Effects of the Financial Crisis in the Propagation of the Great Depression," *American Economic Review,* June 1983, pp. 257–276. This explanation apparently differs from our emphasis in previous chapters that the advantage of banks lies in their ability to provide liquid funds. In addition, banks can have an advantage as lenders in gathering information about borrowers. Our emphasis on liquidity provision is based on recent observations of the behavior of fairly large banks in the much more competitive modern environment. Because of greater access to communications and transportation, there are fewer local banking monopolies than in the Depression era. Also, even in a competitive environment, the sudden elimination of a large number of interme-diaries may take time to restore even if other in-stitutions are perfect substitutes in gathering in-formation about borrowers.

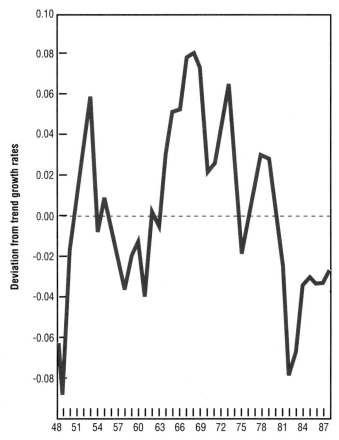

Figure 21.8a POSTWAR FLUCTUATIONS IN DETRENDED REAL GNP

The average growth rate over the period for each variable is calculated to represent the trend growth rate. The trend growth rate is then subtracted from the actual growth rate. Such deviations from trend split the sample for each variable into positive and negative deviations from trend. The term **business cycle** refers to the observation that all these variables tend to deviate simultaneously from their trends. For example, in 1967, unemployment was unusually low, whereas the other variables grew at above their trend growth rates. In contrast, in 1982, unemployment was unusually high, whereas the other variables grew at well below their trend rates.

Although most economists generally agree that monetary interventions can

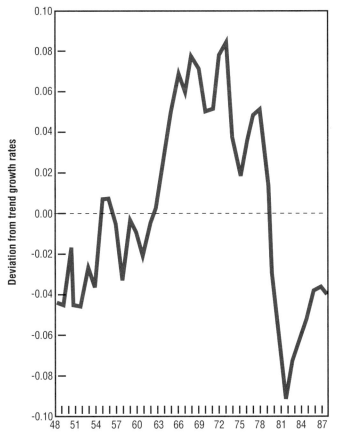

Figure 21.8b POSTWAR FLUCTUATIONS IN DETRENDED REAL CONSUMPTION

affect such real fluctuations, there is great disagreement about how monetary policy should be used to stabilize the economy. First, many economists believe that real fluctuations are generated by nonmonetary disturbances and that monetary and fiscal policy should be used actively to counter their negative impacts. This group would include those who might be called *Keynesians* in the 1960s and 1970s and *neo-Keynesians* in the 1980s. Second, some economists believe that money supply disturbances themselves are major sources of real fluctuations and that monetary policy should aim at minimizing such disturbances. This group would include those who might be called *monetarists*.

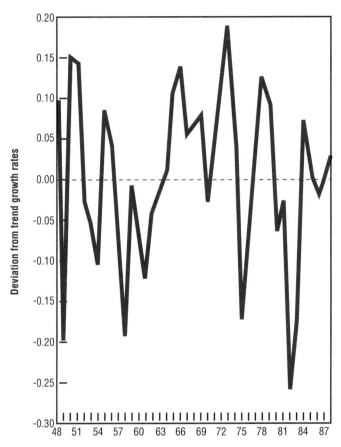

Figure 21.8c   POSTWAR FLUCTUATIONS IN DETRENDED REAL INVESTMENT

While both groups believe that monetary policy has strong effects, they disagree about what policy to follow. Keynesians and neo-Keynesians propose an activist Fed for the improvement of social welfare. Such a Fed, armed with a knowledge of how money affects the economic system and aware that the economy is in an inappropriate equilibrium, can act at its discretion to improve the situation. Monetarists call for a Fed with little discretion, armed with a policy to control only some measure of the stock of money. These economists argue that the Fed lacks enough information about the impact of monetary action on the real economy and of the welfare-maximizing equilibrium for its discretionary actions to improve well-

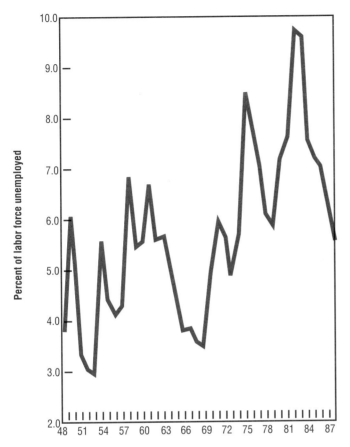

Figure 21.8d POSTWAR FLUCTUATIONS IN UNEMPLOYMENT RATE

being. In fact, quite the contrary, Fed actions will often have a negative impact. See Box 21.2.

Finally, some economists believe that monetary disturbances play a minor role in real economic fluctuations and cannot be used as an effective tool to control such fluctuations. To this group, real fluctuations are caused by changes in technology, tastes for goods and risk, government expenditure and tax policy, and the regulatory environment. Monetary forces play a small role and indeed are themselves driven by these other forces. Since the forces generating cycles arise in the real economy, this view is referred to as *real business cycles theory*.

In the remainder of this chapter we will examine each of these views.

THE MONETARIST VIEW

The observation that the quantity of money strongly affects the price level and real economic activity has driven the policy view known as **monetarism.** Although movements in the quantity of money have powerful real effects, monetarists believe that economic fluctuations are often initiated by sudden monetary shifts that are themselves aimed at controlling real activity. Therefore, monetarists argue that activist and discretionary monetary policy is counterproductive. What is needed is an automatic policy, such as fixing the growth rate of money, to reduce the amount of real and nominal fluctuations in an economy.

monetary policy, and it participates as little as possible as a provider of liquidity to banking markets.

The written goals, however, may be not be implemented in practice. The extent to which the "general economic activity" of the community can be supported without price level instability is highly debatable, as we have seen throughout this chapter. Depending on who gains control of its board of governors, the ECB may indeed become activist. Thus the debate among the central bankers concerns the establishment of means of avoiding such activism.

For example, the draft agreement left unsettled the issue of whether the ECB should be a supervisor and regulator of banks. The Bundesbank wants supervision and regulation to be powers of institutions separate from the ECB. Other central banks wish to regulate the banks through the ECB. If the ECB were to become a creditor of banks through its provision of liquidity to banks, supervision and regulation should naturally be among its activities. Therefore, the Bundesbank position signals an intention that the ECB should provide very little credit to the banks. In addition, the Bundesbank believes that if the ECB supervises the banks, it will tend to extend credit to failing banks to avoid embarrassing political questions about why its supervision was ineffective. Giving some other institution the supervision responsibility is a means of distancing the ECB even farther from the banks.

The birth of this new central banking institution has caused a major debate on the role of a central bank. Is a central bank merely a banker's bank, serving a role in providing liquidity? Is it the keeper of a monetary rule? Should such a monetary rule be activist and discretionary or limited to price level stability? As we have seen throughout this book, the answers that the Europeans find to these questions will determine the organization and liquidity of their banking and financial markets.

We can derive the basis for this view from Figure 21.1. A basic point of departure for monetarism is that the demand for money is a highly stable relationship between the level of real income and wealth and rates of return on a few assets. These rates of return include nominal yields, returns on real assets such as stocks, and the inflation rate or the return on cash in terms of goods. A stable money demand means that knowledge of these few variables allows us to predict tightly the demand for real money.

Suppose in Figure 21.1 that the upward shift in the demand for money results from an immediately observable rise in real income. We determined earlier that a rise in money from M_0 to M_1 would then be associated with no change in the price level or in real income.

Suppose now that real income rises, on average, at a rate of 2.5 percent per year. Then a steady money supply increase at a constant annual percentage rate would be associated with a stable price level and interest rate.

Suppose finally that real income growth fluctuates—in some years it is higher than 2.5 percent and in some years it is lower. Although monetarists believe that in the long run the growth in output is based on changes in the real economy, such as technology, labor, and capital growth, they also believe that in the short run a strong causal relation exists between money creation and real activity. Therefore, there is a temptation to use monetary policy to offset fluctuations in real activity. For example, suppose that in some period output falls by 1 percent, which is 3.5 percent below its normal growth rate. A step-up in the rate of monetary expansion might increase the rate of growth to a more acceptable level.

How would this step-up be transmitted to the real economy? In the monetarist view, the channels of transmission are highly varied. The demand for money depends on the returns from a wide range of assets. When the supply of real money is suddenly increased, there is momentarily an excess supply of money, and prices of other assets must change to generate increased demands sufficient to absorb this supply. These other assets include bonds with fixed nominal coupons, stocks, and consumer durables. Prices of each of these must adjust to shift the demand for money. For example, some people holding excess money will try to reduce their money holdings by buying bonds, so the price of bonds will tend to rise, thereby lowering one of the opportunity costs and increasing the demand for money. The raising of bond prices will lower the cost of financing investments and cause an expansion in demand for investment goods. Similarly, people may increase their demand for consumer durables, thereby raising their prices and causing output to increase.

If monetary expansion will cause an expansion in economic activity in a recession, why is it undesirable to engage in this sort of countercyclical policy? In the monetarist view, such interventions take place in economies whose dynamics are not well understood. In some situations the real effects of a monetary intervention will emerge quickly, for example, within 6 months, but in other situations the real effects will take much longer. The effects of monetary intervention, while powerful, take place with long and variable lags. Thus, by the time such policy interventions take effect, the direction of the economy may have changed. The −1-percent real growth rate may have converted itself to a 3.5-percent real growth rate by the time the added impetus of the monetary change appears. Instead of an expansionary monetary policy in a recession, the policy will add inflationary pressure to an already booming economy.

From the monetarist viewpoint, there is a tendency for activist policy—that is, the active use of central bank actions to expand or contract real economic activity—to worsen cycles in the real economy and not to smooth them. As evidence, monetarists cite data that indicate that downturns in the money supply precede downturns in the business cycle by at least 6 months. From this observation they infer that disturbances in the money supply are a causal force in the business cycle. Their prescription is then to remove this source of disturbance in the business cycle by setting a rate of growth of money at approximately a constant level, typically at a level that matches the growth rate of output, so that the price level would be stabilized.

THE THEORY UNDERPINNING
THE KEYNESIAN MODEL

In the **Keynesian model** monetary policy affects real activity because either prices or wages adjust more slowly than interest rates and output when an economy is disturbed. The analysis centers on behavior in the markets for goods and money, focusing on values of current income and interest rates consistent with the total sources of income and with money market clearing.

The analysis aims ultimately at developing the relationships between aggregate demand and aggregate supply—that is, relationships between price level and output—that can then be used to solve for equilibrium values of the price level and of real output.

The *IS* Curve: Equilibrium in the Goods Market

Aggregate demand behavior is derived by separately analyzing the various uses of goods and the conditions of money market clearing. In the goods market, real income y is, by definition, the total of all the types of expenditures in the economy. These categories include expenditures on the goods used for consumption c, goods used for investment i (that is, adding to the productive capital of the economy), and goods used by the government g. By definition, income is the sum of these categories.[4]

$$y = c + i + g \qquad (21.1)$$

Consumption depends on current income, as shown in Figure 21.9a; a larger current income generates more consumption. An assumption generally used in Keynesian models is that consumption rises by *less* than the increase in income. In addition, taxes T on gross income y reduce personal income available for consumption for any given level of gross income y. Therefore, consumption depends on income *net* of taxes, that is, $y - T$.

Investment i depends negatively on the level of the real interest rate r, as shown in Figure 21.9b. Higher real interest rates mean that firms will have to pay more

4. In an open economy, an additional expenditure "source" is net exports, $x - Im$, where x is real exports and Im is real imports.

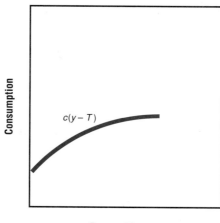

Figure 21.9a   CONSUMPTION VERSUS PERSONAL INCOME

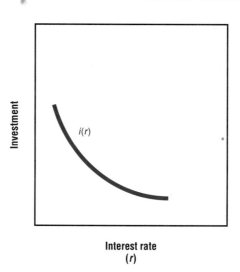

Figure 21.9b   INVESTMENT VERSUS INTEREST RATE

to borrow funds for capital investments. The higher the costs of borrowing, the fewer the projects that will be undertaken.

Government expenditure in this model is taken as a given and is not affected by interest rates and income.

The need to establish equality between income and expenditure generates a relationship between income and the real interest rate known as the **IS curve.** Substituting the behavior of consumption $c(y - T)$ and investment $i(r)$, into the definition of income, we find

$$y = c(y - T) + i(r) + g \qquad (21.2)$$

The difference between income and the sum of consumption and government expenditure is defined as savings, so this definition requires that savings must equal investment. The IS (investment equals savings) curve is defined as all combinations of income y and the real interest rate r that satisfy the relationship expressed in equation 21.2.

Plotting these combinations in Figure 21.10, we generate a negatively sloped curve and label it IS. To convince yourself that the slope is negative, suppose that the income–interest rate pair (y_0, r_0) is such that equation 21.2 is satisfied; that is, the different kinds of expenditure do sum to income. This pair is then a point on the IS curve. Now consider a rise in income to y_1. What must happen to the interest rate for the sources of expenditure to increase sufficiently to absorb the increase in income? We have assumed that consumption itself will rise with income

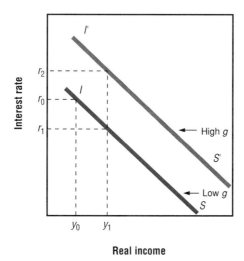

Figure 21.10   IS CURVE

but not sufficiently to absorb the entire increase in income. If government expenditure does not increase, only an increase in investment can absorb the remaining income rise. Investment can rise only if the interest rate is lower. Hence a new pair (y_1, r_1) is also consistent with equation 21.2, so it also lies on the IS curve.

The position of the IS curve itself depends on government expenditure and taxes. Starting with the level of expenditure and taxes associated with IS, suppose that government expenditure increases. What happens to the IS curve? To determine how the IS curve moves, consider what happens to the interest rate at a level of income y_1. Now g is higher, but consumption and income are the same as on the original IS curve. To maintain the equality between income and its uses, investment i must fall to offset the rise in g. However, i declines with a *rise* in the interest rate to r_2. Thus the pair (y_1, r_2) is now on the new IS curve, labeled $I'S'$. You can repeat this analysis for each possible income level to find that rise in g uniformly shifts the IS curve outward.

Now consider a cut in taxes T. Repeating the same method of analysis, you can show that, again, the IS curve shifts outward.

The *LM* Curve: Equilibrium in the Money Market

The LM curve depicts the combination of interest rates and income associated with equilibrium in money markets. In the simple examples in previous chapters, we have described money market equilibrium as

$$\frac{M}{P} = ay - br$$

where the left side is the supply of real money and the right side is the demand. Demand depends positively on real income y, in this case multiplied by a constant coefficient a. Previously, we used the nominal interest rate R in money demand, but in this example, money demand depends on the real interest rate r multiplied by a constant coefficient b. This is consistent with a situation of zero expected inflation. In Keynesian terminology, the right side is a demand for liquidity and the left side is the supply of money. For a given price level and nominal money supply, all the (y, r) pairs that produce money market equilibrium are called the **LM curve** (liquidity demand equals money).

We plot all these pairs in Figure 21.11. Why is the LM curve upward sloping? Suppose again that we begin with a point on the curve (y_0, r_0) for which there is equilibrium in the money market. Now consider a situation in which income is higher at y_1. At a higher income, money demand is higher, but the real supply stays constant. Remember that the position of the curve is determined for a given nominal money stock and price level. Restoring equilibrium requires that money demand be reduced, which can result from a rise in the interest rate to r_1. Thus the pair (y_1, r_1) is also on the LM curve.

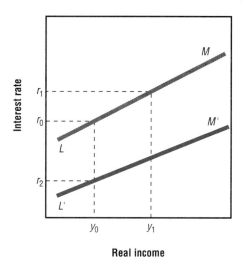

Figure 21.11 *LM* CURVE

The position of the *LM* curve can shift with changes in the nominal money stock or in the price level. For example, suppose that the money stock rises from its level on curve *LM* while the price level stays fixed. This increase in the real supply of money causes the *LM* curve to shift down and to the right to curve $L'M'$. To convince yourself of this, note that for any pair (y_0, r_0) on the original *LM* curve, there is now an excess supply of money. To raise money demand, either income must increase or the interest rate must fall. For a given level of income y_0, only a lower interest rate r_2 clears the money market, and this is true for every possible level of income. Thus a higher money stock moves the *LM* curve to the curve $L'M'$.

Alternatively, a fall in the price level also has the effect of shifting the *LM* curve rightward, because it also raises the supply of real money. Conversely, if the increase in the money stock is associated with an instantaneous and proportionate rise in the price level, there is no movement in the *LM* curve, since the real money stock has not changed.

Aggregate Demand

The next step in our Keynesian model is to combine the *IS* curve and *LM* curve in the same diagram, as in Figure 21.12. Then, by examining the levels of income consistent in both goods and money markets for different price levels, it is possible

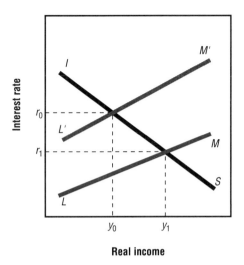

Interest rate

Real income

Figure 21.12 *LM* SHIFT AFTER INCREASE IN PRICE LEVEL

to derive a relationship known as **aggregate demand.** To construct aggregate demand, suppose that the price level is P_1 and that the money stock, government expenditure, and taxation are initially such that the positions of the *IS* and *LM* curves are those labeled in Figure 21.12. The income–interest rate pair (y_1, r_1) lies on both the *IS* and *LM* curves. This pair is then consistent with equilibrium in the money market and with income equaling the sum of expenditures.

Specifically, associated with the price level P_1 is the level of income y_1. Let us plot this pair in Figure 21.13. Now, going back to Figure 21.12, consider what happens if the price level increases to P_0. For a higher price level, we know that the *LM* curve shifts upward and to the left to $L'M'$ because for a given nominal money supply there is a smaller real money supply. Now a new pair (y_0, r_0) lies on both the *IS* curve and the new *LM* curve, with y_0 less than y_1. Plot the new pair (y_0, P_0) in Figure 21.13, and note that it is upward and to the left of (y_1, r_1). Now repeat the analysis for every possible value of the price level, and connect all the plotted points to form the curve labeled *AD* in Figure 21.13.

The downward-sloping curve in Figure 21.13 is known as the aggregate demand curve. For given values of the money stock, taxes, and government expenditure, it shows those combinations of the price level and income that are consistent with the clearing of the money market *and* with the equality of income with the sum of expenditures. It is referred to as aggregate demand because its position is affected by shifts in all those variables that we typically regard as affecting demand—

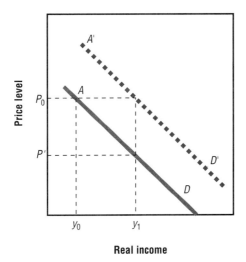

Figure 21.13   AGGREGATE DEMAND

government expenditures and taxes, the money stock, and shifts in the desire for investment and consumption.

In developing monetary policy, the impact of a money supply change on aggregate demand is especially pertinent. Specifically, the aggregate demand curve will shift to the right with an increase in the money stock. To see this, begin with a level of the money stock M_0 and a fixed level of government expenditure and taxes. Suppose that the pair (y_0, P_0) is on the associated aggregate demand curve AD. Now increase the money stock to M_1. From Figure 21.11, we know that this will shift the LM curve to the right, given the original price level P_0. The level of income consistent with both the IS curve and the new LM curve then increases, to y_1, for example. The pair (y_1, P_0) in Figure 21.13 will therefore be a point on the new aggregate demand curve $A'D'$. Now repeat the process for each possible value of the price level on the old aggregate demand curve, and connect to points to produce $A'D'$. Also, repeat the exercise for a fall in the money supply to show that the aggregate demand curve shifts downward to the left.

Aggregate Supply

So far we have ignored the productive side of the economy and effectively have assumed that real income will have a value consistent with the demands for output.

Now to complete the Keynesian model, we must consider how output responds to movements in the price level.

Firms engaged in production choose levels of output and inputs to maximize their profit, which is the difference between the value of their output and the cost of their inputs. Inputs consist of labor and capital, and it is assumed that capital is fixed and that labor can be readily varied. Labor has a diminishing marginal product. That is, each additional unit of labor will cause output to increase by an ever smaller additional amount as labor is increased. A firm will demand labor up to the point where the added real output of the additional unit equals the added real cost, or real wage, of the additional unit of labor. If the market real wage increases, fewer workers will be hired and less output will be produced.

The real wage is the nominal or money wage W divided by the price level P, that is, W/P. This gives the value of the wage in terms of goods. A standard Keynesian model typically presumes that the nominal wage is either fixed or moves sluggishly and that firms can obtain all the labor they demand at the nominal wage W. Therefore, a rise in the price level will reduce the real wage, increase the demand for labor, and increase the production of goods.

The price level is positively related to the supply of goods. We depict this relationship, known as the **aggregate supply,** in Figure 21.14 as the curve AS. Combining aggregate supply with aggregate demand, we can finally determine the equilibrium values of output and the price level, indicated in the figure as the point (y_0, P_0).

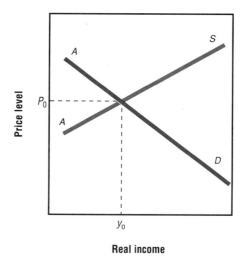

Figure 21.14 DETERMINATION OF PRICE LEVEL AND OUTPUT

THE EFFECT OF MONETARY MOVEMENTS
ON REAL ACTIVITY

We can at last examine how monetary movements affect economic activity in a Keynesian model. The position of the aggregate demand curve AD in Figure 21.15 is determined by given levels of money stock, taxation, and government expenditure. Suppose that the money stock increases from M_0 to M_1, thereby shifting the AD curve to $A'D'$. The new equilibrium will be the point (y_1, P_1), a higher level of output and a higher price level.

An increase in the stock of money has indeed increased the level of economic activity. First, the supply of output increases because the price level increase has reduced the real wage and increased labor demand. The increased output is absorbed partly by an increase in consumption driven by the rise in income. In addition, output is absorbed by an increase in investment driven by the decline in the interest rate. (Recall that an increase in the money stock is associated with a fall in the rate of interest.)

Finally, the rise in the price level must be less than proportional to the rise in the money stock if the real money stock had actually increased. A price level rise brings forth extra goods supply, yet if the price level rises in proportion to the money stock increase, there is no increase in real money and the LM curve shifts back to its original position, as we saw in Figure 21.11. The amount of goods

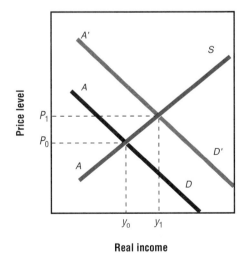

Figure 21.15 SHIFT IN AGGREGATE DEMAND

absorbed by consumption, investment, and government expenditure would then also shift back to the original value y_0. However, then the amount of goods produced would exceed the amount absorbed. The excess supply could then be removed only by a fall in the price level.

STABILIZATION

Finally, using a Keynesian model to see how monetary interventions might reduce the size of economic fluctuations, let us start with an equilibrium situation, as depicted in Figure 21.16, with a given initial level of government expenditure, taxes, and money stock. Suppose that investors suddenly become pessimistic about the future earnings from their investments and reduce their investments at every possible value of the real interest rate. In Figure 21.16a, this would cause the IS curve to shift down to $I'S'$, reducing the level of income and interest rate to (y_1, r_1). Since the original price level P_0 is now associated with a lower income, the aggregate demand curve shifts down and to the left in Figure 21.16b. This lowers the supply of output to y_2 and the price level to P_2. The price level fall in turn causes the LM curve (Figure 12.16a) to shift rightward. In the end, once all the changes stop, the LM curve will have shifted to $L'M'$. Since less income is produced, there will be a smaller level of employment.

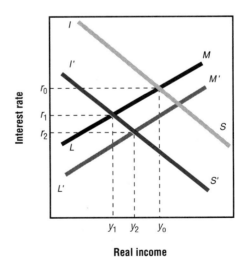

Figure 21.16a   DOWNWARD SHIFT IN INVESTMENT DUE TO INVESTOR PESSIMISM: *AS–AD* EFFECTS

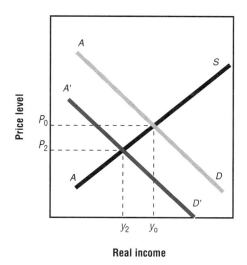

Figure 21.16b   DOWNWARD SHIFT IN INVESTMENT DUE TO INVESTOR PESSIMISM: *IS–LM* EFFECTS

Several policies might prevent this fluctuation in output and employment. First, fiscal policy might be used. The government can increase its expenditures g sufficiently to offset the initial fall in investment. This shifts the *IS* curve back to its original position, and price level, interest rate, output, and employment would stay at their initial levels.

Alternatively, the central bank might increase the money stock. Since we analyzed this case before, we know that this would shift the curve $L'M'$ downward and the aggregate demand curve upward. With a sufficient increase in money, output and the price level can attain their original values. However, the interest rate would fall below its original value.

INFLATION AND ECONOMIC ACTIVITY

In the Keynesian model, monetary policy has a real impact because the real wages move countercyclically—that is, they rise in the downside of the cycle and fall in the upside. Nominal wages are assumed to be a given, or they slowly adjust over the period relevant to the analysis, so a rise in the price level generates added output and employment.

Nominal wages do change, however, and their change must somehow be driven

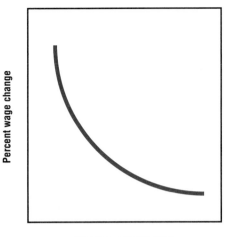

Percent unemployment

Figure 21.17   PHILLIPS CURVE

by market forces. To account for wage movement, an additional relationship, known as the **Phillips curve,** was added to Keynesian models. The idea is that labor market pressure drives the movement of nominal wages. When unemployment levels are low, firms find it difficult to acquire employees and must raise their wage offers. This means that there is a negative relationship between nominal wage changes and the level of unemployment, as depicted in Figure 21.17.[5]

This simple relationship gained support from observations of wage and unemployment relationships from before World War I and from the 1950s and 1960s. Figure 21.18 is a plot of the percentage nominal wage change against unemployment in the United States from 1948 to 1968. Note that in this period there was a negative relation between wage changes and unemployment—that is, when wages grew relatively slowly, unemployment was relatively high.

Economists imagined that it might be possible to exploit the observable empirical relation between wage changes and unemployment to manipulate the level of unemployment through inflation. First, an increase in the money supply in one period would raise the price level, output, and employment by shifting the aggregate demand curve, as in the case studied earlier. The rise in employment, generating an associated fall in unemployment, would put upward pressure on nominal wages in the next period. With no further policy action, this would tend to shift aggregate

5.   This relationship was first documented in British data by A. W. Phillips, "The Relation between Unemployment and the Rate of Change of Money   Wage Rates in the United Kingdom, 1861–1959," *Economica,* November 1958, pp. 283–299.

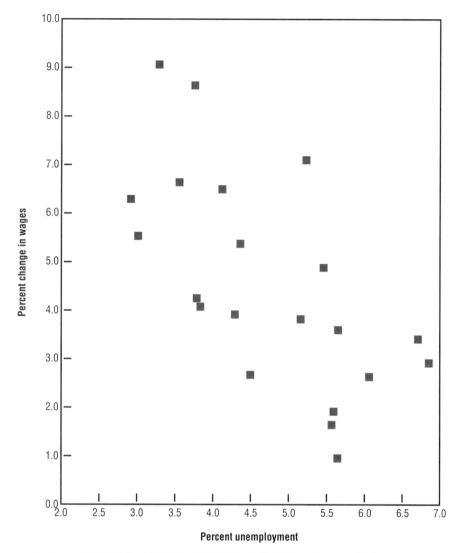

Figure 21.18   PHILLIPS CURVE, UNITED STATES, 1948–1968

supply upward because of the increase in the real wage, thereby tending to reduce output and employment back to their original levels. An additional sufficient increase in the money stock, however, would once more shift the aggregate demand curve outward enough to offset the shift in the aggregate supply curve. The price level rises once again, but output, employment, and unemployment do not change from their newly attained levels. Once again, the low level of unemployment puts upward pressure on wages, and the monetary intervention repeats.

In this framework, it is possible to reduce permanently the level of unemployment in exchange for a permanent increase in the rate of wage and price level inflation. Conversely, a fall in the rate of inflation would be associated with a

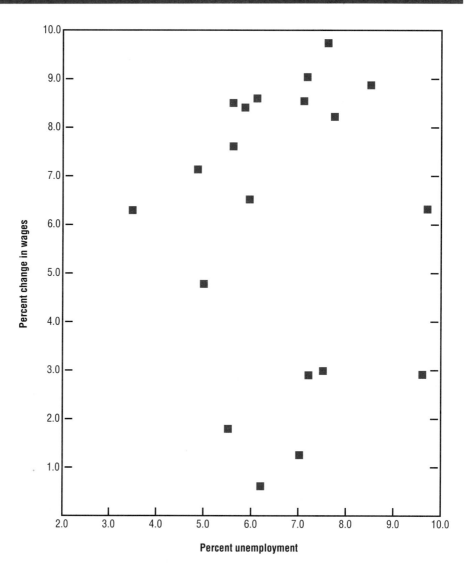

Figure 21.19   PHILLIPS CURVE, UNITED STATES, 1969–1988

CHAPTER 21 MONETARY POLICY AND ECONOMIC ACTIVITY

permanent rise in the level of unemployment. This association was so powerful an idea that it still pervades most macroeconomic policy thinking.

Just as policymakers started attempts to exploit the recognition of this tradeoff between inflation and unemployment, there were warnings that the tradeoff might be illusory.[6] The observed negative relationship between wage changes and unemployment were from periods of relative price stability in which prices were not expected to rise permanently. Under such circumstances, wage-setting behavior in labor markets might not account for possible price level changes, since price changes would be unlikely, so real wages might be affected temporarily by realized price level changes when they actually occurred. Under circumstances of permanent inflation, however, wage-setting agreements would account for such forseeable price level changes and automatically and quickly adjust nominal wages. Hence the inflation-unemployment tradeoff would evaporate the moment an attempt was made to exploit it.

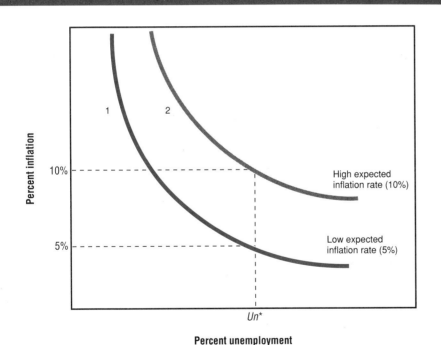

Figure 21.20 INFLATION-ADJUSTED PHILLIPS CURVE

6. The most influential warning was that of Milton Friedman, "The Role of Monetary Policy," *American Economic Review,* March 1968, pp. 7–11.

Events in the 1970s and 1980s confirmed this evaporation. Figure 21.19 plots inflation rates against unemployment during this period. It is evident that the negative relation between inflation and unemployment disappeared. Economists attempted to alter their theory by proposing the "expectations-adjusted Phillips curve," in which the position of the curve shifts with the anticipated rate of inflation, as in Figure 21.20. For a given inflation rate, curve 1 might apply. For a higher expected rate, the curve would shift up to 2. The shift would occur because wage increases would presumably be preprogrammed to match anticipated price level movements. To the extent that anticipations were accurate, there would be no real wage movement and hence no effect of inflation on the level of unemployment.

Still, economists continued to assume that there was some scope for monetary policy to affect real activity. To the extent that price level changes were unanticipated, there would still be a downward slope to the Phillips curve. For example, curve 1 might be associated with an anticipated inflation rate of 5 percent. If inflation were actually 10 percent, there would then be some movement along the curve to a lower level of unemployment. To accomplish this, a central bank would have to accelerate the rate of inflation constantly to keep ahead of changes in expectations.

THE EMERGENCE OF RATIONAL EXPECTATIONS

The breakdown of the Phillips curve relation was momentarily repaired in the early 1970s by adjusting the original Phillips curve for anticipated inflation. This step, however, forced economists to focus on the process by which expectations are formed in an economy. The new emphasis on expectations generated the rise of a school of thought known as **rational expectations,** which assumes that participants in an economy will use all available information to form their expectations, including their knowledge of the objectives of the central bank.

A central bank trying to use monetary policy to make changes in the level of economic activity is in the position of having to trick participants in the economy. Only by causing a deviation of the inflation rate from its anticipated value can a central bank affect economic activity. It is in the interest of people attempting to forecast price level movements to incorporate their knowledge of the objectives of the central bank into their forecasts. If they know that the central bank wants to increase the level of economic activity by expanding the money supply, they will completely expect the associated price level movement. The monetary expansion will have a real impact only if it is a surprise. By their nature, however, surprises cannot be systematic. For example, surprises in the rate of inflation cannot always be positive; if they were, then people would realize that they were consistently underforecasting the inflation rate.

The strong conclusion of the early users of rational expectations theory was

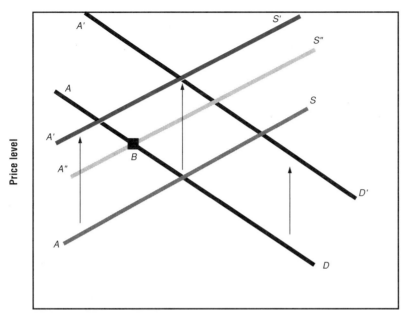

Figure 21.21   SHIFTS WITH CORRECTLY FORECAST INFLATION

that a systematic monetary policy aimed at affecting real economic activity is nec-essarily ineffective.[7] In the context of the aggregate supply–aggregate demand frame-work, an increase in the money stock will still be associated with an upward shift in aggregate demand, as depicted in Figure 21.21. To the extent that the shift in the money stock was forecastable, its impact on the price level will have been foreseen, and nominal wages will have been preprogrammed to rise with the price level to preserve the real wage. This shift in nominal wage by the same percentage as the price level will show up in Figure 21.21 as a shift upward in the aggregate supply curve. Since the real wage will not shift, neither will employment or output. For this to happen, the aggregate supply curve will have to shift upward by exactly the same amount as the aggregate demand curve. The entire monetary shift will then be absorbed by a price level increase.

7.   For a detailed discussion of this ineffectiveness, see Robert E. Lucas, Jr., *Studies in Business Cycle Theory* (Cambridge: MIT Press, 1982).

Multiperiod Wage Contracts

In the case of a surprise increase in the money supply, wages will not have been previously adjusted, and there will be an incomplete upward shift in the aggregate supply curve to a level such as $A''S''$ in Figure 21.21. Then the unexpectedly high price level rise will reduce real wages and bring about a temporary real expansion.

Economists sought to reconcile the Keynesian result of efficacious monetary policy with rational expectations by exploiting the observation that long-term nominal wage contracts were prevalent in labor markets.[8] The contract might prescribe an adjustment for expected inflation during the life of the contract, but the expectation will be based on information available when the contract was signed.

Suppose that labor contracts last for three periods and call for an increase in nominal wages at the expected rate of inflation. Initially, expectations are that there

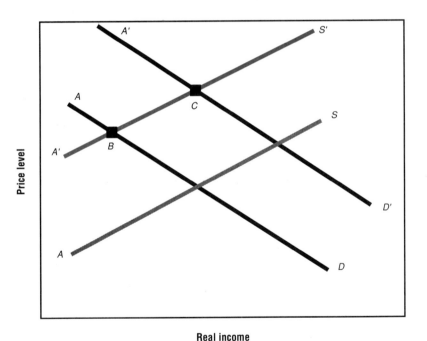

Real income

Figure 21.22   EFFECTIVE MONETARY POLICY DUE TO WAGE CONTRACTS

8.   For details on this literature, see Jo Anna Gray, "Wage Indexation: A Macroeconomic Approach," *Journal of Monetary Economics,* April 1976, pp. 221–236; Stanley Fischer, "Long-Term Contracts, Rational Expectations, and the Optimal Money Supply Rule," *Journal of Political Economy,* February 1977, pp. 191–205; and John Taylor, "Aggregate Dynamics and Staggered Contracts," *Journal of Political Economy,* February 1980, pp. 1–23.

will be no disturbances to aggregate demand and supply and that the central bank will not increase the money stock. This leads to the *AD–AS* combination depicted in Figure 21.22, which is expected to remain constant.

Suppose that in the second period of the contract there is negative disturbance to aggregate supply. For example, the economy experiences an unexpected temporary reduction in the supply of oil. This will shift up the *AS* curve unexpectedly, causing the price level to rise and output and employment to fall to levels indicated by point *B*. The central bank can respond to this unexpected disturbance by increasing the money stock, thereby shifting out aggregate demand, but wages will have been preset without taking this disturbance into account, since it was unexpected. Hence the shift in aggregate supply causes an upward movement along *A'S'* to the point *C*. Output and employment are thus raised above the levels at *B*.

This countercyclical policy works by allowing the central bank to use information not available when the labor contract was signed. Effective monetary policy can then result without assuming predictable errors in expectations. The policy becomes effective, however, through the standard Keynesian assumption of sluggishness in nominal wage movements. This sluggishness implies a countercyclical movement in the real wage. That is, a monetary expansion generates an increase in real economic activity by reducing the real wage.

The Lack of a Countercyclical Real Wage

The standard Keynesian model hinges on the existence of a countercyclical real wage. That is, once we remove the long-term growth rate trends of output and the real wage from the data, we should observe a negative relationship between the real wage and output. This implied relationship has been studied extensively, and the countercyclical implication of the standard Keynesian model for the real wage seems not to hold up in the historical data.[9]

Comparisons of Predepression and Post-World War II Cycles

After World War II, Keynesian policies aimed at stabilizing the real economy were implemented with increasing consistency in the United States. Comparisons of economic fluctuations in the postwar period with those before the Great Depression indicate that the Keynesian policies were associated with a decline in the volatility of real fluctuations. Do these comparisons prove cause and effect? No, but since

9. For recent work on this issue, see Patrick Geary and John Kennan, "The Employment–Real Wage Relationship: An International Study," *Journal of Political Economy*, August 1982, pp. 854–871; Mark Bils, "Real Wages over the Business Cycle: Evidence from Panel Data," *Journal of Political Economy*, August 1985, pp. 666–689; and Scott Sumner and Stephen Silver, "Real Wages, Employment, and the Phillips Curve," *Journal of Political Economy*, June 1989, pp. 706–720.

countercyclical policies were not practiced prior to the Great Depression, this would indicate that whatever its theoretical deficiencies, interventionist fiscal and monetary policies did reduce the magnitude of business cycles.

One indicator of the magnitude of business cycles can be constructed by examining the change in the percentage of unemployment from the peak to the trough of a cycle. Figure 21.23 plots changes in the unemployment rate over a typical cycle. When the economy is booming, the unemployment rate is low; in a succeeding recession, unemployment rises. The amplitude of the change in unemployment is defined as the difference between the peak level of unemployment in a recession and the lowest level of unemployment in the preceding boom.

For a given time period, such as the period 1948–1982 or 1900–1930, we can compute the average amplitude of unemployment changes to produce an indicator of the sharpness of cycles during the period. The first two lines of data in Table 21.1 indicate the average amplitude, that is, the average change in the unemployment percentage during business cycles in each period, for 1900–1930 and 1948–1982 in the United States. These data indeed indicate that the sharpness of the business cycle was reduced in the post-World War II period.

Recently, however, this comparison has been reevaluated by Christina Romer. The unemployment data from the predepression era were not gathered as system-

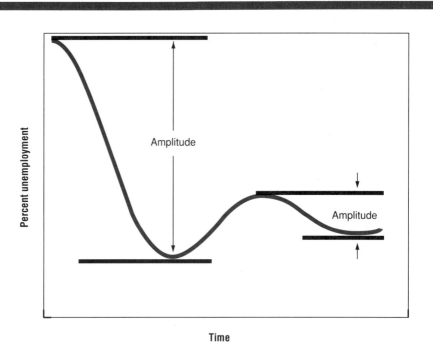

Figure 21.23   DEFINITION OF "AMPLITUDE" OF UNEMPLOYMENT

Table 21.1 AVERAGE AMPLITUDE OF CYCLES IN UNEMPLOYMENT

Period	Data Source	Average Amplitude in Cycle (%)
1900–1930	Lebergott	4.16
1948–1982	BLS	2.65
1948–1978	Romer	4.30

Sources: These results are from Christina Romer, "Spurious Volatility in Historical Unemployment Data," *Journal of Political Economy,* February 1986, pp. 1–37, Table 3. The data labeled "Lebergott" for the period 1900–1930 are from Stanley Lebergott, *Manpower in Economic Growth: The American Record Since 1900* (New York: McGraw-Hill, 1964). The date labeled "BLS" for the period 1948–1982 are the standard Bureau of Labor Statistics unemployment data based on household surveys.

atically as the data from after World War II. Typically, they are based on interpolations of data gathered only in the decennial census, which, by the nature of its construction, can easily overstate the number of people in the labor force and understate employment levels in recessions. Conversely, labor force participation is understated and employment is overstated in booms. Since **unemployment** is defined as

Unemployment = workers in the labor force − workers employed

this earlier method of gathering data tended to overstate unemployment in recessions and understate it in booms. The calculated amplitudes of cyclical movements are therefore too large.

Since we cannot time travel to the past to reconstruct the data properly, Romer has reconstructed modern unemployment data using the same methods used to construct the predepression data.[10] For the period 1948–1978, Romer's calculation of the average amplitude of the unemployment cycle is reported in Table 21.1. Surprisingly, the amplitude of the postwar data constructed with predepression techniques exceeds that for the predepression data. We can conclude, therefore, that the remarkable decline in amplitude that we noticed previously is entirely attributable to a change in statistical method and not to the efficacy of countercyclical policy.[11]

10. The Bureau of Labor Statistics computes the modern unemployment rate by using a monthly survey of a large number of households. A series of questions is designed to indicate whether members of the household are in the labor force and if they are currently employed.

11. Romer also has reconstructed the post-World War II index of industrial production and the gross national product measures with the same methods used to construct predepression data. She similarly finds that the cyclical amplitudes of these data have

not greatly changed between the two eras. See Christina Romer, "Is the Stabilization of the Postwar Economy a Figment of the Data?" *American Economic Review,* June 1986, pp. 314–334, and Christina Romer, "The Pre-War Business Cycle Reconsidered: New Estimates of Gross National Product, 1869–1908," *Journal of Political Economy,* February 1989, pp. 1–37. See also Nathan Balke and Robert Gordon, "The Estimation of Prewar Gross National Product: Methodology and New Evidence," *Journal of Political Economy,* February 1989, pp. 38–92.

THE DECLINE OF KEYNESIAN
AND MONETARIST VIEWS

The struggle between these two views dominated the intellectual debates about monetary policy from the 1940s through the 1970s, and the debates rage even now among their remaining adherents.

Both views, however, have declined: the Keynesian view in the 1970s and monetarism in the 1980s. On a theoretical level, neither theory is very satisfactory, since both assume unchanging behavioral relationships in the presence of different monetary policies. Thus they have been superseded by views that pay more careful attention to tastes, technologies, information availability, and constraints on participants in the economy.

In the 1970s and 1980s, the Keynesian model did not perform well in explaining the inflationary environment, and the monetarist model's dependence on a stable money demand function collapsed in the era of financial deregulation. In addition, as we have seen, new comparisons of pre-World War I and post-World War II business cycles have shown that the interventions aimed at stabilizing the economy have not changed the magnitude of business cycles. This is harmful to both views. First, the countercyclical policy prescribed and pursued by Keynesians in the post-World War II period has left no tracks in the real economy. Second, the discretionary monetary policy condemned by monetarists has not exacerbated real economic disturbances.

Observing this struggle is like touring the battleground of an ancient war. The individual intellectual points on which the battle turned often make little sense to us now. However, the objectives of those involved in the war are always the same: The intellectual debate always serves to provide rhetorical weapons either to those political forces which favor an activist, interventionist government or to those which favor a noninterventionist government. Recent developments in economic thought have now driven the debates in different directions and onto different battlegrounds, but they are merely new incidents in the same political struggle.

The new schools include a group that we may label *neo-Keynesians* because its members still stress the fixity either of wages or prices. Another group, the **real business cycles** school, argues that business cycles are generated primarily by the underlying real forces of technology, taste, taxation, and regulation and are influenced very little by monetary policy.

REAL BUSINESS CYCLES

This school of thought attributes observable cyclical movements in output, employment, and real interest rates to real disturbances that are transmitted through the dynamic operation of the economy. Changes in taste for various goods, in the technology of production, in regulation, in government expenditure, and in financial innovations all would qualify as real disturbances.

Real business cycles theorists generally conduct their analyses by assuming that monetary policy has little or no effect on business cycles. Observed correlations in the movement of the money stock and real variables are attributed to money supplies being driven by the cycles of the real economy. There is assumed to be no feedback from the money supply to the real economy.

One way that real forces may affect the money stock is through the specific intervention strategy of the central bank. For example, a surge in output resulting from a technological shift may generate a monetary expansion if the central bank wants to avoid a deflation. Alternatively, a temporary upsurge in new projects undertaken would lead initially to an increase in the demand for bank financing until more permanent forms of finance could be found. Bank borrowing at the central bank might increase and excess reserves might decline, permitting an expansion of bank deposit liabilities and measured monetary aggregates.

As an example of real business cycles analysis, suppose that labor productivity rises because of a temporary climactic warming trend that makes winters milder. The improvement in productivity increases the demand for labor, raising the real wage. If people recognize the improvement in real wages as temporary, they will enter the labor force, deciding to work more now so that they can have more leisure in the future. Employment thus increases. If entrepreneurs expect the productivity improvement to last for some time, they might expand their investments to take advantage of it, so there will be an investment boom. When the climactic improvement ends, there will be a decline in demand for labor at the high real wage. As planned, people would leave the labor force to take their previously planned leisure in the period of lower wages. The number of employed would not fall immediately to its old level, however. The rise in the capital stock means that labor is more productive until the new capital completely depreciates. The impact of the initial productivity change therefore lasts longer than the initial climactic impulse: The change in the capital stock converts the initial change into a complicated dynamic effect.

You should notice that the real business cycle is analyzed in the context of equilibrium, in which freely flexible prices always clear markets. The variable most worth watching in labor markets is thus the level of employment; unemployment per se has no clear meaning. The analysis always is set up in a dynamic, many period context in which households and entrepreneurs make explicit plans about current and future consumption, outputs, and inputs into the production process. These plans are driven by explicit budget constraints, and government policy can affect the real economy only to the extent that it affects the budget constraints.

CONCLUSION

To account for the major movements in the overall economy, two competing models of macroeconomic activity emerged and dominated attention in the 1960s and 1970s.

First, the Keynesian view, based on the experience of the 1930s, provided useful analytical tools that could be used with facility to describe relations among macroeconomic variables. Within the Keynesian model, both activist monetary policies and fiscal policies were useful in offsetting economic downturns and booms, thereby providing a blueprint for stabilizing the real economy with government intervention. The monetarist view, which emerged in the 1950s and 1960s, opposes activist monetary policy because of its belief that monetary disturbances tend to exacerbate economic fluctuations. Both views have become tarnished because of their inability to predict or explain observed shifts in the economy in the 1970s and 1980s. The Keynesian view lost impetus with the collapse of the inflation-unemployment trade-off. The power of the monetarist argument was reduced with the increased instabilities of money demand in the 1980s. The observation that pre-World War I and post-World War II business cycles were equally severe has indicated that activist monetary policy has neither increased nor decreased economic fluctuations.

The decline of these two dominating views has left the field of macroeconomics, and especially its prescriptions for monetary policy, in disarray. From the hyperinflations and the Great Depression, we know that a central bank should let the money stock grow neither too fast nor too slowly, but the growth rates that define these two extremes are unclear. Attempting to pin them down constitutes the ongoing subject matter of the debate on monetary policy.

KEY TERMS

hyperinflation	*LM* curve
Great Depression	aggregate demand
business cycle	aggregate supply
European Central Bank (ECB)	Phillips curve
monetarism	rational expectations
Keynesian model	unemployment
IS curve	real business cycles

EXERCISES

1. Prior to 1951, the Federal Reserve, in agreement with the Treasury, imposed ceilings on Treasury security yields. The Fed promised to intervene with monetary policy to keep yields from moving beyond the agreed limit. Simultaneously, the Fed wanted to ensure that the price level would not fluctuate beyond certain maximum and minimum limits. Show that the Fed can devise a monetary policy that satisfies both the price level and interest rate constraints.

2. It is possible for a government to collect inflation tax revenue at a maximum steady rate. Suppose that the demand for money is $M/P = \exp(-0.5 \times c)$, where M and P are the nominal money supply and the nominal price level, respectively, and c is the expected percentage rate of inflation. Derive the steady rate of expansion of the money supply that maximizes inflation tax revenue.

3. Countries undertaking large expenditures frequently resort to inflationary policies.

   a. Using central bank balance sheets, describe the mechanics of how money is created and allocated to the Treasury.

   b. How does the creation of money generate "inflation tax" revenue?

4. Suppose that a government running an inflationary policy suddenly alters its rate of money creation to produce price level stability. Show that it can continue to print money for a while with no further inflation.

5. Use the *ISLM,* aggregate supply–aggregate demand framework to analyze the effects of the following disturbances on the price level, the natural level of output, and the short-run level of output.

   a. The advent of a technical change that increases the total productivity of a given amount of labor without affecting its marginal productivity.

   b. A fall in the level of government defense expenditures.

6. For a given level of government spending, will a reduction in taxes cause the price level to rise?

7. Suppose country A and country B are at war. Country A sprays country B's fields with herbicides, thereby permanently reducing country B's income. If country B does not adjust its money supply, show that its price level will rise permanently.

8. The Federal Reserve cannot control the real rate of interest, only the nominal rate. Comment.

9. The Phillips curve shifts with the expected rate of inflation. Can a government permanently reduce unemployment below its natural level by producing an ever-increasing inflation?

10. Suppose that workers make 1-year contracts specifying the exchange of a certain amount of labor at a given nominal wage. Suppose also that workers recognize instantly any change in the price level. What is the shape of the aggregate supply curve?

11. Macroeconomic models are built to mimic the dynamics of macro data rather than the dynamics of the macroeconomy. Discuss how arbitrarily constructed macro data has influenced the choice of macroeconomic models of business cycles.

12. Can the decline in the volatility of the unemployment rate after World War II be explained by a change in data-construction techniques?

FURTHER READING

Barro, Robert. *Macroeconomics*. New York: John Wiley and Sons, 1990.

Bresciani-Turroni, Costantino. *The Economics of Inflation*. Northampton: John Dickens & Co., 1937.

Dotsey, Michael, and Robert King. "Business Cycles," in Eatwell, John, Murray Milgate, and Peter Newman, *The New Palgrave Dictionary of Economics*. London: Macmillan Press, 1987.

Fischer, Stanley. "New Classical Macroeconomics," in Eatwell, John, Murray Milgate, and Peter Newman, *The New Palgrave Dictionary of Economics*. London: Macmillan Press, 1987.

Friedman, Milton, and Anna J. Schwartz. *A Monetary History of the U.S.* Princeton, N.J.: Princeton University Press, 1963.

Gordon, Robert. "What Is New-Keynesian Economics?" *Journal of Economic Literature*, Vol. 28 (September 1990), pp. 1115–1171.

Holtfrerich, Carl-Ludwig. *The German Inflation, 1914–1923*. New York: Walter de Gruyter, 1986.

Kohn, Donald. "Policy Targets and Operating Procedures in the 1990's," *Federal Reserve Bulletin*, January 1990, pp. 2–7.

Mankiw, N. Gregory. "Recent Developments in Macroeconomics: A Very Quick Refresher Course," NBER Working Paper No. 2474, December 1987.

Meulendyke, Ann-Marie. "A Review of Federal Reserve Policy Targets and Operating Guides in Recent Decades," *Federal Reserve Bank of New York Quarterly Review*, Autumn 1988, pp. 6–17.

Romer, Christina. "Spurious Volatility in Historical Unemployment Data," *Journal of Political Economy*, February 1986, pp. 1–37.

Solutions to Odd-Numbered Exercises

Chapter 1 TRADING WITH STRANGERS

1. Prices of bread (and everything else) will be more uniform in a money economy than in a barter economy because it is easier for consumers to compare prices when all sellers are quoting prices in the same unit of measure. This encourages consumers to shop around for the best deal, which makes it harder for a seller to price above the competition.

3. Cash is the physical representation of the unit of account; therefore, cash trades on a one-to-one basis with the unit of account. A one-dollar debt can always be extinguished by paying one paper dollar to the lender. Cash is perfectly liquid because it always maintains its value relative to the unit of account. A paper dollar represents one unit of the dollar unit of account.

5. It is costly to accumulate cash because cash does not pay interest. Accumulating cash has the additional drawback that it might be lost or stolen.

7. A bank issues deposits to savers and makes loans with the proceeds. At maturity, deposits are perfectly liquid in the unit of account. Because the maturity of a bank deposit can be very short, in some cases immediate, bank deposits are, in practice, close substitutes for cash. However, they have several advantages over cash: In most cases bank deposits pay interest, and they provide a convenient, safe means to make large payments. If, instead of holding a deposit, an investor directly holds a loan, he must hold an illiquid asset. Thus the advantage of a bank is that it makes an illiquid asset liquid.

9. A U.S. importer receives dollars for the goods he sells in the United States and must sometimes pay his supplier in the supplier's home currency. If the dollar should decline in value relative to the currency (and unit of account) of the supplier, the importer will have to deliver more dollars to the supplier than he had originally expected. For example, an importer of Audis might sell a car for $20,000. Out of these proceeds, he may owe the German company 30,000 deutschemarks. If there are 2 deutschemarks to the dollar, this is equivalent to $15,000, which leaves the dealer with $5,000 to cover his expenses. If the dollar declines to 1.75 deutschemarks, he owes the German company $17,142.86 (30,000/1.75), which reduces his margin by more than $2,000.

11. Perfectly liquid instruments maintain their value in terms of the unit of account. There must be some device that guarantees to the holders of the liquid instrument that it will maintain its value in terms of the unit of account. The banking systems of the modern industrial economies guarantee liquidity by holding liabilities of the central bank that are perfectly liquid in terms of the unit of account. It is expensive for banks to hold central bank liabilities because they do not pay interest. An obvious question that we did not address in this chapter is why central bank liabilities do not pay interest; we answer it in later chapters of the book.

Chapter 2 AN INTRODUCTION TO CAPITAL MARKETS: DEBT AND EQUITY

1. Let's assume that a firm can issue bonds paying interest of x% per year. (We also assume that the bonds are default free.) The firm can also issue equity with an expected return of $(x + 1)$% per year if it finances entirely with equity. The expected yearly cash flow of the company is $(x + 1)$% of the firm's total assets. No matter what the leverage ratio of the firm, the expected return on the firm's assets must equal the payments that investors expect to receive on their investment in the company.

In our example, this means that the company must expect to pay $(x + 1)$% of its assets to investors every year. If the firm increases its debt outstanding relative to its equity, the return that investors expect on their equity must rise so that ax% $+ b(x + y)$% $= (x + 1)$%, where a and b are the portion of total assets financed by debt and equity, respectively and y is the premium that equity holders must be paid over debt holders for the uncertainty of their return.

We can assume that the capital market is in overall equilibrium—that is, expected payments to investors completely exhaust expected revenues to the firms after payments for labor and material. Bondholders are satisfied with their returns, and stockholders are satisfied with their expected returns.

Now, the stockholders of our firm decide to increase its leverage ratio by issuing bonds to replace equity. Hence they increase a relative to b. Let's assume that with the increase in leverage, $(x + y)\%$ (the market's required expected rate of return on equity) rises because the firm's equity is riskier than before. However, let's assume that it rises by less than is required to absorb the entire expected revenue on the assets of the firm. Hence the expected return on the equity, at current the stock's current price, exceeds $(x + y)\%$.

It now appears that current equity holders can achieve a capital gain by leveraging the firm. The reason is that the market will increase the price of the firm's equity until the expected return on the equity and the required expected return on the equity are equal. That is, the price must rise until the expected revenue available to equity holders equals $(x + y)\%$ of the price of equity.

The increased price of equity makes equity funding look relatively cheap. Other firms can gain by issuing equity to replace debt. As these other firms increase the supply of equity, the required return on equity must rise, reducing the price of equity issued by our firm. In the perfect world of Modigliani-Miller (and with identical firms), capital gains to our firm's shareholders will be wiped out before any transaction ever takes place.

Under the equal-access assumption, the arbitrage takes place through an investor buying all the securities of our firm and reissuing equity for debt.

3. Financial decisions will continue to be irrelevant to the value of the firm if investors can write agreements among themselves to protect the value of their investment. If they cannot, it will be more expensive to use the instrument whose holders are most likely to suffer from a future decision of the firm.

5. The bondholders know that legislatures and governors can change state law. They demand the added legal protection of a bond covenant, which gives them the right to go to court to protect their interests.

7. Firms would fund themselves entirely with debt if equity were subject to a higher tax rate. As long as the two types of instruments are perfect substitutes, a higher tax on one will drive that instrument completely out of the marketplace. Even if the possibility of bankruptcy exists for a firm funded entirely with debt, the problem can be avoided by a financial institution that buys all the liabilities and equity issued by a given firm. For such an institution, default on bond payments does not alter the position it would have had if the firm had partially funded with equity; the financial institution's return would be the same in either case. Tax authorities may treat such a total debt issue as equity finance, however. Thus, companies will not finance themselves totally with debt.

9. In late 1990, the U.S. economy was in a recession whereas, at year-end 1989, it was not. Investors always expect that a higher percentage of risky companies will go bankrupt than will safe companies. They also expect that the relative incidence of bankruptcies among risky companies will rise in a recession. Since an immediate bankruptcy has a higher cost than a future bankruptcy (because of the time value of money), risk premiums should rise in a recession.

11. A firm that issues a short-term liability must return the principal to an investor in a relatively short time-frame. To make good on this promise, the firm must invest in projects with a relatively short payout period. To the extent that the near-term economic picture is better known than that of the distant future, short-term investments are more predictable (and consequently safer) than long-term investments. By demanding that a firm issue short-term liabilities, investors can control the types of projects undertaken by the firm. Thus, short-term liabilities are less risky because the underlying projects they fund are less risky.

13. The issuance of additional equity and the decrease in the leverage ratio can, according to the principal-agent theory, reduce the value of bonds currently outstanding. The additional equity permits management to invest in risky projects. If the increased risk of the underlying assets overwhelms the additional equity protection afforded to bondholders, the price of bonds will decline.

15. When there is a principal-agent problem, a change in the liability structure of the firm often leads to a change in the risk of the underlying assets that the firm holds. If the market thinks the management can manage the risk, the value of the firm and, consequently, the value of its liabilities will rise. If the market does not believe the risky strategy can be successfully executed, the value of the firm's assets and its liabilities will fall. Arbitragers cannot control these market opinions.

Chapter 3 THE DEMAND FOR LIQUID ASSETS

1. As households age, they accumulate financial assets in preparation for retirement; thus, their financial wealth rises relative to current income. This means that the proportion of wealth that they may need to cash in to meet an emergency declines, reducing their relative demand for liquid assets.

This exercise concerns the elasticity, not the level of demand, for liquidity, but the two are related. On the margin, liquidity has much less value for the older household that has accumulated wealth than for the younger household. This implies the older households will pay much greater attention to liquidity premiums in making their investment decisions than younger households. An increase in the liquidity premium will cause older households to hold fewer liquid assets. Of course, the demand for liquidity increases again at very old age, as the potential for a cash emergency increases.

This discussion indicates that the elasticity of demand for liquidity increases with wealth as well as with age because it is the wealth effect that really drives the age effect.

As long as potential cash emergencies are proportional to income, we would not expect the elasticity of demand for liquid assets to vary by income. However, the data indicate that low-income households hold a higher portion of their financial wealth in liquid assets. While part of this results from the fact that Social Security and pension benefits are not included in the definition of wealth, it is probably a fact that high income households, on the margin, have a more elastic demand for liquidity. This fact implies that potential cash emergencies are not proportional to income.

Relative elasticities of demand for liquid assets should show up in the data as the ratio of liquid assets to total financial assets that households of various ages, incomes, and wealth hold. If this ratio is high, the average value placed on liquidity is high. Under most circumstances, a high average value also implies a high marginal value.

3. For the insured, the cost of death not remunerated by the insurance company is very high because he or she will not be around to enjoy the benefits of the insurance payoff. The fire insurance company cannot rely on this outcome. There are cases of suicide motivated by the desire to provide benefits to an heir, but these are rare enough not to cause much concern.

5. Uncertain inflation increases the potential variability of long-term bond contracts, making them less liquid in terms of the unit of account. If households demand liquidity, they will be less willing to hold long-term assets under uncertain inflation.

7. In a Modigliani-Miller world, the firm's liability structure is unaffected by household tastes under the equal access assumption. Under the perfect substitutes hypothesis, the liability structure of firms in the aggregate is determined by taste, but the liability structure of an individual firm is not.

In a world of principal-agent problems, liability structure is used to control the risk of investment decisions. If investors demand safe assets, the economy will take on fewer risky projects, and this decree will be enforced by a change in the liability structure of the firm.

9. Risk-averse households care about risk and return. As long as a single security's expected return is less than perfectly correlated with other securities promising the same expected return, the risk-averse household can reduce risk by creating a portfolio of securities without sacrificing return. We leave it as an exercise to show why this situation is so. (Use the formula for the variance of two partially correlated securities.)

11. There is a tax advantage to home ownership, although it is not the one often referred to in the press, which is the tax-deductibility of interest on mortgages. Landlords are also able to deduct their interest expenses from income earned from rents. The tax benefit they receive should be passed on to renters in the form of lower rents. The real tax benefit to ownership is that landlords must pay tax on rent receipts that exceed their expenses, which amounts to a tax on the equity they have in the property. Homeowners receive an implicit return on the equity they invest in their homes in the form of enjoyment of the house. The implicit income is exempt from taxes.

However, we doubt whether the tax benefit, properly accounted for, is enough of an incentive to explain widespread home ownership. A major factor has to do with principal-agent theory. It is difficult for a renter to capture the gain from improvements he or she makes to a house or apartment. Even if the tenant can receive compensation for the improvement, the landlord is likely to dispute its value. The value of improvements can accrue to the tenant even without compensation if the tenant resides at the property for a long time. However, this diminishes the value of renting, which is the ability to move without risking depreciation of the capital invested in the house.

13. If large investors hold individual securities rather than portfolios, they eschew the benefits of diversification. They might do this because they prefer to hold a large proportion of the stock issued by a single company. For example, investors might prefer to exercise control over management rather than diversify their stock holdings. For investors who prefer to exercise control, the stocks of different companies are not close substitutes. If stocks are not close substitutes, it takes a large movement in the price of a stock to induce investors to switch their investment. Thus, in an undiversified world, the attempt by one investor to sell stock is likely to lead to larger price movements than in a world where the stocks of various companies are close substitutes.

Chapter 4 LIFE INSURANCE COMPANIES AND PENSION PLANS

1. The value of the woman's annuity when she is 65 (30 years from now) must equal the present value of yearly payments to her until her death. Hence, we must determine the present value of $10,000 for the number of years she lives past 65. This dollar amount must equal the present value of the yearly payments she makes from now until age 65. Call the yearly payment x. The present value of yearly payments of x dollars equals $xp_1 + xp_2 + xp_3 + \ldots + xp_{30}$. The present value of $10,000 per year after age 65 is $10,000p_{31} + $10,000p_{32} + \ldots$ until the expected point of death of the annuity holder.

By selling annuity policies to a large number of people, the insurance company can be fairly certain that on average its annuity holders will die at the expected point of death for the population as a whole.

3. Events such as the failure of Executive Life make investors skeptical of the claims of insurance companies. Hence they are likely to look at the insurance company's record of meeting its commitments rather than the quality of the firm's assets in determining the safety of their investment. After all, insurance companies can change their investment policies overnight, leaving the policyholder with a much riskier policy than he or she bargained for. Thus a company with a long record of meeting commitments will be able to sell policies backed by the same assets at a higher price than its new rival. The old company's stockholders will make more profits, which can be considered a reward for meeting past commitments.

For this reason, new companies, such as Take Your Chances, often sell riskier (and lower cost) policies than old insurance companies, such as Old Faithful.

5. If the cost of absorbing risk increases, the risk premium will rise. Hence a shift from corporate pension funds to annuities will cause an increase in the risk premium. Since it is now more expensive to find investors for risky projects, fewer such projects will be undertaken.

7. Insurance companies hold bonds because they sell annuities and life insurance policies with premiums and reserves calculated at a specific interest rate. Hence the value of their liabilities can be calculated accurately. Policyholders and regulators want to know whether the value of a firm's assets equal the value of its liabilities. To make this task easier, they prefer that the insurance company hold assets that promise to pay a specific nominal amount at a specific point in time. Bonds are such an investment. For example, the rate of return on a bond can be compared to the rate of return assumed in calculating an annuity premium to determine whether the insurance company has adequate reserves to meet its annuity obligations.

Of course, the insurance company could offer a product with a variable premium that depended on investment performance. However, the policyholder would have a hard time determining whether a high premium resulted from expenses that are too high or unlucky investment performance. Policyholders avoid these kinds of principal agent problems by insisting that insurance companies hold assets that have a fixed value at the maturity of their policy, such as bonds.

9. If investors increase their demand for liquid assets, corporations must shift their real investment to projects that generate cash quickly; that is, corporations must invest in liquid projects. This happens in both a Modigliani-Miller and principal agent world. However, in a Modigliani-Miller world, the change in types of projects demanded will not change the liability structure of the firm, whereas in a principal agent world it would. The reason is that in a principal agent world, the only way investors can be certain that a corporation will invest in liquid projects is to force it to issue liquid liabilities.

11. In Chapter 2 we noted that if the activities of arbitragers prevent change in the value of the firm, securities markets will be more liquid. The arbitragers can step in and undo any change in a firm's value resulting from a change in its liability structure. This helps stabilize the prices of bonds and equities, making these securities more liquid.

If insurance companies must hold specific types of assets, they can no longer act like the ideal financial institution we introduced in Chapter 2; and hence, they cannot act as arbitragers when a firm changes its liability structure. This decreases the liquidity of financial markets. However, the decrease in liquidity is not necessarily the fault of the regulator who imposes the rule. If he or she is reacting to the demands of the policyholder for protection against misbehavior by the insurance company, the reduction in liquidity is caused by the possibility of misbehavior, not regulation.

Chapter 5 INTEREST RATES

1. The current yield is the coupon payment divided by the bond's price. The coupon rate is defined as the coupon divided by the par value. Since the coupon rate is 5%, the coupon is $5. The current price is $90, so

$$current\ yield = \frac{coupon}{market\ price} = \frac{5}{90} = 5.56\%$$

3. Searching down the column for a coupon bond with maturity of six years, we find that a price of $122.73 corresponds to a yield of 5.5%.

5. In 1994, the holder of the bond will receive $100 and a coupon of $40. Converting to 1993 dollars, the par value received is $50, and the coupon is $20. Thus the holder suffers a $50 capital loss and a total return of $-\$30$. Therefore, the yield is -30%.

7. According to the expectations theory of the term structure, arbitrage profits cannot occur when

$$(1 + I_n)^n = (1 + i_1)(1 + i_2) \ldots (1 + i_n)$$

where I_n is the annualized yield to maturity on an n-period loan and i_j is the one-period yield on a loan originating in j and payable in $j + 1$. Since $I_n = .08$, $n = 2$, $i_1 = .09$, and $i_2 = .05$,

$$(1 + .08)^2 = 1.1664 > (1 + .09)(1 + .05) = 1.1445$$

Alternatively, using the approximation

$$I_n = (i_1 + i_2 + \ldots i_n)/n$$

we see

$$.08 > (.09 + .05)/2 = .07$$

The arbitrage available is to borrow for one year at 9% and use the loan to buy a two-year bond. After one year, roll the loan over at 5%. In two years, the long-term bond will mature, paying 8%. The loan is paid off at an average rate of 7%. The arbitrager pockets the difference.

9. In 1994, a one-period loan payable in 1995 yields 3%. In 1995, the one-period yield will exceed 3% because consumption will return to normal in 1996, and individuals will wish to borrow against 1996 consumption. In 1996 and after, the one-period yield will fall to 3% again. Using this information, by the expectations theory of the term structure we can determine the yield on bonds of longer maturities. A two-period loan originating in 1994 will have the average of the yield of a one-period loan originating in 1994 and one originating in 1995. Thus its yield will exceed 3%. Since after 1995, the one-period yield returns to 3%, the three-period yield will be less than the two-period yield but more than the one-period yield. The longer term yields will be below the three-period yield, and will converge to 3%. We therefore have a hump-shaped yield curve.

11. (a) If $n = 1$, we know

$$\$x(1 + r_1) = \$1$$

Therefore,

$$\$x = 1/(1 + r_1)$$

Similarly, if $n = 2$, r_2 satisfies

$$\$x(1 + r_2)(1 + r_2) = \$1$$

or

$$\$x = 1/(1 + r)^2$$

Generalizing, r_n satisfies:

$$x = 1/(1 + r_n)^n$$

(b) Suppose the coupon bond currently trades in the bond markets for $\$z$. The payoff stream generated by the coupon bond may be represented by

$$\$z = 10/(1 + r) + 10/(1 + r)^2 + \ldots + 10/(1 + r)^{10} + 100/(1 + r)^{10}$$

Now suppose the alert arbitrager purchased ten discount bonds with par value $10 each and maturities from one to ten years. She also purchases ten more of the ten-year pure discount bonds. Suppose the bundle of bonds costs $\$y$, which we assume to be less than $\$z$. If she sells the coupon bonds at $2 and uses the proceeds to buy the bundle, since the payoff stream is identical, she makes a profit. Since this trade is self-financing, she will continue to sell the coupon bond and buy the bundle until the prices of the discount bonds rise and the price of the coupon bond falls enough so that the difference is eliminated.

Chapter 6 MARKET MAKERS, DEALERS, SECURITIES EXCHANGES, AND LIQUIDITY

1. When the market opens, the specialist knows the previous day's closing price of a stock but has no idea how investors will react to information available after the previous day's close. This places the specialist in a bind because he has to identify a price to open the market. The specialist is not an expert at evaluating how news will affect a stock's price; he is only an expert at observing how the market is moving. Since there is no market movement overnight, he cannot rely on his usual signals to establish a price.

The specialist makes money in several ways. He acts as a broker in trades involving orders from the limit book and in many market orders in his stock. From these transactions, he receives a brokerage commission. When he acts as a principal—that is, when he buys for or sells from his inventory, he makes money on the difference between what he sells a stock for and what he buys it for. Of course, from this spread, he must cover his financing costs. To make a profit, the specialist must be very alert to price movements in his stock.

3. The expected return on a NYSE-listed security that market makers actively trade should be lower than a NYSE-listed security that they do not actively trade. The reason is that the market for the second security is less liquid than the market for the first. Investors in the second stock must be compensated for the higher expected cost of having to sell to a market maker who carries high inventory costs. Investors in illiquid securities have a greater expectation that they must sell to a marker maker with such high costs. They must be compensated by earning a higher expected rate of return on the security.

NASDAQ-listed securities (that are not traded on the NYSE) are generally less liquid than NYSE-listed securities. NASDAQ securities do not have active market makers because the cost of holding inventory is just too high. This means that an investor who wishes to sell a NASDAQ stock faces a costly problem of finding a buyer. This investor must receive a relatively high expected return as compensation for the potential cost.

5. An increase in market-maker funding costs will cause a relative increase in the expected selling costs that investors holding illiquid securities face. These investors have a higher expectation of selling to a market maker than investors in liquid securities. Therefore, an increase in the cost of market-maker services will have a larger impact on the cost of selling an illiquid security than on the cost of selling a liquid one. Investors must be compensated by a relative increase in the expected return on illiquid securities—that is, a rise in the liquidity premium.

A key interest rate that determines dealer funding cost is known as the broker-dealer lending rate offered by commercial banks. This rate is determined by the general level of interest rates and banks' perceptions about risk in securities markets. If banks believe that the market will experience a good deal of variability in the near term, the broker-dealer rate will be high relative to other interest rates. Thus, dealer funding costs are really determined by the market's perception of the liquidity of securities markets.

7. On low-volume days, market makers are more likely to buy and sell for their own inventory than on high-volume days because other investors are not so active. Thus the market maker is likely to participate as a principal in a larger portion of the total trades. We assume the market maker has a higher expected return as a principal than as a broker because he takes risk. However, there are also fewer trades on low-volume days. Thus the market maker misses out on brokerage fees. In addition, he may actually engage in more trades as a principal on high-volume days, even though these trades represent a smaller share of the total.

9. We have to distinguish between two types of off-floor trading. The first is trades in NYSE-listed stocks by nonmembers on other exchanges. This is growing in frequency, implying that it is becoming cheaper to supply liquidity off the NYSE. The second type of off-floor trading is block trading by members. This is increasing because institutional trading is becoming a greater force in market trading.

11. Investors hold portfolios that are, of course, made up of individual securities. The expected return on a portfolio is a weighted sum of the expected returns of all the securities making up the portfolio. Thus, if an investor holding a portfolio believes that the expected return on a security in the portfolio has fallen whereas the market does not hold this view, he or she will sell that security, not the whole portfolio. However, if that investor has an opinion about the market rather than an individual stock, he or she will buy or sell all the stocks in the portfolio.

13. An investment bank is a market maker. In the new issues market, it provides a bid price to the security issuer and makes its return by selling the security at a higher offer price to investors. Investment banks also make markets in old securities, just like the specialist on the exchange floor. In addition, investment banks provide advisory services for financial transactions, such as merger and acquisition advice. They also provide hedging services for their customers, a service we shall discuss at length in Chapters 17 and 18.

15. Security Pacific suffered from a credibility problem. The market, rightly or wrongly, believed it provided false information to investors. Security Pacific can restore its credibility by showing the market that it is willing to absorb the loss suffered by investors from perceived misinformation. This cost must be weighed against its expected higher interest cost of selling bonds in a market that places less credibility in the bank's statements.

Chapter 7 MONEY DEMAND AND THE PRICE LEVEL

1. From equation 7.2 in the text, we can calculate the average nominal money balances demanded. The nominal transactions cost, Pb, is $2. The annual nominal cash expenditure, Py, is $12,000. The interest rate forgone by holding cash is 5%, so

$$M^d = \sqrt{\frac{PbPy}{2R}} = \sqrt{\frac{24,000}{.10}} = 489.90$$

3. If the interest rate on deposits falls to .03, we would expect average nominal money balances to increase since their opportunity cost has fallen. Substituting the new lower rate of interest into equation 7.2 in the text we have

$$M^d = \sqrt{\frac{24,000}{.06}} = 632.46$$

As expected, cash holdings increased from 489.90 to 632.46.

5. Consider a bank with Z of capital. Suppose the annual cost per note issued is b. The bank can issue $10Z$ in notes. To back this, they will then buy $11Z$ of U.S. government securities. The yield on government securities is R_T. If

$$11ZR_T > 10b + \text{opportunity cost of capital}$$

then it will be profitable to issue notes.

7. Laundering costs function similarly to transactions costs, b, in the money demand model in the text. Thus, we may examine the impact of an increase in the cost of laundering money by examining an increase in transactions costs. Real money demand is given by

$$\frac{M^d}{P} = \sqrt{\frac{by}{2R}}$$

An increase in real laundering costs b will increase real money demand. Assuming that there is no change in real income or the nominal interest rate and that the nominal money supply is fixed, an increase in real money demand will lead to a fall in the price level. Let us consider the intuition of this result. If the cost of laundering money were to increase, the demand for nominal money balances must increase. The supply of money is fixed, so the price of money is driven up in terms of goods. If the price of money is higher, more goods can be bought with a given amount of money. This implies the price level is lower.

9. A constant 5% growth rate in the money supply will lead to a steady 5% inflation, assuming the real rate of interest and real income are unchanged.

11. The equilibrium in the money market is given by

$$P = \frac{M}{ay - b(r + i)}$$

If the rate of growth of the money supply were to increase to 10%, there would be no instantaneous change in the money supply, nor would this affect real income or the real rate of interest. However, the expected rate of inflation would increase to 10% if the change is well known. Since all other terms are fixed, there must be a sudden increase in the price level to restore the money market to equilibrium.

Chapter 8   THE MONETARY STANDARD

1. Had the United States maintained a bimetallic standard in the latter quarter of the nineteenth century, silver would have chased gold out of circulation, and a steady price inflation would have ensued. Gold stocks were relatively stable during this period, while silver stocks were rapidly increasing. In a short time after 1873, gold's price in terms of silver would have increased. It would have been possible to melt down a dollar's worth of gold coins and to exchange them for more than a dollar's worth of silver. The silver attained through such transactions would be brought to the mint and exchanged for silver coins. The result would be that the gold coins would disappear, and the money supply would be on a silver standard. As silver stocks outpaced the growth of real income, the value of silver in terms of goods would fall. Since the price of silver in terms of dollars is fixed, for the price of silver in terms of goods to fall, the price of goods in terms of dollars had to rise. Thus the implication of reinstating silver would have been inflation.

3. One metal in a bimetallic standard will no longer circulate when its price in terms of goods exceeds the price paid at the mint, even when all the metal is used for nonmonetary purposes. To illustrate, refer to Figure 8.7. We assume that the value at the mint of a unit of gold or silver is $1, and that one unit of goods costs P dollars. When demands for silver and gold are as shown at $D_s{}'$ and D_g, respectively, both gold and silver will circulate. Suppose the demand for silver in nonmonetary uses increases. The supply of silver for nonmonetary purposes increases as silver coins are melted down. This lowers the price level and draws some gold from private uses into coinage. The ratio of gold to silver in circulation as money increases, and the money supply decreases. The new equilibrium will be at a lower price level. If the demand for silver continues to increase to D_s, then even if the entire world supply of silver is converted to nonmonetary uses, the price of silver will still exceed the price offered at the mint. In this case, silver will no longer circulate.

A similar scenario will occur if the demand for gold falls. Suppose initially that D_s' and D_g are as drawn in Figure 8.7, so that both gold and silver circulate as money. If D_g shifts down, gold will be converted from nonmonetary uses to money, decreasing the supply of gold for industry and consumers and restoring the money market to equilibrium. This new equilibrium will have a higher price level. If the demand for gold falls by enough, so that the market for gold and silver would be represented by Figure 8.6, the price of goods will increase by enough that the value of silver in nonmonetary purposes will exceed the value of silver in terms of goods provided by the mint. Then silver will no longer circulate as money.

Similar dynamics would be at work if the world supply of either gold or silver were to increase.

5. The demand for real balances depends negatively on the real interest rate, so an increase in the real interest rate would reduce the demand for real balances. This can be represented by a downward movement in M/P in Figure 8.7, and by a leftward movement in O_M (without having the two meet or cross). Holding D_s and D_g constant, the price level must increase to clear the money market. A negative relationship between the real interest rate and the demands for gold and silver in nonmonetary purposes will generate a reduced demand for silver and gold in other uses. Metal will flow into coinage, raising the price level even more because of the increased nominal money supply.

7. The bimetallic bond has a payoff identical to a portfolio containing a silver bond and a short position of one call option held by the debtor to exchange gold for silver. The option will have a positive value before the maturity of the bond, and it therefore represents a liability of the portfolio. The value of the portfolio is then the value of the silver bond less the value of the option. Since the value of the bimetallic bond is less than the value of the silver bond, the yield to maturity of the bimetallic bond will be higher.

9. Gresham's law holds when two items that serve as legal tender have their values legally fixed in terms of a unit of account. If one item becomes more valuable as a commodity than its fixed monetary value, individuals have an incentive to convert the higher-valued item from its monetary to its commodity uses. Very quickly, the higher-valued item will cease to circulate as money. If, however, the higher-valued item circulating as money is allowed to carry a premium that reflects its greater market value, then it can continue to function as money.

11. (a) If a major supply of gold ore is exhausted, the world supply of gold will increase at a lower rate. Suppose for simplicity that the demand for gold for nonmonetary purposes is stable. Income is constant, and the real interest rate is constant. Under the simple monetary model of Chapter 7, the increase in the world supply of gold every year would translate into inflation. Newly mined gold would be brought into the mint and coined, depressing the price of gold in terms of goods. Since the price of gold is fixed in terms of dollars, the amount of goods that a dollar can buy would fall.

If the supply of gold from a particular deposit is exhausted, the result will be a lower rate of increase of the world gold supply. The impact on the price level depends upon whether the change is expected. If everybody expected the mine to yield a steady supply of gold into the infinite future and then the deposit suddenly plays out, there will be a downward adjustment in the nominal rate of interest (the sum of real interest and the expected rate of inflation). Since money demand depends negatively on the nominal interest rate, there will be an increase in money demand. Since money supply is fixed in the short run, there will be a downward jump in the price level followed by a steady inflation at the new lower level.

Consider what happens to the price of gold. A downward jump in the price level implies that a unit of gold will buy more goods. Thus the value of gold in terms of goods will suddenly increase. This is where expectations enter the calculation. If this appreciation in the value of gold is expected—for example, if it is known that the deposit will play out soon, individuals will want to buy gold in anticipation of its abrupt appreciation. As they buy gold, the goods price of gold must increase, or, stated differently, the gold price of goods must fall. This will continue as long as the possibility of a discontinuous price movement exists. The result is that if the gold ore is known to be almost gone, the price level will slowly fall to the lower level to which it will need to fall when the ore runs out. Thus the expectation of lower inflation in the future will dampen inflation today.

(b) If the demand for industrial gold suddenly falls, gold used in manufacturing will be carried to the mint and exchanged for coins. Thus the value of gold in terms of goods will fall, and the price level will increase.

13. This is an example of Gresham's law. If $P_s > 1$, the market value of silver in terms of gold exceeds its mint value of 1. Since silver is undervalued at the mint, it is the "good money" that is driven out by the "bad money," gold.

15. The issuer of a currency option bond will pay in yen when the dollar is valuable, and in dollars when the yen is valuable. Its payoff is identical to a portfolio containing one dollar bond and short (or liable for) one dollar option. The option allows the debtor to deliver ¥150 and receive a dollar on the exercise date. The payoff on a currency option bond promising to pay either ¥150 or $1 is given in the table.

PAYOFF ON A CURRENCY OPTION BOND AT TWO LEVELS OF THE EXCHANGE RATE

Exchange rate	¥180/$1	¥120/$1
Payoff	.83	$1

When the yen/dollar exchange rate is ¥180/$1, the issuer will pay in yen. A payment of ¥150 when this is the exchange rate will only be worth $.83. When the exchange rate is ¥120/$1, it is the yen that is more valuable. In this case, the payment will be in dollars (a payment worth ¥120 instead of ¥150). The payoff on the dollar discount bond-dollar option portfolio is as follows:

PAYOFF ON A PORTFOLIO LONG ONE BOND AND SHORT ONE OPTION

	¥180/$1	¥120/$1
Exchange rate	¥180/$1	¥120/$1
Dollar bond	$1	$1
Dollar option	$.83—$1	0
Total	$.83	$1

The currency option bond will cost the same as the portfolio. The dollar bond has a price of $(1/1.07) = $.93. The price of the portfolio is .93-G where G denotes the option price (or "premium").

To price the option, we must construct a portfolio of yen and dollar bonds with a payoff identical to the option. The option pays $.17 when the dollar is valuable ($1 = ¥180). The option pays nothing when the dollar is cheap. A dollar bond will deliver $1.00 no matter what the value of the yen. The yen bond will deliver ¥150 in any state, but if the dollar is valuable, this is only worth $.83, and if the dollar is cheap this is worth $1.25. We must determine the number of dollar bonds, x, and yen bonds, y, that will mimic the dollar option.

	¥180	¥120
Dollar option	.17	0
Dollar bond	$1x$	$1x$
Yen bond	$.83y$	$1.25y$

Solving for x and y, we have that $y = -.40$ and $x = .51$. Therefore, one half of a dollar bond combined with 40% of a yen bond short (that is, borrow yen) will have the same payoff as a dollar option. Using this, we can price the dollar option. Letting $P_{¥B}$ denote the price of a yen bond and P_{DB} the price of a dollar bond, the price of the option therefore is

$$G = -.4P_{¥B} + .51P_{DB}$$

The price of a yen bond is $P_{¥B} = 150/1.03 = ¥145.63$ or $.97 at the current exchange rate of ¥150/$1. The price of a dollar bond is $.93. Thus $G = $.09. Finally, the price of the currency option bond is $.84, the current value of a dollar bond, $.93, less the value of the option, $.09. Therefore, the yield on the currency option bond based on a dollar payoff is 19%, considerably higher than the yield on either yen or dollar bonds.

Chapter 9 THE FED FUNDS MARKET
AND SUPPLY AND DEMAND FOR RESERVES

1. Let c denote the currency-to-deposit ratio. If individuals decrease their desired currency, this may be represented as a decrease in c. From the $M1$ multiplier,

$$\frac{M1}{B} = \frac{c + 1}{c + r}$$

we can see that for a fixed monetary base (and assuming $r < 1$), a decrease in the currency-to-deposit ratio leads to an increase in the money supply. If individuals reduced their desired currency holdings, this would increase deposits. Since deposits would not be held as excess reserves, fed funds would become cheaper, and banks would aggressively purchase securities and make loans, thus further increasing the money supply.

3. If the Fed purchases the bond from a Citibank depositor, Citibank's reserves will increase to 30, while its deposits increase to 110. Since it has excess reserves, the portfolio manager purchases 40 billion in T-bills from a Daigin depositor by mid-day. At the end of the day, Citibank must settle with the Fed, so it purchases fed funds from Daigin.

Mid-Day Balance Sheets

CITIBANK				DAIGIN			
Reserves	0	Deposits	110	Reserves	60	Deposits	140
Loans	80	"Due to" Fed	10	Loans	80		
T-bills	40						

End-of-Day Balance Sheets

CITIBANK				DAIGIN			
Reserves	22	Deposits	110	Reserves	28	Deposits	140
Loans	80	Fed funds bought	32	Loans	80		
T-bills	40			Fed funds sold	32		

5. The Federal Reserve's balance sheet will be

ASSETS		LIABILITIES	
US securities	230	Federal Reserve notes	205
Loans	15	Deposits by banks	40

7. During the course of business, a series of large transactions over Fedwire may lead to an overdraft on a bank's account at the Fed. Payments over Fedwire cumulate during the day, and the Fed permits banks to send more net payments than they maintain in their reserve account. In this case, the bank must settle by the end of the day. A later series of Fedwire receipts may provide the funds to eliminate the overdraft. Alternatively, the Fed can purchase (borrow) reserves on the fed funds market from another bank with more reserves than it wants.

9. The Fed is ostensibly a private institution owned by member banks but controlled by the United States government. Its profits are taxed at a rate of 100%.

Chapter 10 BANKS AS FINANCIAL INSTITUTIONS

1. The bank enters your deposit as a demand deposit liability. The offsetting asset item is called a "cash item in the process of collection." However, you usually do not have access to your funds until the check actually clears. If you ask for a balance inquiry, the bank is likely to list your balance including the deposited check but note that your "available balance" is less than the listed balance by the amount of the uncollected check.

3. Demand deposits are subject to a 12% reserve requirement. Thus, when a customer makes a deposit into a demand account, the bank must buy reserves. On the asset side, it holds reserves equal to 12% of the demand deposit. On the liability side, it has fed funds purchased of the same amount. If the customer exchanges a demand deposit for a repurchase agreement, the bank no longer has to hold reserves. It can therefore eliminate its fed funds liability equal to 12% of the former demand deposit. Assets also shrink as the reserve balances at the Fed decline.

5. When interest rates were high and retail deposits were subject to interest rate ceilings, consumers withdrew funds from banks and placed them in money market mutual funds, which, among other investments, bought bank CDs. Thus indirectly, banks were paying open-market interest rates on some consumer deposits. With deregulation, consumer money flowed out of money market mutual funds and back into banks. Consequently, banks reduced their CDs outstanding. While they paid more on consumer deposits after deregulation than before, they continued to pay less for consumer deposits than they paid for money market liabilities such as the CDs bought by money market mutual funds. As a result, their overall cost of funds remained about the same.

7. Banks usually make provisions for loan loss out of current income. This money is added to the loan loss reserve, a contra-item on the asset side of the balance sheet. An increase in the reserve account will therefore reduce assets, but this will be exactly offset by an increase in cash or some other asset that the bank buys with the funds set aside for the reserve account. If provision exceeds net income, there is a shortage of funds available to place in the contra-account and simultaneously invest in an asset. In this case, the bank increases the contra item by the amount of provision, which now causes a decline in assets relative to liabilities. This of course means that the equity account must fall.

9. The conservative bank is better protected against future loan losses because it has, effectively, already retained income to cover future losses. Thus if it faces a major loan loss, it can finance the loss through a reduction in the reserve for loan loss rather than through a decline in earnings. The market will therefore view the earnings of the conservative bank as more stable. Since the two banks have the same current return, the stock of the conservative bank will trade at a higher price.

11. The earnings of the "short-funded" bank are subject to interest-rate risk. When interest rates rise, the cost of liabilities will increase more quickly than the return on assets, and net interest margin will decline. If investors can easily diversify this risk away by holding stocks that exhibit high earnings when interest rates rise, investors will not demand a higher expected return on the stock of the "short-funded" bank. However, it is generally believed that the shares of short-funded banks pay a premium for investors to absorb this risk. This means that investors cannot diversify away interest-rate risk. When interest rates rise, most asset prices fall, so investors demand a premium to absorb this risk.

Chapter 11 THE U.S. RETAIL PAYMENTS SYSTEM

1. When the merchant accepts a check and the check is returned for insufficient funds in the payor's account, the merchant assumes responsibility for the collection of payment. On the other hand, if a customer pays with a credit card and the merchant follows procedures to ensure that the card is acceptable to the credit card company, she is guaranteed payment. However, she pays for this guarantee. The bank that converts the credit card slip into cash discounts the amount shown on the slip. The discount is usually 1 to 2% of the amount of the sale. This discount pays for the cost of processing the transaction and the cost of the funds that are paid to the merchant before the cardholder pays the bill.

3. Because checks take several days to clear, a merchant who accepts a check delivers goods to the customer before she receives cash or a credit to her bank deposit. This, of course, means that the merchant must sacrifice interest on a check transaction compared to one in which she receives payment immediately in the form of cash or a deposit; hence the cost of float. However, the merchant expects some float expenses as part of the normal cost of doing business, and the prices she charges reflect this cost.

This might seem to indicate that all customers pay for the cost of float generated by customers who pay by check. However, accepting a wide variety of means of payment increases the flow of sales, reducing inventory cost and overhead cost per sale.

5. A bank can never be sure that it can collect good funds on a check until the payor's bank actually delivers good funds. If it makes good funds available to the payee's account before good funds are delivered to it, it will have to absorb a loss if good funds are, in fact, not delivered.

7. The Fed operates a nationwide clearing system. It provides banks with a definite funds availability schedule. Thus, after so many days, the Fed automatically credits the payee's bank's reserve account with good funds, whether the check has actually cleared or not. This provides a certainty that is not always available in the private market. Even though the Fed reclaims the good funds for any check that fails to clear, the payee's bank can use the funds like any other deposit in its reserve account. For example, if it has excess reserves, it can lend the good funds in the fed funds market. Because the Fed reclaims funds for unpaid checks, banks usually do not give their customers credit for their check until the check actually clears.

9. Cash customers are the only ones that pay immediately and in full for their purchases. Check customers receive the benefit of float, and credit card customers receive a loan until they pay their bill that is financed by the discount the merchant pays on the credit card sale. However, this does not mean that cash customers are getting charged too much. Merchants offer a wide variety of means of payment to increase sales, which reduces inventory and overhead costs. In addition, a check or credit card sale is usually for a larger amount than a cash sale but may take up approximately the same amount of the merchant's time.

Nevertheless, some establishments do offer cash discounts, indicating that some merchants feel that the cost of servicing cash customers is lower.

11. Under the current technology the Fed uses for making Automated Clearing House payments, the payor institution delivers a tape to the Fed directing its bank to pay funds from its account to the accounts of all the individuals on the tape at their respective banks. The Fed executes the transaction by debiting the payor bank's reserve account and crediting the accounts of all the banks on the tape. It then informs each bank of the account numbers that should be credited or debited. The expense of dealing with lots of transactions on a tape is apparently small relative to the cost of receiving and handling the tape in the first place.

Chapter 12   ELECTRONIC PAYMENTS SYSTEMS AND THE DEMAND FOR RESERVES

1. The Federal Reserve guarantees that good funds will be delivered at the end of the day against payments messages sent over Fedwire, whereas the Fed does not guarantee delivery of good funds against checks received by the payee's bank but not yet returned to the payor's bank for payment. Thus banks are reluctant to credit customers' accounts for checks received but not cleared, whereas they are quite willing to credit customers' accounts for payments messages received over Fedwire even though good funds are not actually delivered until the end of the day.

As a result, customers receiving payments over Fedwire can use expected receipts of good funds to make payments. This permits the banking system to conserve on the use of good funds. For example, a bank customer receiving a payments message over Fedwire can buy a Treasury bill with the good funds he expects to receive at end-of-day settlement. If good funds were not guaranteed, he would not have been able to purchase the Treasury bill until good funds were actually delivered at the end of the day when markets are closed. Thus, he would have had to have held a demand deposit overnight.

Banks pay for the Fed guarantee by holding non-interest-bearing reserves at the Fed. If the Fed forced banks to hold reserves without providing them with the benefit of a guarantee of intraday payments messages, the cost of making payments would increase.

So why shouldn't such a system be applied to checks? In Fedwire payments, even though the Fed guarantees that the sending bank will deliver good funds, the sending bank still guarantees that its customer will deliver good funds. For example, if a bank sends a payments message for its customer, it must deliver good funds as long as it is not bankrupt. If the customer does not have access to good funds, the sending bank must take a loss. To apply this system to checks, the sending bank would have to guarantee the checks of its customers. Checks are generally written for relatively small payments, and it is expensive to make certain that small customers only write checks when they have access to good funds.

3. In a continuous settlement system, banks must deliver reserves against all payments messages. In a periodic net-settlement system, reserves are delivered against a net payments position that is accumulated over a given time period. For example, assume a bank makes a payment for $1 million at 10 A.M. and receives a payment for $900,000 at 3 P.M. Under a continuous settlement system, it delivers $1 million, in reserves at 10 A.M. and receives $900,000 in reserves at 3 P.M. Under a periodic net-settlement system, it would deliver $100,000 in reserves at settlement.

Depositors in a failed bank are better protected under a continuous settlement system than under a net periodic settlement system. The reason for this is that under net periodic settlement, the clearinghouse has the right to offset any of the failed bank's "due from's" with "due to's" it has against the failed bank. Thus, if the failed bank owes $1 million to the clearinghouse and is owed $900,000 by the clearinghouse, the clearinghouse loses only $100,000. If the settlement is continuous, the failed bank borrows $1 million in the interbank market to deliver reserves against its payment. Later in the day it receives $900,000 in reserves and then goes bankrupt. The banks that lent $1 million to the failed bank in the interbank market cannot offset their loans with the $100,000 in reserves just delivered. This asset is available to all creditors, including depositors.

5. Most developing countries do not have an electronic payment system that is guaranteed by the central bank. Thus banks cannot rely on a central bank guarantee that they will be paid. In the payments systems of developing countries, a payee will not receive good funds until the payments draft is delivered to the payor's bank and the two banks exchange good funds. The payee must be concerned with two problems: The solvency of the payor's bank and the solvency of the payor. If the payee wants immediate settlement, he must insist on cash.

7. A private clearinghouse forces its members to hold reserves equal to a fraction of deposits to guarantee payments among the members. Thus, in the event of a bank failure, the clearinghouse seizes the reserves of the failed bank to make good on its "due to's." The clearinghouse also offsets the failed bank's "due to's" with any "due from's." Thus, a fractional reserve banking system actually places depositors in a worse position in the event of failure than if the system had not demanded any reserves at all.

9. It is possible that CHIPS members provided immediate credit on "due to's" because they had a high degree of confidence in each other. However, a more likely reason why CHIPS messages were treated as good funds is that members believed that the Fed would, in fact, make good on a bank's inability to settle its net "due to" position. The basis for this belief was that the failure of a large CHIPS member to settle its net "due to" position could lead to the failure of other CHIPS members. If one bank failed to deliver reserves, the bank to whom it owed reserves might not have been able to settle its position because its net "due to" position would have expanded by the amount of the "due from" that was not paid. This is known as systemic risk.

11. (a) After the interbank lending to top up reserve positions to levels required by the clearinghouse, the balance sheets are as follows:

First National			
Reserves	370	3700	Deposits
Loans	2600	170	Capital
"Due froms"	900		

Daigin			
Reserves	130	1300	Deposits
Loans	1750	450	"Due to" First National
		130	Capital

Midland			
Reserves	40	400	Deposits
Loans	900	450	"Due to" First National
		90	Capital

Clearinghouse			
Cash	540	370	Reserves First National
		130	Reserves Daigin
		40	Reserves Midland

(b) The clearinghouse guarantees the payments from Midland to First National and Daigin even if Midland defaults. The clearinghouse seizes Midland's reserve deposits of 90. The net payment defaulted by Midland is 500. The clearinghouse has then suffered a loss of 410. Equally dividing the loss between the two remaining banks, it debits First National's and Daigin's accounts by 205 each.

In addition, the clearinghouse credits First National with net receipts of 1000 and debits Daigin's account by its net payments of 500, as on a normal day. In all, this leaves First National with reserve deposits of 1065 (= 270 + 1000 − 205) and Daigin with deposits (overdraft) of −525 (= 180 − 500 − 205). Daigin must now borrow from First National in the interbank market to top up its reserve position.

When all adjustments are made, the balance sheets are as follows:

First National			
Reserves	410	3700	Deposits
Loans	2600	− 35	Capital
"Due from"	655		
Daigin			
Reserves	130	1300	Deposits
Loans	1750	655	"Due to" First National
		− 75	Capital
Clearinghouse			
Cash	540	410	Reserves First National
		130	Reserves Daigin

Note that the book value of capital of both First National and Daigin have been wiped out. Both institutions will need injections of capital from outside to remain open. Note also that First National now has excess reserves equal to the amount that Midland would have held if it had stayed liquid.

(c) The amount required of each bank for collateral at CHIPS is 5% of a bank's highest bilateral credit limit to all the other banks. For First National the value of the loans deposited at CHIPS is then 100 = .05 × 2000. Midland must also deposit 100, and Daigin must deposit 75. The sum of the bilateral limits granted by First National and Daigin to Midland is 3000. Of this amount, 2000 is from First National; so First National has an ASO (additional settlement obligation) of 273.33 = 410 × 2/3. Daigin's ASO is 136.67. Once CHIPS assesses the losses, the balance sheets are adjusted as in part (b).

(d) Midland's payments messages are made credible because the clearinghouse can seize both the entire day's payment inflow to Midland and Midland's initial reserve deposits. Thus Midland's payment messages are collateralized. In addition, the clearinghouse can immediately assess the remaining banks according to a loss-sharing formula. For this gain in the credibility of payment orders, however, Midland's depositors suffer in the bankruptcy. If the payment orders coming into the bank and the reserves had not been seized, there would have been more resources for depositors to divide in bankruptcy court.

13. A private clearinghouse can only guarantee delivery of net "due to's" up to the amount of collateral it holds to make good on the promise. Thus, to provide an iron-clad guarantee, the private clearinghouse must hold reserves equal to 100% of net "due to's." A central bank, on the other hand, can print reserves so it can always guarantee delivery of net "due to's" even if they exceed current reserves outstanding. This makes the central bank guarantee more reliable, and banks will be more willing to let their depositors treat payments messages as good funds. As we explained in Exercise 1, this reduces the possibility that bank customers will have to hold a demand deposit overnight.

If the central bank has to create reserves to ensure that "due to's" will be covered, this could lead to inflation if the expansion of reserves must be permanent. Surprise inflation reduces the real value of nominal assets, so holders of these assets would pay for the increased liquidity.

Chapter 13   BANKS IN THE MARKET FOR LIQUIDITY

1. (a) The evidence most often cited that borrowers pay for reserves is that presented by Fama. When large CDs were subject to reserve requirements, they paid the same interest rate as commercial paper, which is not subject to a reserve requirement. Fama reasoned that, since someone must pay for reserves, it must be borrowers who pay. If bank borrowers pay for reserve requirements, bank loans must be a unique form of credit, or bank borrowers would borrow someplace else to avoid paying for reserves. For example, some researchers claim that banks have special information about some borrows; consequently, these borrowers' opportunities are limited to banks.

(b) Commercial paper, bankers acceptances, and repurchase agreements, are, from investors' point of view, perfect substitutes for reservable bank deposits. Since investors can hold these perfect substitutes, they will not pay for bank reserve requirements. This implies that bank borrowers do not pay for reserves, either. Occasionally investors must sell securities to dealers who finance their inventory with bank loans. The cost of selling will incorporate the cost of the dealer's bank loan. In turn, the original return on the security must include the investor's expected cost of selling to a dealer that must use a bank loan. Hence, if investors do not pay for the cost of reserves, neither will bank borrowers.

Since we observe that banks make loans and hold reserves, someone must pay for reserves. Because the above argument indicates that borrowers cannot pay for reserves if depositors do not, both collectively must pay. That is, the cost of reserves must be reflected in both the expected returns on securities and the cost of bank loans. For investors to pay these costs, reserves must be useful. They are useful, as is the banking system, because they guarantee delivery of good funds.

3. If reserve requirements are binding, the cost of settling in demand deposits doubles because reserve costs are now calculated as the fed funds rate times a 20% reserve requirement rather than a 10% requirement. The higher reserve requirement will increase the expected return on securities with a high probability of being sold for a bank deposit relative to those with a low probability. Thus the liquidity premium rises. If reserve requirements are nonbinding, the increase in the reserve requirement will have no effect. Banks will reduce reserves by exchanging demand deposits for repurchase agreements.

5. If, as in the Fama model, reserve requirements are borne by bank borrowers, banks have an incentive only to lend to borrowers that have no alternative to banks and issue liabilities to consumers that are not subject to reserve requirements. If banks issue liabilities both with and without reserves and reserve requirements are binding, they will bid the cost of the nonreservable liability up to the cost of the reservable liability (including the cost of reserves). This contradicts the Fama model because banks would then pay more for consumer deposits (and fed funds) than for CDs by the cost of reserve requirements.

If banks hold loans to borrowers who uniquely use banks as well as to those who do not, banks will have an incentive to equalize the risk-adjusted return on the two types of assets. This means that if the unique loans have returns that include the cost of reserves, banks will have an incentive only to hold the unique loans. Consequently, they will bid the return on unique bank loans down to the return on other assets with similar risk characteristics. Hence our observation of actual bank portfolios makes it highly unlikely that Fama's (and the conventional) conclusion about who pays for reserves is correct.

7. The CP issuer pays for reserves because the CP holder may have to sell the CP to a dealer who must finance inventory with a bank loan. Likewise a CP holder pays for the cost of reserves because the issuer may have to use a bank line to deliver cash when the commercial paper matures. Since commercial paper and certificates of deposit must trade at the same interest rate, the allocation of the cost of reserves must be similar. If the bank cannot roll over its CD at maturity, it will have to issue a demand deposit, which means it will have to call on a fed funds line to borrow additional reserves. CD holders must pay for this expected expense to the bank by receiving a lower interest rate on their deposit.

9. If banks try to lower the interest rate they pay on CDs (relative to that paid on commercial paper), required reserves are greater than desired reserves. Of course, as long as CP is a perfect substitute for a CD, banks will be frustrated in this attempt. Depositors will switch to CP, and bank balance sheets and required reserves will shrink until they reach their desired level.

11. Very liquid assets pay low rates of return because they seldom need to be converted to demand deposits. Thus holding a very liquid asset has an opportunity cost. The opportunity cost is the liquidity premium, which is equal to the cost of holding reserves to make a bank loan of the same size a liquid asset.

13. An increase in the fed funds rate means that the opportunity cost of delivering reserves increases, which will increase the liquidity premium. However, the liquidity premium is also determined by the probability that good funds will have to be delivered. If this probability declines because of the higher cost of settling in good funds and if the decline is large enough, the decline in probability could offset the impact of the higher fed funds rate on the liquidity premium.

15. A decline in reserves relative to immediately available funds will cause an increase in the variability of the fed funds rate because net payment imbalances will not be as well covered by reserve holdings. This will force banks with low reserves and large imbalances suddenly into the fed funds market, causing sharp fluctuations in the fed funds rate. Some banks will see a profit in increasing their holdings of reserves to speculate in the fed funds market. To do this, they reduce repurchase agreements and expand their demand deposits. This offsets the actions of the bank that substituted out of reservable deposits.

17. Generally, the interest rate banks earn on a loan and the interest rate they must pay on a deposit are determined by risk and their liquidity characteristics, not by the noninterest expenses of banks. For example, an illiquid asset will have the same high return whether it is held by a bank or held by another investor. Interest expenses on deposits will be lower than the return on the loan because the deposit is more liquid. All instruments with the same characteristics of the deposit will trade at the same low interest rate. This spread will be maintained as long as it is costly to create liquidity, and investors are willing to pay for liquidity.

The cost of liquidity is determined by the cost incurred by a bank in converting an illiquid loan into a liquid deposit. Even if the bank has no labor or office expenses, it must still hold reserves to guarantee the liquidity of its deposits. These reserves have a cost; so, therefore, does liquidity. Because like instruments must trade at like interest rates, all liquid instruments must bear the same cost as bank deposits. This can only happen if all liquid instruments are equally dependent on the banking system for liquidity.

Chapter 14   THE ROLE FOR BANK LOANS IN THE U.S. ECONOMY

1. A borrower using a short-term loan must have his loan contract renewed frequently. Thus the short-term lender has many opportunities to cut off the borrower's funds, and the borrower must therefore prove the viability of a project at short intervals. Of course, if the lender were to pull funds out in the middle of a project, the borrower might not be able to repay the loan. Hence the lender is, to some extent, forced to renew a short-term loan. However, the short-term lender can adjust the terms of the loan for changes in risk and can control the scope of the project by reducing funding. Thus a short-term lender can exercise greater control over a borrower than a long-term lender.

3. Bonds usually represent claims to specific cash payments, whereas equity represents no specific claim to cash. Even if the company earns a profit, it need not pay cash to its equity holders. PIKs relieve bond issuers of the necessity to deliver cash for a specified period of time because the issuer can pay interest in bonds rather than in cash. Thus a PIK permits the issuer to retain earnings as does an equity issue. However, PIKs must eventually be redeemed for a specific amount of cash so they do not give the issuer as much freedom as an equity contract.

5. Policymakers were concerned that if banks were not willing to lend money, business people would not have the resources to invest in new projects that would create employment and increase spending. Of course, there are many alternative sources of credit in addition to bank loans, so why were policymakers concerned about bank lending? The answer is that they believe banks represent the most likely source of credit for new projects in a risky economic environment. This view is consistent with the notion that banks are special lenders because of their monitoring capability. Banks have the ability to reduce the risk of a project by placing constraints on a borrower.

However, policymakers may be incorrect in assuming that bank lending for new projects was significantly lower in the latest recession compared to the 1982 recession. In 1982 unsold inventories of goods rose much more dramatically than in 1990–91. Inventories have to be financed, and one way to finance them is with bank loans. Lower inventories reduce the need for such funding and increase the likelihood that a recession will be short and mild. If inventories are low, an increase in demand for goods leads to an immediate increase in production.

7. Assume that a bank collects private information about a borrower in the course of making a bank loan. The borrower also issues a security that the bank underwrites and trades. The market makes a judgment about the quality of the security based on publicly available information. The bank knows the public information is incorrect but sells the security anyway at the market price. By the terms of the loan agreement, the bank cannot divulge the private information to the public. If it divulges the information, it is breaching its loan contract; if it does not divulge the information, it is making a profit on private information.

Banks avoid these conflicts of interest by separating securities departments from loan-origination departments. Thus the individuals who determine whether the bank should buy or sell a security do not have access to the private information. Conflict of interest dilemmas also arise in loan sales agreements for the same reasons.

9. If banks sell loans to lenders who do not have the tools available to control borrower behavior, bank loans will be more risky for nonbanks to hold than for banks to hold. The originating bank that does have the tools no longer has an incentive to control borrower behavior. This problem can be avoided by selling loan participations rather than the whole loan. In a participation, the originating bank retains a portion of the loan. Thus the bank has an incentive to continue to control behavior.

Another type of loan sale contract is a syndication in which all the syndicate members agree to share deposits or other assets that are seized in the event of default on the loan. Thus lenders as a group retain the tools to control borrower behavior. However, in a syndication, lenders with small shares in the credit have an incentive to behave contrary to the interest of lenders as a whole. They do this even though it would appear to be against their own interests as well because, by causing trouble, they hope to force lenders with larger shares to buy them out.

11. The market prices all securities according to their risk and liquidity characteristics. Loans should be no different. If they are as liquid as deposits, they should trade at the same interest rate as deposits. If a bank sells a liquid loan instead of funding it with a deposit, the demand for reserves declines as long as the new lender does not fund the loan with a reservable deposit. Thus banks can reduce the reserve to liquid instruments ratio to the desired level through loan sales. However, to make the loan as liquid as the deposit, the bank must attach a line of credit to guarantee delivery of cash at maturity. As we shall see in Chapter 19, these lines must be structured carefully to avoid some costly regulations.

13. A borrower who faces a liquidity squeeze has an incentive to lease rather than borrow for two reasons. The first is that the down payment on a lease is less than that required to make a purchase financed by a loan, so that the immediate cash required to obtain equipment is reduced. Second, the lessee can deduct its entire payment to the lessor from taxable income. On the other hand, if the borrower had purchased the equipment and funded it with a loan, only interest and depreciation would have been tax deductible.

The lessor must provide the cash that the lessee does not provide. The lessor must provide the cash down payment to buy the equipment and must suffer the cash expense of deducting only interest and depreciation from taxable income. (Higher taxes mean lower cash flow.) Of course, the lessee pays the lessor for coming up with the cash early in the contract, but, because the lessor is liquid, this cost is lower than it would be if the lessee had to come up with the cash.

15. Mortgage securitization separated the function of origination from holding. Once this link was broken, mortgage brokers specializing in loan servicing also developed. Fragmentation of the mortgage business along functional lines has increased efficiency and the liquidity of mortgages. Mortgage servicers have been able to take advantage of economies of scale by servicing loan portfolios of many originators, a business that is primarily local in nature. Mortgage-backed securities can be bought and sold much more easily than single mortgages; hence, they are more liquid. This has reduced the interest rates home buyers must pay on mortgages.

Chapter 15   THE DOLLAR
IN THE INTERNATIONAL MARKETPLACE

1. A liquid payments system is one in which a large number of transactions can be settled with only a small transfer of good funds. Thus a good measure of liquidity is the ratio of payments transactions to interbank reserve borrowings. For example, in the domestic market, this would be the ratio of domestic payments to fed funds purchased.

3. Assume an oil exporter purchases a CD of a European branch of an American bank. The money to acquire the CD came from the New York account of an American who purchased a barrel of oil. Thus the New York office loses a deposit on the liability side. It is replaced with a "due to" the European branch. This "due to" will eventually be offset by a "due from" as an asset on the New York office's books when a foreign office of some bank purchases a U.S. asset.

A European branch will end up with a "due to" New York on the liability side of its balance sheet if the oil exporter decides to sell his CD and he cannot find a buyer other than a dealer who must hold inventory. This happens because the dealer must fund his inventory with a bank loan from a European branch of an American bank. This branch funds the loan to the dealer with a "due to" the New York office on the liability side of its balance sheet. Thus the net "due to" position of overseas branches vis-à-vis New York results from the liquidity services that New York provides to the overseas dollar market.

5. The oil exporter obtains the deposit from an American. This creates a "due to" Europe on the New York office balance sheet. However, if a European bank eventually buys a Treasury bill from the New York office, the New York office ends up with a "due from" the European branch, which offsets the earlier "due to." Thus, there is neither a net "due to" nor a net "due from" position between the European branch and the New York office. The balance sheets are as follows:

AMERICAN BANK

"Due from" Europe $100	"Due to" Europe $100

L1

"Due from" L2 $100	CD $100

L2

T-bill $100	"Due to" L1 $100

7. In the domestic market we saw how the commercial paper market helps reduce the burden of reserve requirements. Commercial paper is a perfect substitute for a bank CD, which, until 1991, was subject to a reserve requirement. Thus potential CD holders could not be charged for reserve requirements because, if they were, they would shift their investment to commercial paper. In this chapter we found that, for American investors, Eurodollar CDs are not perfect substitutes for domestic CDs because the difference in the settlement systems prevents them from having the same liquidity characteristics for domestic investors. Thus an arbitrage could not take place between domestic CDs and Eurodollar CDs as occurred between the domestic CD and CP markets.

However, the higher rates available on Eurodollar CDs may have attracted some U.S. investors in domestic CDs who were willing to give up one day's liquidity for higher yields. If the demand for domestic CDs fell by more than the demand for less liquid domestic securities, liquidity premiums in the U.S. market would have declined.

9. Assume that a Japanese company receives $1 million from an American for the sale of goods in the U.S. market. It deposits the money in a London branch of a Japanese bank. Assume that a German company needs a loan of $1 million to finance goods it purchased from the United States. It applies for the loan from a London branch of a German bank. The German bank can get dollars by borrowing them from the Japanese bank's London office. The Japanese bank will have a "due from" the German bank. The German bank will have a "due to" the Japanese bank and a dollar loan on the asset side of its balance sheet. The Eurodollar market will double in size from the original $1 million deposit.

11. In exercises 3 through 6 we saw how a dealer that must fund a Eurodollar CD with a bank loan creates a "due to" New York position. If the dealer could have financed the CD with a repurchase agreement, there would have been no need to borrow good funds. With a liquid foreign exchange market, this could have been done. The dealer could have sold the CD under agreement to repurchase to someone who held deutschemarks. The DM investor could have hedged her dollar position by purchasing the right to swap dollars for DM when the repo matures. Thus the DM investor can maintain her position in DM and still hold the dollar CD. This increases the potential investors for dollar assets, which increases the liquidity of the dollar market.

13. As we learned in Chapter 12, when a central bank creates a payments system that guarantees the delivery of good funds at settlement, it absorbs credit risk that some bank will default on its net "due to" position. It can reduce this credit risk by increasing the cost of its guarantee or by rationing the guarantee through such devices as debit caps. Either policy reduces the liquidity of payments system because participants are less willing to create a net "due to" position that they must pay for. Hence payments will tend to be delayed, and, if there is a backlog of payments at the end of the day, some payments will not be made. Thus, some participants who would have received a payment to offset a payment made will end up with a net "due to" position that must be financed with a bank loan; hence, the demand for reserves will increase.

Thus, from a central bank's point of view, an increase in its compensation for absorbing credit risk leads to a decrease in the liquidity of its payments system. This can be represented by a graph with central bank compensation for credit risk on the vertical axis and liquidity of the payments system on the horizontal axis. The line is downward sloping, which indicates that as central bank revenue rises, liquidity declines.

15. As long as central banks compete to make their currencies the global currency, their decisions about where to locate themselves on the frontier will be affected by the behavior of other central banks. In describing the central bank's objective in exercise 14, you should indicate whether it is worthwhile achieving the status of an international currency.

Chapter 16   MONETARY POLICY IN INTERNATIONAL FINANCIAL MARKETS

1. If the forward rate is 1.9 DM/\$ and the spot rate is 1.7 DM/\$, the three-month depreciation of the deutschmark is 11%. This translates into a 44% annualized depreciation. Plugging into the formula for covered interest parity,

$$1.08 < 1.05 + .44$$

You would borrow 170 deutschmarks and convert them to \$100. In three months, you would receive \$101.25 by lending the funds in the dollar money market. You must repay 173 deutschmarks, but your forward contract permits you to receive 190 deutschmarks for one dollar. After repaying the loan, you have 17 deutschmarks and \$1.25. At 1.9 DM/\$, your profit is \$10.20.

3. If the foreign price level is flexible, we know that the result of an increase in money supply is an inflation in the foreign country's price level that is in proportion to the increase in the money supply. In the domestic economy, there will be a decrease in the nominal interest rate. The nominal interest rate in the foreign country will not change. Letting R_{FI} denote the foreign nominal interest rate in period 1, and defining R_{DI} for the domestic economy similarly,

$$R_{FI} - R_{DI} > 0$$

Letting e denote the nominal exchange rate and e^* the expected exchange rate next period,

$$\frac{e^* - e}{e} > 0$$

The exchange rate is expected to depreciate. Next period when equilibrium is restored in the domestic economy, the price level will increase by the same proportion as the money supply increase this period. The real exchange rate will be restored to its long-term value. The price level in the foreign country, P_F, and the price level in the domestic country, P_D, have increased by the same amount. Therefore, in order to restore the real exchange rate, the nominal exchange rate must return to its original value. Thus, since the exchange rate is expected to rise, it must have fallen when the money supplies increased. Finally, the real exchange rate will also fall (appreciate) in the first period and rise in the second. In the long run, nothing is changed, except that both price levels are higher.

5. Letting $P_\$ = 120$, $P_¥ = 180$, $e = 120$, the real exchange rate is 80.

7. Net reserves are gross reserves minus borrowed reserves. Gross reserves are foreign-denominated securities held by the central bank, while borrowed reserves are foreign currency the central bank owes to other central banks or private firms.

9. Suppose the central bank attempts to increase the amount of base money. Under a floating exchange rate, there is no mechanism by which individuals can dispose of their increased money holdings. In order for real money balances to be unchanged, the price level or the nominal interest rate must adjust. Under a fixed exchange-rate system, the central bank stands ready to exchange foreign funds for domestic money. Thus foreign exchange can be purchased with the increased money holdings. Therefore, increases in base money are offset by sales of foreign exchange.

Chapter 17 FINANCIAL INNOVATION AND THE CREATION OF BANK-LIKE DEPOSITS

1. The formula for the call is given by

$$C = A\,\frac{bA - S}{bA - aA} - \frac{a}{S}\,\frac{bA - S}{b - a}\,\frac{S}{R}$$

Rearranging:

$$C = \frac{bA - S}{b - a} - \frac{a}{R}\,\frac{bA - S}{b - a}$$

We wish to determine the change in the call price when the stock price changes. Therefore, when A changes, the change in C is given by

$$\Delta C = \frac{b\Delta A}{b - a} - \frac{a}{R}\,\frac{b\Delta A}{b - a}$$

When we rearrange again, we find

$$\Delta C = \frac{b\Delta A}{b - a}\left(1 - \frac{a}{R}\right)$$

Since $b>A$, the first term is positive, and since $a<R$, the second term is also positive. Therefore, the change in C is also positive.

We also wish to determine the change in C from a change in the interest rate R. Letting R change to examine the change in the call price we have

$$\Delta C = \frac{a(bA - S)}{b - a} \frac{\Delta R}{R^2}$$

Since $bA>S$ and $b>a$, this is positive.

3. We will assume for simplicity that the stock pays no dividend between today and the expiration date. At expiration, the value of the stock will be either aA or bA where A is the current price and $b>a$. Let R represent one plus the rate of interest for a riskless loan. Let C denote the call price and S the strike price. We will assume $bA>S>aA$. We are interested in determining whether a portfolio consisting of x shares of stocks and y bonds can be constructed such that the return on the portfolio is identical to that on the option. The payoff from the two portfolios at expiration is given by the following:

	$aA < S$	$bA > S$
Call option	0	$bA - S$
Stock	aAx	bAx
Bonds	Ry	Ry

If the stock is below the strike price at expiration, the holder of the option will not wish to buy the stock at a higher price, so the option will not be exercised. If the stock price exceeds the strike price, the option will be exercised, netting a profit of the stock price less the strike price, $bA - S$, for the option holder. With x shares, either the stocks are worth aAx or bAx. The bonds will pay Ry in any state of the world.

To determine the number of shares that must be held we solve

$$aAx + Ry = 0$$

$$bAx + Ry = bA - S$$

The solution to these two equations is

$$y = \frac{-a (bA - S)}{R (b - a)}$$

$$x = \frac{(bA - S)}{(bA - aA)}$$

We assumed $bA>S>aA$, so $0<x<1$, which implies that x is a fraction of shares long. Furthermore, since $bA>S$ and $b>a$, y is negative. Thus the bond position is short, implying the portfolio is partially financed by a loan.

5. (a) Suppose the portfolio to be hedged consists of a basket of all the shares included in the S&P 500. In particular, it is constructed to have a value of $500 times the index value. If the current level of the S&P 500 is 405 and the portfolio manager holds a put with strike price of 400, upside gains will be captured; but if the index falls below 400, the portfolio value is protected. Suppose the option expires on Friday and on Thursday the index falls to 300. The portfolio manager will collect $(400 - 300)500 = $50,000$ on Friday morning. Together with the shares, now worth $150,000, the portfolio is worth $200,000, or the value of the S&P 500 at the strike price.

With the precipitous drop in the index, it is difficult for the exchange to create new options at the strike prices desired. Suppose the lowest strike price available to the portfolio manager is 380. Were she to buy this option, it would almost certainly be exercised. It would be very expensive, probably not much less than the $50,000 just received. If the portfolio manager chooses to buy it, she is essentially converting a large portion of her portfolio into cash. However, if she opts not to buy it, she is unhedged.

(b) She can overcome the problem by constructing a synthetic put in the futures market. The synthetic put consists of a short position in stock and a long position in bonds. If she sells a future on the S&P 500, she essentially acquires the short position in stock, together with a synthetic T-bill of equal value to the short position in stocks. The difference between the bill position and the short position in the put pricing formula is the put price, or premium. This is the equity that she must put in to create the synthetic put. Thus, if she were selling only a futures contract, she would be essentially not long enough in bills. She must buy back more bills, enough to equal the put price. When she does this, she has created a put at a strike price of her choosing. To maintain the hedge, she must now adjust the position as the price of the underlying index changes, a process called dynamic hedging. This process will be self-financing. Increases in the size of the long positions will be identically matched by increased short sales, the latter generating the funds to finance the former.

7. Let A denote the share price and S the strike price. Consider a portfolio long a put, long the stock, and short a call. At expiration, the stock price will be either above or below the strike price.

	Long put	Long stock	Short call	Total
$A > S$	0	A	$-(A - S)$	S
$A < S$	$S - A$	A	0	S

If the exercise date is T, the portfolio has the same payoff as a bond with par value S and maturity T. The value of the bond today is S/R, where R is one plus the interest rate. Therefore, letting P denote the put price and C the call price, the value of the portfolio today is

$$P - C + A = \frac{S}{R}$$

If $P - C + A > S/R$, you would sell a put and a unit of stocks short, and you would use the proceeds to buy a call and a bond. Since $P + A > S/R + C$, the portfolio would be self-financing. On T, the portfolio would pay

	Short put	Short stock	Long call	Bond	Total
$A > S$	0	$-A$	$A - S$	S	0
$A < S$	$-(S - A)$	$-A$	0	S	0

Hence the position cancels the liabilities and returns, but making the trade netted a pure profit for the arbitrager of $P + A - (S/R) - C > 0$.

9. Suppose all margin deposited by customers with XYZ is deposited by XYZ with the clearinghouse.

(a) X is a speculator selling a futures contract. Thus initial margin is $6000. Y is a speculator buying a futures contract. His initial margin will also be $6000. Thus $12,000 is deposited by XYZ Investors with the clearinghouse. The margin is deposited on the morning of March 1.

(b) Y pays variation margin of $1000, and X receives variation margin of $1000. Z is hedger, so her initial margin is $4000.

FUTURES MARKET MARGIN ACTIVITY ON MARCH 2

X	Y	Z
6000	6000	4000
+1000	−1000	

(c) On March 2, the S&P 5 falls five points. Y pays $2500 in variation margin, while X and Z each receive $2500. Notice that Y receives a margin call on the morning of March 3.

FUTURES MARKET MARGIN ACTIVITY ON MARCH 3

X	Y	Z
7000	5000	4000
+2500	−2500	+2500

11. Margin in options is required only for short positions (long positions cannot lose any more than the original premium). For short positions the investor must put up the premium and 15% of the market value of the index plus the amount that the option is out of the money. For a dollar multiplier on the index of $500, the arbitrager must put up $1500 for the put and $7500 (15% of the index value times the dollar multiplier). Notice that the short position is supposed to finance the long position. In this case, no funds are immediately forthcoming from the put sale.

13. Both long and short positions must put up margin on futures contracts. The margin required to open a contract is called initial margin. Every day, the contract is rewritten to reflect the closing futures price that day. Any movement in the price will lead to a gain for one party and a loss for another. In rewriting the contract, margin is subtracted from the loser's account and added to the gainer's. This effectively eliminates debt from the market. If variation margin payments have led to the reduction in value of a customer margin account below the level of maintenance margin, which is less than or equal to initial margin, a margin call is made. The customer must restore the account to the initial margin level. If the customer fails to meet the call, the position is liquidated.

Returning to the problem, if the futures price is F, the margin required against the y contracts is $.1Fy \times 500$. Thus the arbitrager must deliver $.1Fy \times 500$ of initial margin to CMECH.

15. In the example being considered, the arbitrager had to have access immediately to funds to buy a certificate of deposit and a call option and to deliver margin on the short put position and the short stock position. An arbitrage that is self-financing as in this case requires a large extension of funds with no immediate offsetting receipts. (Even if the arbitrager owned the stocks rather than short selling them, it is five days before the money from the sale of a stock clears.) Thus the arbitrage is possible only with access to liquidity. An arbitrager would need to have a line of credit from a bank. This is not costless, but its cost is not considered in the construction of the arbitrage.

Chapter 18 LIQUIDITY CRISES IN FINANCIAL AND BANKING MARKETS

1. During financial panics, market makers need call loans. Individuals who bought securities on margin may find the value of their collateral has declined and may therefore need to meet margin calls. Banks may find the quality of previous loans are hurt by the financial plight of their customers, thus making the banks subject to runs. In general, there is a large increase in the demand for liquidity. If there is no nationalized central bank, the private banking system cannot expand to meet this increased demand for liquidity. Banks may have to liquidate assets, depressing the prices of the assets, and if the increased yields are then passed to the demanders of liquidity, the crisis is aggravated. In addition, if the bulk of reserves is held by a few banks, a money market corner becomes a possibility as those with access to liquidity claim a high price from those who must deliver cash. A nationalized central bank, on the other hand, can expand reserves, contracting them after the liquidity crisis subsides, to minimize the real damage that can occur from bankruptcies, sharply higher interest rates, and shaken confidence in financial institutions.

3. Informed traders have a downward-sloping demand for the security. If the dividend falls, they are willing to hold fewer shares at the original price. As bad news trickles in and informed market participants reduce their estimates of dividends, the informed traders will maintain their holdings of the stock only if the stock price steadily declines to maintain the appropriate dividend yield. When the price reaches the level that triggers the stop-loss strategy, the price will jump discontinuously to a lower level as the uninformed traders dump their shares. Once at this lower level, any further bad news will lead to steady continuous declines in the price. At the lower level, only informed traders hold the stock. They have become willing to hold all the outstanding shares at the lower price because the price fall increased the dividend yield.

5. When liquidity crises emerge, if excess reserves are not available, banks must sell securities to meet the liquidity demand. To induce buyers to exchange deposits for securities, a higher yield on the securities must be offered. Thus interest rates will increase during liquidity crises. A justification for controlling interest rates, then, is that they may signal liquidity crises. Strict control of the money supply during a liquidity crisis may lead to unnecessary real effects, such as bankruptcies of market participants and shaken confidence in financial markets.

7. If banks refuse to lend to buyers of securities when selling volume is high, market makers cannot function as providers of liquidity to the market. Thus the prices are likely to fall lower than their equilibrium price. If, for instance, the triggering of stop-loss strategies is one cause of the selling volume, the lower the price falls, the more stop-loss strategies will be triggered, exacerbating the selling volume, perhaps necessitating margin calls which may bankrupt securities holders. In general, sellers will be hurt by their inability to receive the equilibrium price for the security.

9. Banks are subject to runs because they stand ready to convert one asset, deposits, into another, cash, at a fixed price. If the solvency of the bank and the sustainability of the guarantee are in question, depositors will desire to convert to cash at the fixed price while they can still do so; therefore, they run the bank.

Similarly, insurance companies are subject to runs. Holders of life insurance policies accumulate reserves as they pay premiums on their policies over the years. These reserves are invested by the insurance company, but the company stands ready to convert the reserves to cash, at their cash surrender value, upon demand by the policyholder. When the solvency of the insurance company is in question, policyholders will run the company. It is this characteristic of the liabilities of both insurance companies and banks that makes them subject to runs. Runs can be particularly perilous for these companies because their assets are considerably less liquid than their liabilities. If a run forces a sudden sale of assets to finance the demands of liability holders (depositors or policyholders), asset prices may collapse, rendering the company insolvent.

Central banks may also be subject to runs when they promise to convert a metal to currency at a fixed price to maintain a metallic standard or when they promise to convert foreign currency to domestic currency to maintain a fixed exchange rate. In the latter case, the expansion of domestic credit will lead to an increase in the demand for conversion of the domestic currency to foreign currencies. As the central bank's reserves of foreign currency are depleted, the sustainability of the conversion promise is called into question, a run becomes possible. If domestic credit continues to grow, a run will become inevitable.

11. A corner on the money market occurs when an individual or group is short of cash and its creditor controls all the available cash. The borrower is cornered when the loan is called. Since the group to whom the cash must be delivered also controls the supply, that group names its price and strips the borrower of his or her wealth.

Chapter 19   THE U.S. BANK REGULATORY SYSTEM

1. A private clearinghouse requires its member banks to hold reserves to guarantee that net "due to" positions among the members can be converted to good funds. The clearinghouse does not guarantee that deposits can be converted to good funds. In fact, reserves are typically a small fraction of deposits. Therefore, when depositors have serious doubts about the solvency of their bank, they are not certain that they can cash their deposits in for good funds. This means that depositors must compete with each other for a quantity of good funds that is inadequate to ensure that everyone will get paid. This situation might create a crisis.

3. (a) The purpose of regulation is to protect the central bank from excessive risk-taking by banks that do not have to bear the consequences of failure. In this case, the central bank regulates the system by forcing banks to maintain short-term assets and liabilities. Presumably, the central bank does this to force banks to lend only for liquidity purposes. Since by principal-agent theory the necessity to deliver cash soon constrains management to invest in liquid projects, bank risk-taking should be reduced. It also prevents banks from getting entangled in conflict of interest situations. Long-term funding is provided by the securities markets, and the brokerage houses act as underwriters and dealers in this market.

If regulation were removed, banks would have more opportunities to attempt to take advantage of the government insurance system. They would buy securities but continue to fund with short-term deposits. (The reason for this is that the central bank does not guarantee deposits; it guarantees payments. Depositors prefer to lend short to banks to make sure they can get their money out in case of trouble by making a payment to another bank.) Banks would be willing to hold securities at a lower return than other investors because their risk is partially underwritten by the government. As a result, risk premiums decline, and more risky projects are funded.

(b) If a large number of banks became insolvent, the central bank would have to make good on their net "due to's." This means that the central bank would have to create a large quantity of reserves. The banks failed because the projects that they funded through the securities markets turned out to be worthless. Hence there would be an expansion of reserves at the same time as a decline in real income. The bank failures would be paid for through inflation.

This scenario implies that if the central bank guarantees the liquidity of the payments mechanism, it must prevent banks from cheating on the system. Otherwise, too many risky projects will be undertaken, and when they fail, inflation will ensue.

5. The "too big to fail" doctrine is not precisely defined. No one knows the minimum size of a bank covered by the "too big to fail" doctrine. Also, since the doctrine is really meant to preserve the liquidity of wholesale payments markets, a bank must not only be large, but also it must be an important player in the interbank market. This uncertainty has been enough to cause short-term liability holders to remove their funds from banks in danger of failing. To stop the outflow, the FDIC must make a firm announcement. It must be noted that in major bank failures, the Fed has provided credit until the FDIC has given a firm commitment.

7. Cease and desist orders cannot undo past mistakes. Thus, if a bank made commercial real estate loans in a booming market in 1986 and the market turns bad in 1990, a cease and desist order issued in 1990 cannot save the bank from its mistake. However, the order can place controls on bad management to stop the bank from making more mistakes. If this is done too late to save the bank, at least it might save the FDIC some money by preventing a bad situation from getting worse.

9. The "too big to fail" doctrine does not imply that stockholders will be bailed out if a bank goes under. These uninsured investors, therefore, have a stake in the solvency of the bank. However, the stockholders also have an incentive to encourage a bank to take increased risk—including operating at high leverage ratios and holding risky loans. The reason for this is that the stockholders do not have to pay insured liability holders a higher expected rate of return to put their money in a risky bank. After all, the liability holders are insured. Thus, the stockholders can pocket the relatively high spread between the expected return on the risky portfolio and the cost of insured liabilities. The stockholders have an incentive to hold very risky assets and fund as much of this portfolio with insured liabilities as they can get away with.

By forcing banks to operate at a maximum leverage ratio, the regulators attempt to limit shareholder gain from taking risk at the expense of government insurance.

The lower the leverage ratio, the lower is the percentage of the portfolio that is funded by insured liabilities. This reduces the government's liability, and it reduces the shareholders' expected gain from taking on risk. Shareholders must be compensated for the risk that they bear and therefore must be paid a higher expected return than insured liability holders. A decrease in leverage replaces low-cost insured liabilities with high-cost uninsured equity.

11. The usual argument for permitting banks to underwrite securities is that large corporate customers have abandoned banks because they have gained direct access to securities markets. For example, large corporate customers no longer need to use banks for short-term loans because they have commercial paper. They no longer need to hold demand deposits because they can "repo" securities into assets with overnight maturities. Thus banks have been forced to seek risky clients, thereby weakening the banking system and the government insurance system that supports it.

The contrary argument admits that corporate clients have abandoned banks but makes the point that they have left the banking system because markets have become more liquid. Hence the demand for banking services has declined relative to other financial services. The only real cure for this is shrinkage of the banking system because a bad business cannot be bailed out by a good one.

Proponents of liberalization argue that underwriting securities and commercial banking are complementary businesses because they both utilize the same information about the client. However, banks generally obtain information about clients that is unavailable to the public market. This places them in a potential conflict-of-interest situation. They have an incentive to use the private information to make a killing in the securities market.

13. The purpose of separating banking from commerce is to permit bankers to make judgments about extending credit uninhibited by conflicts of interest. If a bank were owned by an industrial company, it is feared that the parent company would force the bank to make the company a loan at a low interest rate if it is in trouble. Depositors are insured, so they are willing to supply funds to the bank at an interest rate that does not adequately reflect the risk.

Even if regulators prohibit bank loans to parents and affiliated companies (firewalls), the insurance system can still be put at risk when an industrial company owns a bank. For example, if a holding company takes a large loss from a nonbank affiliate, it may have inadequate income to cover its debt payments. To attempt to boost income, it could encourage its banking subsidiary to increase the risk of its portfolio. If this scheme fails, the holding company is no worse off than it would have been if it had failed to meet its debt payment. If it succeeds, it stays in business.

Those in favor of permitting industrial companies to own banks argue that regulators have the power to prevent banks from paying dividends to their parents. However, to make this effective protection, regulators must monitor the creditworthiness of industrial companies as well as of banks. Regulators must be able to spot parent incentives to increase the risk of bank subsidiaries before the solvency of the bank is threatened.

15. Product deregulation will improve the profit opportunities of large banks only if there are synergies with their current business. For example, if there are economies of scope between underwriting securities and commercial banking, there will be a gain from product deregulation. If there are economies of scope between providing insurance and engaging in consumer banking, product deregulation will be beneficial. If these economies of scope do not materialize, regulators will have compounded their problems with product deregulation because the variety of behavior they must police will increase.

Chapter 20   ROGUE BANKS: MORAL HAZARD IN THE BANKING SYSTEM

1. The assets of S&Ls in the early 1980s consisted predominantly of long-term fixed-rate mortgages. When instruments in competition with S&L deposits began to offer higher interest rates, depositors began to invest in these vehicles instead. For the S&Ls to raise interest rates on deposits was an unprofitable proposition. Income from assets would not be sufficient to finance the higher interest costs on liabilities. The S&L capital position would be depleted.

When the S&Ls were permitted to diversify their loan portfolio and take equity positions in real estate, they were already largely insolvent. To turn around their fortunes, many sought out high-risk ventures financed by attracting new deposits with offers of high-interest rates. If the gambles paid off, the high returns would restore their capital. Furthermore, in the short run, fees generated by high-risk investments would permit payment of dividends and high salaries for management.

3. (a) Rapid expansion. A rapid increase in deposits and, therefore, also in loans may signal excessive lending relative to capital. It may also signal the offering of interest rates on deposits that only high-risk lending can finance.

(b) Undiversified loans. When loans are heavily concentrated in one region or in one sector of the economy, the assets of the bank will be more volatile. Diversification across borrowers allows the troubles of one borrower to be separate with the troubles of other borrowers.

(c) Loans to borrowers connected with the bank. This is a signal of potential fraud. One possibility is that the bank is inflating its assets, but there are many other misdeeds that involve loans to cronies.

(d) Mismatch of maturity of assets and liabilities. This subjects the bank to interest-rate risk. If assets are long term and liabilities short, a rise in interest rates may wipe out capital. Even with floating interest rates on both assets and liabilities, an inversion of the yield curve can lead to losses for a bank with a mismatched portfolio. There are also other ways in which a portfolio can be mismatched. One example is lending in one currency and borrowing in another. In this case the bank is exposing itself to exchange-rate risk.

5. By definition, an insolvent bank has a negative capital position. In other words, the value of its liabilities exceeds the value of its assets. In a bailout, or a purchase and acquisition, the insurance fund need pay only this difference. Alternatively, if a payoff or deposit transfer is chosen, the insurance fund assumes the assets and attempts to liquidate them over time. The liabilities are immediately paid off. Since it may be some time before the asset liquidation process is completed, this option requires more money up front. Thus an illiquid insurance fund may opt against it.

7. Since adding to the budget deficit or raising taxes is politically unpopular the RTC is not operated to minimize cost in the long run but to minimize political damage (which is inherently a short-run consideration). The RTC finances itself by issuing bonds. The payment of interest on these bonds is made from payments by thrifts, revenue from liquidating assets, or from the Treasury. The last option has political ramifications, and the first is not sufficient. Therefore, the second option is relied upon more than is optimal. The sale of illiquid assets depresses their prices substantially, increasing the amount that the Treasury will eventually have to pay. Revenue from sales of thrift assets also permits RTC to stay within its debt ceiling of $50 billion.

Chapter 21   MONETARY POLICY AND ECONOMIC ACTIVITY

1. The Fed can place limits on the price level by tightening the money stock when prices tend to rise above the maximum and loosening the money supply when prices tend to fall below the minimum. This policy effectively limits long-term inflation to zero. Shorter-term inflation can be limited by making the zone in which the price level can fluctuate very narrow. If the real rate of interest is below the ceiling set on Treasury securities, controlling inflation in this way will also keep nominal yields below their ceiling. If real yields exceed the ceiling, however, the policy cannot be maintained. The only way to keep nominal yields below the ceiling is to have a steady deflation.

3. (a) Ignoring foreign reserves or deposits of other banks, the central banks assets will consist of Treasury securities, and the liabilities will include currency, and, perhaps, a deposit account of the Treasury that the central bank promises to convert to cash. Suppose the central bank has as assets 100 billion dollars of Treasury bills. Its liabilities are 80 billion dollars of currency and 20 billion dollars of Treasury deposits. Its balance sheet will be given by

Central Bank Balance Sheet

T-bills	100	Currency	80
		Deposit	20

Suppose the Treasury sells 20 billion additional dollars of debt to the central bank. The money is credited to the Treasury deposit account. The balance sheet will now be

Central Bank Balance Sheet After T-Bill Purchase

T-bills	120	Currency	80
		Deposit	40

Finally, as soon as the Treasury draws on the account, the balance sheet will be

Central Bank Balance Sheet

T-bills	120	Currency	120

The outcome of all the activity is an expanded central-bank balance sheet.

(b) Suppose the treasury sells $(M_1 - M_0)$ bonds in Period 1. M_0 denotes the money supply at the beginning of Period 1, and M_1 is the money supply at the beginning of Period 2. If M_0/P_0 is the real money supply before the bond sale, the government receives $(M_1 - M_0)/P_0$ goods for the bonds. This can be rewritten as

$$\frac{(M_1 - M_0)}{M_0} \frac{M_0}{P_0} = (Tax\ Rate)\ Tax\ Base$$

The first term is the percentage growth in the money stock, and the second term is real money holdings. The first term may be interpreted as the tax rate on the second term.

5. (a) If the bubonic plague were to kill one-half the population, this would shift the aggregate supply curve upward. Output falls, and the price level increases both in the short run and in the long run.

(b) If there is a technical change that increases total productivity but does not affect marginal productivity, profit-maximizing firms will increase output. This is an outward shift in aggregate supply. Aggregate demand is unchanged, real interest rates are unchanged, but the price level falls. The level of output increases.

(c) A fall in government defense expenditures will shift the *IS* curve in. The *LM* curve is unchanged, so the real interest rate falls. This increases the amount of investment, but not by enough to offset the fall in government expenditure. As a result of the fall in the *IS* curve, aggregate demand falls, but aggregate supply is unchanged, so the price level must fall.

7. Suppose money demand is given by

$$\frac{M}{P} = ay - br$$

where y denotes real income and r denotes the nominal interest rate. If the money supply is fixed, changes in money demand will translate directly into changes in prices. If the level of real income falls permanently, the real rate of interest will remain unchanged (assuming no change in productivity in the remaining fields), so the price level will have to increase.

9. Suppose that a particular rate of inflation is expected. To drive unemployment below its natural rate, the central bank will have to inflate at a faster rate than is expected. Once this occurs, inflation expectations will adjust to the new higher rate. In order to continue to have unemployment below the natural rate, a higher rate of inflation is required. This process will quickly translate into hyperinflation. If it is known that the government intends to keep unemployment below the natural rate, the economy will immediately begin to hyperinflate. Provided there is some maximum level of inflation, this will be the rate of inflation, and unemployment will remain at its natural rate.

11. On the basis of prewar data and data from the 1950s and 1960s, economists postulated that there was a tradeoff between inflation and unemployment. This relationship, that an increase in inflation will lead to a decrease in unemployment and vice versa, was called the Phillips curve. Economists embraced the theory and incorporated it into their predictions and policy prescriptions. Politicians tried to determine the best mix of fiscal and monetary policy to exploit the tradeoff.

In the 1970s, unemployment jumped, and inflation increased with it. It was realized that if the government tried to increase employment by increasing inflation, workers would foresee the decline in real wages and demand a contract that would protect them. As a result, firms would not find it worthwhile to increase hiring, and all that would occur would be inflation. An empirical relationship alone cannot form the basis for a prediction about the reaction of individuals to the incentives in their economic environment.

To make matters worse, the data are often not reliable. The postwar period was the heyday of the application of countercyclical policy. The fact that during the postwar period, aggregate fluctuations were smaller than they had been before World War II was considered evidence that fiscal and monetary policy can reduce the magnitude of the business cycle. Christina Romer, however, discovered that the data used to support this argument were constructed differently in the two periods. She reconstructed the later data in the style of the earlier data, and discovered that the difference between the size of aggregate fluctuations disappeared.

Glossary

acceleration clause: Clause in a loan agreement giving banks the right to demand full and immediate payment when they determine that a clause in the agreement has been violated.

account payable: The liability item of a company receiving a loan from its supplier. Hence, it is the corresponding liability item to an account receivable.

accounts receivable: The asset item recorded by a business when it sells goods to its customers on credit.

additional settlement obligation (ASO): A procedure undertaken when a bank fails to settle its net debit to CHIPS at the end of a day, which requires that the remaining banks provide the good funds to cover the obligation.

adjustment credit: Credit extended to depository institutions by the Fed to cover unseen events affecting an institution's ability to raise open market funds. It is meant to provide a temporary replacement for market funds.

advance: A loan made directly by the Federal Reserve to a bank collateralized by promissory notes held by the bank, usually U.S. Treasury securities.

aggregate demand: In Keynesian theories, for given values of the money stock, taxes, and government expenditure, aggregate demand is the locus of those combinations of the price level and output that are consistent with the clearing of the money market and with the equality of income with the sum of expenditures.

aggregate supply: In Keynesian theories, a plot of the output that producers are willing to supply at different values of the price level.

alternating standard: An alternative name for a bimetallic standard.

annuity: A contract that promises to pay the owner a fixed amount at specified intervals after a certain date.

arbitrage: The attempt to earn profits by buying a security in a low-priced market and immediately selling it in a high-priced market.

asset: The right to receive payment from another party.

automated clearinghouses (ACH): The institutional arrangements for electronic transfers of funds. They clear electronic payments in a manner analogous to the check-clearing functions of correspondent bank networks.

bailout or open bank assistance: Financial assistance by a deposit insurer to a troubled bank to prevent its failure and to permit its continued operation as an independent entity.

balance of payments: A system of accounts designed to measure a country's payments and receipts to and from other countries for sales of goods, services, and capital, and also for public and private transfers of funds.

balance sheet: A statement of a firm's assets, liabilities, and net worth.

Bank for International Settlements (BIS): An organization jointly owned by the central banks of the major industrial countries. Its purpose is to facilitate coordination of the policies of these central banks.

bank: An institution whose business it is to make loans and securities liquid for investors.

bank account: Another name for a bank deposit (*see* bank deposit).

bank deposit: A contract between a bank and an investor, stating that the investor has the right to withdraw the same amount of cash he or she originally placed in the bank plus accumulated interest at a fixed point in time.

bank examination: A periodic examination made by regulatory agencies to determine the soundness of a bank. These examinations are carried out on an unannounced schedule but are generally done at least every two years.

bank exposure: The amount the bank would lose if an individual or corporate borrower becomes completely unable to repay.

bank holding company (BHC): a legal entity that owns one or more banks.

Bank Insurance Fund (BIF): Deposit insurance fund operated by the FDIC for deposits in commercial banks.

Bank of United States: A bank, with over $200 million in deposits, that failed in December 1930, the largest bank failure during the Great Depression.

banker's acceptance: A short-term credit instrument. When an importer's bank lends money based on its letter of credit, the bank "accepts" its obligation under the letter of credit, and the letter of credit becomes a banker's acceptance.

Banking Holiday of 1933: The week from March 4, 1933, to March 11, 1933, during which the U.S. banking and financial system was closed by President

Roosevelt after massive bank runs and a speculative attack on official gold holdings.

banking panic: A liquidity crisis that occurs when a large segment of a banking system's creditors simultaneously demand delivery of more liquidity than the affected banks can supply.

banking system: A group of banks that depend on each other or on a central bank to provide liquidity.

bankruptcy: The legally declared condition of a company that cannot meet its obligations to creditors.

barter system: A system of trade in which a commodity, such as apples, is exchanged for another commodity, such as oranges.

bid-offer spread: A spread maintained by a market maker between the prices at which the market maker will buy or sell for his or her inventory. The market maker bids to buy at one price and offers to sell at another, hence maintaining a bid-offer spread.

bimetallic standard: A monetary standard in which the unit of account is defined in terms of both gold and silver coins containing precisely defined weights of metal.

block positioning: A process by which member dealers on an exchange originate large trades off the floor of the exchange for their institutional customers; that is, the member dealers are helping a large institutional investor to buy or sell a block of shares.

bond table: A table useful for computing the yield to maturity of a bond given the market price, coupon, and years to maturity of the bond. Alternatively, a bond table can be used to determine the price a purchaser of a bond would be willing to pay for the bond, given that the purchaser wishes to earn a certain yield to maturity.

bond: Securities issued to investors who have made a loan to a firm.

book entry system: A method for centrally registering the ownership and transfers of securities. The system may be one in which physical evidences of claims by security holders are physically held in a depository, with transfers being made by debiting and crediting accounts of security holders. Alternatively, as in the system for U.S. government securities, there may be no physical evidence of a claim on the government; rather, the Federal Reserve, acting as an agent for the government, simply maintains computer entries to keep track of the parties to whom it owes payments. Fedwire is used to transfer U.S. government securities from one owner's account to another.

book value: The acquisition cost of bank assets and the acquisition value of bank liabilities.

borrowed reserves: Central bank liability denominated in foreign currencies.

Bretton Woods system: The system of fixed exchange rates and payments adjustments that operated from the end of World War II through 1971.

bridge bank: A method for dealing with a failed bank in which a new bank owned by the FDIC is set up to operate the failed bank temporarily until its final disposition can be determined.

broker: An individual or firm that buys and sells securities for someone else.

business cycle: The simultaneous deviation from trend over periods of 3 to 5 years of macroeconomic variables such as industrial production, GNP, unemployment, and investment.

call money market: The market in which central reserve city banks invested their bankers' balances and which represented loans to securities brokers and dealers for the purchase of stocks and bonds.

call option: A right that guarantees the purchase of an underlying security at a prearranged price. If the right applies only on a particular date, the right is referred to as a European option. If the right applies on or before a particular date, the option is called an American option.

cap: A limit on the size of the net intraday "due to" that one bank can have with another. The term is shorthand for "sender net debit cap."

capital account: A subaccount in the balance of payments that measures payments and receipts for trade in assets: cash, financial assets, and directly owned real assets such as land, buildings, or machinery.

capital gain: The increase in an asset's value above its purchase price.

capital loss: A fall in the market value of an asset from the price an investor paid for it.

capitalizing: Capitalizing an income stream is the process of discounting the income stream at a given interest rate.

capital market: The market for all financial securities collectively.

capital value: The price of an asset determined by capitalizing its income stream.

cash: The physical representation of the unit of account.

cash items in the process of collection: The situation in which a bank accepts a liability item, such as a deposit in the form of a check, and in which it has not yet actually collected on the funds to be deposited; the bank thus has an asset called a cash item in the process of collection, which is equal in value to the funds not yet collected.

cashier's check: A check that is the liability of the payor's bank rather than the payor. It is used for large transactions to ensure that the payee will be paid.

CD/CP crisis: A settlement crisis in which payees demand that payors deliver commercial paper or CDs. It is a less severe crisis than a DD (demand deposit) crisis.

cease and desist orders: Orders issued by regulatory agencies to stop a depository institution from engaging in unsound banking practices. These orders place severe constraints on what bank management can do without the permission of the regulatory agency.

central bank: A bank that supplies liquid assets to the individual banks tied to it. In the major industrial countries, central banks are government owned.

central reserve cities: The cities of New York and Chicago. Historically, correspondent bank balances tended to pile up in these cities because they were focal points of trade and industry. Under the National Banking Act of 1864, New

York and Chicago were called central reserve cities, and national banks in them had to hold large amounts of required reserves.

certificate of deposit (CD): A bank account that has an original maturity date of at least 2 days; it is also known as a time deposit.

check: The note by which households and businesses typically pay bills; they draft a note, a check, which indicates that they wish to withdraw funds from their transaction account and transfer those funds to the transaction account of the payee.

Chicago Mercantile Exchange Clearinghouse (CMECH): Clearinghouse for options and futures traded on the Chicago Mercantile Exchange. The CMECH guarantees both sides of every future contract.

CHIPS: The Clearing House Inter-Bank Payments System, which is a private clearing network among major international banks. It is the primary international system for clearing large dollar payments.

clearing agent: A bank in which both the payee bank and the payor bank have accounts so that the payor bank can pay the payee bank directly.

clearing balances: Deposits regularly held at the Federal Reserve by some banks in excess of required reserves. The Fed pays interest approximately equal to the fed funds rate for such deposits.

clearinghouse: A netting arrangement for receipts and payments among banks or securities dealers.

collateral: An asset held by a borrower that a lender can seize if the borrower should default on a loan.

commercial and industrial loans (C&I loans): Bank loans to business enterprises.

commercial paper: Short-term marketable debt issued by corporations.

commitments to lend: Agreements to lend in which "material change" conditions are specified in detail. If a bank backs out of a commitment to lend, it will usually find itself in a lawsuit to defend its actions.

compensating balance: Demand deposits that the borrower must hold with the bank. The loan agreement generally specifies what the level of these balances must be. Banks also charge for noncredit services through required demand deposit balances.

Comptroller of the Currency: Official in the U.S. Treasury who is responsible for regulating and examining the financial condition of national banks.

computation period: A two-week period for computing required reserves. Reserves required against transaction deposits are computed against the average end-of-day transaction deposits at the bank during this two-week period, which ends two days before the end of the reserve maintenance period.

confidence problem: A situation that occurred in the late 1960s, when the rise in foreign central bank dollar claims relative to their gold backing in the hands of U.S. authorities generated a well-justified lack of confidence in the ability of the U.S. to make good on its promise to convert the dollar claims to gold.

conflict of interest: A situation created when a person or corporation is in a position to benefit from a decision (or advice) it may make for another party.

consol: A bond issue used by governments to consolidated diverse debt instruments into a standard security. A standard of British finance in the nineteenth century, consols assumed the form of bonds callable at par paying low-coupon yields of 2.5 or 3 percent. Since market yields were generally higher than the coupon yields, it was unlikely that the bonds would ever be called and paid off. For this reason, they were often considered perpetuities.

contagion of fear: The role of crowd behavior in triggering bank runs or panics. Depositors simultaneously awaken with a belief that all other depositors are about to withdraw their funds from banks. Among individual depositors, this leads to a fear that their deposits will be lost or at least frozen if they do not immediately run to the bank and convert their deposits to cash. Given that they believe that all other depositors are also about to run the bank, it is rational for each individual depositor to run the bank; and this belief ratifies the original belief.

continuous settlement: The system in which the rules of a payments system require that each payment message for a given amount be physically accompanied by an identical amount of actual reserves.

cornering the market: A situation in which one person has contracts obliging others to deliver a certain commodity or security on call, yet the person simultaneously controls the entire available supply of the commodity or security.

cost of carry: The cost of acquiring the underlying asset in a futures contract and holding it through expiration of the contract.

coupon bond: A bond that promises the holder a fixed, periodic payment called a coupon.

coupon yield: The annual coupon payment promised by a bond divided by the bond's face or par value.

covariance with a portfolio: The expected value of the deviation of each asset's return from its own mean multiplied by the deviation of the portfolio's return from its mean.

covered interest parity: An arbitrage relation specifying that the interest rate on domestically denominated securities must equal the interest rate on foreign-denominated loans of comparable default risk and maturity plus the percentage by which the forward exchange rate exceeds the spot exchange rate.

Crash of 1929: The most famous of U.S. stock market collapses. At its peak at the beginning of September 1929, the Dow Jones Industrial Average was 381. It reached a low of 230 on October 29, 1929, a fall of about 40 percent in two months.

Crash of 1987: A major worldwide collapse in stock market prices on October 19 and 20, 1987. On October 19 alone, the S&P 500 index fell from 283 to 220.

credit risk: The risk that borrowers may not be able to meet their contractual obligations to the bank.

credit scoring: When credit quality is viewed as a statistical problem, the evaluation method is called credit scoring.

credit union: A consumer bank whose customers jointly own the bank. The bank's "members" often have something in common, such as belonging to the same labor union or working for the same employer.

Crime of '73: Populist reference to a law passed in 1873 governing coinage in the United States. Free coinage of silver dollars was terminated, and their legal tender status was withdrawn. This action was effectively an abandonment of the bimetallic standard.

currency option bond: Bonds that give the debtor the option of paying in one of two currencies.

currency swap: A swap in which streams of interest payments from two securities denominated in different currencies are exchanged.

current account: A record of the dollar value of goods and services purchased from foreigners less how much foreigners purchase from Americans. It also includes how much investment income Americans receive from foreigners (and vice versa), as well as net gifts and grants.

current yield: The annual coupon payment on a bond divided by the bond's current market price.

daylight overdraft: A situation in which a bank's payment orders during the day drive its deposit account at the Federal Reserve below zero.

DD crisis: A settlement crisis in which payees demand that payors deliver demand deposits.

dealer: An individual or firm that buys and sells securities for its own account.

debit card: A card presented by the payor at the point of sale that permits the payee to draw funds directly from the payor's bank account to cover the amount of a purchase.

defaults (at clearinghouses): A situation in which a member of a clearinghouse cannot cover its net "due to" position.

Deferred Credit Items: A liability category on the Federal Reserve's balance sheet indicating that banks have presented the Federal Reserve with checks for clearing but that the Fed has not yet credited the deposit accounts of the banks with the amount of the checks.

demand deposit: The most liquid form of bank deposit (*see* bank deposit). It is payable in cash at the demand of the depositor.

deposit transfer: A method for dealing with a failed bank in which the FDIC makes a cash payment to another institution to accept responsibility for deposit liabilities. The remainder of the bank is liquidated by the FDIC.

Depository Institution Deregulation and Monetary Control Act of 1980 (DIDMCA): The act under which the DIDMCA deregulated depository institutions by gradually terminating regulatory ceilings on deposit interest rates.

depreciation: The loss in value suffered by business and industrial equipment and structures, from the wear and tear of use. The government recognizes this as a tax-deductible business expense.

deviation: The difference in the return of a particular security from its expected value.

discount: An outright Federal Reserve purchase from a bank of a promissory note made by a private borrower or of a U.S. Treasury or agency security.

discount loans: Loans that promise to pay a given amount at maturity but nothing before maturity; also known as zero-coupon loans.

discount rate: Interest rate set by the Federal Reserve on discounts or advances to member banks.

discount window: Credit line offered by the Federal Reserve to banks. Banks may either discount securities—that is, sell them directly to the Federal Reserve—or obtain advances collateralized by their security holdings.

discounting: The process of calculating present value by dividing, for example, next year's value by one plus the interest rate. That is, it is the process of reducing the value of a future payment to account for the time value of money.

diversification: The strategy of holding securities from many firms to reduce the risk that a decline in the fortunes of any one firm will significantly reduce the value of a portfolio.

dividends: Payments from corporate profits distributed as cash to shareholders.

domestic credit: Central bank assets denominated in domestic currency.

draft: An order for the payor's bank to pay the payee the amount specified on the check from the payor's account.

"due from": A "due from" balance represents a payment owed to one bank by another. The bank owed money has an asset, a "due from." On end-of-day balance sheets, a "due from" usually takes the form of a deposit held at another bank.

duration matching: The holding of assets and liabilities whose cash flows are perfectly synchronized.

economies of scope: Gains achieved by performing two or more businesses within the same organization.

escrow account: An account that one party holds for the sole benefit of another.

Eurobond: A bond that is sold and trades outside its home country.

Eurocurrency securities: Securities issued outside the issuer's home country.

Eurodollar deposit: A liability of a bank denominated in dollars when the bank is situated outside the United States.

Eurodollar market: The large dollar market outside the United States, which is centered in London.

European Central Bank (ECB): A central bank proposed in draft statutes of the European Economic Community that will circulate its own currency and regulate and coordinate the monetary operations of each country's national central bank.

European Monetary System (EMS): The system of target zones whereby European currencies are kept in close alignment.

excess reserves: The amount by which a bank's actual reserves exceed its desired reserves. Also, the amount by which a bank's actual reserves exceed its required reserves.

exchange rate: Price of one currency in terms of another currency.

exchange rate overshooting: The change that occurs if money markets are disturbed when price levels adjust sluggishly; there is an initial change in the spot exchange rate that is greater than its ultimate change.

expectations theory of the term structure: A hypothesis that the yield to maturity on n-period loans is simply the average of the expected yields on n one-period loans occurring in sequence during the life of the n-period loan.

expected return (ER): The return on each event multiplied by the probability that the event will occur and summed over all possible events. Formally, the expected return is

$$ER_A = P_1 R_1 + P_2 R_2$$

extended credit: The credit provided by the Fed to prevent a run on an insolvent bank.

factoring: The purchasing by finance companies of the accounts receivable outright. Alternatively, they can extend credit based on accounts receivable as collateral.

fed funds desk: A bank department established to manage the bank's deposits at the Fed. The purpose of the fed funds desk is to minimize the cost of a given level of access to the liquidity of the banking system.

fed funds lines: Lines that represent a contract giving a bank the right to borrow a specified amount in the fed funds market; a bank participating in the market will pay for fed funds lines to avoid incurring the shadow price at the Fed.

fed funds market: The interbank loan market for bank deposits at the Federal Reserve.

Federal Deposit Insurance Corporation (FDIC): Federal agency that insures deposits in commercial and savings banks and in S&Ls. The FDIC operates two separate insurance funds, BIF for commercial banks and SAIF for S&Ls. It also manages the Resolution Trust Corporation.

Federal Home Loan Banks (FHLB): The main regulator of the S&Ls until 1989. Since then, it has been under the control of the Office of Thrift Supervision. It is also the central supplier of credit to the S&Ls. Established in 1932, the FHLB is a federal agency organized like the Fed into twelve district banks spread across the United States. Its purpose is to supply liquidity to S&Ls that are experiencing heavy savings withdrawals.

Federal Reserve Float: The difference between the Items in the Process of Collection and Deferred Credit Items on the Federal Reserve's balance sheet.

Federal Reserve System: The central bank of the United States, often called the Fed.

Federal Savings and Loan Insurance Corporation (FSLIC): The former deposit insurer for S&Ls, dissolved in 1989.

Fedwire: The interbank electronic payment system operated by the Federal Reserve for making large domestic U.S. dollar payments.

fiat currency: A currency that is not backed by promises of convertibility into commodities. Fiat currency circulates through the exercise of the legal power or fiat of the government.

Financial Institutions Reform, Recovery, and Enforcement Act (FIRREA): A 1989 act that reformed the regulatory structure of S&Ls and provided funding for the closing or restructuring of insolvent S&Ls.

financial innovation: The process of creating new financial instruments to reduce reserves to the desired level.

financial intermediary: A firm that buys liabilities or equities issued by many firms and reissues new liabilities to investors based on the pool of financial assets that it has purchased.

financial markets: Another name for securities markets (*see* securities markets).

firewall: The separation of a bank from the other subsidiaries of a holding company.

Fisher equation: The equality of a nominal yield with the expected real yield and the expected rate of inflation.

fixed exchange rates: An exchange rate regime in which central banks intervene to peg an exchange rate at a given level.

floating exchange rates: A regime in which central banks or exchange authorities do not intervene in exchange markets explicitly to fix or to control the movement of exchange rates.

float: The non-interest-bearing loan the payor obtains from the payee during the check clearing process.

foreign reserves: Central bank assets denominated in foreign currencies.

free coinage: A system in which a mint guarantees that if a given metal is delivered to it, the mint in exchange will deliver coins containing the same weight of the metal at no charge.

futures market: An organized market in which a party can contract to buy something at a fixed price for delivery at a future date.

gains from diversification: The benefit of holding more than one kind of security. Holding a portfolio of securities A and B is less risky than holding either A or B separately as long as the returns on securities A and B are only partially correlated.

Garn-St Germain Act of 1982: An act that liberalized the type of deposits that S&Ls could offer, thereby making it easier for S&Ls to attract funds. The act also expanded the range of assets that S&Ls could hold, thereby making it easier for them to take greater risks.

gold clause cases: A series of rulings in 1935 in which the U.S. Supreme Court explicitly upheld the abrogation by the United States government of contractual clauses calling for payment of obligations in gold dollars for private contracts and effectively upheld the abrogation for government bonds.

gold option: An option giving its holder the right to purchase one unit of gold in exchange for one unit of silver from the person who sold the option.

gold standard: A monetary standard in which the unit of account is defined as coins containing a specific weight of gold.

good funds: Assets that banks are always willing to receive from other banks to represent final payment of dollar claims. Currency and especially deposits at the Federal Reserve constitute good funds in the United States.

goodwill: An asset that develops when one company acquires another and pays more for it than the book value of its shares.

Great Depression: The period from 1929 to 1933 in the United States marked by large declines in real output and the price level and extremely high levels of unemployment. The period is also notable for a collapse of the stock market and a sequence of banking panics that led to the closure of thousands of banks.

Gresham's Law: The principle that "bad money" drives out "good money." Gresham's Law operates when two different forms of legal tender are circulated simultaneously and one—the good money—has a market value that exceeds its officially denominated face value. A strict enforcement of legal tender laws will drive the good money out of circulation.

gridlock: A situation in which a payments system holds insufficient reserves to effect settlement of all debits outstanding.

group insurance contract: Life insurance contracts that cover a group of people, such as employees in a large company.

hedger: In a futures market, an investor who holds a position in the underlying asset that is the opposite of its futures position.

holding period yield: Annualized yield of a security computed over the actual period that the security is held and including both interest payments and capital gains.

home equity loans: Bank loans secured by a homeowner's equity in the house. These loans are junior to the original mortgage. If the borrower should default on payments and the house must be sold to pay off the loan, the original mortgage gets paid off first.

hyperinflation: An extreme rate of increase in a country's price level over an extended period of time. Notable examples are the German hyperinflation of 1922 to 1923 and the Hungarian hyperinflation of 1946.

immediacy: Characteristic of a liquid market in which an investor who holds a security can confidently expect to sell or buy a large amount of the security without materially affecting its price.

in the money: A situation in which the value of the underlying security in a call option exceeds the exercise price; alternatively, the situation in which the value of the underlying security in a put option is less than the exercise price.

income statement: A detailed breakdown of a firm's revenues and expenses. It represents change in a firm's condition over a period of time, such as a year.

inflation: A general increase in the prices of all goods and services.

inflation rate: The annual percentage rate of change of the general nominal level of prices, which is typically measured as the percentage change in a price index like the Consumer Price Index, the Producer Price Index, or the GNP Deflator.

inflation tax: The real value of government revenues from inflationary money expansion.

informationless or noise trading: Trading strategies in which stock sales or purchases are triggered purely on the basis of observable stock prices.

initial margin: The amount of collateral required when a position in options, futures, or securities is first established.

insurance principle: The principle that as the number of securities with zero covariance in a portfolio increases, each individual security's weight can move closer to zero, and the variance of the portfolio can approach zero.

insurance reserves: Insurance reserves are liabilities of financial institutions that provide life insurance. They are the liability an insurance company has accumulated to pay off its expected death claims.

interest rate: The percentage by which funds loaned now are marked up when they are repaid in the future. An interest rate represents the price of funds today relative to funds tomorrow.

interest rate gap: The magnitude of the maturity mismatch between assets and liabilities for any one time period.

interest-rate risk: The risk created by the spread between asset maturities and liability maturities.

interest-rate swap: A swap in which interest payments from different types of nominal securities denominated in the same currency are exchanged.

International Monetary Fund (IMF): An international institution established by the Bretton Woods agreement to provide a means of cooperative financing of temporary reserve outflows and of cooperative exchange rate realignments when countries experience chronic reserve outflows or inflows.

investment risk: The risk that cash flow from a security may have to be reinvested at a lower return than that available on the original security.

IS curve: In Keynesian theories, a locus of pairs of output and interest rates for which aggregate demand for output equals the amount of output.

Items in the Process of Collection: An asset category on the Federal Reserve's balance sheet to offset Deferred Credit Items. With this asset category, the Federal Reserve indicates its claim for payment against banks on which checks in process of collection are drawn.

junk bonds: High-risk, high-yield debt securities; they are called junk because of the presumed high risk of the companies that issue them.

Keynesianism: A theory of business cycles that favors active monetary and fiscal policy to counter the perceived negative impacts of cycles.

lead manager: The underwriter who originally assembles a deal.

legal tender: The item whose delivery legally satisfies contracts calling for payment in the unit of account; cash.

legal tender cases: A series of U.S. Supreme Court rulings in the 1870s that upheld the validity of gold clauses—that is, contractual clauses which stated that bonds had to be repaid in U.S. gold coins of a particular gold content or their equivalent value.

lender of last resort: As the only creator of good funds, the central bank assumes the responsibility of lending to the banking system in times of liquidity crisis.

lessee: The party holding a lease.

lessor: The party that lets (rents out) property under a lease.

letter of credit: A letter of credit is a guarantee by an importer's bank that the importer will faithfully pay its bill to the exporter from whom it is purchasing the imported goods.

leverage: The use of credit, or borrowing, to build up a company's resources.

leveraged buyout: A transaction in which a group of investors, often the management of the firm itself, borrows money to purchase shares from the firm's stockholders.

liability: An obligation to pay a specific sum to another party.

LIBOR (London Interbank Offer Rate): A yield (on loans) in a given currency and at a maturity calculated from the average of yields offered by a group of large banks in London.

lines of credit: The weakest form of an agreement to lend, which states that a corporation (or any other borrower) has access to a certain amount of bank funds for a specified period of time. The line can be canceled by the bank at any time. The conditions under which the line will be canceled are specified in a general way by "material change" clauses, which state that if the financial condition of the borrower should change, the line will be canceled.

liquid market: A market in which an individual transaction does not disrupt the continuity of market prices.

liquid security: A security that maintains its value in terms of the unit of account.

liquidity: The quality of having a well-known and stable market value relative to the unit of account.

liquidity event: Massive, though temporary, increases in the demand for the delivery of good funds across a wide range of markets.

listed securities: Securities of companies that have qualified to trade on organized securities exchanges.

LM curve: A curve that depicts the combinations of interest rates and income associated with equilibrium in money markets.

loan: A mechanism for a person accumulating dollars for later use to sell them to someone who wants to use them now.

loan loss reserve: The balance sheet item in which banks set aside reserves to cover possible defaults on loans. The loan loss reserve is a contra item on the asset side of the balance sheet.

loans secured by real estate: Loans collateralized by real estate.

loans to carry securities: Bank accounting category used when a market maker or dealer borrows from the bank to support a securities inventory. These loans help provide the financing that market makers and dealers need to buy securities to maintain liquid markets.

long position: A situation in which a portfolio has a positive quantity of a security or is owed the security. An investor has a long position in a security when he or she would make a profit if the security were to increase in price.

loss provision: The bank's contribution to a reserve to cover losses resulting from defaults on loans. It is an item on the income statement.

M1: A money supply definition that sums assets used as media of exchange; it includes currency in circulation, checkable deposits, and travelers checks.

M2: The sum of M1 and assets that are close substitutes for checkable deposits including savings accounts, small time deposits, and money market mutual funds.

maintenance margin: The minimum amount of margin required in an account. If margin falls to this level, a margin call is triggered.

margin call: A demand for the deposit of additional collateral to secure a position in futures, options, or securities.

margin requirements (futures and options): Collateral required to assure performance by parties to futures contracts, writers of options, and short sellers of stock.

margin requirement (securities): The requirement that a certain percentage of the market value of a security must be financed with cash. The purpose is to prevent defaults on loans collateralized by securities. Currently, an investor in the United States can borrow only up to 50 percent of the market value of his or her security.

market risk: The risk in a security that is correlated with movements in the economy as a whole. The risk cannot be diversified away by holding securities of other firms operating in the same economy.

marking-to-market: In this process, each futures contract outstanding on an exchange is repriced by the exchange clearinghouse at the end of each day according to the futures price established in the day's trading.

match-funding: The process of funding assets with liabilities that have similar repricing characteristics; banks use match-funding to reduce their interest rate gaps.

maturity date: The date when the principal of a loan is due and payable, after which the borrower makes no further contractual payments.

mean return: *See* expected return.

median: The value such that half the numbers on a list are above this value and half are below it.

medium of exchange: An object or mechanism that is useful in facilitating transactions of goods, services, and assets.

Merchandise Trade Account: A subaccount in the current account that encompasses payments and receipts for trade in agricultural and manufactured products.

Mississippi Bubble: The French speculation of 1719–20 that is considered one of the most famous examples of a speculative mania. It is a better example of what happens when a central bank, in this case John Law's Banque Royale, attempts to peg the value of a stock at a level well above its fundamental value than it is an example of a speculative mania.

Modigliani-Miller Theorem: The proposition that the financing costs of an individual firm are independent of its leverage ratio. It is named for the two economists who first presented the arbitrage argument using the equal access assumption.

monetarism: A belief that money supply disturbances are major sources of real fluctuations and that monetary policy should aim at minimizing such disturbances.

monetary base: Deposits by banks at the Federal Reserve plus currency that is in circulation.

Monetary Control Act of 1980: An act making reserve requirements universal on all transaction accounts issued by commercial banks, thrifts, and credit unions.

monetary standard: A set of rules that defines the item serving as the physical manifestation of the unit of account and determines how money is created.

money: An asset that promises to maintain its value in terms of the unit of account and therefore becomes generally acceptable in market transactions.

money center banks: Large banks in New York, and sometimes in Chicago and California. This title was acquired partly because of their role as market makers in currencies and government securities.

money demand: A functional relationship that specifies the real quantity of money desired at given levels of interest rates, real incomes, and real wealth.

money laundering: Use of the banking system to disguise cash earned in illegal activities as legally acquired assets or to move illegally acquired cash from one location to another.

money market instruments: Short-term debt instruments issued by high-quality borrowers; a major type of liquid assets for investors.

money market mutual funds: Mutual funds that hold only short-term money market instruments such as T-bills that are guaranteed to pay off in a short time.

money multiplier: The ratio of a particular money supply definition such as $M1$ or $M2$ to the monetary base.

money trust: A suspected trust in the money and bond markets consisting of important New York commercial and investment banks in the late 1800s and early 1900s; investigated in the Pujo hearings of the U.S. House of Representatives in 1912.

moral hazard: Possibility that the existence of insurance will change the insured's behavior to increase the probability that the insured event will occur.

mortgage banker: Anyone involved in the origination or servicing of a mortgage loan.

multiple expansion of bank deposits: Process whereby banks choose their supply of deposits so that required reserve holdings equal the amount of reserves that banks want to hold.

municipal bonds: Bonds issued by state and local governments in the United States. They are exempt from federal income taxes.

mutual funds: Funds run by investment companies that invest shareholder money in pools of securities of many different companies or governments.

National Association of Securities Dealers Automated Quote System (NAS-DAQ): A nationwide electronic dealer market that lists over-the-counter stocks as well as many of the stocks traded on the New York Stock Exchange and other exchanges.

national banks: Banks chartered by the federal government; their powers are determined by federal law.

negotiable certificate of deposit (CD): A CD that investors can sell to third parties as if it were a bond.

net credit position: A position value for a bank's cumulated net payments—that is, the difference between its total receipts and total payments—in a day's payment operations.

net interest margin: The difference between the gross interest income line and the gross interest expense line.

net reserves: Central bank foreign reserves minus borrowed foreign reserves.

netting: The act of subtracting the amount that Bank A owes to other banks from the amount that Bank A is owed. The difference will be settled with a transfer of cash or good funds. Netting occurs among many different kinds of financial institutions.

New York Stock Exchange (NYSE): The major stock exchange in the United States, located in New York, where most of the equities of major American corporations are traded.

nominal interest rate: The percentage yield or payoff on a security denominated in terms of the unit of account or money.

nontransaction account: A bank deposit from which third party payments are severely restricted or prohibited.

notional principal amount: In an interest rate swap, the principal upon which the amount of cash to be swapped is based.

off-balance sheet items: A commitment by a bank to provide a loan or make a payment that has not yet been funded. Therefore, it does not show up on the bank's balance sheet.

Office of Thrift Supervision (OTS): Established by the FIRRE Act of 1989, the OTS, an office of the U.S. Treasury, that is now the primary regulator of federal and state S&Ls and their holding companies.

open interest parity: A speculative relation specifying that the interest rate on domestically denominated securities equals the interest rate on foreign denominated loans of comparable default risk and maturity plus the percentage by which the exchange rate is expected to depreciate.

open market operation: A process in which the Federal Reserve approaches a securities dealer to sell or buy securities for its own account at market prices.

orderly financial markets: One of the basic goals of central bank policy, that is, to maintain the depth, breadth, and resiliency of financial markets. Central banks aim rather vaguely at assuring price continuity and narrow bid-ask spreads to prevent unnecessary losses arising purely from liquidity problems.

ordinary insurance contract: Life insurance contracts purchased by individuals for a specified period of time, ranging from five years to life.

out of the money: The situation in which the value of the underlying security in a call option is less than the exercise price; alternatively, the situation in which the value of the underlying security in a put option exceeds the exercise price.

overdraft: A payment from an account in excess of the amount on deposit in that account.

owner's equity: That portion of a house financed with savings.

Panic of 1907: A major financial crisis and banking panic in which J. P. Morgan controlled and allocated all available reserves in the banking system. This episode led to the formation of the Federal Reserve in 1913.

par value: The face value of a security. In the case of a bond, this is generally the amount that will be delivered in the final payment by the debtor after subtracting the final coupon payment due.

payee: The seller of a product or service who will receive payment.

payoff: A method for dealing with a failed bank in which the insured depositors are paid and the bank is liquidated.

payor: The purchaser of a product or service who will make a payment.

pension reserves: Liabilities of financial institutions that provide pensions. They are the present value of the pension income that a pension fund promises to pay to individual employees at their retirement.

perfect substitutes: A situation in which an investor is indifferent between holding either of two financial assets when the two are selling for the same price.

periodic net settlement: A process in which a payment system engages in net settlement of gross payments and receipts at periodic intervals such as at the end of the business day.

perpetuity: A security that promises a fixed annual payment forever.

personal loans: Loans typically made to individuals to purchase a car, finance an education, make home improvements, and so on.

Phillips curve: The negative relation between wage changes and unemployment observed in pre-World War II data.

portfolio insurance: A method for placing a floor value on a portfolio by creating a synthetic put through dynamic hedging.

present value: Today's value of a sum of money payable in the future.

price level: The price of a general basket of goods in terms of the unit of account. Index numbers such as the consumer price index or the GNP deflator generally are used to represent the price level.

prime rate: A base interest rate set by banks for lending to business customers.

principal: The face value of a bond, which is paid in one lump sum at maturity.

principal-agent problem: A situation that arises whenever one individual acts on behalf of another. The individual who acts on another's behalf (the agent) may act in his or her own interests rather than in the interests of the other party (the principal).

private placements: Bonds that are not issued publicly, nor sold to the general public after issuance, because they are not registered with the Securities and Exchange Commission.

profit: The income of a firm after all expenses, such as wages for labor, material costs, and so forth, have been paid.

program trader: Traders in stock markets who continuously track the price of stock indexes in the stock market relative to the price in the futures market. If these two prices do not line up in an appropriate manner, these traders take advantage of arbitrage opportunities.

purchase and assumption (P&A): A method for dealing with a failed bank in which another institution purchases some of the bank's assets and assumes the deposit liabilities.

purchasing power parity: An arbitrage relation claiming that if all goods in the consumption baskets of two countries are identical and freely tradeable and if transport costs are minimal, trade should drive their relative price to one.

put option: A right that guarantees the sale of an underlying security at a prearranged price.

put-call parity: An arbitrage condition in which the value of a call option equals the value of a portfolio consisting of one unit of the underlying security, one put option with the same exercise date and exercise price as the call option, and a bank debt in the amount of the exercise price.

rational expectations: The assumption that participants in an economy will use all available information to form their expectations.

reoffering yield: In investment banking parlance, the expected yield of the ultimate investor. A higher offer price implies a lower reoffering yield.

real business cycles theory: A belief that forces arising in the real sectors of the economy drive business cycles and that monetary forces play a small role and indeed are themselves driven by these other forces.

real exchange rate: Units of a foreign consumption basket that exchange for a unit of a domestic consumption basket.

real interest rate: The percentage yield or payoff on a security denominated in terms of goods.

refinancing: The process of taking out a new mortgage at a lower rate than the original mortgage. If interest rates should fall, many mortgage holders will pay off mortgages written at high rates by refinancing.

remote dispersal and lock box system: Procedures to slow and to speed check clearing. Float encourages attempts by payors to slow the process of check clearing and by payees to speed the process of check clearing. Remote dispersal is used by payors and lock boxes are used by payees for this purpose.

repricing schedule: A calculation of the maturity schedules of all assets and liabilities.

repurchase agreements: A means of short-term financing of an asset that consists of a sale of a security, usually a Treasury security, together with a promise to repurchase the security at some specific time in the future at a prearranged higher price.

reserve maintenance period: Two-week period during which the average of the daily reserves held by banks must be greater than or equal to required reserves.

reserve requirement: A rule that requires banks to hold vault cash or deposits at the Federal Reserve equal to a certain percentage of their deposits.

Resolution Trust Corporation (RTC): Corporation established under the FIRRE Act to replace the FSLIC as the conservator and receiver of depository institutions that fail through 1992. The FDIC is the manager of the RTC.

return: The income generated by an asset.

reverse repurchase agreement: The purchase of a security with an agreement to sell later for a given price.

risk averse: Term applied to investors who require a higher expected rate of return to hold a security that has an uncertain payoff than they do to hold a security paying a certain return.

risk neutral: Term applied to investors who are indifferent among securities that have the same expected payoff.

rogue banks: Insolvent banks that acquire risky assets knowing that losses will be at the expense of the deposit insurer.

Savings Association Insurance Fund (SAIF): Separate insurance fund established by the FDIC for S&Ls (note ironic acronym). SAIF will be responsible for managing the closing of thrifts that fail after 1992.

savings deposits: Deposits in banks and thrifts that can be converted to cash at any time. Such claims cannot be transferred by check, so they cannot be used directly for transactions.

seasonal credit: Federal Reserve credit extended to small country banks that do not have access to national money markets to finance agricultural borrowing during the growing season.

securities: Marketable loans and stocks that are sold publicly.

securities affiliate: A subsidiary of a bank holding company engaged in underwriting and dealing in securities.

securities exchange: An organized market in which financial securities are bought and sold in an orderly manner.

securities markets: Markets in which securities are bought and sold.

securities portfolio: A group of securities held by one investor.

sender net debit cap: A device to control the amount of credit risk that the Fed assumes for individual users of CHIPS and Fedwire; the Fed limits the size of a bank's overdraft on these two systems. Known as a participant's sender net debit cap, this limit depends on a bank's capital. A participant that reaches the overdraft limit is not permitted to make further payments until incoming receipts reduce the overdraft.

service account: A subaccount in the current account that includes payments and receipts for direct foreign purchases of domestic labor, earnings on capital previously exported abroad but owned by domestic residents, insurance payments, and payments for shipping.

setoff: A clause in a loan agreement giving the lender the right to seize the debtor's assets in the lender's possession in the event of default.

settlement finality: Characteristic of a payments system if the clearinghouse guarantees that net "due from" positions will be covered by the delivery of reserves at settlement.

shadow price: An unstated price that is higher than the stated price. The Fed's shadow price for borrowing from the discount window exceeds the discount rate, which is the stated price.

short position: A situation in which a portfolio has a negative quantity of a security or owes the security. A short position is the opposite of a long position: The investor gains if the price of the security should fall.

specialist: Member of a stock exchange who is designated to "make a market" in the securities assigned to him or her.

speculative attack: A situation in which holders of domestically denominated assets speculating on an end of a fixed exchange rate regime suddenly exchange the assets with the central bank or exchange rate authority for foreign reserves. This action greatly reduces official holdings of foreign reserves and may coincide with the collapse of the fixed exchange rate.

speculator: A futures market classification for a trader who does not have a position in the underlying asset that balances its futures position.

standard deviation: The positive square root of the variance, which is used as a measure of risk.

standard of deferred payment: A standard unit in which contractual prices for payment in the future can be written; it is usually the unit of account.

standby letters of credit: Irrevocable commitments to lend.

state banks: Banks chartered by the various states. Their powers are determined by state law, subject to certain federal restrictions if they are insured by the FDIC. The states also assume responsibility for examining the financial condition of these institutions, along with the FDIC if they are insured.

static hedging: Hedging a stock or a basket of stocks with a put that exists on the market.

stock index: Weighted average of the prices of a basket of stocks divided by the value of the basket in some base year.

stock index futures: Futures contract whose payoff depends on the value of a basket of stocks.

stocks: Securities representing ownership in a firm. They represent what the owners of the firm owe to themselves and thus correspond to the net worth on a personal balance sheet.

stop-loss trading: A strategy in which a stock sale is triggered when the stock price falls to a certain value.

store of value: A commodity or financial instrument that can be used to transfer purchasing power from the present to the future; one of the functions of money.

strike or exercise price: The contractual price at which a holder has the right to trade the underlying asset in an option.

subsidiary: A company that is wholly owned or controlled by another company.

swap: Exchange of liabilities or cash payments between two parties. Interest rate and currency swaps represent off-balance sheet items.

syndicate (bank): A group of banks formed to divide a loan among themselves to reduce the exposure that each faces. In form, a bank syndicate is similar to an investment-bank underwriting syndicate. The difference is that members of a bank syndicate retain a portion of the loan for their balance sheets, whereas investment banks usually sell the entire issue to investors.

syndicate (investment bank): A group of investment banks, each of which agrees to purchase a portion of a new security issue at the bid price.

synthetic put: A combination of stock and cash loan positions that mimics the payoff of a particular put.

synthetic T-bill, synthetic CD, synthetic commercial paper: The loan equivalent of the cash side of a futures contract.

T-account: A presentation of a balance sheet that lists a firm's assets on the left-hand side and its liabilities and net worth on the right-hand side.

target zone: Well-defined limits beyond which central banks will not allow exchange rates to fluctuate.

tax and loan accounts: Special deposit accounts maintained by the U.S. Treasury in private banks. The Treasury keeps revenue received from taxes or bond sales in these accounts until it is ready to spend the revenue.

term insurance contract: An ordinary life insurance contract that typically agrees to pay a death benefit during a specified number of years, usually five or ten years.

term structure of interest rates: A plot of yields to maturity against remaining time to maturity for bonds unlikely to be defaulted, typically the most liquid U.S. government securities.

third-party payment: Payment made through an intermediary, such as a bank, to the payee's bank.

time deposits: Deposits that have a specific maturity and pay relatively high interest rates.

too big to fail doctrine: Belief that the government will most likely not let a large bank fail and that, consequently, all its liability holders (depositors) are safe, whether technically insured or not.

trade credit: Accounts receivable.

trade debt: Accounts payable.

traders: People who buy and sell securities.

transaction accounts: Deposits that permit the depositor to make third-party payments.

trust fund management: Bank management of long-term investment portfolios for such clients as private pension funds and individuals.

underwriter: A firm that buys new security issues from the firm that issues those securities and sells them to the investment public and other investment banks.

unemployment: The difference between the number of people in the labor force and the number of people employed.

unit of account: The unit in which prices or accounts are generally expressed, such as the U.S. dollar.

variance: The sum of the square of each of the deviations from the expected value, weighted by the probability of occurrence.

variation margin: The amount of collateral required for delivery to top a margin account back up to a satisfactory level.

vault cash: Currency kept on hand by banks to operate their currency business.

walking dead: Name given to insolvent S&Ls that were not closed by the FSLIC because of a lack of resources. They were allowed to maintain their operations in the hope that they might grow out of their insolvency.

weighted risk assets: The value of assets calculated by regulators to determine a bank's required capital-to-asset ratio.

whole life insurance contract: A life insurance policy that agrees to pay a death benefit when the insured party dies, regardless of when death occurs, as long as premiums are up-to-date.

writing an option: Selling an option.

yield to maturity: Annualized, constant yield that equates the discounted present value of all scheduled payments of a bond through maturity to the current market price of the bond.

zero correlation: A situation in which two random variables have a covariance of zero.

Index